EIGHTH EDITION

INSTRUCTOR'S ANNOTATED EDITION

Evergreen

A Guide to Writing with Readings

INSTRUCTOR'S ANNOTATED EDITION

Evergreen
A Guide to Writing with Readings

Susan Fawcett

Houghton Mifflin Company
Boston   New York

Publisher: *Patricia A. Coryell*
Editor-in-Chief, English: *Carrie Brandon*
Senior Sponsoring Editor: *Joann Kozyrev*
Senior Marketing Manager: *Annamarie Rice*
Marketing Assistant: *Bettina Chiu*
Senior Development Editor: *Judith Fifer*
Editorial Assistant: *Daisuke Yasutake*
Senior Project Editor: *Rachel D'Angelo Wimberly*
Editorial Assistant: *Anthony D'Aries*
Art/Design Manager: *Gary Crespo*
Cover Design Director: *Tony Saizon*
Photo Editor: Jennifer Meyer Dare
Composition Buyer: *Chuck Dutton*

Cover image credit: Jan Tove Johansson/Getty Images

Photos: Page 7: Courtesy of National Institute of Drug Abuse. Page 39: Reprinted with permission of The City University of New York. Page 53: Dali, Salvador (1904–1989) © ARS, NY. The Persistence of Memory. 1931. Oil on canvas, 9 1/2 x 13". (162.1934) Given anonymously. The Museum of Modern Art, NY, U.S.A. Digital image © The Museum of Modern Art/Licensed by SCALA/Art Resource, NY. © 2007 Salvador Dali, Gala-Salvador Dali Foundation/Artists Rights Society (ARS), New York. (continued on p. AC-1)

Text: Page 66: Reprinted courtesy of SPORTS ILLUSTRATED: "A New Dawn" by Sam Moses, April 23, 1990. Copyright © 1990. Time Inc. All rights reserved. Page 280: Susan Schindehette and Terry Smith,/People © 1994. ALL RIGHTS RESERVED TIME INC. (continued on p. AC-1)

Printed in the U.S.A.

Library of Congress Control Number: 2006936139

Instructor's Annotated Edition:
ISBN 10: 0–618–87943–9
ISBN 13: 978–0–618–87943–4

For orders, use student text ISBNs:
ISBN 10: 0–618–76644–8
ISBN 13: 978–0–618–76644–4

3 4 5 6 7 8 9 -- WC -- 11 10 09 08 07

Contents

Evergreen
takes another leap forward!

"*I find* Evergreen *refreshing and current.* Evergreen *includes ALL the elements necessary for an instructor to teach an effective course.*"
—Douglas Wilson,
  Department of Human & Academic Development, Richland College, TX

"*The readings are fabulous! The ESL tips are super. It's a very solidly written text. I like the conversational tone that is evident throughout the explanations – very friendly.*"
—Zoe Albright,
  Metropolitan Community College–Longview, MO

Students learn and retain information better when visuals are woven purposefully into instruction, so *Evergreen's* new full-color design and 46 images engage students and prompt them to view and think critically. ▶

"Fawcett's provocative visuals are highly effective to teach critical thinking in a writing class."

—Tsegay Wobado,
Bronx Community College, CUNY

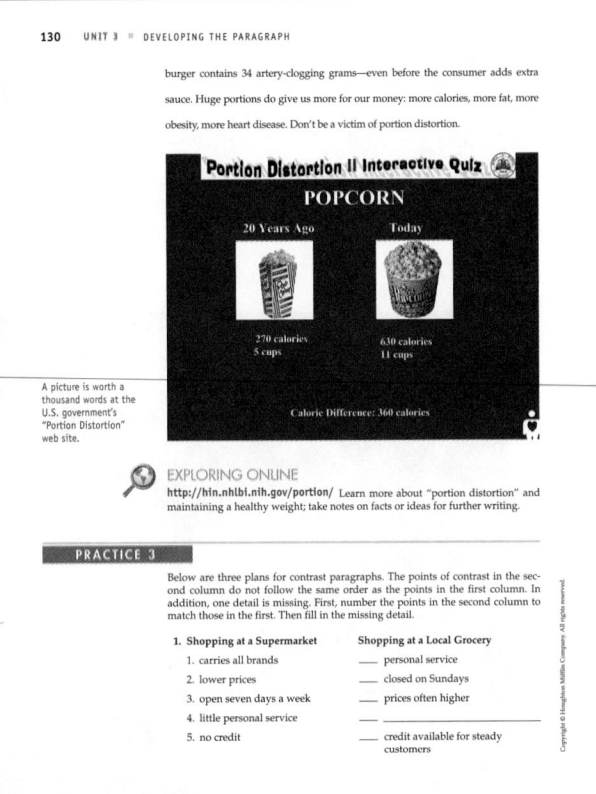

burger contains 34 artery-clogging grams—even before the consumer adds extra sauce. Huge portions do give us more for our money: more calories, more fat, more obesity, more heart disease. Don't be a victim of portion distortion.

Portion Distortion II Interactive Quiz

POPCORN

20 Years Ago — Today

270 calories — 630 calories
5 cups — 11 cups

Calorie Difference: 360 calories

A picture is worth a thousand words at the U.S. government's "Portion Distortion" web site.

EXPLORING ONLINE
http://hin.nhlbi.nih.gov/portion/ Learn more about "portion distortion" and maintaining a healthy weight; take notes on facts or ideas for further writing.

PRACTICE 3

Below are three plans for contrast paragraphs. The points of contrast in the second column do not follow the same order as the points in the first column. In addition, one detail is missing. First, number the points in the second column to match those in the first. Then fill in the missing detail.

1. Shopping at a Supermarket   **Shopping at a Local Grocery**
1. carries all brands   ___ personal service
2. lower prices   ___ closed on Sundays
3. open seven days a week   ___ prices often higher
4. little personal service   ___ _____
5. no credit   ___ credit available for steady
                                             customers

PRACTICE 3   REVIEW

Proofread this essay for preposition errors. Cross out the errors and write corrections above the lines.

Dr. Ben Carson, Pioneer Brain Surgeon

(1) Today, Dr. Benjamin Carson of Johns Hopkins Hospital is internationally known as the man to call from tricky brain surgeries in children. (2) He routinely takes out challenging cases such as removing parts of the brain to stop seizures or repairing deformities of the skull and face. (3) On 1987, he made medical history over successfully separating a pair of conjoined (or Siamese) twins in a twenty-two-hour operation.

(4) This gifted physician was not always a high achiever, however. (5) As a child, he grew up fatherless on Detroit. (6) He now says that, like many off the people he knew, he had a low opinion at himself. (7) Consequently, his grades were poor, and he was prone with violent outbursts and disruptive behavior. (8) Nevertheless, his mother, a high-school dropout who worked two or three jobs

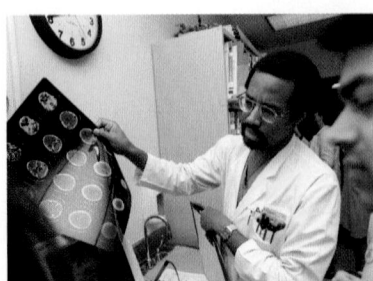

Dr. Benjamin Carson views patient x-rays at Johns Hopkins Hospital.

◀ Because students need extensive practice—and instructors say they can't have too many practices—this edition provides hundreds of carefully crafted practice exercises, both in the text and online. In the text, 65 new practices and models, in addition to many favorites retained from the last edition, keep students involved as they hone their writing skills.

"[Strengths of Evergreen *include] its clear prose, very intelligent exercises, and the Writing Workshops."*

—Marilyn Stachenfeld,
Saddleback College, CA

Evergreen's much-praised readings include nearly 50% fresh selections, ranging from a contrast essay on immigrant experience by Bharati Mukherjee to Christopher Bacorn's challenge to absent fathers. ▶

"Evergreen *does a better job of including interesting readings than any other text I have used.*"

—Elizabeth McCall,
Gaston College, NC

◀ Other authors include Sandra Cisneros, Rick Bragg, Firoozeh Dumas, Alice Walker, Dave Barry, Anna Quindlen, Ana Veciana-Suarez, Arthur Ashe, and Ian Frazier.

"*In Hawaii, everyone is a minority, so the wide range of articles about members of minorities is especially in tune with my students.*"

—Lei Lani Hinds,
Honolulu Community College

xiv

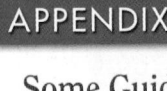

APPENDIX

Some Guidelines for Students of English as a Second Language

Count and Noncount Nouns

Count nouns* refer to people, places, or things that are separate units. You can always count them and often physically point to them. Note that, in English, the following nouns are used as plural count nouns: *police, jeans, pajamas, Middle Ages, scissors, shorts.*

Count Noun	Sample Sentence (Note the underlined words used with count nouns)
television	The marketing department purchased <u>ten</u> large-screen **televisions**.
drive	John had to buy a new flash **drive** to hold the graphics he completed for art class.
assignment	How <u>many</u> **assignments** did you complete last night?
police	The **police** <u>are</u> stationed around the perimeter of the house.

Noncount nouns refer to things that you cannot count separately. Some noncount nouns refer to ideas, feelings, and other things that you cannot see or touch; other noncount nouns refer to food or beverages.

Noncount Noun	Sample Sentence (Note the underlined words used with noncount nouns)
integrity	A politician's **integrity** <u>is</u> frequently tested.
information	We have been waiting for <u>some</u> **information** about the exam.
homework	How <u>much</u> **homework** do you have to finish tonight?
milk	**Milk** <u>is</u> available with 2 percent fat, 1 percent fat, and no fat.

* For more on nouns, see Chapters 30 and 24, Part A.

A-1

"I am not an ESL instructor, but I have many ESL students. For that reason, I value the ESL tips."

—Carolyn Smith Goings,
Broward Community College

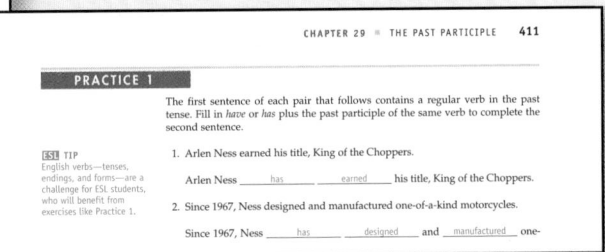

CHAPTER 29 ■ THE PAST PARTICIPLE **411**

PRACTICE 1

The first sentence of each pair that follows contains a regular verb in the past tense. Fill in *have* or *has* plus the past participle of the same verb to complete the second sentence.

ESL TIP
English verbs—tenses, endings, and forms—are a challenge for ESL students, who will benefit from exercises like Practice 1.

1. Arlen Ness earned his title, King of the Choppers.

   Arlen Ness _____ has _____ _____ earned _____ his title, King of the Choppers.

2. Since 1967, Ness designed and manufactured one-of-a-kind motorcycles.

   Since 1967, Ness _____ has _____ _____ designed _____ and _____ manufactured _____ one-

▲ Because more, and more diverse, ESL ▶
students are entering writing classrooms, *Evergreen* offers the most complete, integrated ESL package available, with materials prepared by experts in the field:

- ESL Appendix and more ESL links in the text

- ESL Tips by Linda Fellag, Chair of English, Community College of Philadelphia, and ESL author, plus Teaching Tips in the Instructor's Annotated Edition

- **Evergreen Instructor's Guide to Teaching ESL Students**, with an overview of issues and practical suggestions for *Evergreen* chapters, by Donald L. Weasenforth, Chair of Developmental Reading, Writing, and ESL at Collin County Community College District, and president of TexTESOL V

- Expanded ESL support at the Online Study Center

The *Evergreen* Instructor's Guide to Teaching ESL Students

DONALD L. WEASENFORTH, PH.D.

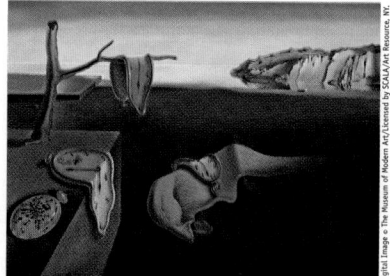

The Persistence of Memory by Salvador Dalí

EXPLORING ONLINE

http://www.vlrtualdali.com/ On this enjoyable site, you can learn more about Dali and view many of his works. Choose one painting; write three things about it that command your attention, arrange them in order of importance, and write a paragraph.

PRACTICE 3

Arrange the ideas that develop each topic sentence in their **order of importance**, numbering them 1, 2, 3, and so on. *Begin with the most important* (or largest, most severe, most surprising) and continue to the *least* important. Or reverse the order if you think that the paragraph would be more dramatic by beginning with the *least* important ideas and building toward a climax, with the most important last.

1. Cynthia Lopez's first year of college brought many unexpected expenses.
   — Her English professor wanted her to own a college dictionary.
   — All those term papers to write required a computer.
   — She had to spend $90 for textbooks.
   — Her solid geometry class required various colored pencils and felt-tip pens.

2. Alcoholic beverages should not be sold at sporting events.
   — Injuries and even deaths caused by alcohol-induced crowd violence would be eliminated.
   — Fans could save money by buying soft drinks instead of beer.
   — Games and matches would be much more pleasant without the yelling, swearing, and rudeness often caused by alcohol.

Evergreen's popular Exploring Online feature now concludes every chapter and selected practices, motivating students to go online for helpful websites–including the *Evergreen Online Study Center*—that provide graded practice, exploration, or research.

"The 'Exploring Online' feature is a great addition to this text. Students love to get away from the paper/pencil activities . . .and 'do something fun for a change.' The online graded quizzes/ activities provide immediate feedback to the students."

—Jennifer Bubb,
Illinois Valley Community College

Student writers must think critically to meet college and work challenges, so more collaborative "Thinking and Writing Together" features, two new Writers' Workshops, and other engaging tasks guide students to problem-solve, analyze, and write. ▶

"[The Thinking and Writing features] are very useful in reinforcing each mode through collaborative activities, and students really respond positively to them."

—Jennifer Ferguson,
Coordinator of Developmental Writing and Reading, Cazenovia College, NY

criminals. (7) For example, crime scene examiners go to the places where crimes have occurred to locate, photograph, collect, and transportation of physical evidence like fingerprints and blood samples. (8) On the other hand, crime laboratory analysts stay in the lab. (9) Using microscopes, DNA tests, firearms tests, and other techniques and equipments to make sense of crime scene evidence.

On television's *CSI*, Gary Dourdan and Marg Helgenberger both examine crime scenes and work in the lab—a departure from reality.

(10) Each of these jobs require a bachelor's degree. (11) Two specialtys requiring a master's degree are forensic anthropology, which involves identifying people from skeletal remains. And psychological profiling. (12) Using behavioral clues to "read" the mind of a killer or other criminal. (13) One specialty, medical examiner, requires a medical degree. (14) Although this is the highest-paid forensics career. (15) It requires a tough personality able to perform autopsies on crime victims to determine exact cause of death. (16) Real-world forensic scientists admit that their

Outlining, whether informal or more formal, is helpful to many writers, so Chapter 14 now includes a new Part D with flexible material on outlining, reinforced in the paragraph and research chapters. ▶

"Outlining is a very difficult concept for novice writers to develop and use. Typically, some less skilled writers want to skip this task completely. This section will help those students resist that urge."

—Glenda Bell,
*University of Arkansas
Community College at Batesville*

written the thesis statement *Hydrogen fuel cell cars, which many experts think will be the automobiles of the future, have strong advantages and disadvantages,* and you plan three paragraphs with these topic sentences:

Because hydrogen cars are clean-running, they will not pollute the environment like cars with gasoline engines.

Hydrogen cell technology costs ten times more than gasoline—a major problem, at least for now.

Hydrogen cars will free America from dependence on foreign oil sources and thus improve national security.

The writer lists three points about hydrogen cell cars. Points one and three both state advantages of hydrogen cars; therefore, it makes sense to order the paragraphs so that those two advantages are grouped together. Point two states a serious disadvantage—high cost. So it would make sense to put this point either first or last—probably last. A logical order of paragraphs, then, might be the following:

1. **INTRODUCTION** and thesis statement	*Hydrogen fuel cell cars, which many experts think will be the automobiles of the future, have strong advantages and disadvantages.*
2. **Topic sentence:**	Because hydrogen cars are clean-running, they will not pollute the environment like cars with gasoline engines.
3. **Topic sentence:**	Hydrogen cars will free America from dependence on foreign oil sources and thus improve national security.
4. **Topic sentence:**	Hydrogen cell technology costs ten times more than gasoline—a major problem, at least for now.
5. **CONCLUSION**	

Student Sung-Yeah Song presents her design for a hydrogen car to General Motors officials at Detroit's College for Creative Studies, 2004.

Dressed head to toe in duct tape, Margaret Roberts and Tyler Mickley won the 2003 Stuck at Prom contest and scored college scholarships.

forty-four states competed the 2005 winners, for example, created an orange harlequin-patterned dress inspired by Pablo Picasso's famous oil painting "Girl Before a Mirror," the matching black tuxedo was stylishly accented with a vest in the same pattern and orange stripes on the pant legs. (8) These dazzling getups required twenty-five rolls of duct tape and four weeks' work to complete. (9) Although the clothes were extremely heavy. (10) The collegebound couple says everyone loved their fashion statement. (11) In addition, the duct tape's insulating qualities made them the hottest couple on the dance floor.

Paragraph 2

(1) Some teenagers seem to start the day tired, they are worn out even before they leave for school. (2) Once in class, they might doze off, even in the middle of an exciting lesson. (3) Are these students lazy, have they stayed out too late partying? (4) Medical research provides a different explanation for the exhaustion of

◀ Humor with an instructional purpose is a hallmark of *Evergreen*, and the Eighth Edition has even more enjoyable humorous subject matter and cartoons to analyze.

"I love the humor in this book! The author uses humor not just to motivate the class, but to advance the lesson."

—Marta Magellan,
Miami Dade College

Evergreen's technology package takes an unprecedented leap forward with an impressive suite of new tools and resources to help teachers and students communicate, organize, and master class material.

WriteSpace for *Evergreen* provides Blackboard-enabled course management with hundreds of exercises and quizzes keyed to *Evergreen*; **HM Assess**, a diagnostic tool that can chart an individualized study path for each student; interactive **multimedia modules** with thinking and writing prompts; an **Online Handbook** for instant grammatical help; plus instructor commentary and peer review tools. ▶

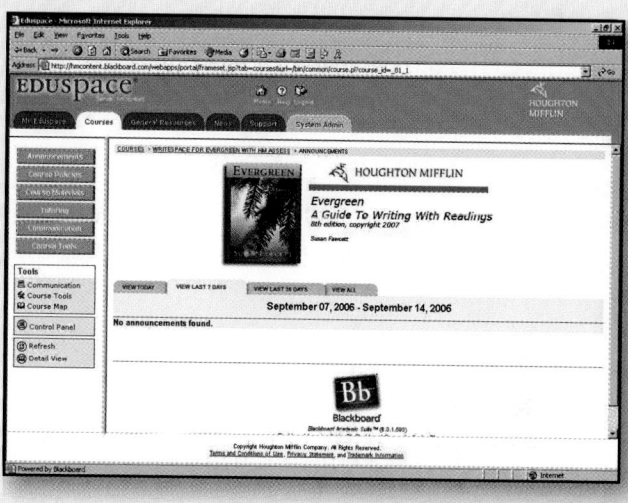

◀ The instructors' **Online Teaching Center** provides

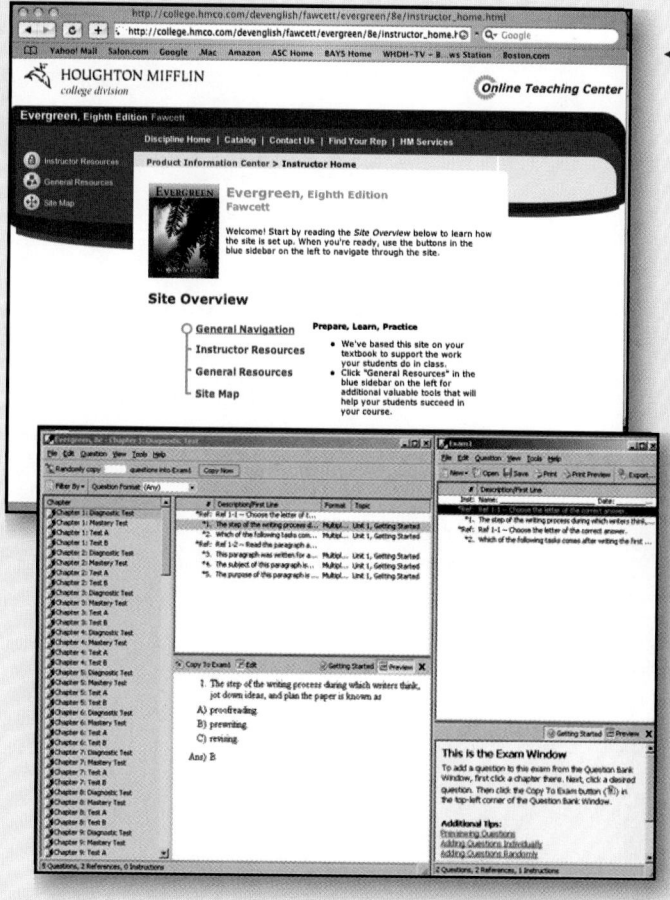

- A 40-page **Instructor's Guide**, with syllabi and author's notes on all chapters and readings

- An expanded **Test Bank** that can be customized, downloaded, and printed; also available in HM Testing format on CD-ROM

- The ***Evergreen* Instructor's Guide to Teaching ESL Students**, by Donald Weasenforth, available both online and in print

- Creative and powerful teaching resources, with teaching strategies, class activities, and resources for preventing plagiarism

- Customizable rubrics for every paragraph and essay type

- PowerPoint slides for classroom use

The student **Online Study Center** for ▶
Evergreen includes

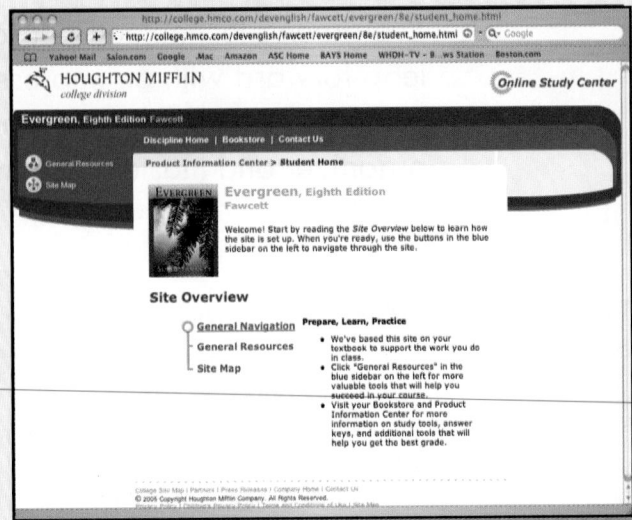

- self-study ACE quizzes for every chapter, providing students with immediate feedback

- live links for every website in the text

- chapter checklists, self-evaluation charts, paragraph- and essay-builder prompts

- ESL practice exercises

- "What's Your Visual IQ?" activities that help students read and analyze visual images, from advertisements to works of art

- Career and Job-Search resources

Evergreen helps students take a leap forward—by improving their writing abilities, making them think, and demonstrating that learning to write can be invigorating, even fun. Do leap into this eighth edition of *Evergreen*. . . .it is the best *Evergreen* yet.

[Evergreen] encompasses all the material needed for the course, and requires that the students (and I) carry only one book. I like the comprehensive approach."

—Kathleen Glidden,
Community College of Vermont–Brattleboro

Preface

"*Evergreen* works." Again and again, I hear this comment from instructors and students alike, and I consider it the greatest possible compliment. Based on my years of classroom experience at Bronx Community College, City University of New York, *Evergreen* is designed for students who need to improve the writing skills so necessary for success in college and in most careers. The text's clear, paced lessons, inspiring student and professional models, many high-interest practices, and varied writing assignments have guided over two million students through the process of writing effectively, from prewriting to final draft. I am proud that *Evergreen with Readings* has won awards for excellence and has continued to be the most widely used developmental writing text in the United States since its first edition.

In this exciting Eighth Edition, I have thoroughly reviewed and updated not only the book, but its technology and supplements, guided by the thoughtful suggestions of faculty across the country. The goal has been to create a text-and-tools package that even more efficiently helps students meet contemporary academic and workplace challenges. The result is, I believe, the best *Evergreen* yet and includes technology offerings that, in the words of one reviewer, "have risen—bravo—to the text's unsurpassed level of excellence."

Specifically, students today must become not only proficient writers but, increasingly, critical thinkers and critical viewers as well. A new four-color design punctuates *Evergreen*'s clear, friendly pedagogy and highlights a new emphasis on critical viewing—with photographs, ads, paintings, and cartoons carefully integrated into the writing instruction. In addition, I have added more critical-thinking assignments, many of them collaborative. *Evergreen*'s Exploring Online feature, with web links for further study and exploration, now concludes every chapter and complements selected practices and tasks.

Greater numbers of students with second-language issues are entering college English classes, yet many instructors have no formal training in ESL instruction. For instructors who want a little expert advice and confidence-boosting information on helping their ESL students, two nationally recognized ESL experts and I have created a suite of useful resources, including ESL and Teaching Tips in the Instructor's Annotated Edition, a practical instructor's resource manual for teaching ESL students in *Evergreen* classrooms, an ESL Appendix with practices in the student text, and enriched online support.

Evergreen's much-praised reading selections have been significantly freshened with seven eloquent essays, combined with ten favorites from the last edition. I also have replaced many models and content-based practices with exciting new subject matter intended to spark and hold students' interest as they learn, and hundreds more new, interactive practice sets and tests written just for *Evergreen* are now available online. Other improvements include new material on outlining, some revision exercises reformatted so that students need not recopy, and more humor.

Special Features of *Evergreen with Readings*, Eighth Edition

New Full Color and Photographs

A four-color design and 46 images expand *Evergreen's* pedagogy. Every image was chosen to engage students and prompt them to view, reflect, and connect more deeply with material they have just studied. For example, Navajo surgeon Dr. Lori Alvord, about whom students have read as they choose synonyms, is shown in a thought-provoking ad for the American Indian College Fund. Other images include NASCAR driver Dale Earnhardt in a HANS safety helmet, a college poetry slam performer, artwork by Salvador Dali and Edvard Munch, *Latina* Magazine's founder Christy Haubegger, and famous pediatric surgeon Dr. Ben Carson.

65 *New* High-Interest Models and Practices

Engaging models and content-based practice sets are vital to *Evergreen's* effectiveness—motivating students to read on and perhaps promoting thinking and writing. Fresh subjects include identity theft, Brazilian capoeira master Edna Lima, hydrogen-fueled cars, Diane Sawyer's career advice, iPods, the Greek myth of Icarus, motorcycle builder Arlen Ness, the creation of Mary Shelley's *Frankenstein*, and the pros and cons of video games.

Nearly 50 Percent *New* Reading Selections

Based on feedback from faculty and students, Unit 8 has been extensively freshened with seven stimulating readings. New to this edition are Rick Bragg's memoir of his near-fatal love for a convertible, Ana Veciana Suarez on choosing generosity over greed, Christopher Bacorn's plea to absentee fathers, Karen Castellucci Cox on four types of courage, and Anna Quindlen's scheme to make Americans vote. Readers' favorite selections from the last edition—those rated most thought-provoking and appealing—have been kept, for a new total of seventeen.

New Integrated ESL Resources

To better meet the needs of native and nonnative students, two nationally recognized ESL experts, Linda Fellag and Donald L. Weasenforth, worked with me to create a customized, integrated ESL package. New ESL Tips in the margins of the Instructor's Annotated Edition were written or vetted by Dr. Fellag, Chair of the Department of English, Community College of Philadelphia and ESL text author; these tips and my Teaching Tips flag trouble spots and suggest ways to best utilize the ESL coverage woven throughout *Evergreen*. A companion teaching guide, *The Evergreen Instructor's Guide to Teaching ESL Students*—authored by Dr. Weasenforth, president of TexTESOL V and chair of Developmental Writing, Reading and English as a Second Language at Collin County Community College District, Plano, Texas—will help instructors better understand and address ESL errors transferred into English. A new ESL Appendix with practices and *Evergreen's* Online Study Center provide students with more assistance and exercises.

More Exploring Online Features

Selected websites throughout the text encourage students to seek additional online study, practice, or information. This Exploring Online feature with links to vetted sites, including top Online Writing Labs (OWLs), now appears at the end of every chapter and *Thinking and Writing Together* task and after selected practices on such topics as ballooning American food portions, Pixar's animated movies, endangered species, Vincent Van Gogh, and the hip-hop community's voter registration drives.

More Critical Thinking Assignments

At the suggestion of instructors, I have added a few more collaborative thinking tasks. The popular Thinking and Writing Together assignments guide students to apply rhetorical strategies to problem solving or critical viewing; new ones prompt discussion of the psychological effects of color, birth order and personality, and the persuasive message of visual images. Two new Writers' Workshops showcase student work for peer critique, and throughout the text, Teaching Tips pose thought-provoking questions or assignments about the lesson.

More on Outlining

Chapter 14, The Process of Writing an Essay, now contains a flexible new Part D, Organizing Your Ideas in an Outline. This material shows students two ways to use outlines, whether informal or more formal, and is reinforced elsewhere in the text.

Other Improvements

Other new or revised material includes a new grammar review practice for conjunctive adverbs, reformatted revision exercises, and the addition of a bit more humor—always with an instructional purpose—in some practices, subject matter, and visuals.

Extensive New Teaching Program

Instructors told us exactly what teaching and learning technology they and their students need. We listened. *Evergreen's* new technology package offers an unprecedented array of tools and resources to meet and surpass those needs:

- *WriteSpace for Evergreen,* a course management system powered by Blackboard, offers hundreds of interactive exercises and quizzes keyed to *Evergreen;* **HM Assess,** a powerful diagnostic tool that can set forth an individualized study path for each student; interactive **multimedia modules** with analytical and writing prompts; an **Online Handbook** offering immediate help with grammar and mechanics; and **Re:Mark** and **Peer Re:Mark,** tools that enable online instructor and peer review of student writing.

- The instructors' **Online Teaching Center for** *Evergreen* provides the **Evergreen Instructor's Guide** with the author's teaching suggestions for the course, each chapter and reading, plus sample syllabi; the expanded and enriched **Test**

Bank—with diagnostic, mastery, unit, and chapter tests (four for each chapter in the book) that can be customized, downloaded, and printed, and which is also available in HM Testing format on a CD-ROM; *The Evergreen Instructor's Guide to Teaching ESL Students* by Donald Weasenforth (also available in print format); **Creative Classroom Links** with teaching strategies and surefire class activities, resources for **preventing plagiarism**, customizable **rubrics** for every paragraph and essay type; and 114 **PowerPoint slides** for classroom use.

■ The student's **Online Study Center for** *Evergreen* provides self-study ACE quizzes keyed to every chapter that provide students with immediate feedback; chapter **checklists**, **self-evaluation** charts, **downloadable outline forms** to help students write 20 types of paragraphs and essays, additional **writing assignments**, and **live links** for all Exploring Online features and other web sites in the book; **What's Your Visual IQ?** exercises that help students to read and analyze visual images, from advertisements to works of art; **Career and Job-Search Resources**; and **ESL Resources** with study, links, and practice.

Organization of the Text

Evergreen's self-contained chapters and units can be taught in any order. Unit 1 provides an overview of the writing process, audience, and purpose and then introduces five prewriting techniques. Unit 2 guides students through the paragraph-writing process: planning, writing topic sentences, generating ideas, organizing, making smooth transitions, and revising. Unit 3 moves on to the rhetorical modes most often required in college writing (illustration, narration, description, process, definition, comparison/contrast, classification, cause/effect, and persuasion). In Unit 4, the techniques of paragraph writing are applied step by step to the process of writing essays, summarizing and quoting from sources, strengthening an essay with research, and answering essay examination questions. Unit 5 covers the more subtle skills of revising for consistency, sentence variety, and language awareness. Unit 6 thoroughly reviews basic grammar, highlighting such major problem areas as verbs, sentence boundaries, punctuation, and mechanics; Unit 7 covers spelling and homonyms. In Unit 8, the instructor can choose from 17 richly varied, thought-provoking reading selections by such authors as Sandra Cisneros, Rick Bragg, Firoozeh Dumas, Ian Frazier, Anna Quindlen, and Brent Staples. Each selection is accompanied by a headnote, glosses, critical thinking questions, and writing assignments. A Quotation Bank of great short quotations and an Appendix of tips and practices for special assistance to ESL students concludes the text.

Evergreen with Reading's full range of materials and flexible organization adapt easily to almost any course design and to a wide range of student needs. Because each chapter is self-contained, the text also works well for tutorials, laboratory work, and self-teaching.

Acknowledgments

Deep thanks to these people whose thoughtful comments and suggestions helped to develop this Eighth Edition.

Zoe Albright, Metropolitan Community College—Longview
Glenda Bell, University of Arkansas Community College at Batesville

Jason Berner, Contra Costa College
Charley Boyd, Genesee Community College
Carla Bradley, Ozarks Technical Community College
Jennifer Bubb, Illinois Valley Community College
Norma Cruz-Gonzales, San Antonio College
Karen F. Dimanche Davis, Marygrove College
Kim Dorfman, Central Connecticut State University
Peg Ehlen, Ivy Tech Community College of Indiana, Evansville
Jennifer Ferguson, Cazenovia College
Janice Filer, Shelton State Community College
Kathleen Glidden, Community College of Vermont—Brattleboro
Carolyn Goings, Broward Community College
LeiLani Hinds, Honolulu Community College
Elizabeth McCall, Gaston College
Sara McLaughlin, South Plains Community College
Ildiko Melis, Lake Superior State University
Theresa Mohamed, Onondaga Community College
Patricia Plasket Osterman, Palm Beach Community College
Jennifer Scheidt, Palo Alto College
Marilyn Stachenfeld, Saddleback College
Leslie Stultz, Ivy Tech Community College of Indiana, Terre Haute
Carmen Subryan, Howard University
Molly Turner, Harold Washington College
Doug Wilson, Richland College
Kirstin May Wiley, Lexington Community College
Jeff Wylie, Maysville Community and Technical College

I am indebted to the team at Houghton Mifflin who contributed to making *Evergreen* quite simply the best book of its kind in the country: Patricia Coryell, Publisher for the Humanities; Carrie Brandon, Editor-in-Chief, English; Joann Kozyrev, Sponsoring Editor; Judith Fifer, Senior Development Editor; Annamarie Rice, Executive Marketing Manager; Bettina Chiu, Marketing Assistant; Tony Saizon, Cover Design Director; Janet Edmonds, Senior Content Manager; Giuseppina Daniel, Senior Media Producer; Rachel D'Angelo Wimberly, Senior Project Editor; Jennifer Meyer Dare, Senior Photo Editor; Anthony D'Aries, Editorial Assistant; and Daisuke Yasutake, Editorial Assistant.

Ann Marie Radaskiewicz contributed high-quality research, writing, and troubleshooting throughout the revision process. With her can-do professionalism and good cheer, she has become a treasured colleague and friend. I owe a great debt of gratitude to Linda Fellag and Donald Weasenforth, who did such a wonderful job creating our new resources both for faculty and the students who enter English classrooms with issues and errors carried over from other languages. I loved working with these gifted teacher-writers. Linda Fellag's ESL Tips received high praise from our reviewers. Don Weasenforth's manual with its Language Transfer Chart will be a much-thumbed *Evergreen* resource; Don also played a major role in crafting a rich, level-appropriate ESL Appendix.

Special thanks to Bronx Community College—English chair Frederick De Naples, my former colleagues in the English Department, President Carolyn Williams, and the resilient and inspiring student body. Many of the student compositions in this text were written for Bronx Community College classes. Karen Castellucci Cox of City College of San Francisco generously shared her creativity and love of teaching. My book group colleagues, many from Miami Dade College, helped me balance fine books, laughter, and food.

For the great gifts of love and discovery on the journey, thank you to my special friends, Maggie Smith, Colleen Huff, Pamela Tudor, and Trisha Nelson, and to the family I am lucky enough to love spending time with—my Mom, Harriet Fawcett, brother David Fawcett, brother-in-law Eddie Brown, and my husband, the English professor, writer, and sports nut Richard Donovan.

S.F.

EIGHTH EDITION

INSTRUCTOR'S ANNOTATED EDITION

Evergreen
A Guide to Writing with Readings

Getting Started

1

Exploring the Writing Process

PART A The Writing Process

PART B Subject, Audience, and Purpose

Did you know that the ability to write well characterizes the most successful college students and employees—in fields from education to medicine to computer science? Skim the job postings in career fields that interest you and notice how many stress "excellent writing and communication skills." Furthermore, reading and writing enrich our daily lives; in surveys, adults always rate reading, writing, and speaking well as the most important life skills a person can possess.

The goal of this book is to help you become a more skilled, powerful, and confident writer. You will see that writing is not a magic ability only a few are born with, but a life skill that can be learned. The first chapter presents a brief overview of the writing process, explored in greater depth throughout the book. Now I invite you to decide to excel in this course. Let *Evergreen* be your guide, and enjoy the journey.

PART A **The Writing Process**

Many people have the mistaken idea that good writers simply sit down and write out a perfect letter, paragraph, or essay from start to finish. In fact, writing is a **process** consisting of a number of steps:

The Writing Process

1 Prewriting

- Thinking about possible subjects
- Freely jotting ideas on paper or computer
- Narrowing the subject and writing your main idea in one sentence
- Deciding which ideas to include
- Arranging ideas in a plan or outline

3

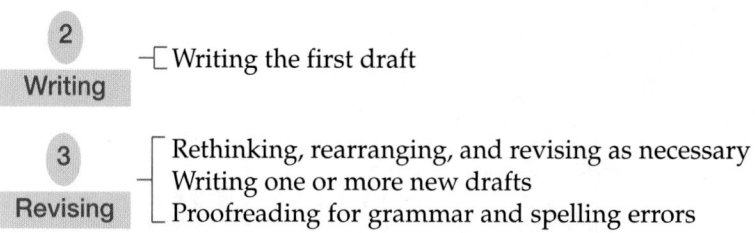

ESL TIP
Nonnative students may fail to understand the importance of *speaking English whenever possible.* Urge them to practice speaking and writing English with a friend or study partner. Stress that this discipline is key to success in this course and in their careers.

Not all writers perform all the steps in this order, but most **prewrite, write, and revise.** Actually, writing can be a messy process of thinking, writing, reading what has been written, and rewriting. Sometimes steps overlap or need to be repeated. The important thing is that writing the first draft is just one stage in the process. "I love being a writer," jokes Peter De Vries. "What I can't stand is the paperwork."

Good writers take time at the beginning to **prewrite**—to think, jot ideas, and plan the paper—because they know it will save time and avoid frustration later. Once they write the first draft, they let it "cool off." Then they read it again with a fresh, critical eye and **revise**—crossing out, adding, and rewriting for more clarity and punch. Good writers are like sculptors, shaping and reworking their material into something more meaningful. Finally, they **proofread** for grammar and spelling errors so that their writing seems to say, "I am proud to put my name on this work." As you practice writing, you will discover your own most effective writing process.

PRACTICE 1

TEACHING TIP
Encourage students to perform similar self-assessments each time they receive feedback on their writing and to use self- and instructor-assessment to set personal goals in this course.

Think of something that you wrote recently—and of which you felt proud—for college, work, or your personal life. Now on paper or with classmates, discuss the *process* you followed in writing it. Did you do any *planning* or *prewriting*—or did you just sit down and start writing? How much time did you spend rewriting and *revising* your work? What one change in your writing process do you think would most improve your writing? Taking more time to prewrite? Taking more time to revise? Improving your grammar and spelling?

PRACTICE 2

Bring in several newspaper help-wanted sections. In a group with four or five classmates, study the ads in career fields that interest you. How many fields require writing and communication skills? Which job ad requiring these skills most surprised you or your group? Be prepared to present your findings to the class. If your class has Internet access, visit *Monster.com* or other job-search web sites and perform the same exercise.

EXPLORING ONLINE

http://www.writingcommission.org. Click "Writing: A Ticket to Work." A survey of business leaders finds that good writing is the key to career success. What two facts or comments in this summary do you find most striking?

PART B Subject, Audience, and Purpose

Early in the prewriting phase, writers should give some thought to their **subject, audience,** and **purpose.**

In college courses, you may be assigned a broad **subject** by your instructor. First, make sure you understand the assignment. Then focus on one aspect of the subject that intrigues you. Whenever possible, choose something that you know and care about: life in Cleveland, working with learning-disabled children, repairing motorcycles, overcoming shyness, watching a friend struggle with drug addiction, playing soccer. You may not realize how many subjects you do know about.

To find or focus your subject, ask yourself:

- What special experience or expertise do I have?

- What inspires, angers, or motivates me? What do I love to do?

- What story in the news affected me recently?

- What campus, job, or community problem do I have ideas about solving?

Your answers will suggest good subjects to write about. Keep a list of all your best ideas.

How you approach your subject will depend on your **audience**—your readers. Are you writing for your professor, classmates, boss, closest friend, youngsters in the community, or the editor of a newspaper?

To focus on your audience, ask yourself:

- For whom am I writing? Who will read this?

- How much do they know about the subject? Are they beginners or experts?

- Will they likely agree or disagree with my ideas?

TEACHING TIP
You might bring in examples of different types of writing—an editorial, a magazine article, a humorous essay, or the text of a web site. Have students determine audience and purpose in each.

Keeping your audience in mind helps you know what information to include and what to leave out. For example, if you are writing about women's college basketball for readers who think that hoops are big earrings, you will approach your subject in a basic way, perhaps discussing the explosion of interest in women's teams. But an audience of sports lovers will already know about this; for them, you would write in more depth, perhaps comparing the technique of two point guards.

Finally, keeping your **purpose** in mind will help you write more effectively. Do you want to explain something to your readers, persuade them that a certain view is correct, entertain them, tell a good story, or some combination of these?

PRACTICE 3

List five subjects that you might like to write about. Consider your audience and purpose: For whom are you writing? What do you want them to know about your subject? Notice how the audience and purpose will help shape your paper. For ideas, reread the boxed questions on page 5.

	Subject	Audience	Purpose
EXAMPLE 1.	my recipe for seafood gumbo	inexperienced cooks	to show how easy it is to make seafood gumbo
2.	_____	_____	_____
3.	_____	_____	_____
4.	_____	_____	_____
5.	_____	_____	_____

TEACHING TIP
Developmental students may think they have nothing to write about. To help counter this myth, ask volunteers to share their answers to some of the boxed questions on page 5. Have them apply the questions to Practice 3.

PRACTICE 4

Jot ideas for the following two assignments, by yourself or in a group with four or five classmates. Notice how your ideas and details differ, depending on the audience and purpose.

1. You have been asked to write a description of your college for local high school students. Your purpose is to explain what advantages the college offers its students. What kinds of information should you include? What will your audience want to know? What information should you leave out?

2. You have been asked to write a description of your college for the governor of your state. Your purpose is to persuade her or him to spend more money to improve your college. What information should you include? What will your audience want to know? What information should you leave out?

PRACTICE 5

In a group with three or four classmates, read these sentences from real job-application letters and résumés, published in *Fortune* magazine. Each writer's *subject* was his or her job qualifications; the *audience* was an employer, and the *purpose* was to get a job. How did each person undercut his or her own purpose? What writing advice would you give each of these job seekers?

TEACHING TIP
Your students will enjoy doing Practice 5 in class. Remind them that the link between good writing and good jobs is strong.

1. I have lurnt Word and computer spreadsheet programs.

2. Please don't misconstrue my 14 jobs as "job-hopping." I have never quit a job.

3. I procrastinate, especially when the task is unpleasant.

4. Let's meet, so you can "ooh" and "aah" over my experience.

5. It is best for employers that I not work with people.

6. Reason for leaving my last job: maturity leave.

7. As indicted, I have over five years of analyzing investments.

8. References: none. I have left a path of destruction behind me.

PRACTICE 6

Study the public service advertisement below and then answer these questions: What *subject* is the ad addressing? Who is the target *audience*? What is the intended *purpose*? In your view, how successful is this ad in achieving its purpose?

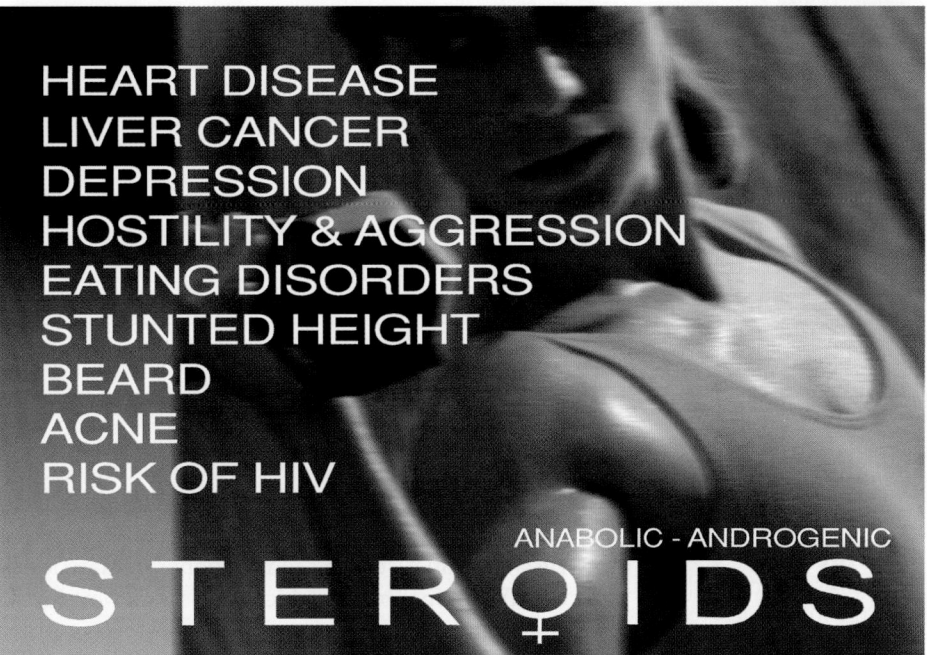

EXPLORING ONLINE

Throughout this book, Exploring Online features will suggest ways to use the Internet to improve your writing and grammar. A number of online writing labs—called OWLs—based at colleges around the country offer excellent additional practice or review in areas where you might need extra help. Here are two good sites to explore:

http://owl.english.purdue.edu/ Purdue University's OWL

http://grammar.ccc.commnet.edu/grammar/ Capital Community College's OWL

Online Study Center college.hmco.com/pic/evergreen8e
Visit the Online Study Center for *Evergreen* for more exercises and quizzes.

2

Prewriting to Generate Ideas

This chapter presents five effective prewriting techniques that will help you get your ideas onto paper (or onto the computer). These techniques can help you overcome the "blank-page jitters" that many people face when they first sit down to write. You can also use them to generate new ideas at any point in the writing process. Try all five to see which ones work best for you.

In addition, if you write on a computer, try prewriting in different ways: on paper and on computer. Some writers feel they produce better work if they prewrite by hand and only later transfer their best ideas onto the computer. Every writer has personal preferences, so don't be afraid to experiment.

TEACHING TIP
Emphasize to students that these prewriting techniques are tools for the *writer*—not meant to be shared with others; therefore, the writer can feel free to explore.

PART A Freewriting

TEACHING TIP
Research indicates that freewriting can be confusing to some students with learning disabilities. Instead, they need to *verbalize* ideas before writing. Suggest that they talk with a partner for two minutes before they start to write.

Freewriting is an excellent method that many writers use to warm up and to generate ideas. These are the guidelines: for five, ten, or fifteen minutes, write rapidly, without stopping, about anything that comes into your head. If you feel stuck, just repeat or rhyme the last word you wrote, but *don't stop writing*. And don't worry about grammar, logic, complete sentences, or grades.

The point of freewriting is to write so quickly that ideas can flow without comments from your inner critic. The *inner critic* is the voice inside that says, every time you have an idea, "That's dumb; that's no good; cross that out." Freewriting helps you tell this voice, "Thank you for your opinion. Once I have lots of ideas and words on paper, I'll invite you back for comment."

After you freewrite, read what you have written, underlining or marking any parts you like.

Freewriting is a powerful tool for helping you turn thoughts and feelings into words, especially when you are unsure about what you want to say. Sometimes freewriting produces only nonsense; often, however, it can help you zoom in on possible topics, interests, and worthwhile writing you can use later. Focused freewriting can help you find subjects to write about.

Focused Freewriting

In **focused freewriting,** you simply try to focus your thoughts on one subject as you freewrite. The subject might be one assigned by your instructor, one you choose, or one you have discovered in unfocused freewriting. The goal of most writing is a polished, organized piece of writing; focused freewriting can help you generate ideas or narrow a topic to one aspect that interests you.

Here is one student's focused freewriting on the topic *someone who strongly influenced you:*

> Mr. Martin, the reason I'm interested in science. Wiry, five-foot-four-inch, hyperactive guy. A darting bird in the classroom, a circling teacher-bird, now jabbing at the knee bone of a skeleton, now banging on the jar with the brain in it. Like my brain used to feel, pickled, before I took his class. I always liked science but everything else was too hard. I almost dropped out of school, discouraged, but Martin was fun, crazy, made me think. Encouragement was his thing. Whacking his pencil against the plastic model of an eyeball in his office, he would bellow at me, "Taking too many courses! Working too many hours in that restaurant! Living everyone else's life but your own!" Gradually, I slowed down, got myself focused. Saw him last at graduation, where he thwacked my diploma with his pencil, shouting, "Keep up the good work! Live your own life! Follow your dreams!"

■ This student later used this focused freewriting—its vivid details about Mr. Martin and his influence—as the basis for an effective paper. Underline any words or lines that you find especially striking or appealing. Be prepared to explain why you like what you underline.

PRACTICE 1

ESL TIP
ESL students may need an explanation of idioms or culturally specific ideas in some exercises. Having native English speakers explain such terms will encourage cross-cultural interaction.

Do a three-minute focused freewriting on three of these topics:

beach	body piercing
friendship	parent (or child)
news	tests

Underline as usual. Did you surprise yourself by having so much to say about any one topic? Perhaps you would like to write more about that topic.

PRACTICE 2

TEACHING TIP
Before having students complete Practice 2, demonstrate the process by verbalizing your thoughts as you examine a freewriting for possible topics.

1. Read over your earlier freewritings and notice your underlinings. Would you like to write more about any underlined words or ideas? Write two or three such words or ideas here:

   Sample answers: _____

   Sometimes I feel closer to my children than to my parents. _____

   I'm often most content on a rainy day. _____

2. Now choose one word or idea. Focus your thoughts on it and do a ten-minute focused freewriting. Try to stick to the topic as you write but don't worry too much about keeping on track; just keep writing.

PART B Brainstorming

ESL TIP
To draw out nonnative students who hesitate to share aloud, try the Anonymous Brainstorming Game, in which each student writes an idea related to the chosen topic (use precut scraps of paper if you wish). Ideas are then chosen randomly and discussed by the class.

Another prewriting technique that may work for you is **brainstorming** or freely jotting down ideas about a topic. As in freewriting, the purpose is to generate lots of ideas so you have something to work with and choose from. Write everything that comes to you about a topic—words and phrases, ideas, details, examples.

After you have brainstormed, read over your list, underlining interesting or exciting ideas you might develop further. As with freewriting, many writers brainstorm on a general subject, underline, and then brainstorm again as they focus on one aspect of that subject.

Here is one student's brainstorm list on the topic *e-mail*:

> everyone has it—really neat
>
> can send mail day or night
>
> not like snail mail—so slow
>
> I hate to write letters but I love to e-mail
>
> I e-mail my friends at their colleges all the time
>
> I even e-mail my little brother at home
>
> more intimate than phone calls—you can share inner thoughts
>
> Mom's always sending me e-mails
>
> she e-mails her old college friends, too
>
> people are more in touch with each other now

With brainstorming, this writer generated many ideas and started to move toward a more focused topic: *People are more in touch with each other now because of e-mail.* With a narrowed topic, brainstorming once more can help the writer generate details and reasons to support the idea.

PRACTICE 3

Choose one of the following topics that interests you and write it at the top of your paper or computer screen. Then brainstorm. Write anything that comes into your head about the topic. Just let ideas pour out fast!

1. a place I want to go back to

2. dealing with difficult people

3. an unforgettable person in politics, sports, or religious life

4. growing up

5. my best/worst job

6. a first or blind date

Once you fill a page with your list, read it over, marking the most interesting ideas. Draw arrows or highlight and move text on your screen to connect related ideas. Is there one idea that might be the subject of a paper?

PART C Clustering

Some writers use still another method—called **clustering** or **mapping**—to get their ideas on paper. To begin clustering, simply write an idea or a topic, usually one word, in the center of a piece of paper. Then let your mind make associations, and write these associations branching out from the center.

TEACHING TIP
Consider modeling the construction of a cluster, or have the class help you create one. Verbalize your mental process as you create it.

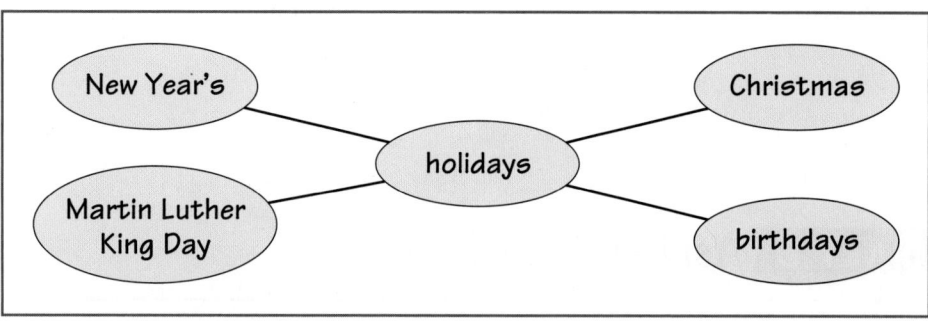

When one idea suggests other ideas, details, and examples, write these around it in a "cluster." After you finish, pick the cluster that most interests you. You may wish to freewrite for more ideas.

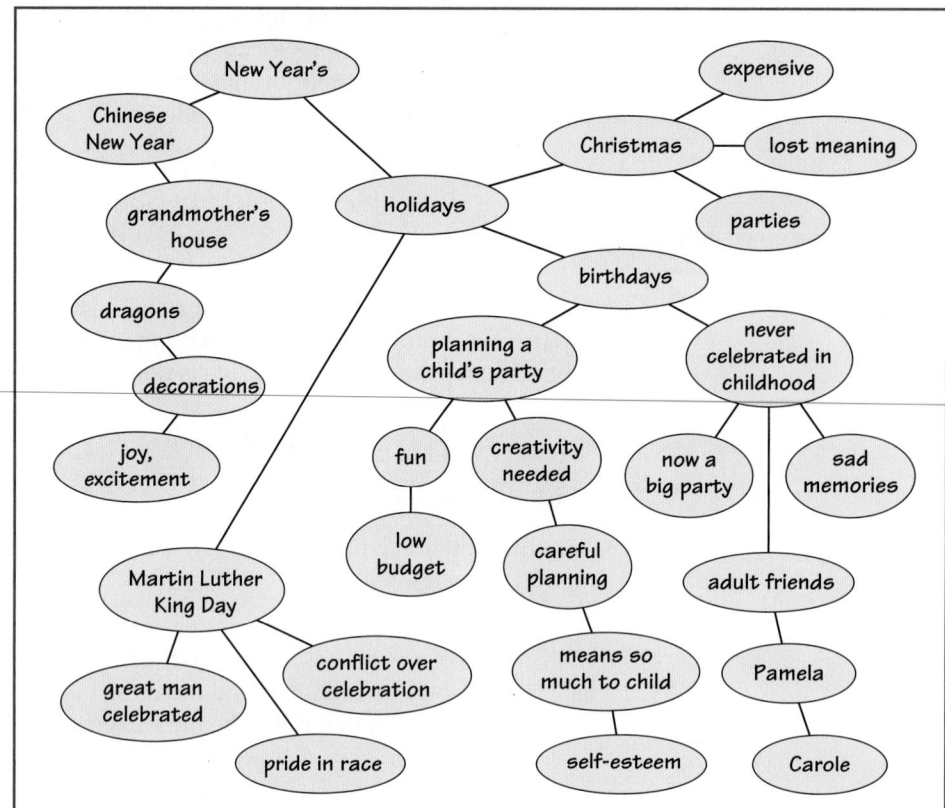

PRACTICE 4

Choose one of these topics or another topic that interests you. Write it in the center of a piece of paper and then try clustering. Keep writing down associations until you have filled most of the page.

1. heroes   4. inspiration

2. holidays   5. a dream

3. food   6. movies

PART D Asking Questions

Many writers get ideas about a subject by asking questions and trying to answer them. This section describes two ways of doing this.

The Reporter's Six Questions

Newspaper reporters often answer six basic questions at the beginning of an article: **Who? What? Where? When? Why? How?** Here is the way one student used these questions to explore the general subject of *sports* assigned by his instructor:

Who?	Players, basketball and football players, coaches, fans. Violence—I'm tired of that subject. Loyal crazy screaming fans—Giants fans.
What?	Excitement. Stadium on the day of a game. Tailgate parties. Cookouts. Incredible spreads—Italian families with peppers, stuff to spread on sandwiches. All-day partying. Radios, TVs, grills, Giants caps.
Where?	Giants Stadium parking lot. People gather in certain areas—meet me in 10-B. Stadiums all over the country, same thing. People party on tailgates, in cars, on cars, plastic chairs, blankets.
When?	People arrive early morning—cook breakfast, lunch. After the game, many stay on in parking lot, talking, drinking beer. Year after year they come back.
Why?	Big social occasion, emotional outlet.
How?	They come early to get space. Some stadiums now rent parking spaces. Some families pass on season tickets in their wills!

Notice the way this writer uses the questions to focus his ideas about tailgate parties at Giants Stadium. He has already come up with many interesting details for a good paper.

Ask Your Own Questions

If the reporter's six questions seem too confining, just ask the questions *you* want answered about a subject. Let each answer suggest the next question.

Here is how one student responded to the subject *a career that interests you* (she chose nursing):

TEACHING TIP
Career planning intrigues most students. You might have them explore a field of interest on **http://stats .bls.gov/oco/** and write about their findings. Alert them to "Career and Job Search Resources" on the *Evergreen* Online Study Center.

What do I know about nursing? I know that hospitals never seem to have enough nurses, so many jobs must be available. Nurses work hard, but their work seems interesting, exciting. The pay is good. Nurses also help people, which is important to me.

What would I like to know? What kind of education and training do nurses need? Is it better to work in a hospital, clinic, doctor's office, school, nursing home? I think nurses specialize in certain areas, like ER medicine or pediatrics. I'd like to know how they pick and how they get specialized training.

Where can I get more information? A friend of my mom's is a nurse in the intensive care unit at Mt. Sinai. I could interview her. I could speak with the career counselor on campus. Kendra told me to check out a great U.S. government web site on careers, **http://stats.bls.gov/oco/**.

What would I like to focus on? Well, I'd like to know more about the real-life experience of being a nurse and the specific knowledge and skills nurses need. What are the rewards and drawbacks of a nursing career?

What is my angle or point? I want to give readers (and myself!) a sense of what it means to be a good nurse and how to prepare for a successful career. I think readers would be interested in practical tips about the education, choices, and what to do to become a nurse.

Who is my audience? I would like to write for people who might be considering nursing as a career.

PRACTICE 5

Answer the reporter's six questions on one of the following topics or on a topic of your own choice.

1. career goals
2. sports
3. stress among students
4. music
5. family get-togethers
6. neighbors/neighborhood

PRACTICE 6

Ask and answer at least five questions of your own about one of the topics in Practice 5. Use these questions if you wish: What do I know about this subject? What would I like to know? Where can I find answers to my questions? What would I like to focus on? What is my point of view about this subject? Who is my audience?

PART E Keeping a Journal

TEACHING TIP
Ask students who are already in the habit of keeping a journal to share with the class the benefits of journaling.

Keeping a journal is an excellent way to practice your writing skills and discover ideas for further writing. Your journal is mostly for you—a private place where you record your experiences and your inner life; it is the place where, as one writer says, "I discover what I really think by writing it down."

You can keep a journal in a notebook or on a computer. If you prefer handwriting, get yourself an attractive notebook with 8½-by-11-inch paper. If you prefer to work on a computer, just open a "Journal" folder or keep a "Journal" disk. Then every morning or night, or several times a week, write for at least fifteen

ESL TIP
ESL students may expect instructors to correct grammatical errors in their journals. Some instructors correct one or two chronic error types; others decline, explaining that a journal's purpose is idea generation and fluency.

minutes in this journal. Don't just record the day's events. ("I went to the store. It rained. I came home.") Instead, write in detail about what most angered, moved, or amused you that day.

Write about what you really care about—motorcycles, loneliness, building web sites, working in a doughnut shop, family relationships, grades, ending or starting a relationship. You may be surprised by how much you know. Write, think, and write some more. Your journal is private, so don't worry about grammar or correctness. Instead, aim to capture your truth so exactly that someone reading your words might experience it too.

You might also carry a little 3-by-5-inch pad with you during the day for "fast sketches," jotting down things that catch your attention: a man playing drums in the street; a baby wearing a bib that reads *Spit Happens*; a compliment you receive at work; something your child just learned to do.

Every journal is unique—and usually private—but here is a sample journal entry to suggest possibilities. The student links a quotation he has just learned to a disturbing "lesson of love":

Apr. 11. Two weeks ago, our professor mentioned a famous quote: "It is better to have loved and lost than never to have loved at all." The words had no particular meaning for me. How wrong I was. Last Sunday I received some very distressing news that will change my life from now on.

My wife has asked me why I never notified any family members except my mother of the birth of our children. My reply has been an argument or an angry stare. Our daughter Angelica is now two months shy of her second birthday, and we were also blessed with the birth of a son, who is five months old. I don't know whether it was maturity or my conscience, but last Sunday I decided it was time to let past grievances be forgotten. Nothing on this green earth would shelter me from what I was to hear that day.

I went to my father's address, knocked on his door, but got no response. Nervous but excited, I knocked again. Silence. On leaving the building, I bumped into his neighbor and asked for the possible whereabouts of my father. I couldn't brace myself for the cold shock of hearing from him that my father had died. I was angry as well as saddened, for my father was a quiet and gentle man whose love of women, liquor, and good times exceeded the love of his son.

Yes, it would have been better to have loved my father as he was than never to have gotten the opportunity to love such a man. A lesson of love truly woke me up to the need to hold dearly the ones you care for and overcome unnecessary grudges. "I love you, Pop, and may you rest in peace. Qué Dios te guíe."

—Anthony Falu (Student)

The uses of a journal are limited only by your imagination. Here are some ideas:

▪ Write down your goals and dreams; then brainstorm steps you can take to make them reality. (Notice negative thoughts—"I can't do that. That will never work." Focus on positive thoughts—"Of course I can! If X can do it, so can I.")

■ Write about a problem you are having and creative ways in which you might solve it.

■ Analyze yourself as a student. What are your strengths and weaknesses? What can you do to build on the strengths and overcome the weaknesses?

■ What college course do you most enjoy? Why?

■ Who believes in you? Who seems not to believe in you?

■ If you could spend time with one famous person, living or dead, who would it be? Why?

■ List five things you would love to do if they didn't seem so crazy.

■ If you could change one thing about yourself, what would it be? What might you do to change it?

■ Use your journal as a place to think about material that you have read in a textbook, newspaper, magazine, or the Internet.

■ What news story most upset you or made you laugh out loud in the past month? Why?

TEACHING TIP
Explain to students that although they may prefer one prewriting technique, they should try using several techniques if they need to generate more ideas about a topic.

■ Write down facts that impress you—the average American child watches 200,000 acts of violence before graduating from high school! Analyzing that one fact could produce a good paper.

■ Read through the Quotation Bank at the end of this book, and copy your five favorite quotations into your journal.

PRACTICE 7

Get a notebook or set up your computer journal. Write for at least fifteen minutes three times a week.

At the end of each week, reread what you have written or typed. Underline sections or ideas you like and put a check mark next to subjects you might like to write more about.

PRACTICE 8

Choose one passage in your journal that you would like to rewrite and let others read. Mark the parts you like best. Now rewrite and polish the passage so you would be proud to show it to someone else.

 EXPLORING ONLINE

http://www.powa.org/discover/index.html
Practical advice on finding a subject you *want* to write about

**http://grammar.ccc.commnet.edu/grammar/composition/
brainstorm_freewrite.htm**
Tips and timed practice on using freewriting to get started

http://depts.gallaudet.edu/englishworks/writing/prewriting.html
Handy prewriting review chart from Gallaudet University

***Online Study Center*   college.hmco.com/pic/evergreen8e**
Visit the Online Study Center for *Evergreen* for more exercises and quizzes.

Writers' Workshop

Using Just One of Your Five Senses, Describe a Place

Readers of a finished paper can easily forget that they are reading the *end result* of someone else's writing process. The writer has already thought about audience and purpose, zoomed in on a subject, and prewritten to get ideas.

Here is one student's response to the following assignment: "Using just one of the five senses—smell, hearing, taste, touch, or sight—describe a special place." In your class or group, read the paper, aloud if possible. As you read, underline words or lines that strike you as especially well written or powerful.

> ### *Noises in My Village*
>
> Orlu, my village in Nigeria, has a population of about five hundred sounds. The sounds range from the clucking of the rooster in the morning to the rumbling of people getting ready for market. You hear the shrill cry of the widow and the squeaking of the rats. At the farm, two men start a fight over land and slam each other on the ground with great thuds. Water flows with a rushing sound from the rocks into the river, and the trees whisper themselves. People fill their earthen pots with water while children splash into the water after washing their clothes. From a distance, a lost goat bleats, "Meeee, meee." At the village square, bamboo drums sound, "Drooom, drooom." This signifies a curfew for the women. A young man tells how his friend bought a car that sounded "Vrooom, vrooom." At dusk people return from the market. One woman shouts at the top of her voice, "I forgot my palm oil keg!" and rushes to get it. After supper children gather at the village square. They clap their hands and listen to folk tales. From distance, the town crier announces the arrival of the new moon.
>
> —Chinwe Okorie (Student)

1. How effective is Ms. Okorie's paper?

   ____Y____ Good topic for a college audience?   ____Y____ Clear main idea?

   ____Y____ Rich supporting details?   ____Y____ Logical organization?

2. Does the first sentence make you want to read on? Why or why not?
   Yes. "Population of five hundred sounds" is interesting.
3. Which of the five senses does the writer emphasize? What words reveal this?
   hearing, sounds
4. Discuss your underlinings with the group or class. Try to explain why a particular word or sentence is effective. For instance, the fourth sentence contains such precise words that we can almost hear the two men "*slam* each other *on the ground* with great *thuds.*"

18

5. Would you suggest that the writer make any improvements? For instance, does the word *cluck* accurately describe the sound roosters make?

6. Last, proofread for grammar, spelling, and omitted words. Do you spot any error patterns (the same type of error made two or more times) that this student should watch out for? Yes, 2 omitted words.

> Of her prewriting process, Chinwe Okorie writes: "I decided to write about my village in Africa because I thought my American classmates (my audience) would find that more interesting than the local neighborhood. This paper also taught me the importance of brainstorming. I filled two whole pages with my brainstorming list, and then it was easy to pick the best details."

GROUP WORK

Imagine that you have been given this assignment: *Using just one of the five senses, describe a special place.* Your audience will be your college writing class. Working as a group, plan a paper and prewrite. First, choose a place that your group will describe; if it is a place on campus, your instructor might even want you to go there. Second, decide whether you will emphasize sound, smell, taste, touch, or sight. Choose someone to write down the group's ideas, and then brainstorm. List as many sounds (or smells, etc.) as your group can think of. Fill at least one page. Now read back the list and put a check next to the best details; does your group agree or disagree about which ones are best?

You are well on your way to an excellent paper. Each group member can now complete the assignment, based on the list. If necessary, prewrite again for more details.

WRITING AND REVISING IDEAS

1. Using one of your five senses, describe a place. You might use a first sentence like this:

   _____ has a population of about five hundred _____.
       (place)   (smells, tastes, etc.)

2. List unusual experiences you have had that your classmates and professor might like to read about (a job, time in another country, and so on). Choose one of these and prewrite; use the prewriting method of your choice and fill at least a page with ideas.

Discovering the Paragraph

3

The Process of Writing Paragraphs

This chapter will guide you step by step from examining basic paragraphs to writing them. The paragraph makes a good learning model because it is short yet contains many of the elements found in longer compositions. Therefore, you easily can transfer the skills you gain by writing paragraphs to longer essays, reports, and letters.

In this chapter, you will first look at finished paragraphs and then move through the process of writing paragraphs of your own.

PART A Defining and Looking at the Paragraph

A **paragraph** is a group of related sentences that develops one main idea. Although there is no definite length for a paragraph, it is often from five to twelve sentences long. A paragraph usually occurs with other paragraphs in a longer piece of writing—an essay, an article, or a letter, for example. Before studying longer compositions, however, we will look at single paragraphs.

A paragraph looks like this on the page:

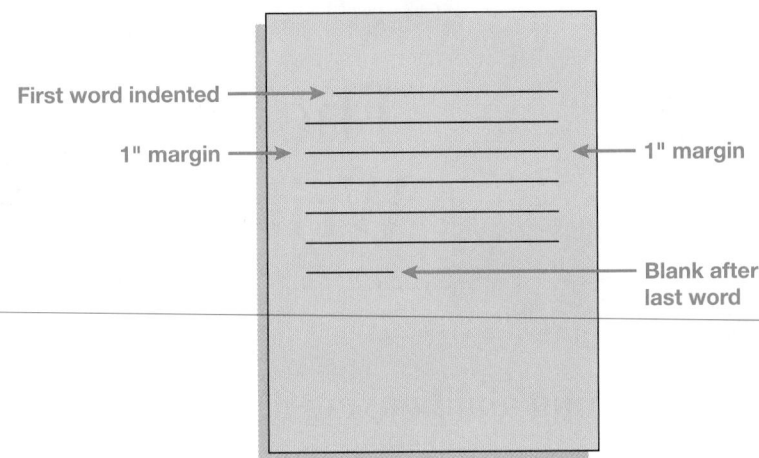

- Clearly **indent** the first word of every paragraph about 1 inch (five spaces on the computer).

- Extend every line of a paragraph as close to the right-hand margin as possible.

- However, if the last word of the paragraph comes before the end of the line, leave the rest of the line blank.

Topic Sentence and Body

Most paragraphs contain one main idea to which all the sentences relate.

The **topic sentence** states this main idea.

The **body** of the paragraph develops and supports this main idea with particular facts, details, and examples:

> I allow the spiders the run of the house. I figure that any predator that hopes to make a living on whatever smaller creatures might blunder into a four-inch-square bit of space in the corner of the bathroom where the tub meets the floor needs every bit of my support. They catch flies and even field crickets in those webs. Large spiders in barns have been known to trap, wrap, and suck hummingbirds, but there's no danger of that here. I tolerate the webs, only occasionally sweeping away the very dirtiest of them after the spider itself has scrambled to safety. I'm always leaving a bath towel draped over the tub so that the big, haired spiders, who are constantly getting trapped by the tub's smooth sides, can use its rough surface as an exit ramp. Inside the house the spiders have only given me one mild surprise. I washed some dishes and set them to dry over a plastic drainer. Then I wanted a cup of coffee, so I picked from the drainer my mug, which was still warm from the hot rinse water, and across the rim of the mug, strand after strand, was a spider web.
>
> —Annie Dillard, *Pilgrim at Tinker Creek*

■ The first sentence of Dillard's paragraph is the **topic sentence.** It states the main idea of the paragraph: that *the spiders are allowed the run of the house.*

■ The rest of the paragraph, the **body,** fully explains and supports this statement. The writer first gives a reason for her attitude toward spiders and then gives particular examples of her tolerance of spiders.

TEACHING TIP
Ask students how paragraphs help the reader follow the writer's ideas. You might bring in a 3- to 5-paragraph passage reformatted as one long paragraph (see the *Evergreen Online Teaching Center* for printable examples).

The topic sentence is more *general* than the other sentences in the paragraph. The other sentences in the paragraph provide specific information relating to the topic sentence. Because the topic sentence tells what the entire paragraph is about, *it is usually the first sentence,* as in the example. Sometimes the topic sentence occurs elsewhere in the paragraph, for example, as the sentence after an introduction or as the last sentence. Some paragraphs contain only an implied topic sentence but no stated topic sentence at all.

As you develop your writing skills, however, it is a good idea to write paragraphs that *begin* with the topic sentence. Once you have mastered this pattern, you can try variations.

PRACTICE 1

Find and underline the **topic sentence** in each of the following paragraphs. Look for the sentence that states the **main idea** of the entire paragraph. Be careful: the topic sentence is not always the first sentence.

Paragraph 1

The summer picnic gave ladies a chance to show off their baking hands. On the barbecue pit, chickens and spareribs sputtered in their own fat and in a sauce whose recipe was guarded in the family like a scandalous affair. However, every true baking artist could reveal her prize to the delight and criticism of the town. Orange sponge cakes and dark brown mounds dripping Hershey's chocolate stood layer to layer with ice-white coconuts and light brown caramels. Pound cakes sagged with their buttery weight and small children could no more resist licking the icings than their mothers could avoid slapping the sticky fingers.

—Maya Angelou, *I Know Why the Caged Bird Sings*

Paragraph 2

In the mid-1980s, 340,000 people in the United States owned cell phones. Today, that number is well over 100 million. Worldwide, more than a billion people have gone wireless, and most of them have no idea that inside the sleek, plastic exterior of every cell phone sits a package of electronics laden with hazardous substances called persistent, bioaccumulative and toxic chemicals (PBTs). When cell users toss their phones into the trash, PBTs like lead, arsenic, and cadmium leak into the land, air, and water, eventually entering the tissues of animals and humans. Every year, 130 million cell phones—complete with batteries and chargers—are pitched into the garbage instead of being recycled or disposed of in a safe manner. As the popularity of cellular phones soars, growing numbers of cell users are creating growing piles of toxic trash.

—Adapted from Rene Ebersole,
"Recycle Cell Phones, Reduce Toxic Trash," *National Wildlife*

Paragraph 3

Eating sugar can be worse than eating nothing. Refined sugar provides only empty calories. It contributes none of the protein, fat, vitamins, or minerals needed for its own metabolism in the body, so these nutrients must be obtained elsewhere. Sugar tends to replace nourishing food in the diet. It is a thief that robs us of nutrients.

A dietary emphasis on sugar can deplete the body of nutrients. If adequate nutrients are not supplied by the diet—and they tend not to be in a sugar-rich diet—they must be leached from other body tissues before sugar can be metabolized. For this reason, a U.S. Senate committee labeled sugar as an "antinutrient."

—Janice Fillip, "The Sweet Thief," *Medical Self-Care*

PRACTICE 2

Each group of sentences below could be unscrambled and written as a paragraph. Circle the letter of the **topic sentence** in each group of sentences. Remember: The topic sentence should state the main idea of the entire paragraph and should be general enough to include all the ideas in the body.

ESL TIP
Because ways of organizing ideas and language vary from culture to culture, Practice 2 is very important. This practice works well in class.

EXAMPLE

    a. Rubies were supposed to stimulate circulation and restore lost vitality.

    b. Clear quartz was believed to promote sweet sleep and good dreams.

    (c.) For centuries, minerals and precious stones were thought to possess healing powers.

    d. Amethysts were thought to prevent drunkenness.

(Sentence c includes the ideas in all the other sentences.)

1. a. The iPod allows people to download—legally—only the songs they want for 99 cents each, instead of entire CDs.

    b. The technologically advanced iPod stores songs in digital format, so the sound is crystal-clear.

    c. Customers are attracted by the modern design and cool colors of the iPod.

    d. Despite its small size, the iPod holds thousands of songs, making an individual's entire music collection easily portable.

    e. Because the iPod provides easy access to different types of music, many people claim it has expanded their musical tastes.

    (f.) By addressing the real needs of music lovers, the iPod digital player has quickly dominated the market.

2. a. Invited to join the space program, she trained as an astronaut and flew on the space shuttle *Endeavor* in 1992.

    b. The young Dr. Jemison headed to West Africa, where she worked in the Peace Corps for two years.

    c. Though a childhood teacher urged her to be a nurse, Mae Jemison knew she wanted to be a scientist and doctor.

    d. After eight years at NASA, she became a professor at Dartmouth College and started a company to help poor countries use solar energy.

    (e.) The life of Dr. Mae Jemison, the first African American female astronaut, is characterized by daring achievements and a strong desire to give back.

    f. A fine student, Jemison entered Stanford University at sixteen and later earned her M.D. degree from Cornell in 1981.

3. a. The left side of the human brain controls spoken and written language.

   b. The right side, on the other hand, seems to control artistic, musical, and spatial skills.

   c. Emotion is also thought to be controlled by the right hemisphere.

   d. The human brain has two distinct halves, or hemispheres, and in most people, each one controls different functions.

   e. Logical reasoning and mathematics are left-brain skills.

   f. Interestingly, the left brain controls the right hand, and vice versa.

4. a. As a Bronx Community College student, Oscar Hijuelos showed his gift for writing.

   b. He researched the Cuban music scene of New York in the '50s for his second novel, *Mambo Kings Play Songs of Love.*

   c. After one year at Bronx Community, he transferred to City College, earning his B.A. in creative writing.

   d. Step by step, Oscar Hijuelos, the son of Cuban immigrants, has become a very successful writer.

   e. While crafting his first two books, Hijuelos earned money selling shoes and writing ad copy for subway cars.

   f. After *Mambo Kings* won the Pulitzer Prize and was made into a film, Hijuelos wrote three more novels and inspired many young writers.

5. a. Male and female insects are attracted to each other by visual, auditory, and chemical means.

   b. Through its chirping call, the male cricket attracts a mate and drives other males out of its territory.

   c. Butterflies attract by sight, and their brightly colored wings play an important role in courtship.

   d. Some female insects, flies among them, release chemicals called *pheromones* that attract males of the species.

6. a. Serious swimmers breast-stroked up and down the pool's blue length, breathing rhythmically, paying no attention to anyone.

   b. Every summer, the municipal pool became the center of activity.

   c. Older children took turns diving or belly flopping off the springy diving board.

   d. Toddlers in little hats splashed in shallow water under their mothers' watchful gaze.

   e. Teenagers lounged in the sun, talking loudly, checking their cell phones, and teasing each other.

7. a. Albert Einstein, whose scientific genius awed the world, did not speak until he was four and could not read until he was nine.

   b. Inventor Thomas Edison had such severe problems reading, writing, and spelling that he was called "defective from birth," taken out of school, and taught at home.

    c. Many famous people have suffered from learning disabilities.

    d. Actor Tom Cruise battles dyslexia, yet he has mastered the scripts of many movies and won awards for his performances.

8. a. Believe it or not, the first contact lens was drawn by Leonardo da Vinci in 1508.

    b. However, not until 1877 was the first thick glass contact actually made by a Swiss doctor.

    c. The journey of contact lenses from an idea to a comfortable, safe reality took nearly five hundred years.

    d. In 1948, smaller, more comfortable plastic lenses were introduced to enthusiastic American eyeglass wearers.

    e. These early glass lenses were enormous, covering the whites of the eyes.

    f. Today, contact lens wearers can choose ultra-thin, colored, or even disposable lenses.

PART B Narrowing the Topic and Writing the Topic Sentence

A writer can arrive at the goal—a finished paragraph—in several ways. However, before writing a paragraph, most writers go through a process that includes these important steps:

1. Narrowing the topic

2. Writing the topic sentence

3. Generating ideas for the body

4. Selecting and dropping ideas

5. Arranging ideas in a plan or an outline

The rest of this chapter will explain these steps and guide you through the process of writing basic paragraphs.

Narrowing the Topic

As a student, you may be assigned broad writing topics by your instructor—success, cheating in schools, a description of a person. Your instructor is giving you the chance to cut the topic down to size and choose one aspect of the topic *that interests you.*

Suppose, for example, that your instructor gives this assignment: "Write a paragraph describing a person you know." The challenge is to pick someone you would *like* to write about, someone who interests you and also would probably interest your readers.

Thinking about your *audience* and *purpose* may help you narrow the topic. In this case, your audience probably will be your instructor and classmates; your purpose is to inform or perhaps to entertain them by describing a person you want to write about.

Many writers find it useful at this point—on paper or on the computer—to brainstorm, freewrite, or ask themselves questions: "What person do I love or hate or admire? Is there a family member I would enjoy writing about? Who is the funniest, most unusual, or most talented person I know?"

Let's suppose you choose Pete, an unusual person and one about whom you have something to say. But Pete is still too broad a subject for one paragraph; you could probably write pages and pages about him. To narrow the topic further, you might ask yourself, "What is unusual about him? What might interest others?" Pete's room is the messiest place you have ever seen; in fact, Pete's whole life is sloppy, and you decide that you could write a good paragraph about that. You have now narrowed the topic to just one of Pete's qualities: *his sloppiness.*

Writing the Topic Sentence

The next important step is to state your topic clearly *in sentence form.* Writing the topic sentence helps you further narrow your topic by forcing you to make a statement about it. The simplest possible topic sentence about Pete might read *Pete is sloppy,* but you might wish to strengthen it by saying, for instance, *Pete's sloppiness is a terrible habit.*

Writing a good topic sentence is an important step toward an effective paragraph because the topic sentence controls the direction and scope of the body. A topic sentence should have a clear *controlling idea* and should be a *complete sentence.*

You can think of the topic sentence as having two parts, a **topic** and a **controlling idea.** The controlling idea states the writer's point of view or attitude about the topic.

	topic	controlling idea
Topic sentence:	Pete's sloppiness	is a terrible habit.

The controlling idea helps you focus on just one aspect or point. Here are three possible topic sentences about the topic *a memorable job.*

1. My job in the complaint department taught me how to calm down angry people.

2. Two years in the complaint department persuaded me to become an assistant manager.

3. Working in the complaint department persuaded me to become a veterinarian.

■ These topic sentences all explore the same topic—working in a complaint department—but each controlling idea is different. The controlling idea in 1 is *taught me how to calm down angry people.*

■ What is the controlling idea in 2?

persuaded me to become an assistant *manager*
_____

What is the controlling idea in 3?

persuaded me to become a veterinarian
_____

■ Notice the way in which the controlling idea lets the reader know what the paragraph will be about. There are many possible topic sentences for any topic, depending on the writer's interests and point of view. If you were assigned the topic *a memorable job,* what would your topic sentence be?

_____

_____

PRACTICE 3

Read each topic sentence below. Circle the topic and underline the controlling idea.

1. (A low-fat diet) provides many health benefits.

2. (Animal Planet) is both entertaining and educational.

3. (Our football coach) works to build players' self-esteem.

4. (This campus) offers many peaceful places where students can relax.

5. (My cousin's truck) looks like something out of *Star Wars.*

As a rule, the more specific and limited your topic and controlling idea, the better the paragraph; in other words, your topic sentence should not be so broad that it cannot be developed in one paragraph. Which of these topic sentences do you think will produce the best paragraphs?

> 4. Five wet, bug-filled days at Camp Nirvana made me a fan of the great indoors.
>
> 5. This town has problems.
>
> 6. Road rage is on the rise for three reasons.

■ Topic sentences 4 and 6 are both specific enough to write a good paragraph about. In each, the topic sentence is carefully worded to suggest clearly what ideas will follow. From topic sentence 4, what do you expect the paragraph to include?

The paragraph will probably discuss how weather and insects ruined the week.
_____

■ What do you expect paragraph 6 to include?

The paragraph will probably discuss three reasons why road rage is on the rise.
_____

■ Topic sentence 5, on the other hand, is so broad that a paragraph could include almost anything. Just what problems does the town have? Strained relations between police and the community? Litter in public parks? Termites? The writer needs to rewrite the controlling idea, focusing on just one problem for an effective paragraph.

TEACHING TIP
An extremely common problem among basic writers is awkwardly announcing the subject of their paper with "This paper will be about . . ." Emphasize the role of the topic sentence as stating a point of view about the subject, not announcing it.

The topic sentence also must be a **complete sentence.** It must contain a subject and a verb, and express a complete thought.* Do not confuse a topic with a topic sentence. For instance, *a celebrity I would like to meet* cannot be a topic sentence because it is not a sentence; however, it could be a title† because topics and titles need not be complete sentences. One possible topic sentence might read, *A celebrity I would like to meet is writer Julia Alvarez.*

Do not write *This paragraph will be about . . .* or *In this paper I will write about. . . .* Instead, craft your topic sentence carefully to focus the topic and let your reader know what the paragraph will contain. Make every word count.

PRACTICE 4

TEACHING TIP
Practice 4 works well as a small-group or full-class behavior.

Put a check beside each topic sentence that is focused enough to allow you to write a good paragraph. If a topic sentence is too broad, narrow the topic according to your own interests and write a new topic sentence with a clear controlling idea.

EXAMPLES ✓ Keeping a journal can improve a student's writing.

Rewrite: _____

_____ This paper will be about my family.

Rewrite: My brother Mark has a unique sense of humor. _____

1. ✓ Eugene's hot temper causes problems at work.

   Rewrite: _____

   _____

2. _____ This paragraph will discuss my two closest friends.

   Rewrite: My two closest friends are alike in three ways. _____

   _____

3. ✓ Learning a foreign language has several benefits.

   Rewrite: _____

   _____

4. _____ Child abuse is something to think about.

   Rewrite: Child abuse can be reduced through parenting classes. _____

   _____

---

* For practice in correcting fragments, see Chapter 26, "Avoiding Sentence Errors," Part B.

† For practice in writing titles, see Chapter 16, "The Introduction, the Conclusion, and the Title," Part C.

5. _✓_ Company officials should not read employees' e-mail.

Rewrite: _____

_____

PRACTICE 5

Here is a list of broad topics. Choose three that interest you from this list or from your own list in Chapter 1, page 6. Narrow each topic, choose your controlling idea, and write a topic sentence focused enough to write a good paragraph about. Make sure that each topic sentence has a clear controlling idea and is a complete sentence.

TEACHING AND ESL TIP
Practice 5 is difficult for some students and might be best done in small groups.

Overcoming fears   Insider's tour of your community

Popular music   Balancing work and play

Credit cards   A person you like or dislike

An act of cowardice or courage   A time when you were (or were not) in control

1. Narrowed topic: _Overcoming fear of flying_____

   Controlling idea: _Daryl boosted his career and calmed his nerves_____

   Topic sentence: _Overcoming his fear of flying boosted Daryl's career and_

   _calmed his nerves._____

2. Narrowed topic: _I dislike Tom_____

   Controlling idea: _his gossiping is destructive_____

   Topic sentence: _I dislike Tom because his gossiping is a destructive habit.__

3. Narrowed topic: _Lack of balance when I worked several jobs_____

   Controlling idea: _during this time I became less productive_____

   Topic sentence: _The more hours a week I worked in part-time jobs, the less_

   _productive I was at school._____

PRACTICE 6

Many writers adjust the topic sentence after they have finished drafting the paragraph. In a group of three or four classmates, study the body of each of these paragraphs to find the main, or controlling, idea. Then, working together, write the most exact and interesting topic sentence you can for each paragraph.

Paragraph 1

Animals occasionally rescue human beings.

A pet parrot recently saved his owner's life. Harry Becker was watching TV in his living room when he suddenly slumped over with a heart attack. The parrot screamed loudly until Mr. Becker's wife awoke and called 911. In another reported case of animal rescue, a family cat saved six-week-old Stacey Rogers. When the cat heard the baby gasping for breath in her crib, it ran howling to alert the baby's mother, who called paramedics. Even more surprising was an event reported in newspapers around the world. In 1996 in a Chicago zoo, a female gorilla rushed to save a three-year-old boy who fell accidentally into the gorilla enclosure. Still carrying her own baby on her back, the 150-pound gorilla gently picked up the unconscious child and carried him to the cage door to be rescued. Though we might not understand why, animals sometimes help and even save us.

Paragraph 2

Digital photography offers the photographer four advantages.

The first advantage of a digital photography is easier picture-taking. Gone are the days of toting film to the store to be processed and waiting to see how the pictures turn out. The digital photographer can see instantly whether a shot is good and then snap more pictures if necessary. Another advantage of digital photography is quick and easy processing. At home on a computer, the digital photographer can size or retouch his or her images, print the good ones, or e-mail them to family and friends. Third, with no film or developing costs, digital photography saves money. The photographer can take hundreds of shots and print only the best. A final advantage is the tiny size and weight of digital cameras. Therefore, when an irresistible photo opportunity arises, the digital photographer is more likely to have a camera handy, tucked in a pocket or handbag. Most people treasure their photographs, and digital cameras offer advantages that can help capture memories with more ease and less frustration.

PART C Generating Ideas for the Body

ESL TIP
Many ESL and other students tend to overuse generalizations. Try the acronym FIRE (fact, incident, reason/result, explanation) to remind them to be specific.

One good way to generate ideas for the body of a paragraph is **brainstorming**—freely jotting on paper or the computer anything that relates to your topic sentence: facts, details, examples, little stories. This step might take just a few minutes, but it is one of the most important elements of the writing process. Brainstorming can provide you with specific ideas to support your topic sentence. Later you can choose from these ideas as you compose your paragraph.

Here, for example, is a possible brainstorm list for the topic sentence *Pete's sloppiness is a terrible habit:*

1. His apartment is full of dirty clothes, books, candy wrappers

2. His favorite candy—M&Ms

TEACHING TIP
List on the board different kinds of supporting detail (facts, examples, anecdotes, expert opinions, testimonials, descriptive details, reasons, effects, etc.). Encourage students to consider all of these possibilities as they are brainstorming ideas for the body of their paragraph.

3. He is often a latecomer or a no-show

4. He jots time-and-place information for dates and appointments on scraps of paper that are soon forgotten

5. Stacks of old newspapers sit on chair seats

6. Socks are on the lampshades

7. Papers for classes are wrinkled and carelessly scrawled

8. I met Pete for the first time in math class

9. His sister is just the opposite, very neat

10. ~~Always late for classes, out of breath~~

11. He is one messy person

12. Papers are stained with coffee or M&Ms

Instead of brainstorming, some writers freewrite or ask themselves questions to generate ideas for their paragraphs. Some like to perform this step on paper, whereas others use a computer. Do what works best for you. The key is to write down lots of ideas during prewriting. If you need more practice in any of these methods, reread Chapter 2, "Prewriting to Generate Ideas."

PRACTICE 7

Now choose the topic from Practice 5 that most interests you. Write your narrowed topic, controlling idea, and topic sentence here.

Narrowed topic: _____

Controlling idea: _____

Topic sentence: _____

_____

Next, brainstorm. On paper or on the computer, write anything that comes to you about your topic sentence. Just let your ideas pour out. Try to fill at least one page.

PART D Selecting and Dropping Ideas

TEACHING TIP
Create a paragraph with the class, honing a topic sentence, brainstorming, and selecting ideas for the body.

Next, simply read over what you have written, **selecting** those ideas that relate to and support the topic sentence and **dropping** those that do not. That is, keep the facts, examples, or little stories that provide specific information about your topic sentence. Drop ideas that just **repeat** the topic sentence but that add nothing new to the paragraph.

If you are not sure which ideas to select or drop, underline the **key word(s)** of the topic sentence, the ones that indicate the real point of your paragraph. Then make sure that the ideas that you select are related to those key words.

Here again is the brainstorm list for the topic sentence *Pete's sloppiness is a terrible habit*. The key word in the topic sentence is *sloppiness*. Which ideas would you keep? Why? Which would you drop? Why?

1. His apartment is full of dirty clothes, books, candy wrappers

2. His favorite candy—M&Ms

3. He is often a latecomer or a no-show

4. He jots time-and-place information for dates and appointments on scraps of paper that are soon forgotten

5. Stacks of old newspapers sit on chair seats

6. Socks are on the lampshades

7. Papers for classes are wrinkled and carelessly scrawled

8. I met Pete for the first time in math class

9. His sister is just the opposite, very neat

10. Always late for classes, out of breath

11. He is one messy person

12. Papers are stained with coffee or M&Ms

You probably dropped ideas 2, 8, and 9 because they do not relate to the topic—Pete's sloppiness. You should also have dropped idea 11 because it merely repeats the topic sentence.

PRACTICE 8

Read through your own brainstorm list from Practice 7. Select the ideas that relate to your topic sentence and drop those that do not. In addition, drop any ideas that just repeat your topic sentence. Be prepared to explain why you drop or keep each idea.

PART E   Arranging Ideas in a Plan or an Outline

TEACHING TIP
Organizing ideas is a key skill that many students lack. You might illustrate the process by "thinking aloud" as you reason out the best order of ideas for a paragraph. That is, model the mental process that writers go through when they plan.

After you have selected the ideas you wish to include in your paragraph, you can begin to make a **plan** or an **outline**. A plan briefly lists and arranges the ideas you wish to present in your paragraph. An outline does the same thing a bit more formally, but in an outline, letters or numbers indicate the main groupings of ideas.

First, group together ideas that have something in common, that are related or alike in some way. Then order your ideas by choosing which one you want to present first, which one second, and so on.

Below is a plan for a paragraph about Pete's sloppiness:

Topic sentence: Pete's sloppiness is a terrible habit.

His apartment is full of dirty clothes, books, candy wrappers

Stacks of old newspapers sit on chair seats

Socks are on the lampshades

He jots time-and-place information for dates and appointments on scraps of paper that are soon forgotten

He is often a latecomer or a no-show

Always late for classes, out of breath

Papers for classes wrinkled and carelessly scrawled

Papers stained with coffee or M&Ms

■ Do you see the logic in this arrangement? How are the ideas in each group above related? Each group includes examples of Pete's sloppiness in one area of his life: home, time management, coursework.

TEACHING TIP
Students often resist outlining, and their papers suffer for it. Discuss with them the pitfalls of skipping outlining (e.g., underdevelopment, rambling, etc.). Outlining is covered in more depth in Chapter 14, "The Process of Writing an Essay."

■ Does it make sense to discuss Pete's apartment first, his lateness second, and his written work third? Why? Yes. The order goes from the personal to the social, which means it goes from what he does in his house to what he does when he's outside his house.

■ Once you have finished arranging ideas, you should have a clear **plan** from which to write your paragraph.*

PRACTICE 9

On paper or on the computer, arrange the ideas from your brainstorm list according to some plan or outline. First, group together related ideas; then decide which ideas will come first, which second, and so on.

Keep in mind that there is more than one way to group ideas. Think about what you want to say; then group ideas according to what your point is.

---

* For more work on order, see Chapter 4, "Achieving Coherence," Part A.

PART F Writing and Revising the Paragraph

Writing the First Draft

The first draft should contain all the ideas you have decided to use in the order you have chosen in your plan. Be sure to start with your topic sentence. Try to write the best, most interesting, or most amusing paragraph you can, but avoid getting stuck on any one word, sentence, or idea. If you are unsure about something, put a check in the margin and come back to it later. Writing on every other line or double-spacing if you write on the computer will leave room for later corrections.

Once you have included all the ideas from your plan, think about adding a concluding sentence that summarizes your main point or adds a final idea. Not all paragraphs need concluding sentences. For example, if you are telling a story, the paragraph can end when the story does. Write a concluding sentence only if it will help to bring your thoughts to an end for your reader.

If possible, once you have finished the first draft, set the paper aside for several hours or several days.

PRACTICE 10

Write a first draft of the paragraph you have been working on.

Revising

TEACHING TIP
Explain the difference between *revising* and *proofreading*.

Revising means rethinking and rewriting your first draft and then making whatever changes, additions, or corrections are necessary to improve the paragraph. You may cross out and rewrite words or entire sentences. You may add, drop, or rearrange details.

As you revise, keep the *reader* in mind. Ask yourself these questions:

■ Is my topic sentence clear?

■ Can a reader understand and follow my ideas?

■ Does the paragraph follow a logical order and guide the reader from point to point?

■ Will the paragraph keep the reader interested?

ESL TIP
Urge your ESL students to use English-only reference materials as they write and revise in English. Using bilingual dictionaries may result in incorrect word choice.

In addition, check your paragraph for adequate support and unity, characteristics that we'll consider in the following pages.

Revising for Support

As you revise, make sure your paragraph contains excellent **support**—that is, specific facts, details, and examples that fully explain your topic sentence.

Be careful, too, that you have not simply repeated ideas—especially the topic sentence. Even if they are in different words, repeated ideas only make the reader suspect that your paragraph is padded and that you do not have enough facts and details to support your main idea properly.

Which of the following paragraphs contains the most convincing support?

Paragraph 1

(1) By making study time a priority every week, I raised my grade-point average from 2.4 to 3.3 in one year. (2) I have a really busy life, so I never studied enough. (3) When my average went down, I knew I had to do something. (4) I made myself study more often. (5) Because I made study time more important, my average went from C to B. (6) I also picked prime times to study, and this made a difference. (7) So sticking to my schedule definitely paid off.

Paragraph 2

(1) By making study time a priority every week, I raised my grade-point average from 2.4 to 3.3 in one year. (2) I work 15 hours a week at the Gap while taking four courses a semester, so finding study time is hard. (3) I used to grab 15 minutes here or 20 there, usually during breaks at work, on the subway to and from school, or right before bedtime. (4) When my average slipped to a C, I knew I had to take action and make my college education count. (5) I decided to make a real commitment to regular, high-quality study time. (6) I scheduled a two-hour study block at least four days a week, either at the library with a classmate from 12:00 to 2:00 P.M. or at home from 7:00 to 9:00 P.M. (7) It was really tough to resist the temptation to go out with friends, gab on the phone, or relax in front of the TV, but I scheduled my study times like appointments I had to keep. (8) As a result, I studied not only regularly but also for longer periods of time. (9) By increasing my study time this way, I began to understand the material much better. (10) In addition, I studied at times when I was more alert—not 10:00 or 11:00 P.M., when I was too tired to concentrate. (11) Soon I was earning more As and Bs, so sticking to my schedule definitely paid off.

TEACHING TIP
Emphasize to students the importance of including adequate supporting details in paragraphs. The number and quality of supporting details often make the difference between a mediocre and an excellent paragraph.

■ *Paragraph 1* contains general statements but little specific information to support the topic sentence.

■ *Paragraph 1* also contains needless repetition. What is the number of the sentence or sentences that just repeat the topic sentence? Sentence 5

■ *Paragraph 2*, however, supports the topic sentence with specific details and examples: *15 hours at the Gap, four courses, two-hour study block four days a week, library with a classmate from 12 to 2 P.M.* What other specific support does it give?

Used to grab 15 minutes here, 20 there, breaks at work, on the subway,

temptation to go out with friends, gab on the phone, relax with TV, scheduled

study times like appointments, times when more alert—not 10 or 11 P.M., soon

earning more As and Bs.

PRACTICE 11

Check the following paragraphs for adequate support. As you read each one, decide which places need more or better support—specific facts, details, and examples. Then rewrite the paragraphs, inventing facts and details whenever necessary and dropping repetitious words and sentences.

Paragraph 1

(1) My uncle can always be counted on when the family faces hardship. (2) Last year, when my mother was very ill, he was there, ready to help in every way. (3) He never has to be called twice. (4) When my father became seriously depressed, my uncle's caring made a difference. (5) Everyone respects him for his willingness to be a real "family man." (6) He is always there for us.

Paragraph 2

(1) Lending money to a friend can have negative consequences. (2) For example, Ashley, a student at Tornado Community College, agreed to lend $200 to her best friend, Jan. (3) This was a bad decision even though Ashley meant well. (4) The results of this loan were surprising and negative for Ashley, for Jan, and for the friendship. (5) Both women felt bad about it but in different ways. (6) Yes, lending money to a friend can have very negative consequences, like anger and hurt.

Paragraph 3

(1) Many television talk shows don't really present a discussion of ideas. (2) Some people who appear on these shows don't know what they are talking about; they just like to sound off about something. (3) I don't like these shows at all. (4) Guests shout their opinions out loud but never give any proof for what they say. (5) Guests sometimes expose their most intimate personal and family problems before millions of viewers—I feel embarrassed. (6) I have even heard hosts insult their guests and guests insult them back. (7) Why do people watch this junk? (8) You never learn anything from these dumb shows.

Revising for Unity

TEACHING TIP
Stress to students that outlining first and then using the outline as a guide while writing will help prevent problems with unity.

It is sometimes easy, in the process of writing, to drift away from the topic under discussion. Guard against doing so by checking your paragraph for unity; that is, make sure the topic sentence, every sentence in the body, and the concluding sentence all relate to one main idea.*

This paragraph lacks unity:

(1) A rival to the Barbie doll aims to provide children with more realistic role models. (2) Named Get Real Girls by their creator, Julz Chavez, the new dolls have pretty faces like Barbie but more realistic measurements and flat, not "high-heeled," feet. (3) Each doll plays a different sport, like soccer or basketball, and comes with realistic equipment. (4) For example, the scuba diving doll has fins, mask, spear gun, and oxygen tank. (5) Chavez patterned the dolls after her real-life friends, so each one is a different ethnicity—Caucasian, African American, Latina, or Asian. (6) Chavez grew up in California with ten brothers and sisters. (7) To inspire children to achieve, each doll has a "life story," including educational goals and personal interests. (9) Chavez hopes to answer complaints from parents all over the world that Barbie seems to care more about shopping and partying than fitness and education.

---

* For more work on revising, see Chapter 23, "Putting Your Revision Skills to Work."

▪ What is the number of the topic sentence in this paragraph?

Sentence 1

▪ Which sentence in the paragraph does not clearly relate to the topic sentence?

Sentence 6

This paragraph also lacks unity:

> (1) Quitting smoking was very difficult for me. (2) When I was thirteen, my friend Janice and I smoked in front of a mirror. (3) We practiced holding the cigarette in different ways and tried French inhaling, letting the smoke roll slowly out of our mouths and drawing it back through our noses. (4) I thought this move, when it didn't incite a fit of coughing, was particularly sexy. (5) At first I smoked only to give myself confidence on dates and at parties. (6) Soon, however, I was smoking all the time.

TEACHING TIP
To find sentences that disrupt unity, some students read backward, one sentence at a time, checking that each one relates directly to the idea in the topic sentence.

▪ Here the topic sentence itself, sentence 1, does not relate to the rest of the paragraph. The main idea in sentence 1, that quitting smoking was difficult, is not developed by the other sentences. Since the rest of the paragraph *is* unified, a more appropriate topic sentence might read, *As a teenager, I developed the bad habit of smoking.*

PRACTICE 12

Check the following paragraphs for unity. If a paragraph has unity, write U in the blank. If not, write the number of the sentence that does not belong in the paragraph.

TEACHING TIP
Practice 12 is fun to do in class.

Paragraph 1

_6_ (1) The first batch of one of the world's most popular soft drinks was mixed in a backyard kettle over a hundred years ago. (2) On May 6, 1886, Dr. John Styth Pemberton heated a mixture of melted sugar, water, coca leaves, kola nuts, and other ingredients. (3) He planned to make one of the home-brewed medical syrups so popular at that time. (4) However, this one tasted so good that Dr. Pemberton decided to sell it as a soda fountain drink for five cents a glass. (5) The first glass of this new drink was sold at Jacob's Pharmacy in Atlanta, Georgia. (6) Atlanta was and still is a wonderful place to live. (7) Pemberton's tasty invention, Coca-Cola, caught on. (8) Today, Coca-Cola is consumed by 140,000 people every minute.

Paragraph 2

_9_ (1) Technology enables people like the famous physicist Dr. Stephen Hawking to continue working despite serious physical disabilities. (2) For thirty-five years, Dr. Hawking has lived with Lou Gehrig's disease, which attacks the muscles, but his brilliant mind works perfectly. (3) He can no longer walk, speak, or feed himself. (4) Nevertheless, a high-tech wheelchair with computer attachments allows him to continue his research and stay in touch with friends and colleagues around the world. (5) His computer is hooked up full-time to the

Internet. (6) To speak, he chooses words displayed on the computer screen, and then an electronic voice machine pronounces each word. (7) A pressure-sensitive joystick even lets Dr. Hawking make his way through traffic. (8) In his home, infrared remote control operates doors, lights, and his personal entertainment center. (9) He had two children with his first wife, Jane. (10) Dr. Hawking continues to search for new ways to overcome his problems through technology.

Paragraph 3

   _5_   (1) Across the country, thousands of college students and others are attending or performing poetry at "poetry slams." (2) A poetry slam is a competitive event in which participants recite one original poem before an audience. (3) With words, rhymes, and dramatic skill as their only tools, these fast-talking bards have just three minutes to win over the audience. (4) After each performance, judges selected from the audience give a numerical score, usually from 1 to 10. (5) Gymnastics competitions are judged using a similar 10 point scoring system. (6) Although most slammers would love to win first prize, they say that poetry slams also are fun, boost their self-esteem, hone their English skills, and connect them with a community of people who "speak from the heart." (7) Poetry slams are gaining popularity as schools, arts organizations, and groups of young writers start poetry clubs or sponsor contests. (8) When Russell Simmons's show *Def Poetry Jam* became an HBO hit, the excitement spread worldwide.

Xavier Smith of Queensborough Community College, N.Y., wins the 2006 Intercollegiate Poetry Slam Finals.

EXPLORING ONLINE

Explore **http://www.poetryslam.com/**. Note the National Poetry Slam. Would you like to attend a poetry slam? Why or why not? What do you think is the reason so many young people attend slams?

Revising with Peer Feedback

You may wish to show or read your first draft to a respected friend. Ask this person to give an honest response, *not* to rewrite your work. Ask specific questions of your own or use this peer feedback sheet.

TEACHING TIP
For printable peer feedback sheets and rubrics for the paragraph, essay, and each rhetorical mode, see the *Evergreen* Online Teaching and Study Centers.

Peer Feedback Sheet

To _____ From _____ Date _____

1. What I like about this piece of writing is _____

_____

2. Your main points seems to be _____

_____

3. These particular words or lines struck me as powerful:

   Words or lines   I like them because

   _____   _____

   _____   _____

   _____   _____

4. Some things aren't clear to me. These lines or parts could be improved (meaning not clear, supporting points missing, order seems mixed up, writing not lively):

   Lines or parts   Need improving because

   _____   _____

   _____   _____

   _____   _____

5. The one change you could make that would make the biggest improvement

   in this piece of writing is _____

   _____

TEACHING AND ESL TIP
Make students aware of the wealth of additional help and practices available at the *Evergreen* Online Study Center. Alert nonnative writers to ESL Corner and to web sites like http://a4esl.org/.

Writing the Final Draft

When you are satisfied with your revisions, recopy your paper or print a fresh copy. If you are writing in class, the second draft will usually be the last one. Be sure to include all your corrections, writing neatly and legibly.

The first draft of the paragraph about Pete, showing the writer's changes, and the revised, final draft follow. Compare them.

First Draft with Revisions

Pete's sloppiness is a terrible habit. He lives by him-

carpeted

self in a <u>small</u> apartment ^with dirty clothes, books, and

candy wrappers. Stacks of papers cover the chair seats.

bake!

Socks are on the lampshades. When Pete makes a date or

an appointment, he may jot down the time and place on a

tucked into a pocket and

scrap of paper that is soon ^forgotten, or—more likely—

As a result,

he doesn't jot down the information at all. ^Pete often ar-

rives late, or he completely forgets to appear. His grades

because

have suffered, too, ^F̶ew instructors will put up with a stu-

ten minutes after class has begun   *wrinkled, scrawled*

dent who arrives out of breath and whose <u>messy</u> papers

punctuated with coffee stains and   *melted M&Ms.*

arrive (late of course) with <u>stains</u> ^on them. Pete's sloppi-

ness really is a terrible habit.

Final Draft

Pete's sloppiness is a terrible habit. He lives by himself in a one-room apartment carpeted with dirty clothes, books, and crumpled candy wrappers. Stacks of papers cover the chair seats. Socks bake on the lampshades. When Pete makes a date or an appointment, he may jot down the time and place on a scrap of paper that is soon tucked into a pocket and forgotten, or—more likely—he doesn't jot down the information at all. As a result, Pete often arrives late, or he completely forgets to appear. His grades have suffered, too, because few instructors will put up with a student who arrives out of breath ten minutes after the class has begun and whose wrinkled, carelessly scrawled papers arrive (late, of course) punctuated with coffee stains and melted M&Ms. The less Pete controls his sloppiness, the more it seems to control him.

- Note that the paragraph contains good support—specific facts, details, and examples that explain the topic sentence.

- Note that the paragraph has unity—every idea relates to the topic sentence.

- Note that the final sentence provides a brief conclusion, so that the paragraph *feels finished.*

TEACHING TIP
Suggest that your students keep lists of their personal error patterns. This will make them better proof-readers. Returned papers, suggestions from you, the practices and links in this text, the *Evergreen* Online Study Center, and the *Evergreen* Online Teaching Center will heighten students' grammatical self-awareness.

Proofreading

Whether you write by hand or on the computer, be sure to **proofread** your final draft carefully for grammar and spelling errors. Pointing to each word as you read it will help you catch errors or words you might have left out, especially small words like *to, the,* or *a.* If you are unsure of the spelling of a word, consult a dictionary and run spell checker if you work on a computer.* Make neat corrections in pen or print a corrected copy of your paper. Chapter 37, "Putting Your Proofreading Skills to Work," and all of Units 6 and 7 in this book are devoted to improving your proofreading skills.

PRACTICE 13

Now read the first draft of your paragraph with a critical eye. Revise and rewrite it, checking especially for a clear topic sentence, strong support, and unity.

PRACTICE 14

Exchange *revised* paragraphs with a classmate. Ask specific questions or use the Peer Feedback Sheet displayed earlier.

When you *give* feedback, try to be as honest and specific as possible; saying a paper is "good," "nice," or "bad" doesn't really help the writer. When you *receive* feedback, think over your classmate's responses; do they ring true?

Now **revise** a second time, with the aim of writing a fine paragraph. Proofread carefully for grammar errors, spelling errors, and omitted words.

 WRITING ASSIGNMENTS

TEACHING AND **ESL** TIP
Advise students to read writing assignments carefully and address all topics included in the prompt. Suggest that they underline all important words.

The assignments that follow will give you practice in writing basic paragraphs. In each, aim for (1) a topic sentence with a clear controlling idea and (2) a body that fully supports and develops the topic sentence.

Remember to **narrow the topic, write the topic sentence, freewrite or brainstorm, select,** and **arrange ideas** in a plan or an outline before you write. Rethink and **revise** as necessary before composing the final version of the paragraph. As you work, refer to the checklist at the end of this chapter.

Paragraph 1

Discuss an important day in your life

Think back to a day when you learned something important. In the topic sentence, tell what you learned. Freewrite or brainstorm to gather ideas. Then describe the lesson in detail, including only the most important steps or events in the learning process. Conclude with an insight.

---

* For tips and cautions on using a computer spell checker, see Chapter 38, Part B.

Paragraph 2

Examine campus fashion

What clothing and hairstyles are currently in fashion on your campus? Update your readers on the look—or looks—of the moment. Focus your topic: You might write about a certain group of students who share one look, hair only, clothing styles only, and so forth. Use humor if you wish. Vivid supporting details, descriptions, and examples will help make your point. Revise your work for good support, unity, and all-around excellent writing.

Paragraph 3

Interview a classmate about an achievement

Write about a time when your classmate achieved something important, like winning an award for a musical performance, getting an A in a difficult course, or helping a friend through a hard time. To gather interesting facts and details, ask your classmate questions like these and take notes: *Is there one accomplishment of which you are very proud? Why was this achievement so important?* Keep asking questions until you feel you can give the reader a vivid sense of your classmate's triumph. In your first sentence, state the person's achievement—for instance, *Being accepted in the honors program improved Gabe's self-esteem.* Then explain specifically why the achievement was so meaningful.

Paragraph 4

Choose an ideal job

Decide what kind of job you are best suited for and, in your topic sentence, tell what this job is. Then give three or four reasons that will convince readers of the wisdom of your choice. Discuss any special qualifications, talents, skills, or attitudes that would make you an excellent _____. Revise your work, checking for support and unity.

Paragraph 5

Discuss a quotation

Look through the quotations in the Quotation Bank before the indexes in this book. Pick a quotation you strongly agree or disagree with. In your topic sentence, state how you feel about the quotation. Then explain why you feel the way you do, giving examples from your own experience to support or contradict the quotation. Make sure your reader knows exactly how you feel.

Paragraph 6

Explain a sports or music fanatic

Do you know a sports or music fan who takes his or her loyalty and enthusiasm to an extreme? Explain this person's behavior to your readers. You might choose several details or actions that best capture his or her fanatic behavior. Or you might wish to discuss why you think a team or musical group is so important to this person. Use humor if you wish. State your controlling idea in the topic sentence and support this idea fully with details, facts, and examples.

✓ CHECKLIST

The Process of Writing Basic Paragraphs

Refer to this checklist of steps as you write a basic paragraph.

☐ 1. Narrow the topic in light of your audience and purpose.

☐ 2. Write a topic sentence that has a clear controlling idea and is a complete sentence. If you have trouble, freewrite or brainstorm first; then narrow the topic and write the topic sentence.

☐ 3. Freewrite or brainstorm, generating facts, details, and examples to develop your topic sentence.

☐ 4. Select and drop ideas for the body of the paragraph.

☐ 5. Arrange ideas in a plan or an outline, deciding which ideas will come first, which will come second, and so forth.

☐ 6. Write the best first draft you can.

☐ 7. Conclude. Don't just leave the paragraph hanging.

☐ 8. Revise as necessary, checking your paragraph for support and unity.

☐ 9. Proofread for grammar and spelling errors.

ESL TIP
Vary your editing responses on student papers. First, correct errors and have ESL students recopy the corrected text. Later, move to editing symbols and eventually, underline or circle errors.

🔍 EXPLORING ONLINE

TEACHING TIP
More practice and assessment are available in the *Evergreen* Test Bank, linked ACE tests on the *Evergreen* Online Teaching and Study Centers, *WriteSpace for Evergreen*, and Exploring Online links in this chapter.

http://owl.english.purdue.edu/handouts/general/gl_proof.html Proofreading strategies to improve your writing and your grade

Online Study Center **college.hmco.com/pic/evergreen8e**
Visit the Online Study Center for *Evergreen* for more exercises and quizzes.

4

Achieving Coherence

| PART A | Coherence Through Order |
| PART B | Coherence Through Related Sentences |

Every composition should have **coherence.** A paragraph *coheres*—holds together—when the sentences are arranged in a clear, logical *order* and when the sentences are *related* like links in a chain.

PART A Coherence Through Order

An orderly presentation of ideas within the paragraph is easier to follow and more pleasant to read than a jumble. *After* jotting down ideas but *before* writing the paragraph, the writer should decide which ideas to discuss first, which second, which third, and so on, according to a logical order.

There are many possible orders, depending on the subject and the writer's purpose. This section will explain three basic ways of ordering ideas: **time order, space order,** and **order of importance.**

Time Order

One of the most common methods of ordering sentences in a paragraph is through **time,** or **chronological, order,** which moves from present to past or from past to present. Most stories, histories, and instructions follow the logical order of time.* The following paragraph employs time order:

---

* For work on narrative paragraphs, see Chapter 6, "Narration," and for work on process paragraphs, see Chapter 8, "Process."

> (1) Most Westerners are fascinated by Japanese sumo wrestling, but few understand the elaborate ritual that begins every bout. (2) *First*, the two *rikishi* (the Japanese term for "sumo wrestlers") step to the edge of the ring opposite each other, squat on their haunches, extend their arms, and clap once. (3) *Then* they go to the center of the ring; each lifts one leg sideways and stomps down on the mat. (4) *Next*, each opponent returns to his side of the ring and receives a dipper of "power-water" to rinse his mouth. (5) *At this point*, an attendant offers each a basket of unrefined salt. (6) The wrestlers walk toward the center of the ring, scattering salt to purify the ring. (7) They stop in the center, squat on their haunches with their fists on their knees, and lean toward each other, eyeball to eyeball. (8) As the fans scream and shout, the wrestlers return to the edge of the ring *one more time*. (9) The referee raises his war fan. (10) *Finally*, the fighters approach each other and begin fighting.

- The events in this paragraph are clearly arranged in the order of time. They are presented as they happen, *chronologically.*

- Throughout the paragraph, key words like *first, then, next,* and *at this point* emphasize time order and guide the reader from event to event.

Careful use of time order helps prevent confusing writing like this: *Oops, I forgot to mention that before the wrestlers scatter salt, they rinse their mouths.*

Occasionally, when the sentences in a paragraph follow a very clear time order, the topic sentence is only implied, not stated directly, as in this example:

ESL TIP
You might use the two model paragraphs on this page to contrast present and past tense. Ask students to identify the verb tense used in each and explain its use.

> (1) <u>In 1905</u>, a poor washerwoman with a homemade hair product started a business—with $1.50! (2) <u>In just five years</u>, Madame C. J. Walker established offices and manufacturing centers in Denver, Pittsburgh, and Indianapolis. (3) The Madame C. J. Walker Manufacturing Company specialized in hair supplies, but Madame Walker specialized in independence for herself and for others. (4) Although she was not formally educated, she developed an international sales force, teaching her African American agents the most sophisticated business skills. (5) <u>Eight years after starting her business</u>, Madame Walker was the first African American woman to become a self-made millionaire. (6) In addition, she drew thousands of former farm and domestic workers into the business world. (7) One of her most original ideas was to establish "Walker Clubs," and she awarded cash prizes to the clubs with the most educational and philanthropic projects in their African American communities. (8) <u>When she died in 1919</u>, Madame Walker left two-thirds of her fortune to schools and charities. (9) Another of her contributions also lived on. (10) <u>After her death</u>, many of her former employees used their experience to start businesses throughout the United States and the Caribbean.

TEACHING TIP
Have students generate examples of academic, professional, and personal writing that might require time order.

- Time order gives coherence to this paragraph. Sentence 1 tells us about the beginning of Madame Walker's career as a businessperson. However, it does not express the main idea of the entire paragraph.

▪ What is the implied topic sentence or main idea developed by the paragraph?

With almost nothing but natural business ability, Madame Walker achieved

success and helped others.

▪ The implied topic sentence or main idea of the paragraph might read, *With nothing but natural business ability and vision, Madame C. J. Walker achieved history-making success for herself and others.*

▪ Because the writer arranges the paragraph in chronological order, the reader can easily follow the order of events in Madame Walker's life. What words and phrases indicate time order? Underline them and list them here:

in 1905; in just five years; eight years after starting her business; when she died in 1919;

after her death.

PRACTICE 1

Arrange each set of sentences in logical time order, numbering the sentences 1, 2, 3, and so on, as if you were preparing to write a paragraph. Underline any words and phrases, like *first, next,* and *in 1692,* that give time clues.

1. __2__ First, lie on your back with your knees comfortably bent.

   __3__ Next, put your hands at your sides or fold them over your chest.

   __5__ Finally, focus on your abs and do your crunches slowly, three sets of 10 each.

   __4__ Lift your torso until the shoulder blades leave the floor, and then slowly roll back down.

   __1__ The perfect crunch should be done slowly and deliberately, working the whole abdominal wall.

2. __4__ In 1957, *The Cat in the Hat* made famous both its hat-wearing tomcat with terrible manners and its author.

   __6__ Before he died in 1991, Dr. Seuss inspired millions to love language with such creations as the Grinch, Nerds, Wockets, Bar-ba-loots, bunches of Hunches, and fox in sox.

   __5__ *Green Eggs and Ham* came out in 1960 and told a memorable story, using only 55 different words.

   __1__ In his long career, Theodor Geisel, better known as Dr. Seuss, wrote 46 wildly imaginative children's books, now read all over the world.

   __2__ His first book was rejected by 28 publishers, who found it "too strange for children."

   __3__ In 1937, when it finally was published, readers loved the rhythmic march of tongue-twisting, invented words and the wacky characters.

3. _5_ The judge later deeply regretted his part, but this murderous chapter in American history has never been forgotten.

   _2_ Two books "proving" that witches existed, by the famous Puritan ministers Increase Mather and his son Cotton Mather, further fanned the hysteria in 1693.

   _3_ The stage was set for the terrible Salem witchcraft trials.

   _4_ Nineteen so-called "witches and wizards" were hanged; one was pressed to death.

   _1_ In 1692, when two girls in Salem Village, Massachusetts, had seizures, they falsely accused neighbors of putting a curse on them.

WRITING ASSIGNMENT 1

Use **time order** to give coherence to a paragraph. Choose one of the following two paragraphs. Compose a topic sentence, freewrite or brainstorm to generate ideas, and then arrange your ideas *chronologically*. You may wish to use transitional words and phrases like these to guide the reader from point to point.*

first, second	before	soon	suddenly
then	during	when	moments later
next	after	while	finally

Paragraph 1

Narrate the first hour of your average day

Start with getting up in the morning and continue to describe what you do for that first hour. Record your activities, your conversations, if any, and possibly your moods as you go through this hour of the morning. As you revise, make sure that events clearly follow time order.

Paragraph 2

Record an unforgettable event

Choose a moment in sports or in some other activity that you vividly remember, either as a participant or as a spectator. In the topic sentence, tell in a general way what happened. *(It was the most exciting touchdown I have ever seen,* or *Ninety embarrassing seconds marked the end of my brief surfing career.)* Then record the experience, arranging details in time order.

Space Order

Another useful way to arrange ideas in writing is through **space order**—describing a person, a thing, or a place from top to bottom, from left to right, from foreground to background, and so on. Space order is often used in descriptive writing because it moves from detail to detail like a movie camera's eye:†

---

* For a more complete list of transitional expressions, see p. 62–63.

† For more work on space order, see Chapter 7, "Description."

(1) A rainforest actually consists of four different layers, each one teeming with life. (2) On the forest's dark floor live a wide variety of creatures, from the smallest insects and spiders to anteaters, wild boars, and even gorillas. (3) Rising a few feet above the ground is a layer of shrubs and seedlings struggling to grow in the deep shadows. (4) Still higher is the forest's *understory*, a cool, shady zone beneath the leaves of the taller trees where beetles, snakes, lizards, and frogs crawl over ferns and vines, and jaguars might lounge in tree branches, watching for prey. (5) The *canopy*—the leafy roof of the forest that is home to many mosses, orchids, birds, reptiles, and monkeys—chirps, squawks, hisses, and howls with life. (6) Bursting through the canopy into the sunlight are a few towering trees of the uppermost *emergent* layer, the habitat of birds like the brilliant red, blue, and yellow scarlet macaw.

- This paragraph uses space order.

- Sentence 1 clearly places the scene: the rainforest.

- Sentence 2 begins at the bottom, *on the forest's dark floor*.

- Sentences 3 and 4 move upward from the forest floor to describe the next two layers: shrubs and new plants and the understory.

- Sentences 5 and 6 move further upward, describing the two highest areas of the rainforest: the canopy and the emergent layer.

Note how phrases like *rising a few feet above the ground, still high, beneath the leaves of the taller trees, leafy roof,* and *bursting through the canopy into the sunlight* help the reader form a mental image of the rainforest as the paragraph moves from bottom to top.

Some paragraphs that are clearly arranged according to space order have only an implied topic sentence:

(1) Just inside the door of Filene's Basement, Boston's famous bargain clothing store, giant hanging signs explain that the longer an item remains in the store, the cheaper it becomes. (2) All around the walls, floor-to ceiling racks are crammed with a random mix of shoes, sneakers, neckties, and handbags. (3) Counters are cluttered with rhinestone rings, plastic sunglasses, and silk scarves. (4) In the center of the floor, huge square bins contain disorganized piles of shoes and clothes. (5) Customers dig into these jumbled bins, pulling out yellow rain hats, pink suede pumps, even cheese graters and other items that belong in a kitchen department. (6) Friends lose each other in the crowded aisles. (7) Frantic shoppers often collide as items fly into the air. (8) Some customers question whether any bargain makes this chaos worthwhile, but they always seem to return.

—Emma Lou Haynes (Student)

▪ The main idea of this paragraph is *implied*, not stated by a topic sentence. What is the main idea?

Filene's discount clothing store is a crowded and frantic place.

▪ The implied topic sentence or main idea of this paragraph might read, *On every side in Filene's, one sees crammed merchandise and frantic bargain hunters.* Because the paragraph is so clearly arranged according to space order, the reader can easily follow it.

▪ Transitional phrases like *just inside the door* and *all around the walls* guide the reader from sentence to sentence. What phrases in sentences 4 and 6 help guide the reader?

in the center of the floor; in the crowded aisles

PRACTICE 2

Following are topics followed by supporting details. Arrange each group of details according to space order, numbering them 1, 2, 3, and so on, as if you were preparing to write a descriptive paragraph. On the line after each topic, tell what kind of space order you used: *left to right, back to front,* and so forth.

1. Describe a firefighter's uniform.   top to bottom

   __4__ fire-retardant pants, called "turnouts"

   __1__ black, hard plastic helmet with flashlight attached

   __5__ steel-reinforced black rubber bunker boots

   __3__ bright yellow, fireproof Kevlar jacket

   __2__ compressed-air face mask

2. Describe the security measures protecting the original Declaration of Independence.   inside to outside (outside to inside)

   _4(2)_ room's perimeter ringed with security cameras and motion sensors

   _3(3)_ two armed guards standing next to the bronze and marble shrine

   _5(1)_ the National Archives building in Washington, D.C.

   _1(5)_ parchment of document touched only by decay-preventing helium gas

   _2(4)_ bulletproof glass case

3. Describe a city scene.   bottom to top

   __1__ dented trash cans in the alley

   __5__ a bird riding the wind in blue sky

   __2__ rusty metal fire escape zigzagging up from the ground

   __3__ laundry flapping on a line near the eighth floor

   __4__ glimpse of the old wooden rooftop water tower

WRITING ASSIGNMENT 2

Use **space order** to give coherence to one of the following paragraphs. Compose a topic sentence, freewrite or brainstorm for more details, and then arrange them in space order. Use transitional words and phrases like these if you wish:*

on the left	above	next to
on the right	below	behind
in the middle	beside	farther out

Paragraph 1

Describe a firefighter's uniform, security around the Declaration of Independence, or a city scene

Choose one group of details from Practice 2, formulate a topic sentence that sets the scene for them all, and use them as the basis of a paragraph. Convert the details into complete sentences, adding words if you wish.

Paragraph 2

Describe a memorable face

Describe the face of someone you know well, perhaps a friend, family member, or person you admire. Study the actual face of the person or visualize it vividly as you jot down the five or six most important or striking details. Then, before writing your paragraph, arrange these details according to space order—moving from left to right or from top to bottom.

Order of Importance

Ideas in a paragraph can also be arranged in the **order of importance.** You may start with the most important ideas and end with the least, or you may begin with the least important idea and build to a climax with the most important one. If you wish to persuade your reader with arguments or examples, beginning with the most important points impresses the reader with the force of your ideas and persuades him or her to continue reading.†

On essay examinations and in business correspondence, be especially careful to begin with the most important idea. In those situations the reader definitely wants your important points first.

Read the following paragraph and note the order of ideas.

> (1) Louis Pasteur is revered as a great scientist for his three major discoveries. (2) Most important, this Frenchman created vaccines that have saved millions of human and animal lives. (3) The vaccines grew out of his discovery that weakened forms of a disease could help the person or animal build up antibodies that would prevent the disease. (4) The vaccines used today to protect children from serious illnesses owe their existence to Pasteur's work. (5) Almost as important was Pasteur's brilliant idea that tiny living beings, not chemical reactions, spoiled beverages. (6) He developed a process, pasteurization, that keeps milk, wine, vinegar, and beer from spoiling. (7) Finally, Pasteur found ways to stop a silkworm disease that threatened to ruin France's profitable silk industry. (8) Many medical researchers regard him as "the father of modern medicine."

---

* For a more complete list of transitional expressions, see p. 62–63.
† See Chapter 5, "Illustration," and Chapter 13, "Persuasion."

▪ The ideas in this paragraph are explained in the **order of importance,** from the *most important to the least important:*

What was Pasteur's most important discovery?_____vaccines_____

_____

What was his next most important discovery?_____pasteurization_____

_____

What was his least important one?_____cure for silkworm disease_____

_____

▪ Note how the words *most important, almost as important,* and *finally* guide the reader from one idea to another.

Sometimes, if you wish to add drama and surprise to your paragraphs, you may want to begin with the least important idea and build toward a climax by saving the most important idea for last. This kind of order can help counter the tendency of some writers to state the most important idea first and then let the rest of the paragraph dwindle away.

Read the following paragraph and note the order of ideas:

> (1) Called a genius by some and a publicity seeker by others, Salvador Dali was one of the best-known painters of the twentieth century. (2) Dali was a *surrealist*—that is, he painted scenes in bizarre or *surreal* ways, trying to express inner realities and shake up the viewer. (3) Recently, shows of his work at major museums have created new Dali admirers, who give at least three reasons for his lasting importance. (4) First, Dali was a larger-than-life creative force—an artist, sculptor, writer, filmmaker, adviser to fashion designers, and international party animal. (5) Even more important, his work strongly influenced younger painters like Andy Warhol, whose brightly colored portraits of Marilyn Monroe and Campbell's Soup cans are known worldwide. (6) But the premiere reason for Dali's importance is that his dreamlike paintings and surreal combinations of images changed people's idea of art. (7) His canvases, like *The Persistence of Memory,* capture unconscious states. Dali continues to inspire, anger, and amuse viewers from the grave, which no doubt would please him.

▪ The reasons for Dali's importance that develop this paragraph are discussed in the **order of importance:** *from the least to the most important.*

▪ The fact that Dali influenced younger painters is more important than his range of talents. However, the fact that his work changed the world's idea of art is the most important of all.

▪ Transitional words like *first, even more important,* and *premiere reason* help the reader follow clearly from one reason to the next.

The Persistence of Memory
by Salvador Dali

 EXPLORING ONLINE

http://www.virtualdali.com/ On this enjoyable site, you can learn more about Dali and view many of his works. Choose one painting; write three things about it that command your attention, arrange them in order of importance, and write a paragraph.

PRACTICE 3

Arrange the ideas that develop each topic sentence in their **order of importance**, numbering them 1, 2, 3, and so on. *Begin with the most important* (or largest, most severe, most surprising) and continue to the *least* important. Or reverse the order if you think that the paragraph would be more dramatic by beginning with the *least* important ideas and building toward a climax, with the most important last.

1. Cynthia Lopez's first year of college brought many unexpected expenses.

    ³ (2) Her English professor wanted her to own a college dictionary.

    ¹ (4) All those term papers to write required a computer.

    ² (3) She had to spend $90 for textbooks.

    ⁴ (1) Her solid geometry class required various colored pencils and felt-tip pens.

2. Alcoholic beverages should not be sold at sporting events.

    ¹ (3) Injuries and even deaths caused by alcohol-induced crowd violence would be eliminated.

    ³ (1) Fans could save money by buying soft drinks instead of beer.

    ² (2) Games and matches would be much more pleasant without the yelling, swearing, and rudeness often caused by alcohol.

3. The apartment needed work before the new tenants could move in.

    3 <u>(2)</u> The handles on the kitchen cabinets were loose.

    1 <u>(4)</u> Every room needed plastering and painting.

    4 <u>(1)</u> Grime marred the appearance of the bathroom sink.

    2 <u>(3)</u> Two closet doors hung off the hinges.

WRITING ASSIGNMENT 3

Use **order of importance** to give coherence to one of the paragraphs that follow. Use transitional words and phrases like these to guide the reader along:*

first	even more	another
next	last	least of all
above all	especially	most of all

Paragraph 1

Describe a day in which everything went right (or wrong)

Freewrite or brainstorm to generate ideas. Choose three or four of the day's best (or worst) events and write a paragraph in which you present them in order of importance—either from the most to the least important, or from the least to the most important.

Paragraph 2

Describe an unusual person

Choose a person you know whose looks or actions are unusual. Write your topic sentence and generate ideas; choose three to five details about the person's looks or behavior. Arrange the details according to the order of importance—either from the most to the least important or from the least to the most important.

PART B Coherence Through Related Sentences

In addition to arranging ideas in a logical order, the writer can ensure paragraph coherence by linking one sentence to the next. This section will present four basic ways to link sentences: **repetition of important words, substitution of pronouns, substitution of synonyms,** and **transitional expressions.**

---

* For a more complete list of transitional expressions, see pages 62–63.

Repetition of Important Words and Pronouns

Link sentences within a paragraph by *repeating important words and ideas*:

(1) An Amber Alert is a notice to the general public that a child has been kidnapped. (2) This notification system was named after Amber Hagerman, a nine-year-old girl abducted from her neighborhood and found murdered a few days later. (3) The term *Amber Alert* is also an acronym for "America's Missing Broadcast Emergency Response." (4) The goal of an Amber Alert is to collect and spread information about the abduction with utmost speed, thus increasing the chances of finding the child alive. (5) First, police confirm that a child is missing and race to collect descriptive details about the child, the suspected abductor, and the suspect's vehicle. (6) Then broadcasts on television, radio, the Internet, and electronic highway signs spread these details and urge people to report any sightings or clues immediately. (7) To date, the program has saved 180 young lives.

■ What important words are repeated in this paragraph?

■ The words *Amber Alert* appear three times, in sentences 1, 3, and 4. The word *child* appears four times, in sentences 1, 4, and 5. The word *abducted* appears in sentence 2, *abduction* in sentence 4, and *abductor* in sentence 5.

■ Repetition of these key words helps the reader follow from sentence to sentence as these terms are defined or the relationships between them are explained.

Although repetition of important words can be effective, it can also become boring if overused.* To avoid *unnecessary* repetition, substitute *pronouns* for words already mentioned in the paragraph, as this author does:

(1) Edna Lima turned *her* childhood problem into personal and professional triumph. (2) This Brazilian American was once so tall, weak, and skinny that *her* mother prayed for Edna to grow strong. (3) At age 12, Edna discovered *capoeira*, a Brazilian martial art, and loved *it*. (4) Karate lessons followed. (5) Today, Lima is the world's first female capoeira master and holds a fifth-degree black belt in karate. (6) The famous capoeira instructor now shares *her* passion for the healthy martial-arts lifestyle with students, helping to build *their* inner strength and confidence.

■ The use of pronouns in this paragraph avoids unnecessary repetition. The pronoun *her* in sentence 1 refers to the antecedent,† *Edna Lima*. In sentence 2, *her* refers to *this Brazilian American*.

---

* For practice in eliminating wordiness (repetition of unimportant words), see Chapter 22, "Revising for Language Awareness," Part B.

† For more work on pronouns and antecedents, see Chapter 31, "Pronouns," Parts A, B, and C.

▪ In sentence 3, the pronoun *it* gives further coherence to the paragraph by referring to what antecedent? _____capoeira_____

▪ The pronoun *her* in the sentence 6 refers to what antecedent? _The famous capoeira instructor_ The pronoun *their* refers to what antecedent? _____students_____

Use pronoun substitution together with the repetition of important words for a smooth presentation of ideas.

PRACTICE 4

What important words are repeated in the following paragraph? Underline them. Circle any pronouns that replace them. Notice the varied pattern of repetitions and pronoun replacements.

I have always considered my father a very intelligent person. His intelligence is not the type usually tested in schools; perhaps he would have done well on such tests, but the fact is that he never finished high school. Rather, my father's intelligence is his ability to solve problems creatively as they arise. Once when I was very young, we were driving through the desert at night when the oil line broke. My father improvised a light, squeezed under the car, found the break, and managed to whittle a connection to join the two severed pieces of tubing; then he added more oil and drove us over a hundred miles to the nearest town. Such intelligent solutions to unforeseen problems were typical of him. In fact, my father's brand of brains—accurate insight, followed by creative action—is the kind of intelligence that I admire and most aspire to.

WRITING ASSIGNMENT 4

Paragraph 1

Explain success

How do you measure *success*? By the money you make, the number or quality of friends you have? Freewrite or brainstorm for ideas. Then answer this question in a thoughtful paragraph. Give the paragraph coherence by repeating important words and using pronouns.

Paragraph 2

Discuss a public figure

Choose a public figure whom you admire—from the arts, politics, media, or sports—and write a paragraph discussing *one quality* that makes that person special. Name the person in your topic sentence. Vary repetition of the person's name with pronouns to give the paragraph coherence.

Synonyms and Substitutions

When you do not wish to repeat a word or use a pronoun, give coherence to your paragraph with a **synonym** or **substitution**. **Synonyms** are two or more words that mean nearly the same thing. For instance, if you do not wish to repeat the word *car*, you might use the synonym *automobile* or *vehicle*. If you are describing a sky and have already used the word *bright*, try the synonym *radiant*.

Or instead of a synonym, **substitute** other words that describe the subject. If you are writing about Manny Ramirez, for example, refer to him as *this powerful slugger* or *this versatile athlete*. Such substitutions provide a change from constant repetition of a person's name or a single pronoun.*

Use synonyms and substitutions together with repetition and pronouns to give coherence to your writing:

> (1) *The main building of Ellis Island* in New York Harbor reopened as a museum in 1990. (2) Millions of people visit *the huge brick and limestone structure* every year. (3) From 1892 to 1954, *this famous immigrant station* was the first stop for millions of newcomers to American shores. (4) In fact, the ancestors of nearly 40 percent of American citizens passed through *this building*. (5) Abandoned in 1954, *it* deteriorated so badly that snow and rain fell on its floor. (6) Today visitors can follow the path of immigrants from a ferryboat, through the great arched doorway, into the room where the weary travelers left their baggage, up the stairway where doctors kept watch, and into the registry room. (7) Here questions were asked that determined if each immigrant could stay in the United States. (8) *This magnificent monument to the American people* contains exhibits that help individuals search for their own relatives' names and that tell the whole immigration history of the United States.

■ This paragraph effectively mixes repetition, pronouns, and substitutions. The important word *building* is stated in sentence 1 and repeated in sentence 4.

■ Sentence 5 substitutes the pronoun *it*.

■ In sentence 2, *the huge brick and limestone structure* is substituted for *building*, and a second substitution, *this famous immigrant station*, occurs in sentence 3. Sentence 8 refers to the building as *this magnificent monument to the American people* and concludes the paragraph.

 EXPLORING ONLINE

http://www.ellisisland.com/ This site has links to Ellis Island immigration records; however, your name or a family story might be fine writing topics, wherever you are from.

To find synonyms, check a **dictionary**. For instance, the entry for *smart* might list *clever, witty, intelligent*. An even better source of synonyms is the **thesaurus,** a book of synonyms. For example, if you are describing a city street and cannot

---

* For more work on exact language, see Chapter 22, "Revising for Language Awareness," Part A.

think of other words meaning "noisy," look in the thesaurus. The number of choices will amaze you.

PRACTICE 5

Read each paragraph carefully. Then write on the lines any synonyms and substitutions that the writer has used to replace the word(s) in italics.

Paragraph 1

According to sports writer Ian Stafford, the British hold the record for winning the world's *oddest competitions*. In one of these bizarre events, contestants contort their faces and are judged on their ugliness. One competitor removed half his dentures and reversed the other half, rolled his eyes, and tucked his nose into his mustache and upper lip to achieve prize-winning ugliness. Another of these eccentric contests is snail racing. Opponents in this case are, of course, snails, which are placed in the center of a thirteen-inch cloth circle. The first to reach the edge of the circle wins. The race often takes four to five minutes, although the all-time champion (owned and trained by an English seven-year-old) finished the course in two minutes. Toe wrestling, bog snorkeling, worm charming—the British have emerged as unconquered rivals in all of these so-called sports. Perhaps you think that sports writer Ian Stafford should win first prize in the Biggest Liar in the World Competition. No, every one of these outlandish games exists. You can check them all out on the Internet.

Oddest competitions are also referred to as __bizarre events__, __eccentric contests__, __so-called sports__, and __outlandish games__.

Paragraph 2

Lori Arviso Alvord spent her childhood playing on the red mesas of a New Mexico Indian reservation. Later, while training to become the first Navajo woman surgeon, she encountered a vary different world, the sterilized steel-and-chrome environment of the modern hospital. There, as she broke her culture's taboos against touching the dead and removing parts of the body, she felt disconnected from her Native American heritage. Yet even as the skilled doctor used the latest medical technology to repair injuries and remove tumors, she felt that something important was missing. Returning to her roots to search for answers, she realized that scientific medicine alone cannot restore the harmony among body, mind, and spirit the Navajos call "walking in beauty." This pioneering healer resolved to integrate her culture's ancient healing traditions with high-tech procedures. Her skill with a scalpel begins a patient's healing process, but her blend of healing ceremonies and the involvement of families and neighbors restores the balance of good health.

Lori Arviso Alvord, M.D., is also referred to as __the first Navajo woman surgeon,__ __the skilled doctor__, and __this pioneering healer__.

Dr. Lori Alvord, surgeon, associate dean, and author, is featured in this ad for the American Indian College Fund. Why does the ad ask, "Have you ever seen a real Indian?"

PRACTICE 6

Give coherence to the following paragraphs by thinking of appropriate synonyms or substitutions for the words in italics. Then write them in the blanks.

Paragraph 1

Christopher Reeve's story includes an extraordinary twist of fate. This *star* played Superman, the fictional hero who inspired fans with his ability to overcome obstacles and save others from harm. How ironic that this Hollywood heartthrob was paralyzed form the neck down in a horse-jumping accident in 1995 and came to personify that superhuman perseverance himself. Before his accident, Reeve was not only a(n) famous actor but a pianist, an athlete who performed his own film stunts, a pilot, and an all-round outdoorsman. After being injured, he depended on a ventilator to breathe and operated his wheelchair by sipping or puffing on a straw. However, this ____brave man____ went on to direct and narrate award-winning films, write the best-selling autobiography *Still Me,* and inspire thousands of people through speeches and interviews. He also raised millions of dollars for research on spinal cord injuries. By the time he died in 2004, Christopher Reeve had become a(n) ____hero____ of a different kind; his heroism depended not on physical strength but on courage, optimism, and a sense of purpose.

Paragraph 2

Much evidence shows that the urge to take a midafternoon *nap* is natural to humans. Sleep researchers have found that volunteer subjects, kept in underground rooms where they cannot tell the time, need a ____sleep break____ about twelve hours after the halfway point of their main sleep. For example, if people sleep from midnight till 6:00 A.M., they'll be ready for a ____relaxing doze____ at 3:00 the next afternoon. Other studies show that people have less trouble taking a ____snooze____ in midafternoon than at any other daylight time. In many countries with warm climates, citizens take their daily ____siesta____ in the afternoon. Even stressed Americans take an average of two afternoon naps a week.

WRITING ASSIGNMENT 5

As you do the following assignments, try to achieve paragraph coherence by using repetition, pronouns, synonyms, and substitutions.

Paragraph 1

Discuss your favorite form of relaxation

Tell what you like to do when you have free time. Do you like to get together with friends? Do you like to go to a movie or to some sporting event? Or do you prefer to spend your time alone, perhaps listening to music, reading, or going fishing? Whatever your favorite free-time activity, name it in your topic sentence. Be sure to tell what makes your activity *relaxing.* Then give your paragraph coherence by using pronouns and synonyms such as *take it easy, unwind* and *feel free.*

Paragraph 2

Describe your ideal mate

Decide on three or four crucial qualities that your ideal husband, wife, or friend would possess, and write a paragraph describing this extraordinary person. Use repetition, pronouns, and word substitutions to give coherence to the paragraph. For example, *My ideal husband . . . he . . . my companion.*

Transitional Expressions

TEACHING TIP
Stress to students that transitional expressions point out specific *relationships* between ideas. Using them helps the reader follow.

Skill in using transitional expressions is vital to coherent writing. **Transitional expressions** are words and phrases that point out the exact relation between one idea and another, one sentence and another. Words like *therefore, however, for example*, and *finally* are signals that guide the reader from sentence to sentence. Without them, even orderly and well-written paragraphs can be confusing and hard to follow.

The transitional expressions in this paragraph are italicized:

> (1) Zoos in the past often contributed to the disappearance of animal populations. (2) Animals were cheap, and getting a new gorilla, tiger, or elephant was easier than providing the special diet and shelter needed to keep captive animals alive. (3) *Recently, however,* zoo directors have realized that if zoos themselves are to continue, they must help save many species now facing extinction. (4) *As a result,* some zoos have redefined themselves as places where endangered animals can be protected and even revived. (5) The San Diego Zoo and the National Zoo, in Washington, D.C., *for example,* have both successfully bred giant pandas, a rapidly disappearing species. (6) The births of such endangered-species babies make international news, and the public can follow the babies' progress on zoo web sites and "animal cams." (7) If zoos continue such work, perhaps they can, like Noah's ark, save some of Earth's wonderful creatures from extinction.

- Each transitional expression in the previous paragraph links, in a precise way, the sentence in which it appears to the sentence before. The paragraph begins by explaining the destructive policies of zoos in the past.

- In sentence 3, two transitional expressions of contrast—*recently* (as opposed to the past) and *however*—introduce the idea that zoo policies have *changed.*

- The phrase *as a result* makes clear that sentence 4 is a *consequence* of events described in the previous sentence(s).

- In sentence 5, *for example* tells us that the National Zoo is *one particular illustration* of the previous general statement, and the San Diego Zoo is another.

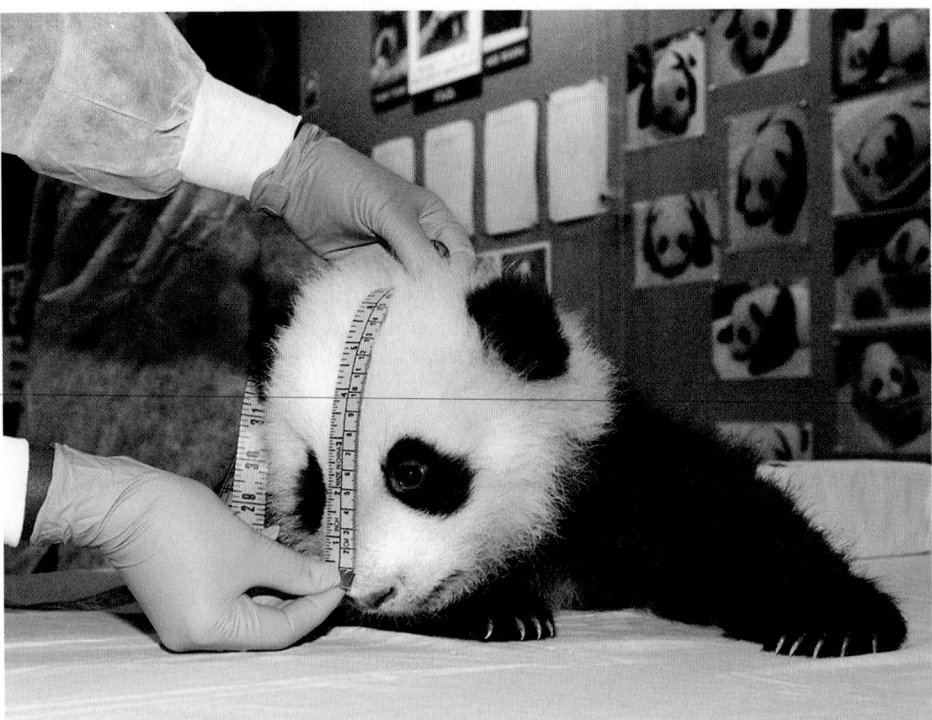

This male giant panda cub, Tai Shan, was born at the National Zoo. He was a healthy three months old when this photo was taken.

EXPLORING ONLINE

On Google or another search engine, type the words, "endangered species, zoos." Take notes on writing ideas, and bookmark web sites that intrigue you.

As you write, use various transitional expressions, together with the other linking devices, to connect one sentence to the next. Well-chosen transitional words also help stress the purpose and order of the paragraph.

Particular groups of transitional expressions are further explained and demonstrated in each chapter of Unit 3. However, here is a combined partial list for handy reference as you write.

Transitional Expressions at a Glance	
Purpose	**Transitional Expressions**
to add	also, and, and then, as well, besides, beyond that, first (second, third, last, and so on), for one thing, furthermore, in addition, moreover, next, what is more
to compare	also, as well, both (neither), in the same way, likewise, similarly
to contrast	although, be that as it may, but, even though, however, in contrast, nevertheless, on the contrary, on the other hand, whereas, yet
to concede (a point)	certainly, granted that, of course, no doubt, to be sure

to emphasize	above all, especially, indeed, in fact, in particular, most important, surely
to illustrate	as a case in point, as an illustration, for example, for instance, in particular, one such, yet another
to place	above, below, beside, beyond, farther, here, inside, nearby, next to, on the far side, opposite, outside, to the east (south, and so on)
to qualify	perhaps, maybe
to give a reason or cause	as, because, for, since
to show a result or effect	and so, as a consequence, as a result, because of this, consequently, for this reason, hence, so, therefore, thus
to summarize	all in all, finally, in brief, in other words, lastly, on the whole, to sum up
to place in time	after a while, afterward, at last, at present, briefly, currently, during, eventually, finally, first (second, and so on), gradually, immediately, in the future, later, meanwhile, next, now, recently, soon, suddenly, then

TEACHING and ESL TIP
Transitional expressions to introduce details and points will be very helpful to both ESL and native students. Encourage them to keep personal lists with a variety of introductory expressions to use in their writing.

PRACTICE 7

Carefully determine the exact relationship between the sentences in each pair below. Then choose from the list a transitional expression that clearly expresses this relationship and write it in the blank. Pay attention to punctuation and capitalize the first word of every sentence.*

TEACHING TIP
As a class or in small groups, have students compare their answers to Practice 7 so that they can see different possibilities.

1. No one inquired about the money found in the lobby. __Consequently__, it was given to charity.

2. First, cut off the outer, fibrous husk of the coconut. __Then__ poke a hole through one of the dark "eyes" and sip the milk through a straw.

3. The English Department office is on the fifth floor. __Next__ to it is a small reading room.

4. Some mountains under the sea soar almost as high as those on land. One underwater mountain in the Pacific, __for example__, is only 500 feet shorter than Mount Everest.

* For practice using conjunctions to join ideas, see Chapter 25, "Coordination and Subordination."

5. All citizens should vote. Many do not, _____however_____.

6. Mrs. Dalworth enjoys shopping in out-of-the-way thrift shops. _____Furthermore_____, she loves bargaining with the vendors at outdoor flea markets.

7. In 1887, Native Americans owned nearly 138 million acres of land. By 1932, _____in contrast_____, 90 million of those acres were owned by whites.

8. Kansas corn towered over the fence. _____Beside_____ the fence, a red tractor stood baking in the sun.

9. Most street crime occurs between 2:00 and 5:00 A.M. _____For this reason_____, do not go out alone during those hours.

10. Dr. Leff took great pride in his work at the clinic. _____Nevertheless_____, his long hours often left him exhausted.

11. Few scientists have worked so creatively with a single agricultural product. _____Besides_____ peanut oil and peanut butter, George Washington Carver developed literally hundreds of uses for the peanut.

12. We waited in our seats for over an hour. _____Finally_____ the lights dimmed, and the Fabulous String Band bounded on stage.

PRACTICE 8

Add **transitional expressions** to this essay to guide the reader smoothly from sentence to sentence. To do so, consider the relationship between sentences (shown in parentheses). Then write the transitional word or phrase that best expresses this relationship.

Oldest Child, Youngest Child—Does It Matter?

TEACHING TIP
Students nearly always love discussing this provocative topic, which also affords an opportunity for critical thinking and writing. See Practice 9.

A number of studies show that birth order—whether a person is the first-born, middle, or last-born child in the family—can affect both personality and career choice. _____For example_____ (illustration), first-borns carry the weight of their parents' expectations and _____frequently_____ (time) are urged to be responsible and set a good example for their younger siblings. _____Consequently_____ (result), they may develop leadership skills and a strong motivation to achieve. Many eldest children _____later_____ (time) become leaders. High percentages of U.S. presidents and CEOs, _____for instance,_____ (illustration) are first-borns.

Middle children, _in contrast_ (contrast), get less attention and applause in childhood. _As a result_ (result), they tend to become flexible and good at resolving conflicts. _In addition_ (addition), some middle children become rebellious or creative as they make their place in the world. _Eventually_ (time), many choose careers as entrepreneurs, negotiators, or businesspeople. _Finally_ (addition), later-born or last-born children, in order to compete with their older siblings, may become rule-breakers or family clowns. Professionally, babies of the family tend to become musicians, adventurers, and comedians. _Of course_ (conceding a point), there are countless exceptions to these general trends; _however_ (contrast) it is interesting to ponder the evidence that our birth order _indeed_ (emphasis) helps shape who we are.

PRACTICE 9 ■ THINKING AND WRITING TOGETHER

In small groups, discuss birth order and personality. What is your place in the family? Do the typical traits apply to you? Take notes for later writing while you describe the classic firstborn, middle-born, or youngest child; then apply these traits to yourself or someone you know well who fills that birth spot. Is the portrait accurate? To learn more, visit **http://en.wikipedia.org/wiki/Birth_order/**.

PRACTICE 10 ■ REVIEW

Most paragraphs achieve coherence through a variety of linking devices: repetition, pronouns, substitutions, and transitional expressions. Read the following paragraphs with care, noting the kinds of linking devices used by each writer. Answer the questions after each paragraph.

Paragraph 1

(1) The blues is the one truly American music. (2) Born in the Mississippi Delta, this twelve-bar cry of anguish found its durable, classic form in the searing soliloquies of poor black men and women who used it to ventilate all the aches and pains of their condition—the great Bessie Smith, Robert Johnson, Ma Rainey, Lightnin' Hopkins and Son House, Mississippi John Hurt, John Lee Hooker and Blind Lemon Jefferson. (3) And, ever since, the blues has served as the wellspring of every major movement in this country's popular music.

—Paul D. Zimmerman with Peter Barnes et al., "Rebirth of the Blues," *Newsweek*

1. What important words appear in both the first and the last sentence?_____

   the blues

2. In sentence 2, *the blues* is referred to as this twelve-bar cry of anguish

   _____

3. What transitional expression is used in sentence 3? and, ever since

   _____

Paragraph 2

(1) In the annals of great escapes, the flight by seventeen-year-old Lester Moreno Perez from Cuba to the United States surely must rank as one of the most imaginative. (2) At 8:30 on the night of Thursday, March 1, Lester crept along the beach in Varadero, a resort town on the north coast of Cuba. (3) Working quickly, he launched his sailboard—a surfboard equipped with a movable sail—into the shark-haunted waters off the Straits of Florida. (4) At first guided by the stars and later by the hazy glow from electric lights in towns beyond the horizon, Lester sailed with 20-knot winds toward the Florida Keys, 90 miles away. (5) All night he balanced on the small board, steering through black waters. (6) Just past daybreak on Friday, Lester was sighted 30 miles south of Key West by the Korean crew of the freighter *Tina D.* (7) The boom on his tiny craft was broken. (8) The astonished sailors pulled him aboard, fed him chicken and rice, and finally radioed the U.S. Coast Guard.

—Adapted from Sam Moses, "A New Dawn," *Sports Illustrated*

1. Underline the transitional expressions in this paragraph.

2. What *order* of ideas does the paragraph employ? time order

   _____

Paragraph 3

(1) *Phishing* is the term for tricking computer users into revealing sensitive information such as passwords or credit-card numbers. (2) A person who goes phishing first sets up a seemingly official web site and e-mail address to pose as a legitimate individual or business. (3) Next, the phisher casts the bait. (4) He or she e-mails unsuspecting individuals to request information, usually threatening account suspension or cancellation if the request is ignored. (5) When an unfortunate recipient takes the bait and sends back the information, the criminal can then reel it in and use it to commit fraud. (6) In one recent phishing case, for example, a young male disguised as an America Online employee sent out messages claiming that members' accounts had problems. (7) The e-mail looked official, with AOL logos and a link to the AOL Billing Center. (8) However, when the victims clicked on that link, they were taken to dummy web page. (9) Anyone who typed in a credit-card number, social security number, bank-account number, or password gave that vital information to the con artist.

1. What important words are repeated in this paragraph? <u>Phishing, e-mail</u>

2. What synonyms and pronouns are used for "a person who goes phishing"?

   <u>the phisher, he or she, the criminal</u>

3. What transitional expressions are used in sentences 6 and 8? <u>for example, however</u>

EXPLORING ONLINE

http://www.powa.org/organize/arranging.html Advice on ordering your ideas in the most powerful way

http://www.powa.org/organize/links.html Review methods of linking sentences within a paragraph

http://web.uvic.ca/wguide/Pages/ParagraphTransitions.html Review transitional expressions

Online Study Center **college.hmco.com/pic/evergreen8e**
Visit the Online Study Center for *Evergreen* for more exercises and quizzes.

Writers' Workshop

Discuss the Pressures to Grow Up Fast

In this unit, you learned that most good paragraphs have a clear topic sentence, convincing support, and an order that makes sense. In your group or class, read this student's paragraph, aloud if possible. Underline any parts you find especially well written. Put a check next to anything that might be improved.

Young Immigrant Translators

~~This paper will discuss children as translators.~~ When immigrant children become translators for their parents, this can change the normal relationship between parent and child. Many immigrant parents do not have the time or opportunity to develop their English skills, even though they know that speaking English is the most important part of surviving in the United States. When they need to understand or speak English, they often ask their school-age children for help. The children must act like little adults, helping their parents with all kinds of problems. They end up taking time away from school and their friends because they are responsible for everything related to English. For example, they might have to answer the phone, fill out forms, pay bills, or shop for groceries. Even in more serious situations, like medical or financial problems, the children might have to translate for the doctor or accountant. Eventually, some children can start to resent their parents for relying on them so much. Instead of turning to their parents for help with homework or personal worries, they might turn instead to friends or teachers who understand the culture better. Although most immigrant children know their parents love them and want a better life for them, the role reversal of being child translators can make them become adults too soon.

—Mandy Li (Student)

---

1. How effective is this paragraph?

   __Y/N__ Clear topic sentence?　　__Y__ Good supporting details?

   __Y__ Logical organization?　　__Y__ Effective conclusion?

2. Which sentence, if any, is the topic sentence? Is sentence 1 as good as the rest of the paragraph? If not, what revision advice would you give the writer?
   No. 2 is topic sentence. Drop No. 1.

3. Does this student provide adequate support for her main idea? Why or why not? Yes. She gives convincing examples.

4. Discuss your underlinings with the group or class. Which parts or ideas in this essay did you find most powerful? As specifically as you can, explain why. For example, the list of possible tasks a child translator must handle vividly supports the main idea of the paragraph.

5. Do you agree with Ms. Li that children being asked to translate for their parents makes children grow up too soon? Have you experienced or witnessed other situations in which children must become adults too soon? What are those situations?

6. Do you see any error patterns (one error made two or more times) that this student needs to watch out for)?   No

GROUP WORK

In your group or class, make a plan of Ms. Li's paragraph. How many points does she use to support her topic sentence? How can a writer know whether a paragraph has good support or needs better support? List three ways. Did this paragraph make you think? How would you rate the ideas in this paragraph? Extremely interesting? Interesting? Not very interesting? Be prepared to explain your rating to the full class.

WRITING AND REVISING IDEAS

1. Discuss the ways in which a child you know had to grow up too soon.

2. What is the most important tool for surviving in the United States, in your view?

UNIT 3

Developing the Paragraph

5

Illustration

To **illustrate** is to explain a general statement by means of one or more specific *examples*.

   Illustration makes what we say more vivid and more exact. Someone might say, "My math professor is always finding crazy ways to get our attention. Just yesterday, for example, he wore a high silk hat to class." The first sentence is a general statement about this professor's unusual ways of getting attention. The second sentence, however, gives a specific example of something he did that *clearly shows* what the writer means.

   Writers often use illustration to develop a paragraph. They explain a general topic sentence with one, two, three, or more specific examples. Detailed and well-chosen examples add interest, liveliness, and power to your writing.

Topic Sentence

Here is the topic sentence of a paragraph that is later developed by examples:

> Great athletes do not reach the top by talent alone but by pushing themselves to the limit and beyond.

- The writer begins an illustration paragraph with a topic sentence that makes a general statement.

- This generalization may be obvious to the writer, but if he or she wishes to convince the reader, some specific examples would be helpful.

Paragraph and Plan

Here is the entire paragraph:

Great athletes do not reach the top by talent alone but by pushing themselves to the limit and beyond. For instance, basketball sensation Lebron James keeps striving to improve. Branded the next Michael Jordan when he was in high school, drafted by the Cleveland Cavaliers, and handed a huge Nike contract on potential, James kept his cool and kept working hard. Despite a rookie-of-the-year award and a U.S. Olympic Team slot in 2004, Lebron undertook a demanding routine to improve his weak outside shots. For hours a day, he practiced shooting—standing, taking passes, cutting off picks—and emerged a 2005–2006 All-Star and leader who brought the Cavaliers to the NBA playoffs. Another example is hard-working golf star Annika Sorenstam. Although she dominates the women's circuit, she presses herself to greater achievement by competing periodically in men's tournaments, with their longer courses and stronger players. To build power and mental toughness, Sorenstam does push-ups with weights on her back and pull-ups with weights tied to her waist. The Associated Press named her Female Athlete of the Year in 2003, 2004, and 2005. Perhaps no player in any sport, however, can match the work ethic of Lance Armstrong. In 1996, this bicycle racer was diagnosed with testicular cancer that had spread to his brain and lungs. After surgery and chemotherapy left him weak and exhausted, Armstrong began a strict diet and training regimen, cycling up to six hours a day. His commitment paid off when he won the Tour de France, cycling's toughest race, every year from 1999 until his retirement in 2005. Like many top athletes, he turned his talent into greatness through sheer hard work.

▪ How many examples does the writer use to develop the topic sentence?

three

▪ Who are they?

Lebron James, Annika Sorenstam, Lance Armstrong

Before completing this illustration paragraph, the writer probably made an **outline** like this:

Topic sentence: Great athletes do not reach the top by talent alone but by pushing themselves to the limit and beyond

Example 1:	Lebron James —worked hard despite early praise, Cavaliers, and Nike contract —demanding routine to improve weak outside shots —improved, won 2006 All-Star and brought Cavs to playoffs
Example 2:	Annika Sorenstam —dominates women's golf —competes in men's tournaments to push herself —does push-ups and pull-ups with extra weight —named Female Athlete of the Year, 2003–2005
Example 3:	Lance Armstrong —1996 cancer diagnosis —after surgery and chemo, strict training (diet, cycling) —won Tour de France, 1999–2005

Conclusion: Like many top athletes, he turned talent into greatness through sheer hard work.

■ Note that each example clearly relates to and supports the topic sentence.

Instead of using three or four examples to support the topic sentence, the writer may prefer instead to discuss one single example:

> Many schools in the twenty-first century will look more like elegant shopping malls than like old-fashioned school buildings. The new Carl Sandburg High School in Chicago is just one example. Now being re-designed, the school will feature a main library with the comfortable, open layout of a superbookstore like Barnes & Noble or Borders. The physical education facilities will include rock-climbing walls and other features now seen in health clubs. Carl Sandburg's cafeteria will be laid out like a food court, not only giving students more choices, but eliminating the long lunch lines that caused delays in the old high school. Retailers have learned how to create attractive, practical public spaces, and many modern school planners think it's time that school officials learned the same lessons.

ESL TIP
ESL students often fail to include specifics in their writing. Ask students to point out the details and facts that enhance each example in this paragraph and the one below.

■ What is the general statement? Many schools in the twenty-first century will
look more like elegant shopping malls than like old-fashioned school buildings.

■ What specific example does the writer give to support the general statement?
Carl Sandburg High School

The single example may also be a **narrative,** a *story* that illustrates the topic sentence:

> Aggressive drivers not only are stressed out and dangerous, but often they save no time getting where they want to go. Recently I was driving south from Oakland to San Jose. Traffic was heavy but moving. I noticed an extremely aggressive driver jumping lanes, speeding up, and slowing down. Clearly, he was in a hurry. For the most part, I remained in one lane for the entire forty-mile journey. I was listening to a new audiotape and daydreaming. I enjoyed the trip because driving gives me a chance to be alone. As I was exiting off the freeway, the aggressive driver crowded up behind me and raced on by. Without realizing it, I had arrived in San Jose ahead of him. All his weaving, rapid acceleration, and putting families at risk had earned him nothing except perhaps some high blood pressure and a great deal of wear and tear on his vehicle.
>
> —Adapted from Richard Carlson, *Don't Sweat the Small Stuff*

---

* For more on narrative, see Chapter 6, "Narration," and Chapter 15, "Types of Essays," Part B.

▪ What general statement does the aggressive driver story illustrate?

Aggressive drivers not only are stressed out and dangerous, but often they save no time

getting where they want to go.

▪ Note that this narrative follows time order.*

Transitional Expressions

The simplest way to tell your reader that an example is going to follow is to say so: *"For instance,* Lebron James . . .*"* or *"The new Carl Sandburg High School is *just one example*."* This partial list should help you vary your use of **transitional expressions** that introduce an illustration:

Transitional Expressions for Illustration	
for instance	another instance of
for example	another example of
an illustration of this	another illustration of
a case in point is	here are a few examples (illustrations, instances)
to illustrate	

▪ Be careful not to use more than two or three of these transitional expressions in a single paragraph.†

PRACTICE 1

Read each of the following paragraphs of illustration. Underline each topic sentence. Note in the margin how many examples are provided to illustrate each general statement.

Paragraph 1 (3 examples)

 Random acts of kindness are those little sweet or grand lovely things we do for no reason except that, momentarily, the best of our humanity has sprung . . . into full bloom. When you spontaneously give an old woman the bouquet of red carnations you had meant to take home to your own dinner table, when you give your lunch to the guitar-playing beggar who makes music at the corner between your two subway stops, when you anonymously put coins in someone else's parking meter because you see the red "Expired" medallion signaling to a meter maid—you are doing not what life requires of you, but what the best of your human soul invites you to do.

—Daphne Rose Kingma, *Random Acts of Kindness*

---

* For more work on time order, see Chapter 4, "Achieving Coherence," Part A.

† For a complete essay developed by illustration, see "Extreme Makeover Library," Chapter 15, Part A.

Paragraph 2 (4 examples)

There are many quirky variations to lightning. A "bolt from the blue" occurs when a long horizontal flash suddenly turns toward the earth, many miles from the storm. "St. Elmo's Fire," often seen by sailors and mountain climbers, is a pale blue or green light caused by weak electrical discharges that cling to trees, airplanes, and ships' masts. "Pearl lightning" occurs when flashes are broken into segments. "Ball lightning" can be from an inch to several feet in diameter. Pearls and balls are often mistaken for flying saucers or UFOs, and many scientists believe they are only optical illusions.

—Reed McManus, *Sierra Magazine*

PRACTICE 2

Each example in a paragraph of illustration must clearly relate to and support the general statement. Each general statement in this practice is followed by several examples. Circle the letter of any example that does *not* clearly illustrate the generalization. Be prepared to explain your choices.

EXAMPLE The museum contains many fascinating examples of African art.

 a. It houses a fine collection of Ashanti fertility dolls.

 b. Drums and shamans' costumes are displayed on the second floor.

 c. The museum building was once the home of Frederick Douglass. (The fact that the building was once the home of Frederick Douglass is *not an example* of African art.)

1. The International Space Station is designed for efficient use of limited space.

 a. Food has been dehydrated so it can be stored in tiny packages.

 b. Special science laboratories onboard are the size of clothes closets.

 c. Daily life in the space station can be observed by 90 percent of the world's population.

 d. Each little "bedroom" can be folded and stored in a single sleeping bag.

2. Today's global companies sometimes find that their product names and slogans can translate into embarrassing bloopers.

 a. Pepsi's slogan "Come alive with the Pepsi Generation" didn't work in Taiwan, where it meant "Pepsi will bring your ancestors back from the dead."

 b. When General Motors introduced its Chevy Nova in South America, company officials didn't realize that *no va* in Spanish means "it won't go."

 c. In Chinese, the Kentucky Fried Chicken slogan "finger-lickin' good" means "eat your fingers off."

 d. Nike runs the same ad campaign in several countries, changing the ad slightly to fit each culture.

3. Many life-enhancing products that we take for granted were invented by women.

 a. Josephine Cochran invented the dishwasher in 1893, declaring that if no one else would build a machine to perform this boring task, she would do it herself.

b. In 1966, chemist Stephanie Louise Kwoleck patented Kevlar, a fabric five times stronger than steel, now used in bulletproof vests and other important products.

c. Lonnie Johnson got the idea for the famous Supersoaker squirtgun after the homemade nozzle on his sink sprayed water across the room.

4. Since a series of tragic accidents in 2000 and 2001 killed several drivers, the National Association of Stock Car Racing (NASCAR) has taken steps to make the sport safe.

a. All new race car seats wrap around the driver's rib cage and shoulders, providing better support during a crash.

b. The fastest NASCAR track is the one in Talledega, Alabama, where the average race speed is 188 miles per hour.

c. All drivers are now required to wear the head and neck support (HANS) device, a collar that prevents the head from snapping forward or sideways during a wreck.

d. NASCAR tracks now have softer walls and barriers that better absorb the impact of cars at high speeds.

NASCAR driver Dale Earnhardt, Jr., dons his helmet and HANS safety device before the 2006 Daytona 500.

5. Some writers use strange tricks to overcome writer's block and keep their ideas flowing.

a. To help himself choose the right word, the German playwright and poet Schiller sniffed rotten apples that he kept inside his desk.

b. Benjamin Franklin believed that he had to write in the nude to do his best work, and he often wrote in the bathtub.

c. Argentinian writer Jorge Luis Borges went blind, but he kept creating brilliant stories packed with learning, philosophy, and magic.

d. To inspire herself before she started writing, Dame Edith Sitwell would lie for a while each morning in an open coffin.

6. Nature has provided us with many powerful medicines.

    a. Aspirin comes from willow bark, penicillin from fungus, and the cancer drug Taxol from the Pacific yew tree.

    (b.) Drugs that lower cholesterol and blood pressure are helping people with heart disease lead longer, healthier lives.

    c. A newly discovered compound from a New Zealand deep-sea sponge, called Halichondrin B, has been eliminating tumors in laboratory tests.

    d. Prialt, a drug that blocks pain signals in the human spinal cord, comes from the venom of the deadly cone snail of the Indian and Pacific oceans.

7. In the Arizona desert, one sees many colorful plants and flowers.

    a. Here and there are patches of pink clover.

    b. Gray-green saguaro cacti rise up like giant candelabra.

    (c.) Colorful birds dart through the landscape.

    d. Bright yellow poppies bloom by the road.

8. Many months in our calendar take their names from Roman gods or heroes.

    a. Mars, the Roman war god, gave his name to March.

    b. January was named for Janus, the god of doorways, whose two faces looked both forward and back.

    c. August honors Augustus, the first Roman emperor and the second Caesar.

    (d.) December took its name from *decem*, the Latin word meaning "ten," and was the tenth month in the Roman calendar.

PRACTICE 3

The secret of good illustration lies in well-chosen, well-written examples. Think of one example that illustrates each of the following general statements. Write out the example in sentence form (one to three sentences) as clearly and exactly as possible.

1. A few contemporary singers work hard to send a positive message.

    Example   Kanye West has made social issues and an appreciation for improving life

    top priorities in his music.

2. In a number of ways, this college makes it easy for working students to attend.

    Example   The college offers many evening and online classes.

3. Believing in yourself is 90 percent of success.

   Example My friend Paco owns a successful restaurant today because his enthusiasm and

   confidence attracted investors.

   _____

4. Many teenagers believe they must have expensive designer clothing.

   Example My nephew has a closet full of Tommy and Nautica clothes that his mother

   cannot really afford.

   _____

5. Growing up in a large family can teach the value of compromise.

   Example The five Hanson children take turns choosing what game they will all play.

   _____

   _____

6. A number of shiny classic cars cruised up and down Ocean Drive.

   Example The robin's egg blue 1955 Thunderbird convertible had gleaming chrome

   bumpers and a white top.

   _____

7. Children say surprising things.

   Example My daughter said that she couldn't sit in her car seat because the Wizard of Oz

   was already sitting there.

   _____

8. Sadly, rudeness seems more and more common in America.

   Example My mother recently called to her neighbor to hold the elevator for her, and he

   shut the door in her face.

   _____

PRACTICE 4   THINKING AND WRITING TOGETHER

Illustrate Acts of Kindness

In the news, we often hear the phrase "random acts of violence"—acts whose unlucky victims are in the wrong place at the wrong time. The phrase "random acts of kindness" reverses this idea in a wonderful way—kind acts whose recipients are often perfect strangers. In a group with four or five classmates, read about random acts of kindness (Practice 1, Paragraph 1, page 74). Now think of one good example of a real-life random act of kindness, performed by you or someone else—either at college or work, or in everyday life. Share and discuss these examples with your group. Which examples are the most striking or moving? Why?

Write up your example in one paragraph. Begin with a clear topic sentence and present the act of kindness as movingly as you can. Refer to the checklist, and ask your group mates for feedback.

EXPLORING ONLINE

http://www.actsofkindness.org/ Click "Inspiration" to read about acts of kindness that people have sent in; click "Contact Us" to submit your group's best writing for possible publication.

✓ CHECKLIST

The Process of Writing an Illustration Paragraph

Refer to this checklist of steps as you write an illustration paragraph of your own.

☐ 1. Narrow the topic in light of your audience and purpose.

☐ 2. Compose a topic sentence that can honestly and easily be supported by examples.

☐ 3. Freewrite or brainstorm to find six to eight examples that support the topic sentence. If you wish to use only one example or a narrative, sketch out your idea. (You may want to freewrite or brainstorm before you narrow the topic.)

☐ 4. Select only the best two to four examples and drop any examples that do not relate to or support the topic sentence.

☐ 5. Make a plan or an outline for your paragraph, numbering the examples in the order in which you will present them.

☐ 6. Write a draft of your illustration paragraph, using transitional expressions to show that an example or examples will follow.

☐ 7. Revise as necessary, checking for support, unity, logic, and coherence.

☐ 8. Proofread for errors in grammar, punctuation, sentence structure, spelling, and mechanics.

Suggested Topic Sentences for Illustration Paragraphs

1. The car a person drives (or the way a person dresses) often makes a statement about him or her.

2. Most people have special places where they go to relax or find inspiration.

3. In my family, certain traditions (or values or beliefs) are very important.

4. Some lucky people love their jobs.

5. Painful experiences can sometimes teach valuable lessons.

6. Many enjoyable activities in this area are inexpensive or even free.

7. Celebrities' behavior and even clothing can negatively affect young people.

8. A sense of humor can make difficult times easier to bear.

9. Sexual harassment is a fact of life for some employees.

10. Eating disorders are a serious problem.

11. College students face a number of pressures.

12. Some unusual characters live in my neighborhood.

13. A true friend is one who sees and encourages the best in us.

14. Choose a quotation from the Quotation Bank at the end of this book. First, state whether you think this saying is true; then use an example from your own or others' experience to support your view.

15. Writer's choice: _____

EXPLORING ONLINE

TEACHING TIP
More practice and assessment are available in the *Evergreen* Test Bank, linked ACE tests on the *Evergreen* Online Teaching and Study Centers, *WriteSpace for Evergreen,* and Exploring Online links in this chapter.

http://www.une.edu.au/tlc/aso/pdf/p-illus.pdf Review of illustration with sample paragraphs

http://writesite.cuny.edu/projects/keywords/example/hand2.html Online practice: brainstorming examples for your paragraph

Online Study Center **college.hmco.com/pic/evergreen8e**
Visit the Online Study Center for *Evergreen* for more exercises and quizzes.

6 Narration

To **narrate** is to tell a story that explains what happened, when it happened, and who was involved.

A news report may be a narrative telling how a man was rescued from icy flood waters or how a brave whistle blower risked her career and perhaps her life to expose an employer's harmful practices. When you read a bedtime story to a child, you are reading a narrative. In a college paper on campus drug use, telling the story of a friend who takes Ecstasy would help bring that subject to life. In an e-mail or letter, you might entertain a friend by narrating your failed attempts to windsurf during a seaside vacation.

We tell stories to teach a lesson, illustrate an idea, or make someone laugh, cry, or get involved. No matter what your narrative is about, every narrative should have a clear **point:** It should reveal what you want your reader to learn or take away from the story.

Topic Sentence

Here is the topic sentence of a **narrative** paragraph:

> The crash of a Brinks truck on a Miami overpass still raises disturbing questions.

- The writer begins a narrative paragraph with a topic sentence that tells or sets up the point of the narrative.

- What is the point of this narrative? <u>to tell the story of a Brinks truck crash that</u>

<u>raises disturbing questions</u>

Paragraph and Plan

Here is the entire paragraph:

> The crash of a Brinks truck on a Miami overpass still raises disturbing questions. January 8, 1997, was just another crowded, rude, and crazy day in Miami traffic until an armored Brinks truck flipped and broke open, sending nearly a million dollars in cash swirling over the highway. Hundreds of motorists screeched to a stop, grabbing whatever money they could. People in nearby houses raced outside, shouting and scooping up bills. When it was over, a tiny handful of people returned some money. Firefighter Manny Rodriguez turned in a huge bale of bills worth $330,000, and one teenager returned some quarters. However, nearly half a million dollars was missing—stolen by everyday people like you and me. In the following days, some rationalized the mass theft as a kind of Robin Hood action because the truck had crashed in a poor area of town. Most people claimed to be shocked. Now we are all left with hard questions: *Why did a few people "do the right thing"? Why did the majority do the "wrong thing"? What causes people to act virtuously, even if no one is watching? What would you or I have done?*

■ The body of a narrative paragraph is developed according to time, or chronological, order.* That is, the writer explains the narrative—the entire incident—as a series of small events or actions in the order in which they occurred. By keeping to strict chronological order, the writer helps the reader follow the story more easily and avoids interrupting the narrative with *But I forgot to mention that before this happened. . . .*

■ What smaller events make up this paragraph? Brinks truck crashes; cash spills on highway; motorists and people in houses grab money; only a few return money, like Manny Rodriguez; half a million dollars gone; people react with excuses or shock.

■ What strong verbs or details help the writing come alive? Crowded, rude, and crazy . . . flipped and broke open . . . cash swirling over the highway . . . motorists screeched . . . grabbing . . . shouting and scooping up bills . . . stolen by everyday people like you and me

■ The writer ends the paragraph with some "hard questions." Do these questions express the point of the story? Yes, the topic sentence says this incident still raises disturbing questions, and the conclusion lists four of them.

---

* For more work on time, see Chapter 4, "Achieving Coherence," Part A.

Before writing this narrative paragraph, the writer may have brainstormed or freewritten to gather ideas, and then she may have made an **outline** like this:

Topic sentence: The crash of a Brinks truck on a Miami overpass still raises disturbing questions.

Event 1:	Brinks truck flips, spilling cash on the highway.
Event 2:	Hundreds of motorists stop, grab money.
Event 3:	People race out of houses, grabbing money.
Event 4:	Later, firefighter Rodriguez returns $330,000.
Event 5:	Just a few others give anything back; half million is gone.
Event 6:	Days after, some call it "Robin Hood" action.
Event 7:	Some say they are shocked.

Conclusion: Now we are all left with hard questions. (Some questions are listed.)

■ Note that all of the events occur in chronological order.

■ Note also that the conclusion provides a strong and thought-provoking ending.

■ Finally, note that the specific details of certain events (like events 2 and 4) make the narrative more vivid.

Transitional Expressions

Because narrative paragraphs tell a story in **chronological** or **time order,** transitional expressions that indicate time can be useful.*

Transitional Expressions for Narratives		
after	finally	soon
as (soon as)	later	then
before	meanwhile	upon
during	next	when
first	now	while

---

* For a complete essay developed by narration, see "Maya Lin's Vietnam War Memorial," Chapter 15, "Types of Essays," Part B.

PRACTICE 1

Read the following narrative paragraph carefully and answer the questions:

> Diane Sawyer is now a world-class television journalist, but when she graduated from college, she had no idea what career to pursue. For a few months, she moped around her parents' house in Kentucky, stewing in self-pity. One day she confessed her turmoil to her father, who posed three questions. "First," he asked, "what do you love to do?" Diane had no trouble answering; she loved storytelling, finding the human tale that brings to life a headline or event. "What is the most exciting place in the world you could do that?" he queried. Television was transforming America, and all the major networks beamed from New York, a thrilling destination yet daunting, too, because few women in TV rose beyond secretary or weather girl. Her father ignored talk of obstacles, however, asking only, "Will this work serve other people?" She believed that a television journalist could help others, by informing them, making them think, even awakening their compassion. Today Sawyer credits this conversation with helping set her life's course. When folks request career advice, she asks the same three questions, adding, "If you can answer the first two and say "yes" to the third, you are ready to work hard and enjoy the ride."

TEACHING TIP
You might want to follow up on this engaging topic by having your students answer Sawyer's three questions in writing. Then share and discuss their answers in class.

1. What is the point of the narrative? This narrative tells how Diane Sawyer used her

   father's three questions to find her career path.

2. What events make up this narrative paragraph? Diane Sawyer graduated from

   college but felt confused about what to do; her father asked her three questions; answering

   these questions helped her decide to become a television journalist; today she tells people

   to answer those questions to find their own path.

PRACTICE 2

Here are three plans for narrative paragraphs. The events in the plans are not in correct chronological order. The plans also contain events that do not belong in each story. Number the events in the proper time sequence and cross out any irrelevant ones.

1. A combination of talent and hard work has propelled Alicia Keys to musical stardom.

   __1__ In 1988, seven-year-old Alicia dazzled her first piano teacher by mastering both classical and jazz pieces.

 4   By 2005, her distinctive voice and blending of soul, jazz, hip hop, and classical styles had won a huge fan base and four more Grammies.

 2   As a teenager in the "Hell's Kitchen" section of New York City, she wrote her first songs and blossomed as a pianist.

——   ~~Every year since 1959, the Grammy, the Academy Award of music, has been given to musicians of outstanding achievement.~~

 3   At age twenty, she released *Songs in A Minor Key*, the debut album that scored five Grammy awards in 2002, including Best New Artist and Song of the Year for her hit single "Fallin."

Alicia Keys performs on MTV's Total Request Live in 2005.

2. In a treasured letter home from the Civil War, my great great grandfather William, then sixteen, describes an evening of surprising calm.

 2   Suddenly, one of William's buddies spotted Confederate soldiers watching from the opposite bank.

——   ~~The Civil War lasted from 1861 to 1865.~~

 4   Yanks and Rebs swam, whooped, and even shared cigarettes together before returning to their camps.

 3   William did not know what signal was given, but instead of shooting, both armies suddenly stripped to their underwear and splashed into the water.

 5   The next morning, these young men continued the slaughter.

 1   After a day of bloody fighting in July 1863, William and his Union company were settling down on a wooded hill above a pond.

3. Some say that the Greek myth of Icarus teaches the importance of moderation and self-control.

   __5__ Just as his father predicted, the blazing sun melted the wax, the wings fell apart, and Icarus plummeted to his death.

   __1__ To escape from a tower prison in the Mediterranean Sea, the inventor Daedalus made wings for himself and his son Icarus out of feathers, thread, and wax.

   __4__ Soaring higher and higher and delighting in his ability to fly toward the sun, Icarus ignored his father's advice.

   __3__ Daedalus and Icarus leapt from the tower and began flying over the sea.

   _____ The study of Greek myths can be rewarding and relevant to modern life.

   __2__ As he strapped on their wings, Daedalus warned his boy not to fly too near the sun, or the heat would melt the wax.

| PRACTICE 3 | THINKING AND WRITING TOGETHER |

Carefully examine this painting. Based on your reading of item 3 above, why does the artist title it "Icarus" instead of "Pear in a Window"? Can you find at least three details in the painting that justify the title?

Icarus by Vladimir Kush.

PRACTICE 4

Here are topic sentences for three narrative paragraphs. Make a plan for each paragraph, placing the events of the narrative in the proper time sequence.

1. When I had trouble with _____, help came from an unexpected source.

   _____

   _____

   _____

   _____

   _____

   _____

2. The accident (or performance) lasted only a few moments, but I will never forget it.

   _____

   _____

   _____

   _____

   _____

   _____

3. Last year, _____ learned something surprising about himself/herself.

   _____

   _____

   _____

   _____

   _____

   _____

TEACHING TIP
Dialogue or quotations can enliven narratives. If students want to include quotations, refer them to Chapter 36, "Mechanics," Part C, to review the rules.

| PRACTICE 5 | THINKING AND WRITING TOGETHER |

Narrate an Experience of Stereotyping

Good narratives have a *point;* they bring to life a moral, lesson, or idea. In a group with four of five classmates, read this narrative passage about "The Latina Stereotype" by Judith Ortiz Cofer and then discuss and answer the questions.

> My first public poetry reading took place at a restaurant where a luncheon was being held before the event. I was nervous and excited as I walked in with a notebook in hand. An older woman motioned me to her table, and thinking (foolish me) that she wanted me to autograph a copy of my newly published slender volume of verse, I went over. She ordered a cup of coffee from me, assuming that I was the waitress. (Easy enough to mistake my poems for menus, I suppose.) I know it wasn't an intentional act of cruelty. Yet of all the good things that happened later, I remember that scene most clearly, because it reminded me of what I had to overcome before anyone would take me seriously.

▪ What is the point of this story? Exactly what *stereotype* did the writer encounter? What did the woman assume about her and why?

▪ Have you ever been stereotyped? That is, has anyone ever treated you a certain way based only on your age, clothing, race, gender, major, accent, piercings or other decoration, or even things you are carrying, like books or a beeper? Share a story with the group. What stereotype was imposed on you, and how did you react? Now narrate vividly in writing your experience of stereotyping. You might wish to place your topic sentence, stating the meaning or point, last. Refer to the checklist, and ask your group mates for feedback.

 EXPLORING ONLINE

http://www.tolerance.org/ Explore this interesting site about increasing tolerance. Take notes on any ideas for further writing.

✔ CHECKLIST

The Process of Writing a Narrative Paragraph

Refer to this checklist of steps as you write a narrative paragraph of your own.

- ☐ 1. Narrow the topic in light of your audience and purpose.
- ☐ 2. Compose a topic sentence that tells the point of the story.
- ☐ 3. Freewrite or brainstorm for all of the events and details that might be part of the story. (You may want to freewrite or brainstorm before you narrow the topic.)
- ☐ 4. Select the important events and details; drop any that do not clearly relate to the point in your topic sentence.
- ☐ 5. Make a plan or an outline for the paragraph, numbering the events in the correct time (chronological) sequence.
- ☐ 6. Write a draft of your narrative paragraph, using transitional expressions to indicate time sequence.
- ☐ 7. Revise as necessary, checking for support, unity, logic, and coherence.
- ☐ 8. Proofread for errors in grammar, punctuation, sentence structure, spelling, and mechanics.

TEACHING TIP
For downloadable rubrics corresponding to each rhetorical mode, go to the *Evergreen* Online Teaching Center.

Suggested Topics for Narrative Paragraphs

1. A favorite family story
2. A lesson in tolerance
3. A fulfilled (or unfulfilled) ambition
4. A few moments that changed someone's life
5. A laugh at yourself
6. A breakthrough (emotional, physical, or spiritual)
7. An experience in a new country
8. A turning point at work
9. A triumphant (or embarrassing) moment
10. The first time you met an important friend
11. A serious choice or decision
12. A visit to the ER (or other interesting place)
13. An encounter with prejudice
14. Something you or another person dared to do
15. Writer's choice: _____

 EXPLORING ONLINE

TEACHING TIP
More practice and assess-
ment are available in the
Evergreen Test Bank, linked
ACE tests on the *Evergreen*
Online Teaching and Study
Centers, *WriteSpace for
Evergreen,* and Exploring
Online links in this chapter.

http://grammar.ccc.commnet.edu/grammar/composition/narrative.htm Review the elements of a good narrative, and read some fine examples.

http://www.healingstory.org/ Do you think that stories can heal? Explore this
web site and decide for yourself. Click "Treasure Chest" and "Discussion Stories."

Online Study Center   **college.hmco.com/pic/evergreen8e**
Visit the Online Study Center for *Evergreen* for more exercises and quizzes.

7

Description

To **describe** something—a person, a place, or an object—is to capture it in words so others can imagine it or see it in their mind's eye.

The best way for a writer to help the reader get a clear impression is to use language that appeals to the senses: sight, sound, smell, taste, and touch. For it is through the senses that human beings experience the physical world around them, and it is through the senses that the world is most vividly described.

Imagine, for instance, that you have just gone boating on a lake at sunset. You may not have taken a photograph, yet your friends and family can receive an accurate picture of what you have experienced if you *describe* the pink sky reflected in smooth water, the creak of the wooden boat, the soothing drip of water from the oars, the occasional splash of a large bass jumping, the faint fish smells, the cool and darkening air. Writing down what your senses experience will teach you to see, hear, smell, taste, and touch more acutely than ever before.

Description is useful in English class, the sciences, psychology—anywhere that keen observation is important.

Topic Sentence

Here is the topic sentence of a descriptive paragraph:

> On November 27, 1922, when archaeologist Howard Carter unsealed the door to the ancient Egyptian tomb of King Tut, he stared in amazement at the fantastic objects heaped all around him.

■ The writer begins a descriptive paragraph by pointing out what will be described. What will be described in this paragraph?

the fantastic objects in King Tut's tomb

■ The writer can also give a general impression of this scene, object, or person. What overall impression of the tomb does the writer provide?

The writer gives the impression that the heaps of fantastic objects in King Tut's tomb were

an amazing sight.

Paragraph and Plan

Here is the entire paragraph:

TEACHING TIP
Point out to students that this paragraph about King Tut's tomb is a good example of how exact, concise, fresh, and figurative language (all discussed in Chapter 22) work together to create vivid mental images in readers' minds.

> On November 27, 1922, when archaeologist Howard Carter unsealed the door to the ancient Egyptian tomb of King Tut, he stared in amazement at the fantastic objects heaped all around him. On his left lay the wrecks of at least four golden chariots. Against the wall on his right sat a gorgeous chest brightly painted with hunting and battle scenes. Across from him was a gilded throne with cat-shaped legs, arms like winged serpents, and a back showing King Tut and his queen. Behind the throne rose a tall couch decorated with animal faces that were half hippopotamus and half crocodile. The couch was loaded with more treasures. To the right of the couch, two life-sized statues faced each other like guards. They were black, wore gold skirts and sandals, and had cobras carved on their foreheads. Between them was a second sealed doorway. Carter's heart beat loudly. Would the mummy of King Tut lie beyond it?

■ The overall impression given by the topic sentence is that the tomb's many objects were amazing. List three specific details that support this impression.

Answers will vary.

wrecks of four golden chariots

chest painted with hunting and battle scenes

gilded throne with cat-shaped legs

ESL TIP
Encourage ESL students to broaden their vocabulary. Ask them to study any unfamiliar words from the sample paragraph with a partner.

■ Note the importance of words that indicate richness and unusual decoration in helping the reader visualize the scene.* List as many of these words as you can:

fantastic, golden, gorgeous, brightly painted, gilded, cat-shaped legs, winged

serpents, animal faces that were half hippopotamus and half crocodile, treasures,

life-sized statues, gold skirts and sandals, cobras carved on their foreheads

■ This paragraph, like many descriptive paragraphs, is organized according to space order.† The author uses transitional expressions that show where things are. Underline the transitional expressions that indicate place or position.

---

* For more work on vivid language, see Chapter 22, "Revising for Language Awareness."

† For more work on space order and other kinds of order, see Chapter 4, "Achieving Coherence," Part A.

Before composing this descriptive paragraph, the writer probably brainstormed and freewrote to gather ideas and then made an **outline** like this:

Topic sentence: On November 27, 1922, when archaeologist Howard Carter unsealed the door to the ancient Egyptian tomb of King Tut, he stared in amazement at the fantastic objects heaped all around him.

1. To the left:	chariots —wrecked —golden	
2. To the right:	a gorgeous chest —brightly painted with hunting and battle scenes	
3. Across the room:	a throne —gilded —cat-shaped legs —arms like winged serpents	
4. Behind the throne:	a couch —decorated with faces that were half hippopotamus and half crocodile	
5. To the right of the couch:	two life-sized statues —black —gold skirts and sandals —cobras carved on foreheads	
6. Between the two statues:	a second sealed doorway	

Conclusion: expectation that King Tut's mummy was beyond the second door

---

■ Note how each detail supports the topic sentence.

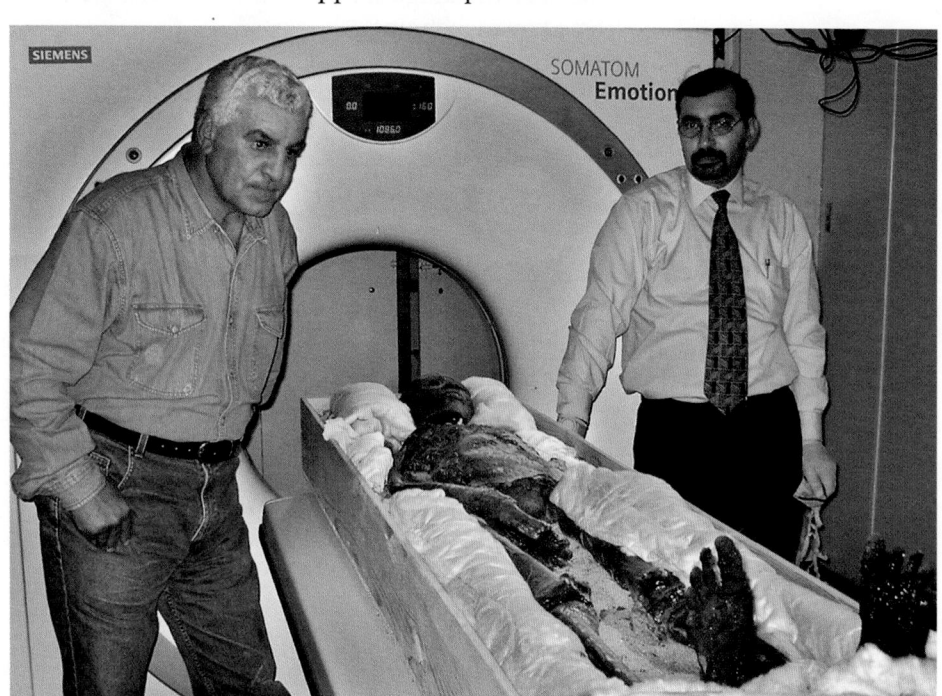

In 2005, a CT scan of Tut's 3300-year-old mummy revealed that the boy king was not murdered, but might have suffered a broken leg before he died.

Transitional Expressions

Since space order is often used in description, **transitional expressions** indicating place or position can be useful:

Transitional Expressions Indicating Place	
next to, near	on top, beneath
close, far	toward, away
up, down, between	left, right, center
above, below	front, back, middle

Of course, other kinds of order are possible. For example, a description of a person might have two parts: details of physical appearance and details of behavior.*

PRACTICE 1

Read the following paragraph carefully and answer the questions.

The woman who met us had an imposing beauty. She was tall and large-boned. Her face was strongly molded, with high cheekbones and skin the color of mahogany. She greeted us politely but did not smile and seemed to hold her head very high, an effect exaggerated by the abundant black hair slicked up and rolled on the top of her head. Her clothing was simple, a black sweater and skirt, and I remember thinking that dressed in showier garments, this woman would have seemed overwhelming.

1. What overall impression does the writer give of the woman?

   The impression is that the woman had a regal and imposing beauty.

   _____

2. What specific details support this general impression? tall; high cheekbones;

   mahogany skin; head held high; hair piled high on head; unsmiling expression

   _____

   _____

3. What kind of order does the writer use? space order _____

---

* For a complete essay developed by description, see "The Day of the Dead," Chapter 15, Part C.

PRACTICE 2

It is important that the details in a descriptive paragraph support the overall impression given in the topic sentence. In each of the following plans, one detail has nothing to do with the topic sentence; it is merely a bit of irrelevant information. Find the irrelevant detail and circle its letter.

1. Leo's dormitory room is uniquely decorated.

    a. dozens of cartoons taped on the door

    b. Leo's car painted with Spider Man designs

    c. lime green junk-shop chair in corner

    d. silver robotic dog guarding the door

    e. bookshelves crammed with computer books

    f. monitor glows with shifting pictures of Einstein

2. The Calle Ocho Festival, named after S.W. 8th Street in Little Havana, is a giant Latino street party.

    a. as far as the eye can see on S.W. 8th Street, thousands of people stroll, eat, and dance

    b. on the left, vendors sell hot pork sandwiches, *pasteles* (spiced meat pies), and fried sweets dusted with powdered sugar

    c. up close, the press of bare-limbed people, blaring music, and rich smells

    d. during the 1980s, Dominican merengue music hit the dance clubs of New York

    e. on the right, two of many bands play mambo or merengue music

3. In the photograph from 1877, Chief Joseph looks sad and dignified.

    a. long hair pulled back, touched with gray

    b. dark eyes gaze off to one side, as if seeing a bleak future

    c. strong mouth frowns at the corners

    d. ceremonial shell necklaces cover his chest

    e. Nez Percé tribe once occupied much of the Pacific Northwest

4. A large pitcher of iced tea sat on the tray.

    a. ice maker humming in the refrigerator

    b. clear glass of the pitcher frosted with cold

    c. large drops running downward, pooling on the tray

    d. clear ice cubes gleaming in rust-brown tea

    e. orange and lemon slices among the ice cubes

5. An illegal dump site has spoiled the field near the edge of town.

    a. fifty or more rusting metal drums, some leaking

b. pools of green-black liquid on the ground

c. in the distance, view of the mountains

d. wildflowers and cottonwood trees dead or dying

e. large sign reading "Keep Out—Toxic Chemicals"

PRACTICE 3

Here are three topic sentences for descriptive paragraphs. Give five specific details that would support the overall impression given in each topic sentence. Appeal to as many of the senses as possible. Be careful not to list irrelevant bits of information. Answers will vary.

EXAMPLE Stopped in time by the photographer, my mother appears confident.

Details: a. her hair swept up in a sophisticated pompadour

b. a determined look in her young eyes

c. wide, self-assured smile

d. her chin held high

e. well-padded shoulders

(These five details support *confident* in the topic sentence.)

1. This was clearly a music lover's room.

a. a grand piano at one end

b. music stand with flute laid across it

c. shelves of books about music

d. CD player and large collection of discs

e. stacks of music on a desk

2. The buildings on that street look sadly run-down.

a. paint peeling from weathered old buildings

b. some windows broken or covered with cardboard

c. other windows covered with dirt and grease

d. sagging roofs with loose tiles

e. screen doors open or attached by only one hinge

3. The beach on a hot summer day presented a constant show.

　　a. children running and splashing in the water

　　b. sunbathers rubbing lotion on themselves

　　c. dogs chasing sticks and balls

　　d. vendors selling soda and ice-cream bars

　　e. sea gulls circling and diving for food

PRACTICE 4

Pick the description you like best from Practice 3. Prewrite for more details if you wish. Choose a logical order in which to present the best details, make a plan or an outline, and then write an excellent descriptive paragraph.

PRACTICE 5　　THINKING AND WRITING TOGETHER

Describe a Painting

In a group with four or five classmates, study the painting below. Your task is to write one paragraph describing this painting so that someone who has never seen it can visualize it. As a group, craft a good topic sentence that gives an *overall impression* of the scene. Your topic sentence might take this form:

"George Tooker's 1950 painting, *Subway*, shows (or captures) _the subway is a_

frightening place, prison-like environment ."

　　Have one person take notes as you brainstorm important details, using rich language to capture the scene. Now decide the best order in which to present your details—right to left, center to sides, or some other. Use transitional expressions to guide the reader's eye from detail to detail. Revise the writing to make it as exact and fresh as possible. Be prepared to read your work to the full class.

Subway by George Tooker

© Whitney Museum of Art, New York; Purchase, with funds from the Juliana Force Purchase Award 50.23.

EXPLORING ONLINE

http://www.artic.edu/aic/ Art Institute of Chicago: Find a work of art that intrigues you and describe it.

http://www.moma.org/ Museum of Modern Art: Find a work of art that intrigues you and write about it.

✔ CHECKLIST

The Process of Writing a Descriptive Paragraph

Refer to this checklist of steps as you write a descriptive paragraph of your own.

☐ 1. Narrow the topic in light of your audience and purpose.

☐ 2. Compose a topic sentence that clearly points to what you will describe or gives an overall impression of the person, object, or scene.

☐ 3. Freewrite or brainstorm to find as many specific details as you can to capture your subject in words. Remember to appeal to your readers' senses. (You may want to freewrite or brainstorm before you narrow the topic.)

☐ 4. Select the best details and drop any irrelevant ones.

☐ 5. Make a plan or an outline for the paragraph, numbering the details in the order in which you will present them.

☐ 6. Write a draft of your descriptive paragraph, using transitional expressions wherever they might be helpful.

☐ 7. Revise as necessary, checking for support, unity, logic, and coherence.

☐ 8. Proofread for errors in grammar, punctuation, sentence structure, spelling, and mechanics.

TEACHING TIP
For downloadable rubrics corresponding to each rhetorical mode, go to the *Evergreen* Online Teaching Center.

Suggested Topics for Descriptive Paragraphs

ESL TIP
Urge your ESL students to try out fresh vocabulary. They may require instructor feedback on word choice.

1. An unusual man or woman: for example, an athlete, an entertainer, someone with amazing hair or clothing, or a teacher you won't forget

2. A food, object, or scene from another country

3. The face of someone in the news

4. A tool or machine you use at work

5. An animal, a bird, or an insect you have observed closely

6. Someone or something you found yourself staring at

7. A photograph of yourself as a child

8. A scene of peace (or of conflict)

9. A room that reveals something about its owner

10. A fascinating or frightening outdoor scene

11. A shop that sells only one type of item: cheese, computer software, Western boots, car parts, flowers

12. An interesting person you have seen on campus

13. A public place: dance club, library, fast-food restaurant, town square, or theater lobby

14. A neighborhood personality

15. Writer's choice: _____

EXPLORING ONLINE

http://leo.stcloudstate.edu/acadwrite/descriptive.html Good tips for improving your descriptive writing, with sample paragraphs

Online Study Center **college.hmco.com/pic/evergreen8e**
Visit the Online Study Center for *Evergreen* for more exercises and quizzes.

8

Process

Two kinds of **process paragraphs** will be explained in this chapter: the how-to paragraph and the explanation paragraph.

The **how-to paragraph** gives the reader directions on how he or she can do something: how to install a software program, how to get to the airport, or how to make tasty barbecued ribs. The goals of such directions are the installed software, the arrival at the airport, or the great barbecued ribs. In other words, the reader should be able to do something after reading the paragraph.

The **explanation paragraph,** on the other hand, tells the reader how a particular event occurred or how something works. For example, an explanation paragraph might explain how an internal combustion engine works or how palm trees reproduce. After reading an explanation paragraph, the reader is not expected to be able to do anything, just to understand how it happened or how it works.

Process writing is useful in history, business, the sciences, psychology, and many other areas.

TEACHING TIP
Ask students to think about their experiences with trying to follow directions and assemble something relatively complex (e.g., a DVD player or barbecue grill). Can they see why clear directions are important?

Topic Sentence

Here is the topic sentence of a **how-to paragraph:**

> Careful preparation before an interview is the key to getting the job you want.

■ The writer begins a how-to paragraph with a topic sentence that clearly states the goal of the process—what the reader should be able to do.

■ What should the reader be able to do after he or she has read the paragraph following this topic sentence?

The reader should be able to prepare for a job interview.

Paragraph and Plan

Here is the entire paragraph:

> "Luck is preparation meeting opportunity," it has been said, and this is true for a job interview. Careful preparation before an interview is the key to getting the job you want. The first step is to learn all you can about the employer. Read about the company in its brochures or in newspaper and magazine articles. A reference librarian can point you to the best sources of company information. You can also find company web sites and other useful material on the Internet. Second, as you read, think about the ways your talents match the company's goals. Third, put yourself in the interviewer's place, and make a list of questions that he or she will probably ask. Employers want to know about your experience, training, and special skills, like foreign languages. Remember, every employer looks for a capable and enthusiastic team player who will help the firm succeed. Fourth, rehearse your answers to the questions out loud. Practice with a friend or a tape recorder until your responses sound well prepared and confident. Finally, select and prepare a professional-looking interview outfit well in advance to avoid the last-minute panic of a torn hem or stained shirt. When a job candidate has made the effort to prepare, the interviewer is much more likely to be impressed.

TEACHING TIP
Alert students to the Career and Job-Search Resources on the *Evergreen* Online Study Center (which stresses the link between good writing and good jobs). Web searches will reveal much online help, including **http://interview.monster. com/archives/tips/.**

■ The topic sentence is the second sentence. In the first sentence, the writer has used a quotation to open the paragraph and spark the reader's interest.

■ The body of the how-to paragraph is developed according to time, or chronological, order.* That is, the writer gives directions in the order in which the reader is to complete them. Keeping to a strict chronological order avoids the necessity of saying, *By the way, I forgot to tell you . . .* , or *Whoops, a previous step should have been to. . . .*

■ How many steps are there in this how-to paragraph and what are they?

There are five steps: (1) Learn about the company, (2) match your talents to the

company's goals, (3) list interviewer questions, (4) practice answering them, and

(5) prepare your outfit.

---

* For more work on order, see Chapter 4, "Achieving Coherence," Part A.

Before writing this how-to paragraph, the writer probably brainstormed or freewrote to gather ideas and then made an **outline** like this:

Topic sentence: Careful preparation before an interview is the key to getting the job you want.

Step 1:   Learn about the employer
— read company brochures, papers, magazines
— reference librarian can help
— check company web site

Step 2:   Think how your talents match company goals

Step 3:   List interviewer questions
— think about experience, training, special skills
— employers want capable team players

Step 4:   Rehearse your answers out loud
— practice with friend or tape recorder

Step 5:   Select your interview outfit
— avoid last-minute panic
— avoid torn hem, stained shirt

Conclusion: Interviewer more likely to be impressed

▪ Note that each step clearly relates to the goal stated in the topic sentence.

The second kind of process paragraph, the **explanation paragraph,** tells how something works, how it happens, or how it came to be:

> Many experts believe that recovery from addiction, whether to alcohol or other drugs, has four main stages. The first stage begins when the user finally admits that he or she has a substance abuse problem and wants to quit. At this point, most people seek help from groups like Alcoholics Anonymous or treatment programs because few addicts can "get clean" by themselves. The next stage is withdrawal, when the addict stops using the substance. Withdrawal can be a painful physical and emotional experience, but luckily, it does not last long. After withdrawal comes the most challenging stage—making positive changes in one's life. Recovering addicts have to learn new ways of spending their time, finding pleasure and relaxation, caring for their bodies, and relating to spouses, lovers, family, and friends. The fourth and final stage is staying off drugs. This open-ended part of the process often calls for ongoing support or therapy. For people once defeated by addiction, the rewards of self-esteem and a new life are well worth the effort.

▪ What process does the writer explain in this paragraph? The writer explains how people recover from addiction.

▪ How many stages or steps are explained in this paragraph? four

■ What are they? <u>(1) deciding to quit, (2) withdrawing from substance,</u>

    <u>(3) changing one's life, (4) staying off drugs</u>

■ Make a plan of the paragraph in your notebook.

    Just as the photographs on this page show each stage in the process of a chick hatching, so your process paragraph should clearly describe each step or stage for the reader. Before you write, try to visualize the process as if it were a series of photographs.*

Transitional Expressions

Since process paragraphs rely on **chronological order,** or **time sequence,** words and expressions that locate the steps of the process in time are extremely helpful.

Transitional Expressions for Process			
Beginning a Process	**Continuing a Process**		**Ending a Process**
(at) first	second, third step	when	finally
initially	until	while	at last
begin by	after(ward)	as soon as	
	then	as	
	next	upon	
	later	during	
	before	meanwhile	

PRACTICE 1

Read the following how-to paragraph carefully and answer the questions.

ESL TIP
ESL students may need help with command verbs in English. Have them point out command verbs in the sample paragraph.

    If your dog barks too much, the Humane Society recommends an easy way to solve the problem. All you need is a plant mister—a small spray bottle—filled with water and kept handy. First and most important, respond immediately every time your dog barks unnecessarily. Instantly say, "Quiet, Pluto," or whatever the dog's name is, giving one or two squirts of water in the dog's face. Be sure to do this while the dog is barking. Waiting until the dog stops barking may confuse it. If the dog moves away, say, "Quiet" again as you move toward the dog and give it one more squirt of water. Second, repeat this procedure every time the dog barks without a good reason. The dog will soon learn that your saying "Quiet" comes with a squirt of water. Usually two days—about five to ten water treatments—are enough. Third, as time goes by, use the spray bottle only if the dog forgets—that is, rarely. Throughout the training process, remember to be consistent, using the spray technique every single time, and don't forget to reassure your dog that you two are still friends by petting it when it is quiet.

—Eleanor Steiger (Student)

1. What should you be able to do after reading this paragraph?

   You should be able to teach your dog to stop unnecessary barking.

   _____

2. Are any "materials" necessary for this process? The only item is a _____

   spray bottle.

3. How many steps are there in this paragraph? List them.

   three: (1) squirt the dog in the face the minute it barks, (2) repeat this every time

   for a day or two, (3) thereafter, squirt only when the dog forgets. Also, the writer

   says, "throughout the process"—be consistent and pet the dog when quiet.

4. What order does the writer employ? time order

PRACTICE 2

Here are five plans for process paragraphs. The steps for the plans are not in the correct chronological order. The plans also contain irrelevant details that are not part of the process. Number the steps in the proper time sequence and cross out any irrelevant details.

1. Monster.com grew quickly into a popular resource for both job seekers and employers.

   _3_ In 1994, before the Internet was used much by the public, Taylor launched the Monster Board to post jobs online.

   _1_ Businessman Jeff Taylor was looking for a way to help his customers find good staff.

   _4_ So many people used the Monster Board that the company soon expanded from 24 to 2,000 employees.

   _2_ One night in a dream, he had a "monster idea"—to use the Internet as a job-search tool.

   ____ ~~Monsters have always been popular in films, from Frankenstein and Dracula to the frightening creatures in the *Alien* series.~~

   _5_ In 1999, Monster.com joined with Online Career Center, adding free help with résumé writing and other career skills.

2. Stress, which is your body's response to physical or mental pressures, occurs in three stages.

   _2_ In the resistance stage, your body works hard to resist or handle the threat, but you may become more vulnerable to other stressors, like flu or colds.

   _3_ If the stress continues for too long, your body uses up its defenses and enters the exhaustion stage.

   ____ ~~Trying to balance college courses, parenthood, and work is sure to cause stress.~~

   _1_ During the alarm stage (also called *fight or flight*), your body first reacts to a threat by releasing hormones that increase your heart rate and blood pressure, create muscle tension, and supply quick energy.

3. Chewing gum is made entirely by machine.

   __3__ Then the warm mass is pressed into thin ribbons by pairs of rollers.

   __1__ First, the gum base is melted and pumped through a high-speed spinner that throws out all impurities.

   _____ ~~The gum base makes the gum chewy.~~

   __2__ Huge machines mix the purified gum with sugar, corn syrup, and flavoring, such as spearmint, peppermint, or cinnamon.

   __5__ Finally, machines wrap the sticks individually and then package them.

   __4__ Knives attached to the last rollers cut the ribbons into sticks.

4. Many psychologists claim that marriage is a dynamic process consisting of several phases.

   __2__ Sooner or later, romance gives way to disappointment as both partners really see each other's faults.

   __1__ Idealization is the first phase, when two people fall romantically in love, each thinking the other is perfect.

   __5__ The last phase occurs as the couple face their late years as a twosome once again.

   __3__ The third phase is sometimes called the productivity period, when two people work at parenting and career development.

   _____ ~~Men and women may have different expectations in a marriage.~~

   __4__ As the children leave home and careers mature, couples may enter a stage when they rethink their lives and goals.

5. Helping to save rare stranded sea turtles, our service learning project, was a rewarding series of steps.

   __3__ Inside, we rubbed Vaseline on each turtle's shell and put saline in its eyes; the sickest turtles needed IV fluids.

   __2__ We gently loaded each tired giant in the front seat of a pickup truck and hurried back to the sanctuary.

   __1__ In the fall, when temperatures dropped, we volunteers at the Wellfleet Wildlife Sanctuary raced to the beaches to find any giant sea turtles that had not swum south.

   _____ ~~Two volunteers so loved working with endangered turtles that they are now pursuing careers in marine biology.~~

   __4__ Within 12 hours, we drove our patients to the aquarium in Boston, to spend the winter and get well before their release in warm Florida seas.

PRACTICE 3

Here are topic sentences for three process paragraphs. Make a plan for each paragraph, listing in proper time sequence all the steps that would be necessary to complete the process. Now choose one plan and write an excellent process paragraph. Answers will vary.

TEACHING TIP
An enjoyable way to help students anticipate readers' questions about their process writing is to have them write and exchange how-to paragraphs with a classmate. Each reader should re-create the process, based *only* on what is written, and then report any unanswered questions to the writer.

1. Although I'm still not the life of the party, I took these steps to overcome my shyness at parties.

   Two weeks before the next party, I told myself that others were as shy as I was.

   One week before the party, I selected clothes I feel comfortable in to wear

   to the party.

   On my way to the party, I rehearsed some conversation topics.

   At the party, I introduced myself to three new people.

   _____

   _____

2. Good kids turning bad: it is a process occurring all over the country.

   It usually begins with a good kid in a bad situation, in a dangerous

   neighborhood or school.

   The child may do the right thing but be mocked or beaten up by peers for

   studying or even attending class.

   After a while, the pressure or effort may be too much, and the child stops

   caring about schoolwork or joins a gang.

   Now, without skills, he or she has no future, and easy money from drug sales or

   other crimes may start to look good.

3. Registration _____ is/was a very complicated (or simple) process.

   I picked the four courses I wanted to take.

   My adviser was in her office when I went to get her signature.

   The line at the registrar's office was short when I arrived.

   None of the courses I wanted was full, so I didn't have to choose alternatives.

   _____

   _____

| PRACTICE 4 | THINKING AND WRITING TOGETHER |

Explain the Process of Intoxication

ESL TIP
For Practice 4, ESL students may need extra help choosing correct word forms.

In a group with four or five classmates, study and discuss these percentages that show rising blood alcohol content (BAC), a measure of intoxication. Now plan and write a paragraph that describes what happens as BAC rises. Your purpose is to inform the public about this process. Write a topic sentence that gives an overview; in the body, include three or four percentages if you wish. In your concluding sentence or sentences, you might wish to emphasize the dangerous human meaning of these numbers. Be prepared to read your paragraph to the full class.

BAC	Effect
0.03%	relaxation, mood change
0.05%	decrease in motor skills; legal driving limit in New York
0.07%	legal driving limit in sixteen states
0.09%	delayed reaction time, decreased muscle control, slurred speech
0.15%	blurred vision, unsteadiness, impaired coordination
0.18%	difficulty staying awake
0.30%	semi-stupor
0.50%	coma and risk of death

Now assume your purpose is to write another paragraph convincing young people not to binge drink. Would BAC percentages help persuade your audience, or would you take another approach? What might that approach be?

 EXPLORING ONLINE

http://www.hsph.harvard.edu/cas/ College Alcohol Study

http://www.dui.com/drunk_driving_research/under_the_influence.html
Defining drunk driving

✓ CHECKLIST

The Process of Writing a Process Paragraph

Refer to this checklist of steps as you write a process paragraph of your own.

☐ 1. Narrow the topic in light of your audience and purpose.

☐ 2. Compose a topic sentence that clearly states the goal or end result of the process you wish to describe.

☐ 3. Freewrite or brainstorm to generate steps that might be part of the process. (You may want to freewrite or brainstorm before you narrow the topic.)

☐ 4. Drop any irrelevant information or steps that are not really necessary for your explanation of the process.

☐ 5. Make an outline or a plan for your paragraph, numbering the steps in the correct time (chronological) sequence.

☐ 6. Write a draft of your process paragraph, using transitional expressions to indicate time (chronological) sequence.

☐ 7. Revise as necessary, checking for support, unity, logic, and coherence.

☐ 8. Proofread for errors in grammar, punctuation, sentence structure, spelling, and mechanics.

TEACHING TIP
For downloadable rubrics corresponding to each rhetorical mode, go to the *Evergreen* Online Teaching Center.

Suggested Topics for Process Paragraphs

1. How to break up with (or attract) someone

2. How to prepare your favorite dish

3. How someone landed a wonderful job

4. How to relax or meditate

5. How to establish credit (or improve your credit score)

6. How an important discovery was made

7. How to find information in the library's electronic card catalogue (or reference book section)

8. How to be a true friend

9. How to shop on a budget for a computer (or clothes, housewares, and so on)

10. How to appear smarter than you really are

11. How to break an unhealthy habit

12. How to motivate someone to _____

13. How to get the most out of a visit to the doctor

14. How to choose a major

15. Writer's choice: _____

EXPLORING ONLINE

TEACHING TIP
More practice and assessment are available in the *Evergreen* Test Bank, linked ACE tests on the *Evergreen* Online Teaching and Study Centers, *WriteSpace for Evergreen,* and Exploring Online links in this chapter.

http://www.ehow.com/how_1323_make-peanut-butter.html Do you think you can make a scrumptious peanut butter and jelly sandwich? Read these clear instructions.

http://www.howstuffworks.com/ This intriguing site tells how to do all sorts of things.

Online Study Center   **college.hmco.com/pic/evergreen8e**
Visit the Online Study Center for *Evergreen* for more exercises and quizzes.

9

Definition

| PART A | Single-Sentence Definitions |
| PART B | The Definition Paragraph |

To **define** is to explain clearly what a word or term means.

As you write, you will sometimes find it necessary to explain words or terms that you suspect your reader may not know. For example, *net profit* is the profit remaining after all deductions have been taken; a *bonsai* is a dwarfed, ornamentally shaped tree. Such terms can often be defined in just a few carefully chosen words. However, other terms—like *courage, racism,* or *a good marriage*—are more difficult to define. They will test your ability to explain them clearly so that your reader knows exactly what you mean when you use them in your writing. They may require an entire paragraph for a complete and thorough definition.

In this chapter, you will learn to write one-sentence definitions and then whole paragraphs of definition. The skill of defining clearly will be useful in such courses as psychology, business, the sciences, history, and English.

PART A Single-Sentence Definitions

There are many ways to define a word or term. Three basic ways are **definition by synonym**, **definition by class**, and **definition by negation**.

Definition by Synonym

TEACHING TIP
Students might wish to keep a thesaurus nearby while writing definitions. For an online thesaurus, go to **http://thesaurus.reference. com**.

The simplest way to define a term is to supply a **synonym,** a word that means the same thing. A good synonym definition always uses an easier and more familiar word than the one being defined.

1. *Gregarious* means *sociable.*

2. *To procrastinate* means *to postpone needlessly.*

> 3. A *wraith* is a *ghost* or *phantom*.
>
> 4. *Adroitly* means *skillfully*.

Although you may not have known the words *gregarious, procrastination, wraith,* and *adroitly* before, the synonym definitions make it very clear what they mean.

A synonym should usually be the same part of speech as the word being defined, so it could be used as a substitute. *Gregarious* and *sociable* are both adjectives; *to procrastinate* and *to postpone* are verb forms; *wraith, ghost,* and *phantom* are nouns; *adroitly* and *skillfully* are adverbs.

> 5. Quarterback Peyton Manning *adroitly* moved his team up the field.
>
> 6. Quarterback Peyton Manning *skillfully* moved his team up the field.

■ In this sentence *skillfully* can be substituted for *adroitly*.

Unfortunately, it is not always possible to come up with a good synonym definition.

Definition by Class

The **class** definition is the one most often required in college and formal writing—in examinations, papers, and reports.

The class definition has two parts. First, the writer places the word to be defined into the larger **category,** or **class,** to which it belongs.

> 7. *Lemonade* is a *drink* . . .
>
> 8. An *orphan* is a *child* . . .
>
> 9. A *dictatorship* is a *form of government* . . .

Second, the writer provides the **distinguishing characteristics** or **details** that make this person, object, or idea *different* from all others in that category. What the reader wants to know is what *kind* of drink is lemonade? What *specific* type of child is an orphan? What *particular* form of government is a dictatorship?

> 10. *Lemonade* is a drink *made of lemons, sugar, and water.*
>
> 11. An *orphan* is a child *without living parents.*
>
> 12. A *dictatorship* is a form of government *in which one person has absolute control over his or her subjects.*

ESL TIP
ESL students may require additional explanation of relative clauses. Refer them to Chapters 21 and 27 for review.

Here is a class definition of the activity pictured: *The tango is a ballroom dance that originated in Argentina and is characterized by catlike walking steps.*

Think of class definitions as if they were in chart form:

Word	Category or Class	Distinguishing Facts or Details
lemonade	drink	made of lemons, sugar, and water
orphan	child	without living parents
dictatorship	form of government	one person has absolute control over his or her subjects

When you write a class definition, be careful not to place the word or term in too broad or vague a category. For instance, saying that lemonade is a *food* or that an orphan is a *person* will make your job of zeroing in on a distinguishing detail more difficult.

Besides making the category or class as limited as possible, be sure to make your distinguishing facts as specific and exact as you can. Saying that lemonade is a drink *made with water* or that an orphan is a child *who has lost family members* is not specific enough to give your reader an accurate definition.

Definition by Negation

A definition by **negation** means that the writer first says what something is not, and then says what it is.

13. A *good parent* does not just feed and clothe a child but loves, accepts, and supports that child for who he or she is.

14. *College* is not just a place to have a good time but a place to grow intellectually and emotionally.

15. *Liberty* does not mean having the right to do whatever you please but carries the obligation to respect the rights of others.

Definitions by negation are extremely helpful when you think that the reader has a preconceived idea about the word you wish to define. You say that *it is not* what the reader thought, but that *it is* something else entirely.

PRACTICE 1

Write a one-sentence definition by **synonym** for each of the following terms. Remember, the synonym should be more familiar than the term being defined.

1. *irate:* To be irate is to be angry.

2. *to elude:* To elude someone is to keep away from him or her.

3. *pragmatic:* To be pragmatic is to be practical.

4. *fiasco:* A fiasco is a disaster.

5. *elated:* To be elated is to be overjoyed.

PRACTICE 2

Here are five **class definitions.** Circle the category and underline the distinguishing characteristics in each. You may find it helpful to make a chart.

1. A *haiku* is a (Japanese poem) that has seventeen syllables.

2. A *homer* is a (referee) who unconsciously favors the home team.

3. An *ophthalmologist* is a (doctor) who specializes in diseases of the eye.

4. The *tango* is a (ballroom dance) that originated in Latin America and is in 2/4 or 4/4 time.

5. *Plagiarism* is (stealing writing or ideas) that are not one's own.

PRACTICE 3

Define the following words by **class definition.** You may find it helpful to use this form: "A _____ is a _____
                              (noun)   (class or category)

that _____."
                    (distinguishing characteristic)

TEACHING TIP
Point out that effective definitions include exact language. For more on this topic, see Chapter 22.

1. *hamburger:* A hamburger is a sandwich that consists of a split bun and a ground beef patty.

2. *bikini:* A bikini is a two-piece swimsuit that is very scanty.

3. *snob:* A snob is a person who thinks he or she is, and acts as if he or she were, socially superior to others.

4. *mentor:* A mentor is a counselor who guides, teaches, and assists another person.

5. *adolescence:* Adolescence is the period of life between puberty and maturity.

PRACTICE 4

Write a one-sentence definition by **negation** for each of the following terms. First say what each term is not; then say what it is.

1. *hero:* A hero is not someone with great athletic ability or wealth but a person admired for his or her acts of morality and fine character.

2. *final exam:* A final exam is not just a way to make students suffer but an enforced review of everything learned in the course.

3. *self-esteem:* <u>Self-esteem does not mean conceit but rather a healthy respect for oneself.</u>

_____

_____

4. *intelligence:* <u>Intelligence is not knowledge in a specific area; it is the capacity to</u>

<u>acquire and apply knowledge.</u>

_____

5. *freedom of speech:* <u>Freedom of speech is not just a phrase we learn in history class;</u>

<u>it is a right guaranteed to each American to express his or her beliefs in public.</u>

_____

PART B   The Definition Paragraph

Sometimes a single-sentence definition may not be enough to define a word or term adequately. In such cases, the writer may need an entire paragraph in which he or she develops the definition by means of examples, descriptions, comparisons, contrasts, and so forth.

Topic Sentence

The topic sentence of a definition paragraph is often one of the single-sentence definitions discussed in Part A: definition by synonym, definition by class, definition by negation.

Here is the topic sentence of a definition paragraph:

> A *flashbulb memory* can be defined as a vivid, long-lasting memory that is formed at the moment a person learns of a highly emotional event.

▪ What kind of definition does the topic sentence use? <u>class</u>

▪ To what larger category or class does a *flashbulb memory* belong? <u>vivid,</u>

<u>long-lasting memory</u>

▪ What are the distinguishing details about a *flashbulb memory* that make it different from other kinds of memories? <u>It is formed at the moment a person learns of a</u>

<u>highly emotional event.</u>

Paragraph and Plan

Here is the entire paragraph:

> A *flashbulb memory* can be defined as a vivid and long-lasting memory formed at the moment a person experiences a highly emotional event. It is as though a mental flashbulb pops, preserving the moment in great detail. Although flashbulb memories can be personal, they often are triggered by public events. For example, many older Americans recall exactly what they were doing when they learned that Pearl Harbor was bombed in 1941. Time froze as people crowded around their radios to find out what would happen next. Many more people recall in detail the shocking moment on November 11, 1963, when they heard that President John F. Kennedy had been assassinated. Considered the most widely shared flashbulb memory of our time, the image of Kennedy's death is burned into the minds of people the world over. More recently, the terrorist attack on the World Trade Center became a flashbulb memory for millions. Whether they heard the terrible news on their morning commute or were awakened by a panicked voice on the phone telling them to turn on the television, research into memory suggests that they will never forget that day. As these examples show, flashbulb memories mark some of our most permanent and haunting experiences, moments that were scored into our hearts.

- One effective way for a writer to develop the body of a definition paragraph is to provide examples.*

- What three examples does this writer give to develop the definition in the topic sentence? Pearl Harbor, the assassination of J. F. Kennedy, and the terrorist attack on the World Trade Center

- By repeating the word being defined—or a form of it—in the context of the definition paragraph, the writer helps the reader understand the definition better: "Although *flashbulb memories* can be personal . . . ," "Considered the most widely shared *flashbulb memory* of our time . . . ," ". . . on the World Trade Center became a *flashbulb memory* for millions."

- Before writing the paragraph, the writer probably brainstormed or freewrote to gather ideas and then made an **outline** like this:

Topic sentence: A flashbulb memory is a vivid and long-lasting memory formed at the moment a person experiences a highly emotional event.

Example 1: Pearl Harbor
—older Americans recall what they were doing in 1941
—people crowded around radios

Example 2: J. F. Kennedy's assassination
—most widely shared flashbulb memory of our time
—image of Kennedy's death burned into minds all over the world

---

* For more work on examples, see Chapter 5, "Illustration."

Example 3:   World Trade Center attack
—more recent flashbulb memory for millions
—whether on morning commute or phone, will never forget

Conclusion: Flashbulb memories mark our most permanent and haunting experiences.

___

■ Note that each example in the body of the paragraph clearly relates to the definition in the topic sentence.

Although examples are an excellent way to develop a definition paragraph, other methods of development are also possible. For instance, you might compare and contrast* *love* and *lust, assertiveness* and *aggressiveness,* or *the leader* and *the follower.* You could also combine definition and persuasion.† Such a paragraph might begin *College is a dating service* or *Alcoholism is not a moral weakness but a disease.* The rest of the paragraph would have to persuade readers that this definition is valid.

There are no transitional expressions used specifically for definition paragraphs. Sometimes phrases like *can be defined as* or *can be considered* or *means that* can help alert the reader that a definition paragraph will follow.‡

Here cartoonist Gary Larson takes a lighter look at flashbulb memory.

THE FAR SIDE® BY GARY LARSON

More facts of nature: All forest animals, to this very day, remember exactly where they were and what they were doing when they heard that Bambi's mother had been shot.

___

* For more work on contrast, see Chapter 10, "Comparison and Contrast."

† For more work on persuasion, see Chapter 13, "Persuasion."

‡ For an entire essay developed by definition, see "Winning," Chapter 15, Part E.

PRACTICE 5

TEACHING TIP
Stereotyped labels or loaded terms for groups of people often make good topics for definition paragraphs (and definitions by negation). Ask the class for other terms (e.g., *immigrant, soccer mom,* or *rapper*).

Read the following paragraph carefully and then answer the questions.

A feminist is *not* a man-hater, a masculine woman, a demanding shrew, or someone who dislikes housewives. A feminist is simply a woman or man who believes that women should enjoy the same rights, privileges, opportunities, and pay as men. Because society has deprived women of many equal rights, feminists have fought for equality. For instance, Susan B. Anthony, a famous nineteenth-century feminist, worked to get women the right to vote. Today, feminists want women to receive equal pay for equal work. They support a woman's right to pursue her goals and dreams, whether she wants to be an astronaut, athlete, banker, or full-time homemaker. On the home front, feminists believe that two partners who work should equally share the housework and child care. Because the term is often misunderstood, some people don't call themselves feminists even though they share feminist values. But courageous feminists of both sexes continue to speak out for equality.

1. The definition here spans two sentences. What kind of definition does the writer use in sentence 1? <u>definition by negation</u>

2. What kind of definition appears in sentence 2? <u>definition by class</u>

3. The paragraph is developed by describing some key beliefs of feminists. What are these? <u>equal rights, equal pay for equal work, freedom to pursue goals</u>

   <u>and dreams, working couples' sharing housework and child care</u>

   _____

4. Which point is supported by an example? <u>Feminists have fought for</u>

   <u>equality. Example: Susan B. Anthony</u>

5. Make a plan or an outline of the paragraph.

   <u>Topic sentence(s): A feminist is not a man-hater, a masculine woman, a</u>

   <u>demanding shrew, or someone who dislikes housewives. A feminist is simply</u>

   <u>a woman or man who believes that women should enjoy the same rights,</u>

   <u>privileges, opportunities, and pay as men.</u>

   <u>—fights for equal rights</u>

   <u>—wants equal pay for equal work</u>

   <u>—wants freedom for women to pursue goals and dreams</u>

   <u>—believes working partners should share housework, child care</u>

   <u>Conclusion: Courageous feminists of both sexes speak out for equality.</u>

PRACTICE 6

Read the following paragraphs and answer the questions.

Induction is reasoning from particular cases to general principles; that is, the scientific method: you look at a number of examples, then come to a general conclusion based on the evidence. For instance, having known twenty-five people named Glenn, all of whom were men, you might naturally conclude, through induction, that all people named Glenn are men. The problem with inductive reasoning here, however, is Glenn Close, the movie actress.

Deduction is reasoning from the general to the particular. One starts from a statement known or merely assumed to be true and uses it to come to a conclusion about the matter at hand. Once you know that all people have to die sometime and that you are a person, you can logically deduce that you, too, will have to die sometime.

—Judy Jones and William Wilson, "100 Things Every College Graduate Should Know," *Esquire*

1. What two terms are defined? induction and deduction

   _____

2. What kind of definition is used in both topic sentences? class definition

   _____

3. In what larger category do the writers place both induction and deduction?

   reasoning

4. What example of induction do the writers give? Glenn as a man's name

   _____

5. What example shows the *problem* with induction? a woman—the actress

   Glenn Close

6. What example of deduction do the writers give? that every person must die

   _____

PRACTICE 7

Here are some topic sentences for definition paragraphs. Choose one that interests you and make a plan for a paragraph, using whatever method of development seems appropriate.

1. An optimist is someone who usually expects the best from life and from people.

2. Prejudice means prejudging people on the basis of race, creed, age, or sex—not on their merits as individuals.

3. A wealthy person does not necessarily have money and possessions, but he or she might possess inner wealth—a loving heart and a creative mind.

4. Registration is a ritual torture that students must go through before they can attend their classes.

5. Bravery and bravado are very different character traits.

THINKING AND WRITING TOGETHER

Define a Team Player

Whether or not we play sports, most of us know what it means to be a *team player* on a basketball or soccer team. But these days, many employers also want to hire "team players." What, exactly, are they looking for? What qualities does a team player bring to the job?

In a group with four or five classmates, discuss the meaning of *team player*, listing all the qualities that you think a team player has. List at least eight qualities. Now craft a topic sentence of definition; have a group member write it down, using the form, "A team player is a(n) _____ who _____." Choose the three or four most important qualities and write a paragraph defining *team player*. Use examples or details to bring your paragraph to life. Be prepared to share your paragraph with the full class.

EXPLORING ONLINE

http://content.monster.com/tools/quizzes/teamplayer/ Take the team player quiz; write about your results.

✔ CHECKLIST

The Process of Writing a Definition Paragraph

Refer to this checklist of steps as you write a definition paragraph of your own.

☐ 1. Narrow the topic in light of your audience and purpose.

☐ 2. Compose a topic sentence that uses one of the three basic methods of definition discussed in this chapter: synonym, class, or negation.

☐ 3. Decide on the method of paragraph development that is best suited to what you want to say.

☐ 4. Freewrite or brainstorm to generate ideas that may be useful in your definition paragraph. (You may want to freewrite or brainstorm before you narrow the topic.)

☐ 5. Select the best ideas and drop any ideas that do not clearly relate to the definition in your topic sentence.

☐ 6. Make a plan or an outline for your paragraph, numbering the ideas in the order in which you will present them.

☐ 7. Write a draft of your definition paragraph, using transitional expressions wherever they might be helpful.

☐ 8. Revise as necessary, checking for support, unity, logic, and coherence.

☐ 9. Proofread for errors in grammar, punctuation, sentence structure, spelling, and mechanics.

TEACHING TIP
For downloadable rubrics corresponding to each rhetorical mode, go to the *Evergreen* Online Teaching Center.

Suggested Topics for Definition Paragraphs

ESL TIP
Remind ESL students that they should *refer* to but not *plagiarize* dictionary definitions. Refer them to Chapter 17 for review.

1. The night person (or morning person)

2. The gossip (or life of the party, perfectionist, Internet addict)

3. Country and western music (or reggae, rock, gospel, or some other type of music)

4. A term from popular culture (e-mail *spam*, *sampling* in music, *Spanglish*, and so on)

5. Integrity

6. Self-esteem

7. The racing-car (or video game, fashion, football, shopping, or other) fanatic

8. An interesting term you know from reading (*placebo, UFO, Oedipus complex, whistle-blower,* and so forth)

9. Plagiarism

10. A racist (terrorist, sexist, artist, activist, or other *-ist*)

11. Urban legend

12. A dead-end job

13. A technical term you know from work or a hobby

14. A slang term you or your friends use

15. Writer's choice: _____

EXPLORING ONLINE

TEACHING TIP
More practice and assessment are available in the *Evergreen* Test Bank, linked ACE tests on the *Evergreen* Online Teaching and Study Centers, *WriteSpace for Evergreen,* and Exploring Online links in this chapter.

http://www.wordspy.com/ This site gives class definitions for often-funny new words entering the English language. Example: *furkid n. A pet treated as though it were one's child.* Click "Subjects" or "Top 100."

http://depts.gallaudet.edu/englishworks/writing/definition.html Read one student's essay defining *honesty* to see how a definition can be developed.

Online Study Center **college.hmco.com/pic/evergreen8e**
Visit the Online Study Center for *Evergreen* for more exercises and quizzes.

10

Comparison and Contrast

PART A The Contrast and the Comparison Paragraphs

PART B The Comparison and Contrast Paragraph

To **contrast** two persons, places, or things is to examine the ways in which they are different. To **compare** them is to examine the ways in which they are similar.

Contrast and comparison are useful skills in daily life, work, and college. When you shop, you often compare and contrast. For instance, you might compare and contrast two dishwashers to get the better value. In fact, the magazine *Consumer Reports* was created to help consumers compare and contrast different product brands.

Your employer might ask you to compare and contrast two computers, two telephone services, or two shipping crates. Your job is to gather information about the similarities and differences to help your employer choose one over the other. In nearly every college course, you will be expected to compare and contrast—two generals, two types of storm systems, two minerals, or two painters of the same school.

TEACHING TIP
Point out to students that the ability to compare and contrast effectively improves decision-making ability, a useful skill in all areas of life.

PART A The Contrast and the Comparison Paragraphs

Topic Sentence

Here is the topic sentence of a **contrast** paragraph:

> Although soul and hip hop both spring from African American roots, they are very different musical expressions.

- The writer begins a contrast paragraph with a topic sentence that clearly states what two persons, things, or ideas will be contrasted.

- What two things will be contrasted?

soul and hip hop

■ What word or words in the topic sentence make it clear that the writer will contrast soul and hip hop?

very different

Paragraph and Plan

Here is the entire paragraph:

> Although soul and hip hop both spring from African American roots, they are very different musical expressions. Soul music borrows from gospel and rhythm and blues. The singer's voice, backed up by live instruments, soars with emotion, with soul. This music captures the optimism of its time—the civil rights movement of the 1960s and hope for social change. There are two types of soul—the smooth Detroit style of the Supremes, Stevie Wonder, and The Temptations and the more gritty, gospel-driven Memphis style of Otis Redding and Booker T and the MGs. Soul music is upbeat and often joyful; its subjects are love and affirmation of the human condition. On the other hand, hip hop (or rap) draws on hard rock, funk, and techno. The rapper chants rhymes against a driving instrumental background that may be prerecorded. Rap grew out of the New York ghettos in the late 1970s and the 1980s, when crack and guns flooded "the hood" and many dreams seemed broken. Of the rival East and West Coast rappers, New Yorkers include Grandmaster Flash, LL Cool J, and the murdered Biggie Smalls, while Los Angeles rappers include Ice Cube and the murdered Tupac Shakur. The subjects of hip hop are racism, crime, and poverty. Both soul and hip hop claim to "tell it like it is." Hip hop's answer to the soulful Four Tops is the Furious Four. What's in a name? Perhaps the way the listener experiences reality.
>
> —Maurice Bosco (Student)

■ The writer first provides information about (A) soul music and then gives contrasting parallel information about (B) hip hop.

■ What information about (A) soul does the writer provide in the first half of the paragraph? _The writer discusses musical influences, sound, time period, types, and subjects._

■ What contrasting parallel information does the writer provide about (B) hip hop in the second half of the paragraph? _The writer discusses the same five points: influences, sound, time period, types, and subjects._

■ Why do you think the writer chose to present the points of contrast in this

order? It makes sense to describe the sound and historical background of each

kind of music first.

■ Note that the last four sentences provide a thoughtful conclusion. What final

point does the writer make? that the two kinds of music express two views

of reality

Before composing the paragraph, the writer probably brainstormed or freewrote to gather ideas and then made an **outline** like this:

Topic sentence: Although soul and hip hop both spring from African American roots, they are very different musical expressions.

Points of Contrast	A. Soul	B. Hip Hop
1. influences	gospel, R&B	hard rock, funk, techno
2. sound	soaring voice, live instruments	chanted rhymes; instrumentals may be prerecorded
3. time period	1960s, civil rights, hope for change	1970s–1980s, crack, guns
4. types	Detroit, Memphis	New York, Los Angeles
5. subjects	love, affirmation	racism, crime, poverty

Organized in this manner, the plan for this contrast paragraph helps the writer make sure that the paragraph will be complete. That is, if the historical period of soul is discussed, that of hip hop must also be discussed, and so on, for every point of contrast.

Here is another way to write the same paragraph:

Although soul and hip hop both spring from African American roots, they are very different musical expressions. Soul music borrows from gospel and rhythm and blues, whereas hip hop (or rap) draws on hard rock, funk, and techno. The soul singer's voice, backed up by live instruments, soars with emotion, with soul; however, the rapper chants rhymes against a driving instrumental background that may be prerecorded. Soul music captures the optimism of its time—the civil rights movement of the 1960s and hope for social change. On the other hand, hip hop grew out of the New York ghettos in the late 1970s and the 1980s, when crack and guns flooded

TEACHING TIP
Stress to students that outlining is particularly helpful in comparison and contrast writing because of its complexity.

"the hood" and many dreams seemed broken. There are two types of soul—the smooth Detroit style of the Supremes, Stevie Wonder, and The Temptations and the more gritty, gospel-driven Memphis style of Otis Redding and Booker T and the MGs. Of the rival East and West Coast rappers, New Yorkers include Grandmaster Flash, LL Cool J, and the murdered Biggie Smalls, while Los Angeles rappers include Ice Cube and the murdered Tupac Shakur. Whereas soul music's subjects are love and affirmation of the human condition, the subjects of hip hop are racism, crime, and poverty. Both soul and hip hop claim to "tell it like it is." Hip hop's answer to the soulful Four Tops is the Furious Four. What's in a name? Perhaps the way the listener experiences reality.

■ Instead of giving all the information about soul music and then going on to hip hop, this paragraph moves back and forth between soul and hip hop, dealing with *each point of contrast separately.*

Use either one of these **two patterns** when writing a contrast or a comparison paragraph:

1. Present all the information about **A** and then provide parallel information about **B**:

   First all A: point 1
   point 2
   point 3

   Then all B: point 1
   point 2
   point 3

■ This pattern is good for paragraphs and for short compositions. The reader can easily remember what was said about A by the time he or she gets to B.

2. Move back and forth between **A** and **B**. Present one point about **A** and then go to the parallel point about **B**. Then move to the next point and do the same:

   First A, point 1;   **then B,** point 1

   First A, point 2;   **then B,** point 2

   First A, point 3;   **then B,** point 3

■ The second pattern is better for longer papers, where it might be hard for the reader to remember what the writer said about A by the time he or she gets to B a few paragraphs later. By going back and forth, the writer makes it easier for the reader to keep the contrasts or comparisons in mind.

What you have learned so far about planning a contrast paragraph holds true for a comparison paragraph as well. Just remember that *contrast stresses differences* whereas *comparison stresses similarities.*

Here is a **comparison** paragraph:

> In my family, personality traits are said to skip generations, so that might explain why my grandfather and I have so much in common. My grandfather arrived in the United States at sixteen, a penniless young man from Italy looking for a new life and ready to earn it. He quickly apprenticed himself to a shoe cobbler and never stopped working until he retired fifty-three years later. Similarly, when I was fourteen, I asked permission to apply for my first job as a bank teller. My parents smiled and said, "She's just like Grandpa." Though everyone else in my family spends money the minute it reaches their hands, my habit of saving every penny does not seem strange to them. My grandfather also was careful with money, building his own shoe repair business out of nothing. He loved to work in his large vegetable garden and brought bags of carrots and tomatoes to our house on Saturday mornings. Like him, I enjoy the feeling of dirt on my fingers and the surprise of seedlings sprouting overnight. Though I raise zinnias instead of zucchinis, I know where I inherited a passion to make things grow. Only in opportunities, we differed. Although my grandfather's education ended with third grade, I am fortunate to attend college—and hope that education will be my legacy to the generations that come after me.
>
> —Angela De Renzi (Student)

■ What words in the topic sentence does the writer use to indicate that a comparison will follow? so much in common

_____

■ In what ways are the writer and her grandfather similar? They started working young and worked hard; both were careful with money; both were gardeners.

_____

■ What transitional words stress the similarities? Similarly, like Grandpa, also, like him

■ What pattern of presentation does the writer use? The writer uses the A-B, A-B, A-B pattern.

■ What one point of *contrast* serves as a strong punch line for the paragraph?

Although the grandfather only attended third grade, the writer attended college.

_____

■ Make a plan or an outline of this comparison paragraph.

TEACHING TIP
To give students more practice, have them work in small groups to brainstorm and organize ideas for comparison or contrast paragraphs.

Transitional Expressions

Transitional expressions in contrast paragraphs stress *opposition* and *difference*:

Transitional Expressions for Contrast	
although	on the other hand
whereas	in contrast
but	while
however	yet
conversely	unlike

Transitional expressions in comparison paragraphs stress *similarities*:

Transitional Expressions for Comparison	
in the same way	just as . . . so
and, also, in addition	similarly
as well as	like
both, neither	too
each of	the same

As you write, avoid using just one or two of these transitional expressions. Learn new ones from the list and practice them in your paragraphs.*

PRACTICE 1

Read the following paragraph carefully and answer the questions.

Certain personality traits, like whether a person is more reactive or proactive, can predict success or its opposite. In his book *The Seven Habits of Highly Effective People,* Steven Covey writes that reactive people tend to sit back and wait for life or circumstances to bring them opportunities. They react instead of act. When good things happen, they are happy, but when bad things happen, they feel like victims. Reactive people often say things like, "There's nothing I can do," "I can't because . . . ," and "If only." In the short term, reactive people might feel comfortable playing it safe, holding back, and avoiding challenges; in the long term, though, they are often left dreaming. On the other hand, proactive people know that they have the power to choose their responses to whatever life brings. They act instead of react: If things aren't going their way, they take action to help create the outcome they desire. Proactive people can be recognized by their tendency to say things like "Let's consider the alternatives," "I prefer," "We can," and "I will." In the short term, proactive people might face the discomfort of failing because they take on challenges, set goals, and work toward them. But in the long term, Covey says, proactive people are the ones who achieve their dreams.

* For an entire essay developed by comparison or contrast, see "E-Notes from an Online Learner," Chapter 15, Part F.

1. Can you tell from the topic sentence whether a contrast or comparison will

   follow? <u>The words "more reactive or proactive" and "success or its opposite" suggest</u>

   <u>contrast.</u>

2. What two personality types are being contrasted? <u>reactive and proactive</u>

3. What information does the writer provide about reactive people? <u>They sit</u>

   <u>and wait; react not act; say things like "There's nothing I can do"; avoid</u>

   <u>discomfort in the short term but are left dreaming.</u>

4. What parallel information does the writer provide about proactive people?

   <u>They know they have power; take positive action; say things like "We can" and</u>

   <u>"I will"; face discomfort but often achieve their dreams.</u>

5. What pattern does the writer of this paragraph use to present the contrasts?

   <u>all A, then all B</u>

6. What transitional expression does the writer use to stress the shift from A to

   B? <u>On the other hand</u>

PRACTICE 2

This paragraph is hard to follow because it lacks transitional expressions that emphasize contrast. Revise the paragraph, adding transitional expressions of contrast. Strive for variety. Answers may vary.

American restaurant portions have increased dramatically between 1985 and the

present, a trend that worries many nutritionists. The small food servings of twenty

years ago were healthy, according to the U.S. Food and Drug Administration (FDA).

In contrast, modern
~~Modern~~ portions have dangerously ballooned. For example, in 1985, a blueberry

ounces, but today's
muffin weighed just 1.5 ~~ounces. Today's~~ typical muffin is a whopping 5 ounces.

Compared with portions in 1985, today's supersized foods pack excess calories. For

calories, whereas now
instance, a plate of spaghetti once provided 500 ~~calories. Now~~ it delivers 1,025 calo-

While the
ries, over half the fuel a male should consume in one day. ~~The~~ smaller food portions

fat, today's
of years past contained reasonable amounts of dietary ~~fat. Today's~~ portions often

ooze with fat. In 1985, a typical fast-food hamburger delivered 15 fat grams. Today's

burger, on the other hand,

~~burger~~ contains 34 artery-clogging grams—even before the consumer adds extra

sauce. Huge portions do give us more for our money: more calories, more fat, more

obesity, more heart disease. Don't be a victim of portion distortion.

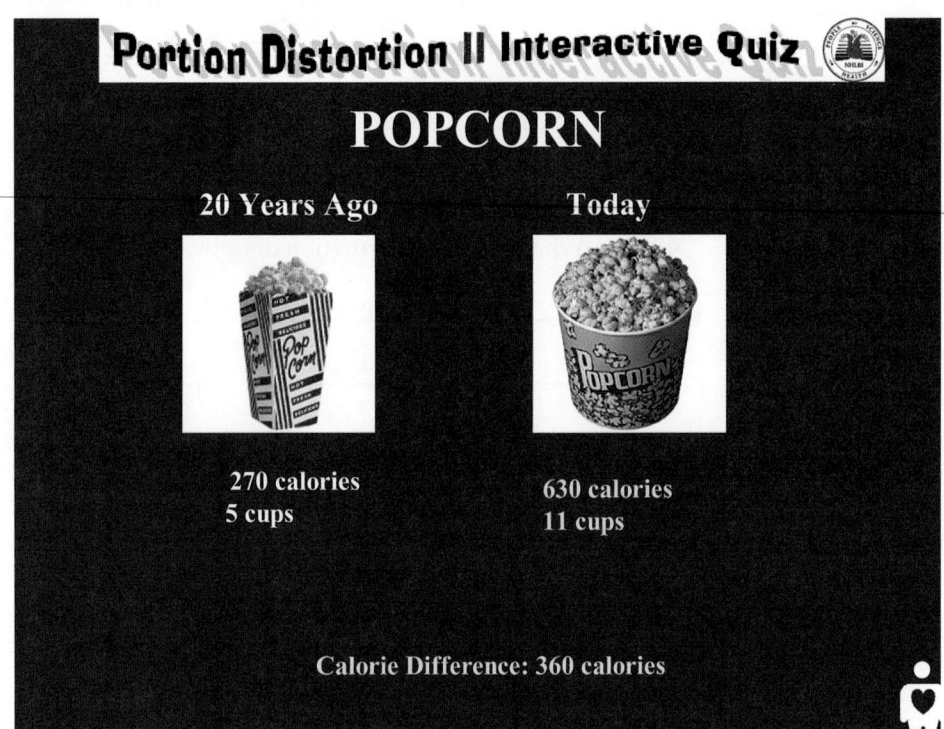

A picture is worth a thousand words at the U.S. government's "Portion Distortion" web site.

EXPLORING ONLINE

http://hin.nhlbi.nih.gov/portion/ Learn more about "portion distortion" and maintaining a healthy weight; take notes on facts or ideas for further writing.

PRACTICE 3

Below are three plans for contrast paragraphs. The points of contrast in the second column do not follow the same order as the points in the first column. In addition, one detail is missing. First, number the points in the second column to match those in the first. Then fill in the missing detail.

1. **Shopping at a Supermarket**	**Shopping at a Local Grocery**
1. carries all brands	_4_ personal service
2. lower prices	_3_ closed on Sundays
3. open seven days a week	_2_ prices often higher
4. little personal service	_1_ doesn't carry all brands
5. no credit	_5_ credit available for steady customers

2. My Son

1. fifteen years old
2. likes to be alone
3. reads a lot
4. is an excellent cook
5. wants to go to chef school

My Daughter

_4_ good at making minor household repairs

_2_ likes to be with friends

_3_ doesn't like to read

_5_ expects to attend a technical college

_1_ seventeen years old

3. Job A

1. good salary
2. office within walking distance
3. two-week vacation
4. work alone
5. lots of overtime
6. no health insurance

Job B

_3_ three-week vacation

_4_ work on a team with others

_2_ one-hour bus ride to office

_6_ health insurance

_5_ no overtime

_1_ low salary

PRACTICE 4

Here are three topics for either contrast or comparison paragraphs. Compose two topic sentences for each topic, one for a possible contrast paragraph and one for a possible comparison paragraph. Answers will vary.

TEACHING AND ESL TIP
Have diverse pairs of students identify and write collaboratively about one cultural difference or similarity (like "Italian Momma or Japanese Okasan"). This builds writing and thinking skills—and it's fun. Read inspiring short-essay examples at **http://www.lclark.edu/~ krauss/advwrf99/ culturecapsules/ culturecapsules.html.**

Topic		Topic Sentences
EXAMPLE	Two members of my family	A. My brother and sister have different attitudes toward exercise.
		B. My parents are alike in that they're easygoing.
	1. Two friends or coworkers	A. Tom Bogyo and Amanda Gill have very different attitudes toward success.
		B. Although Sylvia and Miako excel at different sports, both are talented athletes.
	2. You as a child and you as an adult	A. I am less selfish than I was as a child.

B. As an adult, I have some of the same

dislikes I had as a child.

_____

3. Two vacations

A. Some people like to relax on vacation,

but others like to spend most of their

time sightseeing.

B. My vacations in both Barbados and

Sun Valley included miles of walking.

_____

PRACTICE 5

Here are four topic sentences for comparison or contrast paragraphs. For each topic sentence, think of one supporting point of comparison or contrast and explain that point in one or two sentences. Answers will vary.

1. When it comes to movies (TV shows, books, entertainment), Demetrios and Arlene have totally different tastes.

    Demetrios loves action and violence, whereas Arlene will leave the theater at the first

    sight of blood on the screen.

2. My mother and I have few personality traits in common.

    My mother is extremely temperamental, whereas I pride myself in keeping my cool.

    _____

3. Although there are obvious differences, the two neighborhoods (blocks, homes) have much in common.

    The large house has an extensive and beautiful garden. The smaller house also has a

    garden, less extensive but equally colorful.

4. Paying taxes is like having a tooth pulled.*

    Both are painful. It hurts to write that tax check and to have that tooth pulled. But by

    doing both, we avoid worse pain in the future.

_____

* For more work on this kind of comparison, see Chapter 22, "Revising for Language Awareness," Part D.

PRACTICE 6   **THINKING AND WRITING TOGETHER**

Contrast Toys for Boys and Toys for Girls

Stores like Toys-R-Us frequently recommend toys for different age groups, often dividing their suggestions into "toys for boys" and "toys for girls." In a group with four or five classmates, examine and discuss these typical "great gift ideas" for six-year-olds, made by Etoys.com:

Boys	**Girls**
Pro Pitcher baseball-pitching machine	Patty Playground Interactive doll
Wild Planet wrist walkie-talkies	Barbie Dream Bed and Bath
Fisher-Price pirate ship	My First Phonebook
Nerf Triple Strike arrow shooter	Yoga Kit for Kids
Hot Wheels X-V Racers Daytona 500 Superspeedway Set	Baskin-Robbins ice-cream maker

Based on these lists, what contrasting messages are being sent about what boys and girls supposedly like to do? Do these lists put unfair limits on children of either sex? Now plan and write a comparison or contrast paragraph based on your discussion.

EXPLORING ONLINE

http://www.google.com/ or your favorite search engine; search, "toys, gender roles"

✔ **CHECKLIST**

The Process of Writing a Comparison or Contrast Paragraph

Refer to this checklist of steps as you write a comparison or contrast paragraph of your own.

☐ 1. Narrow the topic in light of your audience and purpose.

☐ 2. Compose a topic sentence that clearly states that a comparison or a contrast will follow.

☐ 3. Freewrite or brainstorm to generate as many points of comparison or contrast as you can think of. (You may want to freewrite or brainstorm before you narrow the topic.)

☐ 4. Choose the points you will use, and drop any details that are not really part of the comparison or the contrast.

☐ 5. List parallel points of comparison or of contrast for both *A* and *B*.

☐ 6. Make a plan or an outline, numbering all the points of comparison or contrast in the order in which you will present them in the paragraph.

☐ 7. Write a draft of your comparison or contrast paragraph, using transitional expressions that stress either differences or similarities.

☐ 8. Revise as necessary, checking for support, unity, logic, and coherence.

☐ 9. Proofread for errors in grammar, punctuation, sentence structure, spelling, and mechanics.

TEACHING TIP
For downloadable rubrics corresponding to each rhetorical mode, go to the *Evergreen* Online Teaching Center.

Suggested Topics for Comparison or Contrast Paragraphs

1. Compare or contrast two attitudes toward money (the spendthrift and the miser) or dating (the confirmed single and the committed partner).

2. Compare or contrast the way you act in two different situations.

3. Compare or contrast a job you hated and a job you loved.

4. Compare or contrast two consumer items of the same type (computers, cars, and so on).

5. Compare or contrast "the blues" and depression.

6. Compare or contrast two high schools or colleges that you have attended (perhaps one in the United States and one in a different country).

7. Compare or contrast two athletes in the same sport (or two entertainers or politicians).

8. Compare or contrast your *expectations* of a person, place, or situation and *reality*.

9. Compare or contrast your best friend and your spouse or partner.

10. Writer's choice: _____

PART B The Comparison and Contrast Paragraph

Sometimes an assignment will ask you to write a paragraph that both compares and contrasts, one that stresses both similarities and differences.

Here is a comparison and contrast paragraph:

> Although contemporary fans would find the game played by the Knickerbockers—the first organized baseball club—similar to modern baseball, they would also note some startling differences. In 1845, as now, the four bases of the playing field were set in a diamond shape, ninety feet from one another. Nine players took the field. The object of the game was to score points by hitting a pitched ball and running around the bases. The teams changed sides after three outs. However, the earlier game was also different. The umpire sat at a table along the third base line instead of standing behind home plate. Unlike the modern game, the players wore no gloves. Rather than firing the ball over the plate at ninety miles an hour, the pitcher gently tossed it underhand to the batter. Since there were no balls and strikes, the batter could wait for the pitch he wanted. The game ended, not when nine innings were completed, but when one team scored twenty-one runs, which were called "aces."

■ How are the Knickerbockers' game and modern baseball similar?

Both have four bases ninety feet apart in a diamond shape, nine players; both score points

by runs; both have three outs.

■ How are these two versions of the game different? In the Knickerbockers'

game, umpire sat at a table on third base line, players wore no gloves, pitcher gently

tossed the ball, there were no balls and strikes, a team needed twenty-one "aces" to win,

and there were no innings. In the modern game, umpire stands at home plate, pitcher fires

the ball, there are balls and strikes, team with the most runs wins, and game is composed

of nine innings.

■ What transitional expressions in the paragraph emphasize similarities and

differences? although, as now, however, unlike, rather than, not when, but when

Before composing this comparison and contrast paragraph, the writer probably brainstormed or freewrote to gather ideas and then made a plan like this:

Topic sentence: Although contemporary fans would find the game played by the Knickerbockers—the first organized baseball club—similar to modern baseball, they would also note some startling differences.

Comparisons	Knickerbockers	Modern Game
Point 1	four bases, ninety feet apart, in diamond shape	
Point 2	nine players	
Point 3	scoring points	
Point 4	three outs	
Contrasts		
Point 1	umpire sat at third base line	umpire at home plate
Point 2	no gloves	gloves
Point 3	pitcher gently tossed ball	pitcher fires ball at plate
Point 4	no balls and strikes	balls and strikes
Point 5	twenty-one "aces" to win, no innings	most runs to win, nine innings

---

- A plan such as this makes it easier for the writer to organize a great deal of material.

- The writer begins by listing all the points of comparison—how the Knickerbockers' game and modern baseball are similar. Then the writer lists all the points of contrast—how they are different.

PRACTICE 7

Here is a somewhat longer comparison and contrast (two paragraphs). Read it carefully and answer the questions.

TEACHING TIP
The distinction between magazines and journals is a useful one for college students to know as they hone research skills or later consult professional journals in their careers.

In nearly every library, popular magazines like *Newsweek, Psychology Today, Essence,* and *Sports Illustrated* sit side by side on the shelves of the periodical section with scholarly journals like the *Journal of the American Medical Association, Poetry,* and the *American Economic Review.* Both magazines and journals are known as *periodicals* because they are published at intervals, such as weekly, monthly, or quarterly. Both contain informative articles. In size and shape, they are roughly the same.

Yet despite these similarities, the two types of publications differ significantly. Supported by bigger budgets, popular magazines are glossier, with color photographs and advertisements, whereas journals are more serious and sober-looking, with visuals like charts and graphs, less color, and fewer ads. A glance inside reveals further contrasts in purpose, audience, and language. The purpose of a magazine is to entertain or provide information for a broad, general audience. Therefore, its articles are written in language that most readers understand. The purpose of a journal, however, is to present in-depth information on a specialized subject or report on original research for scholars (or serious amateurs) in that field. As a result, its language is more technical and includes jargon related to the field. The authors and rules for quoting sources also differ in the two types of publications. Those who contribute articles to popular magazines are typically staff members or freelance writers. They may mention their sources of information, but they don't usually provide full bibliographic details. In scholarly journals, on the other hand, the authors of articles are experts or researchers in the field who painstakingly document all sources of their information with full citations and bibliographies.

1. What two things does this writer compare and contrast? popular magazines

   and scholarly journals

2. What words indicate that both contrast and comparison will follow?

   Despite similarities, differ

3. How are magazines and journals similar? Both are periodicals, both contain

   informative articles, and both have a similar size and shape.

4. How are magazines and journals different? They have two distinct looks.

   They also differ in purpose, audience, language, authors, and handling of sources.

5. On a sheet of paper, make a plan or outline for these paragraphs.

Working Through the Comparison and Contrast Paragraph

You can work through the comparison and contrast paragraph in the same way that you do a comparison or a contrast paragraph. Follow the steps in the earlier checklist, but make certain that your paragraph shows both similarities and differences.

Suggested Topics for Comparison and Contrast Paragraphs

1. Compare and contrast listening to an iPod and live music.

2. Compare and contrast parties, weddings, or funerals in two different cultures.

3. Compare and contrast your life now with your life five years ago.

4. Compare and contrast two films or videos on similar subjects.

5. Compare and contrast learning something from experience and learning something from books.

6. Compare and contrast two singers or musicians.

7. Compare and contrast the requirements for two jobs or careers.

8. Compare and contrast two popular television programs of the same type (newscasts, situation comedies, talk shows, and so on).

9. Compare and contrast two attitudes toward one subject (firearms, education, immigration, and so forth).

10. Writer's choice: _____

EXPLORING ONLINE

TEACHING TIP
More practice and assessment are available in the *Evergreen* Test Bank, linked ACE tests on the *Evergreen* Online Teaching and Study Centers, *WriteSpace for Evergreen,* and Exploring Online links in this chapter.

http://web.uvic.ca/wguide/Pages/ParDevCC.html Review of the comparison/contrast paragraph, with examples

http://muskingum.edu/~cal/database/general/organization.html#Comparison
Print this graphic to help plan your paragraph.

Online Study Center   **college.hmco.com/pic/evergreen8e**
Visit the Online Study Center for *Evergreen* for more exercises and quizzes.

11

Classification

To **classify** is to gather into types, kinds, or categories according to a single basis of division.

Mailroom personnel, for example, might separate incoming mail into four piles: orders, bills, payments, and inquiries. Once the mail has been divided in this manner—according to which department should receive each pile—it can be efficiently delivered.

The same information can be classified in more than one way. The Census Bureau collects a variety of data about the people living in the United States. One way to classify the data is by age group—the number of people under eighteen, between eighteen and fifty-five, over fifty-five, and over seventy. Such information might be useful in developing programs for college-bound youth or for the elderly. Other ways of dividing the population are by geographic location, occupation, family size, level of education, and so on.

Whether you classify rocks by their origin for a geology course or children by their stages of growth for a psychology course, you will be organizing large groups into smaller, more manageable units that can be explained to your reader.

Topic Sentence

Here is the topic sentence for a classification paragraph:

> Gym-goers can be classified according to their priorities at the gym as sweaty fanatics, fashionites, busybodies, or fit normals.

■ The writer begins a classification paragraph with a topic sentence that clearly states what group of people or things will be classified.

■ What group of people will be classified? gym-goers

■ Into how many categories will they be divided? What are the categories?

four: sweaty fanatics, fashionites, busybodies, and fit normals

Paragraph and Plan

Here is the entire paragraph:

> Gym-goers can be classified according to their priorities at the gym as sweaty fanatics, fashionites, busybodies, and fit normals. Sweaty fanatics take gym-going to the extreme. They hog the machines, drip sweat everywhere, and barely look up if someone falls off the treadmill beside them. Occasionally, they will stare at the mirror, admiring the muscle group they are working on. The fashionites also admire their own reflections, but they barely break a sweat. For them, the gym is just another excuse to buy clothes. They wear perfectly matched workout clothes with color-coordinated sport watches and gym shoes. The third group, the busybodies, can't stop talking. Whether it's making idle chitchat or correcting another exerciser's form on a machine, they seem unable to shut up. Not even headphones and one-word answers can stop the busybodies from babbling. Luckily, the fit normals keep things from getting too far out of control. They come to the gym to work out, stay healthy, and go home, but they remember that basic good manners apply in every setting.
>
> —Laurie Zamot (Student)

■ On what basis does the writer classify gym-goers? their priorities at the gym

_____

■ What information does the writer provide about the first type, sweaty fanatics?

They hog machines, drip sweat, and don't notice anyone but themselves.

_____

■ What information does the writer provide about the second type, fashionites?

They admire themselves, barely sweat, and come to show off their outfits.

_____

■ What information does the writer provide about the third type, busybodies?

They can't stop talking, even when others wear headphones and grunt.

_____

■ What information does the writer provide about the fourth type, the fit normals?

They balance things by working out but not forgetting good manners.

_____

■ Why do you think the writer discusses fit normals last? The writer starts with

crazier and funnier types; the normals keep them all from going out of control.

_____

Before composing the paragraph, the writer probably brainstormed or free-wrote to gather ideas and then made an **outline** like this:

Topic sentence: Gym-goers can be classified according to their priorities at the gym as sweaty fanatics, fashionites, busybodies, or fit normals.

Type 1:   Sweaty fanatics
        —hog machines; drip sweat
        —barely look if someone falls
        —stare in mirror, admiring muscles

Type 2:   Fashionites
        —admire themselves but don't sweat
        —excuse to buy clothes
        —matched workout clothes
        —coordinating sport watches and gym shoes

Type 3:   Busybodies
        —can't stop talking, advising
        —headphones, short answers don't work

Type 4:   Fit normals
        —keep things from going out of control
        —work out, go home
        —remember good manners even in gym

■ Note that the body of the paragraph discusses all four types of gym-goers mentioned in the topic sentence and does not add any new ones.

This classification paragraph sticks to a single method of classification: *the priorities of gym-goers at the gym*. If the paragraph had also discussed a fourth category—*left-handed gym-goers*—the initial basis of classification would fall apart because *left-handedness* has nothing to do with *the priorities of different gym-goers*.

The topic sentence of a classification paragraph usually has two parts: the *topic* and the *basis of classification*. The basis of classification is the controlling idea: it *controls* how the writer will approach the topic. Stating it in writing will help keep the paragraph on track.

There is no set rule about which category to present first, second, or last in a classification paragraph. However, the paragraph should follow some kind of **logical sequence** from the most to least outrageous, least to most expensive, from the largest to the smallest category, and so on.*†

---

* For more work on order, see Chapter 4, "Achieving Coherence," Part A.

† For a complete essay developed by classification, see "The Potato Scale," Chapter 15, Part G.

Transitional Expressions

Transitional expressions in classification paragraphs stress divisions and categories:

Transitional Expressions for Classification	
can be divided	the first type
can be classified	the second kind
can be categorized	the last category

PRACTICE 1

Read the following paragraph carefully and answer the questions.

Judges can be divided, on the basis of their written opinions, into three categories: conservative, liberal, and centrist. Although all judges respect the law, conservative judges have an especially strong belief in the importance of the law and the history surrounding it. They believe that real justice comes only from strictly applying the law to the facts of a case, whether or not the outcome seems fair to an individual. On the other hand, liberal judges look beyond a rigid reading to the "spirit of the law" in their search for real justice in a case. They might broadly interpret the law in order to champion individual rights. The outcome of the case matters more to them than the letter of the law. Finally, centrist judges walk the middle ground between conservative and liberal. They do not apply the law as rigidly as conservative judges, yet they are not as willing as liberal judges to apply the law loosely. Having different types of judges helps balance our legal system; their differing views help protect both the law and individual rights.

1. How many categories are there, and what are they?

   three: conservative, liberal, and centrist judges

2. On what basis does the writer classify judges?

   their written opinions

3. Make a plan of the paragraph on a separate sheet of paper.

PRACTICE 2

Each group of things or persons on the following page has been divided according to a single basis of classification. However, one item in each group does not belong—it does not fit that single basis of classification.

Read each group of items carefully; then circle the letter of the one item that does *not* belong. Next write the single basis of classification that includes the rest of the group.

EXAMPLE   Shirts

    a. cotton

    b. suede

    (c.) short-sleeved

    d. polyester

    material they are made of

1. Shoes
   a. flat heels
   b. 2-inch heels
   (c.) patent leather heels
   d. 3-inch heels

   height of heels

2. Dates
   (a.) very good-looking
   b. sometimes pay
   c. always pay
   d. expect me to pay

   financial arrangements

3. Students
   (a.) talkative in class
   b. very hard-working
   c. goof-offs
   d. moderately hard-working

   how hard they work

4. Contact lenses
   (a.) soft
   b. green
   c. brown
   d. lavender

   color

5. Milk
   a. 2 percent fat
   b. whole
   (c.) chocolate
   d. 1 percent fat

   amount of fat

6. Drivers
   a. obey the speed limit
   (b.) teenage drivers
   c. speeders
   d. creepers

   how fast they drive

PRACTICE 3

Any group of persons, things, or ideas can be classified in more than one way, depending on the basis of classification. For instance, students in your class can be classified on the basis of height (short, average, tall) or on the basis of class participation (often participate, sometimes participate, never participate). Both of these groupings are valid classifications of the same group of people.

    Think of two ways in which each of the following groups could be classified.

Answers will vary.

Group	Basis of Classification
EXAMPLE Bosses	(A) *how demanding they are*
	(B) *how generous they are*
1. Members of my family	(A) *how old they are*
	(B) *how emotional they are*
2. Hurricanes	(A) *how much damage they do in dollars*
	(B) *how strong the winds are*

TEACHING TIP
Practice 3 works well as a small-group activity.

ESL TIP
ESL students may prefer to narrow their classification topics by culture, e.g., shopping in Cairo.

3. Fans of a certain sport

(A) how many games they attend

(B) how long they have been fans

4. Vacations

(A) how much activity they involve

(B) how expensive they are

5. Fitness magazines

(A) how much nutrition is covered

(B) how they seem to define fitness

PRACTICE 4

Listed below are three groups of people or things. Decide on a single basis of classification for each group and the categories that would develop from your basis of classification. Finally, write a topic sentence for each of your classifications.

Answers will vary.

TEACHING TIP
Have students share their answers to Practice 4 so that they can see others' ideas. This will reinforce the fact that, though different bases for classifying exist, the writer chooses one.

	Group	Basis of Classification	Categories
EXAMPLE	Professors at Pell College	methods of instruction	1. lectures
			2. class discussions
			3. both

Topic Sentence: Professors at Pell College can be classified according to their methods of instruction: those who lecture, those who encourage class discussions, and those who do both.

ESL TIP
ESL students may need to review word forms or parts of speech to express categories in parallel form. Use a model topic sentence from Practice 4 to illustrate.

Group	Basis of Classification	Categories
1. Car owners	how clean they keep their cars	very neat
		moderately neat
		not neat at all

Topic Sentence: Most car owners can be classified according to how clean they keep their vehicles: those whose cars are very neat, those whose cars are moderately neat, and those whose cars are not neat at all.

2. Credit-card users   how much they use   use only in emergencies

                          their cards   use in moderation

                                                     charge themselves into

                                                     debt and into trouble

Topic Sentence: Credit-card users fall into three categories: those who use
their cards only in emergencies, those who use their cards in moderation,
and those who charge themselves into debt and into trouble.

3. Ways of reacting   how much emotion   people who cry or yell
   to crisis
                         shown   people who talk calmly

                                                    people who don't

                                                    talk at all

Topic Sentence: People react to crises in very different ways: by crying or yelling, by talking
calmly, or by remaining completely silent.

PRACTICE 5

Now choose the classification in Practice 4 that most interests you and make a
plan or outline for a paragraph on a separate sheet of paper. As you work, make
sure that you have listed all possible categories for your basis of classification. Remember, every car owner or credit-card user should fit into one of your categories. Finally, write your paragraph, describing each category briefly and
perhaps giving an example of each.

PRACTICE 6   THINKING AND WRITING TOGETHER

Classify Students on Campus

In a group with four or five classmates, discuss some interesting ways in which
you might classify the students at your college. List at least five possible ways.
You might focus on students in just one place—like the computer lab, swimming

pool, coffee stand, library, or an exam room during finals week. Then come up with one basis of classification, either serious or humorous. For example, you could classify swimmers according to their level of expertise or splashing, students during finals week according to their fashion statements, or students standing in line for coffee according to their degree of impatience.

Now choose the most interesting basis of classification. Name three or four categories that cover the group, and write a paragraph classifying your fellow students. You might wish to enrich your categories with details and examples. Be prepared to read your paragraph to the full class.

✓ CHECKLIST

The Process of Writing a Classification Paragraph

Refer to this checklist of steps as you write a classification paragraph.

- [ ] 1. Narrow the topic in light of your audience and purpose. Think in terms of a group of people or things that can be classified easily into types or categories.

- [ ] 2. Decide on a single basis of classification. This basis will depend on what information you wish to give your audience.

- [ ] 3. Compose a topic sentence that clearly shows what you are dividing into categories or types. If you wish, your topic sentence can state the basis on which you are making the classification and the types that will be discussed in the paragraph.

- [ ] 4. List the categories into which the group is being classified. Be sure that your categories cover all the possibilities. Do not add any new categories that are not logically part of your original basis of classification.

- [ ] 5. Freewrite, cluster, or brainstorm to generate information, details, and examples for each of the categories. (You may want to prewrite before you narrow the topic.)

- [ ] 6. Select the best details and examples, and drop those that are not relevant to your classification.

- [ ] 7. Make a plan or an outline for your paragraph, numbering the categories in the order in which you will present them.

- [ ] 8. Write a draft of your classification paragraph, using transitional expressions wherever they may be helpful.

- [ ] 9. Revise as necessary, checking for support, unity, logic, and coherence.

- [ ] 10. Proofread for errors in grammar, punctuation, sentence structure, spelling, and mechanics.

TEACHING TIP
For downloadable rubrics corresponding to each rhetorical mode, go to the *Evergreen* Online Teaching Center.

Suggested Topics for Classification Paragraphs

1. Shoppers
2. Ways people cope with bad news
3. Women or men you date
4. Clothing in your closet
5. Friends
6. Dancers at a party or club
7. Problems facing college freshmen or someone new to a job
8. College instructors
9. Ways that students prepare for exams
10. Neighbors or coworkers
11. Kinds of success
12. Performers of one type of music
13. Kinds of marriages
14. Brands of jeans, backpacks, cola drinks, or some other product
15. Writer's choice: _____

 EXPLORING ONLINE

http://www.filmratings.com/ Click "ratings guide" for movie classifications.

http://sln.fi.edu/tfi/units/life/classify/classify.html Introduction to the classification of plants and animals

Online Study Center college.hmco.com/pic/evergreen8e
Visit the Online Study Center for *Evergreen* for more exercises and quizzes.

12

Cause and Effect

The ability to think through **causes and effects** is a key to success in many college courses, jobs, and everyday situations. Daily we puzzle over the **causes** of, or reasons for, events: What caused one brother to drop out of school and another to succeed brilliantly? What causes Jenine's asthma attacks? Why did the stock market plunge 300 points?

Effects are the *results* of a cause or causes. Does playing violent computer games affect a child's behavior? What are the effects of being a twin, keeping a secret, or winning the lottery?

Most events worth examining have complex, not simple, causes and effects. That is, they may have several causes and several effects. Certainly, in many fields, questions of cause and effect challenge even the experts: *What will be the long-term effects of the breakup of the former Soviet Union? What causes the HIV virus to disappear from the blood of some infected babies?* (This one answer could help save millions of lives.)

Topic Sentence

Here is the topic statement of a cause and effect paragraph; the writer has chosen to break the information into two sentences.

> What killed off the dinosaurs—and 70 percent of life on earth—65 million years ago? According to recent research, this massive destruction had three causes.

■ The writer begins a cause and effect paragraph by clearly stating the subject and indicating whether causes or effects will be discussed. What is the subject of this paragraph? Will causes or effects be the focus? <u>what killed the</u>

<u>dinosaurs, causes</u>

■ The writer states the topic in two sentences rather than one. Is this effective? Why or why not? (A single sentence might read, "According to recent research, the massive destruction of dinosaurs and other creatures 65 million years ago had three causes.") <u>Starting with a question sparks reader's interest.</u>

■ Words like *causes, reasons,* and *factors* are useful to show causes. Words like *effects, results,* and *consequences* are useful to show effects.

Paragraph and Plan

Here is the entire paragraph:

> What killed off the dinosaurs—and 70 percent of life on earth—65 million years ago? According to recent research, this massive destruction had three causes. Dr. Peter Ward of the University of Washington reports that the first cause was simple "background extinction." This is the normal disappearance of some animals and plants that goes on all the time. Second, a drop in sea level during this period slowly destroyed about 25 percent more of the world's species. Last and most dramatic, a comet as big as Manhattan smashed into the earth near Mexico's Yucatan peninsula, literally shaking the world. The huge buried crater left by this comet was found in 1991. Now Dr. Ward has proved that ash and a rare metal from that fiery crash fell around the globe. This means that the impact, fires, smoke, and ash quickly wiped out the dinosaurs and much of life on earth. This great "die-off" cleared the way for mammals to dominate the earth.

■ How many causes does this writer give for the destruction of the dinosaurs and other species? What are they? <u>three: background extinction; drop in sea level; huge comet</u>

■ Did the writer make up these ideas? If not, who or what is the source of the information? <u>no; Dr. Peter Ward, University of Washington</u>

■ What transitional words introduce each of the three causes? <u>the first cause; second; last and most dramatic</u>

■ What kind of order is used in this paragraph?* <u>order of importance</u>

---

* For more work on order, see Chapter 4, "Achieving Coherence," Part A.

Before writing the paragraph, the writer probably jotted an outline or plan like this:

Topic sentence: According to recent research, this massive destruction had three causes.

    —write a catchy introductory sentence?
    —mention time, 65 million years ago

Cause 1: "background extinction"
    —normal disappearance of animals and plants
    —give credit to Dr. Ward

Cause 2: drop in sea level
    —25 percent more species destroyed

Cause 3: giant comet hit earth
    —big as Manhattan
    —crater found in 1991 near Yucatan peninsula
    —now Ward proves ash and rare metal circled globe
    —this comet destroyed dinosaurs and others

Conclusion: "die-off" cleared way for mammals—OR tie to current news and films about comet danger

---

Other paragraphs examine *effects*, not causes. Either they try to predict future effects of something happening now, or they analyze past effects of something that happened earlier, as does this paragraph:

ESL TIP

Ask your ESL students to find synonyms for the word *effect* in this model paragraph. Have them brainstorm synonyms for *cause* and *effect* so they do not overuse these terms.

> <u>For Christy Haubegger, the lack of Latina role models had life-changing consequences.</u> As a Mexican American girl adopted by Anglo parents, Christy found no reflection of herself in teen magazines or books. One result of seeing mostly blonde, blue-eyed models was an increase in her adolescent insecurities. A more damaging effect was Christy's confusion as she wondered what career to pursue; there were no Hispanic role models in schoolbooks to suggest possible futures for this excellent student. Even at Stanford Law School, Christy and her friends missed the inspiration and encouragement of professional Latina role models. At Stanford, Christy began to see this problem as an opportunity. She decided to start a national magazine that would showcase talented and successful Latinas. The 27-year-old made a detailed business plan and, incredibly, won the financial backing of the CEO of *Essence* magazine. In 1996, the first issue of *Latina* hit the newstands—the very positive consequence of an old loneliness.

■ Underline the topic sentence in this paragraph.

■ For Ms. Haubegger, the lack of Latina role models caused "life-changing conse-quences." What effects are discussed? <u>increased adolescent insecurities; no</u>

<u>professional role models; her decision to start *Latina* magazine</u>

■ What order does the writer follow? <u>time order</u>

■ Notice that the paragraph first discusses negative effects and then a positive one.

Christy Haubegger founded *Latina* magazine to fill a need for Latina role models.

Before you write about causes or effects, do some mental detective work. First, search out the three most important causes or effects. For example, if you are trying to understand the causes of a friend's skiing accident, you might consider the snow conditions that day, whether he took unnecessary risks, and whether he had been drinking.

Causes	**Effect**	**Further Effects**
ice on the ski slope		can't drive
J. took steep course	J. breaks his leg	can't play sports
had two beers		decides to read more

In exploring the effects of something, consider both short-term and long-term effects and both negative and positive effects. (Although Jay could *not* do many things, perhaps he took advantage of his recovery time to read more or to learn a new computer program.)

Avoiding Problems in Cause and Effect Writing

1. **Do not oversimplify.** Avoid the trap of naming one cause for a complex problem: *Why did they divorce? Because she is a hothead.* Or *The reason that reading scores have fallen in the school is television.* Searching for the three most important causes or effects is a good way to avoid oversimplifying.

2. **Do not confuse time order with causation.** If your eye starts watering seconds after the doorbell rings, you cannot assume that the doorbell made your eye water. Were you peeling onions? Is it allergy season? Do you need to wet your contact lenses?

3. **Do not confuse causes and effects.** This sounds obvious, but separating causes and effects can be tricky. (Is Rita's positive attitude the cause of her success in sales or the result of it?)

Transitional Expressions

These transitional expressions are helpful in cause and effect paragraphs, which often imply order of importance or time order:*

Transitional Expressions	
To Show Causes	**To Show Effects**
the first cause (second, third)	one important effect
the first reason (second, third)	another result
yet another factor	a third outcome
because	as a result
is caused by	consequently
results from	then, next, therefore, thus, so

PRACTICE 1

Read this paragraph and answer the questions.

Sadly, this college is part of a national trend: Date rape is on the rise. To stop date rape, college administrators and students must understand and deal with its possible causes. First, some fraternities and male peer groups on campus promote an attitude of disrespect toward women. This mentality sets the stage for date rape. Second, alcohol and drugs erode good judgment and self-control. The kegs, barrels, and bags consumed at many parties here put students at risk, including the risk of date rape. A third cause of date rape is miscommunication between men and women. Men and women often have different ideas of what date rape is or even if it exists. We need campus workshops in which we can discuss

---

* To read an essay of cause and effect, see "Why I Stayed and Stayed," Chapter 15, Part H.

this issue openly and come to some understanding between the sexes. Date rape is a serious problem that can ruin lives. We can make a difference by addressing the causes of date rape: the male mentality of disrespect, heavy campus use of alcohol and drugs, and the differing views of men and women.

—Michael White Moon (Student)

1. Underline the topic sentence. Does this paragraph discuss the causes or effects of date rape? <u>causes</u>

2. Do you agree with this student's analysis of the problem? Would you name other causes, and if so, which? <u>Answers will vary</u>

3. On a separate sheet of paper, make a plan of this paragraph.

4. Does Mr. White Moon discuss the three causes in a logical order? Why or why not? <u>Yes, causes are "layered": disrespectful attitudes set the scene; alcohol and drugs</u> <u>erode judgment; lack of communication is final factor.</u>

PRACTICE 2

TEACHING TIP
Many conjunctions and transitional expressions express cause and effect relationships. Reviewing these may help students more clearly present their ideas in cause and effect writing. (See pages 62–63; Chapter 21, Part D; and Chapter 25.)

To practice separating cause from effect, write the cause and the effect contained in each item below.

EXAMPLE Fewer people are attending concerts at the Boxcar Theater because ticket prices have nearly doubled.

Cause: <u>ticket prices nearly doubled</u>

Effect: <u>fewer people attending concerts</u>

1. A thunderstorm was approaching, so we moved our picnic into the van.

Cause: <u>thunderstorm approaching</u>

Effect: <u>picnic in the van</u>

2. Seeing my father suffer because he could not read motivated me to excel in school.

Cause: <u>saw my father suffer because he could not read</u>

Effect: <u>I excelled in school.</u>

3. One study showed that laughter extended the lives of cancer patients.

   Cause: laughter

   Effect: extended lives of cancer patients

4. Americans are having fewer children and doing so later in life. Some experts believe this is why they are spending more money every year on their pets.

   Cause: Americans having fewer children later

   Effect: spending more money on pets

5. Many doctors urged that trampolines be banned because of an "epidemic" of injuries to children playing on them.

   Cause: children playing on trampolines

   Effect: epidemic of injuries

6. I bought this glow-in-the-dark fish lamp for one reason only: it was on sale.

   Cause: lamp was on sale

   Effect: I bought it.

7. As more people spend time surfing the Internet, television viewing is declining for the first time in fifty years.

   Cause: more people surfing the Internet

   Effect: first decline in TV viewing in fifty years

8. For years, Charboro cigarettes outsold all competitors as a result of added ammonia. This ammonia gave smokers' brains an extra "kick."

   Cause: Charboro added ammonia.

   First Effect: Smokers got an extra kick.

   Second Effect: Charboro outsold all competitors.

PRACTICE 3

List three causes *or* three effects to support each topic sentence below. First, read the topic sentence to see whether causes or effects are called for. Then think, jot, and list your three best ideas.

TEACHING TIP
Practice 3 works well as a small-group activity.

1. The huge success of Barbie (or some other toy, game, or product) has a number of causes. _____

   _____

   _____

2. There are several reasons why AIDS continues to spread among teenagers, despite widespread knowledge about the deadly nature of the disease.

_____

_____

_____

3. Reading books by authors of many nationalities, instead of just American and English authors, has many positive (or negative) effects on American

students. _____

_____

_____

_____

PRACTICE 4

Now choose one topic from Practice 3 that interests you and write a paragraph of cause or effect on notebook paper. Before you write a draft, think and make a plan. Have you chosen the three most important causes or effects and decided on an effective order in which to present them? As you write, use transitional expressions to help the reader follow your ideas.

PRACTICE 5   THINKING AND WRITING TOGETHER

Analyze the Reasons Why Newspapers Are Losing Readers

In a group of four or five classmates, read this passage aloud. Then follow the directions below.

While many news outlets are losing young audiences, the newspaper industry is doing so at an especially alarming clip. Less than a fifth of eighteen-to thirty-four-year-olds rank newspapers as their primary source of news, a recent study by the Carnegie Foundation found, and 12 percent of the young people surveyed said they "never" read a paper to get news. More significant, the average age of newspaper readers is fifty-three, according to the *Los Angeles Times*.

—Kendra Hurley, Can Teens Save the Newspaper
Business, AlterNet, 9/29/05

What do you think are the causes or reasons why newspapers are losing young readers? Choose a group member to jot your ideas; then discuss and brainstorm possible causes for this phenomenon. List your strongest three causes in the order of importance. Advise newspaper editors about one important step they should take to attract younger readers.

CHECKLIST

The Process of Writing a Cause and Effect Paragraph

Refer to this checklist of steps as you write a paragraph.

- ☐ 1. Narrow the topic in light of your audience and purpose. Think of a subject that can be analyzed for clear causes or effects.

- ☐ 2. Decide whether you will emphasize causes or effects. What information would be most interesting to your audience?

- ☐ 3. Compose a topic sentence that states the subject and indicates whether causes or effects will be discussed.

- ☐ 4. Now freewrite, brainstorm, or cluster to find at least three possible causes or effects. Do your mental detective work. At this stage, think of all possible causes; think of short- and long-term effects, as well as positive and negative effects.

- ☐ 5. Select the best causes or effects with which to develop your paragraph. Drop those that are not relevant.

- ☐ 6. Make a plan or an outline for your paragraph, numbering the causes or effects in the order in which you will present them.

- ☐ 7. Write a first draft of your cause and effect paragraph, explaining each point fully so that your reader understands just how *X* caused *Y*. Use transitional expressions to emphasize these relationships.

- ☐ 8. Revise as necessary, checking for good support, unity, logic, and coherence. Does your paragraph have an interesting opening sentence?

- ☐ 9. Proofread for errors in grammar, punctuation, sentence structure, spelling, and mechanics. Especially watch for your personal error patterns.

TEACHING TIP
For downloadable rubrics corresponding to each rhetorical mode, go to the *Evergreen* Online Teaching Center.

Suggested Topics for Cause and Effect Paragraphs

1. Reasons why someone made an important decision

2. Reasons why some people cheat in college

3. Causes of an act of courage or cowardice

4. Causes of a marriage or divorce (friendship or end of a friendship)

5. Reasons for doing volunteer work

6. Causes or effects of membership in a group (choir, band, sports team, church, or gang)

7. Causes or effects of dropping out of school (or attending college)

8. Effects of e-mail, a computer, or other technology on a person's life

9. Effects of having a certain boss (or teacher, parent, or mentor)

10. Effects of a superstition or prejudice

11. Effects of the death of a loved one

12. Effects (positive or negative) of a habit or practice

13. Effects of living in a repressive country or home

14. Effects of living in a rural (or urban, mountainous, flat, rich, poor, or ethnically diverse) place

15. Writer's choice: _____

 EXPLORING ONLINE

http://www.delmar.edu/engl/wrtctr/handouts/cause_effect.htm Review cause and effect

http://lrs.ed.uiuc.edu/students/fwalters/causeconnect.html Graded quiz helps you choose the right transitional expressions to show cause or effect.

Online Study Center college.hmco.com/pic/evergreen8e
Visit the Online Study Center for *Evergreen* for more exercises and quizzes.

13

Persuasion

To persuade is to convince someone that a particular opinion or point of view is the correct one.

Any time you argue with a friend, you are each trying to persuade, to convince, the other that your opinion is the right one. Commercials and advertisements are another form of persuasion. Advertisers attempt to convince the audience that the product they sell—whether jeans, a soft drink, or an automobile—is the best one to purchase.

You will often have to persuade in writing. For instance, if you want a raise, you will have to write a persuasive memo to convince your employer that you deserve one. You will have to back up, or support, your request with proof, listing important projects you have completed, noting new responsibilities you have taken upon yourself, or showing how you have increased sales.

Once you learn how to persuade logically and rationally, you will be less likely to accept the false, misleading, and emotional arguments that you hear and read every day. Persuasion is vital in daily life, in nearly all college courses, and in most careers.

Topic Sentence

Here is the topic sentence of a **persuasive** paragraph:

> Passengers should refuse to ride in any vehicle driven by someone who has been drinking.

■ The writer begins a persuasive paragraph by stating clearly what he or she is arguing for or against. What will this persuasive paragraph argue against?

This paragraph will argue against riding with a driver who has been drinking.

■ Words like *should, ought,* and *must* (and the negatives *should not, ought not,* and *must not*) are especially effective in the topic sentence of a persuasive paragraph.

Paragraph and Plan

Here is the entire paragraph:

TEACHING TIP
Guide students to see how a fact or statistic improves credibility and helps persuade the reader. Point out the wealth of data available in libraries and online. (See also Chapters 18 and 19 on research.)

> Passengers should refuse to ride in any vehicle driven by someone who has been drinking. First and most important, such a refusal could save lives. The National Council on Alcoholism reports that drunk driving causes 25,000 deaths and 50 percent of all traffic accidents each year. Not only the drivers but the passengers who agree to travel with them are responsible. Second, riders might tell themselves that some people drive well even after a few drinks, but this is just not true. Dr. Burton Belloc of the local Alcoholism Treatment Center explains that even one drink can lengthen the reflex time and weaken the judgment needed for safe driving. Other riders might feel foolish to ruin a social occasion or inconvenience themselves or others by speaking up, but risking their lives is even more foolish. Finally, by refusing to ride with a drinker, one passenger could influence other passengers or the driver. Marie Furillo, a student at Central High School, is an example. When three friends who had obviously been drinking offered her a ride home from school, she refused, despite the driver's teasing. Hearing Marie's refusal, two of her friends got out of the car. Until the laws are changed and a vast re-education takes place, the bloodshed on American highways will probably continue. But there is one thing people can do: They can refuse to risk their lives for the sake of a party.

TEACHING TIP
Prompt critical thinking and writing by pairing alcohol advertising statistics (**http://www.madd.org /stats/1777**) and Adbusters' dark parody ads for vodka (**http://adbusters.org /spoofads/alcohol/**). To grasp the latter, students should be familiar with the slick Absolut campaign.

■ The first reason in the argument **predicts the consequence.** If passengers refuse to ride with drinkers, what will the consequence be?

Lives could be saved.

■ The writer also supports this reason with **facts.** What are the facts?

Drunk driving causes 25,000 deaths and 50 percent of all traffic accidents each year.

■ The second reason in the argument is really an **answer to the opposition.** That is, the writer anticipates the critics. What point is the writer answering?

The writer is answering the point that some people believe they drive well even after

having a few drinks.

■ The writer supports this reason by **referring to an authority.** That is, the writer gives the opinion of someone who can provide unbiased and valuable information about the subject. Who is the authority and what does this person say?

Dr. Burton Belloc of the Alcoholism Treatment Center notes that even one drink affects a

driver's reflexes.

■ The third reason in the argument is that risking your life is foolish. This reason is really another **answer to the opposition.** What point is the writer answering?

The writer is answering the point that people hesitate to be "party poopers."

_____

■ The final reason in the argument is that one passenger could influence others. What **example** does the writer supply to back up this reason?

Marie Furillo refused a ride home from school because the driver had been drinking.

Her refusal influenced the two passengers to get out of the car.

■ Persuasive paragraphs either can begin with the most important reason and then continue with less important ones, or they can begin with the least important reasons, saving the most important for last.* This paragraph begins with what the author considers *most* important. How can you tell?

The writer states that the first point is the most important.

Before composing this persuasive paragraph, the writer probably brainstormed or freewrote to gather ideas and then made an **outline** like this:

_____

TEACHING TIP
Stress the importance of outlining before writing an argument. Urge students to consider carefully the order of their ideas before they write.

Topic sentence: Passengers should refuse to ride in any vehicle driven by someone who has been drinking.

    Reason 1:   Refusal could save lives **(predicting a consequence).**
                   —statistics on deaths and accidents **(facts)**
                   —passengers are equally responsible

    Reason 2:   Riders might say some drinkers drive well—not true **(answering the opposition).**
                   —Dr. Belloc's explanation **(referring to authority)**

    Reason 3:   Others might feel foolish speaking up, but risking lives is more foolish **(answering the opposition).**

    Reason 4:   One rider might influence other passengers.
                   —Marie Furillo **(example)**

Conclusion: Bloodshed will probably continue, but people can refuse to risk their lives.

_____

■ Note how each reason clearly supports the topic sentence.

_____
* For work on order of importance, see Chapter 4, "Achieving Coherence," Part A.

Transitional Expressions

The following transitional expressions are helpful in persuasive paragraphs:

Transitional Expressions for Persuasion		
Give Reasons	**Answer the Opposition**	**Draw Conclusions**
first (second, third)	of course	therefore
another, next	some may say	thus
last, finally	nevertheless	hence
because, since, for	on the other hand	consequently
although		

Methods of Persuasion

The drinking-and-driving example showed the basic kinds of support used in persuasive paragraphs: **facts, referring to an authority, examples, predicting the consequences,** and **answering the opposition.** Although you will rarely use all of them in one paragraph, you should be familiar with them all. Here are some more details:

TEACHING TIP
Students may benefit from reviewing the difference between facts and opinions. Facts are information that can be verified; opinions are personal value judgments that cannot be verified.

1. **Facts: Facts** are simply statements of *what is*. They should appeal to the reader's mind, not just to the emotions. The source of your facts should be clear to the reader. If you wish to prove that children's eyesight should be checked every year by a doctor, you might look for supporting facts in appropriate books and magazines, or you might ask your eye doctor for information. Your paper might say, "Many people suffer serious visual impairment later in life because they received insufficient or inadequate eye care when they were children, according to an article in *Better Vision*."*

   Avoid the vague "everyone knows that" or "it is common knowledge that" or "they all say." Such statements will make your reader justifiably suspicious of your "facts."

TEACHING TIP
Engage students in a discussion about what kinds of education, training, or experience qualify someone as an authority on a subject.

2. **Referring to an authority:** An **authority** is an expert, someone who can be relied on to give unbiased facts and information. If you wish to convince your readers that asthma is a far more serious illness than most people realize, you might speak with an emergency-room physician about the numbers of patients treated for asthma attacks, or you might quote experts from the literature of national organizations like the Asthma and Allergy Foundation of America or the American Lung Association. These are all excellent and knowledgeable authorities whose opinions on medical matters would be considered valid and unbiased.

---

* For more work on summarizing and quoting outside sources, see Chapter 18, "Strengthening an Essay with Research."

Avoid appealing to "authorities" who are interesting or glamorous but who are not experts. A basketball player certainly knows about sports, but probably knows little about cameras or cookware.

3. **Examples:** An **example** should clearly relate to the argument and should be typical enough to support it.* If you wish to convince your reader that high schools should provide more funds than they do for women's sports, you might say, "Jefferson High School, for instance, has received inquiries from sixty female students who would be willing to join a women's basketball or baseball team if the school could provide the uniforms, the space, and a coach."

Avoid examples that are not typical enough to support your general statement. That your friend was once bitten by a dog does not adequately prove that all dogs are dangerous pets.

4. **Predicting the consequence: Predicting the consequence** helps the reader visualize what will occur if *something does or does not happen.* To convince your readers that a college education should be free to all qualified students, you might say, "If bright but economically deprived students cannot attend college because they cannot afford it, our society will be robbed of their talents."

Avoid exaggerating the consequence. For instance, telling the reader, "If you don't eat fresh fruit every day, you will never be truly healthy," exaggerates the consequences of not eating fresh fruit and makes the reader understandably suspicious.

5. **Answering the opposition: Answering possible critics** shows that you are aware of the opposition's argument and are able to respond to it. If you wish to convince your readers that your candidate is the best on the ballot, you might say, "Some have criticized him for running a low-key campaign, but he feels that the issues and his stand on them should speak for themselves."

Avoid calling the opposition "fools" or "crooks." Attack their ideas, not their character.

Considering the Audience

In addition to providing adequate proof for your argument, pay special attention to the **audience** as you write persuasively. In general, we assume that our audience is much like us—reasonable people who wish to learn the truth. But because argument can evoke strong feelings, directing your persuasive paper toward a particular audience can be helpful. Consider just *what kind of evidence* this audience would respond to. For instance, if you were attempting to persuade parents to volunteer their time to establish a local Scout troop, you might explain to them the various ways in which their children would benefit from the troop. In other words, show these parents how the troop is important to *them.* You might also say that you realize how much time they already spend on family matters and how little spare time they have. By doing so, you let them know that you understand their resistance to the argument and that you are sympathetic to their doubts. When you take your audience into consideration, you will make your persuasive paragraph more convincing.†‡

---

* For more work on examples, see Chapter 5, "Illustration."

† For more work on audience, see Chapter 1, "Exploring the Writing Process," Part B.

‡ For a complete essay developed by persuasion, see "Stopping Youth Violence: An Inside Job," Chapter 15, Part I.

Building Blocks of Effective Persuasive Writing

Topic: Students should acquire computer skills.

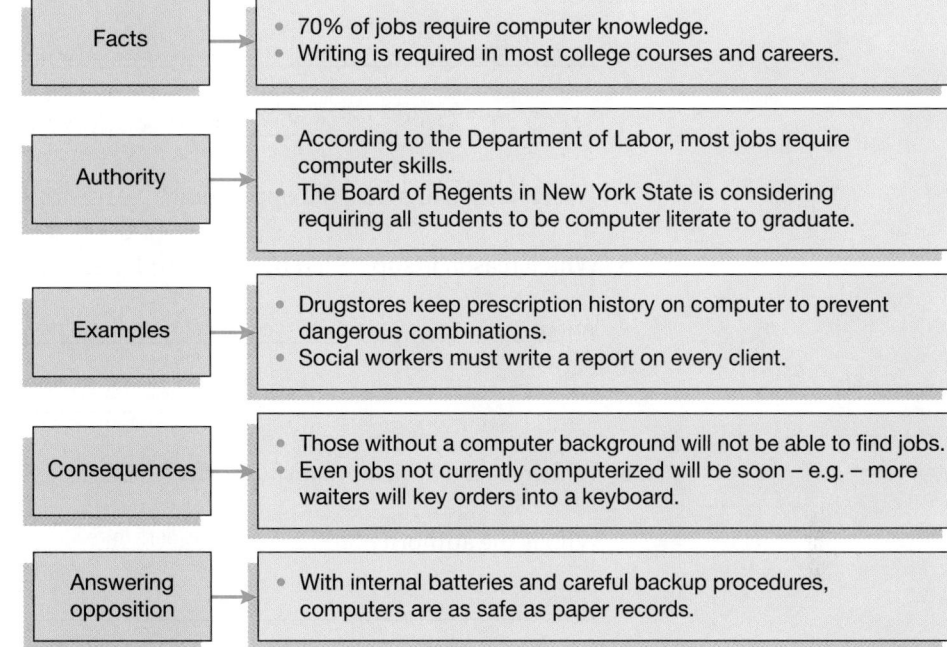

Facts	• 70% of jobs require computer knowledge. • Writing is required in most college courses and careers.
Authority	• According to the Department of Labor, most jobs require computer skills. • The Board of Regents in New York State is considering requiring all students to be computer literate to graduate.
Examples	• Drugstores keep prescription history on computer to prevent dangerous combinations. • Social workers must write a report on every client.
Consequences	• Those without a computer background will not be able to find jobs. • Even jobs not currently computerized will be soon – e.g. – more waiters will key orders into a keyboard.
Answering opposition	• With internal batteries and careful backup procedures, computers are as safe as paper records.

PRACTICE 1

Read the following persuasive paragraph carefully and answer the questions.

American women should stop buying so-called women's magazines because these publications lower their self-esteem. First of all, publications like *Glamour* and *Cosmo* appeal to women's insecurities and make millions doing it. Topics like "Ten Days to Sexier Cleavage" and "How to Attract Mr. Right" lure women to buy 7 million copies a month, reports Claire Ito in *The Tulsa Chronicle,* May 4, 2006. The message: women need to be improved. Second, although many people—especially magazine publishers—claim these periodicals build self-esteem, they really do the opposite. One expert in readers' reactions, Deborah Then, says that almost all women, regardless of age or education, feel worse about themselves after reading one of these magazines. Alice, one of the women I spoke with, is a good example: "I flip through pictures of world-class beauties and six-foot-tall skinny women, comparing myself to them. In more ways than one, I come up short." Finally, if women spent the money and time these magazines take on more self-loving activities—studying new subjects, developing mental or physical fitness, setting goals and daring to achieve them—they would really build self-worth. Sisters, seek wisdom, create what you envision, and above all, know that you can.

—Rochelle Revard (Student)

1. What is this paragraph arguing for or against? The paragraph argues that
   women should stop buying women's magazines.

2. What audience is the writer addressing? women

3. Which reason is supported by facts? the first reason

What are the facts, and where did the writer get them? Women buy 7 million

copies a month, according to Claire Ito, *The Tulsa Chronicle*, May 4, 2006.

4. Which reason answers the opposition? the second reason

5. Which reason is supported by an example? the second reason

What is the example? Alice, one of the women interviewed

6. Which reason appeals to an authority? the second reason

Who is the authority? Deborah Then, expert in readers' reactions

PRACTICE 2

Read the following paragraph carefully and answer the questions.

TEACHING TIP
Explain that writers need
not include *I think* or *I
believe* to preface an
argument.

This state should offer free parenting classes, taught by experts, to anyone who wishes to become a parent. First and most important, such parenting classes could save children's lives. Every year, over 2 million American children are hurt, maimed, or killed by their own parents, according to the National Physicians Association. Some of these tragedies could be prevented by showing parents how to recognize and deal with their frustration and anger. Next, good parenting skills do not come naturally, but must be learned. Dr. Phillip Graham, chairman of England's National Children's Bureau, says that most parents have "no good role models" and simply parent the way they were parented. The courses would not only improve parenting skills but might also identify people at high risk of abusing their children. Third, critics might argue that the state has no business getting involved in parenting, which is a private responsibility. However, the state already makes decisions about who is a fit parent—in the courts, child-protection services, and adoption agencies—but often this is too late for the well-being of the child. Finally, if we do nothing, the hidden epidemic of child abuse and neglect will continue. We train our children's teachers, doctors, day-care workers, and bus drivers. We must also educate parents.

1. What is this paragraph arguing for or against? It is arguing that the state

should offer free parenting courses to all prospective parents.

2. Which reason appeals to an authority for support? <u>reason two</u>

   Who is the authority? <u>Dr. Phillip Graham, chairman of England's National</u>

   <u>Children's Bureau</u>

3. Which reason answers the opposition? <u>reason three</u>

4. Which reason includes facts? What is the source of these facts? <u>reason one;</u>

   <u>the National Physicians Association</u>

5. What consequence does the writer predict if parenting classes are not offered?

   <u>Reason four predicts that the "hidden epidemic of child abuse and neglect"</u>

   <u>will continue.</u>

6. Does this writer convince you that parenting classes might make a difference? If you were writing a persuasion paragraph to oppose or support this writer,

   what would your topic sentence be? _____

   _____

   _____

PRACTICE 3

So far you have learned five basic methods of persuasion: **facts, referring to an authority, examples, predicting the consequence,** and **answering the opposition.** Ten topic sentences for persuasive paragraphs follow. Write one reason in support of each topic sentence, using the method of persuasion indicated.

Answers will vary.

TEACHING TIP
Practice 3 encourages practical application of the persuasive methods students have learned and promotes critical thinking. Try it as a small-group exercise or full-class activity.

Facts

1. A stop sign should be placed at the busy intersection of Hoover and Palm streets.

   Reason: <u>In the last three months, there have been fifteen accidents at this</u>

   <u>intersection.</u>

   _____

2. People should not get married until they are at least twenty-five years old.

   Reason: <u>Statistics show that 75 percent of couples who marry before that</u>

   <u>age eventually divorce.</u>

   _____

Referring to an Authority

(If you cannot think of an authority offhand, name the kind of person who would be an authority on the subject.)

3. These new Sluggo bats will definitely raise your batting average.

   Reason: According to coach Bill Bartlett of the Madison College baseball

   team, the design and weighting of these bats allow for a better swing—by

   any batter.

   _____

4. Most people should get at least one hour of vigorous exercise three times a week.

   Reason: Dr. Pamela Lu of the Fitness Research Corporation notes that

   regular exercise can help prevent heart attacks and other life-threatening

   afflictions.

Examples

5. Pet animals should be allowed in children's hospital rooms because they speed healing.

   Reason: Adam, a six-year-old cancer patient who was deeply depressed,

   began to recover once his doctor allowed his silky terrier, Cola, to visit him.

   _____

   _____

6. Mace and pepper spray should be legalized because they can prevent crime without causing permanent injury.

   Reason: My cousin was given pepper spray by her police-officer father.

   When a man grabbed her at a bus stop, she was able to spray him and get

   away safely.

   _____

Predicting the Consequence

7. Companies should (should not) be allowed to conduct random drug testing on employees.

   Reason: If companies can perform such tests, innocent people will be

   embarrassed, inconvenienced, and insulted.

   _____

   _____

8. The federal government should (should not) prohibit the sale of handguns through the mail.

   Reason: Without such a prohibition, anyone, no matter how unstable, could

   obtain a handgun.

   _____

   _____

Answering the Opposition

(State the opposition's point of view and then refute it.)

9. This college should (should not) drop its required-attendance policy.

   Reason: Although some might argue that students would quickly stop going

   to class, most students would make responsible decisions to attend classes and

   to get an education.

   _____

10. Teenagers should (should not) be required to get their parents' permission before being allowed to have an abortion.

    Reason: Although some teenagers may make mature and informed decisions,

    not all teenagers are able to make such important decisions by themselves.

    _____

    _____

PRACTICE 4

Each of the following sentences tells what you are trying to persuade someone to do. Beneath each sentence are four reaons that attempt to convince the reader that he or she should take this particular course of action. Circle the letter of the reason that *seems irrelevant, illogical,* or *untrue.*

TEACHING TIP
Practice 4 is instructive and enjoyable as a class exercise. The humor of some statements helps students see the fallacies. Have them verbalize the rationale behind their choices.

1. If you wanted to persuade someone to do holiday shopping earlier, you might say that

   a. shopping earlier saves time.

   b. more gifts will be in stock.

   c. stores will not be overly crowded.

   d. Ja Rule shops early.

2. If you wanted to persuade someone to buy a particular brand of cereal, you might say that it

   a. is inexpensive.

   b. contains vitamins and minerals.

   c. comes in an attractive box.

   d. makes a hearty breakfast.

3. If you wanted to persuade someone to move to your town, you might say that

   a. two new companies have made jobs available.

   b. by moving to this town, he or she will become the happiest person in the world.

   c. there is a wide selection of housing.

   d. the area is lovely and still unpolluted.

4. If you wanted to persuade someone to vote for a particular candidate, you might say that she

   a. has always kept her promises to the voters.

   b. has lived in the district for thirty years.

   c. has substantial knowledge of the issues.

   d. dresses very fashionably.

5. If you wanted to persuade someone to learn to read and speak a foreign language, you might say that

   a. knowledge of a foreign language can be helpful in the business world.

   b. he or she may want to travel in the country where the language is spoken.

   c. Enrique Iglesias sings in two languages.

   d. being able to read great literature in the original is a rewarding experience.

6. If you wanted to persuade someone to quit smoking, you might say that

   a. smoking is a major cause of lung cancer.

   b. smoking stains teeth and softens gums.

   c. ashtrays are often hard to find.

   d. this bad habit has become increasingly expensive.

PRACTICE 5

As you write persuasive paragraphs, make sure that your reasons can withstand close examination. Here are some examples of *invalid* arguments. Read them carefully. Decide which method of persuasion is being used and explain why you think the argument is invalid. Refer to the list on pages 161–162.

1. Men make terrible drivers. That one just cut right in front of me without looking.

   Method of persuasion: example

   Invalid because the example of one careless male driver isn't enough to

   support a general statement about all male drivers.

2. Many people have become vegetarians during the past ten or fifteen years, but such people have lettuce for brains.

   Method of persuasion: answering the opposition

   Invalid because the writer attacks the opposition rather than countering the

   benefits of vegetarianism.

3. Candy does not really harm children's teeth. Tests made by scientists at the Gooey Candy Company have proved that candy does not cause tooth decay.

   Method of persuasion: referring to an authority

   Invalid because the scientists are employed by a candy company and may

   therefore be biased.

4. Stealing pens and pads from the office is perfectly all right. Everyone does it.

   Method of persuasion: example

   Invalid because saying "everyone does it" is vague and does not justify

   stealing.

5. We don't want _____ in our neighborhood. We had a _____

   family once, and they made a lot of noise.

   Method of persuasion: example

   Invalid because generalizations about an entire ethnic, religious, etc., group

   based on one family's behavior are stereotypical and not convincing.

6. If our city doesn't build more playgrounds, a crime wave will destroy our homes and businesses.

Method of persuasion: predicting the consequence

Invalid because this argument exaggerates the consequence.

7. Studying has nothing to do with grades. My brother never studies and still gets *A*s all the time.

Method of persuasion: example

Invalid because one person's experience doesn't adequately support such a

broad statement.

8. Women bosses work their employees too hard. I had one once, and she never let me rest for a moment.

Method of persuasion: example

Invalid because a single example cannot justify this sweeping statement.

9. The Big Deal Supermarket has the lowest prices in town. This must be true because the manager said on the radio last week, "We have the lowest prices in town."

Method of persuasion: referring to an authority

Invalid because the "authority" cited was advertising the store, not stating

research findings.

TEACHING TIP
Bring in print advertisements for students to evaluate. Find some that are based on facts and logic and some that attempt to sell nonessential or harmful products (e.g., perfume, cigarettes, alcoholic beverages). Ask students to identify the method of persuasion used in each ad. Are the arguments valid or bogus?

10. If little girls are allowed to play with cars and trucks, they will grow up wanting to be men.

Method of persuasion: predicting the consequence

Invalid because the writer cannot support such a sweeping prediction

with facts.

| PRACTICE 6 | **THINKING AND WRITING TOGETHER** |

Persuade Through Humor

Advertisements bombard us every day—through TV, newspapers, magazines, billboards, store windows, and the labels on people's clothing and possessions. The billions of dollars that Americans spend on brand-name products tell us that ads are very persuasive, usually making their argument with a strong visual image and a

TEACHING TIP
Students love this group task, which is not only fun but prompts application of methods of argument to visual images. The Exploring Online activity below makes an effective follow-up.

few catchy words. To expose the great power of advertising, a group called Adbusters creates stylish spoof ads for real products. The goal is to expose the truth that real-life ads often hide. In a group of four or five classmates, study the ad below and then answer the questions.

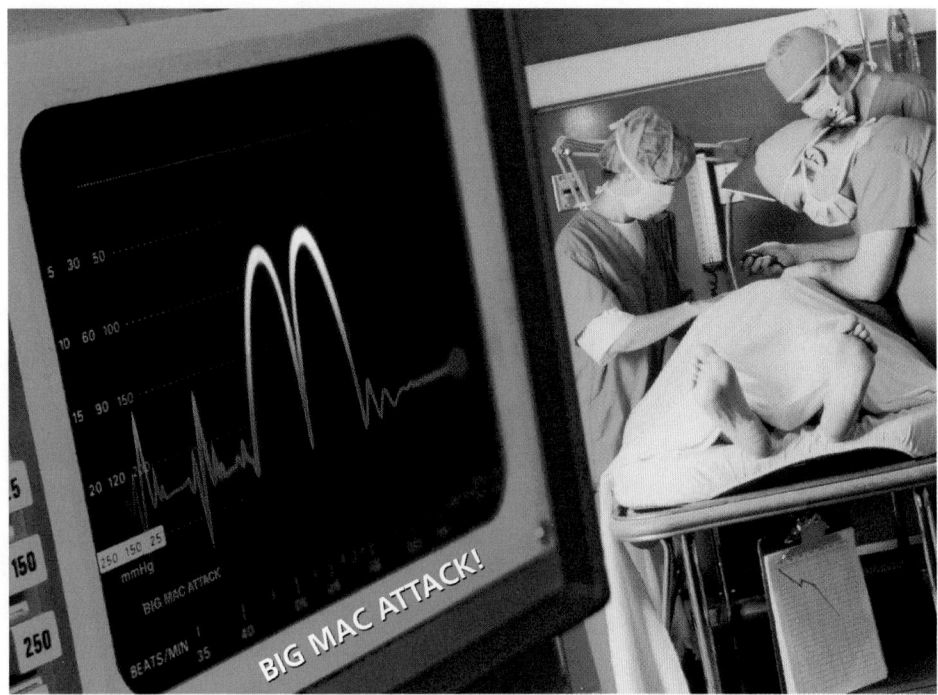

What hugely popular product is being "busted" by this Adbusters spoof? What is the persuasive message of this ad? Working together, write down the ad's "topic sentence" and argument. How effective is Adbuster's ad? Does it successfully answer the "opposition"—that is, McDonald's worldwide campaign to convince us to buy more Big Macs?

EXPLORING ONLINE

http://www.adbusters.org/spoofads/ Study other Adbuster spoof ads, especially those for fashion, alcohol, and tobacco. Pick the funniest and write about its persuasive message. Or click "Create your own print ad." In your group, create a persuasive ad, perhaps using the slogan, "Got _____?"

WRITING ASSIGNMENT

To help you take a stand for a persuasive paragraph of your own, try the following exercises on notebook paper:

1. List five things you would like to see changed at your college.

2. List five things you would like to see changed in your home *or* at your job.

3. List five things that annoy you or make you angry. What can be done about them?

4. Imagine yourself giving a speech on national television. What message would you like to convey?

From your lists, pick one topic you would like to write a persuasive paragraph about and write the topic sentence here:

Sample answer: The college library should be open all day on Sundays.

_____

Now make a plan or an outline for a paragraph on a separate sheet of paper. Use at least two of the five methods of persuasion. Arrange your reasons in a logical order, and write the most persuasive paragraph you can.

✔ CHECKLIST

The Process of Writing a Persuasive Paragraph

Refer to this checklist of steps as you write a persuasive paragraph of your own.

☐ 1. Narrow the topic in light of your audience and purpose. What do you wish to persuade your reader to believe or do?

☐ 2. Compose a topic sentence that clearly states your position for or against. Use *should, ought, must*, or their negatives.

☐ 3. Freewrite or brainstorm to generate all the reasons you can think of. (You may want to freewrite or brainstorm before you narrow the topic.)

☐ 4. Select the best three or four reasons and drop those that do not relate to your topic sentence.

☐ 5. If you use *facts*, be sure that they are accurate and that the source of your facts is clear. If you use an *example*, be sure that it is a valid one and adequately supports your argument. If you *refer to an authority*, be sure that he or she is really an authority and *not biased*. If one of your reasons *predicts the consequence*, be sure that the consequence flows logically from your statement. If one of your reasons *answers the opposition*, be sure to state the opposition's point of view fairly and refute it adequately.

☐ 6. Make a plan or an outline for the paragraph, numbering the reasons in the order in which you will present them.

☐ 7. Write a draft of your persuasive paragraph, using transitional expressions wherever they may be helpful.

☐ 8. Revise as necessary, checking for support, unity, logic, and coherence.

☐ 9. Proofread for errors in grammar, punctuation, sentence structure, spelling, and mechanics.

TEACHING TIP
For downloadable rubrics corresponding to each rhetorical mode, go to the *Evergreen* Online Teaching Center.

Suggested Topic Sentences for Persuasive Paragraphs

A list of possible topic sentences for persuasive paragraphs follows. Pick one statement and decide whether you agree or disagree with it. Modify the topic sentence accordingly. Then write a persuasive paragraph that supports your view, explaining and illustrating from your own experience, your observations of others, or your reading.

1. Companies should not be allowed to read their employees' e-mail.

2. Occasional arguments are good for friendship.

3. A required course at this college should be _____ (Great American Success Stories, Survey of World Art, How to Use PowerPoint, or another).

4. The families of AIDS patients are the hidden victims of AIDS.

5. Condom machines should be permitted on campus.

6. People should laugh more because laughter heals.

7. Expensive weddings are an obscene waste of money.

8. Gay people should be allowed to adopt children.

9. Some college football (soccer, basketball, and so on) programs send the message that academic excellence is not important.

10. TV talk shows trivialize important social issues.

11. _____ is the most _____ (hilarious, educational, mindless, racist) show on television.

12. To improve academic achievement, this town should create same-sex high schools (all boys, all girls).

13. No one under the age of 21 should be allowed to have body piercing (tattoos, cosmetic surgery, or other).

14. _____ (writer, singer, or actor) has a message that more people need to hear.

15. Writer's choice: _____

EXPLORING ONLINE

http://www.readwritethink.org/materials/persuasion_map/ This online persuasion map helps you create your argument.

http://www.geocities.com/frankie_meehan/ArgVocab.htm Practice using the vocabulary of argument.

http://www.made-you-look.ca/quiz.htm Do you think you are not affected by advertising? Take this quiz to hear the slogans in your head!

Online Study Center **college.hmco.com/pic/evergreen8e**
Visit the Online Study Center for *Evergreen* for more exercises and quizzes.

UNIT 3

Writers' Workshop

Give Advice to College Writers

When you are assigned a writing task, take a few minutes to think about the different types of paragraphs you have studied in this unit. Could a certain type of paragraph help you present your ideas more forcefully? You might ask yourself, "Would a paragraph developed by examples work well for this topic? How about a paragraph of cause and effect?"

When he received the assignment "Give advice to other college writers," this student not only made use of one paragraph pattern he had learned, but he added something of his own—humor. In your class or group, read his work, aloud if possible, underlining any lines that you find especially funny or effective.

English Students, Listen Up!

You may think that years of school have taught you how to put off writing a paper; however, true procrastination is an art form, and certain steps must be followed to achieve the status of Master Procrastinator. The first step is to come up with a good reason to put off writing the paper. Reasons prevent others from hassling you about your procrastination. A reason should not be confused with an excuse. An excuse would be, "I am too tired." A reason would be, "It is important that I rest in order to do the best possible job." The second step is to come up with a worthwhile task to do before starting the paper. If you put off writing your paper by watching *Baywatch, you* will feel guilty. On the other hand, if you put off writing your paper by helping your child do his or her homework or by doing three weeks' worth of laundry or by organizing your sock drawer, there will be no guilt. After completing your worthwhile task, you will be hungry. In order to have the energy necessary to write the paper, you will need to eat something. The true artist can make this third step last even longer by either cooking a meal or going out for food. It is important not to risk your energy level by simply eating a bowl of cereal or a ketchup sandwich. After you eat, the fourth step is to prepare the space in which you will write the paper. This includes cleaning all the surfaces, sharpening pencils, and making sure the lighting is exactly right. You may think that after this fourth step is completed, you will have no choice but to start your paper, but you do if you have done the other steps correctly. It is now too late in the day to start your paper. The fifth step is, of course, to go to bed and start over with step one in the morning.

—Thomas Capra (Student)

---

1. How effective is this paragraph?

__Y__ Clear topic sentence?   __Y__ Good supporting details?

__Y__ Logical organization?   __Y__ Effective conclusion?

2. What type of paragraph development does Capra use here? How do you know? Does the topic sentence indicate what kind of paragraph will follow? process; topic sentence says "certain steps must be followed"

3. One step in the process of becoming a Master Procrastinator contains a *contrast*. Which step? What two things are contrasted? step one; reason and excuse

4. Discuss your underlinings with the group or class. Tell what parts of the paragraph you like best, explaining as specifically as possible why. For example, the mention of a ketchup sandwich in step three adds an extra dash of humor.

5. Although this writer is having fun, procrastination is a serious problem for some people. Do you think Capra is writing from experience? Why or why not?

6. This otherwise excellent writer makes the same grammar error three times. Can you spot and correct the error pattern that he needs to avoid? three sentence fragments

GROUP WORK

In your group or class, make a chart like the one below, listing all the types of paragraph development that you have studied. Now suppose that you have been assigned the topic *procrastination*. Discuss how different paragraphs could be developed on the subject of procrastination, each one using a different paragraph pattern. For instance, you could *illustrate* procrastination by discussing examples of procrastinators you have known. Fill in the chart with one idea per paragraph type. Then share your group's ideas with the whole class.

Topic: Procrastination

Method of development: A paragraph could

Illustration   give two to three examples of procrastinators.

Narration

Description

Process

Definition

Comparison and contrast

Classification

Cause and effect

Persuasion

WRITING AND REVISING IDEAS

1. Give advice to college writers. Use humor if you wish.

2. Discuss procrastination, using one kind of paragraph development that you studied this term.

UNIT 4

Writing the Essay

14

The Process of Writing an Essay

Although writing effective paragraphs will help you complete short-answer exams and do brief writing assignments, much of the time—in college and in the business world—you will be required to write essays and reports several paragraphs long. Essays are longer and contain more ideas than the single paragraphs you have practiced so far, but they require many of the same skills that paragraphs do.

This chapter will help you apply the skills of paragraph writing to the writing of short essays. It will guide you from a look at the essay and its parts through planning and writing essays of your own.

PART A   Looking at the Essay

An **essay** is a group of paragraphs about one subject. In many ways, an essay is like a paragraph in longer, fuller form. Both have an introduction, a body, and a conclusion. Both explain one main, or controlling, idea with details, facts, and examples. An essay is not just a padded paragraph, however. An essay is longer because it contains more ideas.

The paragraphs in an essay are part of a larger whole, so each one has a special purpose.

■ The **introductory paragraph*** opens the essay and tries to catch the reader's interest. It usually contains a **thesis statement,** one sentence that states the main idea of the entire essay.

■ The **body** of an essay consists of one, two, three, or more paragraphs, each one making a different point about the main idea.

■ The **conclusion**† brings the essay to a close. It might be a sentence or a paragraph long.

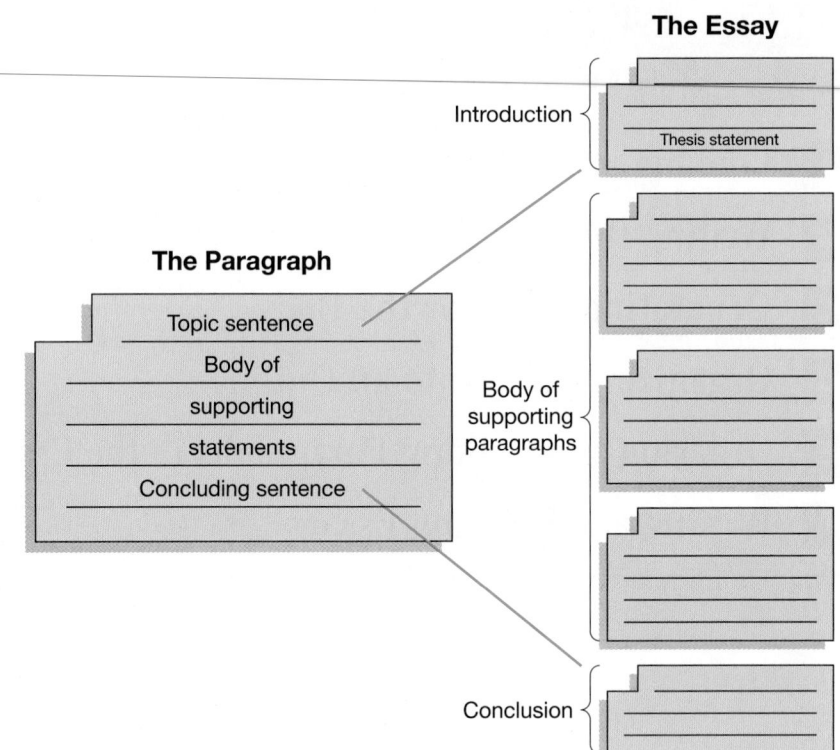

TEACHING TIP
You might want to explain to students the similarities in structure between the paragraph and essay yet show how the essay differs in length and depth. Students often find this graphic very helpful.

Here is a student essay:

Sunlight

TEACHING and ESL TIP
Using color coding to highlight parts of an essay or other written structures can help students—especially visual learners—understand.

(1) An old proverb says, "He who brings sunlight into the lives of others cannot keep it from himself." Students who volunteer through the Center for Community Service often experience this wisdom firsthand. By giving their time and talents to the local community, these students not only enrich the lives of others, but they receive many surprising benefits for themselves.

(2) Most important, volunteering can bring a sense of empowerment, a knowledge that we can make a difference. This is significant because many students feel passive and hopeless about "the way things are." My first volunteer

---

* For more work on introductions, see Chapter 16, "The Introduction, the Conclusion, and the Title."
† For more work on conclusions, see Chapter 16, "The Introduction, the Conclusion, and the Title."

TEACHING TIP
If your students seem interested in this topic, alert them to service learning opportunities on campus or share this site, which matches volunteers and local groups: **http://www.volunteermatch.org/**.

TEACHING TIP
Encourage students to read and study effective essays as models of good writing. The reading selections in Unit 8, the Writers' Workshops concluding each unit, and even some practices in this text offer excellent examples.

assignment was working with a group of troubled teenagers. Together we transformed a dismal vacant lot into a thriving business. The three-acre lot in the South Bronx, surrounded by abandoned buildings, was full of junk and heaps of wood. One teenager kicked a piece of wood and said, "Why don't we chop this up and sell it?" We surprised him by taking his idea seriously. We helped these young men, some of whom already had rap sheets, to chop up the wood, bundle it, contact restaurants with wood-burning ovens, and make deliveries. The restaurants, most of them very elegant, were happy to get cheap firewood, and the teenagers were thrilled to be treated like businesspeople. Most rewarding for me was seeing the changes in Raymond, "Mr. Apathy," as he took on a leading role in our project.

(3) Second, the volunteer often gains a deeper understanding of others. Another student, Shirley Miranda, worked with SHARE, a food cooperative that distributes bulk food once a month to its members. SHARE does not give food as charity; rather, each person does a job like unloading trucks at 5 A.M. on delivery day or packing boxes in exchange for healthy, inexpensive food. For Shirley, SHARE was a lesson in human relationships. Reflecting on her service, she wrote: "I learned that people may sometimes need guidance with dignity rather than total dependency on others. I saw that true teamwork is based on people's similarities, not their differences." SHARE so impressed Shirley that she worked in the program through her graduation.

(4) Finally, volunteering can be a way to "try on" a work environment. Sam Mukarji, an engineering student, volunteers on Saturdays as a docent, or guide, at the Museum of Science and Industry, which he describes as "my favorite place on the planet." Sam admires the creative uses of science in this museum, such as the virtual-reality experience of piloting an airplane. When many visitors asked Sam how the exhibit was put together, he suggested that the museum include signs explaining the technology. His idea was accepted, and he was asked to help implement it. Struggling to explain the exhibit in a clear way taught Sam how important writing skills are, even for an engineering major. Now he is paying closer attention to his English assignments and has discovered that working in a science museum would be his "dream job."

(5) Stories like these are not unusual at the Center for Community Service. Whenever the volunteers meet there, we always seem to end up talking about the positive ways in which volunteering has changed our lives. The Center is in a cinder-block basement without a single window, but it is filled with sunlight.

- The last sentence in the introduction is the **thesis statement**. Just as a topic sentence sets forth the main idea of a paragraph, so the thesis statement sets forth the main idea of the whole essay. It must be *general enough to include the topic sentence of every paragraph in the body.*

- Underline the topic sentence of each supporting paragraph. Each topic sentence introduces one *benefit* that volunteers receive.

- Note that the thesis and topic sentences of paragraphs 2, 3, and 4 make a rough **outline** of the entire essay:

---

1. **INTRODUCTION and thesis statement:**	By giving their time and talents to the local community, these students not only enrich the lives of others, but they receive many surprising benefits for themselves.
2. **Topic sentence:**	Most important, volunteering can bring a sense of empowerment, a knowledge that we can make a difference.
3. **Topic sentence:**	Second, the volunteer often gains a deeper understanding of others.
4. **Topic sentence:**	Finally, volunteering can be a way to "try on" a work environment.
5. **CONCLUSION**	

■ Note that every topic sentence supports the thesis statement. Every paragraph in the body discusses in detail one *benefit* that students receive from volunteering. Each paragraph also provides an *example* to explain that benefit.

■ The last paragraph **concludes** the essay by mentioning sunlight, a reference to the proverb in paragraph 1.

PRACTICE 1

Read this student essay carefully and then answer the questions.

Bottle Watching

(1) Every time I see a beer bottle, I feel grateful. This reaction has nothing to do with beer. The sight reminds me of the year I spent inspecting bottles at a brewery. That was the most boring and painful job I've ever had, but it motivated me to change my life.

(2) My job consisted of sitting on a stool and watching empty bottles pass by. A glaring light behind the conveyor belt helped me to spot cracked bottles or bottles with something extra—a dead grasshopper, for example, or a mouse foot. I was supposed to grab such bottles with my hooked cane and break them before they went into the washer. For eight or nine hours a day that was all I did. I got dizzy and sore in the eyes. I longed to fall asleep. I prayed that the conveyor would break down so the bottles would stop.

(3) After a while, to put some excitement into the job, I began inventing little games. I would count the number of minutes that passed before a broken bottle would come by, and I would compete against my own past record. Or I would see how many broken bottles I could spot in one minute. Once, I organized a contest for all the bottle watchers with a prize for the best dead insect or animal found in a bottle—anything to break the monotony of the job.

(4) After six months at the brewery, I began to think hard about my goals for the future. Did I want to spend the rest of my life looking in beer bottles? I realized that I wanted a job I could believe in. I wanted to use my mind for better

things than planning contests for bleary-eyed bottle watchers. I knew I had to hand in my hook and go back to school.

(5) Today I feel grateful to that terrible job because it motivated me to attend college.

—Pat Barnum (Student)

TEACHING TIP
Questions like these hone students' revising and writing skills. You might ask, whether the one-sentence conclusion works, or is it just too short?

1. Which sentence in the introductory paragraph is the thesis statement?

   That was the most boring and painful job I've ever had, but it motivated me to

   change my life.

2. Did Mr. Barnum's introduction catch and hold your interest? Why or why not? Yes; the first sentence is surprising and makes you want to read on.

3. Underline the topic sentences in paragraphs 2, 3, and 4.

4. What is the controlling idea of paragraph 2? description of his duties on the job

5. What is the controlling idea of paragraph 3? What examples support this idea?

   games Barnum invented to add excitement; examples are competing against his record,

   counting broken bottles, prize for best dead critter

6. What do you like best about this essay? What, if anything, would you change?

PART B ▪ Writing the Thesis Statement

The steps in the essay-writing process are the same as those in the paragraph-writing process: **narrow the topic, write the thesis statement, generate ideas for the body, organize ideas in an outline, draft, and revise.** However, in essay writing, planning on paper, prewriting, and outlining are especially important because an essay is longer than a paragraph and more difficult to organize.

TEACHING TIP
Point out to students that the first step in writing an effective academic essay is understanding the details of the assignment. Before proceeding, they should make sure that the instructor's requirements about the topic, length, and format are clear.

Narrowing the Topic

The essay writer usually starts with a broad subject and then narrows it to a manageable size. An essay is longer than a paragraph and gives the writer more room to develop ideas; nevertheless, the best essays, like the best paragraphs, are often quite specific. For example, if you are assigned a 400-word essay titled "A Trip I Won't Forget," a description of your recent trip to Florida would be too broad a subject. You would need to *narrow* the topic to just one aspect of the trip. Many writers list possible narrowed subjects on paper or on computer:

1. huge job of packing, more tiring than the trip

2. how to pack for a trip with the children without exhausting yourself

3. Disney World, more fun for adults than for children

4. our afternoon of deep-sea fishing: highlight of the trip

5. terrible weather upsetting many of my sightseeing plans

Any one of these topics is narrow enough and specific enough to be the subject of a short essay. If you had written this list, you would now consider each narrowed topic and perhaps freewrite or brainstorm possible ways to support it. Keeping your audience and purpose in mind may also help you narrow your topic. Your audience here might be your instructor and classmates; your purpose might be to inform (by giving tips about packing) or to entertain (by narrating a funny or a dramatic incident). Having considered your topic, audience, and purpose, you would then choose the topic that you could best develop into a good essay.

If you have difficulty with this step, reread Chapter 2, "Prewriting to Generate Ideas."

Writing the Thesis Statement

The **thesis statement**—like the topic sentence in a paragraph—further focuses the narrowed subject because it must clearly state, in sentence form, the writer's **controlling idea**—the main point, opinion, or angle that the rest of the essay will support and discuss.

TEACHING TIP
Students are likely to need extra practice with narrowing topics and writing thesis statements. Consider demonstrating this process with a number of different topics, verbalizing your thoughts as you proceed.

Narrowed subject:	My job at the brewery
Controlling idea:	So bad it changed my life
Thesis statement:	That was the most boring and painful job I've ever had, but it motivated me to change my life.

■ This thesis statement has a clear controlling idea. From it, we expect the essay to discuss specific ways in which this job was boring and painful and how it motivated a change.

The thesis statement and its controlling idea should be as **specific** as possible. By writing a specific thesis statement, you focus the subject and give yourself and your readers a clear idea of what will follow. Here are three ways to make a vague thesis statement more specific.

1. As a general rule, replace vague words with more exact words* and replace vague ideas with more exact information:

---

* For more practice in choosing exact language, see Chapter 22, "Revising for Language Awareness," Part A.

Vague thesis statement:	My recent trip to Florida was really bad.
Revised thesis statement:	My recent trip to Florida was disappointing because the weather upset my sightseeing plans.

■ The first thesis statement above lacks a clear controlling idea. The inexact words *really bad* do not say specifically enough *why* the trip was bad or what the rest of the essay might discuss.

■ The second thesis statement is more specific. The words *really bad* are replaced by the more exact word *disappointing*. In addition, the writer has added more complete information about why the trip was disappointing. From this thesis statement, it is clear that the essay will discuss how the weather upset the writer's plans.

2. Sometimes you can make the thesis statement more specific by stating the natural divisions of the subject. If a subject naturally has two, three, or four divisions, stating these in the thesis can set up an outline for your entire essay:

Vague thesis statement:	The movie *Southern Smoke* seemed phony.
Revised thesis statement:	The costumes, the dialogue, and the plot of the movie *Southern Smoke* all seemed phony.

■ The first thesis statement above gives little specific direction to the writer or the reader.

■ The second thesis statement, however, actually sets up a plan for the whole essay. The writer has divided the subject into three parts—the costumes, the dialogue, and the plot—and he or she will probably devote one paragraph to discussing the phoniness of each one, following the order in the thesis statement.

3. Avoid a heavy-handed thesis statement that announces, "Now I will write about . . ." or "This essay will discuss. . . ." Don't state the obvious. Instead, craft a specific thesis statement that will capture the reader's interest and control what the rest of your essay will be about. Make every word count.

PRACTICE 2

Revise each vague thesis statement, making it more specific. Remember, a good thesis statement should have a clear controlling idea and indicate what the rest of the essay will be about.   Answers will vary.

EXAMPLE Watching TV news programs has its good points.

<u>Watching news programs on TV can make one a more informed and responsible</u>

<u>citizen.</u>

TEACHING TIP
Ask students to share their rewritten thesis statements in small groups or with the class. Discuss different ways to narrow the topic or the point about that topic.

1. A visit to the emergency room can be interesting.

   <u>A late-night visit to the emergency room can shed light on the activities and problems</u>

   <u>of teenagers.</u>

2. I will write about my job, which is very cool.

   <u>Working as an administrative assistant at JamVision has allowed me to meet many</u>

   <u>young musicians in the Chicago area.</u>

3. Professors should teach better.

   <u>Some professors at State College should prepare more completely and spend more</u>

   <u>time on difficult material.</u>

4. There are many unusual people in my family.

   <u>My aunt and uncle, who once traveled the world as circus acrobats, are the most</u>

   <u>unusual members of my family.</u>

5. School uniforms are a good idea.

   <u>To reduce competition and school crime, students at Highland Middle School should be</u>

   <u>required to wear uniforms.</u>

PRACTICE 3

Eight possible essay topics follow. Pick three that interest you. For each one, **narrow** the topic, choose your **controlling idea,** and then compose a specific **thesis statement.**   Answers will vary.

TEACHING TIP
Practice 3 works well as a group activity or as the basis for a class discussion.

a volunteer experience	handling anger (or other emotion)
when parents work	a story or issue in the news now
an addictive habit	a problem on campus or at work
the value of pets	advantages or disadvantages of Internet research

EXAMPLE   Subject: <u>handling anger</u>

Narrowed subject: <u>my angry adolescence</u>

Controlling idea: <u>*channeling adolescent anger into art*</u>

Thesis statement: <u>*In a photography workshop for "at-risk" teenagers,*</u>

<u>*I learned that anger can be channeled positively into art.*</u>

1. Subject: _____

    Narrowed subject: _____

    Controlling idea: _____

    Thesis statement: _____

    _____

2. Subject: _____

    Narrowed subject: _____

    Controlling idea: _____

    Thesis statement: _____

    _____

3. Subject: _____

    Narrowed subject: _____

    Controlling idea: _____

    Thesis statement: _____

    _____

PART C   Generating Ideas for the Body

The thesis statement sets forth the main idea of the entire essay, but it is the **body** of the essay that must fully support and discuss that thesis statement. In composing the thesis statement, the writer should already have given some thought to what the body will contain. Now he or she uses one or more prewriting methods—*brainstorming, freewriting, clustering,* or *asking questions*—to generate ideas for the body.

To get enough material to flesh out an essay, many writers brainstorm or freewrite on paper or on the computer screen—jotting down any ideas that develop the thesis statement, including main ideas, specific details, and examples, all jumbled together. Only after creating a long list do they go back over it, drop any ideas that do not support the thesis statement, and then group ideas that might go together in body paragraphs.

Suppose, for instance, that you have written this thesis statement: *Although people often react to stress in harmful ways, there are many positive ways to handle stress.* By brainstorming and then dropping ideas that do not relate, you might eventually produce a list like this:

work out

dig weeds or rake leaves

call a friend

talking out problems relieves stress

jogging

many sports ease tension

go to the beach

take a walk

taking breaks, long or short, relieves stress

talk to a shrink if the problem is really bad

escape into a hobby—photography, bird watching

go to a movie

talk to a counselor at the college

talk to a minister, priest, rabbi, etc.

many people harm themselves trying to relieve stress

they overeat or smoke

drinking too much, other addictions

do vigorous household chores—scrub a floor, beat the rugs, pound pillows

doing something physical relieves stress

some diseases are caused by stress

take a nap

some people blow up to help tension, but this hurts their relationships

Now read over the list, looking for groups of ideas that could become paragraphs. Some ideas might become topic sentences; others might be used to support a topic sentence. How many possible paragraphs can you find in this list?

four _____

PRACTICE 4

Choose one of the thesis statements you wrote on page 185 and generate ideas to develop an essay. Using your favorite prewriting method, try to fill at least a page. If you get stuck, reread the thesis statement to focus your thoughts or switch to another prewriting method.

PART D Organizing Ideas into an Outline

Many writers make an **outline** before they write an essay. Because an essay is longer, more complex, and harder to control than a paragraph, an outline, even a rough one, helps the writer stay on track and saves time later. The outline should include the following:

1. Two to four main ideas to support the thesis statement

2. Two to four topic sentences stating these ideas

3. A plan for each paragraph in the body (developed in any of the ways explained earlier in this book)

4. A logical order in which to present paragraphs

Different writers create such outlines in different ways. Some writers examine their brainstorming or other prewriting, looking for paragraph groups. Others write their topic sentences first and then generate ideas to support these topic sentences.

Reread prewriting and find paragraph groups. In Part C, you read one student's brainstorm list developing the thesis statement, *Although people often react to stress in harmful ways, there are many positive ways to handle stress.* Here is one possible way to group those ideas:

1. <u>many people harm themselves trying to relieve stress</u>

   they overeat or smoke

   drinking too much, other addictions

   some diseases are caused by stress

   some people blow up to help tension, but this hurts their relationships

2. work out

   dig weeds or rake leaves

   jogging

   many sports ease tension

   take a walk

   do vigorous household chores—scrub a floor, beat the rugs, pound pillows

   <u>doing something physical relieves stress</u>

3. call a friend

   <u>talking out problems relieves stress</u>

   talk to a shrink if the problem is really bad

   talk to a counselor at the college

   talk to a minister, priest, rabbi, etc.

4. go to the beach

<u>taking breaks, long or short, relieves stress</u>

escape into a hobby—photography, bird watching

go to a movie

take a nap

■ What is the main idea of each group? Each group contains a possible topic sentence that expresses its main idea. Underline these topic sentences.

Here is the completed outline from which the student wrote her essay:

TEACHING TIP
Explain to students that outlines can range from scratch jottings to formal outlines—whatever will help the writer organize ideas and plan the paper. Make clear what outline form you prefer.

ESL TIP
Many ESL students find it helpful to use outlines. Explain that informal outlines are also useful in timed writing and examinations.

1. INTRODUCTION and thesis statement:	Although people often react to stress in harmful ways, there are many positive ways to handle stress.
2. Topic sentence:	Many people actually harm themselves trying to relieve stress. —overeat, smoke, or drink too much —get stress-induced diseases —blow up at others
3. Topic sentence:	For some people, doing something physical is a positive way to relieve stress. —walk or jog —work out —vigorous household chores —dig weeds or rake leaves
4. Topic sentence:	Taking breaks, long or short, is another positive way to relieve stress. —take a nap —escape into a hobby —go to a movie, to the beach
5. Topic sentence:	Discussing one's problems can relieve stress and sometimes resolve the cause of it. —call a friend —talk to a minister, etc. —talk to a counselor at the college —talk to a therapist if necessary
CONCLUSION:	Stress is a fact of life, but we can learn positive responses—happier, more productive

■ Note that this writer now has a well-organized outline from which to write her paper.

■ She has chosen a new order for the four supporting paragraphs. Does this order make sense? Explain.

harmful ways first, then physical work and breaks, getting help last

Write topic sentences and then plan paragraphs. Sometimes a writer can compose topic sentences directly from the thesis statement without extensive jotting first. This is especially true if the thesis statement itself shows how the body will be divided or organized. Such a thesis statement makes the work of planning paragraphs easy because the writer has already broken down the subject into supporting ideas or parts:

Thesis statement:	Because the student cafeteria has many problems, the college should hire a new administrator to see that it is properly managed in the future.

■ This thesis statement contains two main ideas: (1) that the cafeteria has many problems and (2) that a new administrator should be hired. The first idea states the problem and the second offers a solution.

From this thesis statement, a writer could logically plan a two-paragraph body, with one paragraph explaining each idea in detail. He or she might compose two topic sentences as follows:

Thesis statement:	Because the student cafeteria has many problems, the college should hire a new administrator to see that it is properly managed in the future.
Topic sentence:	Foremost among the cafeteria's problems are unappetizing food, slow service, and high prices.
Topic sentence:	A new administrator could do much to improve these terrible conditions.

These topic sentences might need to be revised later, but they will serve as guides while the writer further develops each paragraph.

The writer might develop the first paragraph in the body by giving **examples*** of the unappetizing foods, slow service, and high prices.

He or she could develop the second paragraph through **process**,† by describing the **steps** that the new administrator could take to solve the cafeteria's problems. This planning will create a clear **outline** from which to write the essay.

PRACTICE 5

Complete this outline as if you were planning the essay. First, state in sentence form each problem that will develop the topic sentence: *unappetizing food, slow service, and high prices.* Then develop each with details and examples.

---

* For more work on developing paragraphs with examples, see Chapter 5, "Illustration."

† For more work on developing paragraphs by process, see Chapter 8, "Process."

1. INTRODUCTION and thesis statement:

Because the student cafeteria has many problems, the college should hire a new administrator to see that it is properly managed in the future.

2. Topic sentence:

Foremost among the cafeteria's problems are unappetizing food, slow service, and high prices.

Problem 1: _____

_____

_____

Problem 2: _____

_____

_____

Problem 3: _____

_____

_____

3. Topic sentence:

A new administrator could do much to improve these terrible conditions.

Step 1. Set minimum quality standards

—personally oversee purchase of healthful food

—set and enforce rules about how long food can be left out

—set cooking times for hot meals

Step 2. Reorganize service lines

—study which lines are busiest at different times of the day

—shift cooks and cashiers to those lines

—create a separate beverage line

Step 3. Lower prices

—better food and faster service would attract more student customers
—cafeteria could then lower prices

4. CONCLUSION

PRACTICE 6

Write from two to four topic sentences to support each of the thesis statements that follow. (First you may wish to brainstorm or freewrite on paper or on the computer screen.) Make sure that every topic sentence really supports the thesis statement and that every one could be developed into a good paragraph. Then arrange your topic sentences in a rough outline in the space provided.   Answers will vary.

EXAMPLE   1. Before you buy a computer, do these three things.

Topic sentence: _Decide how much you can spend, and determine your price_
range.

Topic sentence: _Examine the models that are within your price range._

Topic sentence: _Shop around; all computer dealers are not created equal._

TEACHING TIP
This practice can be done constructively in small groups. Urge groups to brainstorm and choose rich, interesting supporting details.

1. I vividly recall the sights, smells, and tastes of _the baking table at the_
county fair.

Topic sentence: _Everywhere was a smorgasbord of homemade cakes, pies, cookies,_
and bread.

Topic sentence: _The enticing fragrances of yeast, spices, fruit, and chocolate were_
heavy in the air.

Topic sentence: _Some of the bakers proudly offered samples of their freshly_
baked wares.

Topic sentence: _____

_____

2. Living alone has both advantages and disadvantages.

Topic sentence: _When you live alone, you can make spur-of-the-moment decisions_
about what you want to do.

Topic sentence: _Living by yourself, you can keep your apartment as neat or as_
sloppy as you like.

Topic sentence: _Living alone allows you to eat whatever and whenever_
you want.

Topic sentence: _Living alone, however, makes you especially vulnerable to_
loneliness.

3. Doing well at a job interview requires careful planning.

Topic sentence: <u>First, learn as much as possible about the company at which</u>

<u>you are interviewing.</u>

Topic sentence: <u>Try to anticipate the kinds of questions the interviewer</u>

<u>might ask.</u>

Topic sentence: <u>Choose appropriate clothing to wear at the interview.</u>

Topic sentence: <u>Get a good night's sleep and practice relaxation techniques.</u>

PRACTICE 7

Now choose *one* thesis statement you have written, or write one now. Generate ideas for the body and organize them in an outline for an essay of your own. (For ideas, reread the thesis statements you wrote for Practice 3, pages 184–185.) Your outline should include your thesis statement; two to three topic sentences; and supporting details, facts, and examples. Prewrite every time you need ideas; revise the thesis statement and the topic sentences until they are sharp and clear.

PART E Ordering and Linking Paragraphs in the Essay

TEACHING TIP
Review the concept of coherence by referring students back to Chapter 4.

An essay, like a paragraph, should have **coherence.** That is, the paragraphs in an essay should be arranged in a clear, logical order and should follow one another like links in a chain.

Ordering Paragraphs

It is important that the paragraphs in your outline, and later in your essay, follow a **logical order.** The rule for writers is this: Use your common sense and plan ahead. Do *not* leave the order of your paragraphs to chance.

The types of order often used in single paragraphs—**time order, space order, and order of importance***—can sometimes be used to arrange paragraphs within an essay. Essays about subjects that can be broken into stages or steps, with each step discussed in one paragraph, should be arranged according to *time. Space order* is used occasionally in descriptive essays. A writer who wishes to save the most important or convincing paragraph for last would use *order of importance.* Or he or she might wish to reverse this order and put the most important paragraph first.

Very often, however, the writer simply arranges paragraphs in whatever order makes sense in the particular essay. Suppose, for example, that you have

---

* For more work on time order, space order, and order of importance, see Chapter 4, "Achieving Coherence," Part A.

written the thesis statement *Hydrogen fuel cell cars, which many experts think will be the automobiles of the future, have strong advantages and disadvantages,* and you plan three paragraphs with these topic sentences:

> Because hydrogen cars are clean-running, they will not pollute the environment like cars with gasoline engines.

> Hydrogen cell technology costs ten times more than gasoline—a major problem, at least for now.

> Hydrogen cars will free America from dependence on foreign oil sources and thus improve national security.

The writer lists three points about hydrogen cell cars. Points one and three both state advantages of hydrogen cars; therefore, it makes sense to order the paragraphs so that those two advantages are grouped together. Point two states a serious disadvantage—high cost. So it would make sense to put this point either first or last—probably last. A logical order of paragraphs, then, might be the following:

1. INTRODUCTION and thesis statement	*Hydrogen fuel cell cars, which many experts think will be the automobiles of the future, have strong advantages and disadvantages.*
2. Topic sentence:	Because hydrogen cars are clean-running, they will not pollute the environment like cars with gasoline engines.
3. Topic sentence:	Hydrogen cars will free America from dependence on foreign oil sources and thus improve national security.
4. Topic sentence:	Hydrogen cell technology costs ten times more than gasoline—a major problem, at least for now.
5. CONCLUSION	

Student Sung-Yeah Song presents her design for a hydrogen car to General Motors officials at Detroit's College for Creative Studies, 2004.

Finally, if your thesis statement is divided into two, three, or four parts, the paragraphs in the body should follow the order in the thesis; otherwise, the reader will be confused. Assume, for instance, that you are planning three paragraphs to develop the thesis statement *Using an online encyclopedia for the first time can be overwhelming, exciting, and educational.*

Paragraph 2 should discuss <u>its overwhelming aspects</u>

Paragraph 3 should discuss <u>its exciting aspects</u>

Paragraph 4 should discuss <u>its educational aspects</u>

PRACTICE 8

Plans for three essays follow, each containing a thesis statement and several topic sentences in scrambled order. Number the topic sentences in each group according to *an order that makes sense.* Be prepared to explain your choices.

1. **Thesis statement:** The fastest-growing job markets through the year 2012 will be in the computer and medical fields.

   Topic sentences:

   _3_ Numerous job openings will also exist for nurses and health-care aides who look after the elderly in homes or residential-care facilities.

   _1_ The sources of these career opportunities are the ever-expanding computer industry and Internet, as well as a generation of aging baby-boomers needing more medical care.

   _2_ Skilled computer software publishers, Internet service providers, and computer systems designers will find many job opportunities to choose from.

2. **Thesis statement:** The practice of tai chi can improve one's concentration, health, and peace of mind.

   Topic sentences:

   _2_ In several ways, tai chi boosts physical health.

   _3_ Peace of mind increases gradually as one becomes less reactive.

   _1_ Concentrating on the movements of tai chi in practice promotes better concentration in other areas of life.

3. **Thesis statement:** An immigrant who wishes to become a U.S. citizen must complete a three-stage naturalization process.

   Topic sentences:

   _2_ After submitting an application, the would-be citizen interviews with an immigration officer and takes tests on the English language and American civics.

<u>1</u> An immigrant who meets general require-
ments for minimum length of residency and
good moral character begins by filling out
Form N-400, the Application for Naturalization.

<u>3</u> Applicants who perform well in the interview
and on the tests take the Oath of Allegiance to
the United States in a moving group cere-
mony, thus becoming American citizens.

PRACTICE 9

Now, go over the essay outline that you developed in Practice 7 and reconsider
which paragraphs should come first, which second, and so forth. Does time order,
space order, or order of importance seem appropriate to your subject? Number
your paragraphs accordingly.

Linking Paragraphs

Just as the sentences within a paragraph should flow smoothly, so the paragraphs
within an essay should be clearly **linked** one to the next. As you write your essay,
do not make illogical jumps from one paragraph to another. Instead, guide your
reader. Link the first sentence of each new paragraph to the thesis statement or to
the paragraph before. Here are four ways to link paragraphs:

1. Repeat key words or ideas from the thesis statement.

2. Refer to words or ideas from the preceding paragraph.

3. Use transitional expressions.

4. Use transitional sentences.

    1. Repeat key words or ideas from the thesis statement.* The topic sentences
in the following essay plan repeat key words and ideas from the thesis statement.

Thesis statement:	Spending time in nature can promote inner peace and a new point of view.
Topic sentence:	A stroll in the woods or a picnic by the sea often brings feelings of inner peace and well-being.
Topic sentence:	Natural places can even give us a new point of view by putting our problems in perspective.

---

* For more work on repetition of key words, see Chapter 4, "Achieving Coherence," Part B. See also
"Synonyms and Substitutions" in the same section.

■ In the first topic sentence, the words *feelings of inner peace* repeat, in slightly altered form, words from the thesis statement. The words *a stroll in the woods or a picnic by the sea* refer to the idea of *spending time in nature*.

■ Which words in the second topic sentence repeat key words or ideas from the thesis statement?

natural places, new point of view

2. Refer to words or ideas from the preceding paragraph. Link the first sentence of a new paragraph to the paragraph before, especially by referring to words or ideas near the end of the paragraph. Note how the two paragraphs are linked in the following passage:

> (1) Would you rather take the risk of starting your own business than work for someone else? Would you prefer an insecure job with a large income over a secure job with an average income? Do you have a high energy level? If you answered yes to these questions, you might have some of the traits of what Dr. Frank Farley calls the "Type T" personality.
>
> (2) According to Farley, Type T people ("T" stands for "Thrill") are creative risk takers. He believes that as much as 30 percent of the American public falls into this category. "They are the great experimenters of life," declares Farley. "They break the rules."
>
> —Ira Peck and Larry F. Krieger,
> *Sociology: The Search for Social Patterns*

■ What words and groups of words in paragraph 2 clearly refer to paragraph 1?

Farley, Type T people, *and* "T" stands for "Thrill"

3. Use transitional expressions.* Transitional expressions—words like *for example*, *therefore*, and *later on*—are used within a paragraph to show the relationship between sentences. Transitional expressions can also be used within an essay to show the relationships between paragraphs:

> (1) The house where I grew up was worn out and run-down. The yard was mostly mud, rock hard for nine months of the year but wet and swampy for the other three. Our nearest neighbors were forty miles away, so it got pretty lonely. Inside, the house was shabby. The living room furniture was covered in stiff, nubby material that had lost its color over the years and become a dirty brown. Upstairs in my bedroom, the wooden floor sagged a little farther west every year.
>
> (2) *Nevertheless*, I love the place for what it taught me. There I learned to thrive in solitude. During the hours I spent alone, when school was over and the chores were done, I learned to play the guitar and sing. Wandering in the fields around the house or poking under stones in the creek bed, I grew to love the natural world. Most of all, I learned to see and to appreciate small wonders.

---

* For a complete list of transitional expressions, see Chapter 4, "Achieving Coherence," Part B. See also the chapters in Unit 3 for ways to use transitional expressions in each paragraph and essay pattern.

■ The first paragraph describes some of the negative details about the writer's early home. The second paragraph *contrasts* the writer's attitude, which is positive. The transitional expression *nevertheless* eases the reader from one paragraph to the next by pointing out the exact relationship between the paragraphs.

■ Transitional expressions can also highlight the *order* in which paragraphs are arranged.* Three paragraphs arranged in time order might begin: *First . . . , Next . . . , Finally. . . .* Three paragraphs arranged in order of importance might begin: *First . . . , More important . . . , Most important. . . .* Use transitional expressions alone or together with other linking devices.

 4. Use transitional sentences. From time to time, you may need to write an entire sentence of transition to link one paragraph to the next, as shown in this passage:

> (1) Dee Kantner and Violet Palmer were hardly radicals, but they helped bring about a revolution in sports. In 1995, both were experienced referees in women's college basketball and in the newly created Women's National Basketball Association, the WNBA. Although they were the top women in their profession, they wanted the prize all great referees want—to work in the NBA. In 1997, they won that prize, becoming the first women to referee regular-season games in the NBA and in professional football, hockey, and baseball.
>
> (2) *Achieving this goal, however, created a new challenge.* The two women now faced the criticism and even taunts of male players and coaches. Former Chicago Bulls coach Phil Jackson stated publicly that gender got them into NBA, not qualifications. Dennis Rodman shouted negative comments on the court. Kenny Anderson responded to a foul call by telling Kantner to keep her eyes on the game and off his pants. Yet Kantner and Palmer kept their cool, above all, focusing on the game. When asked how they could curb the behavior of quick-tempered players like Rodman, Charles Barkley, and Anthony Mason, Palmer told a reporter, "Confrontation is part of being a referee. If they cross a line, they get a technical foul."

■ In paragraph 1, Kantner and Palmer achieve their goal. In paragraph 2, they face the reaction of the all-male NBA. The topic sentence of paragraph 2 is the second sentence: *The two women now faced the criticism and even taunts of male players and coaches.*

■ The first sentence of paragraph 2 is actually a **sentence of transition** that eases the reader from success to a new challenge. (Note that it includes a transitional expression of contrast, *however.*)

Use all four methods of linking paragraphs as you write your essays.

PRACTICE 10

Read the essay that follows, noting the paragraph-to-paragraph *links*. Then answer the questions.

---

* For more work on transitional expressions of time, space, and importance, see Chapter 4, "Achieving Coherence," Part A.

Skin Deep

(1) What do Johnny Depp, Lady Randolph Churchill, Whoopi Goldberg, and Charles Manson all have in common? Perhaps you guessed tattoos: body decorations made by piercing the skin and inserting colored pigments. In fact, tattoos have a long and nearly worldwide history, ranging from full-body art to a single heart, from tribal custom to pop-culture fad.

(2) The earliest known tattoo was found on the mummy of an Egyptian priestess dating back to 2200 B.C. Tattoos were also used in the ancient world to decorate Japanese noblemen, mark Greek spies, and hide expressions of fear on Maori tribesmen in New Zealand. Full-body tattooing was practiced for centuries in the South Seas; in fact, the word *tattoo* comes from the Tahitian word *tattaw*. In medieval times, small tattoos were common in Europe. For instance, in 1066, after the famous Battle of Hastings, the only way that the body of the Anglo Saxon King Harold could be identified was by the word *Edith* tattooed over his heart.

(3) For the next 600 years, however, Europeans lost interest in tattoos. Then, in the 1700s, explorers and sailors rekindled public excitement. Captain Cook, returning from a trip to Tahiti in 1761, described the wonders of tattoos. Cook enthusiastically paraded a heavily tattooed Tahitian prince named Omai through England's finest drawing rooms. People were intrigued by the colorful flowers, snakes, and geographical maps covering Omai's body. Although large tattoos were too much for the British, the idea of a pretty little bee or royal crest on the shoulder was very appealing. Tattooing remained popular with Europe's royalty and upper classes through the nineteenth century. The Prince of Wales, the Duke of York, Tsar Nicholas of Russia, and Winston Churchill's mother all had tattoos.

(4) When tattooing first reached America, on the other hand, its image was definitely not refined. American soldiers and sailors, feeling lonely and patriotic during World War II, visited tattoo parlors in South Pacific ports and came home with *Mother* or *Death Before Dishonor* inked into their arms. Soon motorcyclists started getting tattoos as part of their rebellious, macho image. The process was painful, with a high risk of infection, so the more elaborate a cyclist's bloody dagger or skull and crossbones, the better.

(5) Tattooing did not remain an outlaw rite of passage for long. Safer and less painful methods developed in the 1970s and 1980s brought tattooing into the American mainstream, especially among the young. Designs ranged from one butterfly to black-and-white patterns like Native American textiles to flowing, multicolored, stained-glass designs. With the media documenting the tattoos of the rich and famous, tattooing became a full-blown fad by the 1990s. Now the one-time symbols of daring have become so common that many rebels are having their tattoos removed. About one-third of all the work performed by tattoo artists in the United States is "erasing" unwanted tattoos.

1. What transitional expressions does this writer use to link paragraphs? (Find at least two.) For the next 600 years, however; on the other hand

_____

2. How does the writer link paragraphs 1 and 2? The key word *tattoo* from

   paragraph 1 is repeated in 2; "earliest known" refers to "long history"

3. How does the writer link paragraphs 4 and 5? Transitional sentence in 5;

   "outlaw rite of passage" refers to motorcyclists in 4

PART F Writing and Revising Essays

Writing the First Draft

Now you should have a clear plan or outline from which to write your first draft. This plan should include your thesis statement, two to four topic sentences that support it, details and facts to develop each paragraph, and a logical order. Write on every other line to leave room for later corrections, including all your ideas and paragraphs in the order you have chosen to present them. Explain your ideas fully, but avoid getting stuck on a particular word or sentence. When you have finished the draft, set it aside, if possible, for several hours or several days.

PRACTICE 11

Write a first draft of the essay you have been working on in Practices 7 and 9.

Revising and Proofreading

TEACHING TIP
Make sure that students understand the difference between revising and proofreading. Encourage them to avoid using the two terms interchangeably.

Revising is perhaps the most important step in the essay-writing process. Revising an essay involves the same principles as revising a paragraph.* Read your first draft slowly and carefully to yourself—aloud if possible. Imagine you are a reader who has never seen the paper before. As you read, underline trouble spots, draw arrows, and write in the margins, if necessary, to straighten out problems.

   Here are some questions to keep in mind as you revise:

1. Is my thesis statement clear?

2. Does the body of the essay fully support my thesis statement?

3. Does the essay have unity; does every paragraph relate to the thesis statement?

4. Does the essay have coherence; do the paragraphs follow a logical order?

5. Are my topic sentences clear?

6. Does each paragraph provide good details, well-chosen examples, and so on?

7. Is the language exact, concise, and fresh?

8. Are my sentences varied in length and type?

9. Does the essay conclude, not just leave off?

---

* For more work on revising, see Chapter 3, "The Process of Writing Paragraphs," Part F, and Chapter 23, "Putting Your Revision Skills to Work."

If possible, ask a **peer reviewer**—a trusted classmate or friend—to read your paper and give you feedback. Of course, this person should not rewrite or correct the essay but should simply tell you which parts are clear and which parts are confusing.

To guide your peer reviewer, you might ask him or her to use the Peer Feedback Sheet on page 40 or to answer these questions in writing:

1. What do you like about this piece of writing?

2. What seems to be the main point?

3. Which parts could be improved (meaning unclear sentences, supporting points missing, order mixed up, writing not lively, and so forth)? Please be specific.

4. What one change would most improve this essay?

Proofreading and Writing the Final Draft

Next, carefully **proofread** the draft for grammar and spelling. Check especially for those errors you often make: verb errors, comma splices, and so forth.* If you are unsure about the spelling of a word, check a dictionary or use the spell checker on your computer.

Finally, neatly recopy your essay or print out a final copy on 8½-by-11-inch paper. Write on one side only. When you finish, proofread the final copy.

The following sample essay by a student shows his first draft, the revisions he made, and the revised draft. Each revision has been numbered and explained to give you a clear idea of the thinking process involved.

First Draft

Portrait of a Bike Fanatic

(1) I first realized how serious Diane was when I joined her on a long trip one Sunday afternoon. Her bike looked new, so I asked her if it was. When she told me she had bought it three years ago, I asked her how she kept it looking so good. She showed me how she took good care of it.

(2) Diane had just about every kind of equipment I've ever seen. She put on her white crash helmet and attached a tiny rearview mirror on it—the kind the dentist uses to check out the backs of your teeth. She put a warning light on her left leg. She carried a whole bag full of tools. When I looked into it, I couldn't believe how much stuff was in there (wrenches, inner tubes, etc.)—tools to meet every emergency. I was tempted to see if it had a false bottom.

(3) I had no idea she was such a bike nut. We rode thirty miles and I was exhausted. Her equipment was something else, but useful because she had a flat and was able to fix it, saving our trip.

(4) She doesn't look like a bike fanatic, just a normal person. You'd never guess that her bike has more than 10,000 miles on it.

---

* For practice proofreading for individual errors, see chapters in Unit 6; for mixed-error proofreading, see Chapter 37, "Putting Your Proofreading Skills to Work."

(5) As we rode, Diane told me about her travels throughout the Northeast (Cape Cod, Vermont, Penn., New York). Riding to work saved her money, kept her in shape. Her goal for the next summer was a cross-country tour over the Rockies!

(6) Our trip was no big deal to her but to me it was something. I might consider biking to work because it keeps you in shape. But basically I'm lazy. I drive a car or take the bus. I do like to walk though.

Revisions

Portrait of a Bike Fanatic

① Add intro and thesis

② *about bicycling*

I first realized how serious Diane was when I joined

③ *thirty-mile*

her on a ~~long~~ trip one Sunday afternoon. Her bike looked

new, so I asked her if it was. When she told me she had

bought it three years ago, I asked her how she kept it

④ Describe in detail

looking so good. ~~She showed me how she took good care of it.~~

Diane had just about every kind of equipment I've

⑤ *For example,*

ever seen. She put on her white crash helmet and attached a tiny rearview mirror on it—the kind the dentist

⑥ *examine*   ⑦ *strapped*

uses to ~~check out~~ the backs of your teeth. She put a warn-

⑧ Mention trip location

to   *, just below the knee*

ing light ~~on~~ her leg.

> She carried a whole bag full of tools. When I looked into it, I couldn't believe how much stuff was in there (wrenches, inner tubes, etc.)—tools to meet every emergency. I was tempted to see if it had a false bottom.

⑨ New ¶ on tools, flat tire

⑩ ~~I had no idea she was such a bike nut. We rode thirty miles and I was exhausted.~~ Her equipment was something else, but useful because she had a flat and was able to fix it, saving our trip.

⑪ Combine into one ¶ on tools

⑫ Move to intro?

She doesn't look like a bike fanatic, just a normal person. You'd never guess that her bike has more than 10,000 miles on it.

As we rode, Diane told me about her travels

throughout the Northeast (Cape Cod, Vermont, Penn.,

New York). Riding to work saved her money, kept her in

shape. Her goal for the next summer was a cross-country

tour over the Rockies!

Our trip was no big deal to her, but to me it was

something. I might consider biking to work because it

keeps you in shape. But basically I'm lazy. I drive a car or

take the bus. I do like to walk though.

Reasons for Revisions

1. No thesis statement. Add catchy introduction. (introduction and thesis statement)

2. Add *bicycling.* What she is serious *about* is not clear. (exact language)

3. Tell *how* long! (exact language)

4. Expand this; more details needed. (support, exact language)

5. Add transition. (transitional expression)

6. Wrong tone for college essay. (exact language)

7. Find more active verb; be more specific. (exact language)

8. Conclude paragraph; stress time order. (order)

9. This section is weak. Add one paragraph on tools. Tell story of flat tire? (paragraphs, support)

10. Drop! Repeats thesis. Not really a paragraph. (unity, paragraphs)

11. Put this in tools paragraph. Order is mixed up. (order)

12. Put this in introduction? (order)

13. Add details; make this interesting! (support, exact language)

14. Write a better conclusion. (conclusion)

15. Drop! Essay is about Diane and biking, not my bad exercise habits. (unity)

Final Draft

Portrait of a Bike Fanatic

(1) You'd never guess that the powder-blue ten-speed Raleigh had more than 10,000 miles on it. And you'd never guess that the tiny woman with the swept-back hair and the suntanned forearms had ridden those miles over the last two years, making trips through eleven states. But Diane is a bicycle fanatic.

(2) I first realized how serious Diane was about bicycling when I joined her on a thirty-mile trip one Sunday afternoon. Her bike looked new, so I asked her if it was. When she told me she had bought it three years ago, I asked her how she kept it looking so good. From her saddlebag she took the soft cloth that she wiped the bike down with after every long ride and the plastic drop cloth that she put over it every time she parked it outdoors overnight.

(3) Diane had just about every kind of bike equipment I've ever seen. For example, she put on her white crash helmet and attached a tiny rearview mirror to it—the kind the dentist uses to examine the backs of your teeth. She strapped a warning light to her left leg, just below the knee. Then we set off on our trip, starting at Walden Pond in Concord and planning to go to the Wayside Inn in Sudbury and back again before the sun set.

(4) We were still in Concord when Diane signaled me to stop. "I think I have a flat," she said. I cursed under my breath. I was sure that would mean the end of our trip; we'd have to walk her bike back to the car and she'd have to take it to the shop the next day. But she reached into her saddlebag again, and out came a wrench and a new tube. Before I knew it, she took the rear wheel off the bike, installed the new tube, and put the wheel back on. I began to wonder what else was in that saddlebag. When I asked, she showed me two sets of wrenches, another spare inner tube, two brake pads, a can of lubricating oil, two screwdrivers, a roll of reflective tape, extra bulbs for her headlight and taillight, and an extra chain. She had so much in the bag, I was tempted to see if it had a false bottom. Diane is one of those bicyclists who have tools to meet any emergency and know how to use them.

(5) As we rode along, Diane told me about her travels throughout the Northeast. She had taken her bike on summer vacations on Cape Cod and fall foliage tours in Vermont. She had ridden all over Pennsylvania and upstate New York, covering as much as seventy miles in a single day. She also rode to and from work every day, which she said saved money, kept her in shape, and helped her start each day feeling good. Her goal for the next summer, she said, was a cross-country tour. "All the way?" I asked. "What about the Rockies?" "I know," she said. "What a challenge!"

(6) Our trip took a little less than three hours, but I'm sure Diane was slowing down to let me keep up with her. When we got back to the parked car, I was breathing hard and had worked up quite a sweat. Diane was already there waiting for me, looking as if she did this every day—which she does. For Diane, riding a bike is as easy and natural as walking is for most people. Look out, Rockies.

PRACTICE 12

Now, carefully read over the first draft of your essay from Practice 11 and **revise** it, referring to the checklist of questions on page 200. You might wish to ask a Peer reviewer for feedback before you revise. Ask specific questions or use the peer Feedback Sheet on page 40. Take your time and write the best essay you can. Once you are satisfied, **proofread** your essay for grammar and spelling errors. Neatly write the final draft or print a final copy.

WRITING ASSIGNMENTS

The assignments that follow will give you practice in writing essays. In each, concentrate on writing a clear thesis statement and a full, well-organized body. Because introductions and conclusions are not discussed until Chapter 16, you may wish to begin your essay with the thesis statement and conclude as simply as possible.

Before you write, make an outline that includes

■ a clear thesis statement

■ two to four topic sentences that support the thesis statement

■ details, facts, and examples to develop each paragraph

■ a logical order of paragraphs

1. Some college students cheat on their papers and exams; some people cheat on the job. Why do people cheat? What are the advantages and disadvantages of cheating? Does cheating pay off? Does it achieve the end that the cheater desires? Focus on cheating at college or at work, and choose one main idea to write about. You might wish to use examples to support your thesis. Plan your essay carefully on paper—before you write it.

2. Interview a classmate (or, if you do this assignment at home, someone with an unusual skill). As you talk to the person, look for a thesis: ask questions, take notes. What stands out about the person? Is there an overall impression or idea that can structure your essay? Use your descriptive powers. Notice the person's looks, clothes, typical expressions, and gestures. Later, formulate a thesis statement about the person, organize your ideas, and write.

3. Do you feel that certain television programs (or music videos) show stereotypical women, African Americans, Hispanics, or members of any other group instead of believable people? Examine and discuss just one such program (or video) and one group of people. What situations, words, and actions by the characters are stereotypical, not real? Focus your subject, make a plan, and write a well-organized essay.

   You might wish to construct a thesis statement divided in this way: On

   the television program __(name show)__ , __(name group)__ are often portrayed as

   being __(name stereotype)__ .

4. Give advice to the weary job hunter. Describe the most creative job-hunting strategies you have ever tried or heard about. Support your thesis statement with examples, or consider using time order to show a successful job-hunting day in the life of the expert, you.

5. For better or worse, sex education begins at home—whether or not parents speak about the subject, whether parents' words reinforce or contradict the message of their own behavior. How do you think a parent should handle this responsibility? Be as specific as possible, including details from your own and your friends' experiences to make your point.

6. Draw upon your romantic misfortunes to give dating advice to others. Think back to the two, three, or four most disastrous dates you ever had. Relive the unhappy details, the disappointment, the shock, and take notes; look for a pattern, a thesis, that can pull these isolated bad times together. Now write an excellent paper in which you tell what happened to you and share your hard-earned wisdom with those seeking love—or at least, a first-run movie and popcorn.

✔ CHECKLIST

The Process of Writing an Essay

☐ 1. Narrow the topic in light of your audience and purpose. Be sure you can discuss this topic fully in a short essay.

☐ 2. Write a clear thesis statement. If you have trouble, freewrite or brainstorm first; then narrow the topic and write the thesis statement.

☐ 3. Freewrite or brainstorm, generating facts, details, and examples to support your thesis statement.

☐ 4. Plan or outline your essay, choosing from two to four main ideas to support the thesis statement.

☐ 5. Write a topic sentence that expresses each main idea.

☐ 6. Decide on a logical order in which to present the paragraphs.

☐ 7. Plan the body of each paragraph, using all you learned about paragraph development in Unit 2 of this book.

☐ 8. Write the first draft of your essay.

☐ 9. Revise as necessary, checking your essay for support, unity, and coherence. Refer to the list of revision questions on page 201.

☐ 10. Proofread carefully for grammar, punctuation, sentence structure, spelling, and mechanics.

Suggested Topics for Essays

1. The career for which I am best suited

2. This college's worst problem (propose a solution)

3. A special or unusual person

4. A valuable discipline or practice (lifting weights, rock climbing, meditating, or other)

5. Why many Americans don't vote (value education, save money for the future, give their all at work, or read poetry)

6. The best (or worst) teacher I ever had

7. Music videos (choose one performer or group, one type of music, or one TV show)

8. A lesson in diversity, race, or difference

9. The joys of homework (or housework or some other supposedly unpleasant task)

10. How to resolve a disagreement peacefully

11. An important film (book, magazine, or program)

12. The best gift I ever gave (or received)

13. Three ways that cigarette ads hook kids

14. Should courts require a one-year "cooling-off" period before a divorce?

15. Writer's choice: _____

 ## EXPLORING ONLINE

TEACHING TIP
More practice and assessment are available in the *Evergreen* Test Bank, linked ACE tests on the *Evergreen* Online Teaching and Study Centers, *WriteSpace for Evergreen,* and Exploring Online links in this chapter.

http://www.powa.org Review the essay writing process.

http://owl.english.purdue.edu/handouts/general/gl_thesis.html Writing a specific thesis statement

http://owl.english.purdue.edu/handouts/general/gl_edit.html Good revising and proofreading strategies from Purdue

Online Study Center college.hmco.com/pic/evergreen8e
Visit the Online Study Center for *Evergreen* for more exercises and quizzes.

15

Types of Essays

TEACHING TIP
Go over the diagram on page 178 to review the similarities and differences between paragraphs and essays. The parts of Chapter 15 dovetail perfectly with the chapters in Unit 3.

Because an essay is like an expanded paragraph, the methods for developing and organizing a paragraph that you learned in Unit 3—illustration, process, and so forth—can also be used to develop an entire essay. The rest of this chapter will show you how.

PART A   The Illustration Essay

The **illustration** essay is one of the most frequently used in college writing and in business. For papers and exams in history, psychology, health, English, and other subjects, you will often be asked to develop a main point with examples. In a letter of job application, you might wish to give examples of achievements that demonstrate your special skills.

Here is an illustration essay:

Extreme Makeover: Library

(1) As information-seekers began turning to computers and the Internet, some people predicted the end of the public library, which supposedly would serve no purpose in an electronic world. But that has not happened. On the contrary, many city planners now think that libraries are more important than ever for busy people in the twenty-first century. In fact, pioneering cities are spending vast sums to reinvent their libraries as community information centers that not only integrate the latest technology but also attract visitors with art, music, comfort, and beautiful design.

(2) For instance, the new library in Seattle, Washington, opened in 2004 to worldwide praise. After studying feedback from residents, librarians, and library users of all ages, architect Rem Koolhaas created—at a cost of $165 million—a modernistic copper and glass building with interior touches of eye-popping color. Employees describe it as so much fun to work in that they never miss a day. Library-goers enter a huge, welcoming "living room" where they can relax, socialize, read, or connect wirelessly to the Internet. Virtual guides on large monitors greet people and later pop up helpfully on screens throughout the library. At the building's core, a continuous, user-friendly spiral of bookshelves holds the library's collection. Patrons can get help from librarians, search for information on 132 computers, or chat online with the "virtual reference service" in a space Koolhaas calls the "mixing chamber." In the teen center, young patrons can enter sound domes and blast ear-splitting music without disturbing anyone else.

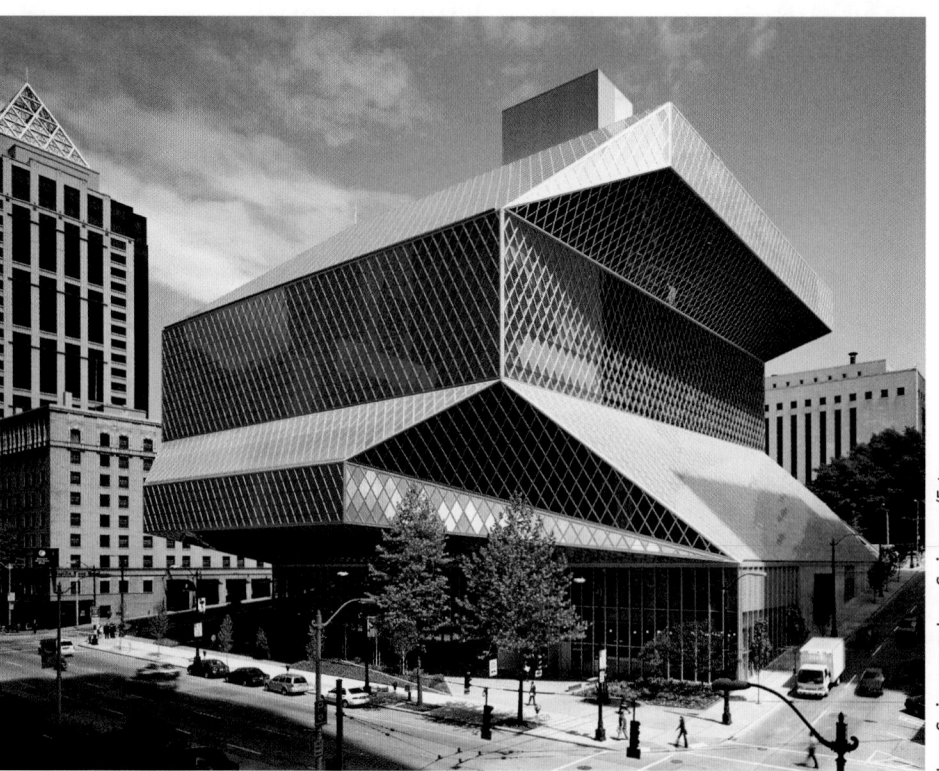

Seattle residents take pride in the new Seattle Central Library, boldly designed by Rem Koolhaas.

(3) A second, even more experimental example is the Salt Lake City Library, which has become one of Utah's top attractions since it opened in 2003. The curved glass skin of the building dazzles visitors with views of the city and the Wasatch Mountains beyond, and a roof garden overlooks for entire Salt Lake Valley. Like Seattle's library, this has won architectural awards, but unlike Seattle, it has been called the "unquietest library in America." Inside, music pumps through speakers, and librarians wear "No Shh!" buttons, although the five floors do get quieter the higher one goes. Patrons can sip coffee at a café, browse a huge CD and DVD collection, surf the Internet on one of 163 computers, stroll through an art gallery, or attend a lecture or concert in the auditorium. Of course, they can also help themselves to one of the books in the library's 500,000-volume collection.

(4) Yet another library breaking the old mold, the Cerritos Public Library in New Mexico strives for a mixed-media experience that reflects modern culture. The first titanium-clad building in the U.S., this sleek library's golden skin changes colors with the weather. Its lobby, where a 15,000-gallon saltwater aquarium reproduces a coral reef, looks more like the inside of a futuristic shopping mall than a library. Video screens flash images such as movie clips, and visitors glide in space-age elevators. Librarians don't sit behind desks; instead, armed with headsets and handheld computers, they greet visitors and move among them to offer assistance and guidance. In the children's library, kids can project themselves onto a video screen beside a life-size replica of a *T. rex* dinosaur. The library aims, through interaction and sensory experience, to stimulate library-goers' imaginations and curiosity, inspiring them to grab one of the library's 300,000 books and start reading.

(5) To achieve the goal of expanding their citizens' knowledge and literacy, savvy library planners know that, first, they must draw people inside. In the case of these three libraries, the plan seems to be working. Library membership at all three has risen dramatically. Residents who never before set foot in a library are regulars, and after school, young people hang out and do homework. As such extreme library makeovers are revealed, old perceptions of libraries as stuffy or boring shatter. *Wired? Enlightening? Gorgeous? Cool?* It might be a library.

■ The **thesis statement** of an illustration essay states the writer's central point—a general statement that the rest of the essay will develop with examples.

■ Which sentence in the introductory paragraph is the thesis statement? Circle it.

In fact, pioneering cities are spending vast sums to reinvent their libraries as community

information centers that not only integrate the latest technology but also attract visitors

with art, music, comfort, and beautiful design.

■ How many **examples** does the writer use to develop the thesis statement? What are they?

three: the Seattle Library; the Salt Lake City Library; and the Cerritos Public Library

■ Underline the topic sentence of each supporting paragraph.

■ The thesis statement and topic sentences setting forth the three examples create an **outline** for this essay. The writer no doubt made an outline well developed with specifics before she wrote the first draft.

TEACHING TIP
Ask students to think critically about how a library's design and features might affect one's studying or learning experience. Would they choose to attend one of these three libraries or a traditional library? Why?

Before writing an illustration essay, you may wish to reread Chapter 5, "Illustration." As you pick a topic and plan your illustration essay, make sure your thesis statement can be richly developed by examples. Then brainstorm or freewrite, jotting down as many possible examples as you can think of; choose the best two or three examples. If you devote one paragraph to each example, each topic sentence should introduce the example to be developed. Use transitional expressions of illustration.* As you revise, make sure you have fully discussed each example, including all necessary details and facts.

PRACTICE 1

Choose a topic from the following list or use a topic that you or your instructor has chosen. Write an illustration essay, referring to the essay checklist at the end of Chapter 14.

Suggested Topics: The Illustration Essay

TEACHING TIP
You may want to have students work together in small groups to practice writing a thesis statement and brainstorming to get strong examples.

ESL TIP
Ask students which suggested topics lend themselves to personal examples and which do not.

1. Good deeds that backfired

2. Inventions that probably will shape the twenty-first century

3. Failure as the best teacher

4. TV talk show hosts who send a positive message (or who _____)

5. Small events that changed lives

6. Memorable neighbors (professors, friends, and so on)

7. Currently cool hairstyles or clothing styles

8. Unusual places to go on dates (or to study, de-stress, get married, and so on)

9. Successful (or unsuccessful) college students

10. Musicians or artists of a particular group (R&B, tropical Latin, surrealist, French impressionist, and so on)

11. Writer's choice: _____

PART B The Narrative Essay

The narrative essay is used frequently in college writing. For instance, in a history course you might be assigned a paper on the major battles of World War I or be given an essay examination on the story of women's struggle to gain the right to vote. An English teacher may ask you to write a composition in which you retell a meaningful incident or personal experience. In all of these instances, your ability to organize facts and details in clear chronological, or time, order—to tell a story well—will be a crucial factor in the success of your paper.

Here is a narrative essay:

---

* For a partial list of transitional expressions showing illustration, see page 74.

Maya Lin's Vietnam Veterans Memorial

(1) The Vietnam War was the longest war in United States history, lasting from 1965 until 1975. Also our most controversial war, it left a deep wound in the nation's conscience. The creation of the Vietnam Veterans Memorial helped heal this wound and put an unknown architecture student into the history books.

(2) In 1980, when the call went out for designs for a Vietnam war memorial, no one could have predicted that as many as 14,000 entries would be submitted. The rules were clear. The memorial had to be contemplative, harmonize with its surroundings, list the names of those dead or missing, and—most important—make no political statement about the war. When the judges, all well-known architects and sculptors, met in April 1981, they unanimously chose entry number 1026. The winner was Maya Lin, a twenty-one-year-old Asian American architecture student who, ironically, was too young to have had any direct experience of the war.

(3) Lin envisioned shining black granite slabs embedded in a long V-shaped trench, with one end pointing toward the Lincoln Memorial and the other toward the Washington Monument. She defined the trench as a cut in the earth, "an initial violence that in time would heal." Names would be carved into the granite in the order of the dates on which the soldiers had died or disappeared. Lin felt that finding a name on the memorial with the help of a directory would be like finding a body on a battlefield.

(4) Although her design satisfied all the contest criteria and was the judges' clear favorite, it aroused much controversy. Some critics called it a "black gash of shame and sorrow," labeling it unpatriotic, unheroic, and morbid. They were upset that the memorial contained no flags, no statues of soldiers, and no inscription other than the names. Privately, some complained that Lin was too young to win the contest—and that she was female besides. She fought back. She claimed that a flag would make the green area around the memorial look like a golf course and that a traditional statue on her modern structure would be like a mustache drawn on someone else's portrait. At last, a compromise was reached: A flag and a statue were added to the memorial, and the critics withdrew their complaints. On Veterans Day, November 11, 1982, the Vietnam Veterans Memorial was finally dedicated.

(5) Since then, the memorial has become the most popular site in Washington, D.C. Some visit to see the monument and pay tribute to those who died in the war. Others come to locate and touch the names of loved ones. As they stand before the wall, they also learn the names of those who served and died with their relatives and friends. When the rain falls, all the names seem to disappear. Visitors often leave memorials of their own—flowers, notes to the departed, bits of old uniforms. A place of national mourning and of love, Maya Lin's monument has helped heal the wounds of the Vietnam War.

■ The **thesis statement** of a narrative essay gives the point of the essay.

■ What is the thesis statement of the essay?

The creation of the Vietnam Veterans Memorial helped heal this wound and put an unknown

architecture student into the history books.

▪ Paragraphs 2, 4, and 5 of this essay tell in chronological order the incidents of the narrative.

▪ What are the incidents?

the call for designs, the judges' decision, the controversy, the dedication, the

healing result

▪ What is the main idea of paragraph 3?

a description of Maya Lin's design

▪ Paragraph 1 provides background information that helps the reader understand the narrative.

▪ What background material is given in this paragraph?

The Vietnam War was the longest and most controversial war in U.S. history.

Before writing a narrative essay, you may wish to reread Chapter 6, "Narration." Make sure that your thesis statement clearly states the point of your narrative. Organize all the incidents and details in chronological, or time, order, in general beginning with the earliest event and ending with the latest. Be sure to supply any necessary background information. As you plan your essay, pay careful attention to paragraphing; if your narrative consists of just a few major incidents, you may wish to devote one paragraph to each one. Use transitional expressions that indicate time order to help your reader follow the narrative easily.*

PRACTICE 2

Choose a topic from the following list or use a topic that you or your instructor has chosen. Write a narrative essay, referring to the essay checklist at the end of Chapter 14.

Suggested Topics: The Narrative Essay

1. A risk that paid off
2. How someone chose his or her career
3. The story behind a key scientific discovery or invention
4. An event that changed your view of yourself
5. An unforgettable incident you witnessed
6. An important historical event
7. A time someone acted with courage or cowardice

---

* For a list of transitional expressions for narratives, see pages 62–63 and 83.

8. The plot line of a movie or TV show you would like to produce

9. Learning a new language (or other subject or skill)

10. Someone's battle with a serious illness

11. Writer's choice: _____

PART C The Descriptive Essay

Although paragraphs of **description** are more common than whole essays, you will sometimes need to write a descriptive essay. In science labs, you may need to describe accurately cells under a microscope or a certain kind of rock. In business, you might have to describe a product, piece of equipment, or the behavior of consumers in a test group. Travel writers frequently use description, and personal letters often call on your descriptive powers.

Here is a descriptive essay:

The Day of the Dead

(1) The most important holiday in Mexico is the Day of the Dead, *El Día de Los Muertos*. Surprisingly, this holiday is anything but depressing. In the weeks before, Mexicans excitedly prepare to welcome the souls of the dead, who come back each year to visit the living. From October 31 through November 2 this year, I attended this fiesta with my roommate Manuel. By sharing Day of the Dead activities in his family's home, in the marketplace, and in a cemetery, I have observed that Mexicans, unlike other North Americans, accept and celebrate death as a part of life.

(2) For this holiday, the home altar, or *ofrenda*, lovingly celebrates the dead. In the Lopez home, a trail of marigold petals and the rich smell of incense led us from the front door to the altar. The bright orange marigold blooms, the flowers of the dead, also trimmed a card table overflowing with everything the dead would need to take up their lives again. For Manuel's Uncle Angel there was a fragrant bowl of *mole*,* a glass of tequila, cigars, playing cards, and two Miles Davis jazz CDs. For Manuel's cousin Lucia, who died at eighteen months, there was a worn stuffed puppy, a coral blanket, and a bowl of the rice pudding she loved. Heavy black and yellow beeswax candles threw a soft glow on photos of Angel and Lucia. It was as if the dead had never left and would always have a place of honor.

(3) While death is given an honored place in the home, it is celebrated with humor and mockery in the marketplace. Here the skeleton, or *calavera*, rules. Shops sell sugar skulls, humorous bone figures, and even skeletons made of flowers. At the candy store, Manuel's niece picked out a white chocolate skull decorated with blue icing and magenta sequins in the eye sockets. In many bakeries, skull-and-crossbones designs decorated the delicious "bread of the dead." Most impressive were the stalls filled with *calacas*, handmade wooden skeletons, some no bigger than my thumb. The shelves showed a lively afterlife where skeleton musicians played in a band, skeleton writers tapped bony fingers on tiny typewriters, and teenage skeletons hoisted boom boxes on their matchstick-sized shoulder bones.

* *mole:* a spicy sauce made with unsweetened chocolate

ESL TIP

ESL students may not be aware that writers can use more than one verb tense in the same paragraph. Illustrate with examples from the essay.

(4) On the evening of November first, reverence and fun combined in an all-night vigil at the cemetery. On a path outside the cemetery gate, rows of vendors sold soft drinks and cotton candy as if it were a sporting event. Men drank a strong fermented cactus beverage called *pulque* and played cards at picnic tables. The loud music of a mariachi band serenaded the dead, who would come back to eat the food laid out for them on the graves. Old grandmothers wearing hand-woven shawls mourned and wept while children chased each other around the pink- and blue-painted graves. Nobody scolded the children. Life and death did not seem so separate.

ESL TIP
Students from Latin and South American countries might wish to share details about Day of the Dead celebrations in their countries. Do these differ from the experience of the student writer?

(5) While I have always felt fearful in cemeteries at home, there I felt excited and hopeful. When a soft breeze made the rows of candles flicker, I wondered if the souls of the children, the *angelitos*, had come back, laughing and giggling. Or was it the real children I heard laughing? I really didn't know. But I felt more alive than ever, waiting for the dead to arrive in a dusty cemetery in Mexico.

—Jason Eady (Student)

▪ The **thesis statement** of a descriptive essay says what will be described and sometimes gives an overall impression of it or tells how the writer will approach the subject. Which sentence in the introductory paragraph is the thesis statement?

By sharing Day of the Dead activities in his family's home, in the marketplace, and in a

cemetery, I have observed that Mexicans, unlike other North Americans, accept and

celebrate death as a part of life.

▪ Each paragraph in the body of this essay describes one scene or aspect of the topic. How many scenes or aspects are described, and what are they?

three scenes: the home altar, the marketplace and shops, and the village cemetery

▪ What kind of order does the writer follow in organizing paragraph 2?

space order: petals leading door to altar, marigolds trim the altar, offerings for Angel

and Lucia, photos

▪ Paragraph 5 completes and **concludes** the essay. How effective is this student's conclusion?

Very effective. He movingly describes the laughter of children—or *angelitos*.

He has so well described the fiesta that we can see why he felt "more alive"

in that cemetery.

▪ Note that the thesis statement and topic sentences make an **outline** for the whole essay.

Before writing an essay of description, you may wish to reread Chapter 7, "Description." Make sure that your thesis statement clearly sets forth the precise subject your essay will describe. Use your senses—sight, smell, hearing, taste, and touch—as you jot down ideas for the body. As you plan, pay special attention to organizing details and observations; space order is often the best way to organize a description.* As you revise, pay special attention to the richness and exactness of your language and details; these are what make good descriptions come alive.

PRACTICE 3

Choose a topic from the following list or use a topic that you or your instructor has chosen. Write an essay of description, referring to the essay checklist at the end of Chapter 14.

Suggested Topics: The Descriptive Essay

1. The decorations and rituals of a holiday you know
2. A person or animal you have closely observed
3. The scene of a historic event or battle as you imagine it
4. A school, landfill, church, prison, store, health club, or other public place
5. A tourist attraction or a place of natural beauty
6. College classrooms in the late twenty-first century
7. A computer, motorcycle, or piece of equipment from your job
8. A place you know from travel or reading
9. Your family portrait
10. A scene you will never forget
11. Writer's choice: _____

PART D The Process Essay

The **process** essay is frequently used in college and business. In psychology, for example, you might describe the stages of personality development. In history, you might explain the process of electing a president or how a battle was won or lost, while in business, you might set forth the steps of an advertising campaign. In science labs, you will often have to record the stages of an experiment.

Here is a process essay:

How to Prepare for a Final Exam

(1) At the end of my first semester at college, I postponed thinking about final examinations, desperately crammed the night before, drank enough coffee to keep the city of Cincinnati awake, and then got Cs and Ds. I have since realized that the students who got As on their finals weren't just lucky; they knew how to *prepare*. There are many different ways to prepare for a final examination, and

---

* For a list of transitional expressions of space order, see page 94.

each individual must perfect his or her own style, but over the years, I have developed a method that works for me.

(2) First, when your professor announces the date, time, and place of the final—usually at least two weeks before—ask questions and take careful notes on the answers. What chapters will be covered? What kinds of questions will the test contain? What materials and topics are most important? The information you gather will help you study more effectively.

(3) Next, survey all the textbook chapters the test will cover, using a highlighter or colored pen to mark important ideas and sections to be studied later. Many textbooks emphasize key ideas with boldface titles or headlines; others are written so that key ideas appear in the topic sentences at the beginning of each paragraph. Pay attention to these guides as you read.

(4) Third, survey your class notes in the same fashion, marking important ideas. If your notes are messy or disorganized, you might want to rewrite them for easy reference later.

(5) Fourth, decide approximately how many hours you will need to study. Get a calendar and clearly mark off the hours each week that you will devote to in-depth studying. If possible, set aside specific times: Thursday from 1 to 2 P.M., Friday from 6 to 8 P.M., and so on. If you have trouble committing yourself, schedule study time with a friend, but pick someone as serious as you are about getting good grades.

(6) Fifth, begin studying systematically, choosing a quiet place free from distractions in which to work—the library, a dorm room, whatever helps you concentrate. One of my friends can study only in his attic; another, in her car. As you review the textbook and your notes, ask yourself questions based on your reading. From class discussions, try to spot the professor's priorities and to guess what questions might appear on the exam. Be creative; one friend of mine puts important study material on cassette tapes, which he plays walking to and from school.

(7) Finally, at least three days before the exam, start reviewing. At the least opportunity, refer to your notes, even if you are not prepared to digest all the material. Use the moments when you are drinking your orange juice or riding the bus; just looking at the material can promote learning. By the night before the exam, you should know everything you want to know—and allow for a good night's sleep!

(8) By following these simple procedures, you may find, as I do, that you are the most prepared person in the exam room, confident that you studied thoroughly enough to do well on the exam.

—Mark Reyes (Student)

TEACHING TIP
Use this essay to illustrate that essays need not be confined to just five paragraphs.

■ The **thesis statement** in a process essay tells the reader what process the rest of the essay will describe.

■ What is the thesis statement in this essay?

There are many different ways to prepare for a final examination, and each individual

must perfect his or her own style, but over the years, I have developed a method that

works for me.

■ What **process** will be described?

preparing for a test

■ How many steps make up this process, and what are they?

six: ask questions about the test, survey the chapters to be tested, survey class notes,

plan studying times, begin studying systematically, review material

■ What kind of **order** does the writer use to organize his essay?

chronological order

Before writing a process essay, you may wish to reread Chapter 8, "Process." The thesis statement should clearly set forth the process you intend to describe. As you plan your essay, jot down all the necessary steps or stages and put them in logical order. Use transitional expressions of time to help the reader follow.* As you revise, make sure you have fully and clearly explained each step so that a reader who may not be familiar with the subject matter can follow easily. Clear language and logical organization are the keys to good process writing. Pay special attention to paragraphing; if the process consists of just three or four steps, you may wish to devote one paragraph to each step. If the steps are short or numerous, you will probably wish to combine two or three steps in each paragraph.

PRACTICE 4

Choose a topic from the list below or use a topic that you or your instructor has chosen. Write a process essay, referring to the essay checklist at the end of Chapter 14.

Suggested Topics: The Process Essay

1. How someone achieved success
2. How to build a web site
3. How to get in shape
4. How a cell phone can ruin a date (or other social occasion)
5. How to get action on a community problem
6. How to teach a child a skill or value
7. The yearly cycle of a crop (corn, wheat, oranges, cocoa, and so on)
8. How to impress the boss
9. A process you learned in another course (stages of human moral development, how a lake becomes a meadow, and so on)
10. How to get an A in _____
11. Writer's choice: _____

---

* For a list of transitional expressions for process writing, see page 104.

PART E The Definition Essay

Although paragraphs of **definition** are more common in college writing than essays are, you may at some time have to write a definition essay. In a computer course, for example, you might be called on to define *Internet*. In psychology, you might need to define the *Oedipus complex,* or in biology, the terms *DNA* or *spontaneous remission*. Sometimes defining at length a term people think they know can be illuminating.

Here is a definition essay:

Winning

ESL TIP
Point out that description, narration, and examples may be used in definition essays.

(1) The dictionary defines winning as "achieving victory over others in a competition, receiving a prize or reward for achievement." Yet some of the most meaningful wins of my life were victories over no other person, and I can remember winning when there was no prize for performance. To me, winning means overcoming obstacles.

(2) My first experience of winning occurred in elementary school gym. Nearly every day, after the preparatory pushups and squat-thrusts, we had to run relays. Although I had asthma as a child, I won many races. My chest would burn terribly for a few minutes, but it was worth it to feel so proud—not because I'd beaten others or won a prize, but because I'd overcome a handicap. (By the way, I "outgrew" my asthma by age eleven.)

(3) In high school, I had another experience of winning. Although I loved reading about biology, I could not bring myself to dissect a frog in lab. I hated the smell of the dead animals, and the idea of cutting them open disgusted me. Every time I tried, my hands would shake and my stomach would turn. Worst of all, my biology teacher reacted to my futile attempts with contempt. After an upsetting couple of weeks, I decided to get hold of myself. I realized that I was overreacting. "The animals are already dead," I told myself. With determination, I swept into my next lab period, walked up to the table, and with one swift stroke, slit open a frog. After that, I excelled in biology. I had won again.

TEACHING TIP
Students may wish to read additional examples of each type of essay at the Guide to Grammar and Writing web site at **http://grammar.ccc .commnet.edu/grammar/** (click on "Essay and Research Paper Level" and scroll down to "Patterns of Organization.")

(4) I consider the fact that I am now attending college winning. To get here, I had to surmount many obstacles, both outside and inside myself. College costs money, and I don't have much of it. College takes time, and I don't have much of that either with a little son to care for. But I overcame these obstacles and a bigger one still—lack of confidence in myself. I had to keep saying, "I won't give up." And here I am, winning!

(5) These examples should clarify what winning means to me. I don't trust anything that comes too easily. In fact, I expect the road to be rocky, and I appreciate a win more if I have to work, sacrifice, and overcome. This is a positive drive for me, the very spirit of winning.

—Audrey Holmes (Student)

■ The **thesis statement** of a definition essay tells the reader what term will be defined and usually defines it as well.

■ Which sentence in the introductory paragraph is the thesis statement?

To me, winning means overcoming obstacles.

■ What is the writer's **definition** of *winning*?

Winning to this writer means overcoming obstacles.

■ Underline the topic sentences of paragraphs 2, 3, and 4.

■ How do paragraphs 2, 3, and 4 develop the thesis statement?

They give examples of how the writer overcame obstacles in her life.

■ What **order** does the writer follow in paragraphs 2, 3, and 4?

time order

Before writing a definition essay, you may wish to reread Chapter 9, "Definition." Choose a word or term that truly interests you, one about which you have something to say. Decide what type of definition you will use and write the thesis statement, which should state and define your term. Then brainstorm ideas to explain your definition. Consider using two or three examples to develop the term—the way the writer does in the preceding essay—devoting one paragraph to each example. As you revise, make sure your writing is very clear, so the reader knows exactly what you mean.

PRACTICE 5

Choose a topic from the following list or one that you or your instructor has chosen. Write a definition essay, referring to the essay checklist at the end of Chapter 14.

Suggested Topics: The Definition Essay

1. A special term from sports, music, art, science, or technology
2. Tolerance
3. A friend
4. An environmental term (*endangered species, biodiversity, wind chill, global warming,* and so on)
5. A breed of dog or other animal
6. Sexual harassment
7. Maturity
8. A slang term in current use

9. A term from another language (*salsa, joie de vivre, machismo, zeitgeist,* and so on)

10. A disease or medical condition

11. Writer's choice: _____

PART F The Comparison or Contrast Essay

Essays of **comparison** or **contrast** are frequently called for in college courses. In an English or a drama class, you might be asked to contrast two of Shakespeare's villains—perhaps Iago and Claudius. In psychology, you might have to contrast the training of the clinical psychologist and that of the psychiatrist, or in history, to compare ancient Greek and Roman religions.

Does the following essay compare or contrast?

E-Notes from an Online Learner

(1) This year I attended my first U.S. history class at midnight, clad in my dancing cow pajamas and fluffy slippers. No, I was not taking part in some bizarre campus ritual. I am enrolled in two courses in the University of Houston's Distance Education Program. Although I took classes on campus at the same college last year, my experiences in the traditional classroom and in the virtual classroom have been vastly different.

(2) Attending online courses has proved more convenient for me than traveling to regular classes each day. Because I live over an hour away from campus, I was often stalled in traffic when my 8:00 A.M. psychology lecture was beginning. Then I spent the last half hour of my afternoon English class praying that the discussion—however lively and interesting—would not go past 4:00 P.M. and make me late to pick up my son at day care. In contrast, my online classes are always convenient to attend because I set my own schedule. Lectures for my history survey course are posted to the class web site, so I can log on whenever I want to read new material or review. My writing seminar is "asynchronous." This means that students and instructors communicate at their convenience on an electronic bulletin board. I can e-mail my questions, file homework, and respond to other students' work at night or on weekends without ever leaving my apartment.

(3) Though some students miss the human energy of a real classroom, the online format actually encourages me to participate more in discussions. As a shy woman who is older than many of my peers, I used to hide in the back row to avoid having to speak. I only answered questions when called upon. On the other hand, writing online, I am more confident. I have time to think about what I want to say, and I know people are not judging me by anything except my ideas. Even though bulletin board discussions can be painfully slow and disjointed compared to the back-and-forth of a great classroom discussion, I like the equality in a virtual classroom. Surprisingly, there I feel freer to be the real me.

(4) The biggest difference in moving from a regular classroom to a virtual one, in my view, is learning to be self-motivated. Attending classes on campus, I was

motivated by the personal involvement of my instructors. I also caught that group adrenaline rush, seeing other students hunched over their notebooks in a lecture hall or coffeehouse. While my online courses still require papers to be written each week and tests to be completed within a certain time, now no instructor is prodding me to get busy. Instead, only the soft bubbling noise of my computer's aquarium screen saver reminds me to tap the keyboard and dive into my coursework. Fortunately, I am self-motivated and focused. As a returning student with a job and a child, I have to be. Honestly, however, I have already seen some of my online classmates post homework assignments later and later until they drop off the screen entirely.

(5) Overall, my experience with online classes has been more positive than my experience on campus, but online learning is not for everyone. So far I find online classes convenient, welcoming for self-expression, and well-suited to my particular personality, which is organized, shy, and prone to bouts of midnight energy. In fact, it's 12:14 A.M. now as I input the final draft of this essay assignment. My son is asleep in the next room and my cat, Miss Fleason, is nuzzling my hot pink fluffy slippers.

—Brenda Wilson (Student)

■ The **thesis statement** of a comparison or contrast essay tells what two persons or things will be compared or contrasted.

■ What is the thesis statement of this essay?

Although I took classes on campus at the same college last year, my experiences in the

traditional classroom and in the virtual classroom have been vastly different.

■ Will this essay **compare** or **contrast** the two kinds of classrooms? What word or words in the thesis indicate this?

contrast; vastly different

■ Does the writer discuss all points about A and then all points about B, or skip back and forth between A and B?

skips back and forth between A and B

■ Note that the thesis statement and topic sentences make an **outline** for this essay.

Before you plan or outline your essay, you may wish to reread Chapter 10, "Comparison and Contrast." Bear in mind, as you choose a subject, that the most interesting essays usually compare two things that are different or contrast two things that are similar. Otherwise, you run the risk of saying the obvious ("Cats and dogs are two different animals").

Here are a few tips to keep in mind as you write your thesis statement: Don't just say that A and B are similar or different; instead, say *in what way* A and B are similar or different, as the writer does on pages 220–221. You may wish to use this form for a contrast thesis: *Although A and B have this similarity, they are different in these ways.* And for a comparison: *Although A and B are unlike in this way, they are similar in these ways.*

Outlining is especially important in comparison and contrast. As you plan the body of your essay, you may wish to make a chart of all your points of comparison or contrast. In any case, if you discuss the food, service, price, and atmosphere of Restaurant A, you must discuss the food, service, price, and atmosphere of Restaurant B as well.

In your essay, you can first discuss A (one paragraph), then discuss B (one paragraph), or you can skip back and forth between A and B (one paragraph on point one, A and B, one paragraph on point two, A and B, and one paragraph on point three, A and B). Refer to the charts in Chapter 10, page 126. Use transitional expressions to help the reader follow.*

PRACTICE 6

Choose a topic from the list below or use a topic that you or your instructor has chosen. Write either a comparison or a contrast essay, referring to the essay checklist at the end of Chapter 14.

Suggested Topics: The Comparison or Contrast Essay

TEACHING TIP
To give students more practice with comparison and/or contrast, have them work together in small groups to practice writing a thesis statement and outline for one of these topics.

1. Shopping at a mall and shopping online

2. Your mother's or father's childhood and your own

3. Two cultural attitudes about one subject

4. A neighborhood store and a chain store (bookstore, restaurant, music store, and so on)

5. Two entertainers, athletes, philosophers, politicians, or other public figures

6. Two views on a controversial issue

7. Two houses or apartments that you know well

8. A traditional doctor and an alternative healer

9. A book and a movie made from that book

10. Two pets

11. Writer's choice: _____

PART G The Classification Essay

The **classification** essay is useful in college and business. In music, for example, you might have to classify Mozart's compositions according to the musical periods of his life. A retail business might classify items in stock according to popularity—how frequently they must be reordered. All plants, animals, rocks, and stars are classified by scientists. A recent book even classified L.A. gangs and their tattoos.

Although the classification essay is usually serious, the pattern can make a good humorous essay, as this essay shows:

---

* For a list of transitional expressions for comparison contrast, see page 128.

The Potato Scale

(1) For years, television has been the great American pastime. Nearly every household has at least one TV, which means that people are spending time watching it, unless, of course, they bought it to serve as a plant stand. Television viewers can be grouped in many ways—by the type of shows they watch (but there is no accounting for taste) or by hours per week of watching (but that seems unfair since a working, twelve-hour-a-week viewer could conceivably become a fifty-hour-a-week viewer if he or she were out of a job). So I have developed the Potato Scale. The four major categories of the Potato Scale rank TV viewers on a combination of leisure time spent watching, intensity of watching, and the desire to watch versus the desire to engage in other activities.

(2) First, we have the True Couch Potatoes. They are diehard viewers who, when home, will be found in front of their televisions. They no longer eat in the dining room, and if you visit them, the television stays on. *TV Guide* is their Bible. They will plan other activities and chores around their viewing time, always hoping to accomplish these tasks in front of the tube. If a presidential address is on every channel but one, and they dislike the president, they will tune in that one channel, be it Bugs Bunny reruns or Polynesian barge cooking. These potatoes would never consider turning off the box.

(3) The second group consists of the Pseudo Couch Potatoes. These are scheduled potatoes. They have outside interests and actually eat at the table, but for a certain period of time (let's say from seven to eleven in the evening), they will take on the characteristics of True Couch Potatoes. Another difference between True and Pseudo Potatoes deserves note. The True Potato must be forced by someone else to shut off the television and do something different; however, if the Pseudo Potato has flipped through all the channels and found only garbage, he or she still has the capacity to think of other things to do.

(4) Third, we have the Selective Potatoes. These more discriminating potatoes enjoy many activities, and TV is just one of them. They might have a few shows they enjoy watching regularly, but missing one episode is not a world-class crisis. After all, the show will be on next week. They don't live by *TV Guide,* but use it to check for interesting specials. If they find themselves staring at an awful movie or show, they will gladly, and without a second thought, turn it off.

(5) The fourth group consists of Last Resort Potatoes. These people actually prefer reading, going to the theater, playing pickup basketball, walking in the woods, and many other activities to watching television. Only after they have exhausted all other possibilities or are dog tired or shivering with the flu, will they click on the tube. These potatoes are either excessively choosy or almost indifferent to what's on, hoping it will bore them to sleep.

(6) These are the principal categories of the Potato Scale, from the truly vegetable to the usually human. What type of potato are you?

—Helen Petruzzelli (Student)

■ The **thesis statement** in a classification essay tells the reader what group will be classified and on what basis.

▪ This entire essay **classifies** people on the basis of their television viewing habits. Which sentence is the thesis statement?

The four categories of the Potato Scale rank TV viewers . . . to engage in other activities.

▪ Into how many categories are TV viewers divided?

four

▪ Each paragraph in the body of the essay discusses one of four categories, which the writer names. What are they?

1. True Couch Potatoes

2. Pseudo Couch Potatoes

3. Selective Potatoes

4. Last Resort Potatoes

▪ The thesis statement and the topic sentences setting forth the four categories create an **outline** for the essay. The writer no doubt made the outline before she wrote the first draft.

▪ Can you see the logic in the writer's *order* of paragraphs? That is, why does she present True Couch Potatoes first, Pseudo Potatoes second, Selective Potatoes third, and Last Resort Potatoes last?

She moves from people who watch TV the most to those who watch it the least.

Before writing your classification essay, you may wish to reread Chapter 11, "Classification." Choose a topic that lends itself to classification and carefully determine your basis of classification. Your thesis statement should state clearly the group you will classify and your basis of classification. As you plan, make sure that all your categories (three or four is a good number) reflect that basis of classification. Discuss one category per paragraph, including enough examples, details, and facts to let the reader completely understand your ideas. Use transitional expressions to guide the reader smoothly along.*

PRACTICE 7

Choose a topic from the following list or use a topic that you or your instructor has chosen. Write a classification essay, referring to the essay checklist at the end of Chapter 14.

Suggested Topics: The Classification Essay

1. Members of your family

2. People studying in the library

---

* For a list of transitional expressions of classification, see page 142.

3. Stories on the front page of the newspaper

4. Drivers

5. Music videos

6. Teenagers whom you interview about their hopefulness or the lack of it (or their belief in education, thoughts about intolerance, and so on)

7. Items in your desk drawer, car trunk, or bureau drawer

8. Shoplifters

9. Your coworkers

10. People in a movie theater or mall

11. Writer's choice: _____

PART H The Cause and Effect Essay

Essays of **cause and effect** are among the most important kinds of essays to master because knowing how to analyze the causes and consequences of events will help you succeed in college, at work, and in your personal life. What *caused* a historic battle, an increase in urban homelessness, or two friends' breaking apart? How will a certain child be *affected* by owning a computer, spending time at Sunshine Day Care, or being teased because he loves to dance? In business, the success of every company and product relies on a grasp of cause and effect in the marketplace. Why does this brand of athletic shoe outsell all others? What causes employees to want to work hard? How will the Internet affect business in 2030?

Here is an essay of cause and effect. As you will see, this writer's eventual understanding of causes and effects might have saved her life.

Why I Stayed and Stayed

TEACHING TIP
Students are likely to want to discuss this powerful essay in class. The writer seeks reasons for her self-destructive behavior—a model of self-reflective critical thinking. You might ask why people engage in self-destructive actions—smoking, having unprotected sex, and so forth.

(1) It has been proven that about 1.8 million women are battered each year, making battery the single largest cause of injury to women in the United States. Domestic violence can be physical, emotional, verbal, financial, or sexual abuse from a partner you live with. I suffered from most of these abuses for almost ten years. I have had black eyes, busted lips, bruises, and scars on my face. He had affairs with other women, yet he claimed that he loved me. People ask, "Why did you wait so long to leave him?" I stayed for many reasons.

(2) First, I was born in a country that is male-dominated. Many of my people accept violence against women as a part of life. I grew up seeing hundreds of women staying in violent relationships for the sake of their children. They wanted their children to grow up with a father at home. Relatives convinced these women to try to make their marriages work. This was all I knew.

(3) Another reason I stayed was that I was afraid to make changes in my life. I had been with him so long that I thought I had nowhere to go. I depended on him to provide me and my child with food and shelter. How could I manage on my own? Of course, the longer I believed these things, the more my self-confidence withered.

(4) Finally, I stayed because I was isolated. I felt ashamed to talk about the problem, believing it was somehow my fault. Fear was isolating, too. Living in a violent home is very frightening. Like many women, I was afraid to say anything to anyone, thinking he would get upset. If I just kept quiet, maybe he wouldn't hurt me. But nothing I did made any difference.

(5) When I finally realized that the abuse was not going to stop, I decided to do something about it. I was finally ready to end my pain. I began to talk to people and learn about ways to get help.

(6) On April 24 of this year, I fought back. When he punched me in the eye, I called 911. Thank God for changes in the way domestic violence cases are now being handled. The police responded quickly. He was arrested and taken to jail, where he waited for two days to go to court. The next day, I went to the courthouse to press charges. I spoke to the district attorney in charge, asking for an order of protection. This order forbids him from having any verbal or physical contact with me.

(7) It is very hard to see someone you love being taken away in handcuffs, but I had to put my safety and my child's well-being first. Although he is now out of jail, I feel safe with my order of protection; however, I understand that court orders sometimes do not stop abusers. These are very difficult days for me, but I pray that time will heal my wounds. I cry often, which helps my pain. But an innocent life depends on me for guidance, and I cannot let her down.

(8) Every case is different, and you know your partner better than anyone, but help is out there if you reach for it. Most cities have a twenty-four-hour hotline. There is help at this college at the PASS Center and the Department of Student Development. You can go to a shelter, to a friend, to your family. These people will not fail you. You too can break the chain.

—Student, name withheld by request

▪ The **thesis statement** in a cause and effect essay identifies the subject and tells whether causes or effects will be emphasized. What is this writer's thesis statement? Will she emphasize causes or effects?

I stayed for many reasons; causes
_____

▪ How many **causes** does the writer discuss, and what are they?

three: upbringing, fear of change, isolation
_____

▪ Although some essays discuss either causes or effects, this one does both. Paragraph 5 marks a turning point, her decision to take action. What positive effects of this new decision does she discuss? Are there any negative effects?

reached out for help and information, fought back by calling 911 and getting order of
_____

protection, acted for her daughter's welfare; negative feelings, sadness and guilt
_____

_____

■ Before she wrote this essay, the writer probably made a **plan** or **outline** like this:

Introduction and thesis statement

Reasons for staying with abusive partner ⎧ upbringing
⎨— fear of change
⎩ isolation

Decision to leave

Effects of leaving abusive partner ⎧ reached out for help
⎨— fought back (911, order of protection)
⎩ acted for daughter

Advice for women in the same situation   sadness, guilt

■ What order does this essay follow?

time

■ Do you think paragraph 8 makes an effective **conclusion**?

good information but might seem anticlimactic after dramatic personal story

Before writing an essay of cause or effect, reread Chapter 12, "Cause and Effect," especially the section called "Avoiding Problems in Cause and Effect Writing." Choose a subject that lends itself to analysis of causes or effects; see the topic lists in Chapter 12 and this chapter for ideas. Think on paper or on the computer screen listing many possible causes or effects; then choose the best three or four. Don't forget to consider short- and long-term effects, as well as positive and negative effects. Decide on a logical order—probably time order or order of importance—and use transitional expressions to introduce your points.*

PRACTICE 8

Choose a topic from the following list or one that your instructor has chosen. Write a cause and effect essay, referring to the checklist at the end of Chapter 14.

Suggested Topics: The Cause and Effect Essay

1. What are the reasons for the popularity of a product, musical group, or game?

2. What caused you to do something you are not proud of?

3. Analyze the main causes of a serious problem in society.

4. Analyze the effects of shyness on someone's life (or anger, pride, curiosity or the lack of it, and so on).

5. What are the effects of a divorce, death, or other loss?

6. What are the effects of a new experience (a trip, military service, living in another country, dorm life)?

7. What causes a hurricane, tornado, or other natural disaster?

8. Choose an event in history that interests you and analyze its causes.

9. What effects did an early failure or success (in public speaking, sports, and so on) have on someone you know?

* For a list of transitional expressions for cause effect, see page 152.

10. How does being unusual looking affect one's daily life?

11. Writer's choice: _____

PART I   The Persuasive Essay

Persuasive essays are the essay type most frequently called for in college, business, and daily life. That is, you will often be asked to take a stand on an issue—censorship on the Internet, capital punishment, whether a company should invest in on-site child care—and then try to persuade others to agree with you. Examination questions asking you to "agree or disagree" are really asking you to take a stand and make a persuasive case for that stand—for example, "The 9-11 terrorist attacks marked a new kind of war. Agree or disagree." You are asked to muster factual evidence to support your stand.

Here is a persuasive essay:

Stopping Youth Violence: An Inside Job

TEACHING TIP
Stress to students the importance of persuasive writing skills to career advancement. Ask for examples of career-related persuasive writing. Point out that documents like job-application letters, which are persuasive in nature, will help them get a job and then advance within an organization.

(1) Every year, nearly 1 million twelve- to nineteen-year-olds are murdered, robbed, or assaulted—many by their peers—and teenagers are more than twice as likely as adults to become the victims of violence, according to the Children's Defense Fund. Although the problem is far too complex for any one solution, teaching young people conflict-resolution skills—that is, nonviolent techniques for resolving disputes—seems to help. To reduce youth violence, conflict-resolution skills should be taught to all children before they reach junior high school.

(2) First and most important, young people need to learn nonviolent ways of dealing with conflict. In a dangerous society where guns are readily available, many youngsters feel they have no choice but to respond to an insult or an argument with violence. If they have grown up seeing family members and neighbors react to stress with verbal or physical violence, they may not know that other choices exist. Robert Steinback, a *Miami Herald* columnist who works with at-risk youth in Miami, writes that behavior like carrying a weapon or refusing to back down gives young people "the illusion of control," but what they desperately need is to learn real control—for example, when provoked, to walk away from a fight.

(3) Next, conflict-resolution programs have been shown to reduce violent incidents and empower young people in a healthy way. Many programs and courses around the country are teaching teens and preteens to work through disagreements without violence. Tools include calmly telling one's own side of the story and listening to the other person without interrupting or blaming—skills that many adults don't have! Conflict Busters, a Los Angeles public school program, starts in the third grade; it trains students to be mediators, helping peers find their own solutions to conflicts ranging from "sandbox fights to interracial gang disputes," according to *Youthwatch: Statistics on Violence,* May 2005. Schools in Claremont, Connecticut, run a conflict-resolution course written by Dr. Luz Rivera, who said in a phone interview that fewer violent school incidents have been reported since the course began. Although conflict resolution is useful at any age, experts agree that students should first be exposed before they are hit by the double jolts of hormones and junior high school.

(4) Finally, although opponents claim that this is a "Band-Aid" solution that does not address the root causes of teen violence—poverty, troubled families, bad schools, and drugs, to name a few—in fact, conflict-resolution training saves lives now. The larger social issues must be addressed, but they will take years to solve, whereas teaching students new attitudes and "people skills" will empower them immediately and serve them for a lifetime. For instance, fourteen-year-old Verna, who once called herself Vee Sinister, says that Ms. Rivera's course has changed her life: "I learned to stop and think before my big mouth gets me in trouble. I use the tools with my mother, and guess what? No more screaming at home."

(5) The violence devastating Verna's generation threatens everyone's future. One proven way to help youngsters protect themselves from violence is conflict-resolution training that begins early. Although it is just one solution among many, this solution taps into great power: the hearts, minds, and characters of young people.

■ The **thesis statement** in a persuasive essay clearly states the issue to be discussed and the writer's position on it. What is the thesis statement?

To reduce youth violence, conflict-resolution skills should be taught to all children

before they reach junior high school.

■ This introduction includes *facts*. What is the source of these facts and why does the writer include them here?

Children's Defense Fund. These facts show how serious a problem youth crime is.

■ Sometimes a writer needs to define terms he or she is using. What term does the writer define?

conflict-resolution skills

■ How many reasons does this writer give to back up the thesis statement?

three

■ Notice that the writer presents one reason per paragraph.

■ Which reasons refer to an *authority*?

reason 1 and reason 2

■ Who are these authorities?

Robert Steinback, *Miami Herald* columnist who works with youth, and Dr. Luz Rivera,

who wrote a conflict-resolution course

■ How is the second reason supported?

by examples

■ What is the source of information on Conflict Busters?

Youthwatch: Statistics on Violence, May 2005

■ Which reason is really an *answer to the opposition*?

reason 3

■ This reason also uses an *example*. What or who is the example?

Verna, a student whose life has changed

■ Note that the thesis statement and topic sentences make up a **plan** or an **outline** for the whole essay.

Before writing an essay of persuasion, reread Chapter 13, "Persuasion." Craft your thesis statement carefully. Devote one paragraph to each reason, developing each paragraph fully with facts and discussion. Use some of the methods of persuasion discussed in Chapter 13: *facts, referring to an authority, examples, predicting the consequence,* and *answering the opposition.* Revise for clarity and support, and remember, ample factual support is the key to successful persuasion. An excellent way to find interesting factual support is to do some basic **research**—for example, to find books or magazine articles by or about experts on your subject or even to conduct your own interviews, as does the author of "Stopping Youth Violence: An Inside Job."* Guide the reader through your argument with transitional expressions.†

PRACTICE 9

In a group of four or five classmates, discuss the meaning of this cartoon. Like many cartoons, this one expresses a strong point of view. What issue is this cartoonist commenting on? What point is he making? Working together, write down the cartoon's "thesis statement" and argument. Do you agree or disagree with the cartoonist?

---

* For information on summarizing and quoting outside sources and on using research in an essay, see Chapter 17, "Avoiding Plagiarism, Summarizing, and Quoting " and Chapter 18, "Strengthening an Essay with Research."

† For a list of transitional expressions for persuasion, see page 161.

PRACTICE 10

Choose a topic from the list below or one that your instructor has chosen. Make sure your thesis statement takes a clear stand. Write a persuasive essay, referring to the checklist at the end of Chapter 14.

Suggested Topics: The Persuasive Essay

1. Parents should routinely test their children's urine for evidence of drug use.

2. Computer and Internet classes should be given to every child in this state.

3. All animal testing of medicines should be banned, even if it will save human lives.

4. Every college student should be required to give three credit hours' worth of community service a year.

5. Only minority police should patrol minority neighborhoods.

6. A college education is (not) worth the time and money.

7. Gay couples should be allowed to adopt children.

8. Naturalized citizens should be allowed to run for president.

9. To better prepare students for the world of work, this college should do three things.

10. The United States must find and deport all illegal aliens, including students with expired visas.

11. Writer's choice: _____

EXPLORING ONLINE

TEACHING TIP
More practice and assessment are available in the *Evergreen* Test Bank, linked ACE tests on the *Evergreen* Online Teaching and Study Centers, *WriteSpace for Evergreen*, and Exploring Online links in this chapter.

http://depts.gallaudet.edu/englishworks/tablecontent.html Scroll down to review "Types of Essays" and read sample students' papers.

http://leo.stcloudstate.edu/acadwrite/comparcontrast.html Helpful advice on writing a comparison contrast essay

http://grammar.ccc.commnet.edu/grammar/composition/argument.htm Excellent tips on developing and supporting an argument

Online Study Center **college.hmco.com/pic/evergreen8e**
Visit the Online Study Center for *Evergreen* for more exercises and quizzes.

16

The Introduction, the Conclusion, and the Title

PART A	The Introduction
PART B	The Conclusion
PART C	The Title

PART A The Introduction

An **introduction** has two functions in an essay. First, it contains the **thesis statement** and, therefore, tells the reader what central idea will be developed in the rest of the paper. Since the reader should be able to spot the thesis statement easily, it should be given a prominent place—for example, the first or the last sentence in the introduction. Second, the introduction has to interest the reader enough that he or she will want to continue reading the paper.

Sometimes the process of writing the essay will help clarify your ideas about how best to introduce it. So once you have completed your essay, you may wish to revise and rewrite the introduction, making sure that it clearly introduces the essay's main idea.

There is no best way to introduce an essay, but you should certainly avoid beginning your work with "I'm going to discuss" or "This paper is about." You needn't tell the reader you are about to begin; just begin!

Here are six basic methods for beginning your composition effectively. In each example, the thesis statement is italicized.

1. Begin with a single-sentence thesis statement. A single-sentence thesis statement can be effective because it quickly and forcefully states the main idea of the essay:

Time management should be a required course at this college.

232

▪ Note how quickly and clearly a one-sentence thesis statement can inform the reader about what will follow in the rest of the essay.

2. **Begin with a general idea and then narrow to a specific thesis statement.** The general idea gives the reader background information or sets the scene. Then the topic narrows to one specific idea—the thesis statement. The effect is like a funnel, from wide to narrow.

> Few Americans stay put for a lifetime. We move from town to city to suburb, from high school to college in a different state, from a job in one region to a better job elsewhere, from the home where we raise our children to the home where we plan to live in retirement. *With each move we are forever making new friends, who become part of our new life at that time.*
>
> —Margaret Mead and Rhoda Metraux, "On Friendship," in *A Way of Seeing*

▪ What general idea precedes the thesis statement and then leads the reader to focus on the specific main point of the essay?

Americans move often.

3. **Begin with an illustration.** One or more brief illustrations in the introduction of an essay make the thesis statement more concrete and vivid:

> The other day I was watching a Reebok commercial. It was about a young male who, after purchasing a pair of sneakers, was walking down the street to a smooth jazz tune. As this "pretty boy" walked in his new pair of sneakers, he drew the attention of all in his path, especially the females. For a second I was envious of this "dude." I've been purchasing sneakers for over eighteen years, and I haven't had one girl look at me the way they did him during his thirty-second stroll down some dark and filthy sidewalk. As I watched this ad and others like it, I started to analyze the ads' underlying message. *I wondered why the majority of sneaker ads are geared to inner-city youth, especially ads for brand-name sneakers.*
>
> —Saladin Brown (Student) "The Illusion of Ads"

▪ Mr. Brown's thesis poses a question that his essay will try to answer.

▪ What example does the writer provide to make the thesis statement more concrete?

the example of a young male who had just bought new sneakers

4. **Begin with a surprising fact or idea.** A surprising fact or idea arouses the reader's curiosity about how you will support this initial startling statement.

> *Millions of law-abiding Americans are physically addicted to caffeine—and most of them don't even know it.* Caffeine is a powerful central nervous system stimulant with substantial addiction potential. When deprived of their caffeine, addicts experience often severe withdrawal symptoms, which may include a throbbing headache, disorientation, constipation, nausea, sluggishness, depression, and irritability. As with other addictive drugs, heavy users develop a tolerance and require higher doses to obtain the expected effect.
>
> —Tom Ferguson and Joe Graedon, "Caffeine," *Medical Self-Care*

■ Why are the facts in this introduction likely to startle or surprise the reader?

So many people drink caffeine-containing beverages that they think caffeine

is harmless.

5. **Begin with a contradiction.** In this type of introduction, your thesis statement contradicts what many or most people believe. In other words, your essay will contrast your opinion with the widely held view.

> Millions of parents take it as an article of faith that putting a bicycle helmet on their children, or themselves, will keep them out of harm's way.
>
> But new data on bicycle accidents raise questions about that. The number of head injuries has increased 10 percent since 1991, even as bicycle helmet use has risen sharply, according to figures compiled by the Consumer Product Safety Commission. But given that ridership has declined over the same period, the rate of head injuries per active cyclist has increased 51 percent just as bicycle helmets have become widespread. What is going on here?
>
> —Julian E. Barnes, "A Bicycling Mystery: Head Injuries Piling Up," *New York Times*

■ What widely held view does the author open with?

the view that bike helmets protect children and adults from biking injuries

■ How does he contradict this idea?

He gives new facts from the Consumer Product Safety Commission showing that

head injuries have increased even as bicycle helmet use has increased.

6. **Begin with a direct quotation.** A direct quotation is likely to catch your reader's attention and to show that you have explored what others have to say about the subject. You can then proceed to agree or to disagree with the direct quotation.

TEACHING TIP
Refer students to the
Quotation Bank at the end
of this text for ideas they
could use in introductions.

> "Speech is silver; silence is golden," according to an old Swiss saying. In a close relationship, however, silence often loses value. If we speak about certain issues, we may endanger the relationship; but if we do not speak, the relationship may become static and tense until the silence takes on a life of its own. Such silences are corrosive. They eat at the innards of intimacy until, often, *the silence itself causes the very rupture or break-up that we've tried to avoid by keeping silent.*
>
> —Adapted from Michael Ventura,
> "Don't Even Think About It," *Psychology Today*

▪ Does the author agree or disagree with the Swiss saying?

The author seems to disagree when it involves close relationships.

TEACHING TIP
Have students review their
recently written essays to
improve the introductions.

Of course, definitions, comparisons, or any of the other kinds of devices you have already studied can also make good introductions. Just make sure that the reader knows exactly which sentence is your thesis statement.

WRITING ASSIGNMENT 1

Here are five statements. Pick three that you would like to write about and compose an introduction for each one. Use any of the methods for beginning compositions discussed in this chapter thus far.

1. Cell phones in cars can be dangerous.

2. Noise is definitely a form of pollution.

3. Serious illness—our own or a loved one's—sometimes can bring surprising blessings.

4. Studying with someone else can pay off in better grades.

5. The college cafeteria should offer vegetarian meals.

PART B   The Conclusion

TEACHING TIP
Conclusions are often
difficult for students
because they feel as though
they've already said
everything that they wanted
to say. These three methods
for concluding an essay will
give them ideas for writing
satisfying endings.

A conclusion signals the end of the essay and leaves the reader with a final thought. As with the introduction, you may wish to revise and rewrite the conclusion once you have completed your essay. Be certain your conclusion flows logically from the body of the essay.

Like introductions, conclusions can take many forms, and the right one for your essay depends on how you wish to complete your paper—with what thought you wish to leave the reader. However, never conclude your paper with "As I said in the beginning," and try to avoid the overused "In conclusion" or "In summary." Don't end by saying you are going to end; just end!

Here are three ways to conclude an essay.

1. **End with a call to action.** The call to action says that in view of the facts and ideas presented in this essay, the reader should *do something*.

> Single-gender schools work. As we have seen, boys-only and girls-only middle and high schools help steer young people toward academic achievement and higher self-esteem. Showing off for the opposite sex, dating too early, and, especially in the case of girls, failing to raise their hands for fear of outshining the boys, are problems avoided altogether in single-gender environments. Parents and concerned citizens must contact their representatives and school boards to demand the option of single-gender schools. We owe it to our children to fight for the schools that truly serve them.

■ What does the writer want the reader to do?

The writer wants the reader to contact representatives and school boards to demand the

option of single-gender schools.

2. **End with a final point.** The final point can tie together all the other ideas in the essay; it provides the reader with the sense that the entire essay has been leading up to this one final point.

> Some estimate that millions of Earth-like planets may be in our Milky Way galaxy alone. The Milky Way is just one of about 100 billion galaxies in the universe. So chances are, plenty of not-too-big, not-too-small, not-too-hot, not-too-cold planets are out there, with water and sunshine—and, perhaps, life.
>
> —Kathy Wollard, "Millions of Unseen Planets
> May Hide in Galaxies," *Milwaukee Journal Sentinel*

■ With what final point does Wollard end her article?

She concludes by stating that, chances are, some other planets in the universe might have

life on them.

3. **End with a question.** By ending with a question, you leave the reader with a final problem that you wish him or her to think about.

> Yes, it is embarrassing to speak with our children about sex. We will feel awkward not knowing what to say, stymied as they resist the discussion. However, knowing the pressures that kids today face, the terrible examples bombarding them from popular culture, and the real threat of diseases, can we afford not to?
>
> —Amelia Garcia (Student), "Talking to Kids about Sex"

TEACHING TIP
Bring in an essay with the conclusion removed. Have students, either individually or in groups, write two concluding paragraphs, each one using a different technique.

■ What problem does the writer's final question point to?

the problem of parents' difficulty in talking to kids about sex

WRITING ASSIGNMENT 2

Review two or three essays that you have written recently. Do the conclusions bring the essays to clear ends? Are those conclusions interesting? How could they be improved? Using one of the three strategies taught in this section, write a new conclusion for one of the essays.

PART C   The Title

If you are writing just one paragraph, chances are that you will not need to give it a title, but if you are writing a multiparagraph essay, a title is definitely in order.

The title is centered on the page above the body of the composition and separated from it by several blank lines (about 1 inch of space), as shown here.

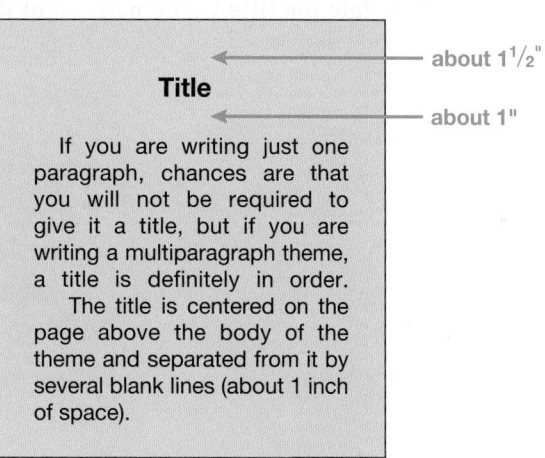

about 1½"

about 1"

Title

If you are writing just one paragraph, chances are that you will not be required to give it a title, but if you are writing a multiparagraph theme, a title is definitely in order.

The title is centered on the page above the body of the theme and separated from it by several blank lines (about 1 inch of space).

■ Do *not* put quotation marks around the title of your own paper.

■ Do *not* underline or italicize the title of your own paper.

■ Remember, unlike the topic sentence, the title is not part of the first paragraph; in fact, it is usually only four to five words long and is rarely an entire sentence.

A good title has two functions: to suggest the subject of the essay and to spark the reader's interest. Although the title is the first part of your essay the reader sees, the most effective titles are usually written *after* the essay has been completed.

To create a title, reread your essay, paying special attention to the **thesis statement** and the **conclusion**. Try to come up with a few words that express the main point of your paper.

Here are some basic kinds of titles.

1. **The most common title used in college writing is the no-nonsense descriptive title.** In this title, stress key words and ideas developed in the essay:

Copyright © Houghton Mifflin Company. All rights reserved.

TEACHING TIP
Have students browse through the reading selections in Unit 8. Ask them to identify the titles that pique their interest and make them want to read on.

> Anger in the Work of Jamaica Kincaid
>
> Advantages and Disadvantages of Buying on Credit

2. **Two-part titles are also effective.** Write one or two words stating the general subject, and then add several words that narrow the topic:

> Rumi: Poet and Mystic
>
> Legal Gambling: Pro and Con

3. **Write the title as a rhetorical question.** Then answer the question in your essay:

> What Can Be Done About the High Price of Higher Education?
>
> Are Athletes Setting Bad Examples?

TEACHING TIP
Have fun by asking students to think of weak or bad titles they have given to past papers. Have volunteers share their worst title and suggest a new, better title—or they can ask the class to help them come up with a "grabber" title.

4. **Relate the title to the method of development used in the essay** (see Unit 3 and Chapter 15):

Illustration:	Democracy in Action Three Roles I Play
Narration:	The Development of Jazz Edwige Danticat: The Making of a Storyteller
Description:	Portrait of a Scientist A Waterfront Scene
Process:	How to Start a Book Group How to Get in Shape Fast
Definition:	What It Means to Be Unemployed A Definition of Respect
Comparison:	Two Country Stars Who Crossed Over Strange Realities: *Star Wars* and *X Files*
Contrast:	Pleasures and Problems of Owning a Home Montreal: City of Contrasts
Classification:	Three Types of Soap Operas What Kind of E-mail User Are You?
Cause and Effect:	What Causes Whales to Beach Themselves? The Effects of Divorce on Children
Persuasion:	Internet Pornography Should Be Banned The Need for Metal Detectors in Our Schools

Use this list the next time you title a paper.*

---

* For more on how to capitalize in titles, see Chapter 36, "Mechanics," Part B.

WRITING ASSIGNMENT 3

Review two or three essays that you have written recently. Are the titles clear and interesting? Applying what you've learned in this chapter, write a better title for at least one paper.

EXPLORING ONLINE

http://www.powa.org/thesis/intros.html Read more about writing strong introductions and conclusions

http://grammar.ccc.commnet.edu/grammar/intros.htm Lively examples of introductions, plus tips for the writer.

http://www.ccc.commnet.edu/sensen/part3/sixteen/techniques_conclusions.html Write an effective conclusion for a sample paragraph and one for an essay, using online text boxes.

Online Study Center college.hmco.com/pic/evergreen8e
Visit the Online Study Center for *Evergreen* for more exercises and quizzes.

17

Summarizing, Quoting, and Avoiding Plagiarism

PART A	Avoiding Plagiarism
PART B	Writing a Summary
PART C	Using Direct and Indirect Quotation

Now more than ever before, it is important for you to know how to find, evaluate, and use information from **outside sources**—that is, sources outside yourself (for example, books, articles, Internet sites, or other people). In some college courses, you will write papers with no outside sources. However, many courses and jobs will require you to refer to outside sources as you write reports, essays, and research papers. Besides, information from outside sources can vastly enrich your writing with facts, statistics, experts' ideas, and more.

In this chapter, you will learn what **plagiarism** is and how to avoid it. You will also learn and practice three excellent ways to use outside sources in your writing: **summarizing, quoting directly,** and **quoting indirectly.**

PART A Avoiding Plagiarism

Before we discuss how to summarize or quote from an outside source, it is all-important that you understand—so you can avoid—**plagiarism.** Plagiarism is failing to give proper credit to an author whose words or ideas you have used. That is, plagiarism means passing off someone else's words or ideas as your own. Whether intentional or careless, plagiarism is stealing. A college student who plagiarizes a paper may be expelled from the course or from college. In the business world, publishing material copied from someone else is a crime.

To avoid plagiarism, you must give proper credit to the original author, as this chapter and the next will explain. Meanwhile, keep this simple rule in mind: **Always tell your reader the source of any words and ideas not your own. Give enough information so that a reader who wants to find your original source can do so.**

PRACTICE 1

What is your college's policy on plagiarism? That is, what consequences or penalties follow if a student is found to have plagiarized a paper or other work? The reference librarian can help you find this information.

PART B Writing a Summary

A **summary** presents the main idea and supporting points of a longer work *in much shorter form*. A summary might be one sentence, one paragraph, or several paragraphs long, depending on the length of the original and the nature of your assignment.

Summarizing is important both in college and at work. In a persuasive essay, you might summarize the ideas of an expert whose views support one of your points. A professor might ask you to summarize a book, a market survey, or even the plot of a film—that is, to condense it in your own words, presenting only the highlights. Of course, many essay exams also call for written summaries.

Compare this short newspaper article—the *source*—with the *summary* that follows:

Source

Fido may be cute, cuddly, and harmless. But in his genes, he's a wolf.

Researchers tracing the genetic family tree of man's best friend have confirmed that domestic dogs, from petite poodles to huge elkhounds, descended from wolves that were tamed 100,000 years ago.

"Our data show that the origin of dogs seems to be much more ancient than indicated in the archaeological record," said Robert K. Wayne of UCLA, the leader of a team that tested the genes from 67 dog breeds and 62 wolves on four continents.

Wayne said the study showed so many DNA changes that dogs had to have diverged genetically from wolves 60,000 to more than 100,000 years ago.

The study suggests that primitive humans living in a hunting and gathering culture tamed wolves and then bred the animals to create the many different types of dogs that now exist.

—Recer, Paul. "Dogs Tamed 100,000 Years Ago." The Herald 13 June 1997: 9A

Summary

Dogs began evolving from wolves between 60,000 and 100,000 years ago, reports Paul Recer in *The Herald*. Apparently, humans tamed wolves far earlier than was previously thought. Researchers at UCLA, led by Robert K. Wayne, came to these conclusions after studying the genes of 67 breeds of dogs and 62 wolves on four continents (9A).

■ Notice that sentence 1 states the author and source of the original article. Sentence 1 also states the main idea of the article. What is its main idea?

Dogs began evolving from wolves 60,000 to 100,000 years ago.

▪ What evidence supports this idea?

a recent UCLA study

▪ The original is short, so the summary is very short—just three sentences long.

▪ The summary writer does not add his own opinions about dogs or evolution but simply states the main ideas of the source. Unlike many kinds of writing, a summary should not contain your personal opinions and feelings.

▪ Note that the page number of the original source appears in parentheses at the end of the summary.*

Preparing to Write a Summary

The secret of writing a good summary is clearly understanding the original. If you doubt this, try to summarize out loud Chapter 3 of your biology book. To summarize well, you have to know the subject matter.

Before you summarize a piece of writing, notice the title and subtitle (if there is one); these often state the main idea. Read quickly for meaning; then carefully read the work again, underlining or jotting down notes for yourself. What is the author's thesis or main point? What points does he or she offer in support? Be careful to distinguish between the most and least important points; your summary should include only the most important ones.

To help you understand *what the author thinks is important*, notice which ideas get the most coverage. Read with special care the topic sentence of each paragraph and the first and last paragraphs of the work. If you are summarizing a magazine article or a textbook chapter, the subheads (often in boldface type) point out important ideas.

> Your written summary should include the following:
>
> 1. The author, title, and source of the original
>
> 2. The main idea or thesis of the original, in your own words
>
> 3. The most important supporting ideas or points of the original, in your own words

Try to present the ideas in your summary in proportion to those in the original. For instance, if the author devotes one paragraph to each of four ideas, you might give one sentence to each idea. To avoid plagiarism, when you finish, compare your summary with the original; that is, make sure you have not just copied the phrasing and sentences of the original.

A summary differs from much other writing in that it should *not* contain your feelings or opinions—just the facts. Your job is to capture the essence of the original, with nothing added.

Following are two summaries of the student essay in Chapter 15, "Types of Essays," Part F, of this book. Which do you think is the better summary, A or B? Be prepared to say specifically why.

---

* For more precise information on how to cite sources, see Chapter 18, "Strengthening an Essay with Research," Part C.

Summary A

(1) In the essay "E-Notes from an Online Learner," printed in Fawcett, *Evergreen*, Eighth Edition, student and mother Brenda Wilson contrasts her learning experiences in traditional and online classrooms. (2) Whereas Wilson's long commute to campus once made her late to class or anxious, she finds online classes more convenient because she can read lectures or submit coursework any time, from home. (3) Next, Ms. Wilson says that other students might prefer the energy of live class discussion, but she feels freer online, writing her thoughts with less self-consciousness. (4) Finally, she stresses that online students must be self-motivated, unlike regular students who can rely on professors to prod them or on the "group adrenaline rush [of] seeing other students hunched over their notebooks." (5) Less focused students might procrastinate and drop out. (6) Overall, Wilson prefers distance learning (223–224).

Summary B

(1) This excellent essay is by Brenda Wilson, student. (2) I enjoyed reading about online learning because I have never taken a course online. (3) This year Ms. Wilson attended her history class dressed in dancing cow pajamas and fluffy slippers. (4) This was not a bizarre college ritual but part of the University of Houston's Distance Education Program. (5) Virtual courses are very different. (6) She has a job and a son, so she is very busy, like many students today. (7) Online classes are great for this type of student, more convenient. (8) Students have to motivate themselves, and Ms. Wilson has only the soft bubbling noise of her aquarium screen saver to remind her to work. (9) She ends by saying it is 12:14 A.M. and her cat is nuzzling her fluffy pink slippers. (10) I also liked her cat's name.

TEACHING TIP
Engage students in a discussion about their answers. They should be able to explain their rationale for choosing Summary A as better. Stress the *objectivity* of a good summary—no opinions added.

ESL TIP
If your ESL students struggle with finding main ideas in a reading, refer them to Chapters 3 and 14 to review paragraph and essay organization.

■ The test of a good summary is how well it captures the original. Which better summarizes Ms. Wilson's essay, A or B?

A is better because it summarizes the original and does not insert the opinions of the

summarizer.

■ If you picked A, you are right. Sentence 1 states the author and title of the essay, as well as the name and edition of the book in which it appears. Sentence 1 also states the main idea of the original, which *contrasts* the author's experience of traditional classes and virtual classes. Does any sentence in B state the main idea of the original essay? no

■ Compare the original with the two summaries. How many points of contrast does A include? B? A includes three points of contrast; B includes one point, confusingly stated.

■ Does each writer summarize the essay *in his or her own words*? If not, which sentences might seem plagiarized? A does; B plagiarizes sentences 3, 4, 8, and 9.

■ Writer A once quotes Ms. Wilson directly. How is this shown? Why do you think the summary writer chose this sentence to quote? <u>Quotation marks</u>

<u>set off Ms. Wilson's words in sentence 4; these words are richly descriptive and somewhat</u>

<u>humorous.</u>

■ Do both summaries succeed in keeping personal opinion out? If not, which sentences contain the summary writer's opinion? <u>A succeeds, but B inserts</u>

<u>personal opinion in sentences 1, 2, and 10.</u>

■ Note that summary writer A includes the source page number in parentheses at the end of the summarized material. On the other hand, writer B refers to Brenda Wilson but does not name her essay or the source in which it appears.

PRACTICE 2

TEACHING TIP
Part C of this chapter discusses paraphrasing. Students may find it helpful to review that information before they complete Practice 2.

In a group with three or four other classmates, choose just one of the following essays to summarize: "Extreme Makeover: Library" (Chapter 15, Part A); "The Day of the Dead" (Chapter 15, Part C); "Stopping Youth Violence: An Inside Job" (Chapter 15, Part I); or "Skin Deep" (Chapter 14, Part E). Read your chosen essay in the group, aloud if possible. Then each person should write a one-paragraph summary of it, referring to the checklist below (15–20 minutes).

Now read your finished summaries aloud to your group. How well does each writer briefly capture the meaning of the original? Has he or she kept out personal opinion? What suggestions for improvement can you offer? Your instructor may wish to have the best summary in each group read aloud to the whole class.

PRACTICE 3

Flip through a copy of a current magazine: *Newsweek, People, Essence, Wired,* or another. Pick one article that interests you, read it carefully, and write a one- to three-paragraph summary of the article, depending on the length of the article. The points you include in your summary should reflect the emphasis of the original writer. Try to capture the essence of the article. Remember to give your source at the beginning, to keep out personal opinion, and to check your summary for plagiarism. Refer to the checklist.

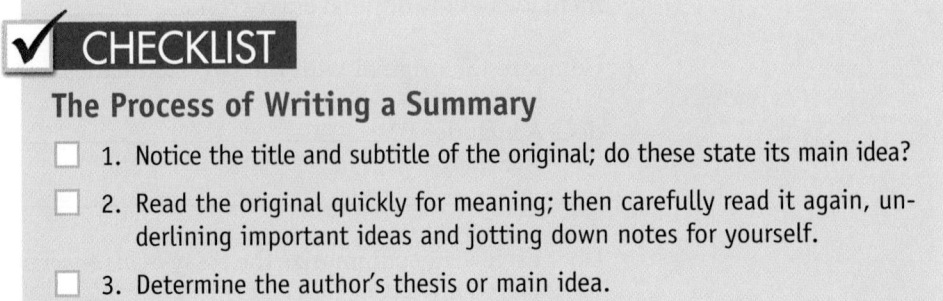

✔ CHECKLIST

The Process of Writing a Summary

☐ 1. Notice the title and subtitle of the original; do these state its main idea?

☐ 2. Read the original quickly for meaning; then carefully read it again, underlining important ideas and jotting down notes for yourself.

☐ 3. Determine the author's thesis or main idea.

☐ 4. Now find the main supporting points. Subheads (if any), topic sentences, and the first and last paragraphs of the original may help you find key points.

☐ 5. Write your topic sentence or thesis statement, stating the author's thesis, title, source, and date of the original.

☐ 6. In your own words, give the author's most important supporting points, in the same order in which the author gives them. Keep the same proportion of coverage as the original.

☐ 7. Write your summary, skipping lines so you will have room to make corrections.

☐ 8. Now revise, asking yourself, "Will my summary convey to someone who has never read the original the author's main idea and key supporting points?"

☐ 9. Proofread, making neat corrections above the lines.

☐ 10. Compare your final draft with the original to avoid plagiarism.

PART C Using Direct and Indirect Quotation

Sometimes you will want to quote an outside source directly. A quotation might be part of a summary or part of a longer paper or report. Quoting the words of others can add richness and authority to your writing; in fact, that is why we include a Quotation Bank at the end of this book—a kind of minireader of great thoughts. Use short quotations in these ways:

▪ Use a quotation to stress a key idea.

▪ Use a quotation to lend expert opinion to your argument.

▪ Use a quotation to provide a catchy introduction or conclusion.

▪ Use a quotation about your topic that is wonderfully written and "quotable" to add interest.

However, avoid using very long quotations or too many quotations. Both send the message that you are filling up space because you don't have enough to say. Of course, to avoid plagiarism, you always must credit the original author or speaker.

Here are some methods for introducing quotations:

Ways to Introduce Quotations

Mr. Taibi says, . . .	Ms. Luboff writes, . . .
One expert had this to say:	. . . , one authority reported.
In a recent *Times* column, Maureen Dowd observes . . .	According to Dr. Haynes, . . .

Following are a passage from a well-known book and two ways that students quoted the author:

Source

> On film or videotape, violence begins and ends in a moment. "Bang bang, you're dead." Then the death is over. This sense of action-without-consequences replicates and reinforces the dangerous "magical" way many children think. Do the twelve- and fourteen-year-olds who are shooting each other to death in Los Angeles, Chicago, or Washington, D.C., really understand that death is permanent, unalterable, final, tragic? Television certainly is not telling them so.
>
> Prothrow-Stith, Deborah. <u>Deadly Consequences</u>.
> New York: Harper Perennial, 1991: 34.

Two students who wrote about the effects of TV violence correctly quoted Dr. Prothrow-Stith as follows:

Direct Quotation

> "This sense of action-without-consequences replicates and reinforces the dangerous 'magical' way many children think," writes Dr. Deborah Prothrow-Stith in <u>Deadly Consequences</u> (34).

Indirect Quotation

> In <u>Deadly Consequences</u>, Prothrow-Stith points out that TV and movie violence, which has no realistic consequences, harms children by reinforcing the magical way in which they think (34).

TEACHING TIP
Consider demonstrating for students how to include a partial quotation, such a phrase or part of a longer sentence.

TEACHING TIP
Remind the class that these quoting techniques are the way to avoid plagiarism.

▪ The first sentence gives Dr. Prothrow-Stith's exact words inside quotation marks. This is **direct quotation.** Note the punctuation.

▪ The second sentence uses the word *that* and gives the *meaning* of Prothrow-Stith's words without quotation marks. This is **indirect quotation,** or **paraphrase.** Note the punctuation.

▪ Both students correctly quote the writer and credit the source. Both include the page number in parentheses after the quoted material and before the period. (See Chapter 18, Part C, for more information on this style of citing sources.)

Now read this passage from a third student's paper:

Plagiarism

> On film and television, violence begins and ends in a minute, and then the death is over. Teenagers killing each other across the country don't realize that death is "unalterable, final, and tragic" because they do not see its consequences on TV.

▪ Can you see why this passage is plagiarized (and why the student received a failing grade)?

▪ Both the ideas and many of the words are clearly Prothrow-Stith's, yet the student never mentions her or her book. Four words from the original are placed in quotation marks, but the reader has no idea why. Instead, the student implies that all the ideas and words are his own. What exact words are plagiarized from the source? What ideas are plagiarized?

"Violence begins and ends . . . then the death is over"; "that death is unalterable, final,

and tragic." The idea that film violence is quick and has no consequences, giving teens a

magical idea of death.

■ Revise this passage as if it were your own, giving credit to the original author and avoiding plagiarism.

PRACTICE 4

Following are passages from two sources. Read each one, and then, as if you were writing a paper, quote two sentences from each, one directly quoting the author's words and one indirectly quoting the author's ideas. Review the boxed ways to introduce quotations and try several methods. Finally, write a brief summary of each passage. Check your work to avoid plagiarism.   Answers will vary.

Source 1

In most cultures throughout history, music, dance, rhythmic drumming, and chanting have been essential parts of healing rituals. Modern research bears out the connection between music and healing. In one study, the heart rate and blood pressure of patients went down when quiet music was piped into their hospital coronary care units. At the same time, the patients showed greater tolerance for pain and less anxiety and depression. Similarly, listening to music before, during, or after surgery has been shown to promote various beneficial effects—from alleviating anxiety to reducing the need for sedation by half. When researchers played Brahms' "Lullaby" to premature infants, these babies gained weight faster and went home from the hospital sooner than babies who did not hear the music. Music may also affect immunity by altering the level of stress chemicals in the blood. An experiment at Rainbow Babies and Children's Hospital found that a single thirty-minute music therapy session could increase the level of salivary IgA, an immunoglobulin that protects against respiratory infections.

Institute of Noetic Sciences with William Poole. <u>The Heart of Healing</u>.
Atlanta: Turner Publishing, 1993: 134.

Direct quotation: _____

_____

Indirect quotation: _____

_____

Summary:

_____

_____

_____

_____

_____

_____

Source 2

Assuming they reach maturity with consciousness intact, the current crop of teenagers will have spent years watching commercials. No one has done the numbers on what happens if you factor in radio, magazine, newspaper advertisements, and billboards, but today's teens probably have spent the equivalent of a decade of their lives being bombarded by bits of advertising information. In 1915, a person could go entire weeks without observing an ad. The average adult today sees three thousand every day.

James B. Twitchell, Adcult USA, New York:
Columbia University Press, 1996:2.

TEACHING TIP
Refer students to Chapter 36, "Mechanics," for information about punctuating direct quotations.

Direct quotation: _____

_____

Indirect quotation: _____

_____

Summary:

_____

TEACHING TIP
If students need more practice with paraphrasing, bring in short passages from books and magazines and ask them to put the information in their own words. Point out any wording that is too close to that of the original source.

_____

_____

_____

_____

_____

PRACTICE 5

Following are four sources and four quotations from student papers. If the student has summarized, directly quoted, or indirectly quoted the source correctly, write C. If you believe the source is plagiarized, write P; then revise the student's work as if it were your own to avoid plagiarism.

■ Does each student clearly distinguish between his or her ideas and the source's?

■ Does each student give enough information so that a reader could locate the original source?

Source 1

"Binge drinking, according to criteria used in periodic surveys by the Harvard researchers, is defined as five or more drinks on one occasion for a man or four or more drinks on one occasion for a woman. Students who reported one or two such episodes in the two weeks preceding the survey were classified as occasional binge drinkers; those reporting three or more were considered frequent binge drinkers."

Okie, Susan. "Survey: 44% of College Students Are Binge Drinkers."
The Washington Post 25 Mar. 2002: A6.

Student's Version

<u>P</u>   Binge drinking is a dangerous problem on campuses, but college administrators are not doing enough to stop it. *According to Susan Okie in The Washington Post,* An amazing 44 percent of college students are binge drinkers. ~~Let us define~~ *Using Harvard's definition, she defines* binge drinking as five or more drinks on one occasion for a man or four or more drinks on one occasion for a woman. *(A6)* College officials need to ask why so many students are drinking dangerously.

Source 2

"The image of the Kitchen God (alternatively known as the Hearth God) usually stood above the family stove, from where he would observe the household. Every New Year he was said to visit heaven to give an account of the behavior of the family in the past year."

Willis, Roy. <u>Dictionary of World Myth</u>. London: Duncan Baird Publishers, 1995: 116.

Student's Version

<u>P</u>   My Chinese grandmother has a Kitchen God above her stove. *Willis's Dictionary of World Myth says that this* ~~It says in the dictionary that this is~~ a special god ~~who~~ observes the household and then visits heaven every New Year to report on the behavior of the family in the past year. *(116)*

Source 3

"Although astronomers often speak of the 'solar surface,' the Sun actually has no surface at all. The Sun is gaseous throughout its volume because of its high internal temperature. If you were somehow able to enter the Sun without vaporizing, you would encounter only denser and denser gases as you went to greater depths."

Kaufmann, William J., and Roger A. Freedman. <u>Universe</u>. 5th ed. New York: W.H. Freeman and Co., 1999: 422.

Student's Version

<u>C</u>   As Kaufmann and Freedman explain in <u>Universe</u>, the sun is too hot to have a solid surface but is made up instead of very dense gases (422).

Source 4

"As alpine glaciers around the world succumb to warming, scientists are reaping grand harvests of frozen organic objects—and with them previously unavailable information on past wildlife, human culture, genetics, climate and more. Tissues with intact DNA and archaeological objects of wood and bone provide pictures that stone tools only hint at, and because they can all be radio-carbon dated, there is little guessing about chronology."

Krajick, Kevin. "Melting Glaciers Release Ancient Relics." <u>Science</u> 19 Apr. 2002: 454–456.

Student's Version

___C___ There might be a positive side to global warming after all. Kevin Krajick

reports in Science, April 19, 2002, that melting glaciers are providing scientists

with many objects and tissue samples that will give them "previously unavailable

information on past wildlife, human culture, genetics, climate and more."

EXPLORING ONLINE

TEACHING TIP
More practice and assessment are available in the *Evergreen* Test Bank, linked ACE tests on the *Evergreen* Online Teaching and Study Centers, *WriteSpace for Evergreen,* and Exploring Online links in this chapter.

http://owl.english.purdue.edu/handouts/research/r_plagiar.html Helpful examples of what constitutes plagiarism and what is properly quoted

http://owl.english.purdue.edu/handouts/research/r_quotprsum.html Purdue's review of quotation and summary

Online Study Center college.hmco.com/pic/evergreen8e
  Visit the Online Study Center for this book for more exercises and quizzes.

18

Strengthening an Essay with Research

PART A Improving an Essay with Research

PART B Finding and Evaluating Outside Sources: Library and Internet

PART C Adding Sources to Your Essay and Documenting Them Correctly

You will have opportunities in college to prepare formal research papers with many outside sources. However, you should not limit your definition of "research" to just such assignments. Whenever you have a question and seek an answer from a source outside yourself, you are doing **research.** Most of us research every day, whether or not we call it that—when we gather facts and opinions about the cheapest local restaurant, the college with the best fire science program, the safest new cars, or various medical conditions. In this chapter, you will learn skills valuable both in college and at work: how to improve your writing with interesting information from outside sources.

PART A Improving an Essay with Research

TEACHING TIP
Stress to students that outside source material does not substitute for their own ideas; instead, it provides additional support for their ideas. Use the "Drastic Plastic: Credit-Card Debt on Campus" essay at the end of this chapter, for example, to point out that thesis statements and topic sentences do not refer to outside sources. They state the writer's ideas, and then the source material helps prove or support those ideas.

Almost any essay, particularly one designed to *persuade* your reader, can benefit from the addition of outside material. In fact, even one outside source—a startling statistic or a memorable quote—can enrich your essay. Supporting your main points with outside sources can be an excellent way to establish your credibility, strengthen your argument, and add power to your words. Compare two versions of this student's paragraph

> Inexperienced hikers often get in trouble because they worry about rare dangers like snakebites, but they minimize the very serious dangers of dehydration and exposure to cold. For example, my brother-in-law once hiked into the Grand Canyon with only a granola bar and a small bottle of water. He became severely dehydrated and was too weak to climb back up without help.

251

▪ This paragraph makes an important point about the dangers that inexperienced hikers can face. The example of the brother-in-law supports the main point, but the paragraph needs more complete support.

Now read the paragraph strengthened by some relevant facts from an outside source.

> Inexperienced hikers often get in trouble because they worry about rare dangers like snakebites, but they minimize the very serious dangers of dehydration and exposure to cold. For example, my brother-in-law once hiked into the Grand Canyon with only a granola bar and a small bottle of water. He became severely dehydrated and was too weak to climb back up without help. He was lucky. According to the National Park Service web site (www.nps.gov), over a hundred hikers die every year because they are not properly prepared for the environment. In addition, the NPS reports that over $3.5 million was spent in 2003 to perform 3,108 search-and-rescue operations, 1,264 of them to save poorly prepared hikers like my brother-in-law (Search and Rescue Report, 2004).

TEACHING TIP
Have your students work in dyads to brainstorm ways to introduce quotations, including reporting verbs. Have them start with the list on page 245.

▪ What facts from the National Park Service web site support the main point and add to the persuasive power of this paragraph?

Over 100 hikers die every year; $3.5 million spent for 3,108 rescue operations

▪ What sentence of transition does the writer use to connect his example of the brother-in-law with facts from the outside source? What transitional words connect the fact about hikers' deaths each year?

He was lucky. According to the National Park Service . . .

▪ Remember that just one well-chosen outside source can improve and enliven a paper.

Consider the facts in this chart from the U.S. Census:

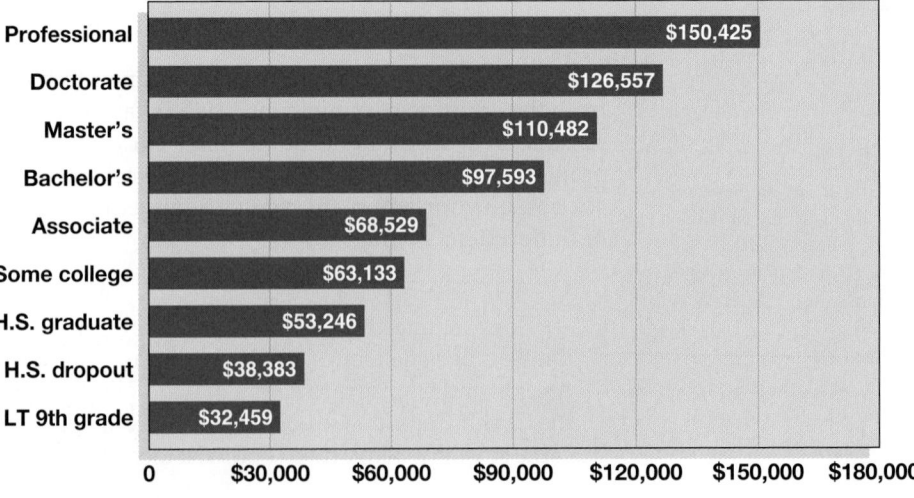

Average Family Income by Education of Householder, 2001

Professional	$150,425
Doctorate	$126,557
Master's	$110,482
Bachelor's	$97,593
Associate	$68,529
Some college	$63,133
H.S. graduate	$53,246
H.S. dropout	$38,383
LT 9th grade	$32,459

0    $30,000 $60,000 $90,000 $120,000 $150,000 $180,000

▪ What patterns do you see in this chart?

▪ How might you use this information in an essay?

Facts and statistics can make a strong statement, but there are many other ways to enhance your writing. Consider adding a good quotation to emphasize one of your key points. You can begin by looking through the Quotation Bank at the end of this book or an online version of *Bartlett's Quotations* at **http://www.bartleby.com/100/**. Or find and quote an expert on the subject you are writing about. For example, if your subject is the lack of recycling receptacles on your campus, an opinion from a Sierra Club official would give authority to your essay. And don't forget experts closer to home; details about a student you know who has begun a recycling campaign on campus would add life and emotion to your work. If your essay is about your family history or the school's registration system, you could interview a relative or a school administrator and use that material to add authority to your paper.

A good way to begin using research is to pick an essay you have recently written. Reread it, marking any places where outside sources might make it even better. Write down any questions you want answers to or information that you would like to find:

TEACHING TIP
Ask students to form dyads, exchange papers, and highlight the statements they feel could use additional support.

▪ What would I like to know more about?

▪ What outside source might make my essay more interesting?

▪ What information—fact, statistic, detail, or quotation—would make my essay more convincing?

▪ What people are experts on this topic? Where can I find them or their opinions?

Carmen's Research Process

Student Carmen Gevana is learning to use outside sources. She plans to add research support to a favorite essay. She selects a cause-and-effect paper that examines the reasons her best friend went into credit-card debt and the devastating effects this debt had on her friend's life. In her paper, Carmen named two causes: credit-card companies using gifts to encourage students to apply for cards and students getting higher credit lines than they can realistically handle. The consequences Carmen discussed were unmanageable debt and ruined credit. Now Carmen wants to add two or three sources to support her own ideas. Her first question is whether heavy credit-card debt is a problem unique to her friend or more widespread among college students. She also wonders how much debt a typical college student carries. Finally, she hopes to find an expert opinion about the effects on college students.

PRACTICE 1

Choose one of the following: either your favorite paper written this term or a paper on a topic assigned by your instructor. Then read through your paper, marking any spots where an outside source—fact, statistic, expert opinion, or quotation—might strengthen your essay. Write down any questions that you want to answer.

PART B Finding and Evaluating Outside Sources: Library and Internet

The next step is finding the information you seek—or something even better. This section will show you how to find sources in the library and on the Internet.

Doing Research at the Library

Visit your college library, with your notes from Practice 1 in hand. Ask about any print guides, workshops, or web sites that show you how to use the library facilities. Introduce yourself to the reference librarian, tell him or her what subject you are exploring, and ask for help finding and using any of these resources in your search:

1. **Online Catalog or Card Catalog.** This will show you what books are available on your topic. For every book that looks like it might be interesting, jot down its title, author, and call number (the number that lets you find the book in the library).

2. **Periodical Indexes.** The more current your topic, the more likely you are to find interesting information in periodicals—magazines, journals, and newspapers—rather than books. *The Readers' Guide to Periodical Literature* is a print resource, listing articles by subject. The library will also have computerized indexes like *InfoTrac, EBSCOhost,* and *Lexis-Nexus.* Ask the librarian to help you explore these exciting resources.

3. **Statistical Sources.** If you are looking for statistics and facts, the library has volumes like *The Statistical Abstract of the United States* with fascinating information on population, education, immigration, crime, economic issues, and so on.

4. **Encyclopedias and Reference Books.** General books on subjects like geology or psychology can be helpful. Special reference books and encyclopedias exist for almost every area—for example, world soccer statistics, terrorism, or the birds of South America.

As you explore, you might see why experienced researchers often love what they do. They never know what they will find, and they learn the darnedest, most interesting things. However, they must **evaluate** each source. If you are writing about the space shuttle, a current article in The *Chicago Tribune* would more likely impress readers as a truthful source than, say, a story in The *National Enquirer* called "Space Aliens Ate My Laundry." Look at the date of a book or article; if your subject is current, your sources should be too. Is the author a respected expert on this subject? Is the information balanced and objective? The librarian can help you find strong sources.

Once you discover good information that will strengthen your essay, take clear and careful notes, using 4×6 note cards or your notebook. Use the techniques you learned in Chapter 17 to summarize and quote directly and indirectly;

these will help you avoid accidental plagiarism. Write down everything you might need later. Print or buy copies of an article or book pages that are important. Don't leave the library without this information:

Book: Author name(s), title and subtitle, year of publication, publisher and location of publisher, exact pages of material quoted or summarized.

Magazine: Author name(s), title of article, title of magazine or journal, year, month, day of publication, volume and number, page numbers.

Carmen's Research Process

Carmen visits her college library and gets help from the librarian using the computerized database *EBSCOhost*. Because Carmen's topic—student credit-card debt—is current, she assumes that newspapers and magazines will give her the most up-to-date information. Searching "credit-card debt," she finds a recent *Business Week* article called "Congratulations, Grads—You're Bankrupt." She is surprised and excited to learn that credit problems like her friend's are a growing national problem. She copies the article and adds it to her source folder.

PRACTICE 2

TEACHING TIP
Scavenger hunts like the one in Practice 2 are both fun and useful for familiarizing students with the library's different resources. For more ideas, ask the librarian or search "library scavenger hunt" online.

In your college or local library, find the answers to the following questions; write the answers and the complete source for each piece of information. Your instructor might wish to have you work in competing teams.

1. List the full titles of five novels by Toni Morrison. What major prize did she win and in what year?

2. How many acres of rain forest are destroyed every day in Brazil?

3. What is the average hourly wage of men in the United States? Of women?

4. How many murders were committed in your town or city last year? Is the number up or down from ten years ago?

5. What was the newspaper headline in your hometown or city on the day and year of your birth? What stories dominated page 1?

PRACTICE 3

In your college or local library, find at least two excellent additions from outside sources that will improve your essay: a fact, statistic, example, quotation, or expert opinion. Write the information from each source precisely on 4 × 6 note cards, using quotation marks as you learned in Chapter 17, Part C, or make copies. Write down everything you will need later to cite the source: the book or magazine, article name, author name(s), and so on. Spell everything perfectly; copy exact punctuation of titles, and don't forget page numbers.

Doing Research on the Internet

The Internet is a wonderful source of information on just about everything—a great place to brainstorm, get ideas as you research, and find certain facts. However, it is harder to evaluate information on the web than in print, as this section will explain, so be careful.

If you have Internet access at the library or at home, use one of the search engines below. Type in search words that narrow your subject the same way you narrow a topic in writing—for example, *credit-card debt, college students.* Spell correctly, and try different words if necessary. Chances are, you will have too many "hits," rather than too few.

Google	http://google.com
Yahoo!	www//yahoo.com
AltaVista	http://www.altavista.com

Evaluate each web site carefully. Who sponsors the site? How balanced and unbiased is the information? Notice also the date of the site and article; many web sites come and go in the night. With practice, web researchers get better at spotting good and not-so-good sources of information. One tip is the web address, or Uniform Resource Locator (URL) of each site. The last part of a URL says who owns the site:

TEACHING TIP
Many magazines' web sites end in .com (e.g., the *U.S. News & World Report* site is **www.usnews.com**). Yet the information on such sites is generally thought to be credible and fair.

.com	=	company (aims to sell something and make a profit)
.org	=	nonprofit organization (aims to promote a cause)
.gov	=	government (provides many public information sites)
.edu	=	college or educational institution (aims to inform the public and promote itself)

For instance, if you are researching *asthma in children, treatments,* a government-sponsored health site might give more unbiased information than a company that sells asthma medications or a personal web site called *Troy's Asthma Story.* For more help evaluating web sites, search "evaluating web sources" or visit **http://lib.nmsu.edu/instruction/evalcrit.html.**

As in the library—to avoid plagiarism later—take good notes, clearly marking words and ideas taken from your sources. Before you leave a web site you wish to quote, cut and paste or print the material you want to refer to, and make sure you have full information to cite the source later in your paper:

Web site: URL address, owner of site, author name(s), title of article, date written (if available), and date you accessed the web site.

TEACHING TIP
Students who conduct research online will no doubt copy and paste information from web sites and electronic documents into their papers. Warn students who use this procedure to be extra careful about citing sources and adequately paraphrasing source material.

Carmen's Research Process

Carmen chooses the Google search engine and types the search words, "college students, credit-card debt." The search engine returns several thousand sources! Carmen scrolls quickly through many different "hits," until she finds one that looks promising. It's the web site for Nellie Mae, a federal loan provider for college students. Carmen takes notes on a number of useful statistics and makes sure she has the URL address and other pertinent information before she logs off the computer.

This web site sponsored by the Federal Trade Commission is one of the sites on credit-card debt that Carmen visited.

PRACTICE 4

Go to **www.fedstats.gov** and learn how to find statistics quickly and easily. Answer these questions:

1. How many people live in the United States?

2. What is the leading cause of death in American men? Women?

3. What is the leading export from your state?

4. How many different ethnic groups live in your state?

5. How many new AIDS cases were reported in your state last year? What groups were hardest hit?

PRACTICE 5

Using one of the suggested search engines, find at least two good pieces of information to strengthen your essay—facts, statistics, expert opinions, and so on. Hone your search words and evaluate what you find. Take careful notes, and cut and paste or print the information you need. Did you find any good material that you were not expecting? (Did you find exciting information on another subject that you might use in another paper? Be sure to take down any information you might use in the future.)

PART C Adding Sources to Your Essay and Documenting Them Correctly

Now, reread your original essay and the new material you found in your research process. Did you find other or better material than you looked for? Where in the paper will your outside sources be most effective? The next step is to use any of the three methods you learned in Chapter 17, Parts B and C—summary, direct quotation, or indirect quotation (paraphrase)—as you revise your essay and add your outside sources. This section will show you how.

The **MLA style** (named after the Modern Language Association) is a good method for documenting sources quickly and clearly. MLA style is also called *parenthetical* documentation because it puts source information in the body of the essay, in parentheses, rather than in cumbersome footnotes or endnotes.

A correct citation does two things:

TEACHING TIP
If you teach the full research paper, excellent guidance exists online for every phase of the process. For more on a documentation style, search "MLA or APA style guidelines."

TEACHING TIP
Survey your students on their majors. Explain that those majoring in science disciplines should eventually learn American Psychological Association (APA) documentation style.

■ It tells your reader that the material is from an outside source.

■ It gives your reader enough information to find the original source.

A correct citation appears in *two places* in your essay:

■ **inside** the essay in parentheses

■ **at the end** in a Works Cited list

Inside Your Essay: Summarize or Quote and Give Credit

When you quote an outside source in an essay, indicate that the material is not yours by introducing the quote with one of the phrases that you practiced in Part C of Chapter 17. If you use the author's name in this phrase, you will put only the page number in parentheses. If you leave the author unnamed, be sure to include both the author's last name and the page number in parentheses. If your source is a web site, no page number is needed—just the author or first word of the title.

Here is the introductory paragraph from Carmen's original essay about credit-card debt.

> In her second year of college, when she was supposed to declare her major, my best friend Maya almost had to declare bankruptcy. In just two years, she had racked up $7,000 in credit-card debt. Starting with necessities such as textbooks and car repairs, Maya soon began charging everything from midnight pizza parties to shopping sprees at the mall. It didn't take long before she had accrued a debt far greater than her part-time campus job could cover. What caused this intelligent student and perhaps others like her to get into so much debt?

■ This is a catchy introduction on a good topic. You can probably see why Carmen chose to do more with this paper.

Now read the same paragraph, strengthened and expanded by facts that Carmen found on the Internet:

TEACHING TIP
Point out that Carmen wrote and revised her essay in 2001. The dates of her outside sources reflect this.

TEACHING TIP
Make sure students know that MLA documentation not only indicates the sources of material but also shows where that material begins and ends so that readers can distinguish outside information from the writer's ideas.

> In her second year of college, when she was supposed to declare her major, my best friend Maya almost had to declare bankruptcy. In just two years, she had racked up $7,000 in credit-card debt. Starting with necessities such as textbooks and car repairs, Maya soon began charging everything from midnight pizza parties to shopping sprees at the mall. It didn't take long before she had accrued a debt far greater than her part-time campus job could cover. Yet Maya's is not an isolated case of bad financial management. According to a 2001 report on the web site of Nellie Mae, the student loan provider, 78 percent of all college students had credit cards in 2000, and the typical student's credit-card balance grew 46 percent, to $2,748, just from 1998 to 2000 ("Credit"). What has caused this jump in credit-card debt among college students nationwide and what can be done about it?

■ Through her research online, Carmen learned that students all over the country are carrying higher credit-card balances. This information adds power to Maya's story.

■ What transitional sentence moves the paragraph from Maya's personal story to the bigger picture? Yet Maya's is not an isolated case of bad financial management.

■ What transitional expression introduces the Nellie Mae report?
According to a 2001 report on the web site of Nellie Mae, . . .

■ Because this article has no listed author, the first word of the title, "Credit," is shown in parentheses. The full title and web site will be listed in Works Cited.

Note: Electronic resources do not have set page numbers because everyone's printer is different, so no page number is shown in parentheses, as it would be with a book or article.

At the End of Your Essay: List Works Cited

The last page of your essay will be a list of all the sources you summarized, directly quoted, or indirectly quoted in your essay, in alphabetical order by the author's last name. If there is no named author, list the entry alphabetically by its title (in quotation marks). Title the page Works Cited, and center the title. Use the models below to format each source properly. (Don't worry about memorizing the forms; even experienced writers often have to check an MLA manual for the correct form.) If a citation goes beyond one line, indent any following lines five spaces to make it clear that the information belongs together.

Books

One author:

Didion, Joan. The Year of Magical Thinking. New York: Alfred A. Knopf, 2006.

More than one author:

McClelland, Deke, and Katrin Eismann. Real World Digital Photography. Berkeley, CA: Peachpit Press, 1999.

Encyclopedia:

"Panama Canal." Encyclopedia Britannica. 2004.

Periodicals

Article in a newspaper:

Asimov, Eric. "Peruvian Cuisine Takes On the World." New York Times 26 May 1999, late ed.: F1.

Article in a magazine:

Adler, Jerry. "The New Fight Over Fat." Newsweek 20 Feb. 2006: 69+.

Article in a journal:

Lockwood, C. J. "Predicting Premature Delivery—No Easy Task." New England Journal of Medicine 346 (2002): 299–300.

Electronic Sources

Because the World Wide Web is a rapidly changing environment, include the date the source was published or updated, as well as the date you accessed the information.

TEACHING TIP
Templates for electronically composing a research paper with MLA documentation exist online. If you want your students to use one, search "research paper templates, MLA (or APA)."

Web site:

Advertising World. 2005. Department of Advertising, University of Texas, Austin. 3 Jul. 2006 <http://advertising.utexas.edu/world/index.asp>.

Article in an online periodical:

Thurer, Shari. "The Working Mom Myth." Salon.com 6 April 1999. 12 August 2002 <http://www.salon.com/mwt/feature/1999/04/06/childcare_study/index.html>.

Work from a subscription service (give the name of the library you used):

Schacter, Daniel. "The Seven Sins of Memory: How the Mind Forgets and Remembers." Psychology Today May 2001: 90–99. Expanded Academic ASAP. InfoTrac. City College of San Francisco Lib., San Francisco, CA. 22 Jan. 2002.

Multimedia

Film or video:

March of the Penguins. Dir. Luc Jacquet. Narr. Morgan Freeman. DVD. Warner Independent Pictures, 2005.

Radio or television program:

"Machismo." Sixty Minutes. Narr. Morley Safer. CBS. WCBS, New York. 6 Aug. 1993.

Personal interview:

Santos, Mariela. Personal Interview. Oct. 31, 2006.

These models cover the most common outside sources you will encounter in your research. If you need assistance with another source, you can find other models in one of the many web sites that publish MLA guidelines. Try Purdue's Online Writing Lab at **http://owl.english.purdue.edu/handouts/research/r_mla. html.** (If your instructor requires APA style instead of MLA, click *APA* at the site above or try **http://www.wisc.edu/writing/Handbook/DocAPA.html**.)

Carmen's Research Process

During her library and Internet research, Carmen had carefully copied the quotes and facts that she wanted to use in her essay onto index cards or copied relevant pages. Now, as she revises her essay to add these sources, she makes sure that she quotes her sources accurately and avoids unintentional plagiarism. As she rewrites her essay, she refers to Chapters 17 and 18. She uses transitional expressions to weave the outside sources smoothly into her essay. Then she prepares a Works Cited list, referring to the models above, as the last page of her paper.

Read Carmen's completed essay with research, "Drastic Plastic: Credit-Card Debt on Campus," at the end of this chapter.

PRACTICE 6

Below are five sources a student has compiled for a research essay on the history of the Olympics. Using the models above to guide you, prepare a Works Cited list for the paper that includes all five sources, properly formatted and in alphabetical order.

■ A book by Susan Wels called The Olympic Spirit: 100 Years of the Games that was published in Del Mar, California, by Tehabi Books in 1995

■ An article in the February 25, 2002, issue of Newsweek called "Going Extreme: Snowboarding and Moguls" written by Devin Gordon and T. Trent Gegax and appearing on page 48

■ A web site called The Ancient Olympic Games Virtual Museum that was presented by Dartmouth College and last updated on January 11, 2004 (the student viewed it on March 12, 2006 at http://minbar.cs.Dartmouth.edu/greecom/ olympics/)

■ A book by Allen Guttman titled The Olympics: A History of the Modern Games published by the University of Illinois Press in the city of Champaign in 2002, 248 pages long

■ An article from the Christian Science Monitor called "Olympic Leaps" that was written by Ross Atkin and appeared on page 18 on Aug. 10, 2004.

Works Cited

The Ancient Olympic Games Virtual Museum. 11 Jan. 2004. Dartmouth College. 12

Mar. 2006. <http://minbar.cs.Dartmouth.edu/greecom/olympics/>.

Atkin, Ross. "Olympic Leaps." Christian Science Monitor. 10 Aug. 2004: 18.

Gordon, Devin, and T. Trent Gegax. "Going Extreme: Snowboarding and Moguls."

Newsweek 25 Feb. 2002: 48.

Guttman, Allen. The Olympics: A History of the Modern Games. Champaign:

University of Illinois Press, 2002.

Wels, Susan. The Olympic Spirits: 100 Years of the Games. Del Mar, CA: Tehabi

Books, 1995.

TEACHING TIP
Have students form small groups to check their answers to Practice 6.

PRACTICE 7

TEACHING TIP
Students might work in dyads to check their essays for plagiarism and correct citation style. Have them bring their original source material to class.

Now, using two of the three methods—summary, direct quotation, or indirect quotation—add your research findings to your essay. Review Chapters 17 and 18 if you need to. Aim to achieve two things: First, try to add the new material gracefully, using introductory phrases so that it relates clearly to your ideas in the essay. Second, be careful to avoid plagiarism by documenting your sources correctly, both inside the essay and in your Works Cited list.

Following is Carmen's final essay strengthened by research.

Gevana 1

Every essay or research paper should begin on a new page.

Carmen Gevana
Professor Fawcett
English 100
22 May 2006

introduction

Drastic Plastic: Credit-Card Debt on Campus

Indirectly quoted facts from Nellie Mae expand the topic; short title given, no page for web site.

Thesis statement, phrased as a question

Topic sentence: cause #1

In her second year of college, when she was supposed to declare her major, my best friend Maya almost had to declare bankruptcy. In just two years, she had racked up $7,000 in credit-card debt. Starting with necessities such as textbooks and car repairs, Maya soon began charging everything from midnight pizza parties to shopping sprees at the mall. It didn't take long before she had accrued a debt far greater than her part-time campus job could cover. Yet Maya's is not an isolated case of bad financial management. According to a 2001 report on the web site of Nellie Mae, the student loan provider, 78 percent of all college students had credit cards in 2000, and the typical student's credit-card balance grew 46 percent to $2,748, just from 1998 to 2000 ("Credit"). What has caused this jump in credit-card debt among college students nationwide and what can be done about it?

Developed by author's ideas, observations

A major cause of growing student debt is that credit-card companies bombard college students the minute they step on campus. Targeting a profitable market of young consumers, these credit companies use many tactics to lure new college students into applying for their cards. Smiling salespeople stand behind tables offering free goodies like candy bars, school sweatshirts, and even airline tickets. They flood students' mailboxes with credit-card offers and pay the college bookstore to stuff applications into every plastic book bag. For my friend Maya, the temptation was too great. Before she had been in college a week, she had already applied for two cards, each with a large credit limit.

Topic sentence: cause #2

Developed by author's ideas, observations

Maya's credit-card behavior illustrates the second cause for the widespread crisis in college debt—most college students spend more than they can repay. Companies that extend credit typically offer higher limits than their customers can handle. After all, the company makes its profit through charging interest, and interest only accrues if the customer cannot pay off the full balance every month. New credit-card users, especially college students who don't have a lot of extra cash and often lack training in how to handle money responsibly, may rapidly build a balance beyond their means. When this occurs, students may be able to cover little more than the minimum monthly payment of $15 to $25. With high average interest rates, the outstanding balance can grow quickly until the student ends up paying more interest than she originally charged.

Topic sentence: effects of heavy debt

Developed by author's ideas; suicide case source is author's cousin

The drastic effects of a reliance on plastic are clear. Some students end up with debts in the thousands that trail them for years. If they have to default on their cards or declare bankruptcy, a bad credit report can follow them into adulthood, hurting their chances to rent an apartment or purchase a home or car. Some students have even fallen into depression and, in one or two extreme cases, suicide. At my cousin's college, the University of Oklahoma, a student committed suicide after being overwhelmed by a $3,000 credit-card debt. Thankfully, Maya avoided such serious consequences; however, her dependence on credit seriously affected

Gevana 2

her education. To avoid bankruptcy, she had to leave college for a semester to work full-time and pay off her debt.

Topic sentence: consequences gaining attention and actions taken

Indirect quote from Business Week article and direct quote from Kobliner's book clearly cited

Advice to credit-card users forms conclusion

Fortunately, the consequences of students' ever-increasing credit-card debt are gaining more widespread attention. Lawmakers and colleges are taking action. A May 21, 2001, article in Business Week entitled "Congratulations, Grads— You're Bankrupt," reports that over a dozen schools have simply banned all credit-card marketers from campuses (48). Yet students should not wait for others to act on their behalf. Financial expert Beth Kobliner, in her book Get a Financial Life, advises, "Limiting your access to credit is a smart move whether you're a binge shopper or a model of self-control" (49). In short, any student can practice self-discipline with credit by following three simple rules: 1) carry just one card, 2) use it only for emergencies, and 3) pay your entire balance every month.

Gevana 3

Works Cited should start on a new page

Works Cited

"Congratulations, Grads—You're Bankrupt." Business Week 21 May 2001: 48.

Credit Card Usage Continues among College Students. Nellie Mae. 2001. 26 Apr. 2002 <http://www.nelliemae.com/library/cc_use.html>.

Kobliner, Beth. Get a Financial Life. New York: Fireside/Simon & Schuster, 1996.

EXPLORING ONLINE

TEACHING TIP
More practice and assessment are available in the *Evergreen* Test Bank, linked ACE tests on the *Evergreen* Online Teaching and Study Centers, *WriteSpace for Evergreen,* and Exploring Online links in this chapter.

http://www.csuohio.edu/writingcenter/mla.html Clear, practical examples of how to insert material from outside sources in your papers

Online Study Center **college.hmco.com/pic/evergreen8e**
Visit the Online Study Center for *Evergreen* for more exercises and quizzes.

19

Writing Under Pressure: The Essay Examination

Being able to write under pressure is a key skill both in college and in the workplace. Throughout your college career, you will be asked to write **timed papers** in class and to take **essay examinations.** In fact, many English programs base placement and passing on timed essay exams. Clearly, the ability to write under pressure is crucial.

An **essay question** requires the same writing skills that a student uses in composing a paragraph or an essay. Even in history and biology, how well you do on an essay test depends partly on how well you write; yet many students, under the pressure of a test, forget or fail to apply what they know about good writing. This chapter will improve your ability to write under pressure. Many of the sample exam questions on the following pages were taken from real college examinations.

PART A Budgeting Your Time

To do well on a timed essay or an essay test, it is not enough to know the material. You must also be able to call forth what you know, organize it, and present it in writing—all under pressure in a limited time.

Since most essay examinations are timed, it is important that you learn how to **budget** your time effectively so that you can devote adequate time to each question *and* finish the test. The following six tips will help you use your time well.

1. **Make sure you know exactly how long the examination lasts.** A one-hour examination may really be only fifty minutes; a two-hour examination may last only one hour and forty-five minutes.

264

2. **Note the point value of all questions and allot time accordingly to each question.** That is, allot the most time to questions that are worth the most points and less time to ones that are worth fewer.

3. **Decide on an order in which to answer the questions.** You do not have to begin with the first question on the examination and work, in order, to the last. Instead, you may start with the questions worth the most points. Some students prefer to begin with the questions they feel they can answer most easily, thereby guaranteeing points toward the final grade on the examination. Others combine the two methods. No matter which system you use, be sure to allot enough time to the questions that are worth the most points—whether you do them first or last.

4. **Make sure you understand exactly what each question asks you to do; then quickly prewrite and plan your answer.** It is all-important to take a breath, study the question, and make a quick scratch outline or plan of your answer *before you start to write.* Parts B through D of this chapter will guide you through these critical steps.

5. **Time yourself.** As you begin a particular question, calculate when you must be finished with that question in order to complete the examination, and note that time in the margin. As you write, check the clock every five minutes so that you remain on schedule.

6. **Finally, do not count on having enough time to recopy your work.** Skip lines and write carefully so that the instructor can easily read your writing as well as any neat corrections you might make.

PRACTICE 1

Imagine that you are about to take the two-hour history test shown below. Read the test carefully, noting the point value of each question, and then answer the questions that follow the examination.   Answers may vary.

Part I   Answer both questions. 15 points each.

1. Do you think that the Versailles Peace Treaty was a "harsh" one? Be specific.

2. List the basic principles of Karl Marx. Analyze them in terms of Marx's claim that they are scientific.

Part II   Answer two of the following questions. 25 points each.

3. Describe the origins of, the philosophies behind, and the chief policies of either Communist Russia or Fascist Italy. Be specific.

4. What were the causes of Nelson Mandela's presidential victory in South Africa in 1994?

5. European history of the nineteenth and twentieth centuries has been increasingly related to that of the rest of the world. Why? How? With what consequences for Europe?

> Part III   Briefly identify ten of the following. 2 points each.
>
> a. John Locke
> b. Franco-Prussian War
> c. Stalingrad
> d. Cavour
> e. Manchuria, 1931
> f. Entente Cordiale
> g. Existentialism
> h. Jacobins
> i. The Opium Wars
> j. Social Darwinism
> k. The Reform Bill of 1832
> l. The most interesting reading you have done this term (from the course list)

TEACHING TIP
Lead a class discussion about students' answers to the questions in Practice 1. They should be able to explain why they answered as they did.

1. Which part would you do first and why? <u>I would do Part II first because it is worth the most points (50).</u>

   How much time would you allot to the questions in this part and why?

   <u>I would allot approximately half of my time because it is half of the exam.</u>

2. Which part would you do second and why? <u>I would do Part I second because it is worth 30 points.</u>

   How much time would you allot to the questions in this part and why?

   <u>I would allot about half my remaining time because this part is about one-fourth of the exam.</u>

3. Which part would you do last and why? <u>I would do Part III last because it is worth the least number of points (20).</u>

   How much time would you allot to the questions in this part and why?

   <u>I would allot most of my remaining time, answering all of the questions I could. I'd save some time to review my other answers.</u>

PART B   Reading and Understanding the Essay Question

Before you begin writing, carefully examine each question to decide exactly what your purpose is: that is, what the instructor expects you to do.

■ This question contains three sets of instructions.

> *Question:*   Using <u>either</u> Communist China or Nazi Germany as a model, (a) <u>describe</u> the characteristics of a totalitarian <u>state</u>, and (b) <u>explain</u> how such a state was <u>created</u>.

▪ First, you must use "either Communist China or Nazi Germany as a model." That is, you must **choose** *one or the other* as a model.

▪ Second, you must **describe,** and third, you must **explain.**

▪ Your answer should consist of two written parts, a **description** and an **explanation.**

It is often helpful to underline the important words, as shown in the previous box, to make sure you understand the entire question and have noted all its parts.

> *The student must* (1) choose to write about either Communist China or Nazi Germany, not both; (2) describe the totalitarian state; (3) explain how such a state was created.

PRACTICE 2

Read each essay question and underline key words. Then, on the lines beneath the question, describe in your own words exactly what the question requires: (1) What directions does the student have to follow? (2) How many parts will the answer contain?

TEACHING TIP
Consider having students complete Practice 2 in small groups so that they can talk through their answers.

EXAMPLE What were the causes of the Cold War? What were its chief episodes? Why has there not been a "hot" war?

Student must (1) tell what caused the Cold War (two or more causes),

(2) mention main events of Cold War, (3) give reasons why we haven't had a

full-scale war. The essay will have three parts: causes, main events, and reasons.

1. State Newton's First Law and give examples from your own experience.

   Student must (1) write out Newton's First Law and (2) give examples of the law from

   his or her own experience. The essay will have two parts: the law and examples.

2. Choose one of the following terms. Define it, give an example of it, and then show how it affects *your* life: (a) freedom of speech, (b) justice for all, (c) equal opportunity.

   Student must (1 and 2) define and give an example of one term: freedom of speech,

   justice for all, or equal opportunity and (3) show how it affects his or her life. The essay

   will have three parts: a definition, an example, and effects.

3. Shiism and Sunni are the two great branches of Islam. Discuss the religious beliefs and the politics of each branch.

Student must (1) discuss the religious beliefs and the politics of Shiism and

(2) discuss the religious beliefs and the politics of Sunni. The essay will have two parts:

Shiism and Sunni.

4. Name and explain four types of savings institutions. What are three factors that influence one's choice of a savings institution?

Student must (1) identify and describe four types of savings institutions and (2) name

three factors influencing one's choice of a savings institution. The essay will have

two parts: types and factors.

5. Steroids: the athlete's "unfair advantage." Discuss.

Student must (1) explain what advantage steroids offer to athletes and (2) explain

why the advantage is considered unfair. The essay will have two parts: explanation of

advantage and explanation of why advantage is unfair.

6. Discuss the causes and consequences of the Broad Street cholera epidemic in mid-nineteenth-century London. What was the role of Dr. John Snow?

Student must (1) discuss the causes of the Broad Street cholera epidemic, (2) discuss

its consequences, and (3) explain Dr. Snow's role. The essay will have three parts: causes,

effects, and role of Snow.

7. Define the Monroe Doctrine of the early nineteenth century and weigh the arguments for and against it.

Student must (1) define the Monroe Doctrine, (2) evaluate the arguments for it, and

(3) evaluate the arguments against it. The essay will have three parts: definition,

arguments for, and arguments against.

8. The sixteenth century is known for the Renaissance, the Reformation, and the Commercial Revolution. Discuss each event, showing why it was important to the history of Western civilization.

Student must discuss the historical importance of (1) the Renaissance, (2) the

Reformation, and (3) the Commercial Revolution. The essay will have three parts: the

Renaissance, the Reformation, and the Commercial Revolution.

9. Erik Erikson has theorized that adult actions toward children may produce either (a) trust or mistrust, (b) autonomy or self-doubt, (c) initiative or guilt. Choose one of the pairs above and give examples of the kinds of adult behavior that might create these responses in a child.

Student must (1) choose one pair of terms, (2) give examples of adult behavior that might create trust (autonomy, initiative) in a child, and (3) give examples of adult behavior that might create mistrust (self-doubt, guilt) in a child. The essay will have two parts: behavior creating positive traits and behavior creating negative traits.

10. Simón Bolívar may not have been as great a hero as he was believed to be. Agree or disagree.

Student must (1) state the "heroic" traits that Bolívar was believed to have had and (2) give reasons supporting or contradicting that portrayal. The essay will have two parts: an explanation of Bolívar's "heroic" traits and the supporting or opposing evidence.

PART C Choosing the Correct Paragraph or Essay Pattern

Throughout this book, you have learned how to write various types of paragraphs and compositions. Many examinations will require you simply to **illustrate, define, compare,** and so forth. How well you answer questions may depend partly on how well you understand these terms.

---

1. *Illustrate* "behavior modification."
2. *Define* "greenhouse effect."
3. *Compare* Agee and Nin as diarists.

■ The key words in these questions are *illustrate, define,* and *compare*—**instruction words** that tell you what you are supposed to do and what form your answer should take.

Here is a review list of some common instruction words used in college examinations.

TEACHING TIP
You can reduce students' test anxiety by reviewing these terms, most of which they now know.

1. Classify:	Gather into categories, types, or kinds according to a single basis of division (see Chapter 11).
2. Compare:	Point out similarities (see Chapter 10). Instructors often use *compare* to mean point out both *similarities* and *differences*.
3. Contrast:	Point out differences (see Chapter 10).
4. Describe:	Give an account of or capture pictorially (see Chapter 7).

5. **Define:** State clearly and exactly the meaning of a word or term (see Chapter 9). You may be required to write a single-sentence definition or a full paragraph. Instructors may use *identify* as a synonym for *define* when they want a short definition.

6. **Discuss:** Often an instructor uses these terms to mean "thoughtfully examine a subject, approaching it from different angles." These terms allow the writer more freedom of approach than many of the others.
   (analyze,
   describe,
   or explain)

7. **Discuss causes:** Analyze the reasons or causes for something; answer the question, Why? (see Chapter 12).

8. **Discuss effects:** Analyze the effects, consequences, or results of something (see Chapter 12).

9. **Evaluate:** Weigh the pros and cons, advantages and disadvantages (see Chapters 10 and 13).

10. **Identify:** Give a capsule who-what-when-where-why answer. Sometimes *identify* is a synonym for *define.*

11. **Illustrate:** Give one or more examples (see Chapter 5).

12. **Narrate:** Follow the development of something through time, event by event (see Chapters 6 and 8).
    (trace)

13. **Summarize:** Write the substance of a longer work in condensed form (see Chapter 17, Part B).

14. **Take a stand:** Persuade; argue for a particular position (see Chapter 13).

PRACTICE 3

You should have no trouble deciding what kind of paragraph or composition to use if the question uses one of the terms just defined—*contrast, trace, classify,* and so on. However, questions are often worded in such a way that you have to discover what kind of paragraph or essay is required. What kind of paragraph or essay is required by each of the following questions?

EXAMPLE What is *schizophrenia?*
(*Write a paragraph to. . . .*) ___define___

1. In one concise paragraph, give the main ideas of Simone de Beauvoir's famous book *The Second Sex.* ___summarize___

2. What is the difference between veins and arteries? ___contrast___

3. Follow the development of Wynton Marsalis's musical style. ___narrate___

4. How do jet- and propeller-driven planes differ? ___contrast___

5. Who or what is each of the
following: the Gang of Four,
Ho Chi Minh, Tiananmen Square?   <u>identify or define</u>

6. Explain the causes of the
American Civil War.   <u>discuss causes</u>

7. Explain what is meant by
"magical realism."   <u>define</u>

8. Take a stand for or against
legalizing marijuana in this country.
Give reasons to support your stand.   <u>persuade, give reasons</u>

9. Give two recent instances of military
hazing that you consider "out of control."   <u>illustrate</u>

10. Divide into groups the
different kinds of web sites
giving out medical information.   <u>classify</u>

PART D Writing the Topic Sentence or the Thesis Statement

A good way to ensure that your answer truly addresses itself to the question is to compose a topic sentence or a thesis statement that contains the key words of the question.

> *Question:* How do fixed-rate and adjustable-rate mortgages differ?

- The key words in this question are *fixed-rate* and *adjustable-rate mortgages*, and *differ*.

- What kind of paragraph or essay would be appropriate for this question?

  a paragraph or essay of contrast
  _____

> *Topic sentence* or *thesis statement of answer:* Fixed-rate and adjustable-rate mortgages differ in three basic ways.

- The answer repeats the key words of the question: *fixed-rate, adjustable-rate, mortgages*, and *differ*.

PRACTICE 4

Here are eight examination questions. Write a topic sentence or thesis statement for each question by using the question as part of the answer. Pretend that you know all the material. Even though you may not know anything about the subjects, you should be able to formulate a topic sentence or thesis statement based on the question.   Answers may vary.

1. Contrast high school requirements in Jamaica with those in the United States.

   Topic sentence or thesis statement: High school requirements in Jamaica are more demanding than those in the United States.

2. Do you think that the terrorist attacks of September 11, 2001, had any positive effects on Americans?

   Topic sentence or thesis statement: The terrorist attacks of September 11, 2001, traumatic as they were, had three positive effects on Americans.

3. What steps can a busy person take to reduce the destructive impact of stress in his or her life?

   Topic sentence or thesis statement: A busy person can take several steps to help reduce the destructive impact of stress in his or her life.

4. Gay couples should be allowed to adopt children. Agree or disagree with this statement.

   Topic sentence or thesis statement: Gay couples definitely should be allowed to adopt children.

5. Assume that you manage a small shop that sells men's apparel. What activities would you undertake to promote the sale of sportswear?

   Topic sentence or thesis statement: As manager of a small shop that sells men's apparel, I would do three things to promote the sale of sportswear.

6. The U.S. government should cover the medical costs of AIDS. Agree or disagree with this statement.

   Topic sentence or thesis statement: The U.S. government should cover the medical costs of AIDS.

7. The state should subsidize students in medical school because the country needs more doctors. Agree or disagree with this statement.

Topic sentence or thesis statement: <u>The state should not subsidize students in</u>

<u>medical school.</u>

8. Does religion play a more vital role in people's lives today than it did in your parents' generation?

Topic sentence or thesis statement: <u>Religion plays a more vital role in people's lives</u>

<u>today than it did in my parents' generation.</u>

✓ **CHECKLIST**

The Process of Answering an Essay Question

- ☐ 1. Survey the test and note the point value for each question.
- ☐ 2. Calculate how much time you need for each question. Then check the clock as you write so that you complete all the questions.
- ☐ 3. Read each question carefully, underlining important words.
- ☐ 4. Determine how many parts the answer should contain.
- ☐ 5. Considering your audience (usually the teacher) and purpose, choose the paragraph or essay pattern that would best answer the question.
- ☐ 6. Write a topic sentence or a thesis statement that repeats the key words of the question.
- ☐ 7. Quickly freewrite or brainstorm ideas on scrap paper and arrange them in a logical order, making a scratch outline or plan.
- ☐ 8. Write your paragraph or essay neatly, skipping lines so you will have enough room to make corrections.

 **EXPLORING ONLINE**

http://www.yorku.ca/cdc/lsp/eponline/exam5.htm Don't get nervous; get an A. Advice for essay-test takers

http://owl.english.purdue.edu/handouts/general/gl_essay.html More good advice, plus practice

Online Study Center college.hmco.com/pic/evergreen8e
Visit the Online Study Center for *Evergreen* for more exercises and quizzes.

UNIT 4

Writers' Workshop

Analyze a Social Problem

Because essays are longer and more complex than paragraphs, organizing an essay can be a challenge, even for experienced writers. Techniques like having a clear *controlling idea*, a good *thesis statement*, and a *plan or an outline* all help an essay writer manage the task. Another useful approach is dividing the subject into three parts, as one student does here. In your group or class, read the essay, aloud if possible, underlining the parts you find most powerful and paying special attention to organization.

It's Great to Get Old

(1) I knock at the door and patiently await an answer. I listen and hear the thump of a cane on the hard wood floor, edging slowly toward the door. "It's great to get old," my grandmother says facetiously[1] as she opens the door, apologizing for making me wait. Through her I learn firsthand the problems of the aged. Loneliness, lack of money, and ailing health are just some of the problems old people must deal with.

(2) For one thing, loneliness seems endemic[2] among old people in America. With difficulty getting around, many spend most of their time confined to their apartments, awaiting visits from family or friends. Through my grandmother, I realize that as much as old people's families may care about them, the family members obviously have lives of their own and cannot visit as much as old persons would like. And when people are very old, most of their friends have already died, so they spend most of their time alone.

(3) Poor health is also a major problem. Any number of physical ailments create a problem. Cataracts, for example, are a common eye problem among old people. Health problems can make life very difficult for an old person.

(4) Last but not least is the financial burden old people must cope with. The rising costs of basic necessities such as food, housing, and health care are especially difficult for old people to meet. Sadly, most are forced to compromise what they need for what they can afford. Take, for example, an old person who buys pounds of inexpensive pasta for dinner every night. While the person may need other nutrients, the person forfeits this need for what the person can afford. Financial problems also make life very difficult for an old person.

(5) There is no easy way to ease the problems of the aged. Simply being aware of them is an important step in the right direction. If we turn our attention and compassion toward the elderly, we can begin to help them find solutions.

—Denise Nelley (Student)

---

[1]facetiously: humorously

[2]endemic: typical in a certain place or population

1. How effective is Ms. Nelley's essay?

   _____Y_____ Strong thesis statement? _____Y/N_____ Good supporting details?
   (see 5 below)

   _____Y/N_____ Logical organization? _____Y_____ Effective conclusion?
   (see 4 below)

2. Did the introductory paragraph catch your interest? Explain why or why not.

3. What is the controlling idea of the essay? What is the thesis statement?
   last sentence in first paragraph

4. This writer has skillfully organized her ideas. Her thesis names three problems facing the elderly. What are they? Does the body of the essay discuss these three problems in the same order that the thesis names them? If not, what changes would you suggest? No. Discuss money second, health third.

5. Are the three problems fully explained in paragraphs 2, 3, and 4? That is, does Ms. Nelley provide enough support for each problem? If not, what revision suggestions would you give the writer, especially for paragraph 3?*

6. This student movingly presents some problems of the elderly. Do you think she should have included solutions? Why or why not?

7. Can you spot any error patterns (the same error two or more times) that this student should watch out for? No

GROUP WORK

In your group or class, evaluate (or grade) Ms. Nelley's essay. Then, based on your evaluation, decide what changes or revisions would most improve the essay, and revise it accordingly, as if it were your own. If your group wishes to add any new ideas or support, brainstorm together and choose the strongest ideas. Rewrite as needed.

When you are done, evaluate the essay again, with your changes.

WRITING AND REVISING IDEAS

1. Discuss the ways in which a loved one's experience has taught you about a problem (addiction, AIDS, disability, and so on).

2. Analyze a social problem (racial profiling or shoplifting, for example).

---

* Prewrite again for more support on health problems. Develop paragraph 3 as fully as 2 and 4. Revise to avoid using the word "problem" four times.

Improving Your Writing

20

Revising for Consistency and Parallelism

PART A	Consistent Tense
PART B	Consistent Number and Person
PART C	Parallelism

All good writing is **consistent.** That is, each sentence and paragraph in the final draft should move along smoothly without confusing shifts in **tense, number,** or **person.** In addition, good writing uses **parallel structure** to balance two or more similar words, phrases, or clauses.

Although you should be aware of consistency and parallelism as you write the first draft of your paragraph or essay, you might find it easier to **revise** for them—that is, to write your first draft and then, as you read it again later, check and rewrite for consistency and parallelism.

PART A Consistent Tense

Consistency of tense means using the same verb tense whenever possible throughout a sentence or an entire paragraph. Do not shift from one verb tense to another—for example, from present to past or from past to present—unless you really mean to indicate different times.

1. Inconsistent tense:	We *stroll* down Bourbon Street as the jazz bands *began* to play.
2. Consistent tense:	We *strolled* down Bourbon Street as the jazz bands *began* to play.
3. Consistent tense:	We *stroll* down Bourbon Street as the jazz bands *begin* to play.

TEACHING TIP
Ask the class to discuss cases where present or past tense might be more effective (for an example of each, see page 46).

■ Sentence 1 begins in the present tense with the verb *stroll* but then slips into the past tense with the verb *began*. The tenses are inconsistent since both actions (strolling and beginning) occur at the same time.

■ Sentence 2 is consistent. Both verbs, *strolled* and *began,* are now in the past tense.

■ Sentence 3 is also consistent, using the present tense forms of both verbs, *stroll* and *begin.* The present tense here gives a feeling of immediacy, as if the action is happening now.*

Of course, you should use different verb tenses in a sentence or paragraph if they convey the meaning that you wish to convey:

4. Last fall I *took* English 02; now I am taking English 13.

■ The verbs in this sentence accurately show the time relationship between the two classroom experiences.†

PRACTICE 1

Read the following sentences carefully for meaning. Then correct any inconsistencies of tense by changing the verbs that do not accurately show the time of events.

EXAMPLE I took a deep breath and opened the door; there stands a well-dressed man with a large box.

Consistent: I took a deep breath and opened the door; there ~~stands~~ *stood* a well-dressed man with a large box.

or

Consistent: I ~~took~~ *take* a deep breath and ~~opened~~ *open* the door; there stands a well-dressed man with a large box.

1. Two seconds before the buzzer sounded, Lebron James sank a basket from midcourt, and the crowd ~~goes~~ *went* wild.

2. Nestlé introduced instant coffee in 1938; it ~~takes~~ *took* eight years to develop this product.

3. We ~~expand~~ *expanded* our sales budget, doubled our research, and soon saw positive results.

4. For twenty years, Dr. Dulfano observed animal behavior and ~~seeks~~ *sought* clues to explain the increasing violence among human beings.

---

* For more work on spotting verbs, see Chapter 24, "The Simple Sentence," Part C.
† For more work on particular verb tenses and forms, see Chapters 27, 28, and 29.

5. I knew how the system ~~works~~. [worked]

6. I was driving south on Interstate 90 when a truck ~~approaches~~ [approached] with its high beams on.

7. Two brown horses ~~graze~~ [grazed] quietly in the field as the sun rose and the mist disappeared.

8. Lollie had a big grin on her face as she ~~walks~~ [walked] over and kicked the Coke machine.

9. Maynard ~~stormed~~ [storms] down the hallway, goes right into the boss's office, and shouts, "I want curtains in my office!"

10. The nurses quietly paced the halls, making sure their patients ~~rest~~ [rested] comfortably.

PRACTICE 2

Inconsistencies of tense are most likely to occur within paragraphs and longer pieces of writing. Therefore, it is important to revise your writing for tense consistency. Read this paragraph for meaning. Then revise, correcting inconsistencies of tense by changing incorrect verbs.

TEACHING TIP
Tell the class to beware of tense shifts in narrative writing. As writers relive past events in their minds, they may shift from past to present verbs.

It was 1850. A poor German-born peddler named Levi Strauss came to San Francisco, trying to sell canvas cloth to tent makers. By chance he met a miner who complained that sturdy work pants ~~are~~ [were] hard to find. Strauss had an idea, ~~measures~~ [measured] the man, and ~~makes~~ [made] him a pair of canvas pants. The miner loved his new breeches, and Levi Strauss ~~goes~~ [went] into business. Although he ordered more canvas, what he ~~gets is~~ [got was] a brown French cloth called *serge de Nîmes*, which Americans soon called "denim." Strauss liked the cloth but had the next batch dyed blue. He became successful selling work pants to such rugged men as cowboys and lumberjacks. In the 1870s, hearing about a tailor in Nevada adding copper rivets to a pair of the pants to make them stronger, Strauss ~~patents~~ [patented] the idea. When he died in 1902, Levi Strauss was famous in California, but the company ~~keeps~~ [kept] growing. In the 1930s, when Levi's jeans became popular in the East, both men *wore*

and women ~~wear~~ them. By 2000, people all over the world had purchased 2.5 billion

pairs of jeans.

PRACTICE 3

TEACHING TIP
Transforming activities like
Practice 3 promote verbal
agility.

The following paragraph is written in the past tense. Rewrite it in consistent present tense. Cross out each past tense verb and write the present tense form above it. Make sure all verbs agree with their subjects.*

   In the late afternoon light on the plains of Botswana, Dereck and Beverly Joubert

   spot   *appears*   *is*

~~spotted~~ what ~~appeared~~ to be a gray boulder a thousand yards away. It ~~was~~ a bull

                    grabs

elephant, about 40 years old, in his prime. Dereck ~~grabbed~~ his movie camera

       swoops   *begin*

while Beverly ~~swooped~~ up her Nikon. They barely ~~began~~ to shoot when the five-

   becomes   *trumpets* *spreads*   *charges*

ton bull ~~became~~ enraged, ~~trumpeted~~, ~~spread~~ his ears, and ~~charged~~ full-speed. The

     continue   *digs*

Jouberts ~~continued~~ filming—even as the elephant suddenly ~~dug~~ both front legs

        skids   *comes*

into the ground, ~~skidded~~ forward in a cloud of dust, and ~~came~~ to a halt within

                  admit

yards of the couple. Later, in their Land Cruiser, the Jouberts ~~admitted~~ that while

     comes   *love*

danger sometimes ~~came~~ a bit too close, they ~~loved~~ their lives as documentary fil-

           live   *write* *produce* *shoot*

makers in Africa. Together they ~~lived~~ in tents in the wild, ~~wrote~~, ~~produced~~, ~~shot~~,

 edit   *help*

and ~~edited~~ award-winning films. By educating the public, they ~~helped~~ stop the

poaching of lions, elephants, and other big game.

—Based on Susan Schindehette and Terry Smith,
"Animal Passions," *People*

PRACTICE 4

TEACHING TIP
Ask students to color-code
the verb tenses in their
compositions with
highlighters. This graphic
presentation may enhance
their awareness of a tense-
shifting problem.

The following paragraph is written in the present tense. Rewrite it in consistent past tense,† crossing out each present tense verb and writing the past tense form above it.

                shared

   In the summer of 1816, four friends ~~share~~ a house in Switzerland. Days of rain

forced   *began*

~~force~~ them to stay indoors. They ~~begin~~ telling ghost stories to ease the boredom.

        read

For awhile, they ~~read~~ aloud from *Tales of the Dead*, a collection of horror stories

---

* For more work on agreement, see Chapter 27, "Present Tense (Agreement)."

† For more work on the past tense, see Chapter 28, "Past Tense."

full of eerie graveyards, swirling fog, and restless spirits. Then one night, they

decided

decide to hold a contest to see who can write the most frightening ghost story. All

felt

four feel eager to compete. Two of the friends—Percy Bysshe Shelley and Lord

were

Byron—are already famous poets. The other two—Dr. John Polidori and Mary

were   passed

Wollstonecraft Godwin, Shelley's wife-to-be—are also writers. Midnight passes,

retired   closed   took

and they retire to their bedrooms. Mary closes her eyes, and imagination takes

saw

over. In her mind's eye, she sees a science student kneeling beside a creature he

was   twitched

constructed. It is a hideous corpse of a man, but suddenly, it twitches with life.

ran

Horror-stricken, the young man runs away from his creation, hoping that the spark

would   woke

of life will sputter and die. Later, though, he wakes to find the monster standing

wrote

over his bed. Following this nightmare, Mary writes her novel *Frankenstein* in a

became

two-month rush. Published in 1818, *Frankenstein* becomes a classic, read by people

around the world.

PRACTICE 5

Longer pieces of writing often use both the past tense and the present tense. However, switching correctly from one tense to the other requires care. Read the following essay carefully and note when a switch from one tense to another is logically necessary. Then revise verbs as needed.

A Quick History of Chocolate

Most of us now take solid chocolate—especially candy bars—so much for

granted that we find it hard to imagine a time when chocolate didn't exist. How-

became

ever, this delicious food becomes an eating favorite only about 150 years ago.

The ancient peoples of Central America began cultivating cacao beans almost

was

3,000 years ago. A cold drink made from the beans is served to Hernando Cortés,

arrived

the Spanish conqueror, when he arrives at the Aztec court of Montezuma in 1519.

liked

The Spaniards took the beverage home to their king. He likes it so much that he

kept the formula a secret. For the next 100 years, hot chocolate was the private

TEACHING TIP
Suggest that students read the passage in Practice 5 aloud, listening and marking switches in tense. Then, they can go back and make the necessary corrections to the verbs they marked.

drink of the Spanish nobility. Slowly, it ~~makes~~ ^{made} its way into the fashionable courts

of France, England, and Austria. In 1657, a Frenchman living in London opened a

shop where devices for making the beverage ~~are~~ ^{were} sold at a high price. Soon choco-

late houses appeared in cities throughout Europe. Wealthy clients met in them,

sipped chocolate, conducted business, and ~~gossip~~ ^{gossiped}.

During the 1800s, chocolate became a chewable food. The breakthrough

~~comes~~ ^{came} in 1828 when cocoa butter was extracted from the bean. Twenty years later,

an English firm mixed the butter with chocolate liquor, which ~~results~~ ^{resulted} in the first

solid chocolate. Milton Hershey's first candy bar ~~come~~ ^{came} on the scene in 1894, and

Tootsie Rolls hit the market two years later. The popularity of chocolate bars ~~soar~~ ^{soared}

during World War I when they ~~are~~ ^{were} given to soldiers for fast energy. M&Ms gave

the industry another boost during World War II; soldiers needed candy that

wouldn't melt in their hands.

On the average, Americans today eat ten pounds of hard chocolate a year.

Their number-one choice is Snickers, which ~~sold~~ ^{sells} more than a billion bars every

year. However, Americans consume far less chocolate than many Western Euro-

peans. The average Dutch person ~~gobbled~~ ^{gobbles} up more than fifteen pounds a year

while a Swiss ~~packed~~ ^{packs} away almost twenty pounds. Chocolate is obviously an in-

ternational favorite.

PART B Consistent Number and Person

Just as important as verb tense consistency is consistency of **number** and **person.**

Consistency of Number

Consistency of number means avoiding confusing shifts from singular to plural
or from plural to singular within a sentence or paragraph. Choose *either* singular
or plural; then be *consistent.*

> 1. Inconsistent number: *The wise jogger* chooses *their* running shoes with care.
>
> 2. Consistent number: *The wise jogger* chooses *his or her* running shoes with care.
>
> 3. Consistent number: *Wise joggers* choose *their* running shoes with care.

- Since the subject of sentence 1, *the wise jogger,* is singular, use of the plural pronoun *their* is *inconsistent.*

- Sentence 2 is *consistent.* The singular pronoun *his* (or *her*) now clearly refers to the singular *jogger.*

- In sentence 3, the plural number is used *consistently. Their* clearly refers to the plural *joggers.*

   If you begin a paragraph by referring to a web site designer as *she,* continue to refer to *her* in the **third person singular** throughout the paragraph:

> The web site designer _____ ; she _____
>
> _____ . The law may not protect *her* _____
>
> _____ . Therefore, *she* _____ .

   Do not confuse the reader by shifting unnecessarily to *they* or *you.*

PRACTICE 6

Correct any inconsistencies of **number** in the following sentences.* Also make necessary changes in verb agreement.

EXAMPLE   1. A singer must protect ~~their~~ voice.   *his or her*

1. An individual's self-esteem can affect ~~their~~ performance.   *his or her*

2. Jorge started drinking diet sodas only last November, but already he hates the taste of ~~it~~.   *them*

3. The headlines encouraged us, but we feared that ~~it wasn't~~ accurate.   *they weren't*

4. The defendant has decided that he will represent ~~oneself~~.   *himself*

---

* For more practice in agreement of pronouns and antecedents, see Chapter 31, "Pronouns," Part B.

5. Dreams fascinate me; <s>it is</s> **they are** like another world.

6. If <s>a person doesn't</s> **people don't** know how to write well, they will face limited job opportunities.

7. Oxford University boasts of the great number of ancient manuscripts <s>they own</s> **it owns**.

8. Always buy corn and tomatoes when <s>it is</s> **they are** in season.

9. The average American takes <s>their</s> **his or her** freedom for granted.

10. <s>Women have</s> **A woman has** more opportunities than ever before. She is freer to go to school, get a job, and choose the kind of life she wants.

Consistency of Person

TEACHING TIP
You might want to explain how the three "persons," or points of view, differ. First person is informal and is not welcomed in some courses and most workplaces. Second person usually should be avoided except in "how-to" writing. Third person is often the best choice for academic writing.

Consistency of person—closely related to consistency of number—means using the same *person,* or indefinite pronoun form, throughout a sentence or paragraph whenever possible.

First person is the most personal and informal in written work: (singular) I, (plural) *we*

Second person speaks directly to the reader: (singular and plural) *you*

Third person is the most formal and most frequently used in college writing: (singular) *he, she, it, one, a person, an individual, a student,* and so on; (plural) *they, people, individuals, students,* and so on

---

Avoid confusing shifts from one person to another. Choose one, and then be *consistent.* When using a noun in a general way—*a person, the individual, the parent*—be careful not to slip into the second person, *you,* but continue to use the third person, *he or she.*

ESL TIP
Some ESL instructors advise students to avoid verb and article errors by sticking to third person *plural.*

---

4. Inconsistent person	A *player* collects $200 when *you* pass "Go."
5. Consistent person:	A *player* collects $200 when *he or she* passes "Go."
6. Consistent person:	*You* collect $200 when *you* pass "Go."

■ In sentence 4, the person shifts unnecessarily from the third person, *a player,* to the second person, *you.* The result is confusing.

■ Sentence 5 maintains consistent third person. *He or she* now clearly refers to the third person subject, *a player.*

■ Sentence 6 is also consistent, using the second person, *you,* throughout.

Of course, inconsistencies of person and number often occur together, as shown in the next box.

TEACHING TIP
Students might ask you about the use of "one," as in "One should practice the piano every day." Share your policy on person with the class—whether you prefer "one," the most formal, or some other, and whether you discourage second person, except in instructions.

7. Inconsistent person and number:	Whether *one* enjoys or resents commercials, *we* are bombarded with them every hour of the day.
8. Consistent person and number:	Whether *we* enjoy or resent commercials, *we* are bombarded with them every hour of the day.
9. Consistent person and number:	Whether *one* enjoys or resents commercials, *he or she* (or *one*) is bombarded with them every hour of the day.

■ Sentence 7 shifts from the third person singular, *one*, to the first person plural, *we*.

■ Sentence 8 uses the first person plural consistently.

■ Sentence 9 uses the third person singular consistently.

PRACTICE 7

Correct the shifts in **person** in these sentences. If necessary, change the verbs to make them agree with any new subjects.

EXAMPLE   One should eliminate saturated fats from ~~your~~ *one's* diet.

1. Sooner or later, most addicts realize that ~~you~~ *they* can't just quit when ~~you~~ *they* want to.

2. One problem facing students on this campus is that ~~a person doesn't~~ *they don't* know when the library will be open and when it will be closed.

3. One should rely on reason, not emotion, when ~~they are~~ *he or she is* forming opinions about such charged issues as abortion.

4. I have reached a time in my life when what others expect is less important than what ~~one~~ *I* really ~~wants~~ *want* to do.

5. Members of the orchestra should meet after the concert and bring ~~your~~ *their* instruments and music.

6. The wise mother knows that she is asking for trouble if ~~you let~~ *she lets* a small child watch violent television shows.

7. The student who participates in this program will spend six weeks in Spain and Morocco. ~~You~~ *He or she* will study the art and architecture firsthand, working closely with an instructor.

TEACHING TIP
If your students need to review pronoun agreement, refer them to Chapter 31 for more help and practice.

8. You shouldn't judge a person by the way ~~they dress~~.
   he or she dresses

9. If you have been working that hard, ~~one needs~~ a vacation.
   you need

10. People who visit the Caribbean for the first time are struck by the lushness of
    the landscape. The sheer size of the flowers and fruit amazes ~~you~~.
    them

PRACTICE 8

The following paragraph consistently uses third person singular—*the job appli-cant, the job seeker, he or she.* For practice in revising for consistency, rewrite the paragraph in **consistent third person plural.** Begin by changing *the job applicant* to *job applicants.* Then change verbs, nouns, and pronouns as necessary.

In a job interview these days, the job applicant should stress his or her personal skills, rather than only technical skills. This strategy could increase his or her chances of getting hired. The job seeker should point out such skills as speaking and writing confidently, working well on a team, solving problems quickly, or manag-ing people. These days, many employers assume that if an applicant has excellent "soft skills" like these, he or she can be trained in the technical fine points of the job.

In a job interview these days, job applicants should stress their personal skills,

rather than only technical skills. This strategy could increase their chances of getting

hired. Job seekers should point out such skills as speaking and writing confidently,

working well on a team, solving problems quickly, or managing people. These days,

many employers assume that if applicants have excellent "soft skills" like these,

they can be trained in the technical fine points of the job.

TEACHING TIP
To give students practice writing in third person, preferred in much college and professional writing, you might distribute paragraphs written in first or second person, and have students rewrite them in third person.

PRACTICE 9

Revise the following essay for inconsistencies of person and number. Correct any confusing shifts (changing words if necessary) to make the writing clear and *con-sistent* throughout.

Immortality In Wax

"Madame Tussaud's. Come and find out who's in. And who's out." That's

how English advertisers lure visitors to a most unusual show—a display of the

rich, the famous, and the infamous in the form of lifelike wax statues. Nearly

3 million people line up each year to rub shoulders with the images of historic

They

and contemporary celebrities. ~~You~~ make Madame Tussaud's the most popular paid tourist attraction in England.

their

Visitors can see and have ~~one's~~ photograph taken with more than 400 eerily lifelike statues of such people as Princess Di, Joan of Arc, Elvis Presley, Naomi Campbell, the Dalai Lama, and Britney Spears. The popular Chamber of Horrors displays the most notorious criminals of all time.

Recently two new Tussaud Museums have opened. In New York, tourists now can mingle with the likes of Whoopi Goldberg, Nicolas Cage, Martin Luther *they* King, Jr., and Buffalo Bill. In Las Vegas, ~~we~~ can pose with Muhammad Ali, Liberace, Gloria Estefan, Lenny Kravitz, and nearly 100 others.

Each month, a committee decides who is in and who is out of the collections. *his or her* A celebrity is chosen for ~~your~~ fame, recognizability, and publicity potential. *He or she is* ~~You are~~ invited to sit for moldings, a process that takes six months and costs $45,000. Mother Teresa was one of the few persons ever to decline an invitation from Madame Tussaud's.

PART C Parallelism

Parallelism, or **parallel structure,** is an effective way to add smoothness and power to your writing. **Parallelism** is a balance of two or more similar words, phrases, or clauses.

Compare the two versions of each of these sentences:

1. She likes dancing, swimming, and to box.
2. She likes *dancing, swimming,* and *boxing.*
3. The cable runs across the roof; the north wall is where it runs down.
4. The cable runs *across the roof* and *down the north wall.*
5. He admires people with strong convictions and who think for themselves.
6. He admires people *who have strong convictions* and *who think for themselves.*

Copyright © Houghton Mifflin Company. All rights reserved.

TEACHING TIP
Most students are completely unaware of the concept of parallelism. Explain that, once grasped and put to use, parallel structures add sophistication and grace to one's writing.

■ Sentences 2, 4, and 6 use **parallelism** to express parallel ideas.

■ In sentence 2, *dancing, swimming,* and *boxing* are parallel; all three are the *-ing* forms of verbs, used here as nouns.

■ In sentence 4, *across the roof* and *down the north wall* are parallel prepositional phrases, each consisting of a preposition and its object.

■ In sentence 6, *who have strong convictions* and *who think for themselves* are parallel clauses beginning with the word *who.*

Sometimes two entire sentences can be parallel:

TEACHING TIP
Remind students to be alert for parallelism errors in sentences that contain coordinating conjunctions, particularly *and, or, but,* and *nor.*

> In a democracy we are all equal before the law. In a dictatorship we are all equal before the police.
>
> —Millor Fernandes

■ In what way are these two sentences parallel? Both use the same format:

"In a ——— we are all equal before the ———."

Certain special constructions require parallel structure:

7. The fruit is *both* tasty *and* fresh.

8. He *either* loves you *or* hates you.

9. Yvette *not only* plays golf *but also* swims like a pro.

10. I would *rather* sing in the chorus *than* perform a solo.

ESL TIP
The regularity and predictability of parallel structures makes the concept fairly easy for ESL students to learn.

■ Each of these constructions has two parts:
  both . . . and
  (n)either . . . (n)or
  not only . . . but also
  rather . . . than

■ The words, phrases, or clauses following each part must be parallel:
  tasty . . . fresh
  loves you . . . hates you
  plays golf . . . swims like a pro
  sing in the chorus . . . perform a solo

PRACTICE 10

Rewrite each of the following sentences, using parallel structure to accent parallel ideas.

EXAMPLE The summer in Louisiana is very hot and has high humidity.

The summer in Louisiana is very hot and humid.

TEACHING TIP
Suggest that students read this chapter's examples and exercise items aloud so that they can better "hear" the parallel and nonparallel structures.

1. Teresa is a gifted woman—a chemist, does the carpentry, and she can cook.

   Teresa is a gifted woman—a chemist, a carpenter, and a cook.
   _____

2. The shape of the rock, how big it was, and its color reminded me of a small turtle.

   The rock's shape, size, and color reminded me of a small turtle.
   _____

3. He is an affectionate husband, a thoughtful son, and kind to his kids.

   He is an affectionate husband, a thoughtful son, and a kind father.
   _____

4. Marvin was happy to win the chess tournament and he also felt surprised.

   Marvin was happy and surprised to win the chess tournament.
   _____

TEACHING TIP
Point out to students that correcting parallelism errors often eradicates wordiness. Ask which version of sentence 5 is more concise—the original or the revised.

5. Dr. Tien is the kindest physician I know; she has the most concern of any physician I know.

   Dr. Tien is the kindest and most concerned physician I know.
   _____

6. Joe would rather work on a farm than spending time in an office.

   Joe would rather work on a farm than spend time in an office.
   _____

7. Every afternoon in the mountains, it either rains or there is hail.

   Every afternoon in the mountains, it either rains or hails.
   _____

8. *Sesame Street* teaches children nursery rhymes, songs, how to be courteous, and being kind.

   Sesame Street teaches children nursery rhymes, songs, courtesy, and kindness.
   _____

9. Alexis would rather give orders than taking them.

   Alexis would rather give orders than take them.
   _____

10. His writing reveals not only intelligence but also it is humorous.

His writing reveals not only intelligence but also humor.

PRACTICE 11

Write one sentence that is parallel to each sentence that follows, creating pairs of parallel sentences.   Answers will vary.

TEACHING TIP
Have students compare
their answers to Practice 11
and help each other
identify any inconsistent
structures.

EXAMPLE On Friday night, she dressed in silk and sipped champagne.

On Monday morning, she put on her jeans and crammed for a history test.

1. When he was twenty, he worked seven days a week in a fruit store.

   When he was forty, he worked four days a week as the owner of a chain of fruit stores.

2. The child in me wants to run away from problems.

   The adult in me knows I must face them.

3. The home team charged enthusiastically onto the field.

   The visiting team sat dejectedly in the dugout.

TEACHING TIP
Students are often intrigued
to learn that good orators—
and good writers—use
parallelism to help the
audience follow their ideas.
If you can, bring in Martin
Luther King's "I Have a
Dream" speech or Abraham
Lincoln's "Gettysburg
Address." Let students find
and analyze uses of
parallelism.

4. "Work hard and keep your mouth shut" is my mother's formula for success.

   "Nothing ventured, nothing gained" is mine.

5. The men thought the movie was amusing.

   The women thought it was insulting.

PRACTICE 12

The following paragraph contains both correct and faulty parallel structures. Revise the faulty parallelism.

During World War II, United States Marines who fought in the Pacific possessed a powerful weapon ~~that was also unbeatable~~ and unbeatable: Navajo Code Talkers. Creating a secret code, Code Talkers sent and ~~were translating~~ translated vital military information. Four hundred twenty Navajos memorized the code, ~~and it was used by them~~ and used. It consisted of both common Navajo words and ~~there were also~~ about 400 invented words. For example, Code Talkers used the Navajo words for *owl, chicken hawk,* and *swallow* to describe different kinds of aircraft. Because Navajo is a complex language ~~that is also uncommon~~ and uncommon, the Japanese military could not break the code. Although Code Talkers helped the Allied Forces win the war, their efforts were not publicly recognized until the code was declassified in 1968. On August 14, 1982, the first Navajo Code Talkers Day honored these heroes, who not only had risked their lives but also ~~been developing~~ had developed one of the few unbroken codes in history.

TEACHING TIP
Ask students to use a highlighter to mark parallel elements (words, phrases, and clauses) in a piece of their own writing.

PRACTICE 13

The following essay contains both correct and faulty parallel structures. Revise the faulty parallelism.

Vincent Van Gogh

Vincent Van Gogh sold only one painting in his lifetime, but his oil paintings later influenced modern art and ~~establishing~~ established him as one of the greatest artists of all time. Born in Holland in 1853, Van Gogh struggled to find an inspiring career. After failing as a tutor and ~~being~~ a clergyman, he began to paint. Van Gogh's younger brother Theo supported him with money and ~~also sending~~ art supplies. Eventually, Van Gogh went to live with Theo in Paris, where the young artist was introduced to Impressionism, a style of painting that emphasizes light at different times of day. Using vivid colors and ~~also with~~ broad brush strokes, Van Gogh made powerful pictures full of feeling. His favorite subjects were landscapes, still lifes, sunflowers, and ~~drawing~~ everyday people. Perhaps his most famous picture, *Starry Night*, shows a wild night sky over a French village, with the moon and stars swirling in fiery circles.

Starry Night, Vincent Van Gogh

    When mental illness or ~~feeling~~ depressed clouded Van Gogh's spirit, Theo gentle and firmly urged him to keep painting. Gradually, however, the penniless Van Gogh sank into insanity and ~~feeling~~ despair. *Wheatfield with Crows*, completed shortly before his death, shows a darkening sky spattered black with crows. Van Gogh committed suicide in 1890; his devoted brother died six months later. Theo's widow Johanna took the paintings back to Holland and ~~working~~ worked hard to get recognition for her brother-in-law's genius. Thanks to Theo's encouragement during Vincent's lifetime and ~~Johanna who made~~ Johanna's efforts after his death, the dynamic paintings of Van Gogh today are admired, studied, and ~~receive love~~ loved all over the world.

EXPLORING ONLINE

http://www.vangoghmuseum.nl Visit the Van Gogh Museum in the Netherlands and explore. Take notes on your experience.

http://www.vangoghgallery.com/ Find *Wheatfield with Crows*. Do you see any details in the painting that would suggest it was made just before the artist committed suicide?

EXPLORING ONLINE

http://grammar.ccc.commnet.edu/grammar/consistency.htm Review consistency with examples, "repairs," and self tests.

http://grammar.ccc.commnet.edu/grammar/parallelism.htm Write more stylishly with parallel words and phrases.

Online Study Center **college.hmco.com/pic/evergreen8e**
Visit the Online Study Center for *Evergreen* for more exercises and quizzes.

21

Revising for Sentence Variety

TEACHING TIP
Tell students that mixing different sentence types and lengths has two important effects:
1. Sentence variety adds sophistication to one's writing.
2. Sentence variety makes writing more interesting to read, thus engaging readers and improving their comprehension.

Good writers pay attention to **sentence variety.** They notice how sentences work together within a paragraph, and they seek a mix of different sentence lengths and types. Experienced writers have a variety of sentence patterns from which to choose. They try not to overuse one pattern.

This chapter will present several techniques for varying your sentences and paragraphs. Some of them you may already know and use, perhaps unconsciously. The purpose of this chapter is to make you more conscious of the **choices** available to you as a writer.

Remember, you achieve sentence variety by practicing, by systematically **revising** your papers, and by trying out new types of sentences or combinations of sentences.

PART A Mix Long and Short Sentences

One of the basic ways to achieve sentence variety is to use both long and short sentences. Beginning writers tend to overuse short, simple sentences, which quickly become monotonous. Notice the length of the sentences in the following paragraph:

294

(1) There is one positive result of the rising crime rate. (2) This has been the growth of neighborhood crime prevention programs. (3) These programs really work. (4) They teach citizens to patrol their neighborhoods. (5) They teach citizens to work with the police. (6) They have dramatically reduced crime in cities and towns across the country. (7) The idea is catching on.

The sentences in the paragraph above are all nearly the same length, and the effect is choppy and almost childish. Now read this revised version, which contains a variety of sentence lengths:

(1) One cause of the falling crime rate in some cities is the growth of neighborhood crime prevention programs. (2) These programs really work. (3) By patrolling their neighborhoods and working with the police, citizens have shown that they can dramatically reduce crime. (4) The idea is catching on.

This paragraph is more effective because it mixes two short sentences, 2 and 4, and two longer sentences, 1 and 3. Although short sentences can be used effectively anywhere in a paragraph or an essay, they can be especially useful as introductions or conclusions, like sentence 4 above. Note the powerful effect of short sentences used between longer ones in the paragraph that follows. Underline the short sentences:

(1) Biting into a tabasco pepper is like aiming a flame-thrower at your parted lips. (2) There might be little reaction at first, but then the burn starts to grow. (3) A few seconds later the chili mush in your mouth reaches critical mass and your palate prepares for liftoff. (4) <u>The message spreads.</u> (5) The sweat glands open, your eyes stream, your nose runs, your stomach warms up, your heart accelerates, and your lungs breathe faster. (6) <u>All this is normal.</u> (7) But bite off more than your body can take, and you will be left coughing, sneezing, and spitting. (8) Tears stripe your cheeks, and your mouth belches like a dragon celebrating its return to life. (9) <u>Eater beware!</u>

—Jeremy MacClancy, *Consuming Culture: Why You Eat What You Eat*

PRACTICE 1

Revise and rewrite the following paragraph in a variety of sentence lengths. Recombine sentences in any way you wish. You may add connecting words or drop words, but do not alter the meaning of the paragraph. Compare your work with a fellow student's.   Answers will vary.

The park is alive with motion today. Joggers pound up and down the boardwalk. Old folks watch them from the benches. Couples row boats across the lake. The boats are green and wooden. Two teenagers hurl a Frisbee back and forth. They yell and leap. A shaggy white dog dashes in from nowhere. He snatches the red disk in his mouth. He bounds away. The teenagers run after him.

The park is alive with motion today. Joggers pound up and down on the
boardwalk, and old folks watch them from the benches. Couples row green wooden
boats across the lake. On the nearby grass, two teenagers hurl a Frisbee back and
forth, yelling and leaping. Suddenly, a shaggy white dog dashes in from nowhere,
snatches the red disk in his mouth, and bounds away. The teenagers run after him.

PART B   Use a Question, a Command, or an Exclamation

The most commonly used sentence is the **declarative sentence,** which is a statement. However, an occasional carefully placed **question, command,** or **exclamation** is an effective way to achieve sentence variety.

The Question

> *Why did I become a cab driver?* First, I truly enjoy driving a car and exploring different parts of the city, the classy avenues and the hidden back streets. In addition, I like meeting all kinds of people, from bookmakers to governors, each with a unique story and many willing to talk to the back of my head. Of course, the pay isn't bad and the hours are flexible, but it's the places and the people that I love.

This paragraph begins with a question. The writer does not really expect the reader to answer it. Rather, it is a **rhetorical question,** one that will be answered by the writer in the course of the paragraph. A rhetorical question used as a topic sentence can provide a colorful change from the usual declarative sentences: *Is America really the best-fed nation in the world? What is courage? Why do more young people take drugs today than ever before?*

The Command and the Exclamation

> (1) Try to imagine using failure as a description of an animal's behavior. (2) Consider a dog barking for fifteen minutes, and someone saying, "He really isn't very good at barking, I'd give him a C." (3) How absurd! (4) It is impossible for an animal to fail because there is no provision for evaluating natural behavior. (5) Spiders construct webs, not successful or unsuccessful webs. (6) Cats hunt mice; if they aren't successful in one attempt, they simply go after another. (7) They don't lie there and whine, complaining about the one that got away, or have a nervous breakdown because they failed. (8) Natural behavior simply is! (9) So apply the same logic to your own behavior and rid yourself of the fear of failure.
>
> —Dr. Wayne W. Dyer, *Your Erroneous Zones*

The previous paragraph begins and ends with **commands, or imperative sentences.** Sentences 1, 2, and 9 address the reader directly and have as their implied subject *you.* They tell the reader to do something: *(You) try to imagine . . . , (you) consider . . . , (you) apply. . . .* Commands are most frequently used in giving directions,* but they can be used occasionally, as in the previous paragraph, for sentence variety.

Sentences 3 and 8 in the Dyer paragraph are **exclamations,** sentences that express strong emotion and end with an exclamation point. These should be used very sparingly. In fact, some writers avoid them altogether, striving for words that convey strong emotion instead.

Be careful with the question, the command, and the exclamation as options in your writing. Try them out, but use them—especially the exclamation—sparingly.

WRITING ASSIGNMENT 1

Write a paragraph that begins with a rhetorical question. Choose one of the questions below or compose your own. Be sure that the body of the paragraph really does answer the question.

1. How has college (or anything else) changed me?

2. Should people pamper their pets?

3. Is marriage worth the risks?

PART C   Vary the Beginnings of Sentences

Begin with an Adverb

Since the first word of many sentences is the subject, one way to achieve sentence variety is by occasionally starting a sentence with a word or words other than the subject.

For instance, you can begin with an **adverb:**†

1. He *laboriously* dragged the large crate up the stairs.

2. *Laboriously*, he dragged the large crate up the stairs.

3. The contents of the beaker *suddenly* began to foam.

4. *Suddenly*, the contents of the beaker began to foam.

■ In sentences 2 and 4, the adverbs *laboriously* and *suddenly* are shifted to the first position. Notice the difference in rhythm that this creates, as well as the slight change in meaning: Sentence 2 emphasizes *how* he dragged the crate—*laboriously;* sentence 4 emphasizes the *suddenness* of what happened.

---

*For more work on giving directions, see Chapter 8, "Process."

†For more work on adverbs, see Chapter 33, "Adjectives and Adverbs."

> ▪ A comma usually follows an adverb that introduces a sentence; however, adverbs of time—*often, now, always*—do not always require a comma. As a general rule, use a comma if you want the reader to pause briefly.

PRACTICE 2

Rewrite the following sentences by shifting the adverbs to the beginning. Punctuate correctly.

EXAMPLE   He skillfully prepared the engine for the race.

Skillfully, he prepared the engine for the race.

1. Two deer moved silently across the clearing.

   Silently, two deer moved across the clearing.

2. The chief of the research division occasionally visits the lab.

   Occasionally, the chief of the research division visits the lab.

3. Proofread your writing always.

   Always proofread your writing.

4. Children of alcoholics often marry alcoholics.

   Often children of alcoholics marry alcoholics.

5. Jake foolishly lied to his supervisor.

   Foolishly, Jake lied to his supervisor.

PRACTICE 3

Begin each of the following sentences with an appropriate adverb. Punctuate correctly.   Answers may vary.

1. _____Cautiously,_____ the detective approached the ticking suitcase.

2. _____Enthusiastically,_____ Maria Sharapova powered a forehand past her opponent.

3. _____Yesterday_____ she received her check for $25,000 from the state lottery.

4. _____Reluctantly,_____ he left the beach.

5. _____Slowly,_____ the submarine sank out of sight.

PRACTICE 4

Write three sentences of your own that begin with adverbs. Use different adverbs from those in Practices 2 and 3; if you wish, use *graciously, furiously, sometimes.* Punctuate correctly.   Sample answers:

1. Graciously, Rosa offered us use of her vacation home.

2. Furiously, she slammed the door.

3. Sometimes I go for long walks on the beach.

Begin with a Prepositional Phrase

A **prepositional phrase** is a group of words containing a **preposition** and its **object** (a noun or pronoun). *To you, in the evening,* and *under the old bridge* are prepositional phrases.*

Preposition	Object
to	you
in	the evening
under	the old bridge

Here is a partial list of prepositions:

Common Prepositions			
about	beneath	into	throughout
above	beside	near	to
across	between	of	toward
against	by	on	under
among	except	onto	up
at	for	out	upon
behind	from	over	with
below	in	through	without

For variety in your writing, begin an occasional sentence with a prepositional phrase:

5. Charles left the room *without a word.*

6. *Without a word,* Charles left the room.

7. A fat yellow cat lay sleeping *on the narrow sill.*

8. *On the narrow sill,* a fat yellow cat lay sleeping.

* For work on spotting prepositional phrases, see Chapter 32, "Prepositions."

ESL TIP
English prepositions are particularly confusing for ESL students. If they need additional help and exercises, refer them to the *ESL Guidelines* at the end of the book and to ESL help on the *Evergreen* Online Study Center.

TEACHING TIP
Does word order affect meaning? Ask students whether placing an adverb or prepositional phrase first instead of last in a sentence changes the emphasis. (Words in first position often receive the greatest emphasis.)

▪ In sentences 6 and 8, the prepositional phrases have been shifted to the beginning. Note the slight shift in emphasis that results. Sentence 6 stresses that Charles left the room *without a word,* and 8 stresses the location of the cat, *on the narrow sill.*

▪ Prepositional phrases that begin sentences are usually followed by commas. However, short prepositional phrases need not be.

Prepositional phrases are not always movable; rely on the meaning of the sentence to determine whether they are movable:

> 9. The dress *in the picture* is the one I want.
>
> 10. Joelle bought a bottle *of white wine for dinner.*

▪ *In the picture* in sentence 9 is a part of the subject and cannot be moved. *In the picture the dress is the one I want* makes no sense.

▪ Sentence 10 has two prepositional phrases. Which one *cannot* be moved to the beginning of the sentence? Why?

"Of white wine" cannot be moved because it describes the word *bottle* and

should therefore follow it.

PRACTICE 5

Underline the prepositional phrases in each sentence. Some sentences contain more than one prepositional phrase. Rewrite each sentence by shifting a prepositional phrase to the beginning. Punctuate correctly.

EXAMPLE   A large owl <u>with gray feathers</u> watched us <u>from the oak tree.</u>

From the oak tree, a large owl with gray feathers watched us.

1. The coffee maker turned itself on <u>at seven o'clock sharp.</u>

At seven o'clock sharp, the coffee maker turned itself on.

2. A growling Doberman paced <u>behind the chainlink fence.</u>

Behind the chainlink fence, a growling Doberman paced.

3. A man and a woman held hands <u>under the street lamp.</u>

Under the street lamp, a man and a woman held hands.

4. They have sold nothing <u>except athletic shoes for years.</u>

For years, they have sold nothing except athletic shoes.

5. A group <u>of men</u> played checkers and drank iced tea <u>beside the small shop.</u>

Beside the small shop, a group of men played checkers and drank iced tea.

PRACTICE 6

Begin each of the following sentences with a different prepositional phrase. Refer to the list and be creative. Punctuate correctly.   Answers will vary.

TEACHING TIP
Have students examine a piece of their own writing for adverbs or prepositional phrases that could be shifted to the beginnings of sentences.

1. From the à la carte menu, we ordered potato skins, salad, and beer.

2. _____At the far table,_____ a woman in horn-rimmed glasses balanced her check-book.

3. _____After work,_____ everyone congratulated Jim on his promotion.

4. _____In the museum,_____ one can see huge sculptures in wood, metal, and stone.

5. _____Over our heads,_____ three large helium-filled balloons drifted.

PRACTICE 7

Write three sentences of your own that begin with prepositional phrases. Use these phrases if you wish: *in the dentist's office, under that stack of books, behind his friendly smile.* Punctuate correctly.   Answers will vary.

1. In the dentist's office, the patients waited nervously.

2. Under that stack of books, you'll find the grocery list.

3. Behind his friendly smile, he is a dishonest salesman.

PART D Vary Methods of Joining Ideas*

Join Ideas with a Compound Predicate

A sentence with a **compound predicate** contains more than one verb, but the subject is *not* repeated before the second verb. Such a sentence is really composed of two simple sentences with the same subject:

---

* For work on joining ideas with coordination and subordination, see Chapter 25, "Coordination and Subordination."

TEACHING TIP
Sentence-combining exercises like these expose students to variant structures and underscore the choices that good writers make as they write. Tell your students that the combining techniques in this section will add style and concisesness to their writing.

1. The nurse entered.

2. The nurse quickly closed the door.

3. The nurse *entered* and quickly *closed* the door.

▪ *The nurse* is the subject of sentence 1, and *entered* is the verb; *the nurse* is also the subject of sentence 2, and *closed* is the verb.

▪ When these sentences are combined with a compound predicate in sentence 3, *the nurse* is the subject of both *entered* and *closed* but is not repeated before the second verb.

▪ No comma is necessary when the conjunctions *and, but, or,* and *yet* join the verbs in a compound predicate.

A compound predicate is useful in combining short, choppy sentences:

4. He serves elaborate meals.

5. He never uses a recipe.

6. He serves elaborate meals yet never uses a recipe.

7. Aviators rarely get nosebleeds.

8. They often suffer from backaches.

9. Aviators rarely get nosebleeds but often suffer from backaches.

▪ Sentences 4 and 5 are joined by *yet*; no comma precedes *yet*.

▪ Sentences 7 and 8 are joined by *but*; no comma precedes *but*.

PRACTICE 8

Combine each pair of short sentences into one sentence with a compound predicate. Use *and, but, or,* and *yet*. Punctuate correctly.   Answers will vary.

EXAMPLE   Toby smeared peanut butter on a thick slice of white bread. He devoured the treat in thirty seconds.

Toby smeared peanut butter on a thick slice of white bread and devoured the

treat in thirty seconds.

ESL TIP
ESL students may overuse *and*. Illustrate the appropriate use of this connector.

1. Americans eat more than 800 million pounds of peanut butter. They spend more than $1 billion on the product each year.

Americans eat more than 800 million pounds of peanut butter and spend more

than $1 billion on the product each year.

2. Peanut butter was first concocted in the 1890s.
   It did not become the food we know for thirty years.

   Peanut butter was first concocted in the 1890s but did not become the food we

   know for thirty years.

3. George Washington Carver did not discover peanut butter.
   He published many recipes for pastes much like it.

   George Washington Carver did not discover peanut butter yet published many

   recipes for pastes much like it.

4. The average American becomes a peanut butter lover in childhood.
   He or she loses enthusiasm for it later on.

   The average American becomes a peanut butter lover in childhood but loses

   enthusiasm for it later on.

5. Older adults regain their passion for peanut butter.
   They consume great quantities of the delicious stuff.

   Older adults regain their passion for peanut butter and consume great

   quantities of the delicious stuff.

PRACTICE 9

Complete the following compound predicates. Do *not* repeat the subjects.   Answers
will vary.

1. Three Korean writers visited the campus and met with aspiring novelists.

   _____.

2. The singer breathed heavily into the microphone but didn't sing a note.

   _____

3. Take these cans to the recycling center or move to a hotel.

   _____

4. The newspaper printed the story yet didn't check the facts first.

   _____

5. Three men burst into the back room and threw confetti on the surprised

   card players.

PRACTICE 10

Write three sentences with compound predicates. Be careful to punctuate correctly.

Sample answers:

1. Many people like to cook but do not like to clean up.

2. We could see a movie or go out to dinner.

3. Renée can drive a car but has never parallel parked.

Join Ideas with an *-ing* Modifier

An excellent way to achieve sentence variety is by occasionally combining two sentences with an *-ing* **modifier.**

> 10. He peered through the microscope.
>
> 11. He discovered a squiggly creature.
>
> 12. *Peering through the microscope*, he discovered a squiggly creature.

▪ Sentence 10 has been converted to an *-ing* modifier by changing the verb *peered* to *peering* and dropping the subject *he. Peering through the microscope* now introduces the main clause, *he discovered a squiggly creature.*

▪ A comma sets off the *-ing* modifier from the word it refers to, *he.* To avoid confusion, the word referred to must appear in the immediately following clause.

An *-ing* modifier indicates that two actions are occurring at the same time. The main idea of the sentence should be contained in the main clause, not in the *-ing* modifier. In the preceding example, the discovery of the creature is the main idea, not the fact that someone peered through a microscope.

Be careful; misplaced *-ing* modifiers can result in confusing sentences: *He discovered a squiggly creature peering through the microscope.* (Was the creature looking through the microscope?)*

Convert sentence 13 into an *-ing* modifier and write it in the blank:

> 13. We drove down Tompkins Road.
>
> 14. We were surprised by the number of "for sale" signs.
>
> 15. Driving down Tompkins Road _____, we were surprised by the number of "for sale" signs.

▪ The new *-ing* modifier is followed directly by the word to which it refers, *we.*

TEACHING TIP

Misplaced and dangling modifiers are discussed more thoroughly in Part E of this chapter.

* For more work on avoiding confusing modifiers, see Part E of this chapter.

PRACTICE 11

Combine the following pairs of sentences by converting the first sentence into an *-ing* modifier. Make sure the subject of the main clause directly follows the *-ing* modifier. Punctuate correctly.

EXAMPLE Jake searched for his needle-nose pliers.
He completely emptied the tool chest.

Searching for his needle-nose pliers, Jake completely emptied the tool chest.

1. She installed the air conditioner.
She saved herself $50 in labor.

   Installing the air conditioner, she saved herself $50 in labor.

2. The surgeons raced against time.
The surgeons performed a liver transplant on the child.

   Racing against time, the surgeons performed a liver transplant on the child.

3. They conducted a survey of Jackson Heights residents.
They found that most opposed construction of the airport.

   Conducting a survey of Jackson Heights residents, they found that most

   opposed construction of the airport.

4. Three flares spiraled upward from the little boat.
They exploded against the night sky.

   Spiraling up from the little boat, three flares exploded against the night sky.

5. Virgil danced in the Pennsylvania Ballet.
Virgil learned discipline and self-control.

   Dancing in the Pennsylvania Ballet, Virgil learned discipline and self-control.

6. The hen squawked loudly.
The hen fluttered out of our path.

   Squawking loudly, the hen fluttered out of our path.

7. The engineer made a routine check of the blueprints.
   He discovered a flaw in the design.

   Making a routine check of the blueprints, the engineer discovered a flaw in the

   design.

8. Dr. Jackson opened commencement exercises with a humorous story.
   He put everyone at ease.

   Opening commencement exercises with a humorous story, Dr. Jackson put

   everyone at ease.

PRACTICE 12

Add either an introductory *-ing* modifier *or* a main clause to each sentence. Make sure that each *-ing* modifier refers clearly to the subject of the main clause.

Answers will vary.

EXAMPLE Reading a book a week _____ Jeff increased his vocabulary.

Exercising every day, I lost five pounds _____.

1. Finally finishing her report _____, she felt a sense of accomplishment.

2. Growing up in Hollywood, he was not dazzled by movie stars. _____.

3. Talking over their differences at last _____, the father and son were reconciled.

4. Interviewing his relatives, Jason collected many family stories. _____.

5. Moving slowly on its long chain _____, the wrecking ball swung through the air and smashed into the brick wall.

PRACTICE 13

Write three sentences of your own that begin with *-ing* modifiers. Make sure that the subject of the sentence follows the modifier and be careful of the punctuation.

Answers will vary.

1. Giving myself a pep talk, I sat down to study Japanese.

2. Practicing with her roommate's manual, Ellen finally learned to use PowerPoint.

3. Rummaging through his drawers, Joe found a stack of unpaid bills.

_____

Join Ideas with a Past Participial Modifier

Some sentences can be joined with a **past participial modifier.** A sentence that contains a *to be* verb and a **past participle*** can be changed into a past participial modifier:

ESL TIP
The use of participles as adjectives is often troublesome for ESL students. This concept might have to be reviewed throughout the term.

16. Judith *is trapped* in a dead-end job.

17. Judith decided to enroll at the local community college.

18. *Trapped in a dead-end job,* Judith decided to enroll at the local community college.

TEACHING TIP
For a review of past participle formation, see Chapter 29.

■ In sentence 18, sentence 16 has been made into a past participial modifier by dropping the helping verb *is* and the subject *Judith.* The past participle *trapped* now introduces the new sentence.

■ A comma sets off the past participial modifier from the word it modifies, *Judith.* To avoid confusion, the word referred to must directly follow the modifier.

Be careful; misplaced past participial modifiers can result in confusing sentences: *Packed in dry ice, Steve brought us some ice cream.* (Was Steve packed in dry ice?)†

Sometimes two or more past participles can be used to introduce a sentence:

TEACHING TIP
Misplaced and dangling modifiers are discussed more thoroughly in Part E of this chapter.

19. The term paper *was revised* and *rewritten.*

20. It received an A.

21. *Revised and rewritten,* the term paper received an A.

■ The past participles *revised* and *rewritten* become a modifier that introduces sentence 21. What word(s) do they refer to?

the term paper _____

PRACTICE 14

Combine each pair of sentences into one sentence that begins with a past participial modifier. Convert the sentence containing a form of *to be* plus a past participle into a past participial modifier that introduces the new sentence.

EXAMPLE   Duffy was surprised by the interruption.
    He lost his train of thought.

Surprised by the interruption, Duffy lost his train of thought.

_____

* For more work on past participles, see Chapter 29, "The Past Participle."

† For more work on avoiding confusing modifiers, see Part E of this chapter.

1. My mother was married at the age of sixteen.
   My mother never finished high school.

   Married at the age of sixteen, my mother never finished high school.

2. The 2:30 flight was delayed by an electrical storm.
   It arrived in Lexington three hours late.

   Delayed by an electrical storm, the 2:30 flight arrived in Lexington three

   hours late.

3. The old car was waxed and polished.
   It shone in the sun.

   Waxed and polished, the old car shone in the sun.

4. The house was built by Frank Lloyd Wright.
   It has become famous.

   Built by Frank Lloyd Wright, the house has become famous.

5. The Nineteenth Amendment was ratified in 1920.
   It gave women the right to vote.

   Ratified in 1920, the Nineteenth Amendment gave women the right to vote.

6. The manuscript seems impossible to decipher.
   It is written in code.

   Written in code, the manuscript seems impossible to decipher.

7. Dr. Bentley will address the premed students.
   He has been recognized for his contributions in the field of immunology.

   Recognized for his contributions in the field of immunology, Dr. Bentley will

   address the premed students.

8. Mrs. Witherspoon was exhausted by night classes.
   She declined the chance to work overtime.

   Exhausted by night classes, Mrs. Witherspoon declined the chance to

   work overtime.

PRACTICE 15

Complete each sentence by filling in *either* the past participial modifier *or* the main clause. Remember, the past participial modifier must clearly refer to the subject of the main clause.   Answers will vary.

EXAMPLE   Wrapped in blue paper and tied with string, <u>the gift arrived</u>.

Chosen to represent the team , Phil proudly accepted the trophy.

ESL TIP
It is beneficial for ESL students to recognize sentences joined by participles even if they cannot yet produce them.

1. Made of gold and set with precious stones, <u>the snuffbox was a wonder</u>
   <u>to behold.</u>

2. Overwhelmed by the response to her ad in *The Star,* <u>Marietta limited</u>
   <u>the number of people she would interview to ten.</u>

3. <u>Tired of junk mail</u>, Tom left no
   forwarding address.

4. <u>Laden with parcels from a shopping trip</u>, we found a
   huge basket of fresh fruit on the steps.

5. Astonished by the scene before her, <u>Consuela reached for the telephone</u>
   <u>and dialed 911.</u>

PRACTICE 16

Write three sentences of your own that begin with past participial modifiers. If you wish, use participles from this list:

shocked	dressed	hidden	bent
awakened	lost	stuffed	rewired

Make sure that the subject of the sentence clearly follows the modifier.
Sample answers:

1. <u>Awakened by the fire alarm, the hotel guests rushed outside.</u>

2. <u>Dressed in her ballet costume, the little girl performed for her parents.</u>

3. <u>Lost for several hours, the hikers were cold and tired when they were rescued.</u>

Join Ideas with an Appositive

A fine way to add variety to your writing is to combine two choppy sentences with an appositive. An **appositive** is a word or group of words that renames or describes a noun or pronoun:

> 22. Carlos is the new wrestling champion.
> 23. He is a native of Argentina.
> 24. Carlos, *a native of Argentina*, is the new wrestling champion.

- ▪ *A native of Argentina* in sentence 24 is an appositive. It renames the noun *Carlos*.

- ▪ An appositive must be placed either directly *after* the word it refers to, as in sentence 24, or directly *before* it, as follows:

> 25. *A native of Argentina,* Carlos is the new wrestling champion.

- ▪ Note that an appositive is set off by commas.

Appositives can add versatility to your writing because they can be placed at the beginning, in the middle, or at the end of a sentence. When you join two ideas with an appositive, place the idea you wish to stress in the main clause and make the less important idea the appositive:

> 26. Naomi wants to become a fashion model.
> 27. She is the daughter of an actress.
> 28. *The daughter of an actress,* Naomi wants to become a fashion model.
>
> 29. FACT made headlines for the first time only a few years ago.
> 30. FACT is now a powerful consumer group.
> 31. FACT, *now a powerful consumer group,* made headlines for the first time only a few years ago.
>
> 32. Watch out for Smithers.
> 33. He is a dangerous man.
> 34. Watch out for Smithers, *a dangerous man.*

Using an appositive to combine sentences eliminates unimportant words and creates longer, more fact-filled sentences.

PRACTICE 17

Combine the following pairs of sentences by making the *second sentence* an appositive. Punctuate correctly.

These appositives should occur at the *beginning* of the sentences.

TEACHING TIP
As students work on Practice 17, they may try to turn one of the sentences in each pair into a relative clause. If so, review the difference between relative clauses and appositives. A discussion of relative clauses begins on page 312.

EXAMPLE My uncle taught me to use watercolors.
He is a well-known artist.

A well-known artist, my uncle taught me to use watercolors.

1. Dan has saved many lives.
He is a dedicated firefighter.

A dedicated firefighter, Dan has saved many lives.

2. Acupuncture is becoming popular in the United States.
It is an ancient Chinese healing system.

An ancient Chinese healing system, acupuncture is becoming popular in the United States.

3. The Cromwell Hotel was built in 1806.
It is an elegant example of Mexican architecture.

An elegant example of Mexican architecture, the Cromwell Hotel was built in 1806.

These appositives should occur in the *middle* of the sentences. Punctuate correctly.

EXAMPLE His American history course is always popular with students.
It is an introductory survey.

His American history course, an introductory survey, is always popular with students.

4. The Korean Ping-Pong champion won ten games in a row.
She is a small and wiry athlete.

The Korean Ping-Pong champion, a small and wiry athlete, won ten games in a row.

5. The pituitary is located below the brain.
It is the body's master gland.

The pituitary, the body's master gland, is located below the brain.

6. The elevator shudders violently and begins to rise.
It is an ancient box of wood and hope.

The elevator, an ancient box of wood and hope, shudders violently and begins to rise.

These appositives should occur at the *end* of the sentences. Punctuate correctly.

EXAMPLE I hate fried asparagus.
It is a vile dish.

I hate fried asparagus, a vile dish.

7. Jennifer flaunted her new camera.
It was a Nikon with a telephoto lens.

Jennifer flaunted her new camera, a Nikon with a telephoto lens.

8. At the intersection stood a hitchhiker.
He was a young man dressed in a tuxedo.

At the intersection stood a hitchhiker, a young man dressed in a tuxedo.

9. We met for pancakes at the Cosmic Cafe.
It was a greasy diner on the corner of 10th and Vine.

We met for pancakes at the Cosmic Cafe, a greasy diner at the corner of 10th

and Vine.

PRACTICE 18

Write three sentences using appositives. In one sentence, place the appositive at the *beginning*; in one sentence, place the appositive in the *middle*; and in one sentence, place it at the *end*. Sample answers:

1. An avid sailor, my brother-in-law dreams of owning a thirty-foot sailboat.

2. We serve vichyssoise, a cold potato soup, on hot summer days.

3. The tall woman standing on the dock is Isabel, my mother's neighbor.

Join Ideas with a Relative Clause

Relative clauses can add sophistication to your writing. A **relative clause** begins with *who, which,* or *that* and describes a noun or pronoun. It can join two simple sentences in a longer, more complex sentence:

ESL TIP
ESL students face formidable challenges with relative clauses. In English and most European languages, the relative clause *follows* the noun being modified, but in several languages (e.g., Japanese, Chinese, and Korean), the relative clause *precedes* the noun being modified.

35. Jack just won a scholarship from the Arts Council.

36. He makes wire sculpture.

37. Jack, *who makes wire sculpture*, just won a scholarship from the Arts Council.

▪ In sentence 37, *who makes wire sculpture* is a relative clause, created by replacing the subject *he* of sentence 36 with the relative pronoun *who.*

▪ *Who* now introduces the subordinate relative clause and connects it to the rest of the sentence. Note that *who* directly follows the word it refers to, *Jack.*

The idea that the writer wishes to stress is placed in the main clause, and the subordinate idea is placed in the relative clause. Study the combinations in sentences 38 through 40 and 41 through 43.

TEACHING TIP
Students will need to memorize that the pronoun *that* is not used with a comma and the pronoun *which* is.

38. Carrots grow in cool climates.

39. They are high in vitamin A.

40. Carrots, *which* are high in vitamin A, grow in cool climates.

41. He finally submitted the term paper.

42. It was due six months ago.

43. He finally submitted the term paper *that* was due six months ago.

▪ In sentence 40, *which are high in vitamin A* is a relative clause, created by replacing *they* with *which.* Which word in sentence 40 does *which* refer to?

carrots

▪ What is the relative clause in sentence 43?

that was due six months ago

▪ Which word does *that* refer to?

term paper

Punctuating relative clauses can be tricky; therefore, you will have to be careful:*

ESL TIP
For ESL students and visual learners, color coding can help show how relative clauses can be embedded in the main sentence or independent clause.

44. Claude, *who grew up in Haiti,* speaks fluent French.

▪ *Who grew up in Haiti* is set off by commas because it adds information about Claude that is not essential to the meaning of the sentence. In other words, the sentence would make sense without it: *Claude speaks fluent French.*

* For more practice in punctuating relative clauses, see Chapter 35, "The Comma," Part D.

TEACHING TIP
A caution for students: improper punctuation of relative pronoun clauses can create fragments, and wrong placement can create dangling or misplaced modifiers.

ESL TIP
Spanish does not distinguish between personal *(who)* and impersonal *(which, that)* pronouns. Furthermore, a relative pronoun cannot be omitted in Spanish, as it has been in the sentence *The girls we saw looked so happy.*

■ *Who grew up in Haiti* is called a **nonrestrictive clause.** It does not restrict or provide vital information about the word it modifies.

> 45. People *who crackle paper in theaters* annoy me.

■ *Who crackle paper in theaters* is not set off by commas because it is vital to the meaning of the sentence. Without it, the sentence would read, *People annoy me;* yet the point of the sentence is that people *who crackle paper in theaters* annoy me, not all people.

■ *Who crackle paper in theaters* is called a **restrictive clause** because it restricts the meaning of the word it refers to, *people.*

Note that *which* usually begins a nonrestrictive clause and *that* usually begins a restrictive clause.

PRACTICE 19

Combine each pair of sentences by changing the second sentence into a relative clause introduced by *who, which,* or *that.* Remember, *who* refers to persons, *that* refers to persons or things, and *which* refers to things.

These sentences require **nonrestrictive relative clauses.** Punctuate correctly.

EXAMPLE   My cousin will spend the summer hiking in the Rockies.
She lives in Indiana.

My cousin, who lives in Indiana, will spend the summer hiking in the Rockies.

1. Scrabble has greatly increased my vocabulary.
It is my favorite game.

Scrabble, which is my favorite game, has greatly increased my vocabulary.

2. Contestants on game shows often make fools of themselves.
They may travel thousands of miles to play.

Contestants on game shows, who may travel thousands of miles to play, often

make fools of themselves.

3. Arabic is a difficult language to learn.
It has a complicated verb system.

Arabic, which has a complicated verb system, is a difficult language to learn.

The next sentences require **restrictive relative clauses.** Punctuate correctly.

EXAMPLE   He described a state of mind.
I have experienced it.

He described a state of mind that I have experienced.

4. The house is for sale.
I was born in it.

The house that I was born in is for sale.

5. My boss likes reports.
They are clear and to the point.

My boss likes reports that are clear and to the point.

6. People know how intelligent birds are.
They have owned a bird.

People who have owned a bird know how intelligent birds are.

PRACTICE 20

Combine each pair of sentences by changing one into a relative clause introduced by *who*, *which*, or *that*. Remember, *who* refers to persons, *that* refers to persons or things, and *which* refers to things.

Be careful of the punctuation. (Hint: *Which* clauses are usually set off by commas and *that* clauses are usually not.)

1. Her grandfather enjoys scuba diving.
He is seventy-seven years old.

Her grandfather, who is seventy-seven years old, enjoys scuba diving.

2. You just dropped an antique pitcher.
It was worth two thousand dollars.

You just dropped an antique pitcher that was worth two thousand dollars.

3. Parenthood has taught me acceptance, forgiveness, and love.
It used to terrify me.

Parenthood, which used to terrify me, has taught me acceptance, forgiveness,

and love.

4. James Fenimore Cooper was expelled from college.
   He later became a famous American novelist.

   James Fenimore Cooper, who was expelled from college, later became a famous

   American novelist.

5. The verb *to hector* means "to bully someone."
   It derives from a character in Greek literature.

   The verb *to hector,* which derives from a character in Greek literature, means

   "to bully someone."

PART E Avoid Misplaced and Confusing Modifiers

ESL TIP
ESL learners may be more likely to misplace phrases and clauses because of differences in word order between English and their native languages. These errors often occur more frequently when students think in their native language and then try to translate a thought into English.

As you practice varying your sentences, be sure that your modifiers say what you mean! Revise your work to avoid **misplaced, confusing,** or **dangling modifiers.**

> 1. Perching on a scarecrow in the cornfield, the farmer saw a large crow.

■ Probably the writer did not mean that the farmer was perching on a scarecrow. Who or what, then, was *perching on a scarecrow in the cornfield*?

■ *Perching* refers to the *crow,* of course, but the order of the sentence does not show this. This misplaced modifier can be corrected by turning the ideas around:

> The farmer saw a large crow perching on a scarecrow in the cornfield.

Do these sentences say what they mean? Are the modifiers misplaced or correct?

TEACHING TIP
Ask students to explain the errors in these sentences. Ask, for example, "Who or what was covered with whipped cream?"

> 2. Covered with whipped cream, Tyrone carried a chocolate cake.
> 3. I sold the tin soldiers to an antique dealer that I found in the basement.
> 4. A homeless teenager, the nun helped the girl find a place to live.

■ In sentence 2, does the past participial modifier *covered with whipped cream* refer to Tyrone or the cake? Rewrite the sentence so that the modifier is placed correctly:

Tyrone carried a chocolate cake covered with whipped cream.

■ In sentence 3, who or what does the relative clause *that I found in the basement* refer to? Rewrite the sentence so that the modifier is placed correctly:

I sold the tin soldiers that I found in the basement to an antique dealer.

■ In sentence 4, the misplaced appositive totally changes the meaning of the sentence. What did this writer mean to say?

The nun helped the girl, a homeless teenager, find a place to live.

Sometimes a modifier is confusing because it does not refer to anything in the sentence. This is called a **dangling modifier** and must be corrected by rewriting.

5. Drilling for oil in Alaska, acres of wilderness were destroyed.
6. Tired and proud, the web site was completed at midnight.

■ In sentence 5, who or what was *drilling for oil*? The sentence doesn't tell us.

■ *Drilling for oil* is a dangling modifier. It can be corrected only by rewording the sentence:

7. Drilling for oil in Alaska, the EndRun Company destroyed acres of wilderness.

■ In sentence 6, *tired and proud* is a dangling modifier. Surely the web site isn't tired and proud, so who is? Rewrite the sentence to say what the writer probably intended.

Tired and proud, we completed the web site at midnight.

PRACTICE 21

Correct any confusing, misplaced, or dangling modifiers. Rearrange words or rewrite as necessary.

1. Plump sausages, the dinner guests looked forward to the main course.

   The dinner guests looked forward to the main course, plump sausages.

2. Soaring over the treetops in a hot air balloon, the view was spectacular.

   Soaring over the treetops in a hot air balloon, they enjoyed the spectacular view.

3. Powered by hydrogen, the engineers designed a new kind of car.

   The engineers designed a new kind of car, powered by hydrogen.

4. I introduced my boyfriend to my father, who wanted to marry me.

   I introduced my boyfriend, who wanted to marry me, to my father.

5. Revised to highlight his computer expertise, Marcelo was proud of his new résumé.

   Marcelo was proud of his new résumé, revised to highlight his computer

   expertise.

6. Jim, who loved to lick car windows, drove his dog to the vet.

   Jim drove his dog, who loved to lick car windows, to the vet.

   _____

7. Banging inside the dryer, Carla heard the lost keys.

   Carla heard the lost keys banging inside the dryer.

   _____

8. We complained about the proposed building to the mayor, which we found ugly and too large for the neighborhood.

   We complained to the mayor about the proposed building, which we found ugly

   and too large for the neighborhood.

PART F Review and Practice

Before practicing some of the techniques of sentence variety discussed in this chapter, review them briefly:

1. Mix long and short sentences.

2. Add an occasional question, command, or exclamation.

3. Begin with an adverb: _Unfortunately,_ the outfielder dropped the fly ball.

4. Begin with a prepositional phrase: _With great style,_ the pitcher delivered a curve.

5. Join ideas with a compound predicate: The fans _roared and banged_ their seats.

6. Join ideas with an _-ing_ modifier: _Diving chin first onto the grass,_ Beltran caught the ball.

7. Join ideas with a past participial modifier: _Frustrated by the call,_ the batter kicked dirt onto home plate.

8. Join ideas with an appositive: Beer, _the cause of much rowdiness,_ should not be sold at games.

9. Join ideas with a relative clause: Box seats, _which are hard to get for important games,_ are frequently bought up by corporations.

Of course, the secret of achieving sentence variety is practice. Choose one, two, or three of these techniques to focus on and try them out in your writing. Revise your paragraphs and essays with an eye to sentence variety.

PRACTICE 22

Revise and then rewrite this essay, aiming for sentence variety. Vary the length and pattern of the sentences. Vary the beginnings of some sentences. Join two sentences in any way you wish, adding appropriate connecting words or dropping unnecessary words. Punctuate correctly.   Answers will vary.

Little Richard, the King of Rock 'n' Roll

With "A Wop-Bop-A-Loo-Bop-A-Lop-Bam-Boom," Little Richard hit the U.S. music scene on September 14, 1955. It has never been the same since. He had almost insane energy. He wore flamboyant clothes. He defined the rebellious behavior at the heart of rock 'n' roll. He has influenced countless performers. These performers include the Beatles, the Rolling Stones, Prince, and Michael Jackson.

Richard Wayne Penniman was born on December 5, 1932, in Macon, Georgia. He was the third of thirteen children. He sang gospel music with his siblings. Richard was a wild and independent child. He left home at fourteen. He traveled through Georgia with musical shows of all kinds. He sang with B. Brown and his orchestra. He was called "Little Richard" for the first time.

By 1955, Richard had developed his own musical style. It combined gospel with rhythm and blues. At its center was a wild scream of pure joy. He had developed a stage style as well. It combined outrageous costumes, a mile-high pompadour, thick mascara, manic piano-playing, and uninhibited hip-swinging. "Tutti Frutti" made him an overnight sensation. Over the next two years, he produced one hit after another. His hits included "Long Tall Sally," "Slippin' and Slidin'," "Lucille," and "Good Golly Miss Molly."

Richard's fans loved him. In 1957, he stopped performing. He had a spiritual awakening. He quit alcohol, drugs, and sexual promiscuity. In 1962, he resurfaced. He became a cult figure over the next thirteen years. He was called "The King of Rock 'n' Roll." His behavior on and off-stage became more outrageous. He dressed as Queen Elizabeth or the pope. He once wore a suit completely covered with small mirrors. In 1986, Richard's contribution to music history was recognized. He was one of the first inductees to the Rock and Roll Hall of Fame and Museum.

Today Richard is still going strong. In 1993, he performed at the presidential inauguration. In 2000, he was the subject of a made-for-television biography. In 2001, his All-Time Greatest Hits CD was issued. It's easy to believe Richard when he proclaims, "Rock still lifts my spirit and gives me joy and an energy force."

Little Richard, the King of Rock 'n' Roll

With "A Wop-Bop-A-Loo-Bop-A-Lop-Bam-Boom," Little Richard hit the U.S.

music scene on September 14, 1955. It has never been the same since. With his

almost insane energy and flamboyant clothes, he defined the rebellious behavior

at the heart of rock 'n' roll. He has influenced countless performers, including the
Beatles, the Rolling Stones, Prince, and Michael Jackson.

Richard Wayne Penniman was born on December 5, 1932, in Macon, Georgia.
The third of thirteen children, he sang gospel music with his siblings. Richard was a
wild and independent child who left home at fourteen. He traveled through Georgia
with musical shows of all kinds. Singing with B. Brown and his orchestra, he was
called "Little Richard" for the first time.

By 1955, Richard had developed his own musical style that combined gospel
with rhythm and blues. At its center was a wild scream of pure joy. He had
developed a stage style as well; it combined outrageous costumes, a mile-high
pompadour, thick mascara, manic piano-playing, and uninhibited hip-swinging.
"Tutti Frutti" made him an overnight sensation. Over the next two years, he
produced one hit after another, including "Long Tall Sally," "Slippin' and Slidin',"
"Lucille," and "Good Golly Miss Molly."

Richard's fans loved him, but in 1957, he stopped performing. He had a spiritual
awakening, quitting alcohol, drugs, and sexual promiscuity. In 1962, he resurfaced
and became a cult figure over the next thirteen years. He was called "The King of
Rock 'n' Roll." His behavior on and off-stage became more outrageous. He dressed as
Queen Elizabeth or the pope and once wore a suit completely covered with small
mirrors. In 1986, Richard's contribution to music history was recognized when he
was one of the first inductees to the Rock and Roll Hall of Fame and Museum.

Today Richard is still going strong. In 1993, he performed at the presidential
inauguration. In 2000, he was the subject of a made-for-television biography, and in
2001, his All-Time Greatest Hits CD was issued. It's easy to believe Richard when he
proclaims, "Rock still lifts my spirit and gives me joy and an energy force."

 EXPLORING ONLINE

http://grammar.ccc.commnet.edu/grammar/combining_skills.htm Add sophistication to your writing. Review and scroll down for interactive, sentence-combining quizzes.

http://owl.english.purdue.edu/handouts/grammar/g_dangmod.html Are your modifiers dangling? Don't blush; revise.

Online Study Center **college.hmco.com/pic/evergreen8e**
Visit the Online Study Center for *Evergreen* for more exercises and quizzes.

Revising for Language Awareness

Although it is important to write grammatically correct English, good writing is more than just correct writing. Good writing has life, excitement, and power. It captures the attention of the reader and compels him or her to read further.

The purpose of this chapter is to increase your awareness of the power of words and your skill at making them work for you. The secret of effective writing is **revision.** Do *not* settle for the first words that come to you, but go back over what you have written, replacing dull or confusing language with exact, concise, fresh, and sometimes figurative language.

PART A Exact Language: Avoiding Vagueness

Good writers express their ideas as *exactly* as possible, choosing *specific, concrete,* and *vivid* words and phrases. They do not settle for vague terms and confusing generalities.

Which sentence in each of the following pairs gives the more *exact* information? That is, which uses specific and precise language? Which words in these sentences make them sharper and more vivid?

1. A car went around the corner.
2. A battered blue Mustang careened around the corner.

3. Janet quickly ate the main course.
4. Janet devoured the plate of ribs in two and a half minutes.

5. The president did things that caused problems.
6. The president's military spending increased the budget deficit.

■ Sentences 2, 4, and 6 contain language that is *exact*.

■ Sentence 2 is more exact than sentence 1 because *battered blue Mustang* gives more specific information than the general term *car*. The verb *careened* describes precisely how the car went around the corner, fast and recklessly.

■ What specific words does sentence 4 substitute for the more general words *ate*, *main course*, and *quickly* in sentence 3?

■ _____devoured_____, _____plate of ribs_____, and

_____in two and a half minutes_____

Why are these terms more exact than those in sentence 3?

They tell exactly how Janet ate, what she ate, and how quickly she ate it.

_____

■ What words in sentence 6 make it clearer and more exact than sentence 5?

military spending; increased the budget deficit _____

_____

Concrete and detailed writing is usually exciting as well and makes us want to read on, as does this passage by Toni Morrison, who won the Nobel Prize for literature:

> It is called the suburbs now, but when black people lived there it was called the Bottom. One road, shaded by beeches, oaks, maples, and chestnuts, connected it to the valley. The beeches are gone now, and so are the pear trees where children sat and yelled down through the blossoms at passersby. Generous funds have been allotted to level the stripped and faded buildings that clutter the road from Medallion up to the golf course. They are going to raze the Time and a Half Pool Hall, where feet in long tan shoes once pointed down from chair rungs. A steel ball will knock to dust Irene's Palace of Cosmetology, where women used to lean their heads back on sink trays and doze while Irene lathered Nu Nile into their hair. Men in khaki work clothes will pry loose the slats of Reba's Grill, where the owner cooked in her hat because she couldn't remember the ingredients without it.
>
> —Toni Morrison, *Sula*

Now compare a similar account written in general and inexact language:

> It is called the suburbs now, but when black people lived there it was called the Bottom. One road, shaded by big trees, connected it to the valley. Many of the trees are gone now. Generous funds have been allotted to level the buildings on the road from Medallion up to the golf course. They are going to knock down the pool hall, the beauty parlor, and the restaurant.

You do not need a large vocabulary to write exactly and well, but you do need to work at finding the right words to fit each sentence. As you revise, cross out vague or dull words and phrases and replace them with more exact terms. When you are tempted to write *I feel good*, ask yourself exactly what *good* means in that sentence: *relaxed? proud? thin? in love?* When people walk by, do they *flounce, stride, lurch, wiggle,* or *sneak?* When they speak to you, do people *stammer, announce, babble, murmur,* or *coo?* Question yourself as you revise; then choose the right words to fit that particular sentence.

PRACTICE 1

Lively verbs are a great asset to any writer. The following sentences contain four overused general verbs—*to walk, to see, to eat,* and *to be*. In each case, replace the general verb in parentheses with a more exact verb *chosen to fit the context of the sentence*. Use a different verb in every sentence. Consult a dictionary or thesaurus* if you wish.   Answers will vary.

EXAMPLES   In no particular hurry, we _____strolled_____ (walked) through the botanical gardens.

Jane _____fidgets_____ (is) at her desk and watches the clock.

1. With guns drawn, three police officers _____crept_____ (walked) toward the door of the warehouse.

2 As we stared in fascination, an orange lizard _____crawled_____ (walked) up the wall.

3. The four-year-old _____teetered_____ (walked) onto the patio in her mother's high-heeled shoes.

4. A furious customer _____strode_____ (walked) into the manager's office.

5. Two people who _____witnessed_____ (saw) the accident must testify in court.

6. We crouched for hours in the underbrush just to _____spy_____ (see) a rare white fox.

7. Three makeshift wooden rafts were _____spotted_____ (seen) off the coast this morning.

8. For two years, the zoologist _____studied_____ (saw) the behavior of bears in the wild.

9. There was the cat, delicately _____munching_____ (eating) my fern!

10. Senator Gorman astounded the guests by loudly _____slurping_____ (eating) his soup.

11. All through the movie, she _____crunched_____ (ate) hard candies in the back row.

* A thesaurus is a book of *synonyms*—words that have the same or similar meanings.

12. Within seconds, Dan had bought two tacos from a street vendor and
_____gulped_____ (eaten) them both.

13. During rush hour, the temperature hit 98 degrees, and dozens of cars
_____stalled_____ (were) on the highway.

14. A young man _____lies_____ (is) on a stretcher in the emergency room.

15. Workers who _____sit_____ (are) at desks all day should make special
efforts to exercise.

16. Professor Nuzzo _____paced_____ (was) in front of the blackboard, excited
about this new solution to the math problem.

PRACTICE 2

The following sentences contain dull, vague language. Revise them using vivid
verbs, specific nouns, and colorful adjectives. As the examples show, you may
add and delete words. Answers will vary.

EXAMPLES   A dog lies down in the shade.

A mangy collie flops down in the shade of a parked car.

My head hurts.

My head throbs.

I have shooting pains in the left side of my head.

1. Everything about the man looked mean.

Even the angle of the shifty-eyed stranger's hat looked mean.

2. I feel good today for several reasons.

I feel giddy today because it's Saturday, it's springtime, and I'm in love.

3. A woman in unusual clothes went down the street.

A six-foot-tall woman in flowing African robes strode regally down the street.

4. The sunlight made the yard look pretty.

The streaming sunlight painted every corner of the yard in technicolor.

5. What the company did bothered the townspeople.

   The company's dumping practices enraged the townspeople.

   _____

6. The pediatrician's waiting room was crowded.

   The pediatrician's waiting room overflowed with whining children and impatient parents.

   _____

7. As soon as he gets home from work, he hears the voice of his pet asking for dinner.

   The minute he walks in the door from work, his ears are assailed by Rover's piteous yelps

   begging for dinner.

8. The noises of construction filled the street.

   A cacophony of jackhammers, diesel engines, and rumbling dump trucks rose from the

   construction site.

9. When I was sick, you were helpful.

   When I had the flu for a week, you brought me chicken soup every day.

   _____

10. This college does things that make the students feel bad.

    The inadequate security in the college's dormitories worries and angers many students.

    _____

ESL TIP
Many nonnative writers are still learning basic English vocabulary even as we urge them to choose exact and nonclichéd language. These ESL sites offer additional vocabulary building help: **http://iteslj.org /links/TESL/Vocabulary/** or **http://depts.gallaudet .edu/englishworks/reading /main/vocabulary.htm.**

PRACTICE 3

TEACHING and ESL TIP
Before asking students to complete Practice 3, you might want to review the concept of *context*. Show them examples of sentences that contain words with multiple meanings (e.g., *dressing* and *fast*) in different contexts. Ask students to determine from the context which meaning of the word is intended.

A word that works effectively in one sentence might not work in another sentence. In searching for the right word, always consider the **context** of the sentence into which the word must fit. Read each of the following sentences for meaning. Then circle the word in parentheses that *most exactly fits* the context of the sentence.

EXAMPLE Machu Picchu, which means "old peak" in the Quechua (words, (language,) lingo), is known as the "Lost City of the Incas."

1. Ever since the ruins of Machu Picchu were (buried, invented, (discovered)) in 1911 by Yale archaeologist Hiram Bingham, people all over the world have been fascinated by this mysterious site.

2. The ancient city ((perches,) hangs, wobbles) high atop a peak in the rugged Andes Mountains of Peru.

3. In the 1400s, using gray Andes granite, the Inca people (arranged, (constructed,) piled) the palace, temples, baths, and houses of Machu Picchu.

ESL TIP
ESL students may benefit from *collocation* study. Choose five to ten target words from Practice 3. Ask students to list words that commonly occur before and after the target words, e.g., *accidentally fell.*

4. The carved stone blocks are so (strong, massive, humongous) that thousands of men would have been needed to move just one of them into place.

5. The city served not only as (hideout, getaway, retreat) and fortress for the nobility but also as an observatory.

6. Many ceremonies took place around the Intihuatana stone, a kind of sundial that (casts, manufactures, emits) no shadow at noon on the two equinoxes, in March and in September.

7. According to legend, when spiritually sensitive people touch their foreheads to the Intihuatana stone, it (magically, accidentally, weirdly) opens their vision to the spirit world.

8. In 1533, Spanish conquistadors (ruthlessly, destructively, properly) destroyed the Inca civilization, but the invaders never found Machu Picchu.

9. Nevertheless, the cloud-capped city was (abandoned, missed, set aside) for 400 years.

10. Today, however, many tourists (enjoy, battle, are awed by) altitude sickness just to trek up the mountain and gaze upon this beautiful, well-preserved sanctuary.

View of Machu Picchu, Peru.

PRACTICE 4

The following paragraph begins a mystery story. Using specific and vivid language, revise the paragraph to make it as exciting as possible. Then finish the story; be careful to avoid vague language.   Answers will vary.

TEACHING TIP
Read aloud the best three to four revisions of the paragraph in Practice 4.

The weather was bad. I was in the house alone, with a funny feeling that something was going to happen. Someone knocked at the door. I got up to answer it and found someone outside. She looked familiar, but I didn't know from where or when. Then I recognized her as a person from my past. I let her in although I was not sure I had done the right thing.

_____

_____

_____

_____

_____

_____

_____

PART B Concise Language: Avoiding Wordiness

TEACHING TIP
Explain to students that many people write a wordy and imprecise first draft. Revising later includes searching for the right words to express one's thoughts.

Concise writing comes quickly to the point. It avoids **wordiness**—unnecessary and repetitious words that add nothing to the meaning.

Which sentence in each of the following pairs is more *concise*? That is, which does *not* contain unnecessary words?

ESL **TIP**
Many world dialects of English, i.e., African and Indian English, value wordy, flowery language. You may need to stress that U.S. English writers prefer conciseness.

1. Because of the fact that the watch was inexpensive in price, he bought it.

2. Because the watch was inexpensive, he bought it.

3. In my opinion I think that the financial aid system at Ellensville Junior College is in need of reform.

4. The financial aid system at Ellensville Junior College needs reform.

5. On October 10, in the fall of 2003, we learned the true facts about the Peruvian mummies.

6. On October 10, 2003, we learned the facts about the Peruvian mummies.

▪ Sentences 2, 4, and 6 are *concise*, whereas sentences 1, 3, and 5 are *wordy*.

▪ In sentence 1, *because of the fact that* is really a *wordy* way of saying *because*. *In price* simply repeats information already given by the word *inexpensive*.

▪ The writer of sentence 3 undercuts the point with the wordy apology of *in my opinion I think*. As a general rule, leave out such qualifiers and simply state the opinion; but if you do use them, use either *in my opinion* or *I think*, not both! Sentence 4 replaces *is in need of* with one direct verb, *needs*.

■ *In the fall of* in sentence 5 is *redundant;* it repeats information already given by which word?

October

■ Why is the word *true* also eliminated in sentence 6?

Facts are always true.

Concise writing avoids wordiness, unnecessary repetition, and padding. Of course, conciseness *does not mean* writing short, bare sentences, but simply cutting out all deadwood and never using fifteen words when ten will do.

PRACTICE 5

The following sentences are *wordy*. Make them more *concise* by crossing out or replacing unnecessary words or by combining two sentences into one concise sentence. Rewrite each new sentence on the lines beneath, capitalizing and punctuating correctly.

EXAMPLES The U.S. Census uncovers many interesting facts that have a lot of truth to them.

The U.S. Census uncovers many interesting facts.

In the year 1810, Philadelphia was called the cigar capital of the United States. The reason why was because the census reported that the city produced 16 million cigars each year.

In 1810, Philadelphia was called the cigar capital of the United States because

the census reported that the city produced 16 million cigars each year.

1. The Constitution requires and says that the federal government of the United States must take a national census every ten years.

The Constitution requires the federal government to take a national census every

ten years.

2. At first, the original function of the census was to ensure fair taxation and representation.

The original function of the census was to ensure fair taxation and representation.

3. Since the first count in 1790, however, the census has been controversial. There have been several reasons why it has been controversial.

Since the first count in 1790, however, the census has been controversial for several

reasons.

4. One reason why is because there are always some people who aren't included.

    One reason is that some people aren't included.

5. The 1990 census, for example, missed almost 5 million people, many of whom were homeless with no place to live.

    The 1990 census, for example, missed almost 5 million people, many of whom were

    homeless.

6. For the 2000 census, the Census Bureau considered using statistical methods. The statistical methods would have been used instead of the traditional direct head count.

    For the 2000 census, the Census Bureau considered using statistical methods instead of

    the traditional direct head count.

7. The Bureau would have directly counted about 90 percent of U.S. residents who live in the United States and then estimated the number and characteristics of the remainder of the rest of the people.

    The Bureau would have directly counted about 90 percent of U.S. residents and then

    estimated the number and characteristics of the remainder.

8. Those who opposed the idea believed that in their opinion statistical methods would have introduced new errors that were mistaken into the count.

    Those who opposed the idea believed that statistical methods would have introduced

    new errors into the count.

9. The distribution of $100 billion in money, as well as the balance of power in the House of Representatives, depended on how and in which manner the census was conducted.

    The distribution of $100 billion, as well as the balance of power in the House of

    Representatives, depended on how the census was conducted.

TEACHING TIP
You may wish to review with the class a list of common wordy expressions. For one such list, see **http://owl .english.purdue.edu /handouts/general /gl_concise.html**.

10. Despite controversy, the U.S. census still continues to serve a beneficial purpose that is for the good of the United States.

    Despite controversy, the census serves a beneficial purpose for the United States.

PRACTICE 6

Rewrite this essay *concisely*, cutting out all unnecessary words. Reword or combine sentences if you wish, but do not alter the meaning.   Answers may vary.

Dr. Alice Hamilton, Medical Pioneer

At the age of forty ~~years old~~, Dr. Alice Hamilton became a pioneer in ~~the field of~~ industrial medicine. In 1910, the governor of Illinois appointed her to investigate rumors that ~~people who were doing the work~~ workers in Chicago's paint factories were dying from lead poisoning. The result of her investigation was the first state law ~~that was passed~~ to protect workers.

The following year, the U.S. Department of Labor hired ~~this woman,~~ Dr. Hamilton to study industrial illness throughout the country ~~of the United States.~~ In the next decade, she researched ~~and studied~~ many occupational diseases, including tuberculosis among quarry workers and silicosis—clogged lungs— among sandblasters. To gather information, Dr. Hamilton went to the workplace— deep in mines, quarries, and underwater tunnels. She also spoke to the workers in their homes ~~where they lived~~.

With great zeal, Dr. Hamilton spread her message about poor health conditions on the job. ~~What happened with her reports is that they~~ Her reports led to new safety regulations, workmen's compensation insurance, and improved working conditions in many industries. She wrote many popular articles and spoke to groups of interested citizens. In ~~the year of~~ 1919, she became the first woman to ~~hold courses and~~ teach at Harvard University. Her textbook ~~which she wrote~~, *Industrial Poisons in the U.S.*, became the standard book on the subject. By the time she died in 1970—she was 101—she had done much to improve the plight of many working people. ~~The reason why she~~ She is remembered today ~~is~~ because she cared at a time when many others seemed not to care at all.

PART C   Fresh Language: Avoiding Triteness

Fresh writing uses original and lively words. It avoids **clichés,** those tired and trite expressions that have lost their power from overuse.

Which sentence in each pair that follows contains fewer expressions that you have heard or read many times before?

> 1. Some people can relate to the hustle and bustle of city life.
>
> 2. Some people thrive on the energy and motion of city life.
>
> 3. This book is worth its weight in gold to the car owner.
>
> 4. This book can save the car owner hundreds of dollars a year in repairs.

▪ You probably found that sentences 2 and 4 contained fresher language. Which words and phrases in sentences 1 and 3 have you heard or seen before, in conversation, on TV, or in magazines and newspapers? List them:

can relate to; the hustle and bustle; worth its weight in gold

Clichés and trite expressions like the following have become so familiar that they have almost no impact on the reader. Avoid them. Say what you mean in your own words:

Cliché:	She is pretty as a picture.
Fresh:	Her amber eyes and wild red hair mesmerize me.

Or occasionally, play with a cliché and turn it into fresh language:

Cliché:	. . . as American as apple pie.
Fresh:	. . . as American as a Big Mac.
Cliché:	The grass is always greener on the other side of the fence.
Fresh:	"The grass is always greener over the septic tank."—Erma Bombeck

The following is a partial list of trite expressions to avoid. Add to it any others that you overuse in your writing.

TEACHING TIP
Ask students for other examples of overused expressions. Write these on the board and have students think of fresher and more interesting ways to say the same thing.

Trite Expressions and Clichés

at this point in time	in this day and age
awesome	last but not least
better late than never	living hand to mouth
break the ice	one in a million
cold cruel world	out of this world
cool, hot	sad but true
cry your eyes out	tried and true
easier said than done	under the weather
free as a bird	work like a dog
hustle and bustle	green with envy

PRACTICE 7

Cross out clichés and trite expressions in the following sentences and replace them with fresh and exact language of your own.   Answers may vary.

ESL TIP
Your ESL students may not recognize trite language. Have them partner with native English speakers to complete Practice 7.

1. Many men and women would like to propose marriage to ~~the love of their life~~ *their loved one* in a ~~way that is out of this world~~ *unique and memorable way*.

2. However, coming up with a special idea is ~~easier said than done~~ *not easy*, especially for people who are busy, unimaginative, or "romantically challenged."

3. Fortunately, resources exist to help them ~~pop the question~~ *propose* in style.

4. Several web sites, for example, make the process ~~easy as pie~~ *easier* by offering creative proposal ideas ~~for a fee that is just a drop in the bucket~~ *for a small fee*.

5. At **www.2propose.com,** one sees "Dinner on the Beach"—the suitor taking the fiancée-to-be for a sunset stroll along the shore, "discovering" a violinist and a candlelit dinner for two, and then kneeling to offer ~~a ring that will take her breath away~~ *a lovely ring*.

6. In "Reverse Surprise Party," a relative convinces the unsuspecting loved one to throw a surprise party for the would-be spouse, who walks in ~~dressed to the nines~~ *handsomely dressed* and ~~asks, cool as a cucumber~~ *calmly asks*, "Will you marry me?"

7. According to **www.romancestuck.com,** the beloved will be ~~one happy camper~~ *delighted* if his or her sweetheart persuades all the neighbors in an apartment building to turn on or off their lights, spelling out MARRY ME.

8. The proposal stories in books like Michael Webb's *The RoMANtic's Guide to Popping the Question* will ~~bring a tear to the eye of~~ *move* even the most unromantic fellow and help him overcome ~~the butterflies in his stomach~~ *his nervousness*.

9. ~~Last but not least~~ *Finally*, proposers can hire consultants to think up one-of-a-kind splashy or romantic moments and then ~~get the ball rolling~~ *help make them happen*.

10. One consultant, for instance, arranged for a client to fly his girlfriend to a secluded Hawaiian waterfall, where he proposed, vowing that they'd ~~live happily ever after~~ *share a joyful life*.

TEACHING and ESL TIP
Urge your students to learn and use new words systematically. Alert them to the challenging vocabulary site at the end of the chapter or have them google "free SAT vocabulary."

PART D Figurative Language: Similes and Metaphors

One way to add sparkle and exactness to your writing is to use an occasional simile or metaphor. A **simile** is a comparison of two things using the word *like* or *as*:

ESL TIP
Point out that using figurative language may be an accessible tool for improving writing because similes and metaphors exist in most languages.

> "He was *as ugly as* a wart." —Anne Sexton
>
> "The frozen twigs of the huge tulip poplar next to the hill clack in the cold *like* tinsnips." —Annie Dillard

A **metaphor** is a similar comparison without the word *like* or *as*:

> "My soul is a dark forest." —D. H. Lawrence
>
> Love is a virus.

■ The power of similes and metaphors comes partly from the surprise of comparing two apparently unlike things. A well-chosen simile or metaphor can convey a lot of information in very few words.

■ Comparing a person to a wart, as Sexton does, lets us know quickly just how ugly that person is. And to say that *twigs clack like tinsnips* describes the sound so precisely that we can almost hear it.

■ What do you think D. H. Lawrence means by his metaphor? In what ways is a person's soul like a *dark forest*?

It is a tangle of emotions containing scary, unexplored areas.

_____

_____

■ The statement *love is a virus* tells us something about the writer's attitude toward love. What is it? In what ways is love like a virus?

The writer thinks that love is contagious; love is a kind of sickness with predictable

symptoms.

_____

Similes and metaphors should not be overused; however, once in a while, they can be a delightful addition to a paper that is also exact, concise, and fresh.

PRACTICE 8

The author of the following paragraph describes a lake as winter turns to spring. She uses at least two similes and two metaphors. Underline the similes and circle the metaphors.

Mornings, a transparent (pane of ice) lies over the meltwater. I peer through and see some kind of water bug—perhaps a leech—paddling <u>like a sea turtle</u> between (green ladders of lakeweed.) Cattails and sweetgrass from the previous summer are bone dry, marked with black mold spots, and <u>bend like elbows</u> into the ice.

—Gretel Erlich, "Spring," *Antaeus*

PRACTICE 9

Think of several similes to complete each sentence that follows. Be creative! Then underline your favorite simile, the one that best completes each sentence.

Answers will vary.

EXAMPLE My English class is like   <u>an orchestra.</u>
the Everglades.
an action movie.
a vegetable garden.

TEACHING TIP
This practice is great fun to do in class.

1. Job hunting is like _____

   <u>a game of chess.</u>

   rock climbing.

   a plunge into cold water.

2. My room looks like _____

   yesterday's scrambled eggs.

   a shipwreck.

   a supernova.

3. Writing well is like _____

   riding down the freeway.

   sailing in a stiff wind.

   reaching the top of a mountain.

4. Marriage is like _____

   a broken record.

   a trip around the world.

   completing a puzzle.

PRACTICE 10

Think of several metaphors to complete each sentence that follows. Jot down three or four ideas, and then underline the metaphor that best completes each sentence. Answers will vary.

EXAMPLE Love is <u>a blood transfusion.</u>
a sunrise.
a magic mirror.
a roller coaster ride.

1. The Internet is _____

a bottle of sedatives.

a palace with many rooms.

an undiscovered continent.

3. My car is _____

a two-eyed monster.

a goldfish bowl.

another child.

2. Registration is _____

a battlefield.

a snakepit.

a lesson in patience.

4. Courage is _____

a taut rope.

a doorway.

a searchlight.

WRITING ASSIGNMENTS

1. Good writing can be done on almost any subject if the writer approaches the subject with openness and with "new eyes." Take a piece of fruit or a vegetable—a lemon, a green pepper, a cherry tomato. Examine it as if for the first time. Feel its texture and parts, smell it, weigh it in your palm.

   Now capture your experience of the fruit or vegetable in words. First jot down words and ideas, or freewrite, aiming for the most *exact* description possible. Don't settle for the first words you think of. Keep writing. Then go back over what you have written, underlining the most exact and powerful writing. Compose a topic sentence and draft a paragraph that conveys your unique experience of the fruit or vegetable.

2. In the paragraph that follows, Rick Bragg describes his home state in such rich, exact detail that it comes to life for the reader. Read his paragraph, underlining language that strikes you as *exact* and *fresh*. Can you spot the two similes? Can you find any especially vivid adjectives or unusual verbs?

   My mother and father were born in the most beautiful place on earth, in the foothills of the Appalachians along the Alabama-Georgia line. It was a place where gray mists hid the tops of low, deep-green mountains, where redbone and bluetick hounds flashed through the pines as they chased possums into the sacks of old men in frayed overalls, where old women in bonnets dipped Bruton snuff and hummed "Faded Love and Winter Roses" as they shelled purple hulls, canned peaches and made biscuits too good for this world. It was a place where playing the church piano loud was near as important as playing it right, where fearless young men steered long, black Buicks loaded with yellow whiskey down roads the color of dried blood, where the first frost meant hog killin' time, and the mouthwatering smell of cracklin's would drift for acres from giant, bubbling pots. It was a place where the screams of panthers, like a woman's anguished cry, still haunted the most remote ridges and hollows in the dead of night, where children believed they could choke off the cries of night birds by circling one wrist with a thumb and forefinger and squeezing tight, and where the cotton blew off the wagons and hung like scraps of cloud in the branches of trees.

—Rick Bragg, *All Over But the Shoutin'*

Write a paragraph or essay in which you describe a place you know well and perhaps love. As you freewrite or brainstorm, try to capture the most precise and minute details of what you experienced or remember. Now revise your writing, making the language as *exact*, *concise*, and *fresh* as you can.

 EXPLORING ONLINE

http://www.ccc.commnet.edu/sensen/part3/sixteen/techniques_using.html
Practice choosing exact language.

http://grammar.ccc.commnet.edu/grammar/concise.htm Practice pruning excess words.

http://grammar.ccc.commnet.edu/grammar/vocabulary.htm Build a powerful, college-level vocabulary: tips, quizzes, links.

Online Study Center college.hmco.com/pic/evergreen8e
Visit the Online Study Center for *Evergreen* for more exercises and quizzes.

23

Putting Your Revision Skills to Work

In Units 2 and 3, you learned to **revise** basic paragraphs, and in Unit 4, you learned to revise essays. All revising requires that you rethink and rewrite with such questions as these in mind:

> Can a reader understand and follow my ideas?
>
> Is my topic sentence or thesis statement clear?
>
> Does the body of my paragraph or essay fully support the topic or thesis statement?
>
> Does my paragraph or essay have unity? That is, does every sentence relate to the main idea?
>
> Does my paragraph or essay have coherence? That is, does it follow a logical order and guide the reader from point to point?
>
> Does my writing conclude, not just leave off?

Of course, the more writing techniques you learn, the more options you have as you revise. Unit 5 has moved beyond the basics to matters of style: consistency and parallelism, sentence variety, and clear, exact language. This chapter will guide you again through the revision process, adding questions like the following to your list:

> Are my verb tenses and pronouns consistent?
>
> Have I used parallel structure to highlight parallel ideas?
>
> Have I varied the length and type of my sentences?
>
> Is my language exact, concise, and fresh?

Many writers first revise and rewrite with questions like these in mind. They do *not* worry about grammar and minor errors at this stage. Then in a separate, final process, they **proofread*** for spelling and grammatical errors.

---

* For practice in proofreading for particular errors, see individual chapters in Units 6 and 7. For practice in proofreading for mixed errors, see Chapter 37, "Putting Your Proofreading Skills to Work."

Here are two sample paragraphs by students, showing the first draft, the revisions made by the student, and the revised draft of each. Each revision has been numbered and explained to give you a clear idea of the thinking process involved.

Writing Sample 1

First Draft

I like to give my best performance. I must relax completely before a show. I often know ahead of time what choreography I will use and what I'll sing, so I can concentrate on relaxing completely. I usually do this by reading, etc. I always know my parts perfectly. Occasionally I look through the curtain to watch the people come in. This can make you feel faint, but I reassure myself and say I know everything will be okay.

Revisions

(1) In order
~~I like~~ to give my best performance. I must relax completely before a show.

(2) and vocals
I often know ahead of time what choreography I will use, and ~~what I'll sing;~~

(3) during that long, last hour before curtain,   (4)
so I can concentrate on relaxing. ~~completely.~~ I usually do this by reading.

(5) an action-packed mystery, but sometimes I joke with the
other performers or just walk around backstage.

~~etc.~~ I always know my parts perfectly. Occasionally I ~~look~~ through the curtain to   (7) peek

(6)   audience file   (8) me
watch the people ~~come in.~~ This can make ~~you~~ feel faint, but I reassure myself.

(9) "Vickie," I say, "the minute you're out there singing to the people, everything will be okay."
~~and say I know everything will be okay.~~

Reasons for Revisions

1. Combine two short sentences. (sentence variety)

2. Make *choreography* and *vocals* parallel and omit unnecessary words. (parallelism)

3. Make time order clear: First discuss what I've done during the days before the performance, and then discuss the hour before performance. (time order)

4. Drop *completely*, which repeats the word used in the first sentence. (avoid wordiness)

5. This is important! Drop *etc.*, add more details, and give examples. (add examples)

6. This idea belongs earlier in the paragraph—with what I've done during the days before the performance. (order)

7. Use more specific and interesting language in this sentence. (exact language)

8. Use the first person singular pronouns *I* and *me* consistently throughout the paragraph. (consistent person)

9. Dull—use a direct quotation, the actual words I say to myself. (exact language, sentence variety)

TEACHING TIP
Go over these reasons with students as they examine the changes to this paragraph and to Writing Sample 2. Use these examples as opportunities to review anything they don't yet fully understand.

Revised Draft

In order to give my best performance, I must relax completely before a show. I often know ahead of time what choreography and vocals I will use, and I always know my parts perfectly, so during that long, last hour before curtain, I can concentrate on relaxing. I usually do this by reading an action-packed mystery, but sometimes I joke with the other performers or just walk around backstage. Occasionally I peek through the curtain to watch the audience file in. This can make me feel faint, but I reassure myself. "Vickie," I say, "the minute you're out there singing to the people, everything will be okay."

—Victoria DeWindt (Student)

Writing Sample 2

First Draft

My grandparents' house contained whole rooms that my parents' house did not (pantry, a parlor, a den where Grandpa kept his loot). The furniture and things always fascinated me. Best of all was the lake behind the house. Grandpa said that Evergreen Lake had grown old just like Grandma and him, that the game fish are gone and only a few bluegills remained. But one day he let me fish. No one thought I'd catch anything, but I caught a foot-long goldfish! Grandpa said it was a goddam carp, but it was a goldfish to me and I nearly fainted with ecstasy.

Revisions

(1) Visiting my grandparents at Evergreen Lake was always an exotic adventure.

(2) Their cavernous (3)

~~My grandparents'~~ house contained whole rooms that my parents' house did

(4) —a pantry,   with a big black grand piano, and   (5) The rooms were furnished

not (pantry, a parlor, a den where Grandpa kept his loot). ~~The furniture and things~~

with musty deer heads, hand-painted candlesticks, and velvet drapes.

~~always fascinated me.~~ Best of all was the lake behind the house. Grandpa said

that Evergreen Lake had grown old just like Grandma and him, that the game fish

(6) were   (7) Add new section below*

~~are~~ gone and only a few bluegills remained. ~~But one day he let me fish. No one~~

~~thought I'd catch anything, but I caught a foot-long goldfish. Grandpa said it was~~

                                                                    B   (8)

~~a goddam carp,~~ but it was a goldfish to me, and I nearly fainted with ecstasy.

*Add: But one day he rigged up a pole for me and tossed my line into the water. I sat motionless for several hours, waiting for a miracle. Suddenly I felt a tug on my line. I screeched and yanked upward. By the time Grandpa arrived on the dock, there on the surface lazily moving its fins was the biggest goldfish I had ever seen, nearly a foot long! Grandpa reached down with the net and scooped the huge orange fish out of the water. "Bring down the pail," he shouted. "It's a goddam carp."

Reasons for Revisions

1. No topic sentence; add one. (topic sentence)

2. Now *grandparents'* repeats the first sentence; use *their*. (pronoun substitution)

3. Add a good descriptive word to give the feeling of the house. (exact language)

4. Expand this; add more details. (details, exact language)

5. More details and examples needed for support! Try to capture the "exotic" feeling of the house. (details, exact language)

6. Verb shifts to present tense; use past tense consistently. (consistent tense)

7. This section is weak. Tell the story of the goldfish; try to create the sense of adventure this had for me as a kid. Quote Grandpa? (details, exact language, direct quotation)

8. Revised paragraph is getting long. Consider breaking into two paragraphs, one on the house and one on the lake.

Revised Draft

Visiting my grandparents at Evergreen Lake was always an exotic adventure. Their cavernous house contained whole rooms that my parents' house did not—a pantry, a parlor with a big black grand piano, and a den where Grandpa kept his loot. The rooms were furnished with musty deer heads, hand-painted candlesticks, and velvet drapes.

Best of all was the lake behind the house. Grandpa said that Evergreen Lake had grown old just like Grandma and him, that the game fish were gone and only a few bluegills remained. But one day he rigged up a pole for me and tossed my line into the water. I sat motionless for several hours, waiting for a miracle. Suddenly I felt a tug on my line. I screeched and yanked upward. By the time Grandpa arrived on the dock, there on the surface lazily moving its fins was the biggest goldfish I had ever seen, nearly a foot long! Grandpa reached down with the net and scooped the huge orange fish out of the water. "Bring down the pail," he shouted. "It's a goddam carp." But it was a goldfish to me, and I nearly fainted with ecstasy.

PRACTICE

Because revising, like writing, is a personal process, the best practice is to revise your own paragraphs and essays. Nevertheless, here is a first draft that needs revising.

Revise it *as if you had written it*. Mark your revisions on the first draft, using and building on the good parts, crossing out unnecessary words, rewriting unclear or awkward sentences, adding details, and perhaps reordering parts. Then, recopy your final draft on the lines. Especially, ask yourself these questions:

Are my verb tenses and pronouns consistent?

Have I used parallel structure?

Have I varied the length and type of my sentences?

Is my language exact, concise, and fresh?

First Draft

Breaking the Yo-Yo Syndrome

For years, I was a yo-yo dieter. I bounced from fad diets to eating binges when I ate a lot. This leaves you tired and with depression. Along the way, though, I learned a few things. As a result, I personally will never go on a diet again for the rest of my life.

TEACHING TIP
Consider having students work together in groups on their revisions to this essay. Encourage them to talk through their ideas for improvement.

TEACHING TIP
Encourage students to
double-space their first
drafts, allowing space for
revisions.

First of all, diets are unhealthy. Some of the low carbohydrate diets are high in fat. Accumulating fat through meat, eggs, and the eating of cheese can raise blood levels of cholesterol and led to artery and heart disease. Other diets are too high in protein and can cause kidney ailments, and other things can go wrong with your body, too. Most diets also leave you deficient in essential vitamins and minerals that are necessary to health, such as calcium and iron.

In addition, diets are short-term. I lose about ten pounds. I wind up gaining more weight than I originally lost. I also get sick and tired of the restricted diet. On one diet, I ate cabbage soup for breakfast, lunch, and dinner. You are allowed to eat some fruit on day one, some vegetables on day two, and so on, but mostly you are supposed to eat cabbage soup. After a week, I never want to see a bowl of cabbage soup again. Because the diet was nutritionally unbalanced, I ended up craving bread, meat, and all the other foods I am not supposed to eat. Moreover, in the short-term, all one loses is water. You cannot lose body fat unless you reduce regularly and at a steady rate over a long period of time.

The last diet I try was a fat-free diet. On this diet I actually gained weight while dieting. I am surprised to discover that you can gain weight on a fat-free diet snacking on fat-free cookies, ice cream, and cheese and crackers. I also learn that the body needs fat—in particular, the unsaturated fat in foods like olive oil, nuts, avocados, and salad dressings. If a dieter takes in too little fat, you are constantly hungry. Furthermore, the body thinks it is starving, so it makes every effort to try to conserve fat, which makes it much harder for one to lose weight.

In place of fad diets, I now follow a long-range plan. It is sensible and improved my health. I eat three well-balanced meals, exercise daily, and am meeting regularly with my support group for weight control. I am much happier and don't weigh as much than I used to be.

Revised Draft

Breaking the Yo-Yo Syndrome

For years, I was a yo-yo dieter, bouncing from fad diets to eating binges that left me tired and depressed. Along the way, though, I learned a few things. As a result, I will never go on a diet again.

First, diets are unhealthy. Some of the low carbohydrate diets are high in fat, and fat from meat, eggs, and cheese can raise blood levels of cholesterol and lead to artery and heart disease. Other diets are too high in protein and can cause kidney ailments and other disorders. Most diets also leave a person deficient in essential vitamins and minerals, such as calcium and iron.

In addition, diets are short-term. I lose about ten pounds; then I wind up gaining more weight than I originally lost. I also get bored on the restricted diet. On one diet, I ate cabbage soup for breakfast, lunch, and dinner. I was allowed to eat some fruit on day one, some vegetables on day two, and so on, but mostly I was supposed to eat cabbage soup. After a week, I never wanted to see a bowl of cabbage soup again. Because the diet was nutritionally unbalanced, I ended up craving bread, meat, and all the other foods I was not supposed to eat. Moreover, in the short term, all you lose is water. You cannot lose body fat unless you reduce steadily over a long period of time.

The last diet I tried was a fat-free diet. I was surprised to discover that you can actually gain weight snacking on fat-free cookies, ice cream, and cheese and crackers. I also learned that the body needs fat—in particular, the unsaturated fat in foods like olive oil, nuts, avocados, and salad dressings. If you take in too little fat, you are constantly hungry. Furthermore, the body thinks it is starving, so it tries to conserve fat, which makes losing weight much harder.

In place of fad diets, I now follow a long-range plan that is sensible and healthful. I eat three well-balanced meals, exercise daily, and meet regularly with my support group for weight control. I am much happier and thinner than I used to be.

 EXPLORING ONLINE

http://owl.english.purdue.edu/handouts/general/gl_edit.html Guidance for the writer about to revise and proofread

Online Study Center   college.hmco.com/pic/evergreen8e
Visit the Online Study Center for *Evergreen* for more exercises and quizzes.

TEACHING TIP
More practice and assessment are available in the *Evergreen* Test Bank, linked ACE tests on the *Evergreen* Online Teaching and Study Centers, *WriteSpace for Evergreen,* and Exploring Online links in this chapter.

Writers' Workshop

Examine Something That Isn't What It Appears to Be

Revising is the key to all good writing—taking the time to sit down, reread, and rethink what you have written. In this unit, you have practiced revising for consistent verb tense, consistent person, parallelism, sentence variety, and language awareness.

In your group or class, read this student's essay, aloud if possible. Underline the parts that strike you as especially effective, and put a checkmark by anything that might need revising.

Behind the Face of Beauty

(1) Beauty is her name. She walks with her head up high, five foot three ~~in height,~~ a hundred and ten pounds ~~in weight,~~ small waist and figure ~~round in shape.~~ *round figure* Her hair is as long as a Native American's, with light brown eyes and a "killer smile." She has a caramel complexion that turns bronze ~~in color~~ during the summer.

(2) She has style and ~~wore~~ *wears* flashy jewelry that will make you stare in amazement. She has a ton of clothing that would make a movie star jealous. She ~~was~~ *is* very sociable and ~~did~~ *does* not have any trouble getting people to like her, mainly because of her sense of humor. Everyone ~~enjoyed~~ *enjoys* being around her, just as she enjoys having everyone around her. Men want to marry her, and women would just about do anything to have her confidence and strength.

(3) Heavenly is what she seems, but she is only disguised as an angel. She does not pay attention to men on foot, meaning, men without cars. Everything and everybody has to be within her control. If she can't dictate to you, she will try to destroy you and do it in a way you won't first recognize. She'll criticize your brand new shoes so that you will return them. Once you have returned the shoes, you will see her wearing the same pair. Blasphemy is what she will accuse you of if you ever call her envious.

(4) Well into her thirties, the oldest of five, and raised in a broken home with her careless teenaged mother, she ran away and chose a life of so-called freedom. Self-hate is inside her soul, but she covers it up with a smile and a bag full of tricks ~~and trades.~~ Using manipulation and deceit is the only way she feels she can get her vengeance.

(5) When I was a girl, I used to watch different sweethearts shower her with gifts. The family adored her. She was my mother's first born. Her young friends catered to her. To them, she was a goddess. I cherished the ground she walked on. I had every intention of being just like her someday.

She said she loved her "baby sis," but the minute ~~you~~ ^I showed signs of confidence, she would make ~~you~~ ^{me} cry by saying ~~you were~~ ^{I was} not strong.

(6) Now, tears are what I shed for her because she is lost. Until she finds the right path, she will continue to cover up with lavishness and luxury. She will hypnotize both men and women into being under her control. With time, others will learn that she is shallow and, to those who open their hearts to her, even dangerous.

—Tyesha Wiggins (Student)

1. How effective is Ms. Wiggins's essay?

   _____Y_____ Strong thesis statement?   _____Y_____ Good supporting details?

   _____Y_____ Logical organization?   _____Y_____ Effective conclusion?

2. What do you like best about this essay? What details or sections most command your attention or make you think?

3. Although this student writes about someone she knows, she is also trying to make sense for herself and the reader of her sister's outward beauty and inner ugliness. Do you think she succeeds?

4. According to one study of thousands of women in ten countries, only 2 percent believe they are beautiful (**www.campaignforrealbeauty.com**). Fifty-seven percent of those surveyed agreed that society defines female beauty too narrowly. How do you think the author of this essay would define beauty?

5. Are all the verb tenses correct, or do you notice any inconsistent tense?
   Inconsistent tense in paragraph 2

6. Are there any places where short, choppy sentences detracted from the excellent content? Yes, paragraph 5

7. Can you spot any error patterns (the same error two or more times) that this student should watch out for?
   Yes, wordiness in paragraph 1 and inconsistent person in paragraph 5. See corrections in blue.

GROUP WORK

In your group, revise Ms. Wiggins's essay as if it were your own. First, decide what problems need attention. Then rewrite those parts, sentence by sentence, aiming for a truly fine paper. Share your revision with the class, explaining why you made the changes you did.

WRITING AND REVISING IDEAS

1. Examine something that isn't what it appears to be or someone whose presentation contrasts with his or her character.

2. Write a definition of the word *beauty* or *ugliness*.

UNIT 6

Reviewing the Basics

24

The Simple Sentence

PART A Defining and Spotting Subjects

PART B Spotting Prepositional Phrases

PART C Defining and Spotting Verbs

PART A Defining and Spotting Subjects

Every sentence must contain two basic elements: a **subject** and a **verb.**

A subject is the *who* or *what* word that performs the action or the *who* or *what* word about which a statement is made:

> 1. Three *hunters* tramped through the woods.
>
> 2. The blue *truck* belongs to Ralph.

- In sentence 1, *hunters,* the *who* word, performs the action—"tramped through the woods."

- In sentence 2, *truck* is the *what* word about which a statement is made—"belongs to Ralph."

Some sentences have more than one subject, joined by *and*:

> 3. Her *aunt and uncle* love country music.

- In sentence 3, *aunt and uncle,* the *who* words, perform the action—they "love country music."

- *Aunt and uncle* is called a **compound subject.**

ESL TIP
If you have many nonnative students, you might discuss possible differences between their language and English, such as word order or singulars and plurals, that might confuse them as they write sentences in English.

Sometimes an *-ing* word can be the subject of a sentence:

> 4. *Reading* strains my eyes.

■ *Reading* is the *what* word that performs the action—"strains my eyes."

PRACTICE 1

Circle the subjects in these sentences.

1. Do (you) know the origin and customs of Kwanzaa?

2. This African-American (holiday) celebrates black heritage and lasts for seven days—from December 26 through January 1.

3. (Maulana Karenga) introduced Kwanzaa to America in 1966.

4. In Swahili, (Kwanzaa) means "first fruits of the harvest."

5. During the holiday, (families) share simple meals of foods from the Caribbean, Africa, South America, and the American South.

6. Specific (foods) have special meanings.

7. For instance, certain (fruits and vegetables) represent the products of group effort.

8. Another important (symbol) is corn, which stands for children.

9. At each dinner, (celebrants) light a black, red, or green candle and discuss one of the seven principles of Kwanzaa.

10. These seven (principles) are unity, self-determination, collective work and responsibility, cooperative economics, purpose, creativity, and faith.

PART B Spotting Prepositional Phrases

TEACHING TIP
Part B anticipates and addresses a common problem: many basic writers confuse the object of a preposition with the subject of the sentence.

One group of words that may confuse you as you look for subjects is the prepositional phrase. A **prepositional phrase** contains a **preposition** (a word like *at, in, of, from,* and so forth) and its **object.**

ESL TIP

Explain, perhaps with a simple drawing, that prepositions express relationships: *on the lake, in the lake, beside the lake.* Ask students for more examples.

Preposition	Object
at	the beach
on	time
of	the students

The object of a preposition *cannot* be the subject of a sentence. Therefore, spotting and crossing out the prepositional phrases will help you find the subject.

ESL TIP

ESL students have trouble with English prepositions. Alert them to Chapter 32, "Prepositions," and ESL Corner on the *Evergreen* Online Study Center and its many ESL practice links, for example, **http://a4esl.org/**.

1. The sweaters in the window look handmade.
2. The sweaters ~~in the window~~ look handmade.
3. ~~On Tuesday,~~ a carton ~~of oranges~~ was left ~~on the porch.~~

■ In sentence 1, you might have trouble finding the subject. But once the prepositional phrase is crossed out in sentence 2, the subject, *sweaters,* is easy to spot.

■ In sentence 3, once the prepositional phrases are crossed out, the subject, *carton,* is easy to spot.

Here are some common prepositions that you should know:

Common Prepositions			
about	before	in	through
above	behind	into	to
across	between	like	toward
after	by	near	under
along	during	of	until
among	for	on	up
at	from	over	with

PRACTICE 2

Cross out the prepositional phrases in each sentence. Then circle the subject of the sentence.

TEACHING TIP

After students have completed Parts A and B, they might highlight all subjects in a recent paragraph of their own, exchange work, and check each other's answers.

1. ~~From 6 A.M. until 10 A.M.,~~ (Angel) works out.

2. Local (buses) ~~for Newark~~ leave every hour.

3. (Three) ~~of my friends~~ take singing lessons.

4. That (man) ~~between Ralph and Cynthia~~ is the famous actor Hank the Hunk.

5. ~~Near the door,~~ a (pile) ~~of laundry~~ sits ~~in a basket.~~

6. ~~Toward evening, the~~ (houses) ~~across the river~~ disappear ~~in the thick fog.~~

7. ~~Before class,~~ (Helena and I) meet ~~for coffee.~~

8. ~~In one corner of the lab,~~ (beakers) ~~of colored liquid~~ bubbled ~~and boiled.~~

PART C   Defining and Spotting Verbs

Action Verbs

In order to be complete, every sentence must contain a **verb.** One kind of verb, called an **action verb,** expresses the action that the subject is performing:

> 1. The star quarterback *fumbled.*
>
> 2. The carpenters *worked* all day, but the bricklayers *went* home early.

■ In sentence 1, the action verb is *fumbled.*

■ In sentence 2, the action verbs are *worked* and *went.**

Linking Verbs

Another kind of verb, called a **linking verb,** links the subject to words that describe or identify it:

> 3. Don *is* a fine mathematician.
>
> 4. This fabric *feels* rough and scratchy.

■ In sentence 3, the verb *is* links the subject *Don* with the noun *mathematician.*

■ In sentence 4, the verb *feels* links the subject *fabric* with the adjectives *rough* and *scratchy.*

Here are some common linking verbs:

Common Linking Verbs	
appear	feel
be (am, is, are, was, were, has been, have been, had been . . .)	look
become	seem

---

* For work on compound predicates, see Chapter 21, "Revising for Sentence Variety," Part D.

Verbs of More Than One Word—Helping Verbs

So far you have dealt with verbs of only one word—*fumbled, worked, is, feels,* and so on. But many verbs consist of more than one word:

> 5. He *should have taken* the train home.
>
> 6. *Are* Tanya and Joe *practicing* the piano?
>
> 7. The lounge *was painted* last week.

■ In sentence 5, *taken* is the main verb; *should* and *have* are the **helping verbs.**

■ In sentence 6, *practicing* is the main verb; *are* is the helping verb.

■ In sentence 7, *painted* is the main verb; *was* is the helping verb.*

PRACTICE 3

TEACHING TIP
Practices 3 and 4 make enjoyable full-class exercises.

ESL TIP
ESL students may be confused by the variety of verb forms and tenses in Practice 3. Be prepared to refer them to Chapters 27 and 28 for explanations.

Underline the verbs in these sentences.

1. She <u>exposes</u> insurance cheats and lying spouses.

2. She <u>spies</u> on suspected nannies with a tiny camera.

3. Theresa Coleman-Negast <u>might have become</u> a police officer.

4. However, wearing a uniform every day <u>did</u> not <u>appeal</u> to her.

5. Instead, she <u>became</u> a private investigator.

6. Only one of every ten private investigators <u>is</u> a woman.

7. Women in this business <u>might face</u> criticism or even sexual harassment.

8. On the other hand, many clients <u>prefer</u> a female P.I. and <u>can talk</u> more freely with her.

9. Theresa <u>enjoys</u> her lack of routine and even the spy equipment.

10. Thanks to technology, cameras and tape recorders <u>have gotten</u> small enough to fit into a Beanie Baby, a pair of sunglasses, or even a ballpoint pen.

---

* For more work on verbs in the passive voice, see Chapter 29, "The Past Participle," Part E.

PRACTICE 4   REVIEW

Circle the subjects and underline the verbs in the following sentences. First, cross out any prepositional phrases.

1. Can (you) name America's top female snowboarder?

2. That (honor) goes ~~to Hannah Teter~~, Olympic gold medalist ~~at the 2006 Winter Games~~.

3. Just nineteen years old, (Hannah) soared ~~to victory~~ ~~in the women's halfpipe competition~~.

4. Following ~~in the footsteps~~ ~~of her four older brothers~~, (she) had started snowboarding lessons ~~at age eight~~.

5. Little (sister) was soon stepping confidently ~~onto winners' podiums~~.

6. Breathtakingly flexible, (Hannah) is called the Gumby Girl.

7. Her frontside (900s and) double overhead (airs) always amaze spectators.

8. (Teter) is constantly expanding her list ~~of skills and tricks~~.

9. Her (adventurousness and love) ~~of snowboarding~~ shine ~~in each performance~~.

10. Consequently, the talented (snowboarder) has become a driving force ~~in her sport~~.

American snowboarder Hannah Teter soars toward gold at the 2006 Olympic Games.

EXPLORING ONLINE

TEACHING TIP
More practice and assessment are available in the *Evergreen* Test Bank, linked ACE tests on the *Evergreen* Online Teaching and Study Centers, *WriteSpace for Evergreen,* and Exploring Online links in this chapter.

http://grammar.ccc.commnet.edu/grammar/quizzes/subjector.htm Interactive subject quiz

http://www.dailygrammar.com/archive.shtml Click "Verbs 6–10" and "11–15" for a verb review.

http://a4esl.org/a/g3.html Interactive preposition quizzes: scroll down to "prepositions."

Online Study Center **college.hmco.com/pic/evergreen8e**
Visit the Online Study Center for *Evergreen* for more exercises and quizzes.

25

Coordination and Subordination

PART A Coordination

A **clause** is a group of words that includes a subject and a verb. If a clause can stand alone as a complete idea, it is an **independent clause** and can be written as a **simple sentence.***

Here are two independent clauses written as simple sentences:

> 1. The dog barked all night.
>
> 2. The neighbors didn't complain.

You can join two clauses together by placing a comma and a **coordinating conjunction** between them:

> 3. The dog barked all night, *but* the neighbors didn't complain.
>
> 4. Let's go to the beach today, *for* it is too hot to do anything else.

---

* For more work on simple sentences, see Chapter 24, "The Simple Sentence."

■ The coordinating conjunctions *but* and *for* join together two clauses.

■ Note that *a comma precedes each coordinating conjunction.*

Here is a list of the most common coordinating conjunctions:

Coordinating Conjunctions			
and	for	or	yet
but	nor	so	

Be sure to choose the coordinating conjunction that best expresses the *relationship* between the two clauses in a sentence:

5. It was late, *so* I decided to take a bus home.

6. It was late, *yet* I decided to take a bus home.

■ The *so* in sentence 5 means that the lateness of the hour caused me to take the bus. (The trains don't run after midnight.)

■ The *yet* in sentence 6 means that despite the late hour I still decided to take a bus home. (I knew I might have to wait two hours at the bus stop.)

■ Note that a comma precedes the coordinating conjunction.

PRACTICE 1

Read the following sentences for meaning. Then fill in the coordinating conjunction that *best* expresses the relationship between the two clauses. Don't forget to add the comma.

1. In 1853, a customer at Moon Lake Lodge in Saratoga, New York, thought his fried potatoes were too thick and soggy___, so___he sent them back to the kitchen.

2. The Native American/African-American chef, George Crum, took offense at this criticism of his cooking___, for___he was a confident and cranky fellow.

3. Crum wanted to annoy his fussy customer___, so___he angrily sliced some potatoes very thin, poured salt all over them, and fried them hard.

4. The chef expected the complaining patron to leave in a huff___, but___he didn't.

5. Instead, the crispy potato thins pleased the customer immensely ___, so/and___ he ordered more.

6. Crum, who soon opened his own restaurant, called his lucky invention "potato crunches" ___, but___he later renamed them "Saratoga Chips."

7. In the 1920s, traveling salesman Herman Lay began selling potato chips out of the trunk of his car___, and___other companies began manufacturing them, too.

8. Now customers could order the tasty treat in restaurants___, or___they could munch them at home.

9. However, chips at the bottom of the barrel or tin packaging would not stay fresh ___, nor___ would they stay crispy.

10. Entrepreneur Laura Scudder solved this problem by putting the chips between sheets of wax paper that she ironed together___, and___the potato chip quickly became America's favorite snack.

TEACHING TIP
After students complete Practice 1, consider discussing their answers as a class so that they can see which conjunctions work in a sentence and which don't.

PRACTICE 2

Combine these simple sentences with a coordinating conjunction. Punctuate correctly.

TEACHING TIP
Students may try to combine these sentences using subordinating conjunctions like *because* and *then*. Remind them to use only the conjunctions in the list on page 355.

1. My daughter wants to be a mechanic. She spends every spare minute at the garage.

   My daughter wants to be a mechanic, so she spends every spare minute

   at the garage.

2. Ron dared not look over the edge. Heights made him dizzy.

   Ron dared not look over the edge, for heights made him dizzy.

   _____

3. Tasha's living room is cozy. Her guests always gather in the kitchen.

   Tasha's living room is cozy, but/yet her guests always gather in the kitchen.

   _____

4. Meet me by the bicycle rack. Meet me at Lulu's Nut Shop.

   Meet me by the bicycle rack, or meet me at Lulu's Nut Shop.

   _____

TEACHING TIP
Have students apply what they have learned by looking for short, choppy sentences in a paragraph they have written and then revising, using coordinating conjunctions.

5. In 1969, the first astronauts landed on the moon. Most Americans felt proud.

   In 1969, the first astronauts landed on the moon, and most Americans

   felt proud.

PART B Subordination

TEACHING TIP
To begin a lesson on subordinating conjunctions, you might review with students the meanings of the terms *coordinate* and *subordinate*.

Two clauses can also be joined with a **subordinating conjunction.** The clause following a subordinating conjunction is called a **subordinate** or **dependent clause** because it depends on an independent clause to complete its meaning:

> 1. We will light the candles *when Flora arrives.*

▪ *When Flora arrives* is a subordinate or dependent clause introduced by the subordinating conjunction *when.*

▪ By itself, *when Flora arrives* is incomplete; it depends on the independent clause to complete its meaning.*

Note that sentence 1 can also be written this way:

ESL TIP
ESL students tend to write dependent clause fragments. In some languages, like Japanese, freestanding dependent clauses are accepted as correct. Further, ESL students often duplicate English oral patterns, in which freestanding dependent clauses are common.

> 2. *When Flora arrives,* we will light the candles.

▪ The meaning of sentences 1 and 2 is the same, but the punctuation is different.

▪ In sentence 1, because the subordinate clause *follows* the independent clause, *no comma* is needed.

▪ In sentence 2, however, because the subordinate clause *begins* the sentence, it is followed by a *comma.*

Here is a partial list of subordinating conjunctions:

TEACHING TIP
Remind students that conjunctions express precise *relationships* between ideas. Discuss the meanings of any conjunctions that confuse them; for definitions, refer them to the transitional expressions chart on pages 62–63.

Subordinating Conjunctions		
after	if	unless
although	if only	until
as	in order that	when
as if	once	whenever
as though	provided that	where
because	rather than	whereas
before	since	wherever
even if	so that	whether
even though	though	while

---

* For more work on incomplete sentences, or fragments, see Chapter 26, "Avoiding Sentence Errors," Part B.

Be sure to choose the subordinating conjunction that *best expresses the relationship* between the two clauses in a sentence:

> 3. This course was excellent *because* Professor Green taught it.
>
> 4. This course was excellent *although* Professor Green taught it.

▪ Sentence 3 says that the course was excellent *because* Professor Green, a great teacher, taught it.

▪ Sentence 4 says that the course was excellent *despite the fact that* Professor Green, apparently a bad teacher, taught it.

PRACTICE 3

TEACHING TIP
After students complete Practice 3, consider discussing the answers as a class so that students can see which conjunctions work in the sentence and which don't.

Read the following sentences for meaning. Then fill in the subordinating conjunction that *best* expresses the relationship between the two clauses.

1. We could see very clearly last night _____because_____ the moon was so bright.

2. Violet read *Sports Illustrated* _____while_____ Daisy walked in the woods.

3. _____Whenever_____ it is cold outside, our new wood-burning Franklin stove keeps us warm.

4. The students buzzed with excitement _____when_____ Professor Hargrave announced that classes would be held at the zoo.

5. _____Until_____ his shoulder loosens up a bit, Ron will stay on the bench.

PRACTICE 4

TEACHING TIP
For Practice 4, encourage students to locate and circle the subordinating conjunction before deciding if the sentence needs a comma.

Punctuate the following sentences by adding a comma where necessary. Put a *C* after any correct sentences.

1. Thousands of low-income children in Venezuela have been given a new life because Jose Antonio Abreu taught them to play classical music. C

2. While some people only talked about the poverty and drugs destroying many young Venezuelans, Abreu took action.

3. After he convinced government leaders that musical training builds self-worth, Abreu got funding to start children's orchestras. C

4. The results have been amazing as communities proudly support their young musicians. C

5. When the children practice their violins or oboes they are also learning discipline, valuable skills, and the joys of musical teamwork.

6. The program ignores pop and tropical musicians like Christina Aguilera and Oscar de Leon because Abreu wants his students to master classical artists like Mozart and Beethoven. C

7. Since the program was launched a generation of talented Venezuelan musicians is already performing, composing, and teaching classical music.

8. Because the program has been so successful it is the model for new youth orchestras now being formed throughout the world.

Brothers Wilfredo and Onil Galarraga received instruments and new opportunities, thanks to the Venezuelan Children's Orchestra.

PRACTICE 5

Combine each pair of the following ideas by using a subordinating conjunction. Write each combination twice, once with the subordinating conjunction at the beginning of the sentence and once with the subordinating conjunction in the middle of the sentence. Punctuate correctly.

EXAMPLE   1. We stayed on the beach.
            The sun went down.

We stayed on the beach until the sun went down.

Until the sun went down, we stayed on the beach.

1. This cactus has flourished.

2. I talk to it every day.

Because I talk to it every day, this cactus has flourished.

This cactus has flourished because I talk to it every day.

_____

_____

3. Ralph takes the train to Philadelphia.

4. He likes to sit by the window.

Whenever Ralph takes the train to Philadelphia, he likes to sit by the window.

Ralph likes to sit by the window whenever he takes the train to Philadelphia.

_____

_____

5. I had known you were coming.

6. I would have vacuumed the guest room.

If I had known you were coming, I would have vacuumed the guest room.

I would have vacuumed the guest room if I had known you were coming.

_____

_____

7. He was the first person to eat a slice of meat between two pieces of bread.

8. The sandwich was named after the Earl of Sandwich.

The sandwich was named after the Earl of Sandwich because he was the first

person to eat a slice of meat between two pieces of bread.

Because he was the first person to eat a slice of meat between two pieces of

bread, the sandwich was named after the Earl of Sandwich.

9. Akila was about to answer the final question.

10. The buzzer sounded.

Akila was about to answer the final question when the buzzer sounded.

When the buzzer sounded, Akila was about to answer the final question.

_____

_____

11. Few soap operas remain on the radio.

12. Daytime television is filled with them.

Daytime television is filled with soap operas although few of them remain on

the radio.

Although few soap operas remain on the radio, daytime television is filled

with them.

13. She connected the speakers.

14. The room filled with glorious sound.

When she connected the speakers, the room filled with glorious sound.

The room filled with glorious sound when she connected the speakers.

_____

_____

TEACHING TIP
For more practice, recommend that students try online practices and quizzes such as those found at **http://a4esl.org/q/h/vm/conj02.html**.

15. The chimney spewed black smoke and soot.

16. Nobody complained to the local environmental agency.

Nobody complained to the local environmental agency although the chimney

spewed black smoke and soot.

Although the chimney spewed black smoke and soot, nobody complained to the

local environmental agency.

PART C   Semicolons

You can join two independent clauses by placing a **semicolon** between them. The semicolon takes the place of a conjunction:

> 1. She hopes to receive good grades this semester; her scholarship depends on her maintaining a 3.5 average.
>
> 2. Tony is a careless driver; he has had three minor accidents this year alone.

■ Each of the sentences above could also be made into two *separate sentences* by replacing the semicolon with a period.

■ Note that the first word after a semicolon is *not* capitalized (unless, of course, it is a word that is normally capitalized, like someone's name).

PRACTICE 6

Combine each pair of independent clauses by placing a semicolon between them.

1. The senator appeared ill at ease at the news conference ; he seemed afraid of saying the wrong thing.

2. The new seed catalogue, a fifteen-hundred-page volume, was misplaced ; the volume weighed ten pounds.

3. On Thursday evening, Hector decided to go camping ; on Friday morning, he packed his bags and left.

4. This stream is full of trout ; every spring men and women with waders and fly rods arrive on its banks.

5. Not a single store was open at that hour ; not a soul walked the streets.

PRACTICE 7

Each independent clause that follows is the first half of a sentence. Add a semicolon and a second independent clause. Make sure your second thought is also independent and can stand alone.   Answers will vary.

1. At 2 A.M. I stumbled toward the ringing telephone ; it was a wrong number. _____

   _____

2. *People* magazine published my letter to the editor ; I am finally an author! _____

   _____

3. The officer pulled over the speeding pickup truck ; the driver had three _____

   outstanding moving violations. _____

4. Cameras are not permitted in the museum ; I will check mine in the coatroom. _____

   _____

5. Computer skills are increasingly important in many careers; learning these _____

   skills is an important investment in one's future. _____

PART D　Conjunctive Adverbs

TEACHING TIP
Point out to students that using conjunctive adverbs correctly will significantly increase the sophistication of their writing.

A **conjunctive adverb** placed after the semicolon can help clarify the relationship between two clauses:

1. I like the sound of that stereo; *however,* the price is too high.
2. They have not seen that film; *moreover,* they have not been to a theater for three years.

■ Note that a comma follows the conjunctive adverb.

Here is a partial list of conjunctive adverbs.

Conjunctive Adverbs		
consequently	in fact	nevertheless
furthermore	indeed	then
however	moreover	therefore

PRACTICE 8

TEACHING TIP
Use sets of closely related sentences to demonstrate how the lack of a conjunctive adverb forces readers to discern the relationship between the two ideas on their own. Thus, readers are more likely to miss the connection or to misunderstand it.

Punctuate each sentence correctly by adding a semicolon, a comma, or both, where necessary. Put a *C* after any correct sentences.

1. I hate to wash my car windows nevertheless it's a job that must be done.

2. Sonia doesn't know how to play chess however she would like to learn.

3. Dean Fader is very funny in fact he could be a professional comedian.

4. Deep water makes Maurice nervous therefore he does not want to join the scuba dive team.

5. I like this painting; the soft colors remind me of tropical sunsets.   C

6. The faculty approved of the new trimester system; furthermore, the students liked it too.   C

7. Bill has an iPod plugged into his ear all day ; consequently ^ he misses a lot of good conversations.

8. We toured the darkroom ; then ^ we watched an actual photo shoot.

PRACTICE 9

Proofread this paragraph for run-ons, comma splices, fragments, and for conjunctive adverbs that do not express the right relationship between ideas. In your corrections, aim for a mix of semicolons and semicolons plus conjunctive adverbs.

(1) The chronograph is a watch that can measure time in different ways. (2) Its dial has two, three, or even four smaller subdials for this purpose. (3) A dial at the 9 o'clock mark might measure continuous seconds ; one at six o'clock might count total hours up to twelve. (4) Invented in France in 1821, the chronograph was introduced as a wristwatch in 1910 ; it has gained in popularity ever since. (5) Chronographs are used by people like pilots, athletes, and military officers, who must measure time with great accuracy; ~~nevertheless~~ consequently, these timepieces project an active, competent, outdoor image. (6) Different features on a chronograph reflect the profession. (7) Divers, for instance, need a waterproof timepiece, rubber gasket rings, and perhaps an extra dial to mark the ~~tides on the other hand~~ tides; on the other hand, race-car drivers need a tachometer to measure the speed of formula one racers. (8) Military personnel conducting operations at night need a radium dial with luminous numbers and hands. (9) In 1990, the Swatch company introduced affordable chronographs and launched a major fashion ~~trend consequently~~ trend; consequently, every watch company now has chronographs in its line. (10) Many of them—for both women and men—play up the contrast between a large, technical watch and such fashion details as a blue, pink, or green leather strap and diamonds around the face. (11) Consumers pay extra for all those fancy dials; however, most people never use them.

PART E Review

In this chapter, you have combined simple sentences by means of a **coordinating conjunction,** a **subordinating conjunction,** a **semicolon,** and a **semicolon** and **conjunctive adverb.** Here is a review chart of the sentence patterns discussed in this chapter.*

Coordination

Option 1   *Independent clause*   { , and / , but / , for / , nor / , or / , so / , yet }   *independent clause.*

Option 2   *Independent clause*   ;   *independent clause.*

Option 3   *Independent clause*   { ; consequently, / ; furthermore, / ; however, / ; in addition, / ; indeed, / ; in fact, / ; moreover, / ; nevertheless, / ; then, / ; therefore, }   *independent clause.*

Subordination

Option 4   *Independent clause*   { after / although / as (as if) / because / before / if / since / unless / until / when(ever) / whereas / while }   *dependent clause.*

Option 5   { After / Although / As (As if) / Because / Before / If / Since / Unless / Until / When(ever) / Whereas / While }   *dependent clause, independent clause.*

---

* For more ways to combine sentences, see Chapter 21, "Revising for Sentence Variety," Part D.

PRACTICE 10

Read each pair of simple sentences to determine the relationship between them. Then join each pair in three different ways, using the conjunctions or conjunctive adverbs in parentheses at the left. Punctuate correctly.   Answers will vary.

EXAMPLE   The company picnic was canceled.
Rain started to fall in torrents.

(for) The company picnic was canceled, for the rain started to fall in torrents.

(because) Because the rain started to fall in torrents, the company

picnic was canceled.

(therefore) The rain started to fall in torrents; therefore, the company

picnic was canceled.

1. My grandmother is in great shape.
   She eats right and exercises regularly.

   (for) My grandmother is in great shape, for she eats right and exercises regularly.

   (because) Because my grandmother eats right and exercises regularly, she is

   in great shape.

   (therefore) My grandmother eats right and exercises regularly; therefore, she

   is in great shape.

2. We just put in four hours paving the driveway.
   We need a long break and a cold drink.

   (since) Since we just put in four hours paving the driveway, we need a long

   break and a cold drink.

   (because) We need a long break and a cold drink because we just put in four

   hours paving the driveway.

   (consequently) We just put in four hours paving the driveway; consequently,

   we need a long break and a cold drink.

3. The bus schedule was difficult to read.
   Penny found the right bus.

   (but) The bus schedule was difficult to read, but Penny found the right bus.

(although) <u>Although the bus schedule was difficult to read, Penny found the</u>

<u>right bus.</u>

(however) <u>The bus schedule was difficult to read; however, Penny found the</u>

<u>right bus.</u>

4. Don is an expert mechanic.
   He intends to open a service center.

(and) <u>Don is an expert mechanic, and he intends to open a service center.</u>

_____

(because) <u>Because Don is an expert mechanic, he intends to open a service</u>

<u>center.</u>

(furthermore) <u>Don is an expert mechanic; furthermore, he intends to open a</u>

<u>service center.</u>

5. We haven't heard from her.
   We haven't given up hope.

(but) <u>We haven't heard from her, but we haven't given up hope.</u>

_____

(although) <u>Although we haven't heard from her, we haven't given up</u>

<u>hope.</u>

(nevertheless) <u>We haven't heard from her; nevertheless, we haven't given up</u>

<u>hope.</u>

PRACTICE 11

In your writing, aim for variety by mixing coordination, subordination, and simple sentences.* Revise the following paragraphs to eliminate monotonous simple sentences. First, read the paragraph to determine the relationships between ideas; then choose the conjunctions that best express these relationships, making your corrections above the lines. Punctuate correctly.

Paragraph 1

Dating has always been a risky business. Television shows like *Blind Date*
succeed because they
succeed. They let viewers leer at other people's embarrassing dates. Now the

_____

* For more work on sentence variety, see Chapter 21, "Revising for Sentence Variety."

Internet is opening a whole new social ~~frontier. It~~ also is creating new dangers. [frontier; however, it]

Online, it is harder to spot nuts, flakes, and predators. ~~We~~ meet someone through [When we]

~~e-mail.~~ We lose our usual ways of judging people. According to Internet safety ex- [e-mail, we]

pert Parry Aftab, it is hard to gauge the truth of someone's ~~statements. We~~ cannot [statements when we]

see, hear, and experience that person's eye contact, body language, dress, per-

sonal hygiene, and voice. Furthermore, most people ~~lie. They~~ begin to date online. [lie when they]

Aftab says that men often fib about their income, fitness level, or amount of

~~hair. Women~~ shave pounds off their weight or years off their age. Cyber daters [hair, and women]

must remain skeptical, ask questions, and watch for red-flag comments. ~~Your~~ on- [If your]

line love keeps calling herself Gilda, Bat Goddess of the Red ~~Planet. It's~~ probably [Planet, it's]

time to log off.

"*On the Internet, nobody knows you're a dog.*"

Paragraph 2

Businessman Robert Johnson has blazed new trails throughout his career. No

existing television network targeted African ~~Americans. Johnson~~ created the [Americans, so Johnson]

Black Entertainment Television network. ~~The~~ *Although the* company started with a tiny budget and just two hours of daily ~~programming. It~~ *programming, it* became a huge success. ~~BET~~ *As BET* grew to be the largest black-owned and -operated company in the ~~country. Johnson~~ *country, Johnson* created new jobs for hundreds of people. He himself became America's first African-American billionaire. In 2005, he achieved yet another ~~first. He~~ *first when he* became the first African American to gain controlling interest in an NBA team, the Charlotte Bobcats. One of his lifelong dreams had come ~~true. He~~ *true, but he* says that he is even prouder of another accomplishment. He wanted to create more economic opportunities for ~~minorities. He~~ *minorities, and he* has succeeded.

Paragraph 3

Cleopatra became Queen of Egypt at ~~seventeen. She~~ *seventeen; nevertheless, she* displayed a flair for ruling and was soon worshipped by her subjects. ~~Julius~~ *When Julius* Caesar, ruler of Rome, was sent to calm civil wars in Egypt in 51 ~~B.C. Cleopatra~~ *B.C., Cleopatra* was in hiding. She directed her servants to roll her up inside a large rug and smuggle her into the palace. Caesar was fifty-two and the most powerful man in the ~~world. He~~ *world, but he* was amazed to receive a giftwrapped queen. Their relationship became one of history's greatest love

In the sunken ruins of Cleopatra's palace, Franck Goddio finds a sphinx believed to be Cleopatra's father, Ptolemy XII.

stories, and it
~~stories. It~~ lasted until Caesar's enemies murdered him. Later, Marc Antony came

to Egypt to add African lands to the Roman Empire. He, too, fell in love with the
queen, and he
spirited ~~queen. He~~ moved into her palace on the island of Antirhodos. This be-
Romans; their
trayal was too much for the ~~Romans. Their~~ navy attacked Cleopatra's fleet. Both
themselves because they
Antony and Cleopatra killed ~~themselves. They~~ would not bow in defeat. The Ro-
queen, and an
mans smashed all statues of the ~~queen. An~~ earthquake sank her palace into the
passed before undersea
Mediterranean Sea. Fifteen hundred years ~~passed. Undersea~~ explorer Franck

Goddio discovered Cleopatra's lost palace in 1996. Neither the Roman Empire nor

the forces of nature could erase one of the most powerful and intriguing women

who ever lived.

EXPLORING ONLINE

TEACHING TIP
More practice and assessment are available in the *Evergreen* Test Bank, linked ACE tests on the *Evergreen* Online Teaching and Study Centers, *WriteSpace for Evergreen,* and Exploring Online links in this chapter.

http://owl.english.purdue.edu/handouts/grammar/g_commacompEX1.html
Paper quiz: combine clauses correctly.

http://grammar.ccc.commnet.edu/grammar/quizzes/nova/nova1.htm
Interactive coordination quiz

Online Study Center **college.hmco.com/pic/evergreen8e**
Visit the Online Study Center for *Evergreen* for more exercises and quizzes.

26

Avoiding Sentence Errors

PART A Avoiding Run-Ons and Comma Splices

PART B Avoiding Fragments

PART A Avoiding Run-Ons and Comma Splices

TEACHING TIP
Stress to students that run-ons and comma splices are among the most common—and most serious—grammatical errors. By forcing readers to stop, back up, and try to figure out where one thought ends and another begins, these errors confuse and irritate the audience.

ESL TIP
Modern Arabic now uses a full stop to separate sentences, but your Arabic-speaking ESL students may still make comma splice errors.

Be careful to avoid **run-ons** and **comma splices**.

A **run-on sentence** incorrectly runs together two independent clauses without a conjunction or punctuation. This error confuses the reader, who cannot tell where one thought stops and the next begins:

> 1. Run-on: My neighbor Mr. Hoffman is seventy-five years old he plays tennis every Saturday afternoon.

A **comma splice** incorrectly joins two independent clauses with a comma but no conjunction:

> 2. Comma splice: My neighbor Mr. Hoffman is seventy-five years old, he plays tennis every Saturday afternoon.

The run-on and the comma splice can be corrected in five ways:

> Use two separate sentences. My neighbor Mr. Hoffman is seventy-five years old. He plays tennis every Saturday afternoon.

Use a coordinating conjunction. (See Chapter 25, Part A.)	My neighbor Mr. Hoffman is seventy-five years old, but he plays tennis every Saturday afternoon.
Use a subordinating conjunction. (See Chapter 25, Part B.)	Although my neighbor Mr. Hoffman is seventy-five years old, he plays tennis every Saturday afternoon.
Use a semicolon. (See Chapter 25, Part C.)	My neighbor Mr. Hoffman is seventy-five years old; he plays tennis every Saturday afternoon.
Use a semicolon and a conjunctive adverb. (See Chapter 25, Part D.)	My neighbor Mr. Hoffman is seventy-five years old; however, he plays tennis every Saturday afternoon.

PRACTICE 1

Some of these sentences contain run-ons or comma splices; others are correct. Put a C next to the correct sentences. Revise the run-ons and comma splices in any way you choose. Be careful of the punctuation.   Answers may vary.

ESL TIP
ESL students often benefit from group activities, especially with a mix of native and ESL speakers. Try using Practice 1 as a pair or group activity. Ask the groups to present and explain each of their answers.

1. Identity theft is the fastest-growing crime in the United States it costs society $4 to $5 billion a year.

   Revised: Identity theft is the fastest-growing crime in the United States, and it costs society $4 to $5 billion a year.

2. The identity thief doesn't just steal someone's cash or jewelry, he or she poses as that person to open new accounts, take out loans, or even buy houses.

   Revised: The identity thief doesn't just steal someone's cash or jewelry; he or she poses as that person to open new accounts, take out loans, or even buy houses.

TEACHING TIP
After students complete Practice 1, go over the answers in class so that you can demonstrate how to use all five revision methods for each sentence.

3. For the victim, identify theft can mean the shock of violation, large financial losses, and ruined credit.

   Revised: C

4. Individuals today must protect themselves against identity theft the U.S. Department of Justice recommends the SCAM approach.

   Revised: Because individuals today must protect themselves against identity theft, the U.S. Department of Justice recommends the SCAM approach.

5. S is for *stingy* people should be stingy about giving their valuable social security, bank account, and credit-card numbers to others.

   Revised: S is for *stingy*, for people should be stingy about giving their valuable social security, bank account, and credit-card numbers to others.

6. C stands for *check* all financial statements carefully for unauthorized withdrawals or purchases.

Revised: C _____

_____

7. The A in SCAM reminds everyone to *ask* periodically for a copy of his or her credit report fraudulent accounts and activity will show up there.

Revised: The A in SCAM reminds everyone to *ask* periodically for a copy of his or her

credit report because fraudulent accounts and activity will show up there.

8. The final step is M, *maintaining* careful records of bank and financial accounts, these records can help dispute any problems.

Revised: The final step is M, *maintaining* careful records of bank and financial

accounts; these records can help dispute any problems.

9. Trash cans and dumpsters still provide identity thieves with most of their valuable information, a final S might stand for *shred*.

Revised: Trash cans and dumpsters still provide identity thieves with most of their

valuable information, so a final S might stand for *shred*.

10. Old checks, bank records, and credit-card offers from today's mail should never be tossed out they should be shredded or burned.

Revised: Old checks, bank records, and credit-card offers from today's mail should

never be tossed out; instead, they should be shredded or burned.

PRACTICE 2

Proofread the following paragraph for run-ons and comma splices. Correct them in any way you choose.

Because college

(1) ~~College~~ costs have risen dramatically in recent years, most students choose

to work part-time to help cover their expenses. (2) Surprising new research re-

veals many benefits for college students who are employed a limited number of

hours a week. (3) Part-time jobs can help students explore career fields and de-

velop professional skills; they might even lead to permanent employment after

surprising. Students

graduation. (4) Another benefit is even more ~~surprising students~~ who work the

ideal number of hours, between fifteen and twenty per week, have higher grade-

point averages and better retention rates than their peers. (5) However, working

TEACHING TIP
Students should be able to
recognize that this is a
cause and effect paragraph.
Your employed students may
enjoy discussing how their
experiences support or
refute the conclusions
presented here.

more than twenty hours can have negative consequences⌃ it may interfere with
. It

schoolwork and reduce financial-aid eligibility. (6) Students who work thirty-five

hours or more often have lower grade-point averages,⌃ they are also less likely to
and

complete their degrees. (7) College students who can keep their working hours

within the ideal range will enjoy the greatest benefits of part-time employment.

PRACTICE 3

Proofread the following essay for run-ons and comma splices. Correct them in
any way you choose, writing your revised essay on a separate sheet of paper. Be
careful of the punctuation.   Answers will vary.

Will K. Kellogg, Least Likely to Succeed

TEACHING TIP
Because run-ons and comma
splices, like fragments, are
most likely to occur in
longer pieces of writing,
proofreading exercises like
these are especially
important.

(1)⌃ Will Kellogg was an unlikely candidate for fame and fortune, he became
Although

one of America's great successes.

(2) The two Kellogg boys could not have been more different. (3) Will was a

slow learner with few friends and interests. (4) His father pulled him from school

at the age of thirteen⌃ he made Will a traveling broom salesman for the family com-

pany. (5) Eight years older than Will, John Harvey Kellogg was the family genius.

(6) He became a noted surgeon and head of an exclusive health resort. (7) He

treated his patients with exercise and a strict vegetarian diet⌃ he wrote best-selling
; furthermore,

books about healthful living.

(8) In 1880,⌃ Will was twenty years old, Dr. John hired him to work at the re-
when

sort. (9) For the next twenty-five years, Will served as his brother's flunky.

(10) According to rumor, he shaved Dr. John every day and shined his shoes.

(11)⌃ John bicycled to work, Will jogged alongside getting his daily work orders.
While

(12) Dr. John was a wealthy man,⌃ he never paid Will more than eighty-seven dol-
but

lars a month.

(13) One of the special foods at the resort was pressed wheat. (14) The broth-

ers boiled wheat dough⌃ then they pressed it through rollers into thin sheets.
, and

(15) One night, they left the boiled dough out. (16) When they pressed it, it turned into flakes instead of forming sheets. (17) Will suggested that they toast the flakes.
(18) Resort guests loved the new cereal, ^and^ former guests ordered it from their homes. (19) To meet the demand, the brothers opened a mail-order business*;* how-ever, the snobbish Dr. John refused to sell the flakes to grocery stores.

(20) In 1906, Will finally bought out John's share of the cereal patents*. He* struck out on his own. (21) Will turned out to be a business genius. (22) He invented advertis-ing techniques that made his new product, Kellogg's Corn Flakes, a household term. (23) Will K. Kellogg quickly became one of the richest persons in America.

(24) Sadly, the two brothers never reconciled. (25) In 1943, ninety-one-year-old Dr. John wrote Will an apology *, but* John died before the letter reached his younger brother.

PART B Avoiding Fragments

TEACHING TIP
Student should know that sentence fragments are considered a serious and distracting error in college and the workplace. Ask, "Are fragments one of your personal error patterns?" What looks like eight errors might be one error—fragments—repeated eight times!

TEACHING TIP
Many dependent clause fragments could be called "afterthoughts." This idea helps some students. Often, attaching such a fragment to the preceding sentence is the best method of correc-tion.

Another error to avoid is the **sentence fragment.** A **sentence** must contain a sub-ject and a verb and must be able to stand alone as a complete idea. A **sentence fragment** is incomplete. It lacks a subject, a verb, or both—or it does not stand alone as a complete idea.

Here are six common fragments and ways to correct them. The first three are among the most frequently made errors in college and business writing.

Dependent Clause Fragments

A dependent clause fragment often starts with a subordinating conjunction like *although, because, if, when,* and so on.*

Complete sentence:	1. Kirk decided to major in psychology.
Fragment:	2. After his sister was diagnosed with anorexia.

▪ Example 1 is a complete sentence.

▪ Example 2 is a fragment because it is a dependent clause beginning with the subordinating conjunction *after.* Furthermore, it is not a complete idea.

---

* For a longer list of subordinating conjunctions and more work on dependent clauses, see Chapter 25, "Coordination and Subordination," Part B.

This fragment can be corrected in two ways:

ESL TIP
Many ESL students begin
sentences with
subordinators like *because*
and *although*, so this type
of fragment is a common
problem. Some are copying
the oral speech patterns
they hear. Others come from
language backgrounds, like
Japanese, in which this
construction is accepted
written practice.

Corrected:	3.	Kirk decided to major in psychology after his sister was diagnosed with anorexia.
Corrected:	4.	Kirk decided to major in psychology. His sister was diagnosed with anorexia.

▪ In sentence 3, the fragment is combined with the sentence before.

▪ In sentence 4, the fragment is changed into a complete sentence.

Relative Clause Fragments

A dependent clause fragment can also start with *who, whose, which,* or *that.**

Complete sentence:	5.	Mrs. Costa is a popular history professor.
Fragment:	6.	Who never runs out of creative ideas.

▪ Example 5 is a complete sentence.

▪ Example 6 is a fragment because it is a relative clause beginning with *who.** It is not a complete idea.

This fragment can be corrected in two ways:

Corrected:	7.	Mrs. Costa is a popular history professor who never runs out of creative ideas.
Corrected:	8.	Mrs. Costa is a popular history professor. She never runs out of creative ideas.

▪ In sentence 7, it is combined with the sentence before.

▪ In sentence 8, the fragment is changed into a complete sentence.

-ing Fragments

An *-ing* fragment starts with an *-ing* verb form.

Complete sentence:	9.	Joaquin can be seen on the track every morning.
Fragment:	10.	Running a mile or two before breakfast.

---

*For more work on relative clauses, see Chapter 21, "Revising for Sentence Variety," Part D, and Chapter 27, "Present Tense (Agreement)," Part G.

■ Example 9 is a complete sentence.

■ Example 10 is a fragment because it lacks a subject and because an *-ing* verb form cannot stand alone without a helping verb.*

This fragment can be corrected in two ways:

Corrected:	11.	Joaquin can be seen on the track every morning, running a mile or two before breakfast.
Corrected:	12.	Joaquin can be seen on the track every morning. He runs a mile or two before breakfast.

■ In sentence 11, the fragment is combined with the sentence before.

■ In sentence 12, the fragment is changed into a complete sentence.

Watch out for fragments beginning with a subordinating conjunction; *who, which,* or *that;* or an *-ing* verb form. These groups of words cannot stand alone, but must be combined with another sentence or changed into a complete sentence.

PRACTICE 4

Some of these examples are fragments; others are complete sentences. Put a *C* next to the complete sentences. Revise the fragments any way you choose.

Answers will vary.

TEACHING TIP
You might wish to complete Practice 4 in class so that everyone can see the ways each fragment can be corrected and understand why some sentences are correct.

1. When Sandra completes her commercial jet training.

   Revised: When Sandra completes her commercial jet training, she will

   interview with Continental and Southwest Air.

2. Loudly talking on his cell phone, Ivan strolled through the mall.

   Revised: C

3. A city that I have always wanted to visit.

   Revised: Moscow is a city that I have always wanted to visit.

4. If she speaks Portuguese fluently, she will probably get the job.

   Revised: C

---

* For more work on joining ideas with an *-ing* modifier, see Chapter 21, "Revising for Sentence Variety," Part D.

5. The comic strip *Peanuts*, which was created by Charles Schultz.

   Revised: The comic strip *Peanuts*, which was created by Charles Schultz, has become

   the most widely printed comic strip in the world.

6. Interviewing divorced people for her research project.

   Revised: Interviewing divorced people for her research project inspired Belkys to

   become a psychologist.

7. Although some students bring laptop computers to class.

   Revised: Although some students bring laptop computers to class, most still take

   notes in paper notebooks.

8. Frantically, the disc jockey flipping through stacks of CDs.

   Revised: Frantically, the disc jockey was flipping through stacks of CDs.

Prepositional Phrase Fragments

Complete sentence:	13. A huge telescope in Green Bank, West Virginia, scans for signs of life.
Fragment:	14. On stars twenty to thirty light years away.

■ Sentence 13 is a complete sentence.

■ Sentence 14 is a fragment because it is a prepositional phrase beginning with *on*. It lacks both a subject and a verb.

   This fragment can be corrected in two ways:

Corrected:	15. A huge telescope in Green Bank, West Virginia, scans for signs of life on stars twenty to thirty light years away.
Corrected:	16. A huge telescope in Green Bank, West Virginia, scans for signs of life. Its target is stars twenty to thirty light years away.

■ Sentence 15 shows the easiest way to correct this fragment—by connecting it to the sentence before.

■ In sentence 16, the fragment is changed into a complete sentence by adding a subject, *its target*, and a verb, *is*.

Appositive Phrase Fragments

Fragment: 17. A fine pianist.

Complete sentence: 18. Marsha won a scholarship to Juilliard.

■ Example 17 is a fragment because it is an appositive—a noun phrase. It lacks a verb, and it is not a complete idea.*

■ Example 18 is a complete sentence.

This fragment can be corrected in two ways:

Corrected: 19. A fine pianist, Marsha won a scholarship to Juilliard.

Corrected: 20. Marsha is a fine pianist. She won a scholarship to Juilliard.

■ In sentence 19, the fragment is combined with the sentence after it.

■ In sentence 20, the fragment is changed into a complete sentence by adding a verb, *is*, and a subject, *she* (to avoid repeating *Marsha*).

Infinitive Phrase Fragments

Complete sentence: 21. Lauri has always wanted to become a biologist.

Fragment: 22. To protect the environment.

■ Example 21 is a complete sentence.

■ Example 22 is a fragment because it lacks a subject and contains only the infinitive form of the verb—*to* plus the simple form of *protect*.

This fragment can be corrected in two ways:

Corrected: 23. Lauri has always wanted to become a biologist and to protect the environment.

Corrected: 24. Lauri has always wanted to become a biologist. Her goal is to protect the environment.

■ In sentence 23, the fragment is combined with the sentence before it.

■ In sentence 24, the fragment is changed into a complete sentence.

---

* For more work on appositives, see Chapter 21, "Revising for Sentence Variety," Part D.

Watch out for phrase fragments. A prepositional phrase, appositive phrase, or infinitive cannot stand alone, but must be combined with another sentence or changed into a complete sentence.

PRACTICE 5

Now, proofread for fragments. Some of these examples are fragments; others are complete sentences. Put a C next to the complete sentences. Revise the fragments any way you choose. Answers will vary.

TEACHING TIP

Have students share their answers to Practice 5 so that everyone can see possibilities other than the ones they wrote.

1. To earn money for college.

   Revised: Malcolm worked at Starbucks to earn money for college.

   _____

2. Terrence, a graphic designer at *Sports Illustrated*.

   Revised: Terrence, a graphic designer at *Sports Illustrated,* loves his job.

   _____

3. Across the railroad tracks and down the riverbank.

   Revised: The black horse raced across the railroad tracks and down the riverbank.

   _____

4. A born comedian.

   Revised: You are a born comedian.

   _____

5. To answer phones for the AIDS Education Network.

   Revised: We want to answer phones for the AIDS Education Network.

   _____

6. On a coffee plantation in Jamaica.

   Revised: Her lifelong dream is to live on a coffee plantation in Jamaica.

   _____

7. That silver razor scooter.

   Revised: That silver razor scooter belongs to my grandmother.

   _____

8. To find a job that you love.

   Revised: To find a job that you love is a gift and a joy.

   _____

Review Chart: Correcting Sentence Fragments

Type of Fragment	F Fragment C Corrected
1. Dependent clause	F After Jake moved to Colorado. C After Jake moved to Colorado, he learned to ski.
2. Relative clause	F Who loves computer games. C My niece, who loves computer games, repairs my computer.
3. *-ing* modifier	F Surfing the Web. C Surfing the Web, we visited European art museum sites.
4. Prepositional phrase	F Inside the cave. C They found mastodon bones inside the cave.
5. Appositive	F A slow student. C Einstein, a slow student, proved to be a genius.
6. Infinitive	F To go dancing tonight. C She wants to go dancing tonight.

ESL TIP
ESL and visual learners will find this review chart especially useful. Suggest that students keep it handy as they write and revise.

PRACTICE 6

Fragments are most likely to occur in paragraphs or longer pieces of writing. Proofread the paragraph below for fragments. Correct them in any way you choose, either adding the fragments to other sentences or making them into complete sentences.   Answers will vary.

TEACHING TIP
Suggest that students try the bottom-up proofreading technique—reading the last sentence first, then the second to last, and so on, until they reach the first sentence.

(1) The sinking of the *Titanic* in 1912 has inspired fifteen motion pictures over the years. (2) All of them requiring special effects. (3) What set James Cameron's *Titanic* apart, however, was his attention to detail. (4) Following the blueprints and plans for the original ship. (5) Cameron's team created scaled sets and models accurate down to the rivets. (6) Scenes of the ship in the water were made possible through the brilliant use of computer technology and a small model. (7) A larger model of the liner's huge cargo hold was needed. (8) To show the ocean rushing into the ship. (9) Although the model was only a quarter as large as the original. (10) It still had enough room for period luggage and a brand-new Renault. (11) The largest model was a 775-foot replica of the luxury ship. (12) Which reproduced every detail, from the ship's name lettered on the façade to the chairs on

the deck. (13) That set took almost a year to build. (14) ~~And~~ *and* a good chunk of the

$287 million that Cameron spent on the most expensive movie ever made.

PRACTICE 7

Proofread this essay for fragments. Correct them in any way you choose, either adding the fragments to other sentences or making them into complete sentences. Be careful of the punctuation.   Answers will vary.

Her Focus Is Success

TEACHING TIP
Practice 7 challenges students to spot and correct fragments even as Ms. Ibanez's story makes them want to read on. Have them think critically about the qualities that made her successful. Can these qualities be learned?

(1) If the way we react to adversity reveals our true character, (2) Maria Elena Ibanez is extraordinary. (3) This successful computer engineer and business-woman is a master at refusing to let obstacles keep her from a goal.

(4) In 1973, nineteen-year-old Maria Elena left Colombia and arrived alone in Miami, (5) *speaking* ~~Speaking~~ just a few words of English. (6) Her goal was to learn fifty new words a day, (7) *by* ~~By~~ talking to people and reading children's books. (8) Soon she spoke well enough to enroll at Florida International University, earn a computer science degree, and so impress college officials that they hired her as a programmer.

(9) In 1982, Maria Elena started her first company. (10) Because computers cost much more in South America than they did in the United States, (11) ~~She~~ *she* decided to sell reasonably priced computers to South American dealers. (12) When some dealers hesitated to do business with such a young woman, she won their respect with her expertise and willingness to teach them about the new technology. (13) Soon she sold International Micro Systems, (14) ~~The~~ *the* nation's fifty-fifth fastest growing private company, at a huge profit.

(15) In spite of this success, people laughed out loud when Maria Elena announced her new goal, (16) ~~To~~ *to* sell computers throughout Africa. (17) She paid no attention and returned from her first selling trip with handfuls of orders. (18) Then in 1992, disaster struck.

(19) Hurricane Andrew plowed into Miami, exploding Maria Elena's house, (20) *as* ~~As~~ she and her two small children hid in a closet. (21) In the morning, dazed,

she walked to the offices and warehouse of her new company. (22) The building

was a mangled mess of fallen walls, trees, wet paper, and smoking wires. (23) Sit-

ting down on a curb, she cried, but as her employees began arriving. (24) ~~She~~ she

sprang into action.

(25) One worker said the company could set up in his home. (26) ~~Which~~ which had

electricity. (27) Working twenty-four hours a day and using cell phones, the em-

ployees called all their African customers. (28) ~~To~~ to say everything was fine and

their orders would be shipped on time. (29) International High Tech grew 700 percent

that year. (30) ~~Despite~~ despite the most damaging hurricane in U.S. history.

(31) Maria Elena moved her company into its rebuilt offices. (32) Today she

and the children live in an apartment. (33) ~~Not~~ not a house. (34) Asked about losing

every piece of clothing, every picture, every possession in her former home. (35)

~~She~~ she laughs, says that most problems hide opportunities, and adds that now she

has no lawn to mow.

PRACTICE 8   **REVIEW**

Proofread these paragraphs for run-ons, comma splices, and fragments. Correct
the errors in any way you choose.   Answers will vary.

Paragraph 1

(1) In 1970, duct tape helped save the lives of the three astronauts aboard the

damaged *Apollo 13* spacecraft, but this strong, fabric-based adhesive tape is not just

for fixing broken things any more. (2) Now rolls of duct tape, creativity, and more

than a dash of humor can bloom into a college scholarship. (3) In 2001, the Duck

Tape Company sponsored the first national "Stuck at Prom" ~~contest.~~ contest after (4) ~~After~~

managers learned that some high school students were sculpting colored rolls of

duct tape into dresses and tuxedos for their senior proms. (5) The couple who de-

signed the most imaginative and stylish formal wear from duct tape received a

$5,000 scholarship to college. (6) The contest tapped into some goofy national

yearning to design clothes with duct tape—or to laugh. (7) By 2005, 260 couples in

Dressed head to toe in duct tape, Margaret Roberts and Tyler Mickley won the 2003 Stuck at Prom contest and scored college scholarships.

forty-four states ~~competed~~ ^{competed. The} the 2005 winners, for example, created an orange harlequin-patterned dress inspired by Pablo Picasso's famous oil painting "Girl Before a Mirror," ^{and} the matching black tuxedo was stylishly accented with a vest in the same pattern and orange stripes on the pant legs. (8) These dazzling getups required twenty-five rolls of duct tape and four weeks' work to complete. (9) Although the clothes were extremely ~~heavy.~~ ^{heavy, the} (10) ~~The~~ collegebound couple says everyone loved their fashion statement. (11) In addition, the duct tape's insulating qualities made them the hottest couple on the dance floor.

Paragraph 2

(1) Some teenagers seem to start the day tired, ^{. They} they are worn out even before they leave for school. (2) Once in class, they might doze off, even in the middle of an exciting lesson. (3) Are these students lazy, ^{? Have} have they stayed out too late partying? (4) Medical research provides a different explanation for the exhaustion of

these teens. (5) As children become adolescents, they develop an increased need for sleep, especially in the morning. (6) Unfortunately, most American high schools
start around 7:30 A.M. _^ many students have to get up as early as 5:00 A.M. (7) Scientists suggest that if students could start school later in the day_^ (8) They might get the extra sleep they need. (9) To test this theory, many schools have begun to experiment with later hours. (10) Congress is even paying the extra operating costs for schools that start after 9:00 A.M. (11) The hope is that teens will be less tired_^ furthermore, because schools that start later will end later, students will be off the streets and out of trouble during the late afternoon_^ (12) Which is prime mischief time.

TEACHING TIP
Students may enjoy debating or writing about keeping or changing early start times for school and/or work.

PRACTICE 9   REVIEW

Proofread this essay for run-ons, comma splices, and fragments. Correct the errors in any way you choose, writing your revisions above the lines.   Answers will vary.

Words for the Wise

(1) Scrabble has been called America's favorite word game. (2) It was invented by Alfred Butts. (3) An architect who wanted to create a word game that required both luck and skill. (4) In 1938, Butts produced a board with 225 squares and 100 tiles with letters on them. (5) Each letter was worth a certain number of points, depending on how easy it was to use that letter in a word.

(6) Butts made fifty Scrabble sets by hand he gave them to his friends. (7) Who loved playing Scrabble. (8) Strangely, Butts could not interest a manufacturer in the game. (9) A friend of his, James Brunot, asked Butts for permission to manufacture and sell the game. (10) At first, Brunot too had little success. (11) Selling only a few sets a year. (12) Then the president of Macy's discovered the game on a vacation. (13) And stocked some sets for his store. (14) Overnight, Scrabble caught on a million sets sold in 1953.

(15) Butts and Brunot couldn't keep up with the demand they sold the rights to a game company. (16) The rest is history today 100 million Scrabble sets have

been sold worldwide. (17) The game is also a successful learning ~~tool~~ tool. (18) ~~for~~ for

teaching spelling and vocabulary. (19) Half a million schoolchildren play it

in ~~school~~ school, and many adults play in local, national, and international Scrabble

tournaments.

Proofread this essay for run-ons, comma splices, and fragments. Correct the errors
in any way you choose, writing your revisions above the lines.   Answers will vary.

Humor as a Life Skill

TEACHING TIP
This passage provides a
good example of how
research strengthens
writing, the topic of Chapter
18. Point out how the
source material is integrated
in the form of paraphrased
indirect quotations.

(1) Do you love to laugh, ? Can ~~can~~ you find humor in daily life, even when things

are going badly? (2) If so, you might be improving your health and your chances

for success in life. (3) Recent studies are exploring the power of laughter to pro-

mote health and even improve performance in college and at work.

(4) Laughter improves health by lowering stress hormones and boosting the

immune system. (5) Studies by Dr. Lee Berk and Dr. Stanley Tan of Loma Linda

University in California show that (6) ~~That~~ belly laughter reduces at least four hor-

mones associated with high levels of stress. (7) These researchers also found that

laughter increases the body's natural ability to kill diseased cells. (8) Laughter

seems to reduce pain, too. The ~~the~~ *Journal of Holistic Nursing* reported that (9) ~~That~~ patients

who were told jokes or watched comic videos after surgery perceived less pain

than those who did not get a dose of humor. (10) Experts recommend taking time

to laugh each day, especially during stressful times like finals week.

(11) In addition, laughter promotes productivity on the job. People ~~people~~ who de-

scribe their work as fun perform better and have better relationships with their

coworkers, according to David Abramis. (12) ~~A~~ a psychologist in the School of Busi-

ness Administration at California State University—Long Beach, who surveyed

382 people in various professions. (13) Another surprising study found that the

most productive workplaces are those in which employees laugh ten minutes of every hour. (14) Writer Daniel Goleman believes that humor improves problem-solving skills and creativity. (15) Because many employers today recognize the value of humor to improve workers' loyalty, teamwork, and overall morale, (16) They are seeking employees who possess this valuable life skill—a sense of humor.

EXPLORING ONLINE

http://grammar.ccc.commnet.edu/grammar/cgi-shl/quiz.pl/run-ons_add1.htm
Review and quizzes to help you root out run-ons

http://grammar.ccc.commnet.edu/grammar/quizzes/fragment_fixing.htm
Great tips and quizzes to help you find and fix sentence fragments.

Online Study Center college.hmco.com/pic/evergreen8e
Visit the Online Study Center for *Evergreen* for more exercises and quizzes.

27

Present Tense (Agreement)

PART A Defining Subject-Verb Agreement

Subjects and verbs in the present tense must **agree** in number; that is, singular subjects take verbs with singular endings, and plural subjects take verbs with plural endings.

ESL TIP
Many ESL students have trouble with verbs and verb tenses in English. You can tailor this comprehensive unit to your needs by assigning some chapters and parts to the full class and other parts selectively.

ESL TIP
In many languages—such as Chinese, Japanese, and Korean—subject-verb number agreement does not exist. Thus, ESL students may need extra help with the concept.

	Verbs in the Present Tense Sample Verb: *To Leap*			
	Singular		**Plural**	
	If the subject is	the verb is	If the subject is	the verb is
1st person:	I	leap	we	leap
2nd person:	you	leap	you	leap
3rd person:	he she it	leaps	they	leap

388

TEACHING TIP
Write two or three sentences containing subject-verb agreement errors on the board. Explain that, in general, an -s follows *either* the subject *or* the verb, not both, dispelling the common misconception that a subject with an -s requires a verb with an -s.

▪ Use an -s or -es ending on the verb only when the subject is *he*, *she*, or *it* or the equivalent of *he*, *she*, or *it*.

The subjects and verbs in the following sentences agree:

1. He *bicycles* to the steel mills every morning.
2. They *bicycle* to the steel mills every morning.
3. This student *hopes* to go to social work school.
4. The planets *revolve* around the sun.

▪ In sentence 1, the singular subject, *he*, takes the singular form of the verb, *bicycles*. *Bicycles* agrees with *he*.

▪ In sentence 2, the plural subject, *they*, takes the plural form of the verb, *bicycle*. *Bicycle* agrees with *they*.

▪ In sentence 3, the subject, *student*, is equivalent to *he* or *she* and takes the singular form of the verb, *hopes*.

▪ In sentence 4, the subject, *planets*, is equivalent to *they* and takes the plural form of the verb, *revolve*.

Subjects joined by the conjunction *and* usually take a plural verb:

5. Kirk and Quincy *attend* a pottery class at the Y.

▪ The subject, *Kirk and Quincy*, is plural, the equivalent of *they*.

▪ *Attend* agrees with the plural subject.*

PRACTICE 1

TEACHING TIP
Consider doing Practice 1 with the whole class or let smaller groups complete it, competing for the best verb-agreement score.

Underline the subject and circle the correct present tense verb.

1. Many <u>people</u> (thinks, (think)) of scientific research as unrelated to everyday life.

2. <u>Professor John Trinkaus</u> ((challenges), challenge) this idea.

3. <u>He and his business students</u> (investigates, (investigate)) such issues as supermarket manners, driving violations, and people's real feelings about Brussels sprouts.

4. <u>They</u> (observes, (observe)) and (records, (record)) data to shed light on human behavior.

---

* For work on consistent verb tense, see Chapter 20, "Revising for Consistency and Parallelism," Part A.

5. For example, most <u>shoppers</u> (grabs, grab) pastries and rolls with their hands instead of tongs or tissues.

6. Of 100 supermarket shoppers, <u>eighty-five</u> (exceeds, exceed) the express line limit.

7. Thanks to Trinkaus, <u>we</u> (knows, know) more about rude and dangerous drivers.

8. Many <u>drivers</u> (parks, park) in fire zones or illegally (snatches, snatch) handicapped parking spots.

9. Only 6 <u>percent</u> (stops, stop) fully at stop signs.

10. In all these studies, <u>observers</u> (notes, note) the vehicle type and driver's sex.

11. Over and over again, <u>women</u> in vans (ranks, rank) as the worst offenders.

12. With a straight face, <u>Trinkaus</u> (investigates, investigate) baseball cap style and pedestrian shoe color.

13. His <u>writings</u> often (stimulates, stimulate) laughter first, then thinking.

14. The eccentric <u>professor</u> proudly (displays, display) his 2003 IgNobel Prize, a joke award for goofy research.

15. According to admirers, his <u>work</u> (sheds, shed) serious light on modern American culture.

PART B Three Troublesome Verbs in the Present Tense: *To Be, To Have, To Do*

Choosing the correct verb form of *to be, to have,* and *to do* can be tricky. Study these charts:

Reference Chart—*To Be* Present Tense				
	Singular		**Plural**	
	If the subject is	the verb is	If the subject is	the verb is
1st person:	I	am	we	are
2nd person:	you	are	you	are
3rd person:	he she it	is	they	are

Reference Chart—*To Have* Present Tense				
	Singular		**Plural**	
	If the subject is	the verb is	If the subject is	the verb is
1st person:	I	have	we	have
2nd person:	you	have	you	have
3rd person:	he she it	has	they	have

Reference Chart—*To Do* Present Tense				
	Singular		**Plural**	
	If the subject is	the verb is	If the subject is	the verb is
1st person:	I	do	we	do
2nd person:	you	do	you	do
3rd person:	he she it	does	they	do

PRACTICE 2

Write the correct present tense form of the verb in the space at the right of the pronoun.

To be		**To have**		**To do**	
I	am	we	have	it	does
we	are	she	has	they	do
he	is	he	has	she	does
you	are	they	have	you	do
it	is	I	have	he	does
they	are	it	has	we	do
she	is	you	have	I	do

PRACTICE 3

Fill in the correct present tense form of the verb in parentheses.

1. Surfing _____is_____ (to be) an extreme sport that _____has_____ (to have) become very popular.

2. Most beginners _____do_____ (to do) basic moves on dry land—lying on the board, kneeling, and then rising to a hunched standing position.

3. An ocean beach with gentle, regular waves _____is_____ (to be) the ideal place to start surfing.

4. Expert surfers _____have_____ (to have) exceptional skills and _____are_____ (to be) at home in the monster waves off Hawaii or Australia.

5. An expert _____does_____ (to do) a "roller coaster" by soaring from the bottom to the top of a giant wave and down again.

6. "Riding a tube" _____is_____ (to be) a thrilling trip through the transparent green tunnel of a giant wave.

7. Hawaiian coastlines _____have_____ (to have) some of the world's best surfing.

8. Banzai Pipeline in Oahu _____is_____ (to be) a famous surfing break that

_____has_____ (to have) excellent tubes and waves three stories high.

9. Oahu's Sunset Rip, a notorious break, _____has_____ (to have) several international surfing competitions.

10. For the surfer, wipeouts, flying boards, and sharks _____are_____ (to be) constant dangers.

11. Yet the sport _____has_____ (to have) new converts every year.

12. Many say that it _____is_____ (to be) a spiritual experience.

PART C Special Singular Constructions

Each of these constructions takes a **singular** verb:

Special Singular Constructions		
either (of) . . .	each (of) . . .	every one (of) . . .
neither (of) . . .	one (of) . . .	which one (of) . . .

> 1. *Neither* of the birds *has* feathers yet.
>
> 2. *Each* of the solutions *presents* difficulties.

■ In sentence 1, *neither* means *neither one*. *Neither* is a singular subject and requires the singular verb *has*.

■ In sentence 2, *each* means *each one*. *Each* is a singular subject and requires the singular verb *presents*.

However, an exception to this general rule is the case in which two subjects are joined by (*n*)*either* . . . (*n*)*or* . . . . Here, the verb agrees with the subject closer to it:

> 1. Neither the teacher nor the *pupils want* the semester shortened.
>
> 2. Either the graphs or the *map has* to be changed.

■ In sentence 3, *pupils* is the subject closer to the verb. The plural subject *pupils* takes the verb *want*.

■ In sentence 4, *map* is the subject closer to the verb. The singular subject *map* takes the verb *has*.

PRACTICE 4

Underline the subject and circle the correct verb in each sentence.

1. Each of these ferns (needs, need) special care.

2. One of the customers always (forget, forgets) his or her umbrella.

3. Which one of the flights (goes, go) nonstop to Dallas?

4. Every one of those cameras (costs, cost) more than I can afford.

5. Either you or Doris (is, are) correct.

6. Either of these computer diskettes (contain, contains) the information you need.

7. Do you really believe that one of these oysters (holds, hold) a pearl?

8. Neither of the twins (resembles, resemble) his parents.

9. One of the scientists (believes, believe) he can cure baldness.

10. Each of these inventions (has, have) an effect on how we spend our leisure time.

PART D Separation of Subject and Verb

Sometimes a phrase or a clause separates the subject from the verb. First, look for the subject; then make sure that the verb agrees with the subject.

> 1. The economist's *ideas* on this matter *seem* well thought out.
>
> 2. *Radios* that were made in the 1930s *are* now collectors' items.

■ In sentence 1, the *ideas* are well thought out. The prepositional phrase *on this matter* separates the subject *ideas* from the verb *seem.**

■ In sentence 2, *radios* are now collectors' items. The relative clause *that were made in the 1930s* separates the subject *radios* from the verb *are.*

PRACTICE 5

Read each sentence carefully for meaning. Cross out any phrase or clause that separates the subject from the verb. Underline the subject and circle the correct verb.

TEACHING TIP
If students erroneously make the verb agree with the object of the preposition in these constructions, remind them to cross out the intervening prepositional phrase and then verify agreement.

1. The plums in that bowl (tastes, taste) sweet.

2. The instructions on the package (is, are) in French and Japanese.

3. Our new community center, which has a swimming pool and tennis courts, (keeps, keep) everyone happy.

4. The lampshades that are made of stained glass (looks, look) beautiful at night.

5. All the CD players on that shelf (comes, come) with a remote control.

6. A movie that lasts more than three hours usually (puts, put) me to sleep.

7. The man with the dark sunglasses (looks, look) like a typical movie villain.

8. The two nurses who check blood pressure (enjoys, enjoy) chatting with the patients.

9. The function of these metal racks (remains, remain) a mystery to me.

10. The lizard on the wall (has, have) only three legs.

---

* For more work on prepositional phrases, see Chapter 24, "The Simple Sentence," Part B.

PART E Sentences Beginning with *There* and *Here*

ESL TIP
In some languages, *there is* sentences do not exist, so ESL students may need to practice using them. A typical sentence error where *there is* or *there are* should be used is the following: *On the bus had many people.*

In sentences that begin with **there** or **here,** the subject usually follows the verb:

> 1. There *seem* to be two *flies* in my soup.
>
> 2. Here *is* my *prediction* for the coming year.

■ In sentence 1, the plural subject *flies* takes the plural verb *seem.*

■ In sentence 2, the singular subject *prediction* takes the singular verb *is.*

You can often determine what the verb should be by reversing the word order: *two flies seem . . .* or *my prediction is. . . .*

PRACTICE 6

Underline the subject and circle the correct verb in each sentence.

1. There (goes, go) Tom Hanks.

2. There (is, are) only a few seconds left in the game.

3. Here (is, are) a terrific way to save money—make a budget and stick to it!

4. There (has, have) been robberies in the neighborhood lately.

5. Here (is, are) the plantains you ordered.

6. Here (comes, come) Jay, the television talk-show host.

7. There (is, are) no direct route to Black Creek from here.

8. There (seems, seem) to be something wrong with the doorbell.

9. Here (is, are) the teapot and sugar bowl I've been looking for.

10. There (is, are) six reporters in the hall waiting for an interview.

PART F Agreement in Questions

In questions, the subject usually follows the verb:

ESL TIP
ESL students might need to be reminded that normal English word order is inverted in questions.

> 1. What *is* the *secret* of your success?
>
> 2. Where *are* the *copies* of the review?

■ In sentence 1, the subject *secret* takes the singular verb *is*.

■ In sentence 2, the subject *copies* takes the plural verb *are*.

You can often determine what the verb should be by reversing the word order: *the secret of your success is . . .* or *the copies are. . . .*

PRACTICE 7

Underline the subject and circle the correct verb in each sentence.

1. How (does, do) the combustion engine actually work?

2. Why (is, are) Robert and Charity so suspicious?

3. Where (is, are) the new suitcases?

4. Which tour guide (have, has) a pair of binoculars?

5. (Are, Is) Dianne and Bill starting a mail-order business?

6. What (seems, seem) to be the problem here?

7. Why (is, are) those boxes stacked in the corner?

8. (Is, Are) the mattress factory really going to close in June?

9. How (does, do) you explain that strange footprint?

10. Who (is, are) those people on the fire escape?

PART G Agreement in Relative Clauses

A **relative clause** is a subordinate clause that begins with *who, which,* or *that*. The verb in the relative clause must agree with the antecedent of the *who, which,* or *that*.*

> 1. People *who have a good sense of humor* make good neighbors.
>
> 2. Be careful of a scheme *that promises you a lot of money fast*.

■ In sentence 1, the antecedent of *who* is *people*. *People* should take the plural verb *have*.

■ In sentence 2, the antecedent of *that* is *scheme*. *Scheme* takes the singular verb *promises*.

---

* For more work on relative clauses, see Chapter 21, "Revising for Sentence Variety," Part D.

PRACTICE 8

Underline the antecedent of the *who, which,* or *that.* Then circle the correct verb.

1. Most patients prefer <u>doctors</u> who (spends, spend) time talking with them.

2. The gnarled <u>oak</u> that (shades, shade) the garden is my favorite tree.

3. Laptop <u>computers</u>, which (has, have) become very popular recently, are still fairly expensive.

4. My <u>neighbor</u>, who (swims, swim) at least one hour a day, is seventy years old.

5. <u>Planning</u> ahead, which (saves, save) hours of wasted time, is a good way to manage time effectively.

6. Employers often appreciate <u>employees</u> who (asks, ask) intelligent questions.

7. This <u>air conditioner</u>, which now (costs, cost) $800, rarely breaks down.

8. Everyone admires her because she is <u>someone</u> who always (sees, see) the bright side of a bad situation.

9. He is the <u>man</u> who (creates, create) furniture from scraps of walnut, cherry, and birch.

10. <u>Foods</u> that (contains, contain) artificial sweeteners may be hazardous to your health.

PRACTICE 9 REVIEW

Proofread the following essay for verb agreement errors. Correct any errors by writing above the lines.

Chimp Smarts

(1) Chimpanzees sometimes seem uncannily human, especially in their use of tools and language. (2) Neither the gorilla nor the orangutan, both close relatives of the chimp, exhibit such behavior. [*exhibits*]

(3) Chimps employs a number of tools in their everyday lives. [*employ*] (4) They dine by inserting sticks into insect nests and then licking their utensils clean. (5) Each

TEACHING TIP
Students should be able to
recognize that this essay is
developed by illustration.
Ask them to identify the
examples that develop the
topic sentences in the
second and third paragraphs.

of these intelligent animals also ~~crack~~ *cracks* fruit and nuts with stones. (6) What's more,

chimpanzees ~~creates~~ *create* their own tools. (7) They make their eating sticks by cleaning

leaves from branches. (8) They even ~~attaches~~ *attach* small sticks together to make longer

rods for getting at hard-to-reach insects. (9) Some of the other tools chimps make

~~is~~ *are* fly-whisks, sponges of chewed bark, and leaf-rags to clean themselves with.

(10) Scientists on safari ~~has~~ *have* observed infant chimps imitating their parents' use of

these tools.

(11) Recent experiments indicate that chimpanzees probably also ~~understands~~ *understand*

language though they lack the physical ability to speak. (12) There ~~are~~ *is* little doubt

that they can comprehend individual words. (13) Using sign language and key-

boards, some chimps in captivity use nearly 200 words. (14) This vocabulary

~~include~~ *includes* nouns, verbs, and prepositions. (15) Hunger and affection ~~is~~ *are* needs that

they have expressed by punching keyboard symbols. (16) Do chimps ~~has~~ *have* the abil-

ity to string words into sentences? (17) Intriguingly, one chimp named Lucy has

shown that she ~~understand~~ *understands* the difference between such statements as "Roger

tickles Lucy" and "Lucy tickles Roger."

(18) Scientists still argue about just how much language a chimpanzee truly

~~comprehend~~ *comprehends*. (19) However, no one who ~~have~~ *has* watched them closely ~~doubt~~ *doubts* the in-

telligence of these remarkable beings.

EXPLORING ONLINE

TEACHING TIP
More practice and assess-
ment are available in the
Evergreen Test Bank, linked
ACE tests on the *Evergreen*
Online Teaching and Study
Centers, *WriteSpace for
Evergreen,* and Exploring
Online links in this chapter.

http://depts.gallaudet.edu/englishworks/exercises/exgrammar/subver2.htm
Crossword puzzle: Add *-s* or *-es* or no *-s* at all?

http://grammar.ccc.commnet.edu/grammar/quizzes/svagr3.html Click on the
subject-verb agreement error you most need to avoid for interactive practice.

Online Study Center   college.hmco.com/pic/evergreen8e
Visit the Online Study Center for *Evergreen* for more exercises and quizzes.

28

Past Tense

PART A   Regular Verbs in the Past Tense

Regular verbs in the past tense take an *-ed* or *-d* ending:

TEACHING TIP
For students who don't pronounce or hear the *-ed* on regular verbs, these forms can be more problematic than irregulars. Help such students see that this is their error pattern.

> 1. The captain *hoisted* the flag.
> 2. They *purchased* a flat screen TV yesterday.
> 3. We *deposited* a quarter in the meter.

- *Hoisted, purchased,* and *deposited* are regular verbs in the past tense.
- Each verb ends in *-ed* or *-d.*

PRACTICE 1

Fill in the past tense of the regular verbs in parentheses.*

1. In the early 1900s, many Floridians ____insisted____ (insist) on draining the

   Everglades, which they ____believed____ (believe) to be a worthless swamp.

———————

* If you have questions about spelling, see Chapter 38, "Spelling," Parts D, E, and F.

TEACHING TIP
You may wish to review spelling rules for adding -d or -ed. 1. If the verb ends in e, add -d (*lived, skated*). 2. If the verb ends in y, change the y to i and add -ed (*cried, applied*). 3. If the last two letters of the verb are a vowel plus a consonant (except w and y), double the consonant and add -ed (*tapped, committed*). 4. For all other verbs, add -ed (*picked, stayed, followed*).

2. This idea ___horrified___ (horrify) Marjory Stoneman Douglas, a freelance writer.

3. Dazzled as a child by the clean tropical light of Florida, she ___loved___ (love) the wild beauty of the Everglades and ___recognized___ (recognize) its value.

4. In 1947, she ___researched___ (research) and ___published___ (publish) *The Everglades: River of Grass*.

5. Her book ___revealed___ (reveal) the Glades' importance as a vast, slow-moving river that ___supplied___ (supply) South Florida with water and even rain.

6. When the petite Douglas ___appeared___ (appear) onstage, real estate developers often ___hurled___ (hurl) verbal abuse.

7. However, she ___refused___ (refuse) to stay silent and eventually ___inspired___ (inspire) a movement to protect the Glades and its unique wildlife.

8. In her seventies, she ___formed___ (form) the Friends of the Everglades and ___persuaded___ (persuade) Florida's governor to support the Everglades Forever Act.

9. Her lifelong defense of this ecosystem ___earned___ (earn) her the title "Mother of the Everglades."

10. Marjory Stoneman Douglas ___died___ (die) in 1998 at age 108, but she ___proved___ (prove) that one person's passion can change the world.

A lone egret surveys the Everglades as a thunderstorm moves in.

PART B Irregular Verbs in the Past Tense

Irregular verbs do not take an *-ed* or *-d* ending in the past but change internally:

ESL TIP
Irregular verbs can be a problem for ESL students and speakers of languages that do not include irregular verbs (e.g., Chinese). See also Error #6: Irregular Verb Errors, in the "8 Most Common ESL Errors" on the *Evergreen* Online Study Center.

1. I *wrote* that letter in ten minutes.
2. Although the orange cat *fell* from a high branch, she escaped unharmed.
3. The play *began* on time but ended fairly late.

■ *Wrote* is the past tense of *write*.

■ *Fell* is the past tense of *fall*.

■ *Began* is the past tense of *begin*.

Here is a partial list of irregular verbs:

TEACHING TIP
Tell students that many irregular verbs fall into one of three categories. 1. Do not change (*cut/cut, hit/hit*). 2. Change their vowel (*ride/rode, get/got, drink/drank*). 3. Change completely (*teach/taught, think/thought*).

TEACHING TIP
Pair students and ask them to take turns using verbs from this list in spoken sentences. Doing so will give them a chance to hear the correct forms.

Reference Chart
Irregular Verbs in the Past Tense

Simple Form	Past Tense	Simple Form	Past Tense
be	was, were	eat	ate
become	became	fall	fell
begin	began	feed	fed
blow	blew	feel	felt
break	broke	fight	fought
bring	brought	find	found
build	built	fly	flew
buy	bought	forbid	forbade
catch	caught	forget	forgot
choose	chose	forgive	forgave
come	came	freeze	froze
cut	cut	get	got
deal	dealt	give	gave
dig	dug	go	went
dive	dove (dived)	grow	grew
do	did	have	had
draw	drew	hear	heard
drink	drank	hide	hid
drive	drove	hold	held

(continued)

Reference Chart Irregular Verbs in the Past Tense			
(continued)			
Simple Form	**Past Tense**	**Simple Form**	**Past Tense**
hurt	hurt	shake	shook
keep	kept	shine	shone (shined)
know	knew	sing	sang
lay	laid	sit	sat
lead	led	sleep	slept
leave	left	speak	spoke
let	let	spend	spent
lie	lay	split	split
lose	lost	spring	sprang
make	made	stand	stood
mean	meant	steal	stole
meet	met	stink	stank
pay	paid	swim	swam
put	put	take	took
quit	quit	teach	taught
read	read	tear	tore
ride	rode	tell	told
rise	rose	think	thought
run	ran	throw	threw
say	said	understand	understood
see	saw	wake	woke (waked)
seek	sought	wear	wore
seel	sold	win	won
send	sent	write	wrote

PRACTICE 2

Fill in the past tense of the regular and irregular verbs in parentheses. If you are not sure of the past tense, use the chart on pages 401–402. Do not guess.

Hispanic Heroes: Shaking Up Hollywood

(1) For much of the twentieth century, Hispanics in Hollywood __remained__ (remain) a small minority. (2) Many Latin actors either __accepted__ (accept) such

stereotyped roles as the gardener or ___changed___ (change) their names, hoping to snag better roles. (3) Jo Raquel Tejada ___chose___ (choose) the last name Welch, and Ramon Estevez ___became___ (become) Martin Sheen. (4) But the approach of a new century ___brought___ (bring) deeper change—in the form of determined individuals who ___dreamed___ (dream) of making or starring in movies and then ___fought___ (fight) to open doors.

(5) Director Robert Rodriguez, for instance, ___succeeded___ (succeed) after a rocky beginning. (6) As a young Texan, Rodriguez was rejected by the film school to which he ___applied___ (apply). (7) Instead of getting discouraged, the twenty-three-year-old ___took___ (take) off for Mexico with a movie camera, some friends, and $7,000. (8) The result was the film *El Mariachi*, a Spanish-language action comedy that Rodriguez later ___sold___ (sell) to Columbia Pictures for worldwide distribution. (9) After that, he ___kept___ (keep) entertaining moviegoers with low-budget, action-packed English-language films like *Desperado, Spy Kids,* and *From Dusk Till Dawn*. (10) He ___raked___ (rake) in millions with his violent shoot-'em-up scenes and special effects. (11) Perhaps more important, Rodriguez ___put___ (put) Hispanics in top roles—for instance, casting Antonio Banderas as a dad, not a Hispanic dad, in *Spy Kids*. (12) "I find that the best way through a closed door," Rodriguez once ___announced___ (announce), "is to kick it open."

(13) Another Hispanic who ___helped___ (help) make her own opportunities is Mexican-born actress and producer Salma Hayek. (14) Ironically, it was Rodriguez who ___battled___ (battle) Hollywood for approval to cast this unknown actress in one of *Desperado*'s leading roles. (15) She ___did___ (do) not disappoint him, and her performance ___catapulted___ (catapult) her to fame. (16) From the time she was thirteen, Hayek ___admired___ (admire) Frida Kahlo and ___longed___ (long) to play the spirited Mexican painter in a film about her life. (17) Behind the scenes, Salma ___strategized___ (strategize) brilliantly to get the movie made, secure rights, and beat out Madonna for the part. (18) In the end, Hayek ___produced___ (produce) and ___starred___ (star) in

Salma Hayek as Mexican painter Frida Kahlo, the dream role for which she fought

Frida, which ___opened___ (open) in 2002. (19) Her performance in that lead role ___earned___ (earn) her an Academy Award nomination. (20) This movie and Salma's depiction of the brainy scientist in *Spy Kids* ___expanded___ (expand) Hollywood's ideas about "suitable" Hispanic roles.

(21) Rodriguez and Hayek are just two examples of the new infusion of talent in American movies. (22) In 2005, the mentor and his leading lady ___found___ (find) themselves together again—on a magazine cover. (23) Both ___won___ (win) spots on *Time* magazine's list of the 25 Most Influential Hispanics in the United States.

PART C A Troublesome Verb in the Past Tense: *To Be*

To be is the only verb that in the past tense has different forms for different persons. Be careful of subject-verb agreement:

	Reference Chart—*To Be* Past Tense			
	Singular		**Plural**	
	If the subject is	the verb is	If the subject is	the verb is
1st person:	I	was	we	were
2nd person:	you	were	you	were
3rd person:	he she it	was	they	were

■ Note that the first person singular form and the third person singular form are the same—*was*.

Be especially careful of agreement when adding *not* to *was* or *were* to make a contraction:

> was + not = wasn't
>
> were + not = weren't

PRACTICE 3

Circle the correct form of the verb *to be* in the past tense. Do not guess. If you are not sure of the correct form, use the chart on page 405.

1. Oprah Winfrey (**was**, were) always an avid reader.

2. In fact, books (was, **were**) sometimes her only comfort during her difficult childhood and painful adolescence.

3. When her producers (was, **were**) considering a TV book club, the world's most popular talk-show host (**was**, were) sure she could get the whole country reading.

4. Her first book club selection (**was**, were) *The Deep End of the Ocean* by Jacquelyn Mitchard, the story of a kidnapped child; the public's rush to buy books (**wasn't**, weren't) anticipated.

5. Mitchard's publishers (was, were) astonished to have to reprint the book nearly twenty times; all in all, 900,000 hardcovers and over 2 million paperbacks (was, were) sold.

6. Every book club pick (was, were) a huge success, and even people who didn't read found they (was, were) eagerly awaiting Winfrey's next selection.

7. When Oprah closed the club in 2002, her e-mail and phone lines (was, were) flooded with protests.

8. So readers (was, were) delighted in 2003 when Oprah revived the club in a new form, focusing on only classic authors like William Faulkner, John Steinbeck, and Carson McCullers.

9. Thanks to Oprah, Leo Tolstoy's 1875 novel *Anna Karenina* (was, were) catapulted to number 1 on *The New York Times* bestseller list.

10. By 2005, however, this influential woman (was, were) again ready to recommend her favorite living authors of both fiction and nonfiction.

PART D Troublesome Pairs in the Past Tense: *Can/Could, Will/Would*

Use **could** as the past tense of **can.**

> 1. Maria is extraordinary because she *can* remember what happened to her when she was three years old.
>
> 2. When I was in high school, I *could* do two sit-ups in an hour.

■ In sentence 1, *can* shows the action is in the present.

■ In sentence 2, *could* shows the action occurred in the past.

PRACTICE 4

ESL TIP
Point out that *can* does not require an *-s* in third person singular.

Fill in either the present tense *can* or the past tense *could*.

1. Tom is so talented that he _____can_____ play most music on the piano by ear.

2. He _____can_____ leave the hospital as soon as he feels stronger.

3. Last week we _____could_____ not find fresh strawberries.

4. When we were in Spain last summer, we _____could_____ see all of Madrid from our hotel balcony.

5. As a child, I _____could_____ perform easily in public, but I _____can_____ no longer do it.

6. Anything you ___can___ do, he ___can___ do better.

7. Nobody ___could___ find the guard after the robbery yesterday.

8. These days, Fred ___can___ usually predict the weather from the condition of his bunions.

Use **would** as the past tense of **will.**

---

3. Roberta says that she *will* arrive with her camera in ten minutes.

4. Roberta said that she *would* arrive with her camera in ten minutes.

▪ In sentence 3, *will* points to the future from the present.

▪ In sentence 4, *would* points to the future from the past.

PRACTICE 5

Fill in either the present tense *will* or the past tense *would.*

1. Sean expected that he ___would___ arrive at midnight.

2 Sean expects that he ___will___ arrive at midnight.

3. I hope the sale at the used car lot ___will___ continue for another week.

4. I hoped the sale at the used car lot ___would___ continue for another week.

5. When Benny had time, he ___would___ color-code his computer disks.

6. When Benny has time, he ___will___ color-code his computer disks.

7. The chefs assure us that the wedding cake ___will___ be spectacular.

8. The chefs assured us that the wedding cake ___would___ be spectacular.

PRACTICE 6   REVIEW

Proofread the following essay for past tense errors. Then write the correct past tense form above the line.

Video Game Nation

TEACHING AND ESL TIP
This practice works well in class. You might ask volunteers to read one paragraph each aloud, correcting the verbs as they go. Have the class check their work by ear.

(1) In 1972, when Nolan Bushnell introduced the first video game to the mass market, few people imagined what the future hold. (2) Bushnell call his new company Atari; the game was Pong. (3) To play, two people simply bounced a digital

(held) *(called)*

ball back and forth on a black-and-white console, turning knobs to control their

was
paddles. (4) Primitive by today's standards, Pong were a sensation in arcades and

outsold
bars across the United States. (5) In 1975, Atari's home version of Pong outsolded

all other items in the Sears Christmas catalog. (6) But that was just the beginning.

became
(7) Over the next thirty-five years, electronic games becomed one of America's

most popular pastimes, spawning a booming industry and new jobs.

flocked
(8) During the 1980s, the first generation of gamers flock to arcades to play Pac-

Man, Donkey Kong, and Centipede. (9) Far-sighted tech companies like Sony, Nin-

saw   went   created
tendo, and Microsoft seen this growing market and gone to work. (10) They create

home consoles, handheld systems, and of course, more and better games. (11) With

the evolution of eye-popping 3-D graphics, realistic sound and action, and imagina-

began
tive characters, video games begin to look more like television and movies than the

kept
electronic paddle-and-ball game that started it all. (12) The public keeped buying.

totaled
(13) In 2004 alone, sales of game consoles and software total $6.2 billion.

did
(14) As the industry grew, so do controversy. (15) Critics warned that gamers

sat   worried
just set on the couch instead of playing outside. (16) Many worryied about the vio-

lent content of some games. (17) Others argued that the puzzle-based adventure

taught   had
games of the 1990s and early 2000s teached useful skills. (18) Gamers has to reason,

invent strategies, and foresee the consequences of their actions. (19) Despite the con-

troversy, video games are part of life for most American children, teens, and even

rose
adults. (20) In recent years, the average age of the video game player rise to thirty.

(21) Some gamers longed to work in the field, but they needed training.

knew
(22) They knowed that companies, hoping to create the latest, greatest game,

formed development teams composed of graphic designers, artists, musicians,

was
computer programmers, and other technicians. (23) So it were students themselves

clamored
who clamor for degree programs to teach them the necessary skills. (24) Some col-

TEACHING TIP
Urge students to think critically about the pros and cons of video games. Perhaps suggest that they research the cognitive benefits of the games. Do any students want to work in this or another technology field?

leges—like New York's Rensselaer Polytechnic Institute and Pittsburgh's Carnegie

Mellon University—responded quickly. (25) They ~~establish~~ interdisciplinary pro-

established

grams to prepare students for the fast-moving video game industry of the future.

EXPLORING ONLINE

TEACHING TIP
More practice and assessment are available in the *Evergreen* Test Bank, linked ACE tests on the *Evergreen* Online Teaching and Study Centers, *WriteSpace for Evergreen,* and Exploring Online links in this chapter.

http://grammar.ccc.commnet.edu/grammar/cgi-shl/par2_quiz.pl/irregular _quiz.htm. Type in the irregular verbs; the computer checks you.

http://web2.uvcs.uvic.ca/elc/studyzone/330/grammar/pasted.htm Review and quizzes: regular verbs

Online Study Center   **college.hmco.com/pic/evergreen8e**
Visit the Online Study Center for *Evergreen* for more exercises and quizzes.

29

The Past Participle

PART A   Past Participles of Regular Verbs

TEACHING TIP
Past participles are the source of problems for many students. Those who don't pronounce the *-ed* ending of regular verbs are more likely to make written mistakes. Explain that verb errors are a serious blot in college and work.

The **past participle** is the form of the verb that can be combined with helping verbs like *have* and *has* to make verbs of more than one word:

Present Tense	Past Tense	Helping Verb plus Past Participle
1. They *skate*.	1. They *skated*.	1. They *have skated*.
2. Beth *dances*.	2. Beth *danced*.	2. Beth *has danced*.
3. Frank *worries*.	3. Frank *worried*.	3. Frank *has worried*.

- *Skated,* *danced,* and *worried* are all past participles of regular verbs.

- Note that both the *past tense* and the *past participle* of regular verbs end in *-ed* or *-d.*

410

PRACTICE 1

The first sentence of each pair that follows contains a regular verb in the past tense. Fill in *have* or *has* plus the past participle of the same verb to complete the second sentence.

TEACHING TIP
You may wish to review spelling rules for adding -*d* or -*ed*. 1. If the verb ends in *e*, add -*d* (*lived, skated*). 2. If the verb ends in *y*, change the *y* to *i* and add -*ed* (*cried, applied*). 3. If the last two letters of the verb are a vowel plus a consonant (except *w* and *y*), double the consonant and add -*ed* (*tapped, committed*). 4. For all other verbs, add -*ed* (*picked, stayed, followed*).

1. Arlen Ness earned his title, King of the Choppers.

   Arlen Ness _____has_____ _____earned_____ his title, King of the Choppers.

2. Since 1967, Ness designed and manufactured one-of-a-kind motorcycles.

   Since 1967, Ness _____has_____ _____designed_____ and _____manufactured_____ one-of-a-kind motorcycles.

3. The craftsmanship, performance, and eye-popping style of Ness bikes attracted worldwide attention.

   The craftsmanship, performance, and eye-popping style of Ness bikes _____have_____ _____attracted_____ worldwide attention.

4. Shaquille O'Neal and Aerosmith's Steven Tyler ordered custom Ness creations.

   Shaquille O'Neal and Aerosmith's Steven Tyler _____have_____ _____ordered_____ custom Ness creations.

5. A master builder and bike painter, Arlen Ness received many first-place trophies.

   A master builder and bike painter, Arlen Ness _____has_____ _____received_____ many first-place trophies.

6. Crowds lined up just to glimpse his elongated yellow chopper, "Top Banana."

   Crowds _____have_____ _____lined_____ up just to glimpse his elongated yellow chopper, "Top Banana."

7. Ness picked witty names like "Jelly Belly" for many bikes.

   Ness _____has_____ _____picked_____ witty names like "Jelly Belly" for many bikes.

8. The curvy, green beauty, "Smooth-Ness," and the silver monster, "Mach Ness," both played on his famous name.

The curvy, green beauty, "Smooth-Ness," and the silver monster, "Mach Ness," both ____have____ ____played____ on his famous name.

9. Corey Ness joined his father's multimillion dollar company.

Corey Ness ____has____ ____joined____ his father's multimillion dollar company.

10. Custom motorcycles turned into big business.

Custom motorcycles ____have____ ____turned____ into big business.

Arlen Ness rides "Top Banana," one of his eye-popping choppers.

PART B Past Participles of Irregular Verbs

Most verbs that are irregular in the past tense are also irregular in the past participle, as shown in the following chart.

Present Tense	Past Tense	Helping Verb plus Past Participle
1. We *sing*.	1. We *sang*.	1. We *have sung*.
2. Bill *writes*.	2. Bill *wrote*.	2. Bill *has written*.
3. I *think*.	3. I *thought*.	3. I *have thought*.

■ Irregular verbs change from present to past to past participle in unusual ways.

■ *Sung, written,* and *thought* are all past participles of irregular verbs.

■ Note that the past tense and past participle of *think* are the same—*thought*.

TEACHING TIP
Students may want to use flash cards to review the past participle forms of irregular verbs. To find or create flash cards, try **http://flashcardexchange. com/index.php**.

ESL TIP
Some ESL teachers rely on memorization to teach irregular verb forms while others use only practice in context. A variety of approaches will address different learning and teaching styles.

Reference Chart
Irregular Verbs, Past and Past Participle

Simple Form	Past Tense	Past Participle
be	was, were	been
become	became	become
begin	began	begun
blow	blew	blown
break	broke	broken
bring	brought	brought
build	built	built
buy	bought	bought
catch	caught	caught
choose	chose	chosen
come	came	come
cut	cut	cut
deal	dealt	dealt
dig	dug	dug
dive	dove (dived)	dived
do	did	done
draw	drew	drawn
drink	drank	drunk
drive	drove	driven
eat	ate	eaten
fall	fell	fallen
feed	fed	fed
feel	felt	felt

(continued)

TEACHING TIP
You might have students write sentences using past participles from this list, then exchange papers and check each other's work.

ESL TIP
Remind students to keep track of their personal error patterns—including any irregular verbs that give them trouble. They should proofread their writing with these errors in mind.

Reference Chart
Irregular Verbs, Past and Past Participle

Simple Form	Past Tense	Past Participle
fight	fought	fought
find	found	found
fly	flew	flown
forbid	forbade	forbidden
forget	forgot	forgotten
forgive	forgave	forgiven
freeze	froze	frozen
get	got	got (gotten)
give	gave	given
go	went	gone
grow	grew	grown
have	had	had
hear	heard	heard
hide	hid	hidden
hold	held	held
hurt	hurt	hurt
keep	kept	kept
know	knew	known
lay	laid	laid
lead	led	led
leave	left	left
let	let	let
lie	lay	lain
lose	lost	lost
make	made	made
mean	meant	meant
meet	met	met
pay	paid	paid
put	put	put
quit	quit	quit
read	read	read
ride	rode	ridden

(continued)

Reference Chart
Irregular Verbs, Past and Past Participle

Simple Form	Past Tense	Past Participle
rise	rose	risen
run	ran	run
say	said	said
see	saw	seen
seek	sought	sought
sell	sold	sold
send	sent	sent
shake	shook	shaken
shine	shone (shined)	shone (shined)
sing	sang	sung
sit	sat	sat
sleep	slept	slept
speak	spoke	spoken
spend	spent	spent
split	split	split
spring	sprang	sprung
stand	stood	stood
steal	stole	stolen
stink	stank	stunk
swim	swam	swum
take	took	taken
teach	taught	taught
tear	tore	torn
tell	told	told
think	thought	thought
throw	threw	thrown
understand	understood	understood
wake	woke (waked)	woken (waked)
wear	wore	worn
win	won	won
write	wrote	written

PRACTICE 2

The first sentence of each pair that follows contains an irregular verb in the past tense. Fill in *have* or *has* plus the past participle of the same verb to complete the second sentence.

1. Sean took plenty of time buying the groceries.

   Sean _____has_____ _____taken_____ plenty of time buying the groceries.

2. We sent our latest budget to the mayor.

   We _____have_____ _____sent_____ our latest budget to the mayor.

3. My daughter hid her diary.

   My daughter _____has_____ _____hidden_____ her diary.

4. The jockey rode all day in the hot sun.

   The jockey _____has_____ _____ridden_____ all day in the hot sun.

5. Hershey, Pennsylvania, became a great tourist attraction.

   Hershey, Pennsylvania, _____has_____ _____become_____ a great tourist attraction.

6. The company's managers knew about these hazards for two years.

   The company's managers _____have_____ _____known_____ about these hazards for two years.

7. Carrie floated down the river on an inner tube.

   Carrie _____has_____ _____floated_____ down the river on an inner tube.

8. At last, our team won the bowling tournament.

   At last, our team _____has_____ _____won_____ the bowling tournament.

9. Larry and Marsha broke their long silence.

   Larry and Marsha _____have_____ _____broken_____ their long silence.

10. Science fiction films were very popular this past year.

    Science fiction films _____have_____ _____been_____ very popular this past year.

PRACTICE 3

Complete each sentence by filling in *have* or *has* plus the past participle of the verb in parentheses. Some verbs are regular, some are irregular.

1. Soccer _____has_____ _____gained_____ (gain) popularity in the United States ever since the 1994 World Cup was held in Pasadena, California.

2. Sports fans _____have_____ _____seen_____ (see) the enthusiasm and passion that soccer arouses in such countries as Argentina, Brazil, Italy, and Portugal.

3. The United States also _____has_____ ___demonstrated___ (demonstrate) that it can win games in the biggest soccer competition in the world.

4. By advancing to the quarterfinals of the 2002 World Cup, the American soccer team _____has_____ _____won_____ (win) new respect worldwide.

5. But the Women's National Team _____has_____ _____taken_____ (take) the sport by storm and _____risen_____ (rise) to number 1 in the world.

6. In the process, it _____has_____ _____made_____ (make) names like Mia Hamm and Michelle Akers household words.

7. Consequently, television coverage of games and audience attendance _____have_____ ___continued___ (continue) to increase.

8. Major League Soccer _____has_____ _____added_____ (add) more professional teams, and cities like Los Angeles, Dallas, Chicago, and New York _____have_____ _____opened_____ (open) or will open stadiums just for soccer.

9. In particular, the game _____has_____ _____become_____ (become) hugely popular among suburban boys and girls, whose parents _____have_____ ___encouraged___ (encourage) them to play a relatively safe but exciting sport.

10. Experts say that this generation, which _____has_____ _____fallen_____ (fall) in love with the game, will likely change the future of American athletics.

PART C Using the Present Perfect Tense

The **present perfect tense** is composed of the present tense of *to have* plus the past participle. The present perfect tense shows that an action has begun in the past and is continuing into the present.

1. Past tense:	Beatrice *taught* English for ten years.
2. Present perfect tense	Beatrice *has taught* English for ten years.

■ In sentence 1, Beatrice *taught* English in the past, but she no longer teaches it. Note the use of the simple past tense, *taught*.

■ In sentence 2, Beatrice *has taught* for ten years and is still teaching English *now*. *Has taught* implies that the action is continuing.

PRACTICE 4

Read these sentences carefully for meaning. Then circle the correct verb—either the **past tense** or the **present perfect tense**.

1. He (directed, **has directed**) the theater group for many years now.

2. Emilio lifted the rug and (has swept, **swept**) the dust under it.

3. She (**went**, has gone) to a poetry slam last night.

4. For the past four years, I (took, **have taken**) art classes in the summer.

5. We (talked, **have talked**) about the problem of your lateness for three days; it's time for you to do something about it.

6. While he was in Japan, he (**took**, have taken) many photographs of shrines.

7. She (**won**, has won) that contest ten years ago.

8. The boxers (fought, **have fought**) for an hour, and they look very tired.

9. He (**applied**, has applied) to three colleges and attended the one with the best sociology department.

10. The auto mechanics (**had**, have had) a radio show together for five years and are now extremely popular.

PART D Using the Past Perfect Tense

The **past perfect tense** is composed of the past tense of *to have* plus the past participle. The past perfect tense shows that an action occurred further back in the past than other past action.

1. Past tense:	Rhonda *left* for the movies.
2. Past perfect tense:	Rhonda *had* already *left* for the movies by the time we *arrived*.

■ In sentence 1, *left* is the simple past.

■ In sentence 2, the past perfect *had left* shows that this action occurred even before another action in the past, *arrived*.

PRACTICE 5

Read these sentences carefully for meaning. Then circle the correct verb—either the **past tense** or the **past perfect tense.**

1. Tony came to the office with a cane last week because he (sprained, had sprained) his ankle a month ago.

2. As Janice (piled, had piled) the apples into a pyramid, she thought, "I should become an architect."

3. Juan (finished, had finished) his gardening by the time I (drove, had driven) up in my new convertible.

4. The man nervously (looked, had looked) at his watch and then walked a bit faster.

5. Roberto told us that he (decided, had decided) to enlist in the Marines.

6. The caller asked whether we (received, had received) our free toaster yet.

7. Last week he told me that he (forgot, had forgotten) to mail the rent check.

8. As the curtain came down, everyone (rose, had risen) and applauded the Brazilian dance troupe.

9. Scott (closed, had closed) his books and went to the movies.

10. The prosecutor proved that the defendant was lying; until then I (believed, had believed) he was innocent.

ESL TIP
Tense sequence can be especially tricky for ESL learners. Using a tense sequence chart might help them. Try **http://grammar .ccc.commnet.edu/grammar /verbs.htm#sequence.**

PART E Using the Passive Voice (To Be and the Past Participle)

TEACHING TIP
To help students improve their writing style, use these and other examples to show that passive voice sentences are often wordier than active voice sentences. Passive voice also allows for omission of the subject—desirable only when the subject is unknown or diplomacy is required (e.g., *The situation was mishandled*).

The **passive voice** is composed of the past participle with some form of *to be* (*am, is, are, was, were, has been, have been,* or *had been*). In the passive voice, the subject does not act but is *acted upon.*

Compare the passive voice with the active voice in the following pairs of sentences.

1. Passive voice:	This newspaper *is written* by journalism students.
2. Active voice:	Journalism students *write* this newspaper.
3. Passive voice:	My garden *was devoured* by rabbits.
4. Active voice:	Rabbits *devoured* my garden.

■ In sentence 1, the subject, *this newspaper,* is passive; it is acted upon. In sentence 2, the subject, *students,* is active; it performs the action.

■ Note the difference between the passive verb *is written* and the active verb *write.*

■ However, both verbs (*is written* and *write*) are in the *present tense.*

■ The verbs in sentences 3 and 4 are both in the *past tense: was devoured* (passive) and *devoured* (active).

Use the passive voice sparingly. Write in the passive voice when you want to emphasize the receiver of the action rather than the doer.

PRACTICE 6

Fill in the correct **past participle** form of the verb in parentheses to form the passive voice. If you are not sure, check the chart on pages 413–415.

1. The barn was _____built_____ (build) by friends of the family.

2. These ruby slippers were _____given_____ (give) to me by my grandmother.

3. A faint inscription is _____etched_____ (etch) on the back of the old gold watch.

4. At the garden party, Sheila and Una were _____bitten_____ (bite) by mosquitoes and gnats.

5. The getaway car is always _____driven_____ (drive) by a man in a gray fedora.

6. Her articles have been _____published_____ (publish) in the *Texas Monthly.*

PRACTICE 7

Whenever possible, write in the *active* not the *passive* voice. Rewrite these sentences in the active voice, making all necessary verb and subject changes. Be sure to keep the sentence in the original tense.

EXAMPLE   Too many personal questions were asked by the interviewer.

The interviewer asked too many personal questions.

1. The shot was blocked by the goalie.

   The goalie blocked the shot.

2. Her reputation was hurt by her rudeness.

   Her rudeness hurt her reputation.

3. The law boards were passed by Eduardo and Noah.

   Eduardo and Noah passed the law boards.

4. The noisy group was warned by the usher.

   The usher warned the noisy group.

5. We were shown how to create PowerPoint slides by the instructor.

The instructor showed us how to create PowerPoint slides.

PART F Using the Past Participle as an Adjective

The **past participle** form of the verb can be used as an **adjective** after a linking verb:

> 1. The window is *broken*.

■ The adjective *broken* describes the subject *window*.

The **past participle** form of the verb can sometimes be used as an adjective before a noun or a pronoun.

> 2. This *fried* chicken tastes wonderful.

■ The adjective *fried* describes the noun *chicken*.

PRACTICE 8

Use the past participle form of the verb in parentheses as an adjective in each sentence.

TEACHING TIP
Remind students that not pronouncing a final *-ed* can contribute to written errors. Urge them to practice saying *pleased to meet you, case closed, well-dressed,* and so on.

1. My _____used_____ (use) laptop was a great bargain at only $200.

2. Bob is highly _____qualified_____ (qualify) to install a water heater.

3. The _____air-conditioned_____ (air-condition) room was making everyone shiver.

4. The newly _____risen_____ (rise) cinnamon bread smelled wonderful.

5. Were you _____surprised_____ (surprise) to hear about my raise?

6. He feels _____depressed_____ (depress) on rainy days.

7. She knows the power of the _____written_____ (write) word.

8. My gym teacher seems _____prejudiced_____ (prejudice) against short people.

9. The _____embarrassed_____ (embarrass) child pulled her jacket over her head.

10. We ordered _____tossed_____ (toss) salad, _____broiled_____ (broil) salmon, _____mashed_____ (mash) potatoes, and _____baked_____ (bake) apple rings.

PRACTICE 9

Proofread the following paragraph for errors in past participles used as adjectives. Correct the errors by writing above the lines.

(1) To experience the food of another culture is to appreciate that culture in new ways. (2) A fine example is the traditional Chinese wedding banquet, where each beautiful dish is chosen, ~~prepare~~ prepared, and presented to carry a promise for the couple's future. (3) Carefully ~~season~~ seasoned shark's fin soup opens the feast; this rare and expensive treat signifies health and long life to both family lines. (4) Each table receives its own glazed Peking duck to indicate the couple's fidelity. (5) In Chinese tradition, chicken represents the phoenix, a magic bird that rises from the ashes, and lobster represents the dragon. (6) Often ~~combine~~ combined and ~~bake~~ baked in a single dish, these two foods mark the peaceful union of two families. (7) Because the Chinese word for fish sounds like "abundance," a whole steamed fish is offered to the newly ~~marry~~ married couple—a wish for prosperity. (8) At the end of the meal, ~~satisfy~~ satisfied guests enjoy dessert buns filled with lotus seeds, promising fertility and future children. (9) It should come as no surprise that an old-~~fashion~~ fashioned Chinese banquet can last an entire day.

PRACTICE 10   **REVIEW**

Proofread the following essay for past participle errors. Correct the errors by writing above the lines.

Crazy as They Want to Be

(1) *Saturday Night Live,* the wacky late-night comedy program, has ~~entertain~~ entertained generations of television viewers since 1975. (2) The show has ~~took~~ taken aim at presidents, self-help experts, Olympic athletes, and current issues—as when concerns about the environment inspired a Global Warming Christmas Special. (3) The dream job of every aspiring comedian, *SNL* is ~~credit~~ credited with launching many careers. (4) Eddie Murphy, Billy Crystal, Damon Wayans, Mike Meyers, and Chris Rock are just a few of the ~~celebrate~~ celebrated comedians who were introduced to the public in

outrageous *SNL* sketches like the Coneheads, Mr. Robinson's Neighborhood, and Wayne's World.

(5) Although men have ~~outnumber~~ outnumbered women throughout the show's history, *SNL* recently has presented more, funny females. (6) Cheri Oteri is one of the comics whose creative energy has ~~electrify~~ electrified the aging program. (7) She has made her mark with dead-on impressions of Barbara Walters, Mariah Carey, and Judge Judy. (8) Perhaps Oteri's best-~~knowed~~ known character is the clumsy cheerleader Arianna, who fails to make the squad but shows up optimistically at every team event. (9) Another talented comic, Molly Shannon, is ~~recognize~~ recognized for her portrayal of Catholic schoolgirl Mary Katherine Gallagher, a boy-~~craze~~ crazed adolescent who falls through walls. (10) ~~Nominate~~ Nominated for an Emmy, Shannon was ~~ask~~ asked to take Mary Katherine onto the big screen in *Superstar.*

(11) *Saturday Night Live* continues to update its image. (12) In 2001, Tina Fey became the first female head writer in the show's history. (13) With her trademark dark-rimmed glasses and navy suit, the bookish brunette has ~~became~~ become hugely popular in her role as a cheery, poison-~~tongue~~ tongued anchorwoman opposite Amy Poehler on *SNL*'s fake news. (14) When Tom Cruise and Nicole Kidman were ~~divorce~~ divorced, Fey wisecracked that their children would be returned to the studio's prop room. (15) With comics like Fey, *SNL* might have attracted a new generation of viewers.

EXPLORING ONLINE

TEACHING TIP
More practice and assessment are available in the *Evergreen* Test Bank, linked ACE tests on the *Evergreen* Online Teaching and Study Centers, *WriteSpace for Evergreen,* and Exploring Online links in this chapter.

http://online.ohlone.cc.ca.us/~mlieu/participles/review2.htm Crossword puzzle: past participles

http://grammar.ccc.commnet.edu/grammar/quizzes/final-ed_option.htm
To add or not to add *-ed*? This one is tricky; test yourself.

Online Study Center **college.hmco.com/pic/evergreen8e**
Visit the Online Study Center for *Evergreen* for more exercises and quizzes.

30
Nouns

PART A Defining Singular and Plural

Nouns are words that refer to people, places, or things. They can be either singular or plural. **Singular** means one. **Plural** means more than one.

Singular	Plural
the glass	glasses
a lamp	lamps
a lesson	lessons

■ As you can see, nouns usually add *-s* or *-es* to form the plural.

Some nouns form their plurals in other ways. Here are a few examples:

TEACHING TIP
Many students will know some or all of the material in this chapter, so you may wish to assign topics selectively.

Singular	Plural	Singular	Plural
child	children	medium	media
crisis	crises	memorandum	memoranda (memorandums)
criterion	criteria	phenomenon	phenomena
foot	feet	syllabus	syllabi
goose	geese	tooth	teeth
man	men	woman	women

These nouns ending in *-f* or *-fe* change endings to *-ves* in the plural:

Singular	Plural
half	halves
knife	knives
life	lives
scarf	scarves
shelf	shelves
wife	wives
wolf	wolves

Hyphenated nouns form plurals by adding *-s* or *-es* to the main word:

Singular	Plural
brother-in-law	brothers-in-law
maid-of-honor	maids-of-honor
master-at-arms	masters-at-arms

Other nouns do not change at all to form the plural; here are a few examples:

Singular	Plural
deer	deer
equipment	equipment
fish	fish
merchandise	merchandise

If you are unsure about the plural of a noun, check a dictionary. For example, if you look up the noun *woman* in the dictionary, you may see an entry like this:

woman, women

The first word listed, *woman,* is the singular form of the noun; the second word, *women,* is the plural.

Some dictionaries list the plural form of a noun only if the plural is unusual. If no plural is listed, that noun probably adds *-s* or *-es.** Remember:* Do not add an *-s* to words that form plurals by changing an internal letter. For example, the plural of *man* is *men,* not *mens;* the plural of *woman* is *women,* not *womens;* the plural of *foot* is *feet,* not *feets.*

* For more work on spelling plurals, see Chapter 38, "Spelling," Part H.

PRACTICE 1

Make these singular nouns plural.

1. man _____ men _____
2. half _____ halves _____
3. foot _____ feet _____
4. son-in-law _____ sons-in-law _____
5. moose _____ moose _____
6. life _____ lives _____
7. tooth _____ teeth _____
8. medium _____ media _____
9. woman _____ women _____
10. crisis _____ crises _____
11. maid-of-honor _____ maids-of-honor _____
12. criterion _____ criteria _____
13. shelf _____ shelves _____
14. mouse _____ mice _____
15. child _____ children _____
16. father-in-law _____ fathers-in-law _____
17. knife _____ knives _____
18. deer _____ deer _____
19. secretary _____ secretaries _____
20. goose _____ geese _____

PART B Signal Words: Singular and Plural

A **signal word** tells you whether a singular or a plural noun usually follows. These signal words tell you that a singular noun usually follows:

ESL TIP
ESL students need to be careful about using words in English that resemble words in other languages but mean something different—e.g., the French *librairie* means *bookstore* in English.

Signal Words

a(n)
a single
another   } house
each
every
one

These signal words tell you that a plural noun usually follows:

Signal Words

all
both
few
many
most   } houses
several
some
two (or more)
various

PRACTICE 2

Some of the following sentences contain incorrect singulars and plurals. Correct the errors. Put a C after correct sentences.

women
1. By three years old, most children have firm ideas about how men and ~~woman~~ should behave.

2. Children develop their concepts about gender differences through *conditioning*,
others
a process of learning that reinforces certain behaviors while discouraging ~~other~~.

peers
3. Conditioning occurs through the messages delivered by parents, ~~peer~~, and the media.

children
4. Research shows that parents begin to treat their ~~childrens~~ differently as early
hours
as twenty-four ~~hour~~ after birth.

5. Fathers hold their infant girls gently and speak softly to them, but they bounce
feet
baby boys, playing "airplane" and tickling their ~~feets~~.

6. Mothers, too, condition gender roles; they reward little girls who play quietly and help with chores, while excusing the loud play of boys as natural.   C

7. Once in school, children quickly learn that certain kinds of make-believe—such as playing house or having tea parties—are girls' games; boys are
friends
encouraged by their ~~friend~~ to crash cars and shoot toy guns.

8. While the boundaries are less rigid for girls at this stage, most boys who show
activities
any interest in feminine clothes or ~~activity~~ will be mocked by their peers.

ads
9. Many TV ~~ad~~ play a key conditioning role by showing boys involved in sports or jobs and girls playing indoors with toy ovens or dolls.

children   interests
10. By limiting choices for most ~~child~~, perhaps we ignore many talents and ~~interest~~
lives
that might greatly enhance their ~~lifes~~ and society as a whole.

ESL TIP
For an interesting list of discussion questions about gender roles in different cultures, see **http://iteslj.org/questions/gender.html**.

PART C Signal Words with *of*

Many signal words are followed by *of* . . . or *of the.* . . . Usually, these signal words are followed by a **plural** noun (or a collective noun) because they really refer to one or more from a larger group.

TEACHING TIP
The constructions in Part C confuse many students and can lead to both noun and verb agreement errors. Remind students to cross out the prepositional phrase in order to find the subject and determine its number.

one of the each of the	pictures is . . .
many of the a few of the lots of the	pictures are . . .

ESL TIP
ESL students may need extra practice using singular and plural nouns appropriately. Have them write sentences using the signal word charts on page 426 and here.

▪ *Be careful:* The signal words *one of the* and *each of the* are followed by a **plural** noun, but the verb is **singular** because only the signal word (*one* or *each*) is the real subject.*

One of the coats *is* on sale.

Each of the flowers *smells* sweet.

PRACTICE 3

Fill in your own nouns in the following sentences. Use a different noun in each sentence.   Answers will vary.

1. Since Jacob wrote each of his _____exams_____ with care, the As came as no surprise.

2. You are one of the few _____people_____ I know who can listen to the radio and play video games at the same time.

3. Naomi liked several of the new _____rock singers_____ but remained faithful to her long-time favorites.

4. Many of the _____students_____ carried laptops.

5. Determined to win the Salesperson of the Year award, Clyde called on all his _____clients_____ two or three times a month.

6. One of the _____categories_____ makes no sense.

TEACHING TIP
You might wish to review relevant spelling rules, e.g., for words that end in *-y*, drop the *-y* and add *-ies* (*victory, victories*).

PRACTICE 4   REVIEW

Proofread the following essay for errors in singular and plural nouns. Correct the errors above the lines.

The Language of Color, the Color of Cash

(1) Have you ever wondered why, every year, the ~~merchandises~~ merchandise in different stores seems strangely color-coordinated? (2) One year, lavender ~~man's~~ men's shirts

---

* For more work on this type of construction, see Chapter 27, "Present Tense (Agreement)," Part C.

seem to be everywhere, no matter what the brand. (3) The next year, the hot color

might be turquoise or lime green. (4) It is as if all the ~~designer~~ designers met secretly to pick

the season's hues. (5) In fact, this ~~phenomena~~ phenomenon is real, but it is color-trend experts,

not designers, who pick the next new colors. (6) One of the most famous color-

trend ~~company~~ companies is Pantone. (7) Each year, Pantone selects several color palettes for

its long list of ~~client~~ clients—DKNY, Apple Computer, Pottery Barn, Nike, Kitchen Aid,

and more.

(8) Pantone is known for its 1,757 colors, including twenty-seven ~~shade~~ shades of

white. (9) Chances are that the pale yellow of that kitchen mixer and matching

toaster in the store window is a Pantone shade. (10) Those gray and moss green

~~sheet~~ sheets and towels stacked on a department store ~~shelves~~ shelf may well be colors by

Pantone. (11) The company's laboratories create and standardize a formula for

every shade. (12) Each of the special ~~color~~ colors that help sell a brand is kept top-

secret. (13) IBM is known as "Big Blue," after its color, mixed from two Pantone

Color sells: Models at Etro and Bill Blass strut some of Pantone's winter shades for 2006–2007.

shades. (14) Barbie pink is a trademarked Pantone color, and the jewelry store

Tiffany is now working with Pantone to trademark the famous robin's egg blue of

                      boxes   media
its bags, ~~box~~, and ~~medium~~ ads.

(15) At their annual meeting, Pantone's color forecasters consider many

criteria
~~criterion~~. (16) Sand and pale blue are soothing earth tones in times of stress. (17)

Red is exciting and daring; yellow is uplifting. (18) During war years, patriotic

~~colors do well, as do traditional colors like colonial blue and burgundy.~~ (19) Color

                     people
is a language that ~~peoples~~ respond to, whether they are aware of it or not. (20)

Pantone is banking on it.

PRACTICE 5   THINKING AND WRITING TOGETHER

In a group with classmates, decide whether car color matters. Imagine spotting four cars during the day, all the same model but different colors: *red, beige, black,* and *purple.* What assumptions, if any, would you make about the car or driver, based on each car color? Pick one person to jot your group's ideas. Be prepared to share with the class.

If you were born in another country, do these colors mean different things in your culture? For intriguing information, quizzes, and writing ideas about color, visit **www.colormatters.com** or **http://en.wikipedia.org/wiki/Color_psychology**.

 EXPLORING ONLINE

TEACHING TIP
More practice and assessment are available in the *Evergreen* Test Bank, linked ACE tests on the *Evergreen* Online Teaching and Study Centers, *WriteSpace for Evergreen,* and Exploring Online links in this chapter.

http://grammar.ccc.commnet.edu/grammar/quizzes/cross/plurals_gap.htm Interactive noun plurals quiz: test yourself!

http://grammar.ccc.commnet.edu/grammar/quizzes/final-s_option.htm Do you know when to add -s to nouns and verbs? Test yourself.

http://www.smccd.net/accounts/sevas/esl/gramcheck/cntnoncnt.html ESL writers, try this interactive noun exercise.

Online Study Center college.hmco.com/pic/evergreen8e
Visit the Online Study Center for *Evergreen* for more exercises and quizzes.

31

Pronouns

PART A Defining Pronouns and Antecedents

ESL TIP
Pronoun forms usually do not present a learning hardship to ESL students because the English pronoun system is far simpler than that of many other languages.

Pronouns take the place of or refer to nouns, other pronouns, or phrases. The word that the pronoun refers to is called the **antecedent** of the pronoun.

> 1. *Eric* ordered *baked chicken* because *it* is *his* favorite dish.
>
> 2. *Simone and Lee* painted *their* room.
>
> 3. *I* like *camping in the woods* because *it* gives *me* a chance to be alone with *my* thoughts.

▪ In sentence 1, *it* refers to the antecedent *baked chicken*, and *his* refers to the antecedent *Eric*.

▪ In sentence 2, *their* refers to the plural antecedent *Simone and Lee*.

▪ In sentence 3, *it* refers to the antecedent *camping in the woods*. This antecedent is a whole phrase. *Me* and *my* refer to the pronoun antecedent *I*.

431

PRACTICE 1

In each sentence, a pronoun is circled. Write the pronoun first and then its antecedent, as shown in the example.

EXAMPLE   Have you ever wondered why we exchange rings in (our) wedding ceremonies?

our _____ we _____

TEACHING and ESL TIP
Point out to students that animals and inanimate object antecedents are referred to with the pronouns *it* and *its* and, in the case of plurals, *they* and *their*.

1. When a man buys a wedding ring, (he) follows an age-old tradition.

   he _____ man _____

2. Rich Egyptian grooms gave (their) brides gold rings five thousand years ago.

   their _____ grooms _____

3. To Egyptian couples, the ring represented eternal love; (it) was a circle without beginning or end.

   it _____ ring _____

4. By Roman times, gold rings had become more affordable, so ordinary people could also buy (them.)

   them _____ rings _____

5. Still, many a Roman youth had to scrimp to buy (his) bride a ring.

   his _____ youth _____

6. The first bride to slip a diamond ring on (her) finger lived in Venice about five hundred years ago.

   her _____ bride _____

7. The Venetians knew that setting a diamond in a ring was an excellent way of displaying (its) beauty.

   its _____ diamond _____

8. Nowadays, a man and a woman exchange rings to symbolize the equality of (their) relationship.

   their _____ a man and a woman _____

PART B   Making Pronouns and Antecedents Agree

TEACHING TIP
Explain to students that although we might not make our subjects and pronouns agree in casual conversation, we must do so in writing. Students have particular trouble with the special cases covered in Part B and with Part C on vague or repeated pronouns.

A pronoun must *agree* with its antecedent in number and person.*

> 1. When *Tom* couldn't find *his* pen, *he* asked to borrow mine.
>
> 2. The three *sisters* wanted to start *their* own business.

▪ In sentence 1, *Tom* is the antecedent of *his* and *he*. Since *Tom* is singular and masculine, the pronouns referring to *Tom* are also singular and masculine.

▪ In sentence 2, *sisters* is the antecedent of *their*. Since *sisters* is plural, the pronoun referring to *sisters* must also be plural.

---

* For more work on pronoun agreement, see Chapter 20, "Revising for Consistency and Parallelism," Part B.

As you can see from these examples, making pronouns agree with their antecedents is usually easy. However, three special cases can be tricky.

1. Indefinite Pronouns

anybody
anyone
everybody
everyone
nobody
no one
one
somebody
someone

> Each of these words is **singular.** Any pronoun that refers to one of them must also be singular: *he, him, his, she,* or *her.*

3. *Anyone* can quit smoking if *he* or *she* wants to.

4. *Everybody* should do *his* or *her* best to keep the reception area uncluttered.

■ *Anyone* and *everybody* require the singular pronouns *he, she, his,* and *her.*

In the past, writers used *he* or *him* to refer to both men and women. Now, however, many writers use *he or she, his or her,* or *him or her.* Of course, if *everyone* or *someone* is a woman, use *she* or *her*; if *everyone* or *someone* is a man, use *he* or *him.* For example:

5. *Someone* left *her* new dress in a bag on the sofa.

6. *Everyone* is wearing *his* new tie.

PRACTICE 2

Fill in the correct pronoun and circle its antecedent. Make sure each pronoun agrees in number and person with its antecedent.

1. (Anyone) can become a good cook if ___he or she___ tries.

2. (Someone) dropped ___her___ lipstick behind the bookcase.

3. (No one) in the mixed doubles let ___his or her___ guard down for a minute.

4. (Everybody) wants ___his or her___ career to be rewarding.

5. (Everyone) is entitled to ___his or her___ full pension.

6. (Mr. Hernow) will soon be here, so please get _____*his*_____ contract ready.

7. (One) should wear a necktie that doesn't clash with _____*one's*_____ suit.

8. The movie theater was so cold that (nobody) took off _____*his or her*_____ coat.

2. Special Singular Antecedents

each (of) . . .
either (of) . . .
neither (of) . . .
every one (of) . . .
one (of) . . .

Each of these constructions is **singular.** Any pronoun that refers to one of them must also be singular.*

7. *Neither* of the two men paid for *his* ticket to the wrestling match.

8. *Each* of the houses has *its* own special charm.

■ The subject of sentence 7 is the singular *neither,* not *men;* therefore, the singular masculine pronoun *his* is required.

■ The subject of sentence 8 is the singular *each,* not the plural *houses;* therefore, the singular pronoun *its* is required.

PRACTICE 3

Fill in the correct pronoun and circle its antecedent. Make sure each pronoun agrees in number and person with its antecedent.

1. (Each) of the men wanted to be _____*his*_____ own boss.

2. (One) of the saleswomen left _____*her*_____ sample case on the counter.

3. (Every one) of the colts has a white star on _____*its*_____ forehead.

4. (Neither) of the actors knew _____*his or her*_____ lines by heart.

5. (Neither) of the dentists had _____*his or her*_____ office remodeled.

6. (Each) of these arguments has _____*its*_____ flaws and _____*its*_____ strengths.

7. (Every one) of the jazz bands had _____*its*_____ own distinctive style.

8. (Either) of these telephone answering machines will work very well if _____*it*_____ is properly cared for.

* For more work on prepositional phrases, see Chapter 24, "The Simple Sentence," Part B.

3. Collective Nouns

Collective nouns represent a group of people but are usually considered **singular.** They usually take singular pronouns.

> 9. The *jury* reached *its* decision in three hours.
>
> 10. The debating *team* is well known for *its* fighting spirit.

■ In sentence 9, *jury* is a collective noun. Although it has several members, the jury acts as a unit—as one. Therefore, the antecedent *jury* takes the singular pronoun *its*.

■ In sentence 10, why does the collective noun *team* take the singular pronoun *its*?

Here is a partial list of collective nouns:

Common Collective Nouns		
class	family	panel
college	flock	school
committee	government	society
company	group	team
faculty	jury	tribe

TEACHING TIP
A good list of collective nouns often amazes students (*a lounge of lizards, a shuffle of bureaucrats*). See **http://www.vigay.com/nouns/.** Craft a lesson on agreement, using these or collective nouns that your students invent (*an absence of waiters, a wallet of doctors*).

PRACTICE 4

Read each sentence carefully for meaning. Circle the antecedent and then fill in the correct pronoun.

ESL TIP
ESL students may need extra help in choosing appropriate collective nouns, but they will reap new vocabulary from the exercise.

1. My (family) gave me all ____its____ support when I went back to school.

2. The (government) should reexamine ____its____ domestic policy.

3. The (college) honored ____its____ oldest graduate with a reception.

4. (Eco-Wise) has just begun to market a new pollution-free detergent that ____it____ is proud of.

5. The (panel) will soon announce ____its____ recommendations to the hospital.

6. The two (teams) gave ____their____ fans a real show.

7. The (jury) deliberated for six days before _____it_____ reached a verdict.

8. After touring the Great Pyramid, the (class) headed back to Cairo in

_____its_____ air-conditioned bus.

PART C Referring to Antecedents Clearly

A pronoun must refer *clearly* to its antecedent. Avoid vague, repetitious, or ambiguous pronoun reference.

1. Vague pronoun:	At the box office, they said that tickets were no longer available.
2. Revised:	The cashier at the box office said . . .
	or
3. Revised:	At the box office, I was told . . .

■ In sentence 1, who is *they*? *They* does not clearly refer to an antecedent.

■ In sentence 2, *the cashier* replaces *they*.

■ In sentence 3, the problem is avoided by a change of language.*

ESL TIP
Some ESL students tend to double the subject, writing both the subject and a pronoun. Refer them to Error #4: Repeated Subject in the "8 Common ESL Errors" on the *Evergreen* Online Study Center.

4. Repetitious pronoun	In the article, *it* says that Tyrone was a boxer.
5. Revised:	The article says that . . .
	or
6. Revised:	It says that . . .

■ In sentence 4, *it* merely repeats *article*, the antecedent preceding it.

■ Use either the pronoun or its antecedent, but not both.

7. Ambiguous pronoun:	Mr. Tedesco told his son that *his* car had a flat tire.
8. Revised:	Mr. Tedesco told his son that the younger man's car had a flat tire.
9. Revised:	Mr. Tedesco told his son Paul that Paul's car had a flat tire.

■ In sentence 7, *his* could refer either to Mr. Tedesco or to his son.

---

* For more work on using exact language, see Chapter 22, "Revising for Language Awareness," Part A.

PRACTICE 5

TEACHING TIP
Ask students to identify each pronoun error in Practice 5 as either vague, repetitious, or ambiguous.

Revise the following sentences, removing vague, repetitious, or ambiguous pronoun references. Make the pronoun references clear and specific.   Answers will vary.

1. In this book it says that hundreds of boys are injured each year copying wrestling stunts they see on TV.

   Revised: This book says that hundreds of boys are injured each year copying wrestling stunts they see on TV.

2. On the radio they warned drivers that the Interstate Bridge was closed.

   Revised: The radio announcer warned drivers that the Interstate Bridge was closed.

3. Sandra told her friend that she shouldn't have turned down the promotion.

   Revised: Sandra told her friend Janet that Janet shouldn't have turned down the promotion.

4. In North Carolina they raise tobacco.

   Revised: Tobacco is raised in North Carolina.

5. The moving van struck a lamppost; luckily, no one was injured, but it was badly damaged.

   Revised: The moving van struck a lamppost; luckily, no one was injured, but the lamppost was badly damaged.

6. Professor Grazel told his parrot that he had to stop chewing telephone cords.

   Revised: Professor Grazel told his parrot to stop chewing telephone cords.

7. On the news, it said that more Americans than ever are turning to nontraditional medicine.

   Revised: The news broadcast reported that more Americans than ever are turning to nontraditional medicine.

8. Keiko is an excellent singer, yet she has never taken a lesson in it.

   Revised: Keiko is an excellent singer, yet she has never taken a voice lesson.

9. Vandalism was once so out of control at the local high school that they stole sinks and lighting fixtures.

    Revised: <u>Vandalism was once so out of control at the local high school that</u>

    <u>sinks and lighting fixtures were stolen.</u>

    _____

10. Rosalie's mother said she was glad she had decided to become a paralegal.

    Revised: <u>Rosalie's mother said she was glad Rosalie had decided to become</u>

    <u>a paralegal.</u>

    _____

PART D Special Problems of Case

Personal pronouns take different forms depending on how they are used in a sentence. Pronouns can be **subjects, objects,** or **possessives.**

Pronouns used as **subjects** are in the **subjective case:**

ESL TIP
Point out to your ESL students that in compound constructions with a noun and a pronoun, the noun goes first, i.e., Do not write: *I and my friend went shopping.*

> 1. *He* and *I* go snowboarding together.
>
> 2. The peaches were so ripe that *they* fell from the trees.

■ *He, I,* and *they* are in the subjective case.

Pronouns that are **objects of verbs** or **prepositions** are in the **objective case.** Pronouns that are **subjects of infinitives** are also in the **objective case:**

> 3. A sudden downpour soaked *her*. (object of verb)
>
> 4. Please give this card to *him*. (object of preposition)
>
> 5. We want *them* to leave right now. (subject of infinitive)

■ *Her, him,* and *them* are in the objective case.

Pronouns that **show ownership** are in the **possessive case:**

> 6. The carpenters left *their* tools on the windowsill.
>
> 7. This flower has lost *its* brilliant color.

ESL TIP
Although most languages have a way of signaling possession, they don't all regard the same nouns as "possessable." In Spanish, one refers to parts of the body using the definite article, whereas in English, we use a possessive form. One would say, in Spanish, *I have broken the leg.*

■ *Their* and *its* are in the possessive case.

ESL TIP
Having students write
sentences using each of the
pronoun cases listed in the
chart will help them
identify any personal error
patterns. Some students
keep a copy of this chart
handy as they write.

TEACHING TIP
Create a quiz on pronoun
cases by removing the
pronouns from this chart
and having students fill
them in.

TEACHING TIP
Crossing out the noun half
of a compound construction
is a good way to choose the
correct case: e.g., *Luke and
I* work out; join *Luke and
me*.

Pronoun Case Chart

Singular	Subjective	Objective	Possessive
1st person	I	me	my (mine)
2nd person	you	you	your (yours)
3rd person	he	him	his (his)
	she	her	her (hers)
	it	it	its (its)
	who	whom	whose
	whoever	whomever	

Plural	Subjective	Objective	Possessive
1st person	we	us	our (ours)
2nd person	you	you	your (yours)
3rd person	they	them	their (theirs)

Using the correct case is usually fairly simple, but three problems require special care.

1. Case in Compound Constructions

A **compound construction** consists of two nouns, two pronouns, or a noun and a pronoun joined by *and*. Make sure that the pronouns in a compound construction are in the correct case.

> 8. *Serge* and *I* went to the pool together.
>
> 9. Between *you* and *me*, this party is a bore.

▪ In sentence 8, *Serge* and *I* are subjects.

▪ In sentence 9, *you* and *me* are objects of the preposition *between*.

Never use *myself* as a substitute for either *I* or *me* in compound constructions.

PRACTICE 6

Determine the case required by each sentence, and circle the correct pronoun.

1. (He, Him) and Harriet plan to enroll in the police academy.

2. A snowdrift stood between (I, me) and the subway entrance.

3. Tony used the software and then returned it to Barbara and (I, me, myself).

4. The reporter's questions caught June and (we, us) off guard.

5. By noon, Julio and (he, him) had already cleaned the garage and mowed the lawn.

6. These charts helped (she, her) and (I, me) with our statistics homework.

7. Professor Woo gave Diane and (she, her) extra time to finish the geology final.

8. Between you and (I, me), I have always preferred country music.

2. Case in Comparisons

Pronouns that complete **comparisons** may be in the **subjective, objective,** or **possessive** case:

10. His son is as stubborn as *he.* (subjective)

11. The cutbacks will affect you more than *me.* (objective)

12. This essay is better organized than *mine.* (possessive)

To decide on the correct pronoun, simply complete the comparison mentally and then choose the pronoun that naturally follows:

13. She trusts him more than I . . . (trust him).

14. She trusts him more than . . . (she trusts) . . . me.

■ Note that in sentences 13 and 14, the case of the pronoun in the comparison can change the meaning of the entire sentence.

PRACTICE 7

Circle the correct pronoun.

1. Your hair is much shorter than (she, her, hers).

2. We tend to assume that others are more self-confident than (we, us).

3. She is just as funny as (he, him).

4. Is Hanna as trustworthy as (he, him)?

5. Although they were both research scientists, he received a higher salary than (she, her).

6. I am not as involved in this project as (they, them).

7. Sometimes we become impatient with people who are not as quick to learn as (we, us).

8. Michael's route involved more overnight stops than (us, our, ours).

3. Use of *Who* (or *Whoever*) and *Whom* (or *Whomever*)

Who and **whoever** are in the **subjective** case. **Whom** and **whomever** are in the **objective** case.

---

15. *Who* is at the door?

16. For *whom* is that gift?

17. *Whom* is that gift for?

■ In sentence 15, *who* is the subject.

■ The same question is written two ways in sentences 16 and 17. In both, *whom* is the object of the preposition *for*.

Sometimes, deciding on *who* or *whom* can be tricky:

---

18. I will give the raise to *whoever* deserves it.

19. Give it to *whomever* you like.

■ In sentence 18, *whoever* is the subject in the clause *whoever deserves it*.

■ In sentence 19, *whomever* is the object in the clause *whomever you like*.

If you have trouble deciding on *who* or *whom*, change the sentence to eliminate the problem.

---

20. I prefer working with people *whom* I don't know as friends.
    or
    I prefer working with people I don't know as friends.

PRACTICE 8

Circle the correct pronoun.

1. (Who, Whom) will deliver the layouts to the ad agency?

2. To (who, whom) are you speaking?

3. (Who, Whom) prefers hiking to skiing?

4. For (who, whom) are those boxes piled in the corner?

5. The committee will award the scholarship to (whoever, whomever) it chooses.

6. (Who, Whom) do you wish to invite to the open house?

7. At (who, whom) did the governor fling the cream pie?

8. I will hire (whoever, whomever) can use a computer and speak Korean.

PART E Using Pronouns with *-self* and *-selves*

Pronouns with *-self* or *-selves* can be used in two ways—as reflexives or as intensives.

A reflexive pronoun indicates that someone did something to himself or herself:

> 1. My daughter felt very grown up when she learned to dress *herself*.

■ In sentence 1, Miriam did something to *herself;* she *dressed herself.*

An intensive pronoun emphasizes the noun or pronoun it refers to:

> 2. Anthony *himself* was surprised at how relaxed he felt during the interview.

■ In sentence 2, *himself* emphasizes that Anthony—much to his surprise—was not nervous at the interview.

The following chart will help you choose the correct reflexive or intensive pronoun.

TEACHING TIP
Students have no doubt heard the words *hisself* and *theirselves* in casual conversation. Point out that these are not real words.

Antecedent	Reflexive or Intensive Pronoun	
Singular	I	myself
	you	yourself
	he	himself
	she	herself
	it	itself
Plural	we	ourselves
	you	yourselves
	they	themselves

Note that in the plural *-self* is changed to *-selves.*

■ **Be careful:** Do not use reflexives or intensives as substitutes for the subject of a sentence.

> Incorrect: Harry and *myself* will be there on time.
> Correct: Harry and *I* will be there on time.

PRACTICE 9

Fill in the correct reflexive or intensive pronoun. Be careful to make pronouns and antecedents agree.

1. Though he hates to cook, André _____himself_____ sautéed the mushrooms.

2. Rhoda found _____herself_____ in a strange city with only the phone number of a cousin whom she had not seen for years.

3. Her coffee machine automatically turns _____itself_____ on in the morning and off in the evening.

4. The librarian and I rearranged the children's section _____ourselves_____.

5. When it comes to horror films, I know that you consider _____yourself_____ an expert.

6. They _____themselves_____ didn't care if they arrived on time or not.

7. After completing a term paper, I always buy _____myself_____ a little gift to celebrate.

8. Larry _____himself_____ was surprised at how quickly he grew to like ancient history.

PRACTICE 10   REVIEW

Proofread the following essay for pronoun errors. Then correct the pronoun error above the line, in any way you choose.

The Many Lives of Jackie Chan

(1) Few movie stars can claim a career as unusual as ~~him~~ *his*. (2) For one thing, Jackie Chan performs his death-defying stunts ~~hisself~~ *himself*. (3) Although he was a huge star in Asia for more than twenty years, fame eluded him in the United States until recently.

ESL TIP
Pronoun errors often persist even among advanced ESL students. Have your students use Practice 10 as a guide to finding and correcting pronoun errors in their own writing.

(4) Chan was born in Hong Kong in 1954. (5) Because ~~him~~ *he* and his parents were so poor, he was sent to live and study at the Peking Opera School. (6) There, ~~they~~ *experts* trained him in acting, dancing, singing, sword fighting, and kung fu. (7) When the school closed in 1971, ~~their~~ *its* lessons paid off for Chan in an unexpected way.

(8) Chan worked as a stuntman and fight choreographer and landed acting roles in several films, including Bruce Lee's *Enter the Dragon*. (9) Lee~~, he~~ died in 1973, and Chan was the natural choice to fill Lee's shoes. (10) In several films, Chan tried to imitate Lee, but the films were unsuccessful. (11) In 1978, however, Chan came up with the idea of turning Lee's tough style into comedy. (12) *Snake in the Eagle's Shadow* and *Drunken Master* were hilarious hits; ~~it~~ *they* established "kung fu comedy." (13) Jackie Chan became one of Hong Kong's most popular stars.

(14) However, Hollywood directors did not appreciate Chan as a stuntman, actor, comedian, director, and scriptwriter all in one, and ~~its~~ *his* early American films flopped. (15) Chan understood his own strengths better than ~~them~~ *they*. (16) He returned to Hong Kong, but ~~him~~ *he* and his fans always believed he could make a U.S. comeback. (17) This happened when *Rumble in the Bronx*, China's most popular film ever, was dubbed in English. (18) Finally, ~~they~~ *Americans* began to appreciate this manic, bruised, and battered action hero ~~who~~ *whose* films were refreshingly nonviolent.

(19) Since then, Chan's U.S. films, like *Rush Hour, Rush Hour 2*, and *Highbinder*, are being received almost as well as ~~its~~ *their* Hong Kong counterparts.

EXPLORING ONLINE

TEACHING TIP
More practice and assessment are available in the *Evergreen* Test Bank, linked ACE tests on the *Evergreen* Online Teaching and Study Centers, *WriteSpace for Evergreen,* and Exploring Online links in this chapter.

http://grammar.ccc.commnet.edu/grammar/cgi-shl/quiz.pl/pronouns_ add1 .htm Interactive pronoun quiz; click for pronoun review.

http://a4esl.org/q/h/vm/pronouns.html Pronoun quiz: especially helpful for ESL writers.

Online Study Center college.hmco.com/pic/evergreen8e
Visit the Online Study Center for *Evergreen* for more exercises and quizzes.

32

Prepositions

PART A Working with Prepositional Phrases

TEACHING TIP
Illustrate the fact that prepositions show precise *relationships: in the boat, under the boat, against the boat,* and so on.

Prepositions are words like *about, at, behind, into, of, on,* and *with*.* They are followed by a noun or a pronoun, which is called the **object** of the preposition. The preposition and its object are called a **prepositional phrase.**

1. Ms. Fairworth hurried *to the computer lab.*

2. Students *with a 3.5 grade average* will receive a special award.

3. Traffic *at this corner* is dangerously heavy.

ESL TIP
English prepositions often confuse nonnative students, even those who are highly proficient in English. One reason is that some languages (e.g., German, Russian, and Latin) use inflections to perform the work of prepositions. Another reason is the variability of preposition use.

■ In sentence 1, the prepositional phrase *to the computer lab* explains where Ms. Fairworth hurried.

■ In sentence 2, the prepositional phrase *with a 3.5 grade average* describes which students will receive a special award.

■ Which is the prepositional phrase in sentence 3 and what word does it describe?

at this corner; traffic

* For more work on prepositions, see Chapter 24, "The Simple Sentence," Part B.

In/On for Time

Two prepositions often confused are *in* and *on*. Use *in* before months not followed by a specific date, before seasons, and before years that do not include specific dates.

ESL TIP
Suggest that students try practicing with flash cards, memorizing when necessary.

1. *In March*, the skating rink will finally open for business.

2. Rona expects to pay off her car *in 2008*.

ESL TIP
If ESL learners need more practice with prepositions, refer them to *WriteSpace for Evergreen* and to Error #3: Preposition Error in the "8 Common ESL Errors" on the *Evergreen* Online Study Center.

Use *on* before days of the week, before holidays, and before months if a date follows.

3. *On Sunday*, the Kingston family spent the day at the beach.

4. *On January 6*, Bernard left for a month of mountain climbing.

In/On for Place

In means *inside* a place.

1. Tonia put her DVD player *in the bedroom*.

2. Many country groups got their start *in Nashville*.

On means *on top of* or *at a particular place*.

3. That mess *on your desk* needs to be cleared off.

4. Pizza Palace will be opening a new parlor *on Highland Avenue*.

PRACTICE 1

Fill in the correct prepositions in the following sentences. Be especially careful of *in* and *on*.

1. _____In_____ a little town _____on_____ the coast of the Dominican Republic, baseball is a way of life.

2. Once known for cattle and sugar, San Pedro de Macoris has been ex-

porting world-class baseball players _____to_____ the major leagues _____for_____ fifty years.

3. Hall-of-Famer Juan Marichal and slugger Manny Ramirez are just two Dominicans who have made names _____for_____ themselves _____in_____ the majors.

4. Other stars born in or _____near_____ San Pedro de Macoris are Pedro Martinez, Alfonso Soriano, Robinson Cano, and Felipe Alou.

5. Baseball was first introduced _____on_____ the island _____by_____ American mill and plantation owners, who encouraged their workers to learn the game.

6. Because equipment was expensive, boys from poor families often batted _____with_____ a tree branch, using a rolled-up sock _____in_____ place _____of_____ a ball.

7. Each young man dreamed that he would be discovered _____by_____ the baseball scouts and sent to play _____in_____ *las ligas mayores*.

8. Amazing numbers _____of_____ these players succeeded, and many Dominican athletes later returned to invest _____in_____ the local economy.

9. For example, Jose Rijo is building a baseball academy _____for_____ youngsters, and many others donate equipment _____to_____ aspiring players.

10. Major league teams, including the Dodgers, Giants, and Expos, now operate year-round training camps _____on_____ the island, hoping to cultivate the athletes _____of_____ tomorrow.

PART B Prepositions in Common Expressions

Prepositions are often combined with other words to form fixed expressions. Determining the correct preposition in these expressions can sometimes be confusing. Following is a list of some troublesome expressions with prepositions. Consult a dictionary if you need help with others.

Expressions with Prepositions

Expression	Example
according to	*According to* the directions, this flap fits here.
acquainted with	Tom became *acquainted with* his classmates.
addicted to	He is *addicted to* soap operas.
afraid of	Tanya is *afraid of* flying.
agree on (a plan)	Can we *agree on* our next step?
agree to (something or another's proposal)	Roberta *agreed to* her secretary's request for a raise.
angry about or at (a thing)	Jake seemed *angry about* his meager bonus.
angry with (a person)	Sonia couldn't stay *angry with* Felipe.
apply for (a position)	By accident, the twins *applied for* the same job.
approve of	Do you *approve of* bilingual education?
argue about (an issue)	I hate *arguing about* money.
argue with (a person)	Edna *argues with* everyone about everything.
capable of	Mario is *capable of* accomplishing anything he attempts.
complain about (a situation)	Patients *complained about* the long wait to see the dentist.
complain to (a person)	Knee-deep in snow, Jed vowed to *complain to* a maintenance person.
comply with	Each contestant must *comply with* contest regulations.
consist of	This article *consists of* nothing but false accusations and half-truths.
contrast with	The light blue shirt *contrasts* sharply *with* the dark brown tie.
correspond with (write)	We *corresponded with* her for two months before we met.
deal with	Ron *deals* well *with* temporary setbacks.
depend on	Miriam can be *depended on* to say the embarrassing thing.
different from	Children are often *different from* their parents.
differ from (something)	A DVD player *differs from* a VCR in many ways.
differ with (a person)	Kathleen *differs with* you on the gun control issue.
displeased with	Ms. Withers was *displeased with* her doctor's advice to eat less fat.
fond of	Ed is *fond of* his pet tarantula.

(continued)

ESL TIP
Have students think of other verbs that change meaning when their accompanying prepositions change (e.g., *run over, run into, run out of; take on, take up, take in; turn out, turn in, turn over*). Ask them to write sentences to check their understanding.

ESL TIP
Refer students to these interactive quizzes on idioms and phrasal verbs: http://a4esl.org/q/h/idioms.html.

Expressions with Prepositions

Expression	Example
grateful for	Be *grateful for* having so many good friends.
grateful to (someone)	The team was *grateful to* the coach for his inspiration and confidence.
identical with	Scott's ideas are often *identical with* mine.
inferior to	Saturday's performance was *inferior to* the one I saw last week.
in search of	I hate to go *in search of* change at the last moment before the toll.
interested in	Willa is *interested in* results, not excuses.
interfere with	That dripping faucet *interferes with* my concentration.
object to	Martin *objected to* the judge's comment.
protect against	This heavy wool scarf will *protect* your throat *against* the cold.
reason with	It's hard to *reason with* an angry person.
rely on	If Toni made that promise, you can *rely on* it.
reply to	He wrote twice, but the president did not *reply to* his letters.
responsible for	Kit is *responsible for* making two copies of each document.
sensitive to	Professor Godfried is *sensitive to* his students' concerns.
shocked at	We were *shocked at* the graphic violence in that PG-rated film.
similar to	Some poisonous mushrooms appear quite *similar to* the harmless kind.
speak with (someone)	Geraldine will *speak with* her supervisor about a raise.
specialize in	This disc jockey *specializes in* jazz of the 1920s and the 1930s.
succeed in	Oscar *succeeded in* painting the roof in less than five hours.
superior to	It's clear that the remake is *superior to* the original.
take advantage of	Celia *took advantage of* the snow day to visit the science museum.
worry about	Never *worry about* more than one problem at a time.

PRACTICE 2

Fill in the preposition that correctly completes each of the following expressions.

1. The number one goal of 76 percent of college freshmen today is making a lot of money, according ____to____ the annual American Freshman survey.

2. Every year since 1966, the Higher Education Research Institute has been responsible ____for____ this survey of hundreds of thousands of college students.

3. The fascinating results show what students each year hope for, worry ____about____, complain ____about____, depend ____on____, and hold dear.

4. In sharp contrast ____with____ today's freshmen, freshmen surveyed in the 1970s cared most about finding "a meaningful philosophy of life."

5. Although today's freshmen are fond ____of____ money and consumer goods, they are more interested ____in____ volunteer work and politics than recent freshman classes.

6. A record 83 percent took advantage ____of____ volunteer opportunities in high school, and a record 67 percent said they would continue to volunteer.

7. Experts say that both Hurricane Katrina and the Indian Ocean tsunami have made students feel more responsible ____for____ the welfare of others.

8. American students of all races are more sensitive ____to____ the problem of racism and more likely to be closely acquainted ____with____ someone of a different race.

9. Dealing ____with____ many pressures, college students report that their physical and emotional health is at a low point.

10. Experts expect students to rely even more ____on____ finding sources of strength, people, and spiritual beliefs ____on____ which they can depend.

TEACHING TIP
Using questions from the American Freshman survey, poll your class and tally the results. This activity prompts lively discussion and/or writing. Alternatively, your students might create their own student survey poll and analyze the results.

PRACTICE 3   **REVIEW**

Proofread this essay for preposition errors. Cross out the errors and write corrections above the lines.

Dr. Ben Carson, Pioneer Brain Surgeon

(1) Today, Dr. Benjamin Carson of Johns Hopkins Hospital is internationally
                                    for/about
known as the man to call ~~from~~ tricky brain surgeries in children. (2) He routinely
               on
takes ~~out~~ challenging cases such as removing parts of the brain to stop seizures or
                                                          In
repairing deformities of the skull and face. (3) ~~On~~ 1987, he made medical history
by
~~over~~ successfully separating a pair of conjoined (or Siamese) twins in a twenty-

two-hour operation.

(4) This gifted physician was not always a high achiever, however. (5) As a
                                in   of
child, he grew up fatherless ~~on~~ Detroit. (6) He now says that, like many ~~off~~ the
                                                        of
people he knew, he had a low opinion ~~at~~ himself. (7) Consequently, his grades
                                            to
were poor, and he was prone ~~with~~ violent outbursts and disruptive behavior.

(8) Nevertheless, his mother, a high-school dropout who worked two or three jobs

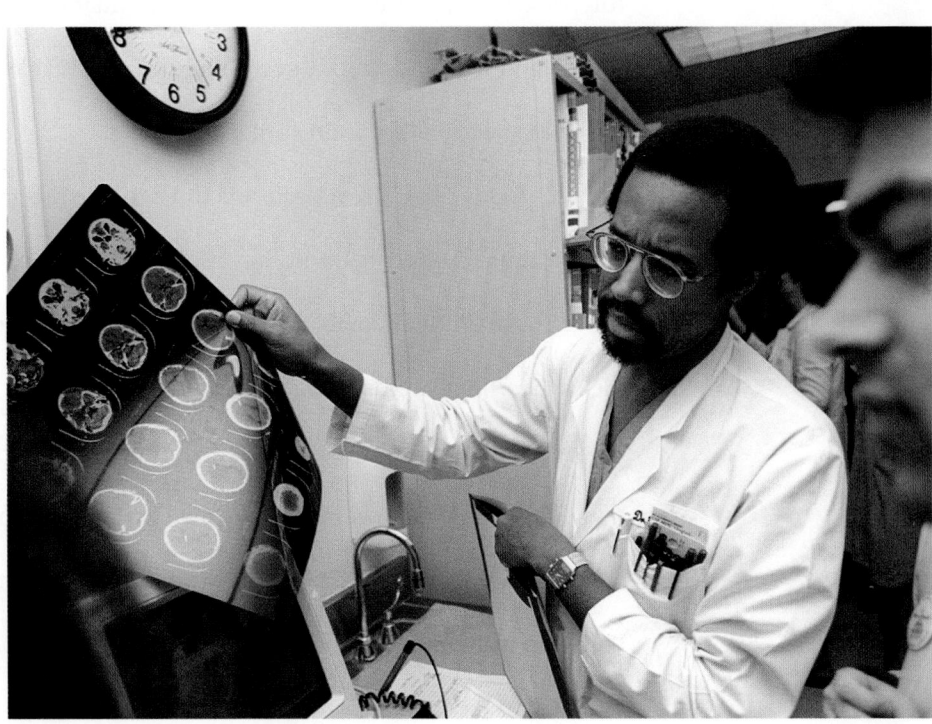

Dr. Benjamin Carson views
patient x-rays at Johns
Hopkins Hospital.

at a time to support her two sons, believed he was capable ~~to~~ *of* doing better and re-fused to give ~~out~~ *up* on him. (9) Convinced that education provides the only escape ~~against~~ *from* poverty, she insisted that Ben and his brother read and complete their homework. (10) Thanks ~~on~~ *to* her encouragement, Ben experienced a turning point one day when a teacher brought rock samples ~~at~~ *to* school. (11) Because of a book he had read, Ben was able to identify all ~~off~~ *of* them. (12) Suddenly, he knew that he wasn't the slow learner he had always thought himself to be. (13) Today Dr. Carson declares, "When I thought I was stupid, I acted like a stupid person. (14) When I thought I was smart, I acted like a smart person and achieved like a smart person." (15) His hunger ~~of~~ *for* knowledge grew, and he rose ~~on~~ *to* the top of his class, going on to attend Yale University.

(16) Nonetheless, Carson would have to overcome another obstacle. (17) Even as late as his first year of medical school, a faculty adviser counseled him to drop ~~off~~ *out* because he wasn't "medical school material." (18) Fortunately, he ignored this advice, by then having discovered his strengths. (19) He knew that he was a careful person with excellent hand–eye coordination. (20) He enjoyed dissecting things, and he could think three dimensionally. (21) With these skills, he decided, he could specialize ~~on~~ *in* brain surgery.

(22) Today Dr. Carson performs three to five life-saving operations a day. (23) ~~On~~ *In* addition, he and his wife have founded the Carson Scholars, a scholarship program for students who succeed ~~on~~ *in* academic subjects. (24) He said he got the idea when he visited schools to speak and saw huge trophies honoring athletic achievements but none for academic achievers. (25) He invested $500,000 of his own money to start rewarding children like he once was ~~about~~ *with* trophies, publicity, and money for college. (26) These scholars are the ones, Carson believes, "who will keep us Number 1, not the guy with the 25-foot jump shot."

EXPLORING ONLINE

http://grammar.ccc.commnet.edu/grammar/quizzes/preposition_quiz1.htm
Graded preposition quiz

http://a4esl.org/q/f/z/zz36mas.htm Interactive quiz: swim with the manatees as you practice prepositions!

Online Study Center **college.hmco.com/pic/evergreen8e**
Visit the Online Study Center for *Evergreen* for more exercises and quizzes.

33

Adjectives and Adverbs

PART A Defining and Using Adjectives and Adverbs

Adjectives and **adverbs** are two kinds of descriptive words. **Adjectives** describe or modify nouns or pronouns. They explain what kind, which one, or how many.

1. A *black* cat slept on the piano.

2. We felt *cheerful*.

3. *Three* windows in the basement need to be replaced.

- The adjective *black* describes the noun *cat*. It tells what kind of cat, a *black* one.

- The adjective *cheerful* describes the pronoun *we*. It tells what kind of mood we were in, *cheerful*.

- The adjective *three* describes the noun *windows*. It tells how many windows, *three*.

   Adverbs describe or modify verbs, adjectives, and other adverbs. They tell how, in what manner, when, where, and to what extent.

4. Joe dances *gracefully*.

5. *Yesterday* Robert left for a weekend of sky diving.

6. Brigit is *extremely* tall.

7. He travels *very* rapidly on that skateboard.

■ The adverb *gracefully* describes the verb *dances*. It tells how Joe dances, *gracefully*.

■ The adverb *yesterday* describes the verb *left*. It tells when Robert left, *yesterday*.

■ The adverb *extremely* describes the adjective *tall*. It tells how tall (to what extent), *extremely* tall.

■ The adverb *very* describes the adverb *rapidly*, which describes the verb *travels*. It tells how rapidly he travels, *very* rapidly.

Many adjectives can be changed into adverbs by adding an *-ly* ending. For example, *glad* becomes *gladly*, *hopeful* becomes *hopefully*, *awkward* becomes *awkwardly*. Note the pairs on this list; they are easily confused:

Adjectives	Adverbs
awful	awfully
bad	badly
poor	poorly
quick	quickly
quiet	quietly
real	really
sure	surely

8. The fish tastes *bad*.

9. It was *badly* prepared.

■ In sentence 8, the adjective *bad* describes the noun *fish*.

■ In sentence 9, the adverb *badly* describes the verb *was prepared*.

PRACTICE 1

Circle the correct adjective or adverb in parentheses. Remember that adjectives modify nouns or pronouns; adverbs modify verbs, adjectives, or adverbs.

1. Have you ever seen (real, really) emeralds?

2. Try to do your work in the library (quiet, quietly).

3. We will (glad, gladly) take you on a tour of the Crunchier Cracker factory.

4. Lee, a (high, highly) skilled electrician, rewired his entire house last year.

5. She made a (quick, quickly) stop at the scanner.

6. It was (awful, *awfully*) wet today; the sleet filled our shoes.

7. The fans from Cleveland (enthusiastic, *enthusiastically*) clapped for the Browns.

8. Are you (*sure*, surely) this bus stops in Dusty Gulch?

9. He (hasty, *hastily*) wrote the essay, leaving out several important ideas.

10. It was a funny joke, but the comedian told it (bad, *badly*).

11. Tina walked (careful, *carefully*) down the icy road.

12. Sam swims (poor, *poorly*) even though he spends hours posing on the beach.

13. Sasha the crow is an (*unusual*, unusually) pet and a (*humorous*, humorously) companion.

14. The painting is not (actual, *actually*) a Picasso; in fact, it is a (real, *really*) bad imitation.

15. It is an (extreme, *extremely*) hot day, and I (sure, *surely*) could go for some (*real*, really) orange juice.

PART B   The Comparative and the Superlative

The **comparative** of an adjective or adverb compares two persons or things:

> 1. Ben is *more creative* than Robert.
> 2. Marcia runs *faster* than the coach.

- In sentence 1, Ben is being compared with Robert.
- In sentence 2, Marcia is being compared with the coach.

The **superlative** of an adjective or adverb compares three or more persons or things:

> 3. Sancho is the *tallest* of the three brothers.
> 4. Marion is the *most intelligent* student in the class.

- In sentence 3, Sancho is being compared with the other two brothers.
- In sentence 4, Marion is being compared with all the other students in the class.

Adjectives and adverbs of one syllable usually form the **comparative** by adding -*er*. They form the **superlative** by adding -*est*.

TEACHING TIP
A trick to help students avoid errors like "more better" is to remember to write just one -*r* in any comparison—either -*er* or *more*, not both.

Adjective	Comparative	Superlative
fast	fast*er*	fast*est*
smart	smart*er*	smart*est*
tall	tall*er*	tall*est*

Adjectives and adverbs of more than one syllable usually form the **comparative** by using *more*. They form the **superlative** by using *most*.

Adjective	Comparative	Superlative
beautiful	*more* beautiful	*most* beautiful
brittle	*more* brittle	*most* brittle
serious	*more* serious	*most* serious

TEACHING TIP
An activity likely to engage students is an analysis of adjectives, comparatives, and superlatives in advertising. Bring in print ads or have students do so. Locate and discuss the use of adjectives. Groups might wish to write ads for a product they use—or for one they invent.

Note, however, that adjectives that end in -*y* (like *happy*, *lazy*, and *sunny*) change the -*y* to -*i* and add -*er* and -*est*.

Adjective	Comparative	Superlative
happy	happ*ier*	happ*iest*
lazy	laz*ier*	laz*iest*
sunny	sunn*ier*	sunn*iest*

PRACTICE 2

Write the comparative or the superlative of the words in parentheses. Remember: Use the comparative to compare two items; use the superlative to compare more than two. Use -*er* or -*est* for one-syllable words; use *more* or *most* for words of more than one syllable.*

1. The ocean is _____colder_____ (cold) than we thought it would be.

2. Please read your lines again, _____more slowly_____ (slowly) this time.

3. Which of these two roads is the _____shorter_____ (short) route?

4. Which of these three highways is the _____shortest_____ (short) route?

---

* If you have questions about spelling, see Chapter 38, "Spelling," Part G.

5. Belkys is the _____busiest_____ (busy) person I know.

6. That red felt hat with feathers is the _most outlandish_ (outlandish) one I've seen.

7. Today is _____warmer_____ (warm) than yesterday, but Thursday was the _____warmest_____ (warm) day of the month.

8. The down coat you have selected is the _most expensive_ (expensive) one in the store.

9. Each one of Woody's stories is _____funnier_____ (funny) than the last.

10. As a rule, mornings in Los Angeles are _____hazier_____ (hazy) than afternoons.

11. Is Paolo _____taller_____ (tall) than Louie? Is Paolo the _____tallest_____ (tall) player on the team?

12. If you don't do these experiments _more carefully_ (carefully), you will blow up the chemistry lab.

13. This farmland is much _____rockier_____ (rocky) than the farmland in Iowa.

14. Therese says that Physics 201 is the _most challenging_ (challenging) course she has ever taken.

15. Mr. Wells is the _____wisest_____ (wise) and _most experienced_ (experienced) leader in the community.

PRACTICE 3

Proofread the following paragraph for comparative and superlative errors. Cross out unnecessary words and write your corrections above the lines.

(1) Wikipedia is a free online encyclopedia that offers information about thousands of topics. (2) Created in 2001, it has become one of the most ~~popularest~~ _popular_ sites on the Internet—and one of the most controversial. (3) Unlike *Britannica* and other encyclopedias of ~~a more early~~ _an earlier_ time, Wikipedia is not an expensive set of books; it exists only online at *www.wikipedia.org.* (4) Its ~~most great~~ _greatest_ innovation is also its ~~most~~ biggest problem: readers can also help write content. (5) The "wiki" software allows anyone who visits the site to add or edit an entry. (6) Supporters believe that thousands of minds produce entries that are often ~~completer~~ _more complete_ and ~~accurater~~ _more accurate_ than those in traditional encyclopedias. (7) Yet mistakes and sabotage have occurred. (8) A U.S. Congressperson changed his Wikipedia profile to make

more positive

it ~~positiver~~. (9) The entry on Harriet Tubman, rescuer of southern slaves, gave the

wrong birthplace and stated as fact several disproved stories. (10) Jokers, vandals,

and even racists have planted lies in some entries. (11) Wikipedia's 800 volunteer

administrators labor to approve each change, making sure that a revised entry

effective

is more ~~effectiver~~ than the previous one. (12) While correcting such errors is

easier   faster

~~more easier~~ and ~~fast~~ than in print encyclopedias, some teachers and professors

caution students not to cite Wikipedia as an information source.

EXPLORING ONLINE

www.wikipedia.org Choose a subject that interests you and evaluate the Wikipedia entry. First, read the Wikipedia article; take notes or print it. Now visit the library and check the facts. Ask the librarian if you need help. Did you find any false information, or is the entry reliable? How would you rate Wikipedia, based on this one entry?

PART C A Troublesome Pair: *Good/Well*

TEACHING TIP
The error most commonly made is using *good* in place of *well* (as in *Julian plays ball very good*). Point out that although we might hear this in casual speech, it is a red flag error in writing. Before students complete Practice 4, you might suggest that they name the missing word's part of speech *before* they choose *good* or *well*.

Adjective	Comparative	Superlative
good	better	best
bad	worse	worst
Adjective	**Comparative**	**Superlative**
well	better	best
badly	worse	worst

Be especially careful not to confuse the adjective **good** with the adverb **well**:

1. Jessie is a *good* writer.
2. She writes *well*.

■ *Good* is an **adjective** modifying *writer.*

■ *Well* is an **adverb** modifying *writes.*

PRACTICE 4

Fill in either the adjective *good* or the adverb *well* in each blank.

1. Corned beef definitely goes _____well_____ with cabbage.

2. How _____well_____ do you understand Spanish?

3. He may not take phone messages very _____well_____, but he is _____good_____ at handling computer problems.

4. Exercise is a _____good_____ way to stay in shape; eating _____well_____ will help you maintain _____good_____ health.

5. Tony looks _____good_____ in his new goatee.

6. This is a _____good_____ arrangement: I wash, you dry.

7. On rainy nights, Sheila loves to curl up with a _____good_____ book.

8. The old Persian carpet and oak desk are a _____good_____ match; they go _____well_____ together.

9. Both teams played _____well_____; it was a _____good_____ game.

10. They are _____good_____ neighbors and are _____well_____ liked in the community.

TEACHING TIP
Have students work in dyads to replace the often overused word *good* (and *well* when appropriate) in Practice 4 with more accurate descriptors.

PRACTICE 5

Fill in the correct comparative or superlative of the word in parentheses.

TEACHING TIP
Students who use *worse* in place of *worst* might not hear the difference in pronunciation between the two words. Have groups create sentences using both words to reinforce their understanding of the difference.

1. Lucinda is a _____better_____ (good) chemist than she is a mathematician.

2. Bascomb was the _____worst_____ (bad) governor this state has ever had.

3. When it comes to staying in shape, you are _____worse_____ (bad) than I.

4. Of the two sisters, Leah is the _____better_____ (good) markswoman.

5. You can carry cash when you travel, but using a credit card is _____better_____ (good).

6. Our goalie is the _____best_____ (good) in the league; yours is the _____worst_____ (bad).

7. When it comes to bad taste, movies are _____worse_____ (bad) than television.

8. Your sore throat seems _____worse_____ (bad) than it was yesterday.

9. Gina likes snorkeling _____better_____ (good) than fishing; she loves scuba diving _____best_____ (good) of all.

10. A parka is the _____best_____ (good) protection against a cold wind; it is certainly _____better_____ (good) than a scarf.

PRACTICE 6 REVIEW

Proofread the following essay for adjective and adverb errors. Correct errors by writing above the lines.

Julia Morgan, Architect

(1) Julia Morgan was one of San Francisco's ~~most~~ finest architects, as well as the first woman licensed as an architect in California. (2) In 1902, Morgan became the first woman to finish ~~successful~~ successfully the program in architecture at the School of Fine Arts in Paris. (3) Returning to San Francisco, she opened her own office and hired and trained a very talented staff that ~~eventual~~ eventually grew to thirty-five full-time architects. (4) Her first major commission was to reconstruct the Fairmont Hotel, one of the city's ~~bestest~~ best-known sites, which had been damaged ~~bad~~ badly in the 1906 earthquake. (5) Morgan earned her reputation by designing elegant homes and public buildings out of ~~inexpensively~~ inexpensive and available materials and by treating her clients ~~real good~~ really well. (6) She went on to design more than 800 residences, stores, churches, offices, and educational buildings, most of them in California.

(7) Her ~~bestest~~ best customer was William Randolph Hearst, one of the country's ~~most rich~~ richest newspaper publishers. (8) Morgan designed newspaper buildings and more than twenty pleasure palaces for Hearst in California and Mexico. (9) She maintained a private plane and pilot to keep her moving from project to project. (10) The ~~most big~~ biggest and ~~famousest~~ most famous of her undertakings was ~~sure~~ surely San Simeon. (11) Morgan worked on it ~~steady~~ steadily for twenty years. (12) She converted a large ranch overlooking the Pacific into a hilltop Mediterranean village composed of three of the ~~beautifullest~~ most beautiful guest houses in the world. (13) The ~~larger~~ largest of the three was designed to look like a cathedral and incorporated Hearst's fabulous art treasures from around the world. (14) The finished masterpiece had 144 rooms and was larger than a football field. (15) San Simeon is now one of the most visited tourist attractions in California and seems to grow ~~popularer~~ more popular each year.

EXPLORING ONLINE

http://owl.english.purdue.edu/handouts/esl/esladjadvEX1.html Choose the correct adjective or adverb, and check your answers.

http://a4esl.org/q/h/9901/gc-advadj.html Interactive practice: comparative and superlative forms

http://grammar.ccc.commnet.edu/grammar/adjectives.htm Everything you wanted to know about adjectives

Online Study Center   college.hmco.com/pic/evergreen8e
Visit the Online Study Center for *Evergreen* for more exercises and quizzes.

34

The Apostrophe

PART A The Apostrophe for Contractions

PART B The Apostrophe for Ownership

PART C Special Uses of the Apostrophe

PART A The Apostrophe for Contractions

Use the **apostrophe** in a **contraction** to show that letters have been omitted.

TEACHING TIP
Students should understand that the apostrophe has just two main uses. (1) to form a contraction, and (2) to indicate possession. A writer should be able to justify every apostrophe with one of these two rules.

1. *I'll* buy that coat if it goes on sale.

2. At nine *o'clock* sharp, the store opens.

- *I'll*, a contraction, is a combination of *I* and *will*. *Wi* is omitted.

- The contraction *o'clock* is the shortened form of *of the clock*.

Be especially careful in writing contractions that contain pronouns:

TEACHING TIP
Your students may be confused about using contractions in academic writing. They should ask their instructors' views before turning in a written assignment.

Common Contractions	
I + am = I'm	it + is or has = it's
I + have = I've	we + are = we're
I + will or shall = I'll	let + us = let's
you + have = you've	you + are = you're
you + will or shall = you'll	they + are = they're
he + will or shall = he'll	they + have = they've
she + is or has = she's	who + is or has = who's

PRACTICE 1

Proofread these sentences and, above the lines, supply any apostrophes missing from the contractions.

1. When Edvard Munch painted *The Scream* in his native Norway in 1893, he couldn't have known that it would become world-famous—and the center of an unsolved mystery.

2. The painting shows an anguished person who's either screaming or covering his ears to muffle a scream.

The Scream by
Edvard Munch

TEACHING TIP
It's/its, they're/their/there, you're/your, and *who's/whose* are some of the most often-confused words in the English language. Take a few moments to cover the differences and perhaps have the class write sentences to demonstrate their mastery.

3. It's become such a powerful symbol of modern stress and anxiety that it's sometimes printed on office mugs as a joke.

4. But art lovers and stressed-out jokers aren't the only ones who've admired *The Scream.*

5. Incredibly, the picture's been stolen twice, and the second time, it wasn't recovered.

6. In 1994, thieves snatched one of four versions of the painting from a gallery in Oslo, Norway, yet they've since been convicted, and the painting was found unharmed.

7. But in August 2004, shocked visitors at Norway's Munch Museum couldn't believe it when two armed bandits ripped another version of the painting out of the wall and escaped.

8. Experts don't agree on an exact figure, but they've guessed that *The Scream* is worth between $50 and $70 million.

9. Thieves usually demand a ransom for such a famous artwork because they can't sell it openly.

10. However, those who've stolen *The Scream* didn't ask for money, and the crime remains one of the great unsolved art heists of all time.

TEACHING TIP
You might take a few moments to have students think critically about the effect of contractions in writing. (They create an informal tone often inappropriate for formal academic assignments and workplace documents.)

PART B The Apostrophe for Ownership

Use the apostrophe to show ownership: Add an *'s* if a noun or an indefinite pronoun (like *someone*, *anybody*, and so on) does not already end in *-s*:

> 1. I cannot find my *friend's* book bag.
> 2. *Everyone's* right to privacy should be respected.
> 3. *John and Julio's* apartment has striped wallpaper.
> 4. The *children's* clothes are covered with mud.

■ The *friend* owns the book bag.

■ *Everyone* owns the right to privacy.

■ Both John and Julio own one apartment. The apostrophe follows the compound subject *John and Julio*.

■ The *children* own the clothes.

Add only an apostrophe to show ownership if the word already ends in *-s*:*

---

* Some writers add an *-'s* to one-syllable proper names that end in *-s*: James's bike.

TEACHING TIP
Many students confuse plurals and possessives—e.g., incorrectly adding an -'s at the end of a noun to form a plural. Take a few minutes to underscore the difference.

> 5. My *aunts'* houses are filled with antiques.
>
> 6. The *knights'* table was round.
>
> 7. *Mr. Jonas'* company manufactures sporting goods and uniforms.

■ My *aunts* (at least two of them) own the houses.

■ The *knights* (at least two) own the table.

■ *Aunts* and *knights* already end in -s, so only an apostrophe is added.

■ *Mr. Jonas* owns the company. *Mr. Jonas* already ends in -s, so only an apostrophe is added.

Note that *possessive pronouns never take an apostrophe: his, hers, theirs, ours, yours, its:*

> 8. *His* car gets twenty miles to the gallon, but *hers* gets only ten.
>
> 9. That computer is *theirs; ours* is coming soon.

PRACTICE 2

Proofread the following sentences and add apostrophes where necessary to show ownership. In each case, ask yourself if the word already ends in -s. Put a C after any correct sentences.

TEACHING TIP
You might enjoy telling students about the Apostrophe Protection Society, which aims to save this mark from bad writers who misuse it: http://www.apostrophe.fsnet.co.uk/.

1. Bill's bed is a four-poster.

2. Martha and David's house is a log cabin made entirely by hand.

3. Somebody's cell phone was left on the sink.

4. During the eighteenth century, ladies' dresses were heavy and uncomfortable.

5. Have you seen the children's watercolor set?

6. Mr. James' fried chicken and rice dish was crispy and delicious.

7. The class loved reading about Ulysses' travels.

8. The Surgeon General's latest report was just released.

9. Our city's water supply must be protected.

10. He found his ticket, but she cannot find hers.   C

11. Every spring, my grandmother's porch is completely covered with old furniture for sale.

12. Jack's car is the same color as ours.

13. Celia's final, a brilliant study of pest control on tobacco farms, received a high grade.

14. The men's locker room is on the right; the women's is on the left.

15. The program is entering its final year.   C

PART C Special Uses of the Apostrophe

Use an apostrophe in certain expressions of time:

> 1. I desperately need a *week's* vacation.

■ Although the week does not own a vacation, it is a vacation of a week—*a week's vacation.*

Use an apostrophe to pluralize lowercase letters, words, and numbers that normally do not have plurals:

> 2. Be careful to cross your *t*'s.
> 3. Your *8*'s look like *f*'s.
> 4. Don't use so many *but*'s in your writing.

Use an apostrophe to show omitted numbers:

> 5. The class of '72 held its annual reunion last week.

PRACTICE 3

Proofread these sentences and add an apostrophe wherever necessary.

1. Cross your *t*'s and dot your *i*'s.

2. I would love a month's vacation on a dude ranch.

3. Too many *and*'s make this paragraph dull.

4. Those 9's look crooked.

5. You certainly put in a hard day's work!

PRACTICE 4 ▋ **REVIEW**

Proofread the following essay for apostrophe errors. Correct the errors by adding apostrophes above the lines where needed and crossing out those that do not belong.

The True Story of Superman

(1) Sometimes, things just don't work out right. (2) That's how the creators of Superman felt for a long time.

(3) Superman's first home wasn't the planet Krypton, but Cleveland. (4) There, in 1933, Superman was born. (5) Jerry Siegel's story, "Reign of Superman," accompanied by Joe Shuster's illustrations, appeared in the boys' own magazine, *Science Fiction*. (6) Later, the teenagers continued to develop their idea. (7) Superman would come to Earth from a distant planet to defend freedom and justice for ordinary people. (8) He would conceal his identity by living as an ordinary person himself. (9) Siegel and Shuster hoped their character's strength and morality would boost people's spirits during the Great Depression.

(10) At first, the creators weren't able to sell their concept; then, Action Comics' Henry Donnenfield bought it. (11) In June of 1938, the first *Superman* comic hit the stands. (12) Superman's success was immediate and overwhelming. (13) Finally, Americans had a hero who wouldn't let them down! (14) Radio and TV shows, movie serials, feature films, and generations of superheroes followed.

(15) While others made millions from their idea, Siegel and Shuster didn't profit from its success. (16) They produced Superman for Action Comics for a mere fifteen dollars a page until they were fired a few years later when Joe Shuster's eyes began to fail. (17) They sued, but they lost the case. (18) For a long time, both lived in poverty, but they continued to fight. (19) In 1975, Siegel and Shuster

finally took their story to the press; the publicity won them lifelong pensions. (20)

The two mens long struggle had ended with success.

EXPLORING ONLINE

http://grammar.ccc.commnet.edu/grammar/quizzes/apostrophe_quiz2.htm
Graded practice: Apostrophe or no apostrophe? This is the question.

http://owl.english.purdue.edu/handouts/grammar/g_apostEX1.html Apostrophe practice makes perfect.

Online Study Center   **college.hmco.com/pic/evergreen8e**
Visit the Online Study Center for *Evergreen* for more exercises and quizzes.

35

The Comma

PART A Commas for Items in a Series

TEACHING TIP
The comma is an often-misused mark, but only because students have not memorized the rules that govern comma usage. Point out that eight basic rules will serve writers well—and all are covered in this chapter.

TEACHING TIP
Students may have been taught that the final comma preceding the conjunction is optional. Encourage them always to insert that last comma to avoid possible confusion or misreading.

Use commas to separate the items in a series:*

1. You need *bolts, nuts,* and *screws.*

2. I will be happy to *read your poem, comment on it,* and *return it to you.*

3. *Mary paints pictures, Robert plays the trumpet,* but *Sam just sits and dreams.*

Do not use commas when all three items are joined by *and* or *or*:

4. I enjoy *biking* and *skating* and *swimming.*

---

* For work on parallelism, see Chapter 20, "Revising for Consistency and Parallelism," Part C.

PRACTICE 1

Punctuate the following sentences:

1. At the banquet, Ed served a salad of juicy red tomatoes, crunchy green lettuce, and stringless snap beans.

2. As a nursing assistant, Reva dispensed medication, disinfected wounds, and took blood samples.

3. Ali visited Santa Barbara, Concord, and Berkeley.

4. Hiking, rafting, and snowboarding are her favorite sports.

5. The police found TV sets, blenders, and blow dryers stacked to the ceiling in the abandoned house.

6. I forgot to pack some important items for the trip to the tropics: insect repellent, sunscreen, and antihistamine tablets.

7. Don't eat strange mushrooms, walk near the water, or feed the squirrels.

8. Everyone in class had to present an oral report, write a term paper, and take a final.

9. We brought a Ouija board, a Scrabble set, and a Boggle game to the party.

10. To earn a decent wage, make a comfortable home, and educate my children—those are my hopes.

PART B **Commas with Introductory Phrases, Transitional Expressions, and Parentheticals**

Use a comma after most introductory phrases of more than two words:*

1. *By four in the afternoon,* everybody wanted to go home.
2. *After the game on Saturday,* we all went dancing.

---

* For more work on introductory phrases, see Chapter 21, "Revising for Sentence Variety," Part C.

Use commas to set off transitional expressions:

> 3. Ferns, *for example,* need less sunlight than flowering plants.
>
> 4. Instructors, *on the other hand,* receive a lower salary than assistant professors.

Use commas to set off parenthetical elements:

> 5. *By the way,* where is the judge's umbrella?
>
> 6. Nobody, *it seems,* wants to eat the nut burgers.

■ *By the way* and *it seems* are called parenthetical expressions because they appear to be asides, words not really crucial to the meaning of the sentence. They could almost appear in parentheses: *(By the way) where is the judge's umbrella?*

Other common parenthetical expressions are *after all, actually, as a matter of fact,* and *to tell the truth.*

PRACTICE 2

Punctuate the following sentences:

1. Frankly I always suspected that you were a born saleswoman.

2. All twelve jurors by the way felt that the defendant was innocent.

3. On every April Fools' Day he tries out a new, dumb practical joke.

4. In fact Lucinda should never have written that poison-pen letter.

5. Close to the top of Mount Washington the climbers paused for a tea break.

6. To tell the truth that usher needs a lesson in courtesy.

7. Near the end of the driveway a large lilac bush bloomed and brightened the yard.

8. He prefers as a rule serious news programs to the lighter sitcoms.

9. To sum up Mr. Choi will handle all the details.

10. During my three years in Minnesota I learned how to deal with snow.

TEACHING TIP

Students who overuse commas, "sprinkling" them throughout their writing, may claim they have been taught to use a comma "to avoid confusion" or wherever they "hear a pause." Stress that the secret of correct comma usage is memorizing and practicing the eight comma rules.

ESL TIP

In some languages, like Spanish, commas are used freely to separate parts of a sentence. Have your ESL students explain comma use in their native language and contrast it with English use.

PART C Commas for Appositives

Use commas to set off appositives:*

> 1. Yoko, *our new classmate,* is our best fielder.
>
> 2. *A humorous and charming man,* he was a great hit with my parents.
>
> 3. This is her favorite food, *ketchup sandwiches.*

■ Appositive phrases like *our new classmate, a humorous and charming man,* and *ketchup sandwiches* rename or describe nouns and pronouns—*Yoko, he, food.*

> 4. Hip hop mogul Simmons launched Def Jam Recordings.
>
> 5. His wife, Kimora, succeeded with her company Baby Phat.

■ A one-word appositive is not set off by commas when it is essential to the meaning of the sentence. Without the appositive *Simmons,* we do not know who launched Def Jam Recordings.

■ A one-word appositive is set off by commas when it is not essential to the meaning of the sentence. The name *Kimora* does not affect the meaning of the sentence.

PRACTICE 3

Punctuate the following sentences.

1. The Rock, the popular wrestler and actor, starred in movies and made a video with musician Wyclef Jean.

2. Long novels, especially ones with complicated plots, force me to read slowly.

3. Rolando, a resident nurse, hopes to become a pediatrician.

4. I don't trust that tire, the one with the yellow patch on the side.

5. Tanzania, a small African nation, exports cashew nuts.

6. Watch out for Phil, a man whose ambition rules him.

7. Ms. Liu, a well-known nutritionist, lectures at public schools.

---

* For more work on appositives, see Chapter 21, "Revising for Sentence Variety," Part D.

8. A real flying ace␣Helen will teach a course in sky diving.

9. We support the Center for Science in the Public Interest␣a consumer education

   and protection group.

10. My husband␣Bill␣owns two stereos.

PART D   Commas with Nonrestrictive and Restrictive Clauses

A **relative clause** is a clause that begins with *who, which,* or *that* and modifies a noun or pronoun. There are two kinds of relative clauses: **nonrestrictive** and **restrictive.***

A **nonrestrictive relative clause** is not essential to the meaning of the sentence:

1. Raj, *who is a part-time aviator,* loves to tinker with machines of all kinds.

▪ *Who is a part-time aviator* is a relative clause describing *Raj.* It is a nonrestrictive relative clause because it is not essential to the meaning of the sentence. The point is that *Raj loves to tinker with machines of all kinds.*

▪ **Commas** set off the nonrestrictive relative clause.

A **restrictive relative clause** is essential to the meaning of the sentence:

2. People *who do their work efficiently* make good students.

▪ *Who do their work efficiently* is a relative clause describing *people.* It is a restrictive relative clause because it is *essential* to the meaning of the sentence. Without it, sentence 2 would read, *People make good students.* But the point is that certain people make good students—*those who do their work efficiently.*

▪ Restrictive relative clauses do *not* require commas.

PRACTICE 4

Set off the nonrestrictive relative clauses in the following sentences with commas. Note that *which* usually begins a nonrestrictive relative clause and *that* usually begins a restrictive clause. Remember: Restrictive relative clauses are *not* set off by commas. Write a *C* after each correct sentence.

---

*For more work on nonrestrictive and restrictive clauses, see Chapter 21, "Revising for Sentence Variety," Part D.

TEACHING TIP
Remind students that *who* refers to persons, *which* and *that* refer to things.

1. Olive who always wanted to go into law enforcement is a detective in the Eighth Precinct.

2. Employees who learn to use the new computers may soon qualify for a merit raise. C

3. Polo which is not played much in the United States is very popular in England.

4. A person who always insists upon telling you the truth is sometimes a pain in the neck. C

5. Statistics 101 which is required for the business curriculum demands concentration and perseverance.

6. Robin who is usually shy at large parties spent the evening dancing with Arsenio who is everybody's favorite dance partner.

7. This small shop sells furniture that is locally handcrafted. C

8. His uncle who rarely eats meat consumes enormous quantities of vegetables, fruits, and grains.

9. Pens that slowly leak ink can be very messy. C

10. Valley Forge which was the site of Washington's winter quarters draws many tourists every spring and summer.

PART E Commas for Dates and Addresses

Use commas to separate the elements of an address. Note, however, that no punctuation is required between the state and ZIP code if the ZIP code is included.

1. Please send the books to *300 West Road, Stamford, CT 06860.*

2. We moved from *1015 Allen Circle, Morristown, New Jersey,* to *Farland Lane, Dubuque, Iowa.*

Use commas to separate the elements of a date:

TEACHING TIP
Have students recall an important day in their lives and then write one sentence stating what happened, the full date, and address. Ask pairs to share what they wrote, exchanging pages to check each other's prowess with commas.

3. The sociologists arrived in Tibet on *Monday, January 18, 1999,* and planned to stay for two years.

4. John DeLeon arrived *from Baltimore in January* and will be our new short-stop this season.

Do not use a comma with a single-word address or date preceded by a preposition:

5. I expect to have completed my B.A. in physical education by June 2010.

PRACTICE 5

Punctuate the following sentences. Write a C after each correct sentence.

1. The unusual names of many American towns reflect our history and sense of humor. C

2. In February 1878, Ed Schieffelin told friends that he was joining the California Gold Rush, and they warned, "The only thing you'll find out there will be your own tombstone." C

3. But Schieffelin found silver in Arizona and named his settlement Tombstone, now famous for the shootout at the O.K. Corral on October 26,1881.

4. The residents of another mining town wanted to honor the chicken-like ptarmigan bird, but an argument about the word's spelling led them to select Chicken,Alaska,instead.

5. It was Christmas Eve, December 24,1849,when residents of a small rural community chose to name their town Santa Claus.

6. Every Christmas since the 1920s, volunteers have replied to the thousands of children's letters that pour into the town's post office, located at 45 N. Kringle Place,Santa Claus,Indiana 47579.

7. Hell, Michigan, got its name when crusty resident George Reeves was asked his opinion and replied, "I don't care. You can name it Hell if you want to." C

8. At a 10K race there on August 13, 2005, runners went home with T-shirts announcing, "I Ran Thru Hell."

9. On January 20, 2000, the town of Halfway, Oregon, became the "World's First Dot Com City" when it officially changed its name to Half.com.

10. Choosing the right name can be difficult, as the folks who founded Nameless, Tennessee, can attest.

PART F Minor Uses of the Comma

Use a comma after answering a question with *yes* or *no*:

> 1. *No,* I'm not sure about that answer.

TEACHING TIP
Commas in direct quotations are covered in Chapter 36.

Use a comma when addressing someone directly and specifically naming the person spoken to:

> 2. *Alicia,* where did you put my law books?

Use a comma after interjections like *ah*, *oh*, and so on:

> 3. *Ah,* these coconuts are delicious.

Use a comma to contrast:

> 4. Harold, *not Roy,* is my scuba-diving partner.*

---

* For help using commas with coordinating and subordinating conjunctions—and help avoiding run-ons, commas splices, and fragments—see Chapters 25 and 26.

PRACTICE 6

Punctuate the following sentences.

1. Yes I do think you will be famous one day.

2. Well did you call a taxi?

3. The defendant ladies and gentlemen of the jury does not even own a red plaid jacket.

4. Cynthia have you ever camped in the Pacific Northwest?

5. No I most certainly will not marry you.

6. Oh I love the way they play everything to a salsa beat.

7. The class feels Professor Molinor that your grades are unrealistically high.

8. He said march not swagger.

9. Perhaps but I still don't think that the carburetor fits there.

10. We all agree Ms. Crawford that you are the best jazz bassist around.

PRACTICE 7　REVIEW

Proofread the following essay for comma errors—either missing commas or commas used incorrectly. Correct the errors above the lines.

Pixar Perfect

(1) A new company that would change the future of animated films was created in January 1986. (2) The founder was Steven Jobs the head of Apple Computer and creator of the iPod. (3) Applying technical imagination to story-telling Pixar has produced some of the most successful and beloved movies ever made. (4) *Toy Story A Bug's Life Monsters, Inc.,* and *Finding Nemo* appealed to both children and adults by combining engaging stories memorable characters, and cutting-edge computer animation.

(5) Pixar's action-packed adventure plots also carry emotional punch. (6) In *Finding Nemo* for instance Nemo's father searches for his missing son in the vast

In Pixar's *Finding Nemo,* Dorie and Marlin face danger in the deep.

ocean and learns about the bonds of family love. (7) *Monsters, Inc.* explores the theme of facing fears as it follows two monsters attempting to return a wayward toddler to her room. (8) In *A Bug's Life* tiny ants take on bullying grasshoppers.

(9) Pixar populates these plots with lovable heroes and diabolical villains. (10) Although none of them is technically a human characters like Woody Buzz Lightyear, Flick Sully Nemo, and Dorie win moviegoers' hearts with their "humanity." (11) Woody is upset when a new toy replaces him as the favorite. (12) Dorie the charming blue fish in *Nemo*, has short-term memory loss. (13) The characters seem even more real because stars like Ellen Degeneres Tom Hanks Tim Allen John Goodman and Billy Crystal bring their voices to life.

(14) Finally Pixar animators use the latest computer-animation technology and meticulous detail to create realistic 3-D images. (15) Monster Sully's shaggy blue coat ripples in the wind, for example because animators created a separate computer model for each of its 2.3 million individual hairs. (16) Before they created *Finding Nemo* animators studied the movements of live fish as well as the facial expressions of the stars who supplied the voices.

(17) Pixar's animated films dazzle critics as well as audiences. (18) In fact, these movies inspired the Academy of Motion Picture Arts and Sciences to create in 2002 a new Academy Awards category Best Animated Feature.

EXPLORING ONLINE

http://www.pixar.com/howwedoit/# This site, "How We Make a Movie," offers a quick tour through the Pixar process. Notice the clear, step-by-step presentation that helps make a complicated series of steps understandable—just as good process writing does.

EXPLORING ONLINE

TEACHING TIP
More practice and assessment are available in the *Evergreen* Test Bank, linked ACE tests on the *Evergreen* Online Teaching and Study Centers, *WriteSpace for Evergreen,* and Exploring Online links in this chapter.

http://owl.english.purdue.edu/handouts/grammar/g_commaEX1.html
Paper quiz with answers: Revise for commas.

http://grammar.ccc.commnet.edu/grammar/quizzes/commas_fillin.htm
Interactive quiz: Where have all the commas gone?

Online Study Center **college.hmco.com/pic/evergreen8e**
Visit the Online Study Center for *Evergreen* for more exercises and quizzes.

36

Mechanics

PART A   Capitalization

TEACHING TIP
You may wish to begin this lesson by reviewing with students the distinction between proper nouns/adjectives and common nouns/adjectives.

Always capitalize the following: *names, nationalities, religions, races, languages, countries, cities, months, days of the week, documents, organizations,* and *holidays.*

> 1. The *Protestant* church on the corner will offer *Spanish* and *English* courses starting *Thursday, June* 3.

TEACHING TIP
Explain to students that although *African American* and *Caucasian* are capitalized, the words *black* and *white* usually are not.

Capitalize the following *only* when they are used as part of a proper noun: *streets, buildings, historical events, titles,* and *family relationships.*

> 2. We saw *Professor Rodriguez* at *Silver Hall,* where he was delivering a talk on the *Spanish Civil War.*

ESL TIP
Your ESL students may need extra practice in forming lowercase and capital letters. Search online for reproducible penmanship guides.

Do not capitalize these same words when they are used as common nouns:

> 3. We saw the professor at the lecture hall, where he was delivering a talk on a civil war.

481

Capitalize geographic locations but not directions:

> 4. The tourists went to the *South* for their winter vacation.
>
> 5. Go south on this boulevard for three miles.

Capitalize academic subjects only if they refer to a specific named and numbered course:

> 6. Have you ever studied psychology?
>
> 7. Last semester, I took *Psychology* 101.

PRACTICE 1

Capitalize wherever necessary in the following sentences. Put a *C* after each correct sentence.

1. Barbara Kingsolver, a well-known novelist, nonfiction writer, and poet, was born on april 8, 1955, in annapolis, maryland.

2. She grew up in rural kentucky and then went to college in indiana; after graduating, she worked in europe and since then has lived in and around tucson, arizona.

3. In college, Kingsolver majored first in music and then in biology; she later withdrew from a graduate program in biology and ecology at the university of arizona to work in its office of arid land studies.

4. Kingsolver's first novel, *The Bean Trees,* has become a classic; it is taught in english classes and has been translated into more than sixty-five languages.

5. The main character, named taylor greer, is considered one of the most memorable women in modern american literature.

6. In a later novel, *The Poisonwood Bible,* Kingsolver follows the family of a baptist minister in its move to the congo.

7. The fanaticism of reverend price brings misery to his family and destruction to the villagers he tries to convert to christianity.

8. Kingsolver's writing always deals with powerful political and social issues, but her novels don't sound preachy because she is a wonderful storyteller. C

9. She has won awards and prizes from the <u>a</u>merican <u>l</u>ibrary <u>a</u>ssociation and many other organizations; she also has earned special recognition from the <u>u</u>nited <u>n</u>ations <u>n</u>ational <u>c</u>ouncil of <u>w</u>omen.

10. This gifted writer, who plays drums and piano, performs with a band called <u>r</u>ock <u>b</u>ottom <u>r</u>emainders; other band members are also notable writers— <u>s</u>tephen <u>k</u>ing, <u>a</u>my <u>t</u>an, and <u>d</u>ave <u>b</u>arry.

PART B Titles

Capitalize words of a title except short prepositions, short conjunctions, and the articles *the*, *an*, and *a*. Always capitalize the first and last words of the title, no matter what they are:

---

1. I liked <u>The Invisible Man</u> but found <u>The House on the River</u> slow reading.

Underline the titles of long works: *books,* newspapers and magazines, television shows, plays, record albums, operas,* and *films.*

Put quotation marks around shorter works or parts of longer ones: *articles, short stories, poems, songs, scenes from plays,* and *chapters from full-length books.*

---

2. Have you read Hemingway's "The Killers" yet?

3. We are assigned "The Money Market" in <u>Essentials of Economics</u> for homework in my marketing course.

▪ "The Killers" is a short story.

▪ "The Money Market" is a chapter in the full-length book <u>Essentials of Economics</u>.

---

* The titles and parts of sacred books are not underlined and are not set off by quotation marks: Job 5:6, Koran 1:14, and so on.

Do not underline or use quotation marks around the titles of your own papers.

PRACTICE 2

Capitalize these titles correctly. Do not underline or use quotation marks in this practice.

1. inside women's college basketball
   (I, W, C, B)

2. the genius of frank lloyd wright
   (T, G, F, L, W)

3. breath, eyes, memory
   (B, E, M)

4. an insider's guide to the music industry
   (A, I, G, M, I)

5. the orchid thief
   (T, O, T)

6. dave barry's guide to marriage and/or sex
   (D, B, G, M, S)

7. how to build a web site
   (H, B, W)

8. a history of violence in american movies
   (A H, V, A, M)

9. harry potter and the goblet of fire
   (H, P, G, F)

10. currents from the dancing river
    (C, D, R)

PRACTICE 3

Wherever necessary, underline or place quotation marks around each title in the sentences below so that the reader will know at a glance what type of work the title refers to. Put a *C* after any correct sentence.

EXAMPLE Two of the best short stories in that volume are "Rope" and "The New Dress."

1. African American writer Langston Hughes produced his first novel, Not Without Laughter, when he was a student at Lincoln University in Pennsylvania.

2. By that time, he had already been a farmer, a cook, a waiter, and a doorman at a Paris nightclub; he had also won a prize for his poem "The Weary Blues," which was published in 1925 in the magazine Opportunity.

3. In 1926 Hughes wrote his famous essay "The Negro Artist and the Racial Mountain," which appeared in the Nation magazine; he wanted young black writers to write without shame or fear about the subject of race.

4. Because he spoke Spanish, Hughes was asked in 1937 by the newspaper the <u>Baltimore Afro-American</u> to cover the activities of blacks in the International Brigades in Spain during the Spanish Civil War.

5. For the rest of his life, he wrote articles in newspapers such as the <u>San Francisco Chronicle</u>, the <u>New York Times</u>, and the <u>Chicago Defender</u>.

6. In fact, for more than twenty years he wrote a weekly column for the <u>Chicago Defender</u>, in which he introduced a character named Simple, who became popular because of his witty observations on life.

7. The stories about Simple were eventually collected and published in five books; two of those books are <u>Simple Speaks His Mind</u> and <u>Simple Takes a Wife</u>.

8. In 1938, Hughes established the Harlem Suitcase Theater in Manhattan, where his play <u>Don't You Want to Be Free?</u> was performed.

9. Because Hughes's poetry was based on the rhythms of African American speech and music, many of his poems have been set to music, including "Love Can Hurt You," "Dorothy's Name Is Mud," and "Five O'Clock Blues."

10. Few modern writers can rival Hughes's enormous output of fine poems, newspaper articles, columns, and novels.   C

PART C Direct Quotations

TEACHING TIP
Remind students that quotation marks are always used in pairs. When they proofread and edit their work, they should verify that they provided the end quotation mark.

1. He said, "These are the best seats in the house."

■ The direct quotation is preceded by a comma or a colon.
■ The first letter of the direct quotation is capitalized.
■ Periods always go *inside* the quotation marks.

2. He asked, "Where is my laptop?"

3. Stewart yelled, "I don't like beans!"

■ Question marks and exclamation points go inside the quotation marks if they are part of the direct words of the speaker.

4. "That was meant for the company," he said, "but if you wish, you may have it."

5. "The trees look magnificent!" she exclaimed. "It would be fun to climb them all."

■ In sentence 4, the quotation is one single sentence interrupted by *he said*. Therefore, a comma is used after *he said*, and *but* is not capitalized.

■ In sentence 5, the quotation consists of two different sentences. Thus a period follows *exclaimed*, and the second sentence of the quotation begins with a capital letter.

PRACTICE 4

Insert quotation marks where necessary in each sentence. Capitalize and punctuate correctly.

1. The sign reads don't even think about parking here.

2. Alexander Pope wrote to err is human, to forgive divine.

3. Well, it takes all kinds she sighed.

4. He exclaimed you look terrific in those jeweled sandals.

5. The article said Most American children do poorly in geography.

6. These books on ancient Egypt look interesting he replied but I don't have time to read them now.

7. Although the rain is heavy she said we will continue harvesting the corn.

8. Give up caffeine and get lots of rest the doctor advised.

9. The label warns this product should not be taken by those allergic to aspirin.

10. Red, white, and blue Hillary said are my favorite colors.

PART D Minor Marks of Punctuation

1. The Colon

Use a colon to show that a direct quotation will follow or to introduce a list:*

1. This is the opening line of his essay: "The airplane is humanity's greatest invention."
2. There are four things I can't resist in warm weather: fresh mangoes, a sandy beach, cold drinks, and a hammock.

Use a colon to separate the chapter and verse in a reference to the Bible or to separate the hour and minute:

3. This quotation comes from Genesis 1:1.
4. It is now exactly 4:15 P.M.

2. Parentheses

Use parentheses to enclose a phrase or word that is not essential to the meaning of the sentence:

5. Herpetology (the study of snakes) is a fascinating area of zoology.
6. She left her hometown (Plunkville) to go to the big city (Fairmount) in search of success.

3. The Dash

Use a dash to emphasize a portion of a sentence or to interrupt the sentence with an added element:

7. This is the right method—the only one—so we are stuck with it.

The colon, parentheses, and the dash should be used sparingly.

---

* Avoid using a colon after any form of the verb *to be* or after a preposition.

PRACTICE 5

Punctuate these sentences with colons, dashes, or parentheses.

1. Calvin asked for the following: two light bulbs, a pack of matches, a lead pencil, and a pound of grapes.

2. They should leave by 11:30 P.M.

3. The designer's newest fashions (magnificent leather creations) were generally too expensive for the small chain of clothing stores.

4. Harvey—the only Missourian in the group—remains unconvinced.

5. She replied, "This rock group (The Woogies) sounds like all the others I've heard this year."

6. If you eat a heavy lunch—as you always do—remember not to go swimming immediately afterward.

7. By 9:30 P.M., the zoo veterinarian (a Dr. Smittens) had operated on the elephant.

8. Note these three tips for hammering in a nail: hold the hammer at the end of the handle, position the nail carefully, and watch your thumb.

9. Whenever Harold Garvey does his birdcalls at parties—as he is sure to do—everyone begins to yawn.

10. Please purchase these things at the hardware store: masking tape, thumbtacks, apple-green paint, and some sandpaper.

PRACTICE 6   REVIEW

Proofread the following essay for errors in capitalization, quotation marks, colons, parentheses, and dashes. Correct the errors by writing above the lines.

The Passion of Thomas Gilcrease

(1) Thomas Gilcrease, a descendent of creek indians, became an instant Millionaire when oil was discovered on his homestead in 1907. (2) He spent most of his fortune collecting objects that tell the story of the american frontier, particularly of the Native American experience. (3) The Thomas Gilcrease institute of american history and arts in Tulsa, oklahoma, is the result of his lifelong passion.

(4) This huge collection more than 10,000 works of art, 90,000 historical documents, and 250,000 native american artifacts spans the centuries from 10,000 B.C. to the 1950s. (5) Awed visitors can view nearly 200 George Catlin paintings of Native American life. (6) They can walk among paintings and bronze sculptures by Frederic Remington with names like *The Coming And Going Of The Pony Express* that call up images of the West. (7) Museumgoers can admire Thomas Moran's watercolors that helped persuade congress to create yellowstone, the first national park. (8) In addition, visitors are treated to works by modern Native Americans, such as the display of wood sculptures by the cherokee Willard Stone.

(9) The museum also houses many priceless documents an original copy of the declaration of independence, the oldest known letter written from the new world, and the papers of Hernando Cortés. (10) A new glass storage area even allows visitors to view the 80 percent of the holdings that are not on display. (11) Thousands of beaded moccasins and buckskin dresses line the shelves, and a collection of magnificent war bonnets hangs from brackets.

(12) When the Gilcrease Institute opened its doors on May 2, 1949, *Life* magazine declared "it is the best collection of art and literature ever assembled on the American frontier and the Indian. (13) Thousands of visitors agree.

EXPLORING ONLINE

TEACHING TIP
More practice and assessment are available in the *Evergreen* Test Bank, linked ACE tests on the *Evergreen* Online Teaching and Study Centers, *WriteSpace for Evergreen,* and Exploring Online links in this chapter.

http://grammar.ccc.commnet.edu/grammar/cgi-shl/par_numberless_quiz .pl/caps_quiz.htm Graded capitalization practice

http://grammar.ccc.commnet.edu/grammar/quizzes/punct_fillin.htm Mixed practice: test your skill with many marks of punctuation.

Online Study Center **college.hmco.com/pic/evergreen8e** Visit the Online Study Center for *Evergreen* for more exercises and quizzes.

37

Putting Your Proofreading Skills to Work

TEACHING TIP
Lead a discussion about the effect that error-filled written work has on the reader, especially in academic and professional settings.

After you have written a paragraph or an essay—once you have prewritten, drafted, and revised—you are ready for the next step—**proofreading.**

Proofreading, which takes place at the sentence level, means applying what you have learned in Units 5 and 6. When you proofread, carefully check each sentence for correct grammar, punctuation, and capitalization. Is every sentence complete? Do all verbs agree with their subjects? Are there any comma errors? Do all proper nouns begin with a capital letter?

This chapter gives you the opportunity to put your proofreading skills to work in real-world situations. As you proofread the paragraphs and essays that follow, you must look for any—and every—kind of error, just as you would in the real world of college or work. The first four practices tell you what kinds of errors to look for; if you have trouble, go back to those chapters and review. The other practices, however, contain a random mix of errors and give you no clues at all.

PRACTICE 1   PROOFREADING

TEACHING TIP
By now, your students should have learned their individual *error patterns* and know to proofread carefully for these. Make sure this is the case. Remember: One error repeated ten times looks like ten errors!

Proofread this paragraph, correcting any errors above the lines. To review, see these chapters:

Chapter 26	run-ons, comma splices, fragments
Chapter 27	present tense problems, subject-verb agreement
Chapter 28	past tense problems
Chapter 29	past participle problems

(1) Mount Everest is the tallest mountain in the world. (2) ~~The~~ the highest point on Earth, and the dangerous dream of every mountain climber. (3) Everest ˄is set in the Himalaya Mountains of central Asia and ~~rise~~ rises 29,028 feet. (4) The deadliest threat to

climbers are not the steep, icy slopes or even the bitter cold and ferocious winds ^{is} it is ^{.It} the lack of air. (5) Air at the top of Everest has only one-third the oxygen of air below, so without preparation, the average person would live less than an hour at the summit. (6) In fact, altitude sickness begin ^{begins} at 8,000 feet, with headache, nausea, and confusion. (7) At 12,000 feet, the brain and lungs starts ^{start} filling with fluid, which can lead to death. (8) How, then, has anyone ever climbed Everest, the answer is acclimatization. ^{?The} (9) Mountaineers climb slowly, about 2,000 feet a day, and they drink huge amounts of water. (10) They also carry oxygen. (11) Amazingly, in 1980, the first person to climb Everest solo was also the first to climb it without oxygen. (12) That was Reinhold Messner from Italy. (13) Who ^{who} later wrote in *Climbing* magazine that the lack of air "saps your judgment and strength, even your ability to feel anything at all. I don't know how I made it." (14) Over 145 climbers have died scaling Mount Everest, nonetheless, this danger keeps tempting others to try their skills and their luck.

The oldest person to climb Mount Everest, seventy-year-old Yuichiro Miura of Japan.

| PRACTICE 2 | PROOFREADING |

ESL TIP
**http://depts.gallaudet
.edu/ESL/** is an especially
helpful site for nonnative
writers. It offers many
helpful practices, including
cloze quizzes.

Proofread this paragraph, correcting any errors above the lines. To review, see these chapters:

Chapter 20	inconsistency of number or person, parallelism problems
Chapter 26	run-ons, comma splices, fragments
Chapter 27	present tense problems, subject-verb agreement
Chapter 29	past participle problems
Chapter 34	apostrophe errors

(1) American culture emphasizes quick results we pick up fast food and do our

banking in drive-through lanes. (2) We buy gadgets that promise to save you time.

(3) We even call ahead for restaurant seating, so we wont have to wait for a table.

(4) Now a new trend know as *speed dating* becoming popular in big cities like Los

Angeles, Chicago, and Boston. (5) Also called pre-dating or "McDating." (6) This

activity is suppose to reduce the time that busy single people spend getting to know

each other. (7) Speed dating events are arranged by companies like HurryDate and

8MinuteDating. (8) At these events, even numbers of men and women are paired

off, each couple chats for eight to ten minutes while trying to determine potential

compatibility. (9) Then a bell rings, and everyone switch partners. (10) At the end of

the session, participants who are interest in each other are provide with each other's

phone and e-mail contacts. (11) Some say that speed dating is ideal for people who

are busy, who dislike the bar scene, or who hope to lessen the pain of rejection.

(12) Others calls it drive-through dating, just another crazy American fad.

| PRACTICE 3 | PROOFREADING |

Proofread this paragraph, correcting any errors above the lines. To review, see these chapters:

Chapter 26	run-ons, comma splices, and fragments
Chapter 28	past tense errors
Chapter 29	past participle problems
Chapter 33	adjective and adverb errors

ESL TIP
A popular ESL proofreading technique is to ask students to check their work *from the end*, starting with the last sentence, proceeding to the next-to-the-last sentence, and so on, to the first sentence. This process requires students to slow down and proof their work carefully.

(1) Lea Salonga, a talented Broadway performer, has became [*become*] a role model for aspiring young actors, both in the United States and her native Philippines. (2) Born in Manila, Salonga began performing at age seven. (3) After she won a small part in a local production of *The King and I*, (4) Her [*her*] popularity grew quickly. (5) She acted in many theater productions, recorded a number of albums, (6) And [*and*] even star [*starred*] in her own children's television show, called *Love, Lea.* (7) Through it all, Salonga's parents focused on her education and good manners rather than her fame. (8) When British talent scouts arrived in Manila, they were charm [*were charmed*] by the gracious young woman with the beautiful soprano voice and cast her immediate [*immediately*] as the lead in their new musical *Miss Saigon.* (9) Salonga was only twenty when she winned [*won*] a Tony award for her sensitive portrayal of a Vietnamese woman who sacrifices her own life to give her child a more [ ] better one. (10) Since then, Salonga has starred in some of the popularest [*most popular*] Broadway musicals, landed a role in *As the World Turns*, and singing [*sung*] the soundtrack for the female leads in the Disney films *Aladdin* and *Mulan.* (11) Despite her success, Salonga remains close to her family and her traditional upbringing. (12) Her first kiss occurred on the set of *Miss Saigon* [*and*] she was chaperoned on dates until she turned twenty-one. (13) Salonga's parents have encouraged her to complete her college education. (14) With her balanced lifestyle and much [*many*] achievements, Lea Salonga encourages other young people to follow their dreams without loosing [*losing*] sight of their roots.

TEACHING TIP
Urge students to review the errors they fail to identify in this chapter's practices. Suggest that they either return to relevant chapters or complete additional online exercises such as those in *WriteSpace for Evergreen*.

PRACTICE 4   PROOFREADING

Proofread this paragraph, correcting any errors above the lines. To review, see these chapters:

Chapter 21	relative clause problems
Chapter 26	run-ons, comma splices, fragments
Chapter 27	present tense problems, subject-verb agreement
Chapter 30	noun errors

Chapter 31   pronoun errors

Chapter 36   capitalization errors

(1) In ^F^ french, its name means "Circus of the Sun," but don't expect Cirque du Soleil to have old-fashioned lion tamers, elephants on parade, or clowns with orange hair. (2) Instead, this innovative Quebec-based company draws on the ancient traditions of ^C^ chinese acrobat^s^. (3) ~~And feature~~ and features strangely beautiful sets and costumes. (4) Dramatic lighting and eerie live music ~~sets~~ set the mood. (5) Then a bare-chested man ~~fly~~ flies through the darkness above the stage, 40-foot wings of red silk flowing from his arms. (6) Four young ^A^ asian ~~woman~~ women contort their tattooed bodies so they resemble flowers, figure eight^s^, or spirals. (7) A giant wheel with human spokes rolls across the stage while acrobats perform. (8) ~~Dangling~~ dangling from an open door ~~who~~ that swings high in the air. (9) In a show called "O," after the ^F^ french word for "water," a 1.5-million-gallon pool of water appears in the stage. Underwater ~~underwater~~ swimmers rise magically from the stage floor, and acrobats near the ceiling dive and disappear into the water. (10) Cirque has grown from a tiny group of street performers in 1984 to an Entertainment Empire of 500 actors and athletes ~~which~~ who perform in twelve shows on three continents. (11) The secret of Cirque du ^S^ soleil's success lies in its ongoing spirit of teamwork. (12) Despite their large numbers, performers from forty different countries still create the shows together. (13) ~~Proposing~~ proposing ideas and designing their own roles. (14) The result is a show that dazzles even those ~~whom~~ who think they have seen it all.

TEACHING TIP
Remind students that although programs like Microsoft Word can help them identify spelling and some grammatical errors in their papers, computers are far from foolproof. Proofreading is still the job of every writer.

PRACTICE 5   PROOFREADING

This paragraph contains many of the errors you have learned to avoid in Unit 6. Proofread each sentence carefully, and then correct each error above the line.

(1) If you want to eat well and do our planet a favor, become a ^v^ Vegetarian.

(2) Most vegetarian's eat eggs, milk, dairy products, and fish. (3) All you're giving

up are leathery steak's and overcooked chicken. (4) A vegetarian dinner might begin with a greek salad of crisp cucumbers, sweet red onion black olives, and a sprinkling of feta cheese. (5) Youll think you're sitting in a little café overlooking the mediterranean sea. (6) For the main course, head to mexico for tamale pie. (7) A rich, flavorful dish made of pinto beans's, brown rice, green peppers and tomatoes. (8) On the table of course is a loaf of warm bread. (9) Do you have room for dessert how about some ben and jerrys ice cream, made in vermont? (10) As you linger over a cup of french espresso coffee think how your vegetarian meal was delicious, nutritious, and a help to our planet. (11) If more people ate vegetarian the land given to raising cattle and crops to feed cattle could be used for raising grain many of the worlds hungry people could be fed. (12) To read about vegetarianism, get the best-known guide *laurels kitchen: a handbook for vegetarian cookery and nutrition.*

PRACTICE 6 PROOFREADING

This paragraph contains many of the errors you have learned to avoid in Unit 6. Proofread each sentence carefully, and then correct each error above the line.

(1) Some of the most popularest programs on television today are the *CSI* dramas, which depict crime scene investigators using state-of-the-art equipment and old-fashioned detective work to solve crimes. (2) These shows not only entertain 60 million viewers a week but have also stimulate great interest in forensics as a career, in fact, demand for training has reached record levels. (3) According to the American academy of forensic sciences, the many jobs in forensics allows people to apply their love of science to the pursuit of justice and public safety.

(4) Forensic scientists are curious, detail-oriented people whom like to think and puts puzzles together. (5) They also need to work good in groups. (6) Unlike *CSI* characters on TV, who perform many varied tasks, real forensic scientists usually specialize on one area and then pool their expertise to help police nab

criminals. (7) For example, crime scene examiners go to the places where crimes have occurred to locate, photograph, collect, and ~~transportation of~~ ^{transport} physical evidence like fingerprints and blood samples. (8) On the other hand, crime laboratory analysts stay in the ~~lab.~~ ^{lab, using} (9) ~~Using~~ microscopes, DNA tests, firearms tests, and other techniques and ~~equipments~~ ^{equipment} to make sense of crime scene evidence.

On television's *CSI*, Gary Dourdan and Marg Helgenberger both examine crime scenes and work in the lab—a departure from reality.

(10) Each of these jobs ~~require~~ ^{requires} a bachelor's degree. (11) Two ~~specialtys~~ ^{specialties} requiring a master's degree are forensic ~~anthropology,~~ ^{anthropology,} which involves identifying people from skeletal ~~remains. And~~ ^{remains, and} psychological ~~profiling.~~ ^{profiling, using} (12) ~~Using~~ behavioral clues to "read" the mind of a killer or other criminal. (13) One specialty, medical examiner, requires a medical degree. (14) Although this is the highest-paid forensics ~~career.~~ ^{career,} ^{it} (15) ~~It~~ requires a tough personality able to perform autopsies on crime victims to determine exact cause of death. (16) Real-world forensic scientists admit that their

jobs are not quite as glamorous as those of their television ~~counterparts~~ [counterparts;] however,

they describe their work as challenging, interesting, and ~~with rewards~~ [rewarding].

PRACTICE 7 PROOFREADING

This essay contains many of the errors you learned to avoid in Unit 6. Proofread each sentence carefully, and then correct each error above the line.

In the Market for a Used Car?

(1) For several year's now, used car sales have exceeded new car sales. (2) Good used cars can be ~~founded~~ [found] at dealers[.] (3) And through newspaper ads. (4) You might also let your friends know ~~your~~ [you're] in the market for a used car[;] they might know of someone who wants to sell ~~their~~ [his or her] car. (5) Wherever you look for a used car[,] keep the following tips in mind.

(6) First[,] shop before you need the car. (7) This way you can decide exactly what type of car ~~suit~~ [suits] you ~~most~~ best. (8) Do you want a compact[?] (9) ~~Or~~ [or] a midsize car? (10) What features are important to you? (11) Should you get an ~~american~~ [A]-made car or a ~~japanese~~ [J], ~~german~~ [G], or other import? (12) If you shop when you ~~are'nt~~ [aren't] desperate, you are more likely to make a good choice and negotiate ~~good~~ [well].

(13) Second[,] narrow your choices to three or four cars, and do some research. (14) Start with the *~~kelley blue book used car price manual~~* [Kelley Blue Book Used Car Price Manual], online at **http:/www.kbb.com.** (15) The blue ~~book~~ [Book] as it's called for short[,] gives the current value by model year[,] and features. (16) It['s] also a good idea to check *~~consumer reports~~* [Consumer Reports] magazine. (17) Every ~~april~~ [April] issue lists good used car buys and cars to avoid. (18) Based on what you learn[,] go back and test-drive the cars that interest you the ~~mostest~~ [most]. (19) Drive each for at least an hour[,] drive in stop-and-go traffic ~~in~~ [on] the highway, ~~in~~ [on] winding roads, and ~~in~~ [on] hills.

(20) When you do decide on a car[,] ask your mechanic to look at it. (21) Be sure to get a written report that ~~include~~ [includes] an estimate of what repair's will cost.

TEACHING TIP
Have students identify the main pattern of organization used in the essays in Practices 7 and 8. They should recognize that "In the Market for a Used Car?" is a process essay, and "Gators and Crocs" is a comparison and contrast essay.

(22) Money spent at this point is money spent wise, if the seller wont allow an inspection take your business elsewhere.

(23) When you buy a used car you want dependability and value. (24) Follow these tip's youll be able to tell a good buy when you see it.

PRACTICE 8 — PROOFREADING

This essay contains many of the errors you learned to avoid in Unit 6. Proofread each sentence carefully, and then correct each error above the line.

Gators and Crocs

(1) With their scaly bodies slit eyes and long tails, alligators and crocodiles look a lot like dinosaurs. (2) In fact alligators and crocodiles descended from the same family as dinosaurs. (3) While its true that alligators and crocodiles look a lot alike, they differ in three ways.

(4) First alligators and crocodiles are found in different parts of the world. (5) Alligators be found in china, central america, and south america. (6) On the other hand, crocodiles are found in africa (especially around the nile river), australia, southeast asia, india, cuba, and the west indies. (7) Only in the southern united states is both alligators and crocodiles found. (8) In all cases however alligator's and crocodile's live in hot, tropical regions. (9) Reptiles are cold-blooded, so at temperatures below 65 degrees, alligators and crocodiles gets sluggish and cannot hunt.

(10) Alligators and crocodiles also differ in appearance. (11) Alligators has broader flatter snouts that are rounded at the end. (12) Crocodiles has narrower, almost triangular snouts. (13) The best way to tell the difference is to view both from the side when they have their mouths closed, you can see only upper teeth on an alligator, but you can also see four lower teeth on a croc. (14) If you get really close you can see that alligators have a space between they're nostrils while the nostrils of crocs are very close together.

(15) Finally⌄ alligators and crocodiles are temperamentally different. (16) Alligators are not aggressive⸴ they are even a bit shy. (17) They will lie in wait along a river bank for prey⌄ when on land, they move slow and uneven. (18) Crocodiles, however, are much more aggressive. (19) They are fast and mean⸴ they often stalk they're prey. (20) The australian freshwater crocodile and the nile crocodile can even run on land, with their front and back legs working together like a dog. (21) Nile crocodiles kill hundred's of people every year.

(22) Alligators and crocodiles have outlived the dinosaurs, but they might not survive hunters who want to turn them into shoes⌄ wallets⌄ briefcases⌄ and belts. (23) In 1967, the u.s. government declared alligators an endangered species. (24) Fortunately⌄ american alligators have repopulated and are now reclassified as threatened. (25) Importing crocodile and alligator skins are banned worldwide, but some species is still threatened. (26) These frightening and fascinating ancient creatures need help worldwide if they are to survive.

EXPLORING ONLINE

http://www.unc.edu/depts/wcweb/handouts/proofread.html Proofreading instruction and practice

http://grammar.ccc.commnet.edu/grammar Interactive grammar and writing help. Explore, learn, review!

http://owl.english.purdue.edu/handouts/general/gl_edit.html Overview of proven revising and proofreading strategies

Online Study Center college.hmco.com/pic/evergreen8e
Visit the Online Study Center for *Evergreen* for more exercises and quizzes.

UNIT 6

Writers' Workshop

Adopt a New Point of View

No matter how excellent the content of an essay, report, or business letter, grammatical errors will diminish its impact. Ironically, errors call attention to themselves. Learning to proofread your writing might not seem terribly exciting, but it is an all-important skill.

When this student received the interesting assignment to *write as if you are someone or something else,* he decided to see what it's like to be a roach. His audience: humans. His tone: wacky. In your group or class, read his essay, aloud if possible. Underline details or sentences that are especially effective or humorous, and **proofread** as you go. If you spot any errors, correct them.

It's Not Easy Being a Roach

(1) It's not easy being a roach. My life ~~consist~~ consists of the constant struggle to survive. We have existed for millions of years, yet we still do not get the respect that we deserve. We have witnessed the dawn of the dinosaur and the building of Rome. We have experienced two world wars, enjoyed the benefits of cable television, and feasted our eyes on many women taking showers. Being small has its advantages, and it doesn't hurt to be quick either. Because we have ~~live~~ lived so long, ~~You~~ you would think that respect would be ours, but that is not the case.

(2) We are looked upon as pests rather than ~~pets, we~~ pets. We are quieter than household pets. We don't eat much, and contrary to popular belief, we are very clean. Sure, some of us ~~prefers~~ prefer the wild life of booze, drugs, and unprotected sex with other insects, but that doesn't mean that most of us are not seeking a happy life that includes love and affection from you humans. I think it's high time that you appreciated our value as insects, pets, and potential lifelong companions.

(3) I might have six legs, but that doesn't mean I can handle all the burdens that come with being a roach. My wife is pregnant again, which means 10,000 more mouths to feed. It's bad enough that I have to find a meal fit for ~~thousands~~ thousands; I also live in fear of becoming a Roach McNugget. For some strange reason, rodents consider us food. Do I look scrumptious to you? Does my body ignite wild fantasies of sinful feasting? I think not. Mice and rats refuse to respect us because they see us as midnight munchies.

(4) I don't ask for much—a home, some food, and maybe an occasional pat on the head. If I can't have these simple things, I would prefer somebody simply step on me. A fast, hard crunch would do—no spraying me

500

with roach spray, no Roach Motel. I may be on the lower end of the species chain, but that doesn't mean I'm not entitled to live out my dreams. I am roach and hear me roar!

(5) When you humans kill each other off with nuclear bombs, we will still be around. With luck on our side, we will grow into big monsters because of exposure to radiation. Then I don't think those of you who ~~remains~~ remain will enjoy being chased around by giant, glowing roaches—all because you humans didn't want to hug a roach when you had the chance.

(6) One more thing: Stop trying to kill us with that pine-scented roach spray. It doesn't kill ~~us it~~ us. It just makes us smell bad. If I want to smell like pine trees, I will go and frolic in some wood, naked and free. You people really tick me off.

—Israel Vasquez (Student)

1. How effective is Mr. Vasquez's essay?

____Y____ Strong thesis statement?   ____Y____ Good supporting details?

____Y____ Logical organization?   ____Y____ Effective conclusion?

2. Discuss your underlinings. What details or lines in the essay did you like the most? Explain as exactly as possible why you like something or why it made you laugh.

3. Mr. Vasquez's sense of humor comes through to readers. Does he also achieve his goal of presenting a roach's point of view?

4. Would you suggest any revisions? Is this essay effective or offensive? Why? Does the final paragraph provide a strong and humorous conclusion, or does it seem like an afterthought?

5. This essay contains several serious grammar errors. Can you find and correct them? What two error patterns does this fine writer need to watch out for? verb agreement and comma splices; one past participle error

GROUP WORK

In writing as in life, it is often easier to spot other people's errors than our own. In your group or class, discuss *your* particular error patterns and how you have learned to catch them. Do you have problems with comma splices, *-ed* verb endings, or prepositional phrases? Discuss any proofreading tricks and techniques you have learned to spot and correct those errors successfully in your own papers. Have someone jot down the best techniques that your group mates have used, and be prepared to share these with the class.

WRITING AND REVISING IDEAS

1. Adopt a new point of view; discuss your life as a bird, animal, insect, or object.

2. Write as a person of another gender, ethnic group, or period in history.

501

Strengthening Your Spelling

38

Spelling

PART A Suggestions for Improving Your Spelling

ESL TIP
To ESL students in particular, English spelling is difficult and unpredictable. Point out that many other languages have more regular spelling rules than English does.

Accurate spelling is an important ingredient of good writing. No matter how interesting your ideas are, if your spelling is poor, your writing will not be effective.

Some Tips for Improving Your Spelling

■ **Look closely at the words on the page.** Use any tricks you can to remember the right spelling. For example, "The *a*'s in *separate* are separated by an *r*," or "*Dessert* has two *s*'s because you want two desserts."

TEACHING TIP
You may want to model for students exactly how to look up an unfamiliar word in the dictionary, especially when you don't know how to spell it. Talk aloud as you think through finding a word like *rhyme*.

ESL TIP
Encourage nonnative students to invest in a good ESL dictionary. The latest versions include a CD-ROM and web site with spelling vocabulary, and grammar activities.

- **Use a dictionary.** Even professional writers frequently check spelling in a dictionary. As you write, underline the words you are not sure of and look them up when you write your final draft. If locating words in the dictionary is a real problem for you, consider a "poor speller's dictionary."

- **Use a spell checker.** If you write on a computer, make a habit of using the spell-check software. See Part B for tips and cautions about spell checkers.

- **Keep a list of the words you misspell.** Look over your list whenever you can and keep it handy as you write.

- **Look over corrected papers for misspelled words (often marked *sp*.).** Add these words to your list. Practice writing each word three or four times.

- **Test yourself.** Use flash cards or have a friend dictate words from your list or from this chapter.

- **Review the basic spelling rules explained in this chapter.** Take time to learn the material; don't rush through the entire chapter all at once.

- **Study the spelling list on pages 512–513, and test yourself on these words.**

- **Read through Chapter 39, "Look-Alikes/Sound-Alikes," for commonly confused words (*their*, *there*, and *they're*, for instance).** The practices in that chapter will help you eliminate some common spelling errors from your writing.

PART B Computer Spell Checkers

TEACHING TIP
Suggest that students who save their papers as electronic files get in the habit of using an online dictionary—like **www.dictionary.com**—to check their spelling during the proofreading phase of the writing process.

Almost all computer programs are equipped with a spell checker. A spell checker picks up spelling errors and gives you alternatives for correcting them. Get in the habit of using this feature as your first and last proofreading task.

What a spell checker cannot do is think. If you've mistyped one word for another—*if* for *it*, for example—the spell checker cannot bring it to your attention. If you've written *then* for *than*, the spell checker cannot help. Proofread your paper *after* using the spell checker. For questions about words that sound the same but are spelled differently, check Chapter 39, "Look-Alikes/Sound-Alikes." Run spell check again after you've made all your corrections. If you've introduced a new error, the spell checker will let you know.

PRACTICE 1

With a group of four or five classmates, read this poem, which "passed" spell check. Can your group find and correct all the errors that the spell checker missed?

Eye halve a spelling check her,

It came with my pea see.

It clearly marques four my revue,

Mistakes   I   cannot   see
Miss steaks eye can knot sea.

through
I've run this poem threw it.

You're surely pleased to know
Your Shirley please too no

It's   its   way
Its letter perfect in it's weigh.

told   so
My checker tolled me sew.

PART C Spotting Vowels and Consonants

To learn some basic spelling rules, you must know the difference between vowels and consonants.

> The **vowels** are *a, e, i, o,* and *u.*
>
> The **consonants** are *b, c, d, f, g, h, j, k, l, m, n, p, q, r, s, t, v, w, x,* and *z.*
>
> The letter *y* can be either a vowel or a consonant, depending on its sound:
>
> **daisy**　　　　**sky**
>
> **yellow**　　　**your**

- In both *daisy* and *sky, y* is a vowel because it has a vowel sound: an *ee* sound in *daisy* and an *i* sound in *sky.*

- In both *yellow* and *your, y* is a consonant because it has the consonant sound of *y.*

PRACTICE 2

Write *v* for vowel and *c* for consonant in the space on top of each word. Be careful of the *y.*

EXAMPLE c v c v c / h o p e d

1. c v c v / r e l y
2. c v c c v c c / p e r h a p s
3. v c c c v v c / i n s t e a d
4. c v c c / y a w n
5. c v c c v / f o r g e
6. c v c c v c c v c / b y s t a n d e r

PART D Doubling the Final Consonant (in Words of One Syllable)

When you add a suffix or an ending that begins with a vowel (like *-ed, -ing, -er, -est*) to a word of one syllable, double the final consonant *if* the last three letters of the word are *consonant-vowel-consonant* or *c-v-c*.

TEACHING TIP
Point out that, for some words, failing to double the consonant correctly creates a word with a different sound and meaning (e.g., *hoped/hopped, riper/ripper, staring/starring*). Ask your students to think of other similar pairs.

plan + ed = planned	swim + ing = swimming
thin + est = thinnest	light + er = lighter

▪ *Plan, swim,* and *thin* all end in *cvc*; therefore, the final consonants are doubled.

▪ *Light* does not end in *cvc*; therefore, the final consonant is not doubled.

PRACTICE 3

Which of the following words should double the final consonant? Check to see whether the word ends in *cvc*. Then add the suffixes *-ed* and *-ing*.

EXAMPLE

Word	Last Three Letters	*-ed*	*-ing*
drop	cvc	dropped	dropping
boil	vvc	boiled	boiling
1. tan	cvc	tanned	tanning
2. brag	cvc	bragged	bragging
3. mail	vvc	mailed	mailing
4. peel	vvc	peeled	peeling
5. wrap	cvc	wrapped	wrapping

PRACTICE 4

Which of the following words should double the final consonant? Check for *cvc*. Then add the suffixes *-er* or *-est*.

EXAMPLE

Word	Last Three Letters	*-er*	*-est*
wet	cvc	wetter	wettest
cool	vvc	cooler	coolest

Word	Last Three Letters	-er	-est
1. deep	vvc	deeper	deepest
2. short	vcc	shorter	shortest
3. red	cvc	redder	reddest
4. dim	cvc	dimmer	dimmest
5. bright	ccc	brighter	brightest

PART E Doubling the Final Consonant (in Words of More Than One Syllable)

TEACHING TIP
Review with students what *suffixes* and *stressed syllables* are.

TEACHING TIP
Have students come up with their own examples in order to reinforce their knowledge of the rule.

When you add a suffix that begins with a vowel to a word of more than one syllable, double the final consonant *if*:

(1) the last three letters of the word are *cvc, and*

(2) the accent or stress is on the *last* syllable.

begin + ing = beginning   **control + ed = controlled**

▦ *Begin* and *control* both end in *cvc.*

▦ In both words, the stress is on the last syllable: *be-gin'*, *con-trol'*. (Pronounce the words aloud and listen for the correct stress.)

▦ Therefore, *beginning* and *controlled* double the final consonant.

listen + ing = listening   **visit + ed = visited**

▦ *Listen* and *visit* both end in *cvc.*

▦ However, the stress is *not* on the last syllable: *lis'-ten, vis'-it.*

▦ Therefore, *listening* and *visited* **do not** double the final consonant.

PRACTICE 5

Which of the following words should double the final consonant? First, check for *cvc*; then check final stress. Then add the suffixes *-ed* and *-ing*.

EXAMPLE

TEACHING TIP
Encourage students to say the words in Practice 5 aloud so they can hear the stressed syllable.

Word	Last Three Letters	-ed	-ing
repel	cvc	repelled	repelling
enlist	vcc	enlisted	enlisting

1. happen ____cvc____ ____happened____ ____happening____

2. admit ____cvc____ ____admitted____ ____admitting____

3. offer ____cvc____ ____offered____ ____offering____

4. prefer ____cvc____ ____preferred____ ____preferring____

5. compel ____cvc____ ____compelled____ ____compelling____

PART F Dropping or Keeping the Final *E*

TEACHING TIP
The rules for keeping or dropping the final *e* should be memorized.

When you add a suffix that begins with a vowel (like *-able, -ence, -ing*), drop the final *e*.

When you add a suffix that begins with a consonant (like *-less, -ment, -ly*), keep the final *e*.

move + ing = moving   pure + ity = purity

■ *Moving* and *purity* both drop the final *e* because the suffixes *-ing* and *-ity* begin with vowels.

home + less = homeless   advertise + ment = advertisement

■ *Homeless* and *advertisement* keep the final *e* because the suffixes *-less* and *-ment* begin with consonants.

TEACHING TIP
Ask students to explain how each of the exceptions deviates from the rules.

Here are some exceptions to memorize:

argument	courageous	knowledgeable	truly
awful	judgment	simply	manageable

PRACTICE 6

Add the suffix indicated for each word.

EXAMPLE hope + ing = ____hoping____

hope + ful = ____hopeful____

1. love + able = ____lovable____

2. love + ly = ____lovely____

3. pure + ly = ____purely____

4. pure + er = ____purer____

5. complete + ing = ____completing____

6. complete + ness = ____completeness____

7. enforce + ment = ____enforcement____

8. enforce + ed = ____enforced____

9. arrange + ing = ____arranging____

10. arrange + ment = ____arrangement____

PRACTICE 7

Add the suffix indicated for each word.

EXAMPLE come + ing = _____coming_____

rude + ness = _____rudeness_____

1. guide + ance = _____guidance_____
2. manage + ment = _____management_____
3. dense + ity = _____density_____
4. polite + ly = _____politely_____
5. motive + ation = _____motivation_____

6. sincere + ly = _____sincerely_____
7. like + able = _____likable_____
8. response + ible = _____responsible_____
9. judge + ment = _____judgment_____
10. fame + ous = _____famous_____

PART G Changing or Keeping the Final *Y*

When you add a suffix to a word that ends in -*y*, change the *y* to *i* if the letter before the *y* is a consonant.

Keep the final *y* if the letter before the *y* is a vowel.

happy + ness = happiness   portray + ed = portrayed

▪ The *y* in *happiness* is changed to *i* because the letter before the *y* is a consonant, *p*.

▪ The *y* in *portrayed* is not changed because the letter before it is a vowel, *a*.

However, when you add -*ing* to words ending in *y*, always keep the *y*:

copy + ing = copying   delay + ing = delaying

Here are some exceptions to memorize:

day + ly = daily   pay + ed = paid

lay + ed = laid   say + ed = said

PRACTICE 8

Add the suffix indicated to each of the following words.

TEACHING TIP
Practicing with flash cards
may help students learn to
apply the rules more
consistently.

EXAMPLE marry + ed = _____married_____

buy + er = _____buyer_____

1. try + ed = _____tried_____
2. vary + able = _____variable_____
3. worry + ing = _____worrying_____

4. pay + ed = _____paid_____
5. enjoy + able = _____enjoyable_____
6. wealthy + est = _____wealthiest_____

7. day + ly = _____daily_____   9. display + s = _____displays_____

8. duty + ful = _____dutiful_____   10. occupy + ed = _____occupied_____

Add the suffix in parentheses to each word.

1. beauty (fy) _____beautify_____   3. betray (ed) _____betrayed_____

        (ful)_____beautiful_____   (ing) _____betraying_____

        (es) _____beauties_____   (al) _____betrayal_____

2. lonely (er) _____lonelier_____   4. study (es) _____studies_____

        (est)_____loneliest_____   (ous) _____studious_____

        (ness)_____loneliness_____   (ing) _____studying_____

PART H Adding -*S* or -*ES*

Nouns usually take an -*s* or an -*es* ending to form the plural. Verbs take an -*s* or -*es* in the third person singular (*he, she,* or *it*).

Add -*es* instead of -*s* if a word ends in *ch, sh, ss, x,* or *z* (the -*es* adds an extra syllable to the word):

    box + es = boxes   **crutch + es = crutches**   **miss + es = misses**

Add -*es* instead of -*s* for most words that end in *o*:

    do + es = does   **hero + es = heroes**

    echo + es = echoes   **tomato + es = tomatoes**

    go + es = goes   **potato + es = potatoes**

Here are some exceptions to memorize:

    pianos   sopranos

    radios   solos

When you change the final *y* to *i* in a word,* add -*es* instead of -*s*:

    fry + es = fries   **marry + es = marries**   **candy + es = candies**

Add -*s* or -*es* to the following nouns and verbs, changing the final *y* to *i* when necessary.

EXAMPLE sketch _____sketches_____

           echo _____echoes_____

_____

* See Part G of this chapter for more on changing or keeping the final *y*.

1. watch _____watches_____   6. piano _____pianos_____

2. tomato _____tomatoes_____   7. donkey _____donkeys_____

3. reply _____replies_____   8. dictionary _____dictionaries_____

4. company _____companies_____   9. boss _____bosses_____

5. bicycle _____bicycles_____   10. hero _____heroes_____

PART I Choosing *IE* or *EI*

Write *i* before *e*, except after *c* or in an *ay* sound like *neighbor* or *weigh*.

achieve, niece   deceive   vein

■ *Achieve* and *niece* are spelled *ie*.

■ *Deceive* is spelled *ei* because of the preceding *c*.

■ *Vein* is spelled *ei* because of its *ay* sound.

However, words with a *shen* sound are spelled with an *ie* after the *c*: *ancient, conscience, efficient, sufficient.*

Here are some exceptions to memorize:

either	seize
neither	society
foreign	their
height	weird

PRACTICE 11

Pronounce each word out loud. Then fill in either *ie* or *ei*.

1. bel _i_ _e_ ve   6. ch _i_ _e_ f   11. h _e_ _i_ ght

2. _e_ _i_ ght   7. soc _i_ _e_ ty   12. ach _i_ _e_ ve

3. effic _i_ _e_ nt   8. rec _e_ _i_ ve   13. v _e_ _i_ n

4. n _e_ _i_ ther   9. fr _i_ _e_ nd   14. for _e_ _i_ gn

5. cash _i_ _e_ r   10. consc _i_ _e_ nce   15. perc _e_ _i_ ve

PRACTICE 12   REVIEW

Test your knowledge of the spelling rules in this chapter by adding suffixes to the following words. If you have trouble, the part in which the rule appears is shown in parentheses.

	Part			Part
1. nerve + ous ___nervous___	(F)	6. occur + ed ___occurred___	(E)
2. drop + ed ___dropped___	(D)	7. carry + ing ___carrying___	(G)
3. hope + ing ___hoping___	(F)	8. tomato + s/es ___tomatoes___	(H)
4. busy + ness ___business___	(G)	9. believe + able ___believable___	(F)
5. radio + s/es ___radios___	(H)	10. day + ly ___daily___	(G)

PRACTICE 13   REVIEW

Circle the correctly spelled word in each pair.

1. writting, (writing)   6. (piece,) peice

2. (receive,) recieve   7. (resourceful,) resourcful

3. begining, (beginning)   8. (argument,) arguement

4. greif, (grief)   9. (marries,) marrys

5. relaid, (relayed)   10. thier, (their)

PART J Spelling Lists

Commonly Misspelled Words

Following is a list of words that are often misspelled. As you can see, they are words that you might use daily in speaking and writing. The trouble spot, the part of each word that is usually spelled incorrectly, has been put in bold type.

To help yourself learn these words, you might copy each one twice, making sure to underline the trouble spot, or copy the words on flash cards and have someone test you.

1. a**cross**	11. crow**ded**	21. envir**on**ment
2. add**ress**	12. defin**ite**	22. exa**gg**erate
3. ans**w**er	13. de**scribe**	23. famil**iar**
4. arg**u**ment	14. desp**erate**	24. fina**lly**
5. ath**lete**	15. di**ff**erent	25. govern**ment**
6. begi**nn**ing	16. dis**app**oint	26. gra**mm**ar
7. beha**vior**	17. dis**app**rove	27. hei**ght**
8. calen**dar**	18. doesn't	28. i**ll**egal
9. car**eer**	19. ei**ghth**	29. imm**ediately**
10. consc**ience**	20. embarr**ass**	30. impor**tant**

"First off, there's no 'y' in resume..."

31. inte**g**ration
32. int**ell**igent
33. int**er**est
34. int**er**fere
35. jew**el**ry
36. ju**dgm**ent
37. knowle**dge**
38. maint**ain**
39. mathematics
40. meant
41. ne**cess**ary
42. nerv**ous**
43. o**cc**asion
44. opin**ion**
45. optimist

46. particular
47. **per**form
48. **per**haps
49. perso**nn**el
50. po**ssess**
51. po**ss**ible
52. **pref**er
53. pre**ju**dice
54. privi**leg**e
55. pro**bably**
56. **psy**chology
57. pursue
58. re**f**erence
59. **rhy**thm
60. ridi**cul**ous

61. sep**arate**
62. simi**lar**
63. **since**
64. speech
65. stren**gth**
66. su**cc**ess
67. **sur**prise
68. tau**ght**
69. temperature
70. tho**rou**gh
71. thought
72. tir**ed**
73. until
74. wei**ght**
75. written

Personal Spelling List

In your notebook, keep a list of words that *you* misspell. Add words to your list from corrected papers and from the exercises in this chapter. First, copy each word as you misspelled it, underlining the trouble spot; then write the word correctly. Study your list often. Use this form:

© www.CartoonStock.com.

TEACHING TIP
Encourage students to keep a list of personal problem words in their notebooks and to review the correct spellings frequently.

ESL TIP
Periodically, ask pairs of
students—an ESL student
and a native speaker—to
quiz each other on the
words in their personal
spelling lists.

	As I Wrote It	**Correct Spelling**
1.	*probly*	*probably*
2.		
3.		

PRACTICE 14   REVIEW

Proofread the following essay for spelling errors. (Be careful: There are misspelled words from both the exercises in this chapter and the spelling list.) Correct any errors by writing above the lines.

Man's Best Clone

(1) Ever since the ~~sucessful~~ *successful* cloning of Dolly the sheep in 1996, scientists have experimented with cloning other animals. (2) Now a Texas company is ~~offerring~~ *offering* cloning services to people who want to copy their favorite cat or dog. (3) Losing a beloved pet is ~~dificult~~ *difficult* for anyone, so it should come as no ~~suprise~~ *surprise* that some ~~greiving~~ *grieving* pet owners are hurrying to resurrect their furry friends.

(4) Genetic Savings & Clone already has preserved the tissue of hundreds of pets whose owners hope one day to cuddle a clone. (5) Freezing a DNA sample from Fido or Fluffy costs over a thousand dollars, with yearly maintenance around $100. (6) Once the cloning process is perfected, creating the ~~replacment~~ *replacement* animal will cost $10,000 more—making Fluffy II one expensive little cat!

(7) Ironically, experts tell owners of pricey purebred animals to forget about ~~cloneing~~ *cloning*. (8) The bloodlines that produce the look and ~~behavor~~ *behavior* of pure breeds work nearly as well as cloning. (9) On the other hand, if Fido has four or five breeds in his blood, he truly is a unique mutt and a good ~~posibility~~ *possibility* for cloning.

(10) Critics say cloning pets is ~~ridiclous~~ *ridiculous*. (11) Because both genes and ~~enviroment~~ *environment* determine animal behavior, ~~puting~~ *putting* a piece of Fido in the fridge will not ~~guarentee~~ *guarantee* good results. (12) Owners who ~~beleive~~ *believe* ~~thier~~ *their* copycat will have the same ~~adoreable~~ *adorable* personality as the original kitty are bound to be ~~disapointed~~ *disappointed*. (13)

TEACHING AND ESL TIP
Tell your students about additional graded spelling quizzes on the *Evergreen* Online Study Center. They also can search "English spelling quizzes"—*e.g.*, at **http://grammar.ccc .commnet.edu/grammar /spelling.htm**.

The Humane Society opposes cloning, urging lonely pet owners to adopt an abandoned animal at their local shelter instead. (14) With thousands of strays needing homes, creating a copy cat or dog seems like a waste of money and scientific resources. (15) But people are so ~~tyed~~ tied to their pets that Genetic Savings & Clone might well remain a booming ~~busyness~~ business.

EXPLORING ONLINE

TEACHING TIP
More practice and assessment are available in the *Evergreen* Test Bank, linked ACE tests on the *Evergreen* Online Teaching and Study Centers, *WriteSpace for Evergreen,* and Exploring Online links in this chapter.

http://grammar.ccc.commnet.edu/grammar/cgi-shl/quiz20.pl/spelling_ quiz3.htm Interactive spelling test: three endings

http://grammar.uoregon.edu/homework/homework8.html Challenging spelling test: Raise your level!

Online Study Center **college.hmco.com/pic/evergreen8e**
Visit the Online Study Center for *Evergreen* for more exercises and quizzes.

39

Look-Alikes/ Sound-Alikes

A/an/and

1. *A* is used before a word beginning with a consonant or a consonant sound.

   a **man**   *a* **house**   *a* **union** (here *u* sounds like the consonant *y*)

2. *An* is used before a word beginning with a vowel (*a, e, i, o, u*) or silent *h*.

   an **igloo**   *an* **apple**   *an* **hour** (*h* in *hour* is silent)

3. *And* joins words or ideas together.

   Edward *and* Ralph are taking the same biology class.
   She is very honest, *and* most people respect her.

PRACTICE 1

Fill in *a, an,* or *and.*

1. The administration building is ____an____ old brick house on top of ____a____ hill.

2. ____An____ artist ____and____ two students share that studio.

3. The computer in my office has ____a____ flat screen ____and____ ____a____ CD burner.

4. For lunch, Ben ate ____a____ tofu sandwich, ____an____ apple, ____and____ two bananas.

Accept/except

1. *Accept* means to receive.

   That college *accepts* only women.   I *accepted* his offer of help.

2. *Except* means other than or excluding.

   Everyone *except* Marcelo thinks it's a good idea.

PRACTICE 2

Fill in *accept* or *except*.

1. Jan has read all of Shakespeare's comedies _____except_____ one.

2. Please _____accept_____ my apologies.

3. Unable to _____accept_____ defeat, the boxer protested the decision.

4. Sam loves all his courses _____except_____ chemistry.

Affect/effect

1. *Affect* (verb) means to have an influence on or to change.

   Her father's career as a lawyer *affected* her decision to go to law school.

2. *Effect* (noun) means the result of a cause or an influence.

   Careful proofreading had a positive *effect* on Carl's grades.

3. *Effect* is also a verb that means to cause.

   The U.S. Senate is attempting to *effect* changes in foreign policy.

PRACTICE 3

Fill in *affect* or *effect*.

1. You are mistaken if you think alcohol will not _____affect_____ your judgment.

2. Attractive, neat clothing will have a positive _____effect_____ on a job.

3. Hot, humid summers always have the _____effect_____ of making me lazy.

4. We will not be able to _____effect_____ these changes without the cooperation of the employees and the union.

TEACHING TIP
To give students more practice with look-alikes /sound-alikes, you might ask them to write sentences using the words they confuse.

Been/being

1. *Been* is the past participle form of *to be*. *Been* is usually used after the helping verb *have*, *has*, or *had*.

   She *has been* a poet for ten years.

2. *Being* is the *-ing* form of *to be*. *Being* is usually used after the helping verb *is*, *are*, *am*, *was*, or *were*.

   They *are being* helped by the salesperson.

PRACTICE 4

Fill in *been* or *being*.

1. Have you _____been_____ to Rib Heaven yet?

2. Pete thinks his phone calls are _____being_____ taped.

3. Are you _____being_____ secretive, or have I _____been_____ imagining it?

4. Yoko has never _____been_____ to Omaha!

Buy/by

1. *Buy* means to purchase.

   My aunt *buys* new furniture every five years.

2. *By* means near, by means of, or before.

   He walked right *by* and didn't say hello.

   By sunset, we had finished the harvest.

PRACTICE 5

Fill in *buy* or *by*.

1. You can't _____buy_____ happiness, but many people try.

2. Lee _____buys_____ sand _____by_____ the ton for his masonry business.

3. Please drop _____by_____ the book store and _____buy_____ some novels; I want to read all weekend.

4. _____By_____ _____buying_____ out his partners, Joe became sole owner of the firm.

TEACHING TIP
Alert students to the exhaustive "Notorious Confusables" bank of explanations, examples, and interactive quizzes: **http://www.grammar.ccc .commnet.edu/grammar /notorious.htm**.

It's/its

1. *It's* is a contraction of *it is* or *it has*. If you cannot substitute *it is* or *it has* in the sentence, you cannot use *it's*.

   It's a ten minute walk to my house.   **It's been a nice party.**

2. *Its* is a possessive and shows ownership.

   Industry must do *its* share to curb inflation.

PRACTICE 6

Fill in *it's* or *its*.

1. Put the contact lens in _____its_____ case, please.

2. _____It's_____ about time H.T. straightened up the rubble in his room.

3. The company offered some of _____*its*_____ employees an early retirement option.

4. You know _____*it's*_____ cold when the pond has ice on _____*its*_____ surface.

Know/knew/no/new

1. *Know* means to have knowledge or understanding.

   Carlos *knows* he has to finish by 6 P.M.

2. *Knew* is the past tense of the verb *know.*

   I *knew* it.

3. *No* is a negative.

   He is *no* longer dean of academic affairs.

4. *New* means recent, fresh, unused.

   I like your *new* hat.

PRACTICE 7

Fill in *know, knew, no,* or *new.*

1. I _____*know*_____ he's _____*new*_____ in town, but this is ridiculous.

2. If I _____*knew*_____ then what I _____*know*_____ now, I wouldn't have made so many mistakes when I was young.

3. Abe and Gabe _____*know*_____ that they have _____*no*_____ chance of winning the marathon.

4. _____*No*_____, I don't _____*know*_____ the way to Grandma's house, you hairy weirdo.

Lose/loose

1. *Lose* means to misplace or not to win.

   Be careful not to *lose* your way on those back roads.

2. *Loose* means too large, not tightly fitting.

   This shirt is not my size; it's *loose.*

PRACTICE 8

Fill in *lose* or *loose.*

1. When Ari studies in bed, he _____*loses*_____ the _____*loose*_____ change from his pockets.

2. Several layers of _____*loose*_____ clothing can warm you in winter.

3. Don't _____lose_____ any sleep over tomorrow's exam.

4. If you _____lose_____ that _____loose_____ screw, the handle will fall off.

Past/passed

1. *Past* is that which has already occurred; it is over with.

   Never let the *past* interfere with your hopes for the future.

2. *Passed* is the past tense of the verb *to pass*.

   The wild geese *passed* overhead.

PRACTICE 9

Fill in *past* or *passed*.

1. As Jake _____passed_____ the barn, he noticed a man talking to the reindeer.

2. To children, even the recent _____past_____ seems like ancient history.

3. Mia _____passed_____ up the opportunity to see a friend from her _____past_____.

4. This Bible was _____passed_____ down to me by my mother; it contains records of our family's _____past_____.

Quiet/quit/quite

1. *Quiet* means silent, still.

   The woods are *quiet* tonight.

2. *Quit* means to give up or to stop doing something.

   Last year I *quit* drinking.

3. *Quite* means very or exactly.

   He was *quite* tired after playing handball for two hours.

   That's not *quite* right.

PRACTICE 10

Fill in *quiet*, *quit*, or *quite*.

1. The stone cottage is a _____quiet_____ place in which to study.

2. Kali is _____quite_____ dedicated to her veterinary career.

TEACHING TIP
This unit can be a springboard for work on vocabulary building. Urge students to make use of online resources like Pop-up Lexicon, a year of new words: **http://grammar .www.ccc.commnet.edu /grammar/definition_list .htm.**

ESL TIP
Many ESL students need vocabulary development work. Consider independent study assignments focusing on prefixes, roots, and suffixes. See **http://depts .gallaudet.edu /englishworks/reading /main/vocabulary.htm** and ESL Corner on the *Evergreen* Online Study Center.

3. Don't _____quit_____ your job, even though you aren't _____quite_____ happy with the working conditions.

4. Each day when he _____quits_____ work, Dan visits a _____quiet_____ spot in the park.

Rise/raise

1. *Rise* means to get up by one's own power.
   The past tense of *rise* is *rose*.
   The past participle of *rise* is *risen*.

   The moon *rises* at 9 P.M.

   Daniel *rose* early yesterday.

   He has *risen* from the table.

2. *Raise* means to lift an object or to grow or increase.
   The past tense of *raise* is *raised*.
   The past participle of *raise* is *raised*.

   ***Raise* your right hand.**

   She *raised* the banner over her head.

   We have *raised* one thousand dollars.

PRACTICE 11

Fill in the correct form of *rise* or *raise*.

1. The loaves of bread have _____risen_____ perfectly.

2. The new mayor _____raised_____ his arms in a victory salute.

3. Once the sun has _____risen_____, Pete _____raises_____ the shades.

4. We all _____rose_____ as the bride walked down the aisle.

Sit/set

TEACHING TIP
Students who speak certain regional or ethnic dialects are more likely to confuse words that they pronounce incorrectly (e.g., in the South, *sit* may be pronounced "set").

1. *Sit* means to seat oneself.
   The past tense of *sit* is *sat*.
   The past participle of *sit* is *sat*.

   ***Sit* up straight!**

   He *sat* down on the porch and fell asleep.

   She has *sat* reading that book all day.

2. *Set* means to place or put something down.
   The past tense of *set* is *set*.
   The past participle of *set* is *set*.

   Don't *set* your workout clothes on the dining room table.

   She *set* the package down and walked off without it.

   He had *set* the timer on the stove.

PRACTICE 12

Fill in *sit* or *set*.

1. Please _____set_____ your briefcase here. Would you like to

   _____sit_____ down?

2. Have they _____sat_____ in on a rehearsal before?

3. Tomas _____set_____ the chair by the window and _____sat_____ down.

4. Sorry, I wouldn't have _____sat_____ here if I had known you were returning.

Suppose/supposed

1. *Suppose* means to assume or guess.
   The past tense of *suppose* is *supposed*.
   The past participle of *suppose* is *supposed*.

   Brad *supposes* that geology will be interesting.

   We all *supposed* she would win first prize.

   I had *supposed* Dan would bring his trumpet.

2. *Supposed* means ought to or should; it is followed by *to*.

   You were *supposed* to wash and wax the car.

   Remember: When you mean *ought to* or *should*, always use the *-ed* ending—
   supposed.

PRACTICE 13

Fill in *suppose* or *supposed*.

1. Why do you _____suppose_____ wolves howl at the moon?

2. I _____suppose_____ you enjoy reggae.

3. Detective Nguyen is _____supposed_____ to address the Citizens' Patrol tonight.

4. Wasn't Erik _____supposed_____ to meet us at five?

Their/there/they're

1. *Their* is a possessive and shows ownership.

   They couldn't find *their* wigs.

2. *There* indicates a direction.

   I wouldn't go *there* again.

   There is also a way of introducing a thought.

   ***There* is a fly in my soup.**

3. *They're* is a contraction: *they + are = they're.* If you cannot substitute *they are* in the sentence, you cannot use *they're.*

If *they're* coming, count me in.

PRACTICE 14

Fill in *their, there,* or *they're.*

1. If ____they're____ not ____there____ on time, we will leave without them.

2. ____They're____ two of the most amusing people I know.

3. ____There____ are two choices, and ____they're____ both risky.

4. Two mail carriers left ____their____ mail bags ____there____ on the steps.

5. The motorcycles roared ____their____ way into town.

6. Don't worry about ____their____ performance in the race because ____they're____ both tough.

Then/than

1. *Then* means afterward or at that time.

First we went to the theater, and *then* we went out for a pizza and champagne.

I was a heavyweight boxer *then*.

2. *Than* is used in a comparison.

She is a better student *than* I.

PRACTICE 15

Fill in *then* or *than.*

1. First, Cassandra kicked off her shoes; ____then____ she began to dance.

2. Jupiter's diameter is eleven times larger ____than____ Earth's.

3. If you're more familiar with this trail ____than____ I, ____then____ you should lead the way.

4. Fran lived in Chicago ____then____; now she lives in Los Angeles.

Through/though

1. *Through* means in one side and out the other, finished, or by means of.

The rain came *through* the open window.

***Through* practice, I can do anything.**

2. *Though* means although. Used with *as, though* means as if.

***Though* he rarely speaks, he writes terrific letters.**

It was *as though* I had never ridden a bicycle before.

PRACTICE 16

Fill in *through* or *though*.

1. _____Through_____ study and perseverance, Charelle earned her degree in three years.

2. Dee usually walks to work, _____though_____ she sometimes rides the bus.

3. Julio strode _____through_____ the bank as _____though_____ he owned it.

4. Clayton is a Texan _____through_____ and _____through_____.

To/too/two

1. *To* means toward.

   We are going *to* the computer lab.

   To can also be combined with a verb to form an infinitive.

   Where do you want *to go* for lunch?

2. *Too* means also or very.

   Roberto is going to the theater *too*.

   They were *too* bored to stay awake.

3. *Two* is the number 2.

   There are *two* new nursing courses this term.

PRACTICE 17

Fill in *to*, *too*, or *two*.

1. Please take my daughter _____to_____ the movies _____too_____.

2. Dan, _____too_____, took _____two_____ hours _____to_____ complete the exam.

3. Luis went _____to_____ Iowa State for _____two_____ semesters.

4. This curry is _____too_____ hot _____to_____ eat and _____too_____

   good _____to_____ resist.

Use/used

1. *Use* means to make use of.
   The past tense of *use* is *used*.
   The past participle of *use* is *used*.

   Why do you *use* green ink?

   He *used* black-and-white film for the project.

   I have *used* that brand of cell phone myself.

2. *Used* means in the habit of or accustomed to; it is followed by *to*.

I am not *used* to getting up at 4 A.M.   They got *used* to the good life.

Remember: When you mean *in the habit of* or *accustomed to,* always use the *-ed* ending—*used*.

PRACTICE 18

Fill in *use* or *used*.

1. Marie _____used_____ to drive a jalopy that she bought at a _____used_____ car lot.

2. We will _____use_____ about three gallons of paint on this shed.

3. Can you _____use_____ a _____used_____ laptop?

4. Pam _____used_____ to _____use_____ a pick to strum her guitar.

Weather/whether

1. *Weather* refers to atmospheric conditions.

   In June, the *weather* in Spain is lovely.

2. *Whether* implies a question.

   ***Whether* or not you succeed depends on you.**

PRACTICE 19

Fill in *weather* or *whether*.

1. In fine _____weather_____, we take canoe rides on the lake.

2. _____Whether_____ or not you like Brazilian food, you'll love this dish.

3. The _____weather_____ person never said _____whether_____ or not it would snow.

4. In 1870 a national _____weather_____ service was established.

Where/were/we're

1. *Where* implies place or location.

   ***Where* have you been all day?**

2. *Were* is the past tense of *are*.

   We *were* on our way when the hurricane hit.

3. *We're* is a contraction: *we* + *are* = *we're*. If you cannot substitute *we are* in the sentence, you cannot use *we're*.

   Since *we're* in the city, let's go to the zoo.

PRACTICE 20

Fill in *where*, *were*, or *we're*.

1. _____We're_____ going to Hawaii _____where_____ the sun always shines.

2. _____Were_____ you standing _____where_____ we agreed to meet?

3. There _____were_____ two high-rise apartment houses _____where_____ the ballpark used to be.

4. _____We're_____ determined to attend college though we don't yet know _____where_____ .

Whose/who's

1. *Whose* implies ownership and possession.

   Whose term paper is that?

2. *Who's* is a contraction of *who is* or *who has*. If you cannot substitute *who is* or *who has*, you cannot use *who's*.

   Who's knocking at the window?

   Who's seen my new felt hat with the red feathers?

PRACTICE 21

Fill in *whose* or *who's*.

1. _____Whose_____ convertible is this?

2. Tanya, _____who's_____ in my history class, will join us for dinner.

3. We need someone in that position _____who's_____ dependable, someone _____whose_____ abilities have already been proven.

4. _____Whose_____ biology textbook is this?

Your/you're

1. *Your* is a possessive and shows ownership.

   Your knowledge astonishes me!

2. *You're* is a contraction: *you* + *are* = *you're*. If you cannot substitute *you are* in the sentence, you cannot use *you're*.

   You're the nicest person I know.

PRACTICE 22

Fill in *your* or *you're*.

1. _____You're_____ sitting on _____your_____ hat.

2. When _____you're_____ ready to begin _____your_____ piano lesson, we'll leave.

3. Let _____your_____ adviser help you plan _____your_____ course schedule.

4. When _____you're_____ with _____your_____ friends, _____you're_____ a different person.

Personal Look-Alikes/Sound-Alikes List

In your notebook, keep a list of look-alikes and sound-alikes that *you* have trouble with. Add words to your list from corrected papers and from the exercises in this chapter; consider such pairs as *adapt/adopt, addition/edition, device/devise, stationery/ stationary,* and so forth.

First, write the word you used incorrectly; then write its meaning or use it correctly in a sentence, whichever best helps you remember. Now do the same with the word you meant to use.

Word	**Meaning**
1. though	means although
through	We hiked through the woods.
2. _____	_____
_____	_____

PRACTICE 23

Write a paragraph using as many of the look-alikes and sound-alikes as possible. Exchange paragraphs with a classmate and check each other's work.

PRACTICE 24   REVIEW

The following essay contains a number of look-alike/sound-alike errors. Proofread for these errors, writing the correct word above the line.

Isabel Allende

(1) Possibly the best-known female writer of Latin-American literature, Isabel

Allende has survived many political and personal tragedies. (2) Most of those

their
events have found ~~there~~ way into her books. (3) Born in 1942, Allende was ~~raise~~ raised

by her mother in Chile after her parents' divorce. (4) When her uncle, President Salvador Allende, was killed during a military coup in 1973, she fled. (5) For the next seventeen years, she lived in Venezuela, ~~were~~ where she was unable to find work and felt trapped in ~~a~~ an unhappy marriage.

(6) One day, learning that her grandfather was dying in Chile, Allende began to write him a long letter; that letter grew until it became her first novel. (7) Still her most famous book, *The House of the Spirits* established Allende's style of writing, which combines political realism and autobiography with dreams, spirits, ~~an~~ and magic. (8) The novel, which was banned in Chile, was translated into more ~~then~~ than twenty-five languages and in 1994 was made into a movie.

(9) ~~Buy~~ By 1988, Allende had divorced, moved to northern California, remarried, and written her fourth novel, *The Infinite Plan,* which is her second husband's story. (10) Her next book traced the profound ~~affect~~ effect on Allende of the death of her daughter, Paula. (11) The book *Paula,* like *The House of the Spirits,* was ~~suppose~~ supposed to be a letter, this time ~~too~~ to her daughter, who lay in a coma in a Madrid hospital.

(12) After *Paula* was published, Allende stopped writing for several years. (13) She started again in 1996, on January 8, the same day of the year that she had begun every one of her books. (14) The result was *Aphrodite,* a nonfiction book about food and sensuality that was ~~quiet~~ quite different from Allende's ~~passed~~ past work. (15) With renewed energy to ~~right~~ write again, Allende spun the tale of an independent woman who leaves her home in Chile to move to San Francisco during the Gold Rush. (16) Two novels, *Daughter of Fortune* and *Portrait in Sepia,* complete her story.

(17) Isabel Allende is famous for ~~been~~ being a passionate storyteller ~~who's~~ whose writing captures both the Latin-American and the universal human experience. (18) As the first Latina to write a major novel in the mystical tradition, she not only created a sensation, but she paved the way for other female Hispanic writers, including Julia Alvarez and Sandra Cisneros.

EXPLORING ONLINE

TEACHING TIP
More practice and assessment are available in the *Evergreen* Test Bank, linked ACE tests on the *Evergreen* Online Teaching and Study Centers, *WriteSpace for Evergreen,* and Exploring Online links in this chapter.

http://owl.english.purdue.edu/handouts/interact/g_spelhomoEX1.html
Look-alikes/sound-alikes quiz

http://a4esl.org/q/h/homonyms.html Confused by English words that sound alike? Practice and learn with these excellent quizzes.

Online Study Center **college.hmco.com/pic/evergreen8e**
Visit the Online Study Center for *Evergreen* for more exercises and quizzes.

UNIT 7

Writers' Workshop

Discuss a Time When You Felt Blessed

Some writers are naturally good spellers, and others are not. If you belong to the latter group, this unit has given you some techniques and tools for overcoming your spelling problems.

In your group or class, read this student's essay, aloud if possible. Underline the ideas and sentences you find especially effective. If you spot any spelling errors, correct them.

Rain

(1) It is interesting to watch the way people act when rain starts falling. Most run for cover, ~~especialy~~ especially the women who just got ~~there~~ their hair done. The guy with the brand new shoes also ~~trys~~ tries to find a dry spot. Many people think, "~~They're~~ There goes the day." That's what I thought before I went to the big sand box.

(2) It happened last year around March. President Bush decided Iraq was a threat to the United States, and of course being a Marine meant I was one of the first to go. Our first weeks were the hardest because we had to get ~~aclimated~~ acclimated to the ~~whether~~ weather. Iraq has got to be one of the ~~hotest~~ hottest places on earth, and I swear that you can be motionless and still be soaked with sweat. The glare almost hurts, even in sunglasses. Those days I prayed for rain as I never thought I would.

(3) It ~~finely~~ finally happened in the middle of June; I was outside my tent doing pushups with a fellow Marine. The sky did not darken or cloud up. Instead, the rain came down in one great splash as if the sky had held on for awhile and just could not hold on any longer. We all smiled at the sky and then ~~noded~~ nodded at each other. At that moment, we felt we were ~~been~~ being blessed. Some guys took ~~there~~ their shirts off, and some started jumping around like little kids. Not one of us ran for cover, and those who were inside ~~there~~ their tents came out to join in the celebration. For a few minutes, we all forgot that we were at war.

(4) That rain gave us new energy and hope. We knew from that day on that everything was going to be all right. Even those who disliked each other shook hands in the name of rain. We felt more ~~then~~ than special because God had shown us his blessings.

(5) When I got back home last August, I took my girlfriend to the movies. As we left the theater, it started to rain. Everybody started ~~runing~~ running

> frustrated
>
> into the subway station, and most looked ~~fustrated~~ because the rain had ru-ined their night. My girlfriend started pulling my arm, but I slowed my pace. She asked if I was crazy because I was not rushing like everyone else. I smiled at her and told her that I wanted to walk in Central Park. She laughed at me; however, she agreed because, as she said, I had just come back from war, and she wanted to please me. During our walk, I felt the same joy I had felt that day in June. I told her how that moment blessed us in the hell of war, and how special rain can be.
>
> —Gayber E. Guzman (Student)

1. How effective is Mr. Guzman's essay?

   _____Y_____ Strong thesis statement? _____Y_____ Good supporting details?

   _____Y_____ Logical organization? _____Y_____ Effective conclusion?

2. Discuss your underlinings. What details or lines in the essay did you like the most? Explain as exactly as possible why something struck you as interesting or moving.

3. Every narrative should have a clear point. What point does Mr. Guzman make by telling this story? Living through war made him appreciate "small things" like rain.

4. Have you had an experience of sudden appreciation for small things or of knowing clearly what really matters? What prompted this insight?

5. This student's spelling errors are distracting in an otherwise thoughtful and well-written essay. What suggestions would you make to him for improving his spelling? Review Chapter 36 on doubling consonants, final *y*, and commonly mis-spelled words. Watch out for look-alike/sound-alike errors.

6. Do you see any error patterns (one error made two or more times) that this student needs to watch out for? He misspells *their* three times; spelling in general is a problem.

GROUP WORK

In your group, find and correct the spelling errors in this essay. See if your group can find every error. Hint: There are fifteen misspelled or confused words.

WRITING AND REVISING IDEAS

1. Discuss a time when you felt blessed.

2. Discuss something you took for granted and fully appreciated only after it was gone.

Reading
Selections

Reading Strategies for Writers

The seventeen enjoyable and thought-provoking reading selections that follow deal with many of the concerns you have as a student, as a worker, and as a member of a family. Your instructor may ask you to read and think about a selection for class discussion or for a composition either at home or in class.

The more carefully you read these selections, the better you will be able to discuss and write about them. Below are ten strategies that can help you become a more effective reader and writer:

1. **Note the title.** A title, of course, is your first clue as to what the selection is about. For example, the title "Strike Out Little League" lets you know that the selection will discuss negative aspects of organized sports for children.

    A title may also tell you which method of development the author is using. For instance, a selection entitled "From Thailand to Houston: My Two Childhoods" might be a comparison/contrast essay; one entitled "Using the Library—Electronically" might be a process piece explaining how to use a computerized library catalogue.

2. **Underline main ideas.** If you read a long or difficult selection, you may forget some of the important ideas soon after you have finished the essay. However, underlining or highlighting these key ideas as you read will later help you review more easily. You may wish to number main ideas to help you follow the development of the author's thesis.

3. **Write your reactions in the margins.** Feel free to express your agreement or disagreement with the ideas in a selection by commenting "yes," "no," "Important—compare with Alice Walker's essay," or "Is he kidding?" in the margins.

    You will often be asked to write a "reaction paper," a composition explaining your thoughts about or reaction to the author's ideas. The comments that you have recorded in the margins will help you formulate a response.

4. **Prepare questions.** As you tackle more difficult reading selections, you may come across material that is hard to follow. Of course, reread the passage to see if a second reading helps. If it does not, put a question mark in the margin.

    Ask a friend or the instructor to help answer your questions. Do not be embarrassed to ask for explanations in class. Instructors appreciate careful readers who want to be sure that they completely understand what they have read.

5. **Note possible composition topics.** As you read, you may think of topics for compositions related to the ideas in the selection. Jot these topics in the margins or write about them in your journal. They may become useful if your instructor asks you for an essay based on the selection.

6. **Note effective writing.** If you are particularly moved by a portion of the selection—a phrase, a sentence, or an entire paragraph—underline or highlight it. You may wish to quote it later in class or use it in your composition.

533

7. **Circle unfamiliar words.** As you read, you will occasionally come across unfamiliar words. If you can guess what the word means from its context—from how it is used in the sentence or in the passage—do not interrupt your reading to look it up. Interruptions can cause you to lose the flow of ideas in the selection. Instead, circle the word and check it in a dictionary later.

8. **Vary your pace.** Some essays can be read quickly and easily. Others may require more time if the material is difficult or if much of the subject matter is unfamiliar to you. Be careful not to become discouraged, skimming a particularly difficult section just to get through with it. Extra effort will pay off.

9. **Reread.** If possible, budget your time so you can read the selection a second or even a third time. One advantage of rereading is that you will be able to discuss or write about the essay with more understanding. Ideas that were unclear may become obvious; you may even see new ideas that you failed to note the first time around.

   Another advantage is that by the second or third reading, your responses may have changed. You may agree with ideas you rejected the first time; you may disagree with ones you originally agreed with. Rereading gives you a whole new perspective!

10. **Do not overdo it.** Marking the selection as you read can help you become a better reader and writer. However, too many comments may defeat your purpose. You may not be able to decipher the mass—or mess—of underlinings, circles, and notes that you have made. Be selective.

The following essay has been marked, or annotated, by a student. Your responses might be different. Use this essay as a model to help you annotate other selections in this book—and reading material for your other courses as well.

How Sunglasses Spanned the World

Could be a process essay

Like many of the world's inhabitants, you probably own at least one pair of sunglasses, chosen as much for the image they project as for their ability to protect your eyes from the sun. In fact, sunglasses have become a staple in almost every country; it is no longer surprising to spot sunglasses on robed Arabian sheiks, Bolivian grandmothers, or Inuit fishermen tramping Arctic snows. The process by which sunglasses have gained worldwide popularity is a fascinating one that began, surprisingly, in the justice system of medieval China.

staple—standard item

Inuit—Eskimo

Dark glasses with smoke-tinted quartz lenses existed for centuries in China prior to 1430, but they were not used for sun protection. Chinese judges wore the darkened lenses in court to conceal their eye expressions and keep secret their reactions to evidence until the end of a trial. In 1430, when vision-correcting

Step 1—really Stage 1

This is a great idea.

glasses were introduced into China from Italy, these lenses, too, were smoke-tinted, but almost entirely for judicial use. Some people wore the darkened lenses for sun protection, but the idea never really caught on.

judicial—relating to court

Stage 2—aviator glasses invented

Five hundred years passed before the popularity of sunglasses began to grow. In the 1930s, the U.S. Army Air Corps asked the optical firm of Bausch & Lomb to produce a highly effective spectacle that would protect pilots from the dangers of high-altitude glare. Company scientists perfected a special dark-green tint that absorbed yellow light from the spectrum. They also designed a slightly drooping metal frame to protect the aviator's eyes, which repeatedly glanced down at the plane's instrument panel.

I own a pair just like this!

3 *I wonder why . . .*

spectrum—range or band (light breaks into a series of colors)

Stage 3

Soon this type of sunglasses was offered to the public as Ray Ban aviators, scientifically designed to ban the sun's rays. For the first time in history, large numbers of people began to purchase sunglasses.

4

Stage 4—sunglasses are chic

The next step in the process—making sunglasses chic—was the result of a clever 1960s advertising campaign by the firm of Foster Grant. Determined to increase its share of the sunglass market, the company began to feature the faces of Hollywood celebrities wearing sunglasses above a slogan that read, "Isn't that . . . behind those Foster Grants?" Big stars of the day like Peter Sellers, Anita Ekberg, and Elke Sommer posed for the ads, and the public love affair with sunglasses took off. Behind those Foster Grants, everyone now could feel like a movie star.

5 *Ah, yes. What makes anything span the world? Advertising.*

Stage 5—designer shades

In the 1970s, the trend escalated further when well-known fashion designers and Hollywood stars introduced their own brand-name lines, charging high prices for status sunglasses in the latest styles. A giant industry developed where only a few decades earlier none had existed, and shades became big business.

6 *True. I know people who spend $200 for wrap-arounds to wear dancing—at night!*

Stage 6

Today sunglasses—like blue jeans and Coca-Cola—circle the globe. Protection against solar radiation is just part of their appeal. As women in ancient times had hidden seductively behind an expanded fan or a tipped parasol, modern women and men all over the world have discovered the mystery, sex appeal, and cosmopolitan cool of wearing sunglasses.

7

parasol—umbrella for the sun

Writing ideas—
- Research the development or origin of another popular item.
- Think more about the power of advertising to influence us.
- Observe sunglass wearers and write about them.

100 Miles per Hour, Upside Down and Sideways

RICK BRAGG

Have you ever wanted to "slingshot" yourself out of your present circumstances? This essay by Pulitzer Prize–winning journalist Rick Bragg narrates his brief love affair with a 1969 convertible, the "mother of all slingshots." It appears in Bragg's memoir, *All Over But the Shoutin'*, which details his experiences of growing up "dirt poor" in Alabama.

Since I was a boy I have searched for ways to slingshot myself into the distance, faster and faster. When you turn the key on a car built for speed, when you hear that car rumble like an approaching storm and feel the steering wheel tremble in your hands from all that power barely under control, you feel like you can run away from anything, like you can turn your whole life into an insignificant speck in the rearview mirror. [1]

In the summer of 1976, the summer before my senior year at Jacksonville High School, I had the mother of all slingshots. She was a 1969 General Motors convertible muscle car[1] with a 350 V-8 and a Holley four-barreled carburetor as long as my arm. She got about six miles to the gallon, downhill, and when you started her up she sounded like Judgment Day. She was long and low and vicious, a mad dog cyclone with orange houndstooth interior and an eight-track tape player, and looked fast just sitting in the yard under a pine tree. I owned just one tape, that I remember, *The Eagles' Greatest Hits*. [2]

I worked two summers in the hell and heat at minimum wage to earn enough money to buy her and still had to borrow money from my uncle Ed, who got her for just nineteen hundred dollars mainly because he paid in hundred-dollar bills. "You better be careful, boy," he told me. "That'un will kill you." I assured him that, Yes, Sir, I would creep around in it like an old woman. [3]

I tell myself I loved that car because she was so pretty and so fast and because I loved to rumble between the rows of pines with the blond hair of some girl who had yet to discover she was better than me whipping in the breeze. But the truth is I loved her because she was my equalizer. She raised me up, at least in my own eyes, closer to where I wanted and needed to be. In high school, I was neither extremely popular nor one of the great number of want-to-bes. I was invited to parties with the popular kids, I had dates with pretty girls. But there was always a distance there, of my own making, usually. [4]

That car, in a purely superficial[2] way, closed it. People crowded around her at the Hardee's. I let only one person drive her, Patrice Curry, the prettiest girl in school, for exactly one mile. [5]

That first weekend, I raced her across the long, wide parking lot of the TG&Y, an insane thing to do, seeing as how a police car could have cruised by at any minute. It was a test of nerves as well as speed, because you actually had to be [6]

---

1. muscle car: a midsize American car with a powerful engine
2. superficial: shallow

slowing down, not speeding up, as you neared the finish line, because you just ran out of parking lot. I beat Lyn Johnson's Plymouth and had to slam on my brakes and swing her hard around, to keep from jumping the curb, the road and plowing into the parking lot of the Sonic Drive-In.

It would have lasted longer, this upraised standing, if I had pampered her. I guess I should have spent more time looking at her than racing her, but I had too much of the Bragg side of the family in me for that. I would roll her out on some lonely country road late at night, the top down, and blister down the blacktop until I knew the tires were about to lift off the ground. But they never did. She held the road, somehow, until I ran out of road or just lost my nerve. It was as if there was no limit to her, at how fast we could go, together.

It lasted two weeks from the day I bought her.

On Saturday night, late, I pulled up to the last red light in town on my way home. Kyle Smith pulled up beside me in a loud-running Chevrolet, and raced his engine. I did not squall out when the light changed—she was not that kind of car—but let her rpm's[3] build, build and build, like winding up a top.

I was passing a hundred miles per hour as I neared a long sweeping turn on Highway 21 when I saw, coming toward me, the blue lights of the town's police. I cannot really remember what happened next. I just remember mashing the gas pedal down hard, halfway through that sweeping turn, and the sickening feeling as the car just seemed to lift and twist in the air, until I was doing a hundred miles per hour still, but upside down and sideways.

She landed across a ditch, on her top. If she had not hit the ditch in just the right way, the police later said, it would have cut my head off. I did not have on my seat belt. We never did, then. Instead of flinging me out, though, the centrifugal force[4]—I had taken science in ninth grade—somehow held me in.

Instead of lying broken and bleeding on the ground beside my car, or headless, I just sat there, upside down. I always pulled the adjustable steering wheel down low, an inch or less above my thighs, and that held me in place, my head covered with mud and broken glass. The radio was still blaring—it was the Eagles' "The Long Run," I believe—and I tried to find the knob in the dark to turn it off. Funny. There I was in an upside-down car, smelling the gas as it ran out of the tank, listening to the tick, tick, tick of the hot engine, thinking: "I sure do hope that gas don't get nowhere near that hot manifold,"[5] but all I did about it was try to turn down the radio.

I knew the police had arrived because I could hear them talking. Finally, I felt a hand on my collar. A state trooper dragged me out and dragged me up the side of the ditch and into the collective glare of the most headlights I had ever seen. There were police cars and ambulances and traffic backed up, it seemed, all the way to Piedmont.

"The Lord was riding with you, son," the trooper said. "You should be dead."

My momma stood off to one side, stunned. Finally the police let her through to look me over, up and down. But except for the glass in my hair and a sore neck, I was fine. Thankfully, I was too old for her to go cut a hickory and stripe my legs with it, but I am sure it crossed her mind.

7

8

9

10

11

12

13

14

15

---

3. rpm's: abbreviation for *revolutions per minute*, which relates to speed

4. centrifugal force: in a rotating object, the force that pushes something away from the center

5. manifold: part of an engine

The trooper and the Jacksonville police had a private talk off to one side, try- 16 ing to decide whether or not to put me in prison for the rest of my life. Finally, they informed my momma that I had suffered enough, to take me home. As we drove away, I looked back over my shoulder as the wrecker dragged my car out of the ditch and, with the help of several strong men, flipped it back over, right-side up. It looked like a white sheet of paper someone had crumpled up and tossed in the ditch from a passing car.

"The Lord was riding with that boy," Carliss Slaughts, the wrecker opera- 17 tor, told my uncle Ed. With so many people saying that, I thought the front page of the *Anniston Star* the next day would read: LORD RIDES WITH BOY, WRECKS ANYWAY.

I was famous for a while. No one, no one, flips a convertible at a hundred 18 miles per hour, without a seat belt on, and walks away, undamaged. People said I had a charmed life. My momma, like the trooper and Mr. Slaughts, just figured God was my copilot.

The craftsmen at Slaughts' Body Shop put her back together, over four 19 months. My uncle Ed loaned me the money to fix her, and took it out of my check. The body and fender man made her pretty again, but she was never the same. She was fast but not real fast, as if some little part of her was still broken deep inside. Finally, someone backed into her in the parking lot of the Piggly Wiggly, and I was so disgusted I sold her for fourteen hundred dollars to a preacher's son, who drove the speed limit.

DISCUSSION AND WRITING QUESTIONS

1. Bragg selects vivid details and interesting words to bring his story to life. Which details and words do you find especially effective?

2. He also employs *similes* and *metaphors*, comparisons of two unlike things: "you hear that car rumble like an approaching storm" (paragraph 1), and "she was . . . a mad dog cyclone" (paragraph 2). Find at least three other similes or metaphors. Which is your favorite? Why?

3. For a short time, this car was the author's social "equalizer" (paragraph 4). What does he mean by this? Have you ever needed an equalizer? What was it and how well did it work for you?

4. What does Bragg seem to think is the point of his narrative? Others conclude after the crash that God was riding with him. Is that what he thinks?

WRITING ASSIGNMENTS

1. With a group of other students, discuss the excessive focus on status or popularity among many high school students. What are some ways that teenagers gain status in high school? Are there healthy and less healthy ways?

2. Write a narrative that begins, "Since I was a boy/girl, I have searched for _____." Fill in the blank, and develop your essay with details and exact description. Use several similes or metaphors if you wish.

3. Did you or your friends ever do something dangerous or foolhardy? What happened, and why did you (or they) do it? Specifically, what aspects of your thinking caused you to ignore the potential consequences and willingly put yourself into harm's way?

Sandra Cisneros chose this photo of herself to use on her web site. What do the clothing, pose, and colors convey about this woman?

Only Daughter

SANDRA CISNEROS

Sandra Cisneros is the author of *The House on Mango Street* and other books. She often writes about the experience of being bicultural, bilingual, and female. Here, she explores the ways in which her birth family helped define who she is—and is not.

Once, several years ago, when I was just starting out my writing career, I was 1 asked to write my own contributor's note for an anthology I was part of. I wrote: "I am the only daughter in a family of six sons. *That* explains everything."

Well, I've thought about that ever since, and yes, it explains a lot to me, but 2 for the reader's sake I should have written: "I am the only daughter in a *Mexican* family of six sons." Or even: "I am the only daughter of a Mexican father and a Mexican-American mother." Or: "I am the only daughter of a working-class family of nine." All of these had everything to do with who I am today.

I was/am the only daughter and *only* a daughter. Being an only daughter in a 3 family of six sons forced me by circumstance to spend a lot of time by myself because my brothers felt it beneath them to play with a *girl* in public. But that aloneness, that loneliness, was good for a would-be writer—it allowed me time to think and think, to imagine, to read and prepare myself.

Being only a daughter for my father meant my destiny would lead me to be- 4 come someone's wife. That's what he believed. But when I was in the fifth grade and shared my plans for college with him, I was sure he understood. I remember my father saying, "*Que bueno, mi'ja,* that's good." That meant a lot to me, especially since my brothers thought the idea hilarious. What I didn't realize was that my father thought college was good for girls—good for finding a husband. After four years in college and two more in graduate school, and still no husband, my father shakes his head even now and says I wasted all that education.

In retrospect, I'm lucky my father believed daughters were meant for husbands. It meant it didn't matter if I majored in something silly like English. After all, I'd find a nice professional eventually, right? This allowed me the liberty to putter about embroidering my little poems and stories without my father interrupting with so much as a "What's that you're writing?" 5

But the truth is, I wanted him to interrupt. I wanted my father to understand what it was I was scribbling, to introduce me as "My only daughter, the writer." Not as "This is only my daughter. She teaches." *Es maestra*—teacher. Not even *profesora*. 6

In a sense, everything I have ever written has been for him, to win his approval even though I know my father can't read English words, even though my father's only reading includes the brown-ink *Esto* sports magazines from Mexico City and the bloody *¡Alarma!* magazines that feature yet another sighting of *La Virgen de Guadalupe* on a tortilla or a wife's revenge on her philandering[1] husband by bashing his skull in with a *molcajete* (a kitchen mortar made of volcanic rock). Or the *fotonovelas*, the little picture paperbacks with tragedy and trauma erupting from the characters' mouths in bubbles. 7

My father represents, then, the public majority. A public who is uninterested in reading, and yet one whom I am writing about and for, and privately trying to woo. 8

When we were growing up in Chicago, we moved a lot because of my father. He suffered bouts of nostalgia. Then we'd have to let go our flat, store the furniture with mother's relatives, load the station wagon with baggage and bologna sandwiches and head south. To Mexico City. 9

We came back, of course. To yet another Chicago flat, another Chicago neighborhood, another Catholic school. Each time, my father would seek out the parish priest in order to get a tuition break, and complain or boast: "I have seven sons." 10

He meant *siete hijos*, seven children, but he translated it as "sons." "I have seven sons." To anyone who would listen. The Sears Roebuck employee who sold us the washing machine. The short-order cook where my father ate his ham-and-eggs breakfasts. "I have seven sons." As if he deserved a medal from the state. 11

My papa. He didn't mean anything by that mistranslation, I'm sure. But somehow I could feel myself being erased. I'd tug my father's sleeve and whisper: "Not seven sons. Six! and *one daughter.*" 12

When my oldest brother graduated from medical school, he fulfilled my father's dream that we study hard and use this—our heads, instead of this—our hands. Even now my father's hands are thick and yellow, stubbed by a history of hammer and nails and twine and coils and springs. "Use this," my father said, tapping his head, "and not this," showing us those hands. He always looked tired when he said it. 13

Wasn't college an investment? And hadn't I spent all those years in college? And if I didn't marry, what was it all for? Why would anyone go to college and then choose to be poor? Especially someone who had always been poor. 14

Last year, after ten years of writing professionally, the financial rewards started to trickle in. My second National Endowment for the Arts Fellowship. A guest professorship at the University of California, Berkeley. My book, which sold to a major New York publishing house. 15

At Christmas, I flew home to Chicago. The house was throbbing, same as always; hot *tamales* and sweet *tamales* hissing in my mother's pressure cooker, and 16

---

1. philandering: unfaithful

everybody—my mother, six brothers, wives, babies, aunts, cousins—talking too loud and at the same time, like in a Fellini[2] film, because that's just how we are.

I went upstairs to my father's room. One of my stories had just been translated 17 into Spanish and published in an anthology of Chicano writing, and I wanted to show it to him. Ever since he recovered from a stroke two years ago, my father likes to spend his leisure hours horizontally. And that's how I found him, watching a Pedro Infante movie on Galavisión and eating rice pudding.

There was a glass filmed with milk on the bedside table. There were several 18 vials of pills and balled Kleenex. And on the floor, one black sock and a plastic urinal that I didn't want to look at but looked at anyway. Pedro Infante was about to burst into song, and my father was laughing.

I'm not sure if it was because my story was translated into Spanish, or because 19 it was published in Mexico, or perhaps because the story dealt with Tepeyac, the *colonia* my father was raised in and the house he grew up in, but at any rate, my father punched the mute button on his remote control and read my story.

I sat on the bed next to my father and waited. He read it very slowly. As if he 20 were reading each line over and over. He laughed at all the right places and read lines he liked out loud. He pointed and asked questions: "Is this So-and-so?" "Yes," I said. He kept reading.

When he was finally finished, after what seemed like hours, my father looked 21 up and asked: "Where can we get more copies of this for the relatives?"

Of all the wonderful things that happened to me last year, that was the most 22 wonderful.

DISCUSSION AND WRITING QUESTIONS

1. In what two ways can the title of this essay, "Only Daughter," be interpreted?

2. What expectations did the author's father have for his daughter? Did his limited expectations create any advantages for her? Why did the father's comment "I have seven sons" bother her so much?

3. In paragraphs 16 through 18, Cisneros describes one of her trips home. She includes vivid details that help the reader "see" and "feel" life inside her parents' house. Which details do you find especially effective? Although the home is in Chicago, which details capture the family's Mexican heritage?

4. For years, the author wanted her father's attention and approval. Why do you think he finally appreciated her achievement as a writer?

WRITING ASSIGNMENTS

1. In a group with three or four classmates, share statements about your personal history like those in Cisneros's opening paragraphs. First, take five minutes working on your own, and then define yourself, using a two- or three-

sentence pattern: "I am _____

_____. That explains everything."

Revise your sentences until you feel they capture a truth about you. Now share and discuss these statements with your group. What is most and least effective or intriguing about each? Use your definition as the main idea for a paper to be written at home.

---

2. Fellini: an Italian movie director whose films were full of strange, unforgettable characters

2. Have you (or has someone you know) wanted another person's approval so badly that it influenced how you conducted your life? Who was the person whose approval you sought, and why was that approval so important? What did you do to please him or her and what happened? Was it worth it?

3. What were your family's expectations for you as you grew up, and how did those expectations affect your life choices? Were the expectations high or low? Did your gender or place in the family (oldest, middle, youngest) affect them? Did you accept or reject the family's vision for you?

My Outing[1]

ARTHUR ASHE

> Arthur Ashe was the first African American male to become a great tennis champion. After a heart attack ended his career, he contracted AIDS through a blood transfusion. He kept his illness private for years while he pursued many business interests and human-rights projects. Then the possibility of a newspaper report forced him to reveal his condition to the public. The press conference he refers to was held in April 1992. Ashe died of AIDS in 1993.

The day after my press conference, I made sure to keep the two appointments on my calendar because I was anxious to see how people would respond to me after the announcement. I was thinking not only about the people I knew personally, even intimately, but also about waiters and bartenders, doormen and taxi drivers. I knew all the myths and fears about AIDS. I also understood that if I hadn't been educated in the harshest possible way—by contracting the disease and living with it—I would probably share some of those myths and fears. I knew that I couldn't spread the disease by coughing or breathing or using plates and cups in a restaurant, but I knew that in some places my plates and cups would receive special attention, perhaps some extra soap and hot water. Perhaps they would be smashed and thrown away.

That morning, I accompanied Donald M. Stewart, head of the College Board Testing Service, on a visit to the offices of the New York Community Trust. We were seeking a grant of $5,000 to support the publication of a handbook aimed at student-athletes. The appointment went well; we got the money. And in the evening, I went in black tie to a gala dinner to celebrate the eightieth birthday of a man I had known for thirty years and regarded as one of my key mentors in New York City, Joseph Cullman III, a former chairman of Philip Morris. At the event, which took place at the Museum of Natural History in Manhattan, I felt anxiety rising as our taxi drew up to the curb. How would the other guests respond to me? The first person I saw was an old friend, John Reese. An investment banker now, in his youth John had been an up-and-coming star with me in junior tennis. He saw me, and hurried over. There was no mistaking the warmth of his greeting, his genuine concern but also his understanding of my predicament. We walked inside together and I had a fine time at the celebration.

---

1. "Outing" someone usually means revealing publicly, without permission, that he or she is homosexual. Although Ashe was not gay, he was "outed" as a person with AIDS.

I was glad, in this context, that I had not concealed my condition from certain people. I had reminded myself from the outset that I had an obligation to tell anyone who might be materially hurt by the news when it came out. I have been both proud of my commercial connections and grateful to the people who had asked me to represent them or work for them in some other way. Several of them had taken a chance on me when they knew full well, from the most basic market research in the early 1970s, that having an African American as a spokesman or an officer might cost them business. ₃

Among these organizations, the most important were the Aetna Life and Casualty Company, where I was a member of the board of directors; Head USA, the sports-equipment manufacturer that had given me my first important commercial endorsement, a tennis racquet with my very own autograph on it; the Doral Resort and Country Club in Florida, where I had directed the tennis program; Le Coq Sportif, the sports-clothing manufacturer; Home Box Office (HBO), the cable-television network for which I worked as an analyst at Wimbledon;[2] and ABC Sports, for which I also served as a commentator. ₄

Not one of these companies had dropped me after I quietly revealed to their most important executives that I had AIDS. Now those executives had to deal with the response of the public. I would have to give them a chance to put some distance between their companies and me because I now carried the most abominable and intimidating medical virus of our age. In business, image is everything. And one would have to go back to leprosy, or the plague, to find a disease so full of terrifying implications as AIDS carries. AIDS was a scientific mystery that defied our vaunted[3] claims for science, and also a religious or spiritual riddle—at least to those who insisted on thinking of it as possibly a punishment from God for our evil on earth, as more than one person had publicly suggested. ₅

I waited for the phone calls and the signs that my services were no longer needed. None came. ₆

I read somewhere that in the two weeks following his announcement that he was HIV-positive, Earvin "Magic" Johnson received thousands of pieces of mail, and that months later he was still receiving hundreds of letters a week. Well, I received nothing approaching that volume of correspondence following my press conference, but I certainly had a mountain of reading and writing to do in its aftermath. And every time I appeared on one of the few television interview shows I agreed to do, such as with Barbara Walters or Larry King, there was another surge of correspondence. I heard from the famous and the completely unknown, people I knew and people I had never met. ₇

The most moving letters, without a doubt, came from people who had lived through an AIDS illness, either their own or that of a loved one. Often the loved one was now dead. These writers, above all, understood why I had made such a fuss about the issue of privacy. Many probably understood better than I did, because they were more vulnerable than I am, and had suffered more. One Manhattan woman wrote to tell me about her father, who had received HIV-tainted blood, as I had, through a blood transfusion following heart surgery. Without knowing it, he had passed the infection on to her mother. For some years, they had kept their illness a secret from their daughter. After they could keep the secret from her no longer, she in turn had worked to keep their secret from other family members and friends, and from the world. Although both parents were now ₈

---

2. Wimbledon: London, England, district where a major tennis tournament is held each year
3. vaunted: boastful

dead, she wrote, "I share your anger at that anonymous person who violated either your trust or their professional ethics."

A grandmother in New England, HIV-positive after a transfusion, shared with me her terror that the company she worked for would dismiss her if they found out; she was awaiting the passage of a law that might protect her. From Idaho, a mother told me about her middle-aged son, who had tried to keep his AIDS condition a secret even from her. "My son kept it to himself for six months before he told me and I'll never forget that day as we cried together." His ordeal included dementia,[4] forced incarceration in a state asylum, and ostracism[5] by relatives and friends. But mother and son had spent his last "four difficult months" together. "I'm so thankful to have had those days with him."

I heard from people whom I had not thought of in years, and some of them had been touched by their own tragedy. A woman I remembered as a stunningly beautiful UCLA coed, as we called them in those days, told me about her younger brother, who had been diagnosed with full-blown AIDS about five years before. "He is gay," she reported, "and I saw how he lost so much self-esteem and hope" because of intolerance. "No one can speak as eloquently[6] as you and Magic to allow the stigma[7] to disperse[8] regarding this situation." Another letter illustrated the power of the stigma. Signed simply, "Sorry I can't identify myself, but you understand," it came from a man who had been diagnosed with HIV three years ago. "I'm the father of six children and many grandchildren. I'm not into needles or the gay life. Don't know where it came from (really)."

As for my daughter, Camera, more than one writer underscored my fears about what she might have to undergo from insensitive people in the future. A woman whose son had died of AIDS about a year before, following the death of his wife, was now bringing up their young son: "I struggle with how this little child is going to deal with the insults and rejections that people will inflict on him when they find out that his father died from AIDS." . . .

Needless to say, I am grateful to all those who have taken the trouble to write. Most of the letters left me humbled.

DISCUSSION AND WRITING QUESTIONS

1. In paragraph 3, Ashe says that he had told some business associates about his illness early on. Why had he done that? How had they reacted? Why, then, was Ashe concerned about the business community's reaction to his *public* announcement?

2. How did the general public react to Ashe's announcement? Which letters did Ashe find most moving? Why?

3. The privacy issue was extremely important to Ashe, who felt that he had been forced by the press to make an announcement he had not wanted to make. One letter he received said, "I share your anger at that anonymous person who violated either your trust or their professional ethics" (paragraph 8). What did the letter writer mean by this statement?

---

4. dementia: insanity

5. ostracism: exclusion, banishment

6. eloquently: skillfully, persuasively

7. stigma: mark of disgrace

8. disperse: disappear

4. Arthur Ashe called his life story *Days of Grace.* On the basis of this essay, why do you think he chose that title? What example or examples of "grace" did he tell about?

WRITING ASSIGNMENTS

1. Have you ever prepared yourself for the worst—the ending of a relationship, a frightening medical test result, or other bad news—only to find that the worst did not happen? Discuss such a time: why you expected the worst, what you did to prepare, and what really happened.

2. Serious illness can force people to reevaluate their lives—their aspirations and their goals. Have you, or has someone you know, looked at life differently because of an illness or accident? Write a short account of your own or the other person's experience.

3. In a group with three or four classmates, discuss Ashe's belief that no newspaper had the right to tell the world that he had AIDS. Do you think the press was justified in revealing Ashe's condition? Why or why not? Ashe believed that his right to privacy was greater than the public's need to know. The press argued that Ashe was a public figure and that whenever a public figure is ill, his or her condition is legitimate news. Write your own essay about this issue, based on the conclusions you come to after your group's discussion.

When Greed Gives Way to Giving

ANA VECIANA-SUAREZ

If you suddenly made millions of dollars, what would you do with the money? Here *Miami Herald* columnist Ana Veciana-Suarez reports one man's surprising response to that situation. Like many newspaper writers, she employs a casual tone and style, but the questions she raises are profound.

In the flurry of life, you probably missed this story. I almost did, and that would 1
have been too bad. Over in Belleville, Minnesota, a 67-year-old man named Bob Thompson sold his road-building company for $422 million back in July. He did not, as we would expect, buy himself a jet or an island, not even a new home. Instead, Thompson decided to share the wealth.

He divided $128 million among his 550 workers. Some checks exceeded an- 2
nual salaries. And for more than 80 people, the bonus went beyond their wildest expectations: They became millionaires. Thompson even included some retirees and widows in his plan. What's more, he paid the taxes on those proceeds—about $25 million.

Employees were so flabbergasted[1] that the wife of an area manager tearfully 3
said: "I think the commas are in the wrong place." The commas were right where they belonged. Thompson had made sure of that, had made sure, too, that not one of the workers would lose his or her job in the buyout.

I sat at the breakfast table stunned. I just don't know too many people or com- 4
panies that would do something like that. Sure, many employers offer profit-sharing

---

1. flabbergasted: astonished; shocked

and stock-option plans. But outright giving? Nah. Employees rarely share in the bounty when the big payoff comes. In fact, many end up losing their jobs, being demoted,[2] seeking transfers, or taking early retirement. Insecurity—or better yet, the concept of every man for himself—is a verity[3] of work life in America.

Yet here is one man defying all of the stereotypes. I search for clues in his life, but find nothing out of the ordinary, nothing that stands out. He started the business in his basement with $3,500, supported by his schoolteacher wife. He has owned the same modest house for 37 years. His wood-paneled office has no Persian rugs or oil paintings, only photos of three children and five grandchildren. He admits to an indulgence or two: a Lincoln and an occasional Broadway show. 5

Yet he possesses something as priceless as it is rare: generosity. And he seems to be sheepishly modest even about that. "It's sharing good times, that's really all it is," he told a reporter. "I don't think you can read more into it. I'm a proud person. I wanted to go out a winner, and I wanted to go out doing the right thing." We all want to do the right thing, but blessed by a windfall,[4] would we have done as Thompson did? Maybe. I don't know. Honestly, I'm embarrassed to say I'm not sure I would have. 6

Perhaps, however, the more appropriate question is this: In our own more limited circumstances, do we share with others in the same spirit Thompson showed? Do we give beyond expectations? For most of us, generosity comes with limits. It is, by and large, a sum without sacrifice, a respectable token. 7

Some might say that Thompson's munificence[5] was token-like. After all, the $153 million is less than a third of his $422 million payoff. That kind of reasoning, however, misses the mark. Few of us give away even 10 percent, and if our income increases, the tendency is not to share more but to buy more, to hoard[6] more. Not Thompson. After finishing with his employees, he plans to continue giving away much of what's left of the $422 million. 8

I suspect he is on to something. In a society where success tends to be measured in what we can acquire, this guy instead is preaching and practicing the opposite. Success, he is telling us, is in the giving back. He seems to have mastered what many of us have yet to understand: the difference between need and want, between the basic essentials and our inchoate[7] desires. He has, by golly, defined *enough*. Maybe that's all the wealth he needs. 9

DISCUSSION AND WRITING QUESTIONS

1. The author first tells the factual story of Bob Thompson's "windfall" and then discusses its meaning. What does she believe is the point, or importance, of his story?

2. Do you agree with the author that generosity is a rare quality in today's society? If so, why do you think this is true? If you know a truly generous person, describe his or her generosity to the class.

3. Buddhism, one of the world's major religions, teaches that the causes of human suffering are greed and selfish desire. Would you agree, or is this overstated? What is wrong with greed and selfish desire?

---

2. demoted: reduced in status or rank

3. verity: truth or reality

4. windfall: sudden, unexpected good fortune or personal gain

5. munificence: great generosity

6. hoard: accumulate in a private supply, usually more than needed

7. inchoate: only partially formed or developed

4. What point does the author make in the last sentence about the concept of "enough"? What is your own personal definition of "enough"?

WRITING ASSIGNMENTS

1. Do you know a person who "gives beyond expectations" or even makes personal sacrifices to help others? Write an essay illustrating that person's generosity with specific examples.

2. Veciana-Suarez discusses two definitions of success: the idea that success is aquiring as much as we can and Bob Thompson's idea that success is "giving back" (paragraph 9). Which of these is closer to the truth for you? Write an essay honestly exploring your personal definition of the word *success*.

3. What career path have you chosen to pursue or are considering now? Will that career lead you to your idea of success? Write about the top three rewards of that career for you (for example, salary, mental stimulation, security, fun, the chance to give back, to travel, and so on).

Build Yourself a Killer Bod with Killer Bees

DAVE BARRY

> Humorist Dave Barry writes that he was "born in Armonk, N.Y., in 1947 and has been steadily growing older ever since without ever actually reaching maturity." He is a Pulitzer Prize–winning columnist with the *Miami Herald*. Although Barry's columns and books often make us laugh out loud, his humor always has a point. Here he takes on America's obsession with the "perfect" body.

If there's one ideal that unites all Americans, it's the belief that every single one of us, regardless of ethnic background, is fat. 1

It was not always this way. There was a time, not so long ago, when Americans did not obsess about fat. In those days, a man could be portly[1] and still be considered attractive. The standards were also more lenient[2] for women: Marilyn Monroe, whom nobody ever called skinny, was a major sex goddess. 2

By today's beauty standards, of course, Marilyn Monroe was an oil tanker. Today's beauty ideal, strictly enforced by the media, is a person with the same level of body fat as a paper clip. Turn on your TV, and all you see are men and women who would rather have both eyeballs removed via corkscrew than eat a slice of pizza. These are genetic mutants:[3] You can see their muscles, veins, and neck bones almost bursting through their fat-free skin. I don't know who decided that the see-through look was attractive; I, personally, have never heard anybody express lust 3

---

1. portly: somewhat stout or fat
2. lenient: tolerant; not strict
3. mutants: individuals who have been biologically changed or altered

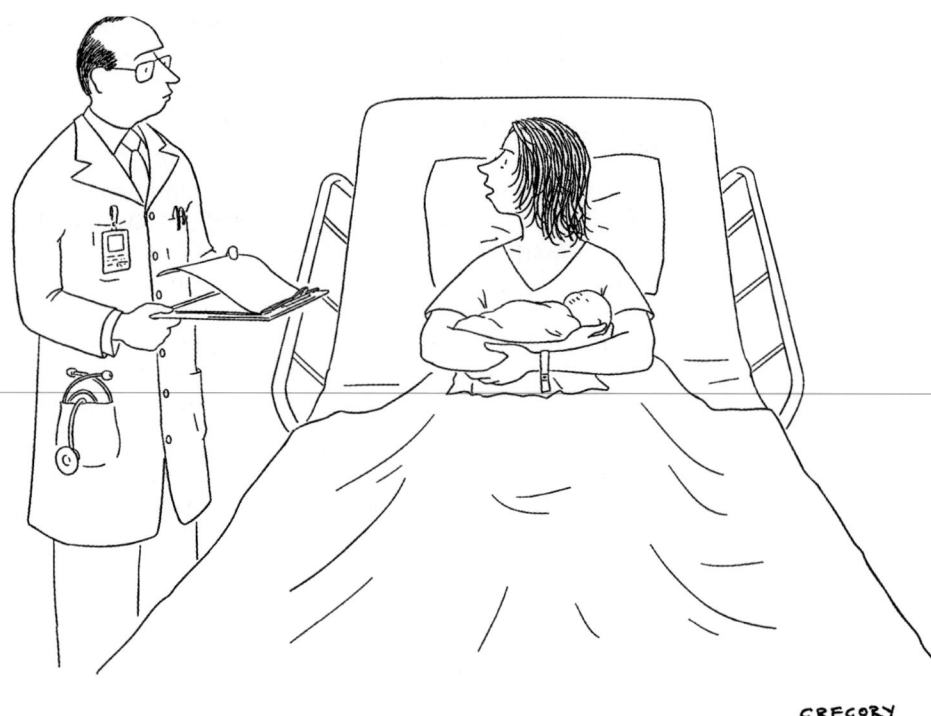

"How soon can I start her on fad diets?"

for anybody else's internal organs. But we normal humans are constantly exposed to the zero-fat mutants in the media, and we naturally assume that we're supposed to look like them. This is of course impossible, but we try. We diet constantly, especially young women, many of whom now start dieting while still in the womb.

And of course we spend millions of dollars on "exercise," defined as "activity designed to be strenuous without accomplishing anything useful." For example, we drive our cars to health clubs so we can run on treadmills. But we do NOT run to the health club, because then we would be accomplishing something useful. We pedal furiously on exercise bicycles that do not go anywhere. We take elevators every chance we get, but we buy expensive machines that enable us to pretend we're climbing stairs. It would not surprise me if yuppies started paying potato farmers for the opportunity to go into the fields and burn fat by pretending to conduct a harvest, taking great care not to dig up any actual potatoes. 4

If you think that's ridiculous, then you haven't seen "Tae-Bo." This was a recent hot fad, advertised extensively on TV by perspiring mutants. As I understand it, Tae-Bo is based on martial arts; the difference is that martial artists actually learn to defend themselves, whereas Tae-Bo people throw pretend punches and kicks strictly for fitness purposes. While they're busy kicking air and checking their abdominals, an actual mugger could walk right up and whack them with a crowbar. 5

But never mind practicality. The point is that Tae-Bo was briefly very, very hot, which means that soon everybody got bored with it. That's what always happens with exercise trends: People realize that, after countless hours of pretending to climb stairs or punching the air, they still bear a stronger resemblance to the Michelin Tire Man than to the TV mutants. So they give up on that particular trend and look for a new one. 6

Will this craziness ever end? Will Americans ever come to their senses and stop wasting millions and millions of dollars on hopeless efforts to look like people who don't really look like people? I hope not, because I'm planning to cash in 7 on this. I got my idea from a wonderful newspaper article, sent in by alert veterinarian Steven Berry, from the *Leader News* of Central City, Kentucky. The article, written by Paul Camplin, is headlined "Cobbs Invented Odd Sport of Bee Fighting as Family Entertainment." It concerns the descendants of Bunn and Betty Cobb of Calhoun, Kentucky, who have gotten together annually for about 70 years to fight wild bees for fun. The article states:

"Without use of protective gear, one of the group approaches the bumble-bee 8 hive and whacks it with a stick. When all of the now angry bees come flying out the group of bee fighters simply fight off the bees as best they can with large clumps of maple leaves."

The article, which I am not making up, is illustrated by photos of members of 9 the extended Bunn family, including grandparents, wildly waving branches at bees.

When I saw those photos, I knew I was looking at a gold mine. I'm talking 10 about the Next Big Fitness Trend: "Tae-Bee." I'm going to make a 30-minute TV infomercial wherein enthusiastic hired mutants stress the benefits of bee-fighting (". . . and while you're OUCH burning fat, your arm motion is also OUCH building those OUCH . . .").

In no time millions of Americans will be ordering the Tae-Bee workout video- 11 tape, along with the Official (Accept No Substitutes!) Tae-Bee Maple Leaf Clump and of course the Official Tae-Bee Box o' Really Mad Bees. And if you don't think Americans will pay good money to get stung, I have one word for you: "ThighMaster."

So laugh if you want: I'm going to get rich on this thing. And then I'm going 12 to hire a personal trainer. His sole job will be to order my pizza.

DISCUSSION AND WRITING QUESTIONS

1. The first sentence of Barry's essay is funny, but it makes a serious point. What is Barry's opinion of the American obsession with weight and fitness?

2. "Today's beauty ideal is a person with the same level of body fat as a paper clip," writes Barry (paragraph 3). What humorous details and comments in this paragraph underscore this point? Why does Barry call people who represent today's ideal of beauty "mutants"?

3. Do you know someone who is truly happy in his or her body, even if it's not perfect? What is the secret of this person's self-acceptance?

4. Is Barry serious about creating a Tae-Bee video and spin-off products? How do you know? What point is he making about the fitness industry and those who buy its products and services?

WRITING ASSIGNMENTS

1. Have you ever tried a diet or fitness fad? Did it work? Write a paragraph or essay about your attempt, or that of someone you know, to build a killer bod. Your approach could be serious or humorous.

2. Do you agree that the media are responsible for fostering unrealistic beauty ideals? Write about the cause (or causes) of Americans' obsession with thinness and fitness.

3. According to the U.S. Centers for Disease Control and Prevention, over half of all Americans really do have a weight problem. About 35 percent are slightly or moderately overweight, and 26 percent are obese, or grossly overweight. Write an essay discussing either the causes of this national epidemic or effective ways to lose weight. For ideas and information, visit **http://win.niddk.nih.gov /publications/understanding.htm/**.

A Brother's Murder

BRENT STAPLES

Brent Staples grew up in a rough, industrial city. He left to become a successful journalist, but his younger brother remained. Staples's story of his brother is a reminder of the grim circumstances in which so many young men of the inner city find themselves today.

It has been more than two years since my telephone rang with the news that my younger brother Blake—just twenty-two years old—had been murdered. The young man who killed him was only twenty-four. Wearing a ski mask, he emerged from a car, fired six times at close range with a massive .44 Magnum, then fled. The two had once been inseparable friends. A senseless rivalry—beginning, I think, with an argument over a girlfriend—escalated[1] from posturing,[2] to threats, to violence, to murder. The way the two were living, death could have come to either of them from anywhere. In fact, the assailant had already survived multiple gunshot wounds from an accident much like the one in which my brother lost his life.

As I wept for Blake I felt wrenched backward into events and circumstances that had seemed light-years gone. Though a decade apart, we both were raised in Chester, Pennsylvania, an angry, heavily black, heavily poor, industrial city southwest of Philadelphia. There, in the 1960s, I was introduced to mortality, not by the old and failing, but by beautiful young men who lay wrecked after sudden explosions of violence. The first, I remembered from my fourteenth year—Johnny, brash lover of fast cars, stabbed to death two doors from my house in a fight over a pool game. The next year, my teenage cousin, Wesley, whom I loved very much, was shot dead. The summers blur. Milton, an angry young neighbor, shot a crosstown rival, wounding him badly. William, another teenage neighbor, took a shotgun blast to the shoulder in some urban drama and displayed his bandages proudly. His brother, Leonard, severely beaten, lost an eye and donned a black patch. It went on.

I recall not long before I left for college, two local Vietnam veterans—one from the Marines, one from the Army—arguing fiercely, nearly at blows about which outfit had done the most in the war. The most killing, they meant. Not much later, I read a magazine article that set that dispute in a context. In the story, a noncommissioned officer—a sergeant, I believe—said he would pass up any number of affluent, suburban-born recruits to get hard-core soldiers from the inner city. They jumped into the rice paddies with "their manhood on their sleeves," I believe he said. These two items—the veterans arguing and the sergeant's words—still characterize for me the circumstances under which black men in their teens and twenties kill one another with such frequency. With a touchy paranoia born of living battered lives, they are desperate to be *real* men. Killing is only machismo taken to the extreme. Incursions[3] to be punished by death were many and minor, and they remain so: they include stepping on the wrong toe, literally; cheating in a drug deal; simply saying "I dare you" to someone holding a gun; crossing territorial lines in a gang dispute. My brother grew

1. escalated: increased
2. posturing: trying to appear tough
3. incursions: attacks, violations

up to wear his manhood on his sleeve. And when he died, he was in that group—black, male and in its teens and early twenties—that is far and away the most likely to murder or be murdered.

I left the East Coast after college, spent the mid- and late 1970s in Chicago as a graduate student, taught for a time, then became a journalist. Within ten years of leaving my hometown, I was overeducated and "upwardly mobile," ensconced[4] on a quiet, tree-lined street where voices raised in anger were scarcely ever heard. The telephone, like some grim umbilical, kept me connected to the old world with news of deaths, imprisonings and misfortune. I felt emotionally beaten up. Perhaps to protect myself, I added a psychological dimension to the physical distance I had already achieved. I rarely visited my hometown. I shut it out.

As I fled the past, so Blake embraced it. On Christmas of 1983, I traveled from Chicago to a black section of Roanoke, Virginia, where he then lived. The desolate public housing projects, the hopeless, idle young men crashing against one another—these reminded me of the embittered town we'd grown up in. It was a place where once I would have been comfortable, or at least sure of myself. Now, hearing of my brother's forays[5] into crime, his scrapes with police and street thugs, I was scared, unsteady on foreign terrain.[6]

I saw that Blake's romance with the street life and the hustler image had flowered dangerously. One evening that late December, standing in some Roanoke dive among drug dealers and grim, hair-trigger losers, I told him I feared for his life. He had affected the image of the tough he wanted to be. But behind the dark glasses and the swagger, I glimpsed the baby-faced toddler I'd once watched over. I nearly wept. I wanted desperately for him to live. The young think themselves immortal, and a dangerous light shone in his eyes as he spoke laughingly of making fools of the policemen who had raided his apartment looking for drugs. He cried out as I took his right hand. A line of stitches lay between the thumb and index finger. Kickback from a shotgun, he explained, nothing serious. Gunplay had become part of his life.

I lacked the language simply to say: Thousands have lived this for you and died. I fought the urge to lift him bodily and shake him. This place and the way you are living smells of death to me, I said. Take some time away, I said. Let's go downtown tomorrow and buy a plane ticket anywhere, take a bus trip, anything to get away and cool things off. He took my alarm casually. We arranged to meet the following night—an appointment he would not keep. We embraced as though through glass. I drove away.

As I stood in my apartment in Chicago holding the receiver that evening in February 1984, I felt as though part of my soul had been cut away. I questioned myself then, and I still do. Did I not reach back soon enough or earnestly enough for him? For weeks I awoke crying from a recurrent dream in which I chased him, urgently trying to get him to read a document I had, as though reading it would protect him from what had happened in waking life. His eyes shining like black diamonds, he smiled and danced just beyond my grasp. When I reached for him, I caught only the space where he had been.

DISCUSSION AND WRITING QUESTIONS

1. Staples says that he was "introduced to mortality" in Chester, Pennsylvania, in the 1960s (paragraph 2). What does he mean?

---

4. ensconced: settled comfortably

5. forays: undertakings, trips

6. terrain: ground

2. What does the author mean when he says his brother grew up to "wear his manhood on his sleeve" (paragraph 3)? Does he imply that there are other ways of expressing masculinity?

3. Staples speaks of a dream in which he holds a document for his brother to read (paragraph 8). What do you suppose that document might say? What does this dream seem to say about communication between the two brothers?

4. Staples begins his narrative by describing the moment at which he hears of Blake's death. Why does he *start* with this event, instead of moving toward it?

WRITING ASSIGNMENTS

1. Write a narrative about a shocking incident that took place in your neighborhood. Like Staples, you may want to start with the incident, and then narrate the smaller events in the story that led up to it. Or you can follow time order and end with the incident.

2. Do you think Brent Staples could have done more to change his brother? Can we really influence others to change their lives?

3. In a group with three or four classmates, discuss the most significant problem facing young people in the inner city today. Is it crime? Drugs? Lack of educational or employment opportunities? Choose one problem and decide how it can be solved. Your instructor may ask you to share your solution with the class. Then write your own paper, discussing the problem you think is most significant and proposing a solution.

Dear Dads: Save Your Sons

CHRISTOPHER N. BACORN

According to the National Fatherhood Initiative, an estimated 24.7 million children (36.3 percent) do not live with their biological fathers. About 40 percent of these children have not seen their fathers during the past year. Psychologist Christopher N. Bacorn puts human faces on these statistics in this provocative *Newsweek* essay. These kids don't need a shrink, he argues; they need a dad.

I had seen a hundred like him. He sat back on the couch, silently staring out the window, an unmistakable air of sullen[1] anger about him. He was 15 and big for his age. His mother, a woman in her mid-30s, sat forward on the couch and, on the edge of tears, described the boy's heartbreaking descent into alcohol, gang membership, failing grades and violence. She was small, thin, worn out from frantic nights of worry and lost sleep waiting for him to come home. She had lost control of him, she admitted freely. Ever since his father had left, four years ago, she had had trouble with him. He had become more and more unmanageable and then, recently, he had hurt someone in a fight. Charges had been filed, counseling recommended.

I listened to the mother's anguished[2] story. "Are there any men in his life?" I asked. There was no one. She had no brothers, her father was dead and her

---

1. sullen: resentful, sulking

2. anguished: feeling terrible physical or mental pain

ex-husband's father lived in another state. She looked up at me, her eyes hopeful. "Will you talk with him?" she asked. "Just speak with him about what he's doing. Maybe if it came from a professional . . ." she added, her voice trailing off. "It couldn't hurt."

I did speak with him. Maybe it didn't hurt, but like most counseling with 15-year-old boys, it didn't seem to help either. He denied having any problems. Everyone else had them, but he didn't. After half an hour of futility,[3] I gave up.

I have come to believe that most adolescent boys can't make use of professional counseling. What a boy can use, and all too often doesn't have, is the fellowship of men—at least one man who pays attention to him, who spends time with him, who admires him. A boy needs a man he can look up to. What he doesn't need is a shrink.

That episode, and others like it, set me thinking about children and their fathers. As a nation, we are racked[4] by youth violence, overrun by gangs, guns and drugs. The great majority of youthful offenders are male, most without fathers involved in their lives in any useful way. Many have never even met their fathers.

What's become of the fathers of these boys? Where are they? Well, I can tell you where they're not. They're not at PTA meetings or piano recitals. They're not teaching Sunday school. You won't find them in the pediatrician's office, holding a sick child. You won't even see them in juvenile court, standing next to Junior as he awaits sentencing for burglary or assault. You might see a few of them in the supermarket, but not many. You will see a lot of women in these places—mothers and grandmothers—but you won't see many fathers.

So, if they're not in these places, where are the fathers? They are in diners and taverns, drinking, conversing, playing pool with other men. They are on golf courses, tennis courts, in bowling alleys, fishing on lakes and rivers. They are working in their jobs, many from early morning to late at night. Some are home watching television, out mowing the lawn or tuning up the car. In short, they are everywhere, except in the company of their children.

Of course there are men who do spend time with children, men who are covering for all those absentee fathers. The Little League coaches, Boy Scout leaders, Big Brothers and schoolteachers who value contact with children, who are investing in the next generation, sharing time and teaching skills. And there are many fathers who are less visible but no less valuable, those who quietly help with homework, baths, laundry and grocery shopping. Fathers who read to their children, drive them to ballet lessons, who cheer at soccer games. Fathers who are on the job. These are the real men of America, the ones holding society together. Every one of them is worth a dozen investment bankers, a boardroom full of corporate executives and all of the lawmakers west of the Mississippi.

Poverty prevention: What would happen if the truant[5] fathers of America began spending time with their children? It wouldn't eliminate world hunger, but it might save some families from sinking below the poverty line. It wouldn't bring peace to the Middle East, but it just might keep a few kids from trying to find a sense of belonging with their local street-corner gang. It might not defuse[6] the population bomb, but it just might prevent a few teenage pregnancies.

If these fathers were to spend more time with their children, it just might have an effect on the future of marriage and divorce. Not only do many boys lack a sense of how a man should behave; many girls don't know either, having little

---

3. futility: uselessness

4. racked: tortured or suffering from

5. truant: absent without permission

6. defuse: to make less dangerous

exposure themselves to healthy male-female relationships. With their fathers around, many young women might come to expect more than the myth that a man's chief purpose on earth is to impregnate them and then disappear. If that would happen, the next generation of absentee fathers might never come to pass.

Before her session ended, I tried to give this mother some hope. Maybe she 11 could interest her son in a sport: how about basketball or soccer? Any positive experience involving men or other boys would expose her son to teamwork, cooperation and friendly competition. But the boy was contemptuous[7] of my suggestions. "Those things are for dorks," he sneered. He couldn't wait to leave. I looked at his mother. I could see the embarrassment and hopelessness in her face. "Let's go, Ma," he said, more as a command than a request. I walked her out through the waiting room, full of women and children, mostly boys, of all ages. Her son was already in the parking lot. I shook her hand. "Good luck," I said, "Thank you," she replied, without conviction. As I watched her go, my heart, too was filled with a measure of hopelessness. But anger was there too, anger at the fathers of these boys. Anger at fathers who walk away from their children, leaving them feeling confused, rejected and full of suffering. What's to become of boys like this? What man will take an interest in them? I can think of only one kind—a judge.

DISCUSSION AND WRITING QUESTIONS

1. At both the beginning and end of this persuasive essay, Bacorn describes a mother and her 15-year-old son. Why does he focus on their story? Would the argument be as effective if he had begun with paragraph 4 and ended with paragraph 10?

2. Do you agree with the author that a boy needs "the fellowship of men" and "a man he can look up to" (paragraph 4)? Does this essay underestimate—or even insult—the millions of single mothers raising healthy sons?

3. In paragraphs 9 and 10, what positive consequences for boys and girls does Bacorn predict if truant fathers spent time with their children? Do you agree with his predictions, or is he exaggerating?

4. The author does not press to see the angry 15-year-old boy again, claiming that professional counseling for adolescent boys is a waste of time. What is your opinion about his decision?

WRITING ASSIGNMENTS

1. Playing sports can save some young men, writes Bacorn. What else could be done? Write an essay discussing other ways to help boys stay out of trouble and succeed. Visit **www.supportingoursons.org** or **www.fatherhood.org** for ideas.

2. Write about your own father's (or mother's) involvement in your upbringing. Was he (or she) an involved parent, an absentee parent, or somewhere in between? Based on your experience, what factors help a child become a healthy man or woman?

3. In a group of four or five classmates, study the following public service advertisement (PSA) recently released by the National Fatherhood Initiative. Can you identify its subject, audience, and purpose? Could this ad persuade some men to change their behavior? Why or why not? Use your notes from the group to plan and write an essay on fathers or mothers who can live at home but still be absentee.

---

7. contemptuous: feeling scorn or disdain

who are you spending your quality time with?

have you been a dad today?

AdCouncil.org   for more ideas call 800-790-DADS or visit www.fatherhood.org   National Fatherhood Initiative™

Two Ways to Belong in America

BHARATI MUKHERJEE

Bharati Mukherjee describes herself as "an American writer born in India." She often writes about immigrants struggling to make a home for themselves in America. Although her sister also moved to the United States, the two women hold different beliefs about who they are, what America owes them, and what they owe America. As the immigration debate grows louder and angrier, this article, first published in the *New York Times* in 1996, may shed light on some enduring issues.

This is a tale of two sisters from Calcutta, Mira and Bharati, who have lived in the United States for some thirty-five years, but who find themselves on different sides in the current debate over the status of immigrants. I am an American citizen and she is not. I am moved that thousands of long-term residents are finally taking the oath of citizenship. She is not.

Mira arrived in Detroit in 1960 to study child psychology and preschool education. I followed her a year later to study creative writing at the University of Iowa. When we left India, we were almost identical in appearance and attitude.

We dressed alike, in saris;[1] we expressed identical views on politics, social issues, love and marriage in the same Calcutta convent-school[2] accent. We would endure our two years in America, secure our degrees, then return to India to marry the grooms of our father's choosing.

Instead, Mira married an Indian student in 1962 who was getting his business administration degree at Wayne State University. They soon acquired the labor certifications necessary for the green card of hassle-free residence and employment.   3

Mira still lives in Detroit, works in the Southfield, Michigan school system, and has become nationally recognized for her contributions in the fields of preschool education and parent-teacher relationships. After 36 years as a legal immigrant in this country, she clings passionately to her Indian citizenship and hopes to go home to India when she retires.   4

In Iowa City in 1963, I married a fellow student, an American of Canadian parentage. Because of the accident of his North Dakota birth, I bypassed labor-certification requirements and the race-related "quota"[3] system that favored the applicant's country of origin over his or her merit. I was prepared for (and even welcomed) the emotional strain that came with marrying outside my ethnic community. In thirty-three years of marriage, we have lived in every part of North America. By choosing a husband who was not my father's selection, I was opting for fluidity,[4] self-invention, blue jeans and T-shirts, and renouncing three thousand years (at least) of caste-observant,[5] "pure culture" marriage in the Mukherjee family. My books have often been read as unapologetic (and in some quarters overenthusiastic) texts for cultural and psychological "mongrelization."[6] It's a word I celebrate.   5

Mira and I have stayed sisterly close by phone. In our regular Sunday morning conversations, we are unguardedly affectionate. I am her only blood relative on this continent. We expect to see each other through the looming crises of aging and ill health without being asked. Long before Vice President Gore's "Citizenship U.S.A." drive, we'd had our polite arguments over the ethics of retaining an overseas citizenship while expecting the permanent protection and economic benefits that come with living and working in America.   6

Like well-raised sisters, we never said what was really on our minds, but we probably pitied one another. She, for the lack of structure in my life, the erasure of Indianness, the absence of an unvarying daily core. I, for the narrowness of her perspective, her uninvolvement with the mythic depths or the superficial pop culture of this society. But, now, with the scapegoating[7] of "aliens" (documented or illegal) on the increase, and the targeting of long-term legal immigrants like Mira for new scrutiny and new self-consciousness, she and I find ourselves unable to maintain the same polite discretion. We were always unacknowledged adversaries, and we are now, more than ever, sisters.   7

"I feel used," Mira raged on the phone the other night. "I feel manipulated and discarded. This is such an unfair way to treat a person who was invited to stay and work here because of her talent. My employer went to the I.N.S. and petitioned for the labor certification. For over thirty years, I've invested my creativity and professional skills into the improvement of *this* country's preschool system. I've obeyed all the rules, I've paid my taxes, I love my work, I love my   8

---

1. saris: lightweight cloth garments worn by the women of India
2. convent school: a school run by a religious organization
3. quota: the maximum number that may be admitted
4. fluidity: ability to move easily
5. caste-observant: following the rules of rigid social class
6. mongrelization: mixing different breeds or races
7. scapegoating: unfairly blaming one person or group for the wrongs of others

students, I love the friends I've made. How dare America now change its rules in midstream? If America wants to make new rules curtailing benefits of legal immigrants, they should apply only to immigrants who arrive after those rules are already in place."

To my ears, it sounded like the description of a long-enduring, comfortable yet loveless marriage, without risk or recklessness. Have we the right to demand, and to expect, that we be loved? (That, to me is the subtext[8] of the arguments by immigration advocates.) My sister is an expatriate,[9] professionally generous and creative, socially courteous and gracious, and that's as far as her Americanization can go. She is here to maintain an identity, not to transform it.

I asked her if she would follow the example of others who have decided to become citizens because of the anti-immigration bills in Congress. And here, she surprised me. "If America wants to play the manipulative game, I'll play it too," she snapped. "I'll become a U.S. citizen for now, then change back to Indian when I'm ready to go home. I feel some kind of irrational attachment to India that I don't to America. Until all this hysteria against legal immigrants, I was totally happy. Having my green card meant I could visit any place in the world I wanted to and then come back to a job that's satisfying and that I do very well."

In one family, from two sisters alike as peas in a pod, there could not be a wider divergence[10] of immigrant experience. America spoke to me—I married it—I embraced the demotion[11] from expatriate aristocrat to immigrant nobody, surrendering those thousands of years of "pure culture," the saris, the delightfully accented English. She retained them all. Which of us is the freak?

Mira's voice, I realize, is the voice not just of the immigrant South Asian community but of an immigrant community of the millions who have stayed rooted in one job, one city, one house, one ancestral culture, one cuisine, for the entirety of their productive years. She speaks for greater numbers than I possibly can. Only the fluency of her English and the anger, rather than fear, born of confidence from her education, differentiate her from the seamstresses, the domestics, the technicians, the shop owners, the millions of hard-working but effectively silenced documented immigrants as well as their less fortunate "illegal" brothers and sisters.

Nearly twenty years ago, when I was living in my husband's ancestral homeland of Canada, I was always well-employed but never allowed to feel part of the local Quebec or larger Canadian society. Then, through a Green Paper that invited a national referendum[12] on the unwanted side effects of "nontraditional" immigration, the Government officially turned against its immigrant communities, particularly those from South Asia.

I felt then the same sense of betrayal that Mira feels now. I will never forget the pain of that sudden turning, and the casual racist outbursts the Green Paper elicited. That sense of betrayal had its desired effect and drove me, and thousands like me, from the country.

Mira and I differ, however, in the ways in which we hope to interact with the country that we have chosen to live in. She is happier to live in America as expatriate Indian than as an immigrant American. I need to feel like a part of the community I have adopted (as I tried to feel in Canada as well). I need to put roots down, to vote and make the difference that I can. The price that the immigrant willingly pays, and that the exile avoids, is the trauma of self-transformation.

---

8. subtext: unstated but implied message

9. expatriate: one who chooses to live in a foreign country, not his or her homeland

10. divergence: difference

11. demotion: reduction in status or rank

12. referendum: a proposal submitted for a public vote

DISCUSSION AND WRITING QUESTIONS

1. How do the title and first paragraph let readers know that this essay will compare and contrast? How are Mira and Bharati alike? How are they different?

2. How does Mukherjee view her decision to become an American citizen (paragraph 5)? With her oath, what did she accept and what did she give up?

3. In paragraph 7, she writes that she and her sister probably pitied each other. What did each pity about the other's life? What change made them feel more like allies and sisters?

4. Mukherjee's last paragraph states her view that immigrants who become citizens must pay a price: the "trauma of self-transformation." In your own words, explain what she means. Do you agree with her?

WRITING ASSIGNMENTS

1. Have you ever experienced a shock or change so radical that you had to transform yourself? Perhaps you immigrated, had a child, divorced, experienced a death, or won the lottery. Describe your process of transformation. What did you gain and lose?

2. In a small group, discuss this topic: *Are immigrants still important to American society? Why or why not?* What positive things do they contribute? What problems can immigration pose? Jot ideas for a paper explaining your answers to these questions.

3. Compare and contrast yourself and a sibling or family member with whom you share important similarities but from whom you differ in a significant way.

Forever Young

FIROOZEH DUMAS

Firoozeh Dumas moved with her to family to America in 1972, when she was seven years old. Her book *Funny in Farsi: A Memoir of Growing up Iranian in America* is filled with humorous tales of learning to assimilate into Western culture. As this story of her father's eightieth birthday party shows, people of differing ethnic heritages may not be so different after all.

On the fourth night of the cruise, we all waited in the main restaurant, Versailles, while my brother escorted my parents from their cabin. The restaurant, complete with gilded[1] columns, sun-patterned wallpaper and enormous chandeliers, highlighted all that has remained in Western culture from the reign of Louis XIV,[2] mainly the words "faux"[3] and "buffet." 1

As soon as my father showed up, we started singing "Happy Birthday" in English. It would have been more natural for us to sing in Persian, but if you are 2

---

1. gilded: coated with a thin layer of gold
2. Louis XIV: French king from 1643 to 1715, called the Sun King
3. faux: fake or artificial

part of a large Middle Eastern contingent[4] these days, you're already scaring people. Add to that a loud song with guttural[5] sounds and clapping, and you have passengers speed-dialing the Department of Homeland Security.

Once we finished singing, my father looked rather pleased. That's when another passenger approached my father, introduced himself as Chuck and said that it was also *his* 80th birthday. "I am not 80." my father declared. This left Chuck a bit confused. My father was, after all, wearing a hat declaring "80!"

"I am 76," my father continued. "Maybe 75." At this point, Chuck left.

My father, Kazem, was born in Ahwaz Iran. That much he knows for sure. His birth date—the year, the month, the day—is anybody's guess. Whenever a child was born in my father's family, my grandfather, Javad, recited a prayer and noted the birth date in the family Koran.[6] The system worked without a glitch until someone lost the Koran. Not a big deal. Back then, you needed only the year of your birth, exact or approximate, to obtain a passport. And birthday parties did not exist.

When my father got an engineering job in America in the early seventies, the immigration forms required a birth date. He picked March 18, my mother's birthday. "Forms will be easier to fill out," he said. "And if I ever forget my birthday, I can ask your mom." (Needless to say, my mother resents the fact that my father is a birthday squatter.[7])

When immigrants come to America, they often have the opportunity to develop in ways not possible in their native lands, perhaps becoming lawyers or owners of Jiffy Lubes. For my father, America meant having perfect strangers sing him "Happy Birthday." It all started innocently one day when my brother told our waitress in Bob's Big Boy that it was my father's birthday. My father had never in his lifetime blown out a birthday candle or had anyone sing him "Happy Birthday."

When the kind waitress appeared with a free slice of cake, a candle and two other waitresses and a busboy as backup singers, a dormant[8] gene awakened. My father's face went from confusion to elation.[9] He was shocked. From then on, several times a year, my father made a point of telling waitresses that it was his birthday. His favorite recurring birthday spot was a local Mexican chain with a particularly rousing rendition of "Feliz Compleaños," complete with maracas[10] and a guitar. As his birthday sombrero collection amassed, so did our objections. "Aren't you embarrassed?" I often asked.

"I have a party deficit,"[11] he always said.

"But it's not your birthday," I reminded him.

"It *could* be," he said.

Then when my father entered his mid-seventies, something strange happened. He decided that his birth certificate was wrong and that he was definitely two, if not four or five, years younger than previously thought. We laughed, but he was adamant.[12] "I can still eat spicy foods before bedtime. No *way* is that late seventies."

---

4. contingent: group

5. guttural: having a harsh, grating quality

6. Koran: the holy book of Islam

7. squatter: a person who occupies a piece of land without owing it

8. dormant: inactive or asleep

9. elation: joy

10. maracas: percussion instruments, hollow gourd rattles often played in pairs

11. deficit: deficiency or lack

12. adamant: stubborn, unyielding

As his eightieth birthday approached, we wanted to celebrate in a place where 13 he would feel too self-conscious to object to the fact of his age. That is why 47 members of my extended family ended up on an Alaskan cruise, with my unsuspecting father in tow. I was responsible for buying the hats before the cruise. I soon discovered that preprinted hats go up to age "50 and Fabulous!" One place had "60 and Sexy!" but nothing higher; "80 and . . . What Was I Saying?" would have been perfect for my father, but that's a winning slogan not yet widely available. I finally purchased hats declaring "30!" With the help of my willing 10-year-old daughter and a permanent marker, the hats become "80!"

None of my aunts wanted to wear the conical hat. "I didn't do my hair and put 14 on hair spray for this," Aunt Fatima declared, getting the rest of my aunts riled up. "He won't even admit he's 80!" added Aunt Sedigeh. As our ship glided past majestic glaciers, a sight that should impress anyone born in the arid[13] climate of Ahwaz, my aunts and uncles continued discussing the hats. My aunts added that if they had bald spots like their brothers', *then* they would wear them. I understood their opposition. Why flatten the do for someone who is aging backward while they, the now much older siblings, age forward every single year?

That evening, my father received not just a free slice but an entire white cake 15 covered with pink roses. There are benefits to turning 80, even if he would never admit it.

DISCUSSION AND WRITING QUESTIONS

1. The author chooses vivid details that help the reader "see" the cruise ship and the birthday party. Were any details especially effective? Why?

2. In paragraph 2, Ms. Dumas says that if her "large Middle Eastern contingent" began singing in Persian, they would "have passengers speed-dialing the Department of Homeland Security." Is she being serious or funny?

3. How does the author feel about her father? How can you tell? Provide details that support your opinion.

4. Do any of Firoozeh's relatives remind you of any of your relatives? In what ways?

WRITING ASSIGNMENTS

1. Write a humorous (or serious) account of one of your own family celebrations, traditions, or stories.

2. Did you or anyone in your family immigrate to the United States? Focus on one event or aspect of the immigration experience and try to capture it in words. You might want to submit your completed essay to this online collection of "immigrant journeys": **http://www.immigrantjourneys.com/**.

3. Do you know someone whose age does not match his or her attitudes, appearance, or pursuits? Choose a person who acts younger (or older) than his or her years. Support your main idea with specific beliefs, actions, or physical details that are unusual for a person of that age.

---

13. arid: dry

On the Rez

IAN FRAZIER

> Do you think a single act of courage or heroism can reverse decades of misunderstanding? In his book *On the Rez,* Ian Frazier tells the true story of SuAnne Marie Big Crow, who faced a taunting crowd and decided to answer its jeers with a surprising gift.

Some people who live in the cities and towns near reservations treat their Indian neighbors decently; some don't. In Denver and Minneapolis and Rapid City police have been known to harass Indian teenagers and rough up Indian drunks and needlessly stop and search Indian cars. Local banks whose deposits include millions in tribal funds sometimes charge Indians higher interest rates than they charge whites. Gift shops near reservations sell junky caricature[1] Indian pictures and dolls, and until not long ago beer coolers had signs on them that said INDIAN POWER. In a big discount store in a reservation-border town a white clerk observes a lot of Indians waiting at the checkout and remarks, "Oh, they're Indians—they're used to standing in line." Some people in South Dakota hate Indians, unapologetically, and will tell you why; in their voices you can hear a particular American meanness that is centuries old.

When teams from Pine Ridge play non-Indian teams, the question of race is always there. When Pine Ridge is the visiting team, usually the hosts are courteous and the players and fans have a good time. But Pine Ridge coaches know that occasionally at away games their kids will be insulted, their fans will feel unwelcome, the host gym will be dense with hostility, and the referees will call fouls on Indian players every chance they get. Sometimes in a game between Indian and non-Indian teams the difference in race becomes an important and distracting part of the event.

One place where Pine Ridge teams used to get harassed regularly was the high school gymnasium in Lead, South Dakota. Lead is a town of about 3,200 northwest of the reservation, in the Black Hills. It is laid out among the mines that are its main industry, and low, wooded mountains hedge it around. The brick high school building is set into a hillside. The school's only gym in those days was small, with tiers of gray-painted concrete on which the spectator benches descended from just below the steel-beamed roof to the very edge of the basketball court—an arrangement that greatly magnified the interior noise.

In the fall of 1988 the Pine Ridge Lady Thorpes[2] went to Lead to play a basketball game. SuAnne was a full member of the team by then. She was a freshman, fourteen years old. Getting ready in the locker room, the Pine Ridge girls could hear the din from the Lead fans. They were yelling fake Indian war cries, a "*woo-woo-woo*" sound. The usual plan for the pre-game warm-up was for the visiting team to run onto the court in a line, take a lap or two around the floor, shoot some baskets, and then go to their bench at courtside. After that the home team would come out and do the same, and then the game would begin. Usually the Thorpes lined up for their entry more or less according to height, which meant that senior Doni De Cory, one of the tallest, went first. As the team waited in the hallway leading from the locker room, the heckling got louder. Some fans were waving food stamps, a reference to the reservation's receiving federal aid. Others yelled,

---

1. caricature: cartoon
2. Lady Thorpes: named for Native American Jim Thorpe, one of the greatest athletes of all time

"Where's the cheese?"—the joke being that if Indians were lining up, it must be to get commodity cheese. The Lead high school band had joined in, with fake Indian drumming and a fake Indian tune. Doni De Cory looked out the door and told her teammates, "I can't handle this." SuAnne quickly offered to go first in her place. She was so eager that Doni became suspicious. "Don't embarrass us," Doni told her. SuAnne said, "I won't. I won't embarrass you." Doni gave her the ball, and SuAnne stood first in line.

She came running onto the court dribbling the basketball, with her teammates 5 running behind. On the court the noise was deafening. SuAnne went right down the middle and suddenly stopped when she got to center court. Her teammates were taken by surprise, and some bumped into each other. Coach Zimiga, at the rear of the line, did not know why they had stopped. SuAnne turned to Doni De Cory and tossed her the ball. Then she stepped into the jump-ball circle at center court, facing the Lead fans. She unbuttoned her warm-up jacket, took it off, draped it over her shoulders, and began to do the Lakota shawl dance. SuAnne knew all the traditional dances (she had competed in many powwows as a little girl), and the dance she chose is a young woman's dance, graceful and modest and show-offy all at the same time. "I couldn't believe it—she was powwowin', like, 'Get down!'" Doni De Cory recalls. "And then she started to sing." SuAnne began to sing in Lakota, swaying back and forth in the jump-ball circle, doing the shawl dance, using her warm-up jacket for a shawl. The crowd went completely silent. "All that stuff the Lead fans were yelling—it was like she *reversed* it somehow," a teammate says. In the sudden quiet all they could hear was her Lakota song. SuAnne dropped her jacket, took the ball from Doni De Cory, and ran a lap around the court dribbling expertly and fast. The audience began to cheer and applaud. She sprinted to the basket, went up in the air, and laid the ball through the hoop, with the fans cheering loudly now. Of course, Pine Ridge went on to win the game.

For the Oglala, what SuAnne did that day almost immediately took on the status of 6 myth. People from Pine Ridge who witnessed it still describe it in terms of awe and disbelief. Amazement swept through the younger kids when they heard. "I was, like, '*What* did she just do?'" recalls her cousin Angie Big Crow, an eighth grader at the time. All over the reservation people told and retold the story of SuAnne at Lead. Anytime the subject of SuAnne came up when I was talking to people on Pine Ridge, I would always ask if they had heard about what she did at Lead, and always the answer was a smile and a nod—"Yeah, I was there," or "Yeah, I heard about that." To the unnumbered big and small slights of local racism that the Oglala have known all their lives SuAnne's exploit made an emphatic reply.

Back in the days when Lakota war parties still fought battles against other 7 tribes and the Army, no deed of war was more honored than the act of counting coup. To "count coup" means to touch an armed enemy in full possession of his powers with a special stick called a coup stick, or with the hand. The touch is not a blow, and serves only to indicate how close to the enemy you came. As an act of bravery, counting coup was regarded as greater than killing an enemy in single combat, greater than taking a scalp or horses or any prize. Counting coup was an act of almost abstract courage, of pure playfulness taken to the most daring extreme. Very likely, to do it and survive brought an exhilaration to which nothing else could compare. In an ancient sense that her Oglala kin could recognize, SuAnne counted coup on the fans of Lead.

And yet this coup was an act not of war but of peace. SuAnne's coup strike 8 was an offering, an invitation. It gave the hecklers the best interpretation, as if their silly, mocking chants were meant only in good will. It showed that their fake Indian songs were just that—fake—and that the real thing was better, as real things usually are. We Lakota have been dancing like this for centuries, the dance said; we've been doing the shawl dance since long before you came, before you got on the boat in Glasgow or Bremerhaven, before you stole this land, and we're still doing it today. And isn't it pretty, when you see how it's supposed to be done? Because finally, what SuAnne proposed was to invite us—us onlookers in the stands, namely, the non-Lakota rest of this country—to dance too. She was in the Lead gym to play, and she invited us all to play. The symbol she used to include us was the warm-up jacket. Everyone in America has a warm-up jacket. I've got one, probably so do you, so did (no doubt) many of the fans at Lead. By using the warm-up jacket as a shawl in her impromptu shawl dance she made Lakota relatives of us all.

"It was funny," Doni De Cory says, "but after that game the relationship between Lead and us was tremendous. When we played Lead again, the games were really good, and we got to know some of the girls on the team. Later, when we went to a tournament and Lead was there, we were hanging out with the Lead girls and eating pizza with them. We got to know some of their parents, too. What SuAnne did made a lasting impression and changed the whole situation with us and Lead. We found out there are some really good people in Lead."   9

America is a leap of the imagination. From its beginning people have had only a persistent idea of what a good country should be. The idea involves freedom, equality, justice, and the pursuit of happiness; nowadays most of us probably could not describe it much more clearly than that. The truth is, it always has been a bit of a guess. No one has ever known for sure whether a country based on such an idea is really possible, but again and again we have leaped toward the idea and hoped. What SuAnne Big Crow demonstrated in the Lead high school gym is that making the leap is the whole point. The idea does not truly live unless it is expressed by an act; the country does not live unless we make the leap from our tribe or focus group or gated community or demographic[3] and land on the shaky platform of that idea of a good country which all kinds of different people share.   10

DISCUSSION AND WRITING QUESTIONS

1. How was the Pine Ridge girls' basketball team usually treated when they played games at Lead? What larger problem between Indians and non-Indians in South Dakota was reflected in this behavior?

2. SuAnne's performance of the Lakota shawl dance to a silent gymnasium full of people is described in powerful detail. What descriptive details does the author include to make that scene come alive for the reader?

3. What did the students at Lead discover during SuAnne's dance that caused them to change their opinions about Lakota Indians? What made the Pine Ridge players decide that "there are some really good people in Lead" (paragraph 9)?

4. The author calls SuAnne's dance an act of courage. What was courageous about her dance that day? Consider in your answer her age, the history between Pine Ridge and Lead, and the behavior of the audience before the game.

---

3. demographic: group of similar people

WRITING ASSIGNMENTS

1. SuAnne Marie Big Crow's actions that day made her a hero for the people of the Pine Ridge reservation. With a group of classmates, brainstorm the qualities that make someone a hero. Then, select two or three of these qualities and write an essay defining heroism. You may wish to illustrate with an anecdote of your own about someone who performed like a hero in a difficult situation.

2. How can we promote tolerance in the world? Think of a conflict that you have experienced or heard about—perhaps between two ethnic groups, gangs, families, or individuals. What specific actions would you recommend to help promote understanding and tolerance between the two sides? Explore the web site **www.tolerance.org** for more ideas.

3. Frazier says that equality and justice do not live until they are expressed in action—until "we make the leap from our tribe or group" into a larger community that "different people share" (paragraph 10). Write an essay in which you describe someone who has made such a leap, such as reaching out to an outsider, standing up against a stereotype, or moving to a new country or community.

Four Types of Courage

KAREN CASTELLUCCI COX

"In these times when many students wonder anxiously what the future will bring, courage may be more important than ever," claims Karen Castellucci Cox, a professor of English at City College of San Francisco. In this inspiring essay, she examines four different kinds of courage first set forth by psychologist Rollo May, applying his categories to contemporary challenges.

Most people think they know what courage is. When asked to name a courageous person, many pick a Hollywood hero like Jack Bauer, the impossibly capable action star of television's *24*. Others choose real-life heroes, often those who confront great physical danger like firefighters or soldiers. Indeed, our culture teaches us to view courage as a kind of Rambo-style bravado. Consider these cases, however: Chardee, a battered wife who finally leaves her husband; Luis, who goes against his family's wishes to pursue his dream of becoming an actor; Ann, who cares for a father with Alzheimer's disease, patiently having the same conversations day after day yet infusing their small apartment with good cheer and kindness. Do any of these people exhibit courage? In his classic book *The Courage to Create*, American psychologist Rollo May invites us to examine more deeply the quality he believes is essential to a meaningful life. Courage, he insists, is not just one emotion among others, but the foundation on which all other virtues and values rest. May divides courage into four distinct types—physical, social, moral, and creative.

Physical courage is familiar to most people: the ability to confront bodily pain or danger with self-possession, usually for a greater goal or good. For example, when Hurricane Katrina hit the Gulf Coast in August 2005, causing devastating floods in New Orleans, local police raced to curb looting and rescue the stranded. These officers had no experience facing such a catastrophic emergency and little training in search-and-rescue. Yet they risked their lives to save desperate and angry citizens amid surging water, threat of disease, and even sniper fire. The

1

2

pressure proved too much for some; several dozen deserted. But the truly remarkable fact was that 1,700 men and women continued to report to work each day, exhibiting the brand of physical courage that May believes capable of transforming society.

Physical courage has lost much of its usefulness in contemporary life, May cautions. Whereas our society once applauded the self-reliant pioneer, now we egg on the Tony Sopranos,[1] who justify their violence with talk of disrespect or frontier justice. What masquerades as physical courage in television, films, music videos, and games is often little better than the bully's swagger on the playground. A more productive physical courage, like that of the New Orleans officers, puts the body on the line, not to overpower or harm others, but to serve and protect them.

The second category, social courage, is the type demanded of us in daily life. This is the courage to have meaningful relationships, to dare to reveal who we really are, to tell the truth in public forums despite the risks. The child who faces peer disapproval to befriend an unpopular classmate demonstrates social courage. The 55-year-old woman who goes back for her college degree though she fears she will feel out of place demonstrates social courage. The employee who volunteers to give a business presentation despite a lifelong terror of public speaking demonstrates social courage. Marriage, parenthood, any relationship that calls for an engagement of the heart and mind invites this brand of courage. May writes, "It is easier in our society to be naked physically than to be naked psychologically or spiritually." But when one chooses to open oneself, despite real risks of embarrassment, rejection, or worse, the reward is the chance of making a profound connection in a world of superficial ones.

Moral courage may exact an even heavier toll. The one who exhibits moral courage usually recognizes the suffering of others and decides to help despite the consequences. Aung San Suu Kyi is such a figure. The daughter of a diplomat and a general who was assassinated after negotiating Burma's independence from Great Britain in 1947, Suu Kyi was inspired by her parents to spend her life promoting democracy and human rights in Burma. When an oppressive military gained control of the government in 1988, Suu Kyi stepped into a leadership position, helping to found a democratic party and speaking publicly throughout Burma. Her inspiring vision drew huge crowds, and when her popularity became a threat, she was followed, harassed, and arrested. Suu Kyi spent a total of eleven years under house arrest, a sacrifice that meant living apart from her grown sons and not being able to visit her dying husband in England. Her moral courage was recognized when she won the Nobel Peace Prize in 1991. Beloved by Burmese citizens and admired worldwide, she continues to lead Burma's National League for Democracy today.

Moral courage is found as well in ordinary people who take a stand. Between April and July 1994, nearly one million people were killed in a mass genocide[2] in Rwanda; Hutu extremists murdered their Tutsi[3] neighbors while the international community looked the other way. But one man, Paul Rusesabagina, did not look the other way. The son of farmers and a modest hotel manager, Rusesabagina at first wanted to protect only his wife and children. Gradually, however, he began to comprehend the scope of the brutality. He devised a way to hide Tutsi refugees in his hotel until they could be carried to safety. In all, Rusesabagina is responsible for single-handedly saving the lives of 1,268 people. His story, told in the film *Hotel Rwanda*, is reminder that moral courage can be found wherever a person chooses action over apathy.[4]

---

1. Tony Soprano: lead character in *The Sopranos*, a dramatic HBO series about a Mafia family

2. genocide: the systematic and planned execution of an entire national, racial, or ethnic group

3. Hutu and Tutsi: two of the three ethnic groups that occupy Rwanda and Burundi

4. apathy: lack of interest or concern

The final category is creative courage, "discovering new forms, patterns" and   7
solutions that no one has yet imagined and that might even promote a better future. A writer, musician, or inventor shows creative courage when he or she re-
jects the status quo,[5] seeing beyond what *is* to create something new. President
Lincoln called Harriet Beecher Stowe, the "little woman who wrote the book that
started this great war." Her 1851 novel *Uncle Tom's Cabin,* while it didn't actually
provoke the Civil War, created a groundswell[6] of public outrage against slavery
through its detailed and moving descriptions. Another example is *Rent,* one of the
longest running shows on Broadway. *Rent* was the first musical to address the
HIV health crisis through life-affirming personal stories aimed at the general public.
An uplifting musical form helped the public face difficult issues.

Not just the arts, but all professions, require creative courage. Tim Berners-   8
Lee, for instance, is credited with inventing the World Wide Web, maybe the most
important innovation of our time. In 1991, he set up the first web site and began
networking his computer with others around the country. Concerned that patent-
ing his discovery would make the growing Web too expensive for general use,
Berners-Lee chose to keep the technology public. In doing so, he passed up a personal fortune and risked mockery for his "foolish" insistence that the World Wide
Web should belong to everyone.

Of course, the four types of courage sometimes overlap. Tobacco executive Jef-   9
frey Wigand was motivated by moral courage when he revealed in the 1990s that Big
Tobacco[7] was hiding the truth about nicotine causing cancer. This whistle blower[8]
demonstrated physical courage as well, refusing to be silenced by veiled threats of
violence. Wigand's social courage was tested as the case hit the media, the business
community shunned[9] him, and his own family deserted him. And when his old life
was shattered, this man somehow found the creative courage to build a new one.

"Courage has many faces," writes Katherine Martin, the author of *Women of*   10
Courage. "We lose much when we dismiss it in ourselves, thinking we don't measure up." The classification that May sets forth invites us to find and cultivate
courage in our own lives, to ask what blocks our daring, and then to stand and try.

DISCUSSION AND WRITING QUESTIONS

1. How does the author classify courage in this essay? That is, what four categories
   of courage does she identify? What is the source of these categories?

2. Provide one additional example of each type of courage. Draw your illustrations
   from your own or loved ones' experiences, the news, history, or this textbook.

3. What are the most common obstacles to behaving courageously? Fear? Apathy?
   Selfishness? What, in your opinion, most often "blocks our daring" (paragraph 10)?

4. A street campaign called "Stop Snitchin" is urging people in urban neighborhoods not to speak to police investigating local crimes—not to share tips and
   information that might solve those crimes. T-shirts, hip hop albums, and other
   marketing devices tell people to keep silent and sometimes threaten them.
   Does it take courage to stop snitching or to keep talking? Why? (To learn
   more, search online for "stop snitchin.")

---

5. status quo: existing condition or state of affairs

6. groundswell: a sudden gathering of force

7. Big Tobacco: nickname for the three most powerful tobacco companies in the United States

8. whistle blower: an employee or member of an organization who exposes misconduct or corruption

9. shunned: rejected, ignored

The "Stop Snitchin" compaign urges people not to cooperate with police. Does it take courage to stop snitching or keep talking?

WRITING ASSIGNMENTS

1. Discuss a time when you or someone close to you displayed one or more of the four types of courage described in this essay.

2. Write a classification essay about another concept, emotion, or term—such as success, friends, mistakes, or lies—and break it into different types or "faces."

3. Are you facing right now a situation or problem that will require courage to confront and correct? First, state the problem. Has a lack of courage in the past made it worse? If you applied true courage to the situation, what might be the outcome?

Cell Yell: Thanks for (Not) Sharing

ERIC A. TAUB

Once considered a luxury, cell phones have become a common and sometimes obnoxious presence in our daily lives—whether we own one or not. In this *New York Times* article, Eric Taub considers the reasons why cell phones—and their users—so often intrude on the people around them.

With just five minutes to takeoff, the young man across the aisle on the Baltimore-bound flight whipped out his cellphone and began a hurried and boisterous conversation, explaining the fine points of marketing his new Christmas-gift Web site to an unseen underling. With glazed eyes staring at the seat in front of him, the executive unconsciously pounded his foot in rhythm to his conversation, oblivious[1] to the 15 surrounding passengers glaring at this human loudspeaker in seat 23B.

1. oblivious: unaware

The harried young executive was engaged in one of the more despised forms 2
of mobile-phone behavior. In the industry it is called cell yell—a tendency of
many cellphone users to speak into their phones more loudly than necessary, un-
wittingly involving surrounding strangers in their personal business.

Cell yell has created a subculture of cell-yell haters. The phenomenon has 3
given rise to a Web site (www.cellmanners.com). An artist, John Detrich, offered a
cell-yell-themed illustration for sale online. And The Register, a British Web site devoted to technology, reported that a mobile phone user in Germany died two years
ago after a beer-garden brawl over his lack of cellular civility.

It is too simplistic to put the blame for this antisocial behavior strictly on tech- 4
nology, social scientists say, because the way society uses new inventions both
defines and reflects the existing culture. In the 1950s, people were used to the privacy of enclosed phone booths when making calls in public places. If cellphones
had been invented then, people would probably have jumped into those same
booths to use them. Today, with more mobile, informal and open societies, many
in Western countries relish the idea of speaking in open spaces, oblivious to the
presence of others, and often in too loud a voice.

Mobile phone design doesn't help temper that arch behavior. Unlike standard 5
corded phones, cellphones provide little in the way of aural[2] feedback; it has long
been known that if you can hear yourself through the earpiece, you are better able
to keep your voice properly modulated. (That's why the hard of hearing often
speak more loudly than others.) Because the mouthpiece of the typical cellphone
barely extends to the cheek, many users act, consciously or not, as if they have to
shout to be heard.

"Cellphones are so small that people don't trust the technology to work," said 6
Timo Kopomaa, a social scientist at the University of Technology in Helsinki and author of a study on cellphone behavior. That is one reason Motorola makes phones
that flip open, according to a company executive: to give people the illusion that the
phone is bigger and the microphone is closer to the mouth.

Add to that loud street sounds, plus the relative novelty of being able to 7
speak to anyone anywhere, and suddenly throngs[3] are shouting above the ambient[4] noise in public squares, restaurants and post offices as they become en-
grossed in personal conversations, consequently "privatizing the public space,"
Dr. Kopomaa said. By doing so, he said, they ignore the needs of the nonphon-
ing public, "denying others the privacy they selfishly appropriate for their own
use."

Perversely, many onlookers find it difficult to withdraw attention from the 8
unwanted cellular intrusion. The ringing phone has long taken precedence over a
conversation between two people in the same physical space; an unanswered
phone expresses urgency and creates tension for the listener.

A ringing cellphone is perceived as even more important than a ringing tradi- 9
tional phone. Sounding in public, it "spreads tension to all those within earshot,
yet because it's not for them, they're powerless to answer the call," said Dr. Sadie
Plant, a researcher in Birmingham, England, who was commissioned by Motorola
to study cultural differences in cellphone use.

Some cellphone owners prominently display even cellphones not in use, for 10
their presence alone creates tension, as bystanders wonder if they are soon going
to ring, Dr. Plant said. Users also often engage in "stage-phoning," making unimportant calls in public just to impress others.

---

2. aural: heard

3. throngs: crowds

4. ambient: surrounding

Dr. Plant found individuals who actually enjoyed listening to strangers' cell 11
calls; a soap opera was created, but one with only half the information available.
It was up to the eavesdropper to fill in the unheard party's responses with fantasy
dialogue. Others found it obnoxious, since they are neither fully admitted to nor
excluded from that cellphone user's world.

The public cellphone user creates what Dr. Kopomaa calls a "black hole" as 12
the user psychologically withdraws from his immediate surroundings to focus on
the call. At the same time, others are forced to suspend their own activities,
whether they were talking with the cellphone user or trying to concentrate on
their own affairs.

"People are forced to remain present both physically and mentally," Dr. 13
Kopomaa wrote in "The City in Your Pocket," a Finnish study of cellphone culture. Since a phone conversation by its nature is the opposite of public speaking,
surrounding people are "disgusted by this forced eavesdropping," he theorized.

Cellphone users tend to answer their phones quickly, but not because they are 14
concerned about annoying their fellow citizens. Rather, a rapid response to a ring
shows bystanders that the users have "telecredibility," Dr. Kopomaa said. They
have mastered this new technology, and they do not have to fumble to figure out
how to answer it.

When Dr. Kopomaa recently discussed the implications of his study in an in- 15
terview on his cellphone while riding a ferry from Finland to Sweden, he did
what few other cellphone users do: he retreated into the ship's bathroom for privacy. In doing so, Dr. Kopomaa, 45, betrayed his age; studies indicate that young
Western people see the cellphone, and the receipt of cellphone calls, as a symbol
of virility and social importance, and therefore something to be flaunted.

In Dr. Plant's view, the cellphone has become a psychosexual[5] symbol of per- 16
formance. When mixed couples dine in restaurants, for example, it is more likely
that the male will place his phone on the table and the female will leave hers in
her purse, according to Dr. Plant. When two women dine together, both tend to
keep them out of sight. But if one woman places her phone on the table, the other
will probably follow suit.

Dr. Plant found this tendency toward display to be as true in Chicago as in 17
London. Indeed, while cell boorishness[6] is not confined to one country, certain
practices are culture-specific. In China, cellphone owners prominently carry them
in crocheted or silk bags, Dr. Plant said, while Japanese users often customize
their phones with stick-on designs and graphically distinctive cases. In many
countries, texting—sending short, coded text messages to another cell user—has
become the communication method of choice, especially for adolescents. It offers
the socially shy the anonymity and immediacy of e-mail.

"Boys can ask girls out by sending a text message, without having to hear the 18
disappointment in their voices," Dr. Plant said. "And I've observed many noncom-
municative teenage boys become much more communicative thanks to texting."

But even where texting is used as a nonintrusive way to communicate, it 19
seems it is not being used enough, judging from the anti-cellphone backlash. A
bagel shop in Westlake Village, Calif., banned the use of cellphones while ordering last year because customers routinely asked for the wrong food when they
were busy jabbering. To stem the jangle of ringing cellphones, Cingular Wireless
is erecting kiosks[7] at 100 Loews movie theaters as a sort of lobby-based cellphone
purgatory where users will be encouraged to place and receive any calls.

---

5. psychosexual: perceived as sexual

6. boorishness: rudeness

7. kiosks: small booths

"People are very upset when they're forced to hear the results of a stranger's [20] medical tests," said Carol Page, a Boston public relations consultant and founder of CellManners.com. The site has so far recruited three "cell spies," volunteers in Boston, San Francisco and Washington who report on bad cellular behavior—like the man who insisted on phoning while using the urinal, or the wedding guest whose phone went off between the words "I" and "do."

As a new consensus[8] develops over the use of cellphones, perhaps the fear of [21] stigma,[9] rather than rules and laws, will do the most to turn the disruptive tide. In Finland, Dr. Kopomaa has noticed that people already use cellphones more often in casual restaurants than in expensive ones. And when they do, they now call not from their table but from outside the establishment, sharing the space with society's other shunned antisocial group of addicts, cigarette smokers.

DISCUSSION AND WRITING QUESTIONS

1. How does the author define "cell yell" (paragraph 2)? What changes in society since the 1950s does the author suggest account for the way people use cell phones today?

2. How does mobile phone design contribute to bad cell phone manners? What part does the cell phone user's sense of self-importance play?

3. Eavesdroppers on cell phone conversations experience various reactions, both positive and negative. According to the author, what are some of these reactions and how do people listening against their will handle their strong feelings?

4. Based on the author's examples, what are the rude cell behaviors that bother people the most? What behaviors bother *you* the most? You might wish to share with the class a humorous or outrageous illustration of bad cell manners that you have encountered.

WRITING ASSIGNMENTS

1. Write an essay in which you argue for or against having a "designated outcast zone" for cell talkers in restaurants, theaters, or other places—the way many establishments now isolate smokers. Develop your thesis with two or three clear supporting points.

2. Is the rudeness of cell phone users just a symptom of a society that has become less considerate and more self-centered? With a group of classmates, brainstorm other possible "symptoms" of this trend. Some ideas might include rude clerks and customers, aggressive drivers, or the dying art of thank-you notes. Then select one of these and write an essay in which you suggest ways to reverse the trend.

3. E-mail is another technology that some people use inconsiderately or even abusively. For instance, some people forward jokes many times a day, and many advertisers send "spam"—ads and e-mail junk. Write an essay in which you suggest rules of web etiquette for online mail. You may wish to look up "netiquette"—the new word for rules to govern online behavior.

---

8. consensus: general agreement
9. stigma: a mark of disgrace

Homeward Bound

JANET WU

At age twelve, American-born Janet Wu learned that her grandmother was still alive in China. From their first meeting, despite the miles and differences separating them, the two developed a powerful bond. Their story underscores the importance of staying connected to our ancestors and our heritage. Janet Wu is television news anchor/reporter for WHDH-TV, Boston.

My grandmother has bound feet. Cruelly tethered[1] since her birth, they are like bonsai trees,[2] miniature versions of what should have been. She is a relic[3] even in China, where foot binding was first banned more than 80 years ago when the country could no longer afford a population that had to be carried. Her slow, delicate hobble betrays her age and the status she held and lost.

My own size 5 feet are huge in comparison. The marks and callouses they bear come from running and jumping, neither of which my grandmother has ever done. The difference between our feet reminds me of the incredible history we hold between us like living bookends. We stand like sentries[4] on either side of a vast gulf.

For most of my childhood, I didn't even know she existed. My father was a young man when he left his family's village in northern China, disappearing into the chaos of the Japanese invasion and the Communist revolution that followed. He fled to Taiwan and eventually made his way to America, alone. To me, his second child, it seemed he had no family or history other than his American-born wife and four children. I didn't know that he had been writing years of unanswered letters to China.

I was still a young girl when he finally got a response, and with it the news that his father and six of his seven siblings had died in those years of war and revolution. But the letter also contained an unexpected blessing: somehow his mother had survived. So 30 years after he left home, and in the wake of President Nixon's visit, my father gathered us up and we rushed to China to find her.

I saw my grandmother for the very first time when I was 12. She was almost 80, surprisingly alien and shockingly small. I searched her wrinkled face for something familiar, some physical proof we belonged to each other. She stared at me the same way. Did she feel cheated, I wondered, by the distance, by the time we had not spent together? I did. With too many lost years to reclaim, we had everything and nothing to say. She politely listened as I struggled with scraps of formal Chinese and smiled as I fell back on "Wo bu dong" ("I don't understand you"). And yet we communicated something strange and beautiful. I found it easy to love this person I had barely met.

The second time I saw her I was 23, arriving in China on an indulgent[5] post-graduate-school adventure, with a Caucasian boyfriend in tow. My grandmother sat on my hotel bed, shrunken and wise, looking as if she belonged in a museum case. She stroked my asymmetrically[6] cropped hair. I touched her feet, and her

---

1. tethered: tied
2. bonsai trees: dwarf trees forced to grow in small pots
3. relic: an object or fragment from the past
4. sentries: guards
5. indulgent: whimsical, unnecessary
6. asymmetrically: unevenly

face contorted with the memory of her childhood pain. "You are lucky," she said. We both understood that she was thinking of far more than the bindings that long ago made her cry. I wanted to share even the smallest part of her life's journey, but I could not conceive of surviving a dynasty[7] and a revolution, just as she could not imagine my life in a country she had never seen. In our mutual isolation of language and experience, we could only gaze in wonder, mystified that we had come to be sitting together.

I last saw her almost five years ago. At 95, she was even smaller, and her frailty frightened me. I was painfully aware that I probably would never see her again, that I would soon lose this person I never really had. So I mentally logged every second we spent together and jockeyed with my siblings for the chance to hold her hand or touch her shoulder. Our departure date loomed like some kind of sentence. And when it came, she broke down, her face bowed into her gnarled[8] hands. I went home, and with resignation[9] awaited the inevitable news that she was gone.

But two months after that trip, it was my father who died. For me, his loss was doubly cruel: his death deprived me of both my foundation and the bridge to my faraway grandmother. For her, it was the second time she had lost him. For the 30 years they were separated, she had feared her son was dead. This time, there was no ambiguity,[10] no hope. When she heard the news, my uncle later wrote us, she wept quietly.

When I hear friends complain about having to visit their nearby relatives, I think of how far away my grandmother is and how untouched our relationship remains by the modern age. My brief handwritten notes are agonizingly slow to reach her. When they do arrive, she cannot read them. I cannot call her. I cannot see, hear or touch her.

But last month my mother called to tell me to brush up on my Chinese. Refusing to let go of our tenuous[11] connection to my father's family, she has decided to take us all back to China in October for my grandmother's 100th birthday. And so every night, I sit at my desk and study, thinking of her tiny doll-like feet, of the miles and differences that separate us, of the moments we'll share when we meet one last time. And I beg her to hold on until I get there.

DISCUSSION AND WRITING QUESTIONS

1. Why does the author start her essay by contrasting her grandmother's feet and her own? What other differences between the two women's lives are revealed through this comparison (paragraphs 1 and 2)?

2. A language barrier exists between the author and her grandmother, yet they communicate "something strange and beautiful" (paragraph 5). What would you say this *something* is?

3. Paragraph 6 describes the author's visit to China with her boyfriend. Did you find any details especially strong or moving? How do these details help us understand what the grandmother means when she says, "You are lucky"?

---

7. dynasty: a family or group that rules for generations
8. gnarled: twisted, bumpy
9. resignation: hopeless acceptance
10. ambiguity: uncertainty
11. tenuous: weak, slender

4. Do you ever complain, like the author's friends, about having to visit relatives? What do you think the author would say to those who do not seek out or appreciate time with family members? What benefits do these relationships offer? What can we learn from older relatives?

WRITING ASSIGNMENTS

1. Do you and a family member have a special relationship in spite of distance, age, or other barriers? Describe this relationship and what makes it unique. You might begin as Wu does with a single contrast that reveals other differences between you.

2. Are any of your cultural traditions or customs being lost through immigration or the passage of time? Write an essay describing one special tradition or custom that is being lost in your family—or a special tradition that your family keeps alive.

3. How do people in the United States tend to regard the elderly? How do these attitudes and beliefs compare with what you were taught—or with the views of some other culture? For ideas on America's increasingly negative view of aging, research "negative images of aging" on your favorite search engine.

Freedom's Just Another Word

ANNA QUINDLEN

> Only about half of eligible Americans bother to vote in presidential elections, and even fewer vote in local elections. Columnist and Pulitzer Prize–winning author Anna Quindlen argues for a new way to get out the vote in this article from *Newsweek*, 2004.

We introduced the Australian exchange students to Honey Nut Cheerios. They introduced us to compulsory[1] voting. In class, they'd heard about the woeful turnout in American elections. "But aren't people concerned about paying the fine?" one of them asked.   1

It turns out that the laid-back country in which our two curious, self-possessed and intelligent houseguests live requires its citizens to vote. Really requires it. If you don't show up at your polling place on Election Day, you are asked to provide an excuse in writing afterward. "The dingo[2] ate my ballot" will not do. Unless you have a good explanation—a heart attack that morning, say—you are fined. The result is that Australia has one of the highest voter-turnout rates in the world, around 90 percent.   2

Lest we forget, only 51 percent of all voting-age Americans bothered to show up in the last presidential election, which means that while Australia may be a forcible democracy, we are barely a participatory one. (Unless you count   3

---

1. compulsory: required
2. dingo: wild dog of Australia

participating in opining[3] without action, an event at which Americans would win the gold medal if it ever became part of the Olympics.) This makes me wonder: Why don't we adopt the compulsory system the Aussies have embraced so successfully? And, on a lesser note, how come you can't get Honey Nut Cheerios in Sydney?

Almost by magic, I feel a hostile horde behind my desk, the many Americans   4 who have made it their life's work to champion reckless abandon masquerading as liberty. Their causes may vary, but the motto is unwavering: "Wanna make me?" That's why some states have been persuaded to weaken their seat-belt laws. That's why there are motorcycle enthusiasts who make the right to ride without a helmet sound like Rosa Parks's[4] moving to the front of the bus. That's why there are all those smokers who complain about the gulag[5] outside the office-building door.

No facts can convince the rugged individualists hellbent[6] on emphysema or   5 spinal injuries. Some 13,000 lives are saved each year because of seat belts. A National Highway Traffic Safety Administration study last year showed that the severity and mortality of motorcycle accidents shot up when helmet laws were repealed. There have been studies on secondhand smoke and its link to such spread-the-death ailments as childhood asthma. Personally, I'm just happy to be able to taste my food in restaurants and not go home with my hair smelling like that classic fragrance, Philip Morris's Eau de Fleur Tabac.[7]

The argument is that you should be allowed to put your own body in harm's   6 way if you choose. The fact that the collateral damage[8] and the costs for the catastrophes and long-term care are spread around among the rest of us is conveniently overlooked. But forgoing the vote is an injury to the body politic,[9] and that's not a personal matter. Low voter turnouts hurt everyone because they erode the notion of government by the people and for the people; when we complain that big corporations and paid lobbyists[10] have taken over politics, we should remember that nature abhors a vacuum.[11] In fact it's astonishing that we've blithely[12] allowed Americans to drop out of the electoral process for so long. There's no argument about this: when we make an act optional, we inevitably suggest that it's not that important.

There's been a real registration boom recently, with election boards in many   7 states being forced to hire additional workers and schedule lots of overtime. As deadlines loomed, there were tsunamis[13] of paper across the country. Philadelphia had its biggest jump in new registrations in 21 years. "It was almost an April 15, IRS post-office type of operation," the elections director in Columbus, Ohio, told a reporter about the atmosphere at his office.

Some credit the work of registration groups like the ones spearheaded by hip   8 hop artists or pro wrestlers; others think voters were galvanized[14] by how tight

---

3. opining: stating opinions

4. Rosa Parks: civil rights activist who refused to give up her seat on a bus in 1955

5. gulag: forced-labor camp or prison

6. hellbent: recklessly determined

7. Eau de Fleur Tabac: French for "tobacco flower perfume"

8. collateral damage: accidental or unintentional harm

9. body politic: the people as a whole, the democracy

10. lobbyists: people who try to influence lawmakers or officials to support an industry or cause

11. vacuum: an empty, airless space

12. blithely: lacking proper concern

13. tsunamis: huge ocean waves caused by earthquakes or volcanic eruptions

14. galvanized: spurred to action

the 2000 race turned out to be, reversing the traditional cynicism[15] about the value of a single vote. But almost everyone who studies voting patterns cautions: just because many have registered does not guarantee that many will actually go to the polls on November 2. Sad, but true: the United States has not had 60 percent of its voting-age citizens turn out since 1968. And 60 percent is not exactly a high-water mark.

What's the price of *freedom*? How about a fine of 50 bucks? I like to be left alone as much as the next person, but there's no point in continuing to be high and mighty about being the cradle of liberty if it's just empty rhetoric.[16] We laud[17] free elections in formerly totalitarian nations,[18] but, like a lot of what's free, fresh air and ocean water and the like, we've learned to devalue the product. Democracy without participation is like a house with two walls: it just doesn't stand up. Maybe our lackluster voting record means we're not really interested in all that anymore, that our new message to the world might be something simpler and more modern: we make a slamming sugared cereal!

DISCUSSION AND WRITING QUESTIONS

1. Do you vote in elections? Why or why not? If not, would a fine make you vote?

2. What are the main points in Quindlen's argument for compulsory voting in the United States? How does she answer the opposition (paragraphs 4–6)?

3. What does Quindlen mean when she says that Americans would win a gold medal if "opining without action" ever became an Olympic sport (paragraph 3)?

4. Is it true that "when we make an act optional, we suggest that it's not that important" (paragraph 6)? Voting for *American Idol* is optional, yet millions of people vote for the contestants on that show, while fewer than half of us vote for our president once every four years. How do you explain this?

WRITING ASSIGNMENTS

1. In a group with classmates, create a plan to persuade more students at your college to vote. Discuss your target audience and whether a fine or other methods would work best. Later, each student should present the plan (or a better one) in writing.

2. Write an essay arguing *against* compulsory voting. Give at least three reasons for your position.

3. Visit one of the registration web sites listed below. Analyze the methods used to persuade people to register—including words, visual images, and sounds. Write an essay discussing these techniques.
   Rock the Vote (**http://www.rockthevote.com/home.php**)
   Choose or Lose (**http://www.mtv.com/chooseorlose/**)
   Smackdown Your Vote! (**http://vote.wwe.com/**).

---

15. cynicism: negative or pessimistic attitude

16. rhetoric: language that is empty or insincere

17. laud: praise

18. totalitarian nations: those ruled by a dictator

The Case for Torture

MICHAEL LEVIN

Leaders like Martin Luther King and Mahatma Ghandi have preached nonviolence no matter what, and many people agree that deliberately injuring another person is wrong. However, philosophy professor Michael Levin argues in this startling essay that torture is sometimes necessary.

1 It is generally assumed that torture is impermissible,[1] a throwback to a more brutal age. Enlightened societies reject it outright, and regimes suspected of using it risk the wrath of the United States.

2 I believe this attitude is unwise. There are situations in which torture is not merely permissible but morally mandatory. Moreover, these situations are moving from the realm of imagination to fact.

3 Suppose a terrorist has hidden an atomic bomb on Manhattan Island which will detonate at noon on July 4 unless . . . (here follow the usual demands for money and release of his friends from jail). Suppose, further, that he is caught at 10 A.M. of the fateful day, but—preferring death to failure—won't disclose where the bomb is. What do we do? If we follow due process—wait for his lawyer, arraign him—millions of people will die. If the only way to save those lives is to subject the terrorist to the most excruciating possible pain, what grounds can there be for not doing so? I suggest there are none. In any case, I ask you to face the question with an open mind.

4 Torturing the terrorist is unconstitutional? Probably. But millions of lives surely outweigh constitutionality. Torture is barbaric? Mass murder is far more barbaric. Indeed, letting millions of innocents die in deference[2] to one who flaunts his guilt is moral cowardice, an unwillingness to dirty one's hands. If *you* caught the terrorist, could you sleep nights knowing that millions died because you couldn't bring yourself to apply the electrodes?

5 Once you concede that torture is justified in extreme cases, you have admitted that the decision to use torture is a matter of balancing innocent lives against the means needed to save them. You must now face more realistic cases involving more modest numbers. Someone plants a bomb on a jumbo jet. He alone can disarm it, and his demands cannot be met (or if they can, we refuse to set a precedent[3] by yielding to his threats). Surely we can, we must, do anything to the extortionist[4] to save the passengers. How can we tell 300, or 100, or 10 people who never asked to be put in danger, "I'm sorry, you'll have to die in agony, we just couldn't bring ourselves to . . . ."

6 Here are the results of an informal poll about a third, hypothetical,[5] case. Suppose a terrorist group kidnapped a newborn baby from a hospital. I asked four mothers if they would approve of torturing kidnappers if that were necessary to get their own newborns back. All said yes, the most "liberal" adding that she would administer it herself.

---

1. impermissible: not allowed
2. deference: respectful submission
3. precedent: a possible example in similar situations
4. extortionist: one who gets something by force or threat
5. hypothetical: assumed to be true for the purposes of argument

I am not advocating torture as punishment. Punishment is addressed to deeds irrevocably[6] past. Rather, I am advocating torture as an acceptable measure for preventing future evils. So understood, it is far less objectionable than many extant[7] punishments. Opponents of the death penalty, for example, are forever insisting that executing a murderer will not bring back his victim (as if the purpose of capital punishment were supposed to be resurrection, not deterrence[8] or retribution).[9] But torture, in the cases described, is intended not to bring anyone back but to keep innocents from being dispatched.[10] The most powerful argument against using torture as a punishment or to secure confessions is that such practices disregard the rights of the individual. Well, if the individual is all that important—and he is—it is correspondingly important to protect the rights of individuals threatened by terrorists. If life is so valuable that it must never be taken, the lives of the innocents must be saved even at the price of hurting the one who endangers them.

Better precedents for torture are assassination and preemptive[11] attack. No Allied[12] leader would have flinched at assassinating Hitler[13] had that been possible. (The Allies did assassinate Heydrich.[14]) Americans would be angered to learn that Roosevelt could have had Hitler killed in 1943—thereby shortening the war and saving millions of lives—but refused on moral grounds. Similarly, if nation A learns that nation B is about to launch an unprovoked attack, A has a right to save itself by destroying B's military capability first. In the same way, if the police can by torture save those who would otherwise die at the hands of kidnappers or terrorists, they must.

There is an important difference between terrorists and their victims that should mute talk of the terrorists' "rights." The terrorist's victims are at risk unintentionally, not having asked to be endangered. But the terrorist knowingly initiated his actions. Unlike his victims, he volunteered for the risks of his deed. By threatening to kill for profit or idealism, he renounces civilized standards, and he can have no complaint if civilization tries to thwart him by whatever means necessary.

Just as torture is justified only to save lives (not extort confessions or recantations),[15] it is justifiably administered only to those *known* to hold innocent lives in their hands. Ah, but how can the authorities ever be sure they have the right malefactor?[16] Isn't there a danger of error and abuse? Won't We turn into Them?

Questions like these are disingenuous[17] in a world in which terrorists proclaim themselves and perform for television. The name of their game is public recognition. After all, you can't very well intimidate a government into releasing your freedom fighters unless you announce that it is your group that has seized

---

6. irrevocably: impossible to change

7. extant: existing

8. deterrence: preventing similar acts

9. retribution: punishment

10. dispatched: killed

11. preemptive attack: striking first, before the enemy does

12. Allied: in World War II, the Allied Powers included the United States, Britain, France, the Soviet Union, and China

13. Hitler: dictator of Nazi Germany who ordered the murder of millions of Jews and others

14. Heydrich: a Nazi organizer of mass executions

15. recantations: taking back of previous statements

16. malefactor: evildoer

17. disingenuous: falsely innocent-seeming

its embassy. "Clear guilt" is difficult to define, but when 40 million people see a group of masked gunmen seize an airplane on the evening news, there is not much question about who the perpetrators are. There will be hard cases where the situation is murkier. Nonetheless, a line demarcating[18] the legitimate use of torture can be drawn. Torture only the obviously guilty, and only for the sake of saving innocents, and the line between Us and Them will remain clear.

There is little danger that the Western democracies will lose their way if they 12 choose to inflict pain as one way of preserving order. Paralysis in the face of evil is the greater danger. Some day soon a terrorist will threaten tens of thousands of lives, and torture will be the only way to save them. We had better start thinking about this.

DISCUSSION AND WRITING QUESTIONS

1. What is the author's main point—his thesis? According to Levin, in what specific circumstances should torture be used? Do you agree that someone who refuses to torture a terrorist is guilty of moral cowardice?

2. What arguments *against* torture does the author answer in paragraph 4? Are his answers convincing? His introduction also answers the opposition (paragraphs 1 and 2). Why do you think Levin spends so much time answering the opposition in this essay?

3. Levin first argues that torturing one person to save millions of lives would be acceptable; then he works down from millions to 300, 100, 10, and finally, a single infant (paragraphs 3–6). Would you, like the four mothers, approve of torturing someone who kidnapped your newborn if this would get your infant back?

4. Why does Levin argue that torture should never be used as punishment (paragraph 7)?

WRITING ASSIGNMENTS

1. Write a reply to Michael Levin's essay. Develop an argument against torture under any circumstances. For ideas visit the United Nations web site on torture at **http:/www.unhchr.ch/html/menu2/i2civtor.htm** or Amnesty International's site at **http://www.amnesty.org** (search "torture").

2. Write an essay called "A Case for (or Against) Racial Profiling." Consider whether authorities should use racial or ethnic profiling to identify possible terrorists at airports and elsewhere. What about profiling on highways (where African Americans are sometimes stopped for DWB, "driving while black")? Carefully plan your argument before you write.

3. Conduct an informal poll of mothers based on a hypothetical kidnap case, as Levin does in paragraph 6. Ask at least five mothers whether they would support torture of the kidnapper and why. Organize your findings and write a paper presenting them.

---

18. demarcating: setting boundaries

Beauty: When the Other Dancer Is the Self

ALICE WALKER

Being physically injured can be terrifying; coming to terms with a permanent disability can be a painful, difficult process. Alice Walker, a noted fiction writer, poet, and author of *The Color Purple*, tells of her feelings and experiences before, during, and after an injury that changed her life.

It is a bright summer day in 1947. My father, a fat, funny man with beautiful eyes and a subversive wit,[1] is trying to decide which of his eight children he will take with him to the county fair. My mother, of course, will not go. She is knocked out from getting most of us ready: I hold my neck stiff against the pressure of her knuckles as she hastily completes the braiding and then beribboning of my hair.

My father is the driver for the rich old white lady up the road. Her name is Miss Mey. She owns all the land for miles around, as well as the house in which we live. All I remember about her is that she once offered to pay my mother thirty-five cents for cleaning her house, raking up piles of her magnolia leaves, and washing her family's clothes, and that my mother—she of no money, eight children, and a chronic earache—refused it. But I do not think of this in 1947. I am two and a half years old. I want to go everywhere my daddy goes. I am excited at the prospect of riding in a car. Someone has told me fairs are fun. That there is room in the car for only three of us doesn't faze[2] me at all. Whirling happily in my starchy frock, showing off my biscuit-polished patent-leather shoes and lavender socks, tossing my head in a way that makes my ribbons bounce, I stand, hands on hips, before my father. "Take me, Daddy," I say with assurance; "I'm the prettiest!"

Later, it does not surprise me to find myself in Miss Mey's shiny black car, sharing the back seat with the other lucky ones. Does not surprise me that I thoroughly enjoy the fair. At home that night I tell the unlucky ones all I can remember about the merry-go-round, the man who eats live chickens, and the teddy bears, until they say: that's enough, baby Alice. Shut up now, and go to sleep.

It is Easter Sunday, 1950. I am dressed in a green, flocked, scalloped-hem dress (handmade by my adoring sister, Ruth) that has its own smooth satin petticoat and tiny hot-pink roses tucked into each scallop. My shoes, new T-strap patent leather, again highly biscuit-polished. I am six years old and have learned one of the longest Easter speeches to be heard that day, totally unlike the speech I said when I was two: "Easter lilies/pure and white / blossom in / the morning light." When I rise to give my speech I do so on a great wave of love and pride and expectation. People in the church stop rustling their new crinolines. They seem to hold their breath. I can tell they admire my dress, but it is my spirit, bordering on sassiness (womanishness), they secretly applaud.

"That girl's a little *mess*," they whisper to each other, pleased.

Naturally I say my speech without stammer or pause, unlike those who stutter, stammer, or, worst of all, forget. This is before the word "beautiful" exists in people's vocabulary, but "Oh, isn't she the *cutest* thing!" frequently floats my way. "And got so much sense!" they gratefully add . . . for which thoughtful addition I thank them to this day.

---

1. subversive wit: sarcastic, sharp sense of humor
2. faze: discourage

It was great fun being cute. But then, one day, it ended.   7

I am eight years old and a tomboy. I have a cowboy hat, cowboy boots, checkered   8
shirt and pants, all red. My playmates are my brothers, two and four years older
than I. Their colors are black and green, the only difference in the way we are
dressed. On Saturday nights we all go to the picture show, even my mother; West-
erns are her favorite kind of movie. Back home, "on the ranch," we pretend we are
Tom Mix, Hopalong Cassidy, Lash LaRue (we've even named one of our dogs
Lash LaRue); we chase each other for hours rustling cattle, being outlaws, deliver-
ing damsels from distress. Then my parents decide to buy my brothers guns.
These are not "real" guns. They shoot "BBs," copper pellets my brothers say will
kill birds. Because I am a girl, I do not get a gun. Instantly I am relegated to[3] the
position of Indian. Now there appears a great distance between us. They shoot
and shoot at everything with their new guns. I try to keep up with my bow and
arrows.

One day while I am standing on top of our makeshift "garage"—pieces of tin   9
nailed across some poles—holding my bow and arrow and looking out toward
the fields, I feel an incredible blow in my right eye. I look down just in time to see
my brother lower his gun.

Both brothers rush to my side. My eye stings, and I cover it with my hand. "If   10
you tell," they say, "we will get a whipping. You don't want that to happen, do
you?" I do not. "Here is a piece of wire," says the older brother, picking it up from
the roof; "say you stepped on one end of it and the other flew up and hit you."
The pain is beginning to start. "Yes," I say. "Yes, I will say that is what happened."
If I do not say this is what happened, I know my brothers will find ways to make
me wish I had. But now I will say anything that gets me to my mother.

Confronted by our parents we stick to the lie agreed upon. They place me on a   11
bench on the porch and I close my left eye while they examine the right. There is a
tree growing from underneath the porch that climbs past the railing to the roof. It
is the last thing my right eye sees. I watch as its trunk, its branches, and then its
leaves are blotted out by the rising blood.

I am in shock. First there is intense fever, which my father tries to break using   12
lily leaves bound around my head. Then there are chills: my mother tries to get
me to eat soup. Eventually, I do not know how, my parents learn what has
happened. A week after the "accident" they take me to see a doctor. "Why did
you wait so long to come?" he asks, looking into my eye and shaking his head.
"Eyes are sympathetic,[4]" he says. "If one is blind, the other will likely become
blind too."

This comment of the doctor's terrifies me. But it is really how I look that both-   13
ers me most. Where the BB pellet struck there is a glob of whitish scar tissue, a
hideous cataract, on my eye. Now when I stare at people—a favorite pastime, up
to now—they will stare back. Not at the "cute" little girl, but at her scar. For six
years I do not stare at anyone, because I do not raise my head.

Years later, in the throes[5] of a mid-life crisis, I ask my mother and sister whether I   14
changed after the "accident." "No," they say, puzzled. "What do you mean?"
What do I mean?   15

---

3. relegated to: assigned

4. sympathetic: closely connected

5. throes: a condition of struggle

I am eight, and, for the first time, doing poorly in school, where I have been some- 16
thing of a whiz since I was four. We have just moved to the place where the "accident"
occurred. We do not know any of the people around us because this is a different
county. The only time I see the friends I knew is when we go back to our old church.
The new school is the former state penitentiary. It is a large stone building, cold and
drafty, crammed to overflowing with boisterous,[6] ill-disciplined children. On the
third floor there is a huge circular imprint of some partition that has been torn out.

"What used to be there?" I ask a sullen girl next to me on our way past it to 17
lunch.

"The electric chair," says she. 18

At night I have nightmares about the electric chair, and about all the people 19
reputedly[7] "fried" in it. I am afraid of the school, where all the students seem to be
budding criminals.

"What's the matter with your eye?" they ask, critically. 20

When I don't answer (I cannot decide whether it was an "accident" or not), 21
they shove me, insist on a fight.

My brother, the one who created the story about the wire, comes to my rescue. 22
But then brags so much about "protecting" me, I become sick.

After months of torture at the school, my parents decide to send me back to 23
our old community, to my old school. I live with my grandparents and the teacher
they board. But there is no room for Phoebe, my cat. By the time my grandparents
decide there *is* room, and I ask for my cat, she cannot be found. Miss Yarborough,
the boarding teacher, takes me under her wing, and begins to teach me to play the
piano. But soon she marries an African—a "prince," she says—and is whisked
away to his continent.

At my old school there is at least one teacher who loves me. She is the teacher 24
who "knew me before I was born" and bought my first baby clothes. It is she who
makes life bearable. It is her presence that finally helps me turn on the one child at
the school who continually calls me "one-eyed bitch." One day I simply grab him
by his coat and beat him until I am satisfied. It is my teacher who tells me my
mother is ill.

My mother is lying in bed in the middle of the day, something I have never seen. 25
She is in too much pain to speak. She has an abscess in her ear. I stand looking
down on her, knowing that if she dies, I cannot live. She is being treated with
warm oils and hot bricks held against her cheek. Finally a doctor comes. But I
must go back to my grandparents' house. The weeks pass but I am hardly aware
of it. All I know is that my mother might die, my father is not so jolly, my brothers
still have their guns, and I am the one sent away from home.

"You did not change," they say. 26

Did I imagine the anguish of never looking up? 27

I am twelve. When relatives come to visit I hide in my room. My cousin Brenda, 28
just my age, whose father works in the post office and whose mother is a nurse,
comes to find me. "Hello," she says. And then she asks, looking at my recent
school picture, which I did not want taken, and on which the "glob," as I think of
it, is clearly visible, "You still can't see out of that eye?"

"No," I say, and flop back on the bed over my book. 29

---

6. boisterous: rowdy and noisy
7. reputedly: supposedly

That night, as I do almost every night, I abuse my eye. I rant and rave at it, in front of the mirror. I plead with it to clear up before morning. I tell it I hate and despise it. I do not pray for sight. I pray for beauty. 30

"You did not change," they say. 31

I am fourteen and baby-sitting for my brother Bill, who lives in Boston. He is my favorite brother and there is a strong bond between us. Understanding my feelings of shame and ugliness he and his wife take me to a local hospital, where the "glob" is removed by a doctor named O. Henry. There is still a small bluish crater where the scar tissue was, but the ugly white stuff is gone. Almost immediately I become a different person from the girl who does not raise her head. Or so I think. Now that I've raised my head I win the boyfriend of my dreams. Now that I've raised my head I have plenty of friends. Now that I've raised my head classwork comes from my lips as faultlessly as Easter speeches did, and I leave high school as valedictorian, most popular student, and *queen,* hardly believing my luck. Ironically, the girl who was voted most beautiful in our class (and was) was later shot twice through the chest by a male companion, using a "real" gun, while she was pregnant. But that's another story in itself. Or is it? 32

"You did not change," they say. 33

It is now thirty years since the "accident." A beautiful journalist comes to visit and to interview me. She is going to write a cover story for her magazine that focuses on my latest book. "Decide how you want to look on the cover," she says. "Glamorous, or whatever." 34

Never mind "glamorous," it is the "whatever" that I hear. Suddenly all I can think of is whether I will get enough sleep the night before the photography session: if I don't, my eye will be tired and wander, as blind eyes will. 35

The writer Alice Walker

At night in bed with my lover I think up reasons why I should not appear on   36
the cover of a magazine. "My meanest critics will say I've sold out," I say. "My
family will now realize I write scandalous books."

"But what's the real reason you don't want to do this?" he asks.   37

"Because in all probability," I say in a rush, "my eye won't be straight."   38

"It will be straight enough," he says. Then, "Besides, I thought you'd made   39
your peace with that."

And I suddenly remember that I have.   40

I remember: 41

I am talking to my brother Jimmy, asking if he remembers anything unusual   42
about the day I was shot. He does not know I consider that day the last time my
father, with his sweet home remedy of cool lily leaves, chose me, and that I suffered and raged inside because of this. "Well," he says, "all I remember is standing by the side of the highway with Daddy, trying to flag down a car. A white man
stopped, but when Daddy said he needed somebody to take his little girl to the
doctor, he drove off."

I remember: 43

I am in the desert for the first time. I fall totally in love with it. I am so over-   44
whelmed by its beauty, I confront for the first time, consciously, the meaning of
the doctor's words years ago: "Eyes are sympathetic. If one is blind, the other will
likely become blind too." I realize I have dashed about the world madly, looking
at this, looking at that, storing up images against the fading of the light. *But I
might have missed seeing the desert!* The shock of that possibility—and gratitude for
over twenty-five years of sight—sends me literally to my knees. Poem after poem
comes—which is perhaps how poets pray.

On Sight

I am so thankful I have seen
The Desert
And the creatures in the desert
And the desert Itself.

The desert has its own moon
Which I have seen
With my own eye.
There is no flag on it.

Trees of the desert have arms
All of which are always up
That is because the moon is up
The sun is up
Also the sky
The stars
Clouds
None with flags.
If there *were* flags, I doubt
the trees would point.
Would you?

But mostly, I remember this: 45

I am twenty-seven, and my baby daughter is almost three. Since her birth I   46
have worried about her discovery that her mother's eyes are different from other
people's. Will she be embarrassed? I think. What will she say? Every day she
watches a television program called "Big Blue Marble." It begins with a picture of

the earth as it appears from the moon. It is bluish, a little battered-looking, but full of light, with whitish clouds swirling around it. Every time I see it I weep with love, as if it is a picture of Grandma's house. One day when I am putting Rebecca down for her nap, she suddenly focuses on my eye. Something inside me cringes, gets ready to try to protect myself. All children are cruel about physical differences, I know from experience, and that they don't always mean to be is another matter. I assume Rebecca will be the same.

But no-o-o-o. She studies my face intently as we stand, her inside and me out-   47 side her crib. She even holds my face maternally between her dimpled little hands. Then, looking every bit as serious and lawyerlike as her father, she says, as if it may just possibly have slipped my attention: "Mommy, there's a *world* in your eye." (As in, "Don't be alarmed, or do anything crazy.") And then, gently, but with great interest: "Mommy, where did you *get* that world in your eye?"

For the most part, the pain left then. (So what, if my brothers grew up to buy   48 even more powerful pellet guns for their sons and to carry real guns themselves. So what, if a young "Morehouse man" once nearly fell off the steps of Trevor Arnett Library because he thought my eyes were blue.) Crying and laughing I ran to the bathroom, while Rebecca mumbled and sang herself to sleep. Yes indeed, I realized, looking into the mirror. There *was* a world in my eye. And I saw that it was possible to love it: that in fact, for all it had taught me of shame and anger and inner vision, I *did* love it. Even to see it drifting out of orbit in boredom, or rolling up out of fatigue, not to mention floating back at attention in excitement (bearing witness, a friend has called it), deeply suitable to my personality, and even characteristic of me.

That night I dream I am dancing to Stevie Wonder's song "Always" (the   49 name of the song is really "As," but I hear it as "Always"). As I dance, whirling and joyous, happier than I've ever been in my life, another bright-faced dancer joins me. We dance and kiss each other and hold each other through the night. The other dancer has obviously come through all right, as I have done. She is beautiful, whole and free. And she is also me.

DISCUSSION AND WRITING QUESTIONS

1. When did the author stop being "cute"? Is she happy about this change?

2. Why do you think her family insists that she did not change after the shooting?

3. Until her operation at age fourteen, Walker speaks of hating her injured eye. By the end of the essay, she dances with another "dancer," who is "beautiful, whole and free. And she is also me." What makes the author change her mind about her "deformity"?

4. The author uses particular words and phrases to indicate time or chronological order in her narrative. Find the words that indicate time order. At one point in her narrative, she breaks this time order to skip back into the past. In which paragraph does this flashback occur?

WRITING ASSIGNMENTS

1. Write about an unpleasant event or experience that resulted in personal growth for you. Your writing need not focus on something as painful as Alice Walker's injury. What is important is how you came to terms with the experience and what you ultimately learned from it.

2 Tell a story about being thrust into a completely unfamiliar situation. You might describe your reaction to attending a new school, starting a new job, or moving to a new city. Present concrete details of your experience. Organize the story around your most vivid memories, like meeting new classmates for the first time, or your first few days on the new job.

3. In a group with three or four classmates, discuss the accident that injured Walker's eye and the children's cover-up (paragraphs 8–11). Her brothers, ten and twelve, were given BB guns. How did these guns change the relationships among siblings even before the accident? Why did this happen? Are BB guns "real guns"? Have you known someone injured by "gun play"? How can such accidents be prevented? Write a paper on your own in which you present one to three ways in which Walker's injury—or one that you know about—could have been prevented.

Quotation Bank

This collection of wise and humorous statements has been assembled for you to read, enjoy, and use in a variety of ways as you write. You might choose quotations that you particularly agree or disagree with and use them as the basis of journal entries and writing assignments. Sometimes when writing a paragraph or an essay, you may find it useful to include a quotation to support a point you are making. Alternatively, you may simply want to read through these quotations for ideas and for fun. As you come across other intriguing statements by writers, add them to the list—or write some of your own.

Education

Knowledge is power.   1
—*Francis Bacon*

Everyone is ignorant, only on different subjects.   2
—*Will Rogers*

Never be afraid to sit awhile and think.   3
—*Lorraine Hansberry*

A mind stretched by a new idea can never go back to its original dimensions.   4
—*Oliver Wendell Holmes, Jr.*

The contest between education and TV . . . has been won by television.   5
—*Robert Hughes*

This thing called "failure" is not the falling down, but the staying down.   6
—*Mary Pickford*

Tell me what you pay attention to, and I will tell you who you are.   7
—*José Ortega y Gasset*

We learn something by doing it. There is no other way.   8
—*John Holt*

Work and Success

He who does not hope to win has already lost.   9
—*José Joaquin de Olmedo*

The harder you work, the luckier you get.   10
—*Gary Player*

Float like a butterfly, sting like a bee.   11
—*Muhammad Ali*

All glory comes from daring to begin.   12
—*Anonymous*

Show me a person who has never made a mistake, and I'll show you a
person who has never achieved much.   13
—*Joan Collins*

Nice guys finish last.
—*Leo Durocher*

14

Do as the bull in the face of adversity: charge.
—*José de Diego*

15

Should you not find the pearl after one or two divings, don't blame the ocean! Blame your diving! You are not going deep enough.
—*P. Yogananda*

16

I merely took the energy it takes to pout and wrote some blues.
—*Duke Ellington*

17

I write when I'm inspired, and I see to it that I'm inspired at nine o'clock every morning.
—*Peter De Vries*

18

Love

If you want to be loved, be lovable.
—*Ovid*

19

After ecstasy, the laundry.
—*Zen saying*

20

The first duty of love is to listen.
—*Paul Tillich*

21

A successful marriage requires falling in love many times, always with the same person.
—*Mignon McLaughlin*

22

Love is a fire, but whether it's going to warm your hearth or burn down your house, you can never tell.
—*Dorothy Parker*

23

The way to love anything is to realize that it might be lost.
—*G. K. Chesterton*

24

It's like magic. When you live by yourself, all your annoying habits are gone!
—*Merrill Marko*

25

Friends and Family

Love is blind; friendship closes its eyes.
—*Anonymous*

26

Friendship with oneself is all important because without it one cannot be friends with anyone else in the world.
—*Eleanor Roosevelt*

27

You do not know who is your friend and who is your enemy until the ice breaks.
—*Eskimo proverb*

28

Your children need your presence more than your presents. 29
—*Jesse Jackson*

Children need love, especially when they do not deserve it. 30
—*Harold S. Hulbert*

Ourselves in Society

America is not a melting pot. It is a sizzling cauldron. 31
—*Barbara Ann Mikulski*

When spider webs unite, they can tie up a lion. 32
—*Ethiopian proverb*

A smile is the shortest distance between two people. 33
—*Victor Borge*

Freedom does not always win. This is one of the bitterest lessons of history. 34
—*A. J. P. Taylor*

If you think you're too small to have an impact, try going to bed with
a mosquito. 35
—*Anita Koddick*

Courage isn't the absence of fear; it is action in the face of fear. 36
—*S. Kennedy*

Racism is still a major issue because it is a habit. 37
—*Maya Angelou*

What women want is what men want: they want respect. 38
—*Marilyn Vos Savant*

Basically people are people . . . but it is our differences which charm,
delight, and frighten us. 39
—*Agnes Newton Keith*

Wisdom for Living

Look within! The secret is inside you! 40
—*Hui Neng*

One who wants a rose must respect the thorn. 41
—*Persian proverb*

To live a creative life, we must lose our fear of being wrong. 42
—*Joseph Chilton Pearce*

People who keep stiff upper lips find that it's damn hard to smile. 43
—*Judith Guest*

Self-pity in its early stages is as snug as a feather mattress. Only when it
hardens does it become uncomfortable. 44
—*Maya Angelou*

When three people call you a donkey, put on a saddle.   45
—*Spanish proverb*

Self-examination—if it is thorough enough—is always the first step
towards change.   46
—*Thomas Mann*

If you can't change your fate, change your attitude.   47
—*Amy Tan*

Time is a dressmaker specializing in alterations.   48
—*Faith Baldwin*

Living in the lap of luxury isn't bad, except you never know when luxury
is going to stand up.   49
—*Orson Welles*

Egoist. A person of low taste, more interested in himself than me.   50
—*Ambrose Bierce*

Envy is a kind of praise.   51
—*John Gay*

What doesn't destroy me strengthens me.   52
—*Friedrich Nietzsche*

Life shrinks and expands in proportion to one's courage.   53
—*Anaïs Nin*

I'm not afraid to die. I just don't want to be there when it happens. 54
—*Woody Allen*

Some Guidelines for Students of English as a Second Language

Count and Noncount Nouns

Count nouns* refer to people, places, or things that are separate units. You can always count them and often physically point to them. Note that, in English, the following nouns are used as plural count nouns: *police, jeans, pajamas, Middle Ages, scissors, shorts*.

Count Noun	Sample Sentence (Note the underlined words used with count nouns)
television	The marketing department purchased ten large-screen **televisions**.
drive	John had to buy a new flash **drive** to hold the graphics he completed for art class.
assignment	How many **assignments** did you complete last night?
police	The **police** are stationed around the perimeter of the house.

Noncount nouns refer to things that you cannot count separately. Some noncount nouns refer to ideas, feelings, and other things that you cannot see or touch; other noncount nouns refer to food or beverages.

Noncount Noun	Sample Sentence (Note the underlined words used with noncount nouns)
integrity	A politician's **integrity** is frequently tested.
information	We have been waiting for some **information** about the exam.
homework	How much **homework** do you have to finish tonight?
milk	**Milk** is available with 2 percent fat, 1 percent fat, and no fat.

---

* For more on nouns, see Chapters 30 and 24, Part A.

Three signs can help you identify noncount nouns: (1) nouns that have the same verb form (e.g., *help, to help; light, to light*), (2) words that occur only in noun form (e.g., *business, vocabulary*), and (3) nouns with certain endings:

Endings on Many Noncount Nouns

-ance/ence: insurance, patience, persistence

-ness: frankness, nervousness

-age: courage, postage, luggage, leverage

-sure or *-ture*: pressure, furniture

-fare: welfare, warfare

-th: health, warmth, wealth, strength, truth

-ice: advice, juice, practice

-tion: information, inspiration, respiration, transportation

-esty/ity: honesty, continuity, integrity

-ware: software, sportswear, silverware

-ment: development, equipment

-work: homework, metalwork (exception: network)

PRACTICE 1

Choose the correct word in each pair in the following sentences. Be prepared to explain your choice.

1. After moving to the condominium, they decided to buy new (furniture, furnitures).

2. An important key to learning a second language is memorizing (vocabulary, vocabularies).

3. The crew took a lot of video (equipment, equipments) to the film shoot.

4. This class was difficult because of all the (homework, homeworks) we had to complete.

5. This class was difficult because of all the (exercise, exercises) we had to complete.

6. The (scissor, scissors) lay on the color copier.

7. Waldo set up some computer (network, networks) for the company.

8. The patient's (respiration, respirations) seemed normal.

Some nouns have both count and noncount meanings. Usually, the count meaning is concrete while the noncount meaning is abstract. Note that the count and noncount meanings of some nouns (e.g., *corn, iron*) differ significantly.

Count Meaning	Noncount Meaning
Almost all of the **lights** in the office went out. Only the exit **light** is still burning.	Technicians can now send messages as pulses of **light** through optic wires
Some loud **sounds** are coming from the street. The last **sound** was a shout of victory from a sports fan.	The speed of **sound** is slower than the speed of light.
I found a great store with **teas** and **cakes** from different countries. I bought a green **tea** and a chocolate **cake** there.	Do you like **tea** with **cake**? Would you prefer green or black **tea**?
Two broken **irons** lay on the washer in the laundry room. One working **iron** sat in the cabinet.	**Iron** is a strong metal used to make heavy machinery.

PRACTICE 2

Circle the correct word in each pair in the following sentences. Be prepared to explain your choice.

1. I always have (**coffee**, coffees) with dessert. Please give us two Persian (coffee, **coffees**) and two orders of baklava.

2. You have work (**experience**, experiences) in this field, I see. Tell me about your various (experience, **experiences**) at the ABC Company, where you held several positions.

3. Ship builders use a lot of (**iron**, irons) to build cruise and war ships.

4. Most modern (iron, **irons**) are made of plastic and steel, so they are light and easy to use.

5. To make Maria's wonderful salsa, you need to grill some fresh (**corn**, corns).

6. He had several (corn, **corns**) from years of wearing tight leather shoes.

7. If all cars had both front and side air bags, more (life, **lives**) would be saved.

8. How (**time**, times) passes! We have met several (time, **times**) by chance since we became engineers.

Articles with Count and Noncount Nouns

Indefinite Articles

The words *a* and *an* are **indefinite articles**. They refer to one *nonspecific* (indefinite) thing. For example, "a woman" refers to *any* woman, not a particular woman. **The article *a* or *an* is used before a singular count noun.***

---

*For information about when to use *an* instead of *a*, see Chapter 39.

Singular Count Noun	With Indefinite Article
music video	a music video
question	a question
umbrella	an umbrella

The indefinite article *a* or *an* is never used before a noncount noun:

Noncount Noun	Sample Sentence
music	*Correct:* I enjoy music. *Incorrect:* I enjoy a music.
courage	*Correct:* She displayed courage. *Incorrect:* She displayed a courage.

Be careful: An indefinite article *can* be used with a quantifier (a word that specifies the noun's quantity) and a noncount noun:

Noncount Noun	Noncount Noun with Quantifier
information	The hackers were looking for *a piece of information* that was classified.
news	Let me give you *a bit of news*.

PRACTICE 3

Cross out *a* or *an* if it is used incorrectly in the sentences below. Be ready to explain your answers.

1. We need *a* special luggage for the camping trip.

2. She gave us *an* advice that helped our project succeed.

3. She gave us *a* piece of advice that helped our project succeed.

4. They are transferring to *a* university located somewhere in Los Angeles.

5. To drive on California freeways, one needs *a* patience.

6. I am in the mood for *a* fish, perhaps *a* piece of salmon and a green vegetable.

7. Mr. Lee will offer *a* help if you give him *a* call.

8. We heard *a* laughter coming from the other room.

Definite Article

The word *the* is the only **definite article** in English. It usually refers to one or more specific (definite) things. For example, "the doctor" refers not to *any doctor* but to a specific doctor. "The doctors" refers to two or more specific doctors. **The article *the* can be used before any singular or plural count noun:** *the moon, the soccer players, the Chinese ambassador.**

The **can be used before a noncount noun** *only* **if that noun is specifically identified, usually by a prepositional phrase† or relative clause.‡**

Noncount Noun	Sample Sentence
food	*Correct: The* food <u>at the party</u> was delicious. (specific food) *Incorrect:* All living things must have *the* food to survive. (nonspecific food)
poetry	*Correct: The* poetry <u>that she writes</u> is richly detailed. (specific poetry) *Incorrect:* He enjoys reading *the* poetry. (nonspecific poetry)

Review of Article Usage

	Count Nouns		Noncount Nouns
	Singular	**Plural**	
Indefinite	Use *a/an*. *A chair would be useful. Let's buy one.* (refers to a nonspecified chair)	No article *Chairs come in many different styles.* (refers to nonspecified chairs)	No article *Furniture comes in many different styles.* (refers to nonspecified furniture)
Definite	Use *the*. *The chair we bought is comfortable.* (refers to a specific chair)	Use *the*. *The chairs we bought are comfortable.* (refers to specific chairs)	Use *the*. *The furniture we bought is comfortable.* (refers to specific furniture)

---

*In fact, every singular count noun must be preceded by a "determiner": that is, by a definite or indefinite article; by a pronoun such as *his, her, their, our,* and *my*; by *this, that, these, those*; or by a word such as *many, most, all, both, every,* or *some*, or by a number.
†For more on prepositional phrases, see Chapter 32.
‡For more on relative clauses, see Chapter 21, Part D.

PRACTICE 4

Write the article *the* where needed in each blank. Write X where no article is needed. Be prepared to explain your answers. (More than one answer is correct in some cases.)

Who said that __X__ life never changes? Recent research has shown that __the__ human body has changed significantly, especially during __the__ past 200 years. Dr. Robert Fogel at __the__ University of Chicago and other scientists around __the__ world have concluded that a significant change in __X__ peoples' physical size has taken place. They note that __X__ modern humans are much taller and heavier than __X__ people were only a couple of centuries ago. __The__ same scientists also found that humans today are much healthier than their ancestors. __X__ Chronic diseases occur 10 to 25 years later than they used to, and older people today experience fewer disabilities. __The__ same trend was also found for __X__ mental health. __The__ average IQ, for example, has increased for decades, and mental illnesses are diagnosed and treated much more effectively today. Because of these changes, we now enjoy __X__ happier, healthier, longer, and more productive lives.

Verbs Followed by a Gerund or an Infinitive

A **gerund** is the *–ing* form of the verb used as a noun.

> *Watching* my weight is harder during the cold months.
> They enjoy *hiking* in the Rocky Mountains.

In the first sentence, *watching* is the simple subject of the sentence.* In sentence two, *hiking* is the object of the verb *enjoy*.† Some common English verbs can be followed by a gerund. Example: Joaquin quit *smoking*.

Verbs That Can Be Followed by a Gerund

appreciate	consider	enjoy	mention	quit	risk
avoid	discuss	finish	mind	recommend	suggest
complete	dislike	keep	postpone	remember	understand

---

*For more on simple subjects, see Chapter 24, Part A.
†For more on objects of verbs, see Chapter 31, Part D.

The verbs in the previous box are never followed by an infinitive (*to* + the simple form of the verb):

Verb	Sample Sentence
dislike	*Correct:* I *dislike* **cooking** on weeknights. *Incorrect:* I *dislike* **to cook** on weeknights.
discuss	*Correct:* Let's *discuss* **taking** a trip to Asia. *Incorrect:* Let's *discuss* **to take** a trip to Asia.

Other English verbs can be followed by an **infinitive** (but never by a gerund). Example: He expects *to graduate* in June.

Verbs That Can Be Followed by an Infinitive					
afford	attempt	demand	hope	mean	offer
agree	choose	expect	intend	need	refuse
appear	dare	fail	learn	plan	wish
ask	decide	forget	like	promise	

Some verbs can be followed by a **noun or pronoun and** an **infinitive** (but never by a gerund). Example: She asked *him to dance.*

Verbs That Can Be Followed by Noun or Pronoun + Infinitive					
advise	caution	expect	invite	persuade	teach
allow	convince	hire	order	remind	tell
ask	encourage	instruct	permit	require	want

The verbs listed above are never followed by a gerund:

Verb	Sample Sentence
afford	*Correct:* They can *afford* **to buy** the tickets. *Incorrect:* They can *afford* **buying** the tickets.
agree	*Correct:* I *agree* **to lend** you $100 this week. *Incorrect:* I *agree* **lending** you $100 this week.
plan	*Correct:* He *plans* **to move** to Ohio this summer. *Incorrect:* He *plans* **moving** to Ohio this summer.

A few verbs can be followed by *either* **a gerund or an infinitive** without a change in meaning. Example: They *began* to **write.** They *began* **writing.**

Verbs That Can Be Followed by a Gerund or an Infinitive		
begin	hate	prefer
continue	like	start
dislike	love	try

Some verbs can be followed by *either* a gerund *or* **an infinitive,** but the meaning of the verb differs depending on the form (gerund or infinitive) used:

He stopped *seeing* her. (**Meaning:** He is not seeing/dating her anymore.)
He stopped *to see* her. (**Meaning:** He made a stop to see/visit her.)

PRACTICE 5

Circle the correct form (gerund or infinitive) to follow the verb in each sentence.

1. Many Americans enjoy (to watch, (watching)) television.

2. Because this is the store's busy season, we will postpone (to visit, (visiting)) our friends until spring.

3. Yuri asked Mia ((to repair,) repairing) the DVD player.

4. Mae Lee regretted (to miss, (missing)) the auto show.

5. Barring any unforeseen problems, the family expects me ((to complete,) completing) my degree by this summer.

6. Ichiro will persuade Edgar ((to join,) joining) us at the library.

7. Please keep (to sing, (singing)). We both want ((to hear,) hearing) another song.

8. Remember that Bruno's party is a surprise, so please do not mention our (to go, (going)) to the bakery and (to buy, (buying)) this huge cake.

PRACTICE 6

Circle the correct verb in each sentence. If you need help, review the verb lists.

1. I ((prefer,) want) listening to NPR during breakfast.

2. Ichiro (suggests, (hopes)) to finish his coursework this semester so that he can graduate in May.

3. Given the high cost of housing, he (plans, (recommends)) sharing an apartment with another serious student.

4. The mayor (hoped, (advised)) the city council not to pass legislation that would hurt local retailers.

5. Now that she has a good job, she can ((afford,) consider) to buy a new car.

6. I enjoyed the evening very much. I ((appreciate,) thank) your inviting me.

7. Several students (decided, (kept)) working after the chemistry lab closed.

8. He ((loves,) anticipates) to get up early and go running along the river.

For more practice and assessment in ESL-related issues in English, visit *Evergreen's* Online Study Center at **college.hmco.com/pic/evergreen8e.**

Acknowledgments

Continued from p. iv

Photos

Page 59: Reprinted with permission of The American Indian College Fund.

Page 62: AP/Wide World Photos.

Page 76: AP/Wide World Photos.

Page 85: Scott Gries/Getty Images.

Page 86: © Vladimir Kush/Kush Fine Art Galleries.

Page 93: AP/Wide World Photos.

Page 97: George Tooker b. 1920/*The Subway*, 1950/Egg tempera on composition board/18 1/8 x 36 1/8 in. (46.04 x 91.76 cm)/© Whitney Museum of Art, New York; Purchase, with funds from the Juliana Force Purchase Award 50.23.

Page 103: (All photos) © Grant Heilman Photography, Inc.

Page 113: AP/Wide World Photos. Page 118: The Far Side ® by Gary Larson © 1993 FarWorks, Inc. All Rights Reserved. The Far Side ® and the Larson ® signature are registered trademarks of FarWorks, Inc. Used with permission.

Page 130: U. S. National Institute of Health. From "Portion Distortion."

Page 151: © *St. Petersburg Times*.

Page 171: Courtesy **www.adbusters.com.**

Page 193: © Justin Munter.

Page 208: © Lara Swimmer/ESTO. All rights reserved.

Page 230: Jim Morin, *Miami Herald*, Cartoon Arts International/Cartoonists & Writers Syndicate.

Page 292: Gogh, Vincent van (1853–1890). *The Starry Night*. 1889. Oil on canvas, 29 x 36 1/4. Acquired through the Lillie P. Bliss Bequest (472.1941). Digital Image © The Museum of Modern Art/Licensed by SCALA/Art Resource, NY.

Page 327: © David Fawcett.

Page 352: AP/Wide World Photos.

Page 359: David Rochkind/Polaris Images.

Page 368: © *The New Yorker Collection 1993*, Peter Steiner from **cartoonbank.com.** All rights reserved.

Page 369: Photo by Christoph Gerigk. © Franck Goddio/Hilti Foundation.

Page 384: Reprinted with permission of Duck ® brand Duct Tape.

Page 400: AP/Wide World Photos.

Page 404: The Everett Collection.

Page 412: From the book: *Arlen Ness, The King Of Choppers* by Michael Lichter. © Michael Lichter.

Page 429: AP/Wide World Photos.

Page 429: AP/Wide World Photos.

Page 451: © Marty Katz Photography.

Page 464: Edvard Munch, "The Scream." © 2007 The Munch Museum/The Munch-Ellingsen Group/Artists Rights Society (ARS), NY. Reprinted with permission The National Museum of Art, Architecture And Design, Oslo, Norway.

Page 479: The Everett Collection.

Page 491: AP/Wide World Photos.

Page 496: The Everett Collection.

Page 513: © **www.cartoonstock.com.**

Page 539: Copyright John Dyer Photography.

Page 548: © *The New Yorker Collection 2002*, Alex Gregory from **cartoonbank.com.** All rights reserved.

Page 555: Reprinted with permission of the National Fatherhood Initiative, **www.fatherhood.org.**

Page 567: Photo by John Beale. Copyright, *Pittsburgh Post-Gazette*, 2006, all rights reserved. Reprinted with permission.

Page 584: AP/Wide World Photos.

Text

Pages 536–538: From ALL OVER BUT THE SHOUTIN' by Rick Bragg, copyright © 1997 by Rick Bragg. Used by permission of Pantheon Books, a division of Random House, Inc.

Pages 539–541: Copyright © 1990 by Sandra Cisneros. First published in *Glamour*, November 1990. Reprinted by permission of Susan Bergholz Literary Services, New York. All rights reserved.

Pages 542–544: From DAYS OF GRACE by Arthur Ashe and Arnold Rampersad, copyright © 1993 by Arthur Ashe and Arnold Rampersad. Used by permission of Alfred A. Knopf, a division of Random House, Inc.

Pages 545–546: MIAMI HERALD by ANA VECIANA-SUAREZ. Copyright 1999 by MIAMI HERALD. Reproduced with permission of MIAMI HERALD in the format Textbook via Copyright Clearance Center.

Pages 547–549: From DAVE BARRY IS NOT TAKING THIS SITTING DOWN by Dave Barry, copyright © 2000 by Dave Barry. Used by permission of Crown Publishers, a division of Random House, Inc.

Pages 550–551: "A Brother's Murder" by Brent Staples, *New York Times*, March 30, 1986 ("About Men" Column). © 1986, The New York Times. Reprinted by permission.

Pages 552–554: "Dear Dads: Save Your Sons" by Christopher N. Bacorn, *Newsweek*, 12/7/92. Reprinted by permission of the author.

Pages 555–557: Bharati Mukherjee, "Two Ways to Belong in America," *New York Times*, September 2, 1996. © 1996, The New York Times. Reprinted by permission.

Pages 558–559: "Forever Young" by Firoozeh Dumas, *New York Times Magazine*, 10/30/05, p. 34. © 2005. Reprinted by permission.

Pages 561–563: Excerpts from ON THE REZ by Ian Frazier. Copyright © 2000 by Ian Frazier. Reprinted by permission of Farrar, Straus and Giroux, LLC.

Pages 564–566: "Four Types of Courage" by Karen Castellucci Cox and Susan Fawcett. Copyright 2006 by Karen Castellucci Cox and Susan Fawcett. Reprinted by permission of the authors.

Pages 567–570: "Cell Yell: Thanks for (Not) Sharing" by Eric A. Taub, *New York Times*, November 22, 2001, pp. G1, G5. Copyright © 2001 by The New York Times Co. Reprinted with permission.

Pages 571–572: "Homeward Bound" by Janet Wu, Television News Anchor/Reporter for WHDH-TV, Boston. Reprinted by permission of the author.

Pages 573–575: Anna Quindlen, "Freedom's Just Another Word," *Newsweek*, October 16, 2004, p. 82. Reprinted by permission of International Creative Management, Inc. Copyright © 2004 by Anna Quindlen.

Pages 576–578: "The Case for Torture" by Michael E. Levin, *Newsweek*, June 1982. Reprinted by permission of the author.

Pages 579–584: "Beauty: When the Other Dancer is the Self" from IN SEARCH OF OUR MOTHERS GARDENS: WOMANIST PROSE, copyright © 1983 by Alice Walker, reprinted by permission of Harcourt, Inc.

Index

Rhetorical Index

The following index first classifies the paragraphs and essays in this text according to rhetorical mode and then according to rhetorical mode by chapter. (Those paragraphs with built-in errors for students to correct are not included.)

Rhetorical Modes

Rhetorical Modes by Chapter

Rhetorical Modes in the Reading Selections

Notes

Notes